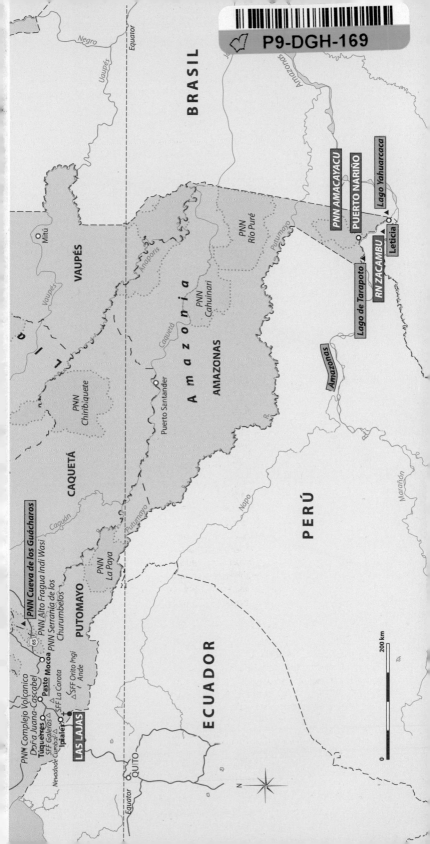

THEGREENGUIDE
Colombia

Parque Nacional Natural Tayrona © graham.klotz/iStockphoto.com

THEGREENGUIDE **COLOMBIA**

Special thanks to **Proexport** for their help in the creation of this guide.

Michelin Colombia

Presidente	Jorge Luis Vega
Vicepresidente Comercial	Alejandro Botero
Gerente de Mercadeo	Elena Sancho
Marketing Comunicaciones	Alberto Telch

Michelin Apa Publications Ltd

General Manager	Cynthia Clayton Ochterbeck
Editorial Manager	Jonathan P. Gilbert
Project Editor	Françoise Klingen
Editor	Gwen Cannon
Contributing Writers	Anna Maria Espaster, Glenn Harper, Françoise Klingen, Claiborne Linvill, Linda Lee, Richard McColl, Sarah Woods
Production Manager	Natasha G. George
Cartography	Peter Wrenn, John Dear, Paul Hopgood, Andrew Thompson, Debbie Wilson
Photo Editor	Yoshimi Kanazawa
Proofreader	Sean Cannon
Interior Design	Chris Bell
Cover Design	Chris Bell, Christelle Le Déan
Layout	Natasha G. George, Françoise Klingen
Cover Layout	Michelin Apa Publications Ltd.

Contact us	The Green Guide Michelin Maps and Guides One Parkway South Greenville, SC 29615, USA www.michelintravel.com Michelin Maps and Guides Hannay House, 39 Clarendon Road Watford, Herts WD17 1JA, UK ☎01923 205240 www.ViaMichelin.com travelpubsales@uk.michelin.com
Special Sales	For information regarding bulk sales, customized editions and premium sales, please contact our Customer Service Departments: USA 1-800-432-6277. UK 01923 205240. Canada 1-800-361-8236

PROMOCIÓN DE EXPORTACIONES, INVERSIÓN Y TURISMO.

Colombia, the only risk is wanting to stay.

www.colombia.travel

ProExport
President Proexport, Maria Claudia Lacouture; Vice President Tourism, Ismael Enrique Ramirez; Holiday Travel Manager, Zully Salazar; Advisor Holiday Tourism Management, Camilo Andrés Díaz; E-Marketing Manager, Laura Ortega.

PLANNING YOUR TRIP

The blue-tabbed PLANNING YOUR TRIP section gives you **ideas for your trip** and **practical information** to help you organize it. You'll find practical information, a host of outdoor activities, a calendar of events, information on shopping, sightseeing and more.

INTRODUCTION

The orange-tabbed INTRODUCTION section explores Colombia's **Nature** and geology. The **History** section spans from Pre-Columbian times through to the present. The **Art and Culture** section covers fine arts and crafts, the performing arts, architecture and literature, while **Colombia Today** delves into modern-day life in the country.

DISCOVERING

The green-tabbed DISCOVERING section features Principal Sights by region, featuring the most interesting local **Sights**, **Walking Tours** and nearby **Excursions**. Admission prices shown are normally for a single adult.

ADDRESSES

We've selected the best hotels, restaurants, cafes, shops, nightlife and entertainment to fit all budgets. See the Legend on the cover flap for an explanation of the price categories. See the back of the guide for an index of hotels and restaurants.

Sidebars

Throughout the guide you will find blue, orange and green-colored text boxes with lively anecdotes, detailed history and background information.

☺ A Bit of Advice ☺

Green advice boxes found in this guide contain practical tips and handy information relevant to the sight in the Discovering section.

STAR RATINGS ★★★

Michelin has given star ratings for more than 100 years. If you're pressed for time, we recommend you visit the ★★★ or ★★ sights first:

★★★ **Highly recommended**
★★ **Recommended**
★ **Interesting**

MAPS

☺ Sights map.
☺ Region maps.
☺ Maps for major cities.
☺ Local tour maps.

All maps in this guide are oriented north, unless otherwise indicated by a directional arrow. The term "Local Map" refers to a map within the chapter or Tourism Region. A complete list of the maps found in the guide appears at the back of this book.

© Jane Sweeney/AWL Images

© Jane Sweeney/AWL Images

PLANNING YOUR TRIP

INTRODUCTION TO COLOMBIA

CONTENTS

IDT Cortesía Germán Montes/Procexport Colombia

DISCOVERING COLOMBIA

Welcome to Colombia

Nowhere else in Latin America will you find such a variety of landscapes and wildlife. Extending from the lost cities and stunning beaches of the Caribbean to the Amazon, frowning over its pristine Pacific forests from the high peaks of three Andean cordilleras, Colombia has much in store for the adventurous traveler. Its warm and hospitable people have a world of friendship to offer all comers.

BOGOTÁ AND SURROUNDINGS
(pp108-147)

Colombia's cosmopolitan capital is a city on the upswing, with sleek high-rise blocks that characterize a forward-thinking modern metropolis. Around Bogotá's paved plazas and leafy parks, a host of designer stores, swank cafes and top-notch restaurants vie for attention. However, it is La Candelaria, Bogotá's colonial core, that forms the city's spiritual heart. On Sundays the capital becomes a traffic-free zone where jugglers and musicians take center stage in this highland plateau, once home to the advanced pre-Columbian Muisca civilization.

NORTHEASTERN COLOMBIA
(pp148-207)

Colombia's breadbasket, the northeast revels in rolling fields planted with potatoes, onions, maize and fruit trees, edged by pastures of grazing dairy cattle. In higher elevations, lilies, roses and carnations provide a riot of color. Villa de Leyva's colonial center is ringed by roadside stalls tended by sombrero-attired peasants. The city of Tunja still evokes the memory of the farmers from the surrounding villages who joined Simón Bolívar's makeshift army, and cleared the way for the nation's independence.

MEDELLÍN AND THE INNER NORTHWEST *(pp208-269)*

Steep, palm-clad slopes rise from humid flatlands to reach cooler highlands and snow-capped peaks. Emerald valleys brimming with sugarcane, plantain and banana crops stretch to the Coffee Zone's outer fringes, where rustic haciendas recall images of rural Spain. Colonial settlements dotting oxen-plowed fields offer sharp contrast to modern Medellín, the region's capital, with its spring-like climate. Here, cutting-edge architecture and urban gentrification embody cultural sophistication born of an indomitable settler's drive.

COFFEE REGION *(pp251-269)*

Located in the Andean highlands of the West, Colombia's coffee-growing triangle encompasses the cities of Manizales, Pereira and Armenia. Comprising only 1 percent of the country's terrain, this region of rolling farmlands, working plantations and verdant slopes is responsible for 50 percent of all Colombian coffee production and 10 percent of the world's coffee supply. A growing sector of tourism is guests' stays at area coffee farms.

Villa de Leyva, Northeastern Colombia

Proexport Colombia

CARTAGENA AND THE CARIBBEAN REGION *(pp270-327)*

Blessed with white-sand isles and a palm-fringed coast, this laid-back region is home to Cartagena, the country's best-preserved colonial city. This jewel in Colombia's architectural crown graces a shoreline famed for its exuberant festivals, Afro-Caribbean cultures and UNESCO-listed sites. From the Andean Mountain range, a massive plain stretches to the Sierra Nevada de Santa Marta and the Guajira Peninsula at Colombia's most northerly point, offering a spectrum of varied terrain, from marshes, jungle and coastal desert to Caribbean islands teeming with coral reefs.

Parque Nacional Natural Corales del Rosario, the Caribbean

Proexport Colombia

THE PACIFIC REGION
(pp328-347)

Rain-nourished and sun-blessed, the verdant jungles and mangrove forests of El Pacifico flourish along Colombia's western flank. Set in rounded bays with silvery beaches and fed by mighty rivers, the region's coastal waters provide fertile feeding grounds for an array of marine life. Vast rain forests form part of the bird-rich Chocó eco-region, filled with magnificent flora and fauna, and extending from the Atrato River near the Panamanian border to the Mataje River on the Ecuadorian frontier.

CALI AND THE INNER SOUTHWEST *(pp348-399)*

Colombia's inner southwest region boasts a dizzying array of elevations, from lofty rugged highlands and dense folds of swamp-heavy jungle to lush valleys, dusty sands and snowy mountain peaks. Among the highlights is the colonial city of Popayán, home to a 400-year-old Holy Week festival. The other-worldly funerary monuments of San Agustín and Tierradentro are some of the most important pre-Columbian sites in the Americas. Vibrant Cali, the country's "Capital of Salsa," pulsates with contagious rhythm and dance.

LOS LLANOS AND AMAZONIA
(pp400-425)

Colombia's cowboy-movie backdrop, these endless plains are the province of gaucho-esque ranchers and vast herds of cattle and a prairie culture that perpetuates rich legends and musical paeans to man, horse, love and land. Farther south, savannas subside where knotted swaths of dense, untouched jungle define Colombia's Amazon Basin. Here, the ink-green, cappuccino-frothed waters of the mighty Amazon support incalculable amounts of the planet's most spectacular flora and fauna.

Parque Nacional Natural Amacayacu, Amazonia

© Sandra Patricia Urrea Camargo/Archivo Parques Nacionales Naturales de Colombia

La Piscina,
Parque Nacional Natural Tayrona
© Jane Sweeney/AWL Images

When and Where to Go

WHEN TO GO

Colombia is a year-round destination, but one of the best times to visit is during the short **summer** (December-March), since these months are the **driest**. Another popular time of year is **mid-June to mid-August**, but bear in mind that these two travel periods are also the time for school holidays in Colombia, so reserve accommodations and domestic travel well in advance. Advance bookings are advised for all big public holidays throughout the country, when many Colombians travel to visit family and friends. Although it can **rain** at any time year-round, it is possible to catch at least some sun whenever and wherever you go. Colombia's **climate** is generally pleasant year-round, with an average temperature of 25°C/77°F. Medellín, in particular, is known as "The City of Eternal Spring," with a 22°C/71.6°F average at any time of year.

That said, temperatures in Colombia are strongly influenced by **altitude**, and what is true for lowlying areas does not apply to more mountainous regions, where temperatures can plunge as low as -10°C/14°F to -15°C/5°F at high altitudes. The opposite is true for the coastal areas and the Amazon, which can be very hot and humid. The latter gets plenty of rain, even when the rest of the country experiences a dry season.

IDEAS FOR YOUR VISIT
MAIN URBAN CENTERS

All of Colombia's main cities have something attractive to visitors, something special and unique. Bogotá, the nation's capital, Medellín and Cali sit amid stunning mountains; Cartagena de Indias, Barranquilla and Santa Marta lie on the shores of the Caribbean's turquoise waters; Leticia, the capital of Amazonia, hides deep within the jungle.

To "city-hop" among these urban centers is to experience different aspects of Colombia.

Bogotá, founded in 1538, has a number of interesting sights to explore, not least of which is a museum showcasing some of the finest gold pieces in the world. Its oldest neighborhood, La Candelaria, teems with Colonial structures. For beautiful views and tranquillity, the peak of Montserrate, a sanctuary near La Candelaria, can be reached by cable car. **Medellín**, a quick 30-minute flight from the capital—but a grueling nine hours by bus—has an altogether more laid-back and modern feel to it. The weather is pleasant year-round, and the famous botanical garden, with its

AVERAGE TEMPERATURES BY QUARTER in both Celsius and Fahrenheit (Composite sources)				
	Jan	**Apr**	**Aug**	**Dec**
Bogotá	13.1	13.9	13.3	13.2
	55.6	57.0	55.9	55.8
Cali	23.7	23.3	23.8	23.2
	74.7	73.9	74.8	73.8
Cartagena	26.7	27.5	28.0	27.1
	80.1	81.5	82.4	80.8
Leticia	27.0	27.0	26.5	27.0
	81.0	81.0	80.0	81.0
Medellín	21.9	21.8	21.9	21.4
	71.4	71.2	71.4	70.5

varied collection of orchids, further adds to the spring-like atmosphere. You will also enjoy good shopping, a hip and happening nightlife and, as it's the culinary capital of Colombia, a great mix of restaurants. Colombia's third-largest city, **Cali,** is slower paced than its two larger counterparts. This hot and muggy town is definitely the place to soak in some Latino ambience. Self-proclaimed capital of salsa music and dancing, Cali is particularly renowned for its nightlife and beautiful women. Founded in 1533 **Cartagena de Indias**, on the Caribbean coast, is currently the Colombian city that is attracting the most international visitors, particularly to its fortifications and Colonial architecture, which have been faithfully restored. The bustling Caribbean port city of **Barranquilla** is famed for its carnival. **Santa Marta** is a gateway to nearby beaches and the archaeological site of **Ciudad Perdida**. In the country's southernmost reaches of Amazonia, **Leticia** is a world unto its own, connected to the rest of Colombia by airplane. Brazil and Peru can be reached from here by boat or overland. The town itself serves as a base for excursions into the Amazon jungle.

TWO COASTS

Blessed with coastlines on two seas and several sun-soaked islands, Colombia offers some relaxing beaches. Best known of the islands are the Caribbean getaways of **San Andrés** and **Providencia**, 775km/465mi west of the Colombian mainland, but only 220km/132mi off the coast of Nicaragua. There are plenty of flights from Colombian main hubs to San Andrés, and from there, it's a short hop to Providencia. Apart from their pleasant beaches and outlying cays, these islands are the place for some serious **diving**. In the waters around the San Andrés archipelago lies one of the largest coral reefs in the world, with a variety

Colombia's Must Sees
(in order of placement in guidebook)

1 **La Candelaria, Bogotá**★★★
2 **Sierra Nevada del Cocuy**★★★
3 **El Centro, Medellín**★★★
4 **Ciudad Amurallada, Cartagena de Indias**★★★
5 **PNN Tayrona**★★★
6 **La Guajira Peninsula**★★★
7 **PNN Sierra Nevada de Santa Marta**★★★
8 **Santuario de Fauna y Flora Malpelo**★★★
9 **Parque Arqueológico de San Agustín**★★★
10 **Puerto Nariño, Amazonia**★★★

of marine life. San Andrés is also great for **birding**, while **hiking** is popular on Providencia. If lazing on the beach becomes too peaceful here, Colombia's mainland Caribbean coast has plenty to offer in terms of lively activities. The beach is never far from the cities of Cartagena, Santa Marta or Barranquilla. Several national parks and protected areas can be found along this coastline as well, such as the coral islands of **Rosario**, the stunning tropical paradise that is **Tayrona National Park** and the archaeological site of **Ciudad Perdida**, carved out of the mountainside.

San Andrés Island, Caribbean Coast

Proexport Colombia

13

Nuquí, Pacific Coast

Proexport Colombia

To the south, Colombia's other coast—the one that edges the Pacific Ocean—has a very different vibe from the sandy beaches of the Caribbean. Here the scenery is mountainous and wild, with dense forests that receive plenty of rainfall. The **biodiversity** of the Colombian Pacific coast, especially its bird life, makes it particularly important for the country's **ecotourism**.

Perhaps one of the greatest natural marvels is that of the annual southern migration of the **humpback whale** along with its offspring; in the areas around **Nuquí** and **Bahia Solano**, in the Chocó department, sightings are frequent.

Around Nuquí, the gateway to **Utría National Park**, you will find a number of award-winning ecolodges. Farther south, the former prison island of **Isla Gorgona**, now also a national park, is home to several endemic species.

Heron in the Cauca River Valley

Miky Calero/Proexport Colombia

THE GREAT PLAINS AND RIVER VALLEYS

Colombia has some spectacular lesser known regions, such as **Los Llanos**, one of the most impressive of places due to sheer size alone. Comparable to the *pampas* in Argentina or the prairies of North America, these wide-open savannas reach the borders of Venezuela in the east, and continue on southward almost all the way into Amazonia. Find the cowboy within you and stay at a **cattle ranch**, where you can saddle up. To get a feel for the folkloric *llanero* culture and its traditional music, visit **Villavicencio**, the "Gate to the Plains." Each year the town hosts the World Coleo Encounter, a picturesque event with rodeo-type competitions.

Rivers are another prominent feature of Colombia's landscape. Just an hour from Cali, the scenic Andean valley of the **Cauca River** holds sugarcane plantations and haciendas. The **Magdalena River** is another great Colombian river. Also stretching across the country's interior, it runs through cattle farmlands and towns as distant from one another as **Honda**, with excellent fishing, or **Mompox**, renowned for its stunning Colonial architecture and Easter celebrations. Colombia's rivers also make for great white-water rafting; **San Gil**, in the Santander's river valley of the Río Fonce, is a prime destination for outdoor water sports.

Colombia's UNESCO World Heritage Sites

CULTURAL SITES

- Port, fortresses and group of monuments in **Cartagena**
- Historic center of **Santa Cruz de Mompox**
- **San Agustín** Archaeological Park
- National Archaeological Park of **Tierradentro**

NATURAL SITES

- **Los Katíos** National Park
- **Malpelo** Fauna/Flora Sanctuary

ON THE TENTATIVE LIST

- Buritaca 200 - **Ciudad Perdida** - Sierra Nevada de Santa Marta
- Colombian **Coffee Cultural landscape**
- **Qhapaq Ñan** Inka road system
- **Chiribiquete** National Park
- **Río San Jorge** pre-Hispanic hydraulic system
- **Seaflower Marine Protected Area** around the archipelago of San Andrés, Providencia and Santa Catalina

MOUNTAINOUS COFFEE ZONE AND SOUTHERN ANDES

One of Colombia's picture-perfect settings, the **Zona Cafetera**, or Coffee Zone, is home to gently rolling green hills where coffee farms are tucked away in the abundant vegetation. The three coffee-growing departments of **Quindío**, **Risaralda** and **Caldas** offer tours and samples and charming overnight stays at coffee *fincas*. The departmental capitals of **Armenia**, **Pereira** and **Manizales**, as well as many smaller towns in the area, such as **Salento** and **Filandia**, all have brightly painted houses in picturesque, tranquil surroundings. Not far from here rise the snow-capped peaks of **Los Nevados National Park**, which offers excellent hiking. There is also a coffee theme park if you want to know more about these magic beans: Parque Nacional del Café. Going south into the Valley of the Cauca River, you reach Cali. Farther south towards Ecuador, the archaeological sites of **Tierradentro** and **San Agustín** reveal Colombia's ancient heritage, while the nearby town of **Popayán** has some of the best Colonial architecture in the country.

JUNGLES OF THE NORTH AND SOUTH

Now deemed safe to visit, **Capurgana**, near the Dairén Gap, a stone's throw from the Panamanian border, is a quiet haven for surfing, snorkeling, kayaking or just relaxing on its two pristine beaches. Diving is popular, and from here it is also possible to visit the 400 islands of San Blas, in neighboring Panama.

In the south the department of **Amazonia** covers a vast 643,000sq km/248,264sq mi of jungle and rivers. The departmental capital of **Leticia** serves as a hub and good starting point for exploring the national parks and seeing the wildlife, especially the birdlife, of the Amazon. It's easiest to get around by an **organized tour** of the area; such tours can be arranged in advance or upon your arrival in Leticia. Most tours last a minimum of four days and often take in parts of Peru and Brazil as well as Colombia, visiting national parks, Indian villages and smaller towns in the basin. There are opportunities for kayaking the Amazon river or one of its 1,100 tributaries, as well as hiking and night safaris to spot the amazing wildlife.

Paddling the Amazon River, Leticia

Proexport Colombia

15

What to See and Do

CULTURAL TOURISM
HISTORICAL ROUTES

If the thought of walking on 18C cobblestone paths built in the time of the Viceroyalty of New Granada appeals to you, read on. If you are interested in learning more about the 1781 Revolt of the Comuneros against the Spanish authorities, retracing the steps of Simón Bolívar's army during the 1819 victorious liberation campaign, or appreciating colonial villages and local architecture; read on. The Colombian authorities have seized upon the 2010 celebrations of the **Bicentennial** of the first Republic of Colombia to revive significant historical routes pertaining, one way or another, to the struggle for independence. This initiative proposes to make opportunities for reliving the past possible, ones that history buffs will really relish.

www.mincultura.gov.co
Visit the website of the **Colombian Ministry of Culture** for more details on these historical routes. Under "Turismo Cultural," then "Destinos Culturales," you will find plenty of maps and extensive background information.

Ruta Libertadora
At the time of writing, only this route was truly operational. It is a fascinating journey into history that allows visitors to discover some significant highlights along the route traveled by Bolívar's troops some 200 years ago.
A comprehensive **online guide** (in Spanish) to this route can now be downloaded in pdf format on the website of the Colombian Ministry of Culture (☝see above). It contains a detailed description of each stop on the route, which is divided into four major sections, through Bogotá and the departments of Cundinamarca, Boyacá, Casanare and Arauca. Some

portions of the route actually lend themselves to **hiking** or **horseback riding**. Among the suggested highlights, you will recognize some of the sights described in this guide, such as Puente de Boyacá or Pantano de Vargas (☝see TUNJA), to name a few.

Ruta Mutis
This route is a very original way to discover some of Colombia's picturesque colonial villages, appreciate the local architecture and rural landscapes, and learn about the amazing biodiversity along the way. The proposed route follows the steps of the **botanical expedition** led by famed **José Celestino Mutis** in 1783, taking you from Bogotá (Cundinamarca) to Ibagué (Tolima).
A downloadable pdf **online guide** (in Spanish), also available on the website of the Colombian Ministry of Culture (☝see above), details the itinerary between **Guaduas** and **Honda** (☝see AROUND BOGOTÁ). This journey is a great opportunity to do some **hiking** on an Important 16C **royal path** (Camino Real) that linked Honda (on the Magdalena River) to Santa Fé de Bogotá, capital of New Granada.

Ruta La Gran Convención
Still in the making at this point, this promising historical route will trace some major political events that occurred in post-independence Colombia. Selected for their historical significance, several places in the departments of Norte de Santander and Cesar will be highlighted, such as **Ocaña** where, in 1828, the National Convention assembled to discuss the future organization of the new republic, and Bolívar suggested that the 1821 constitution should be reformed.

Ruta de Los Comuneros
Close to completion, this historical route will go through the departments of Cundinamarca, Boyacá and Santander where, in 1781, anger over taxation led to New Granada's

Revolt of the Comuneros. This uprising, during which the ideas of self-government were expressed for the first time, foreshadowed the fight for independence. Among the many highlights along this route is Bogotá's Plaza de Bolívar (◐ see BOGOTÁ), where the leaders of the rebellion were publicly executed.

ARCHAEOLOGICAL SITES

First settled by mankind around 12,000 BC, Colombia has been home to a number of great civilizations. Artists, potters, goldsmiths, civil engineers and builders among the **Tayrona**, **Muisca**, **Zenú** and **Quimbaya** people, just to name a few, have left many marks on the country. Modern Colombia realizes the importance of its rich pre-Columbian past, and great efforts are being made to preserve and showcase a wealth of archaeological sites, for the benefit of future generations.

Ciudad Perdida, Sierra Nevada de Santa Marta
IM - Editores/Proexport Colombia

Ciudad Perdida

Believed to be the architectural masterpiece of the Tayrona civilization, the mythical "Lost City" stands between 900m/2,953ft and 1,000m/3,281ft of altitude in the **Sierra Nevada de Santa Marta** (Magdalena department). Currently on the UNESCO's World Heritage **tentative list**, this impressive **ruined**

Colombia's Religious Architecture

The Spaniards left an impressive architectural legacy in many parts of Colombia. Built during the 16C-18C, many of these jewels were churches. Discovering religious buildings from that era and beyond is a good way to experience the religious fervor that is an enduring and essential element of the national character.

ANDEAN REGION
Bogotá (◐ see Bogotá). Santuario del Señor Caído de Monserrate - Nuestra Señora del Carmen - Catedral Primada de Colombia.

Chiquinquirá (◐ see VILLA DE LEYVA). Basílica de Nuestra Señora del Rosario.

Tunja (◐ see TUNJA). Catedral Basílica de Santiago el Mayor.

Villa de Leyva (◐ see VILLA DE LEYVA). Iglesia Parroquial - Iglesia Santuario de la Virgen del Carmen.

Zipaquirá (◐ see AROUND Bogotá). Catedral de Sal.

CARIBBEAN REGION
Cartagena (◐ see CARTAGENA). Convento de la Popa - Iglesia y Convento de Santo Domingo - San Pedro Claver.

Mompox (◐ see CARTAGENA). Iglesia Santa Barbara - La Concepción - Santo Domingo - San Juan de Dios.

SOUTHWEST
Buga (◐ see CALI). Basílica del Señor de los Milagros.

Cali (◐ see CALI). Iglesia de la Merced Iglesia de la Ermita - Iglesia de San Antonio - Catedral San Pedro - Iglesia de San Francisco.

Ipiales (◐ see PASTO). Basílica Santuario de Nuestra Señora de Las Lajas.

Pasto (◐ see PASTO). Iglesia de San Juan Bautista - Iglesia de Cristo Rey.

Popayán (◐ see POPAYÁN). Catedral Basílica Nuestra Señora de la Asunción - Iglesia la Ermita - Iglesia de San Francisco.

city exhibits a complex system of terraces, stone paths, walls and irrigation channels. Located in a once unsafe area, the site was reopened to tourism in 2005. To get there is quite a strenuous **trek** through a dense jungle.

🚶 *See SANTA MARTA and the section on Hiking and Trekking in this chapter for more details on the Parque Arqueológico Ciudad Perdida - Teyuna.*

San Agustín

Located in the Huila department, this archaeological site is perhaps Colombia's best known, and definitely one of the country's must sees. A **UNESCO World Heritage Site** since 1995, San Agustín is a wonderland of mysterious **statues** spread out over a mystic landscape of stunning beauty. It is an impressive part of Colombia's ancient heritage.

🚶 *See SAN AGUSTÍN for more details on the Parque Arqueológico de San Agustín and nearby Parque Arqueológico Alto de los Ídolos y Alto de las Piedras.*

♦ **Chaska Tours**
  Finca El Maco, San Agustín
  ☏ +57 (8) 837 3437 or
  311 271 4802 (mobile)
  www.elmaco.ch/chaska
  Organizes tours to various parts of Colombia, including San Agustín and Tierradentro (🚶 *see below*).

Colombian Institute of Anthropology and History

For excellent, in-depth information on **Ciudad Perdida**, **San Agustín** and **Tierradentro**, you may want to check the official website of the Colombian Institute of Anthropology and History.

www.icanh.gov.co *(look under "Parques y Museos").*

Tierradentro

This famous pre-Columbian necropolis, located in the Cauca department, was also inscribed on the **UNESCO World Heritage Site** in 1995. Its strange **underground tombs**, decorated with colored **drawings** and symbols, are set within a remote, volcanic landscape.

🚶 *See POPAYÁN for more details on the Parque Arqueológico de Tierradentro.*

♦ **Luna Paz Tours**
  Calle 8 # 7-61
  Popayán
  ☏ 315 513 9593 (mobile)

ECOTOURISM
WHALE WATCHING

Colombia's **Caribbean Coast** and **islands** offer whale- and dolphin-watching trips, but it is definitely the annual migration of **humpback whales** off the **Colombian Pacific Coast** that provides the most spectacular sightings.
Migratory whales come from as far as Antarctica to give birth to their calves in the warm waters of Colombia. Occurring from **June** to **November**, the massive presence of these easily spotted migrants—in some places even visible from the shore—draws crowds to Chocó's **Bahía Solano**, **El Valle** or **Nuquí**, and **Parque Nacional Natural Utria** (🚶 *see CHOCÓ REGION*). **Parque Nacional Natural Isla Gorgona** is another great place to be during the whale season. The warm coastal waters of **Bahía de Málaga** (🚶 *see PACIFIC SOUTH COAST*), some 20km/12mi from Buenaventura, have been recorded as having one of the highest birth rates for humpback whales in the world.

♦ On the mainland, **El Almejal** ecolodge (www.almejal.com.co) in El Valle or **El Cantil** (www.el cantil.com) in Guachalito, near Nuquí, stand out in terms of whale-watching trip organization. The main accommodation at Ensenada de Utría is the

NATIONAL PARKS OF COLOMBIA

Among the 55 natural areas belonging to the Colombian park system, here is a selection of sites offering ecotourism activities. For more information, visit **www.parquesnacionales.gov.co**.

Amacayacu (see p418)	canoeing - cultural activities - nature walks - photography - wildlife observation
Corales del Rosario and San Bernardo (see p282)	bird watching - boat rides - cultural activities - nature observation - kayaking - sailing - skin diving - snorkeling - swimming - water sports
El Cocuy (see p174)	camping - climbing - cycling - hang gliding - mountain climbing - rock and ice climbing - nature walks - spelunking - wildlife observation
Flamencos (see p313)	bird watching - cultural activities - environmental education - swimming
Gorgona (see p344)	boat rides - diving - nature walks - photography - snorkeling - whale watching - wildlife observation
Isla de Salamanca (see p296)	boat rides - nature walks - photography - wildlife observation
Los Nevados (see p257)	camping - cycling - fishing - mountain climbing - nature walks - rock and ice climbing - photography - spelunking - wildlife observation
Malpelo (see p344)	bird watching - photography - skin diving
Otún Quimbaya (see p261)	kayaking - nature walks - observation of butterflies - photography wildlife observation
Providencia (see p324)	nature trails - skin diving - snorkeling - swimming - water sports
Tayrona (see p306)	horseback-riding - nature observation - nature walks - nautical sports - skin diving - snorkeling - photography - visiting archaeological sites
Utría (see p335)	bird watching - nature walks - snorkeling - whale watching

Jaibaná visitor center itself; the **Mano Cambiada** community organization (www.nuquipacifico.com) also provides small scale lodgings and guided trip opportunities.

◆ **www.concesionesparques naturales.com/en**
Reaching Isla Gorgona is usually done by launches from Guapi (1hr30mn). Package tours and accommodations are provided by **Aviatur** (1) 607 1597. www.concesionesparques naturales.com.

BIRD WATCHING

Colombia's great diversity of ecosystems attracts a wide variety of birdlife, often within easy reach of enthusiastic birders. Tanagers come in all shapes and color patterns in the tropical forests of the **Pacific Coast**, while more than a hundred species of hummingbirds thrive in the **Andean forests** and altitude plateaus. The **Amazonian canopy** is alive with the cries of all kinds of parrots and toucans, while lowland waterfowl make themselves at home in the **Eastern Llanos** fluvial plains. The **Caribbean Coast** harbors seabirds and shorebirds as well as mangrove swamp dwellers such as herons and pelicans. Good places to look

Colombian Important Bird Areas

A list of the Colombian Important Bird Areas (**IBA**s), classified by **department** and including practical information such as **maps**, how to get there and which **species** and **ecosystems** to expect, is available on the following site:

http://aicas.humboldt.org.co *(Spanish).*

🖑 For specific information on the **Chocó Endemic Bird Area (EBA)**, *see sidebar p333.*

for Andean birds are the **Reserva Río Blanco** near Manizales, the **Parque Regional Natural Ucumarí** (nicknamed "Land of Birds") and the nearby **Santuario de Fauna y Flora Otún Quimbaya** near Pereira (🖑*see ZONA CAFETERA).* **Parque Nacional Natural Amacayacu** (🖑*see LETICIA)* for Amazonian birds and the area around **El Almejal ecolodge** (🖑*see CHOCÓ REGION)* for Pacific lowland birdlife are also worth mentioning. In the Caribbean region, the **Sierra Nevada de Santa Marta** (🖑*see SANTA MARTA)* is definitely a must see, as it possesses the world's highest density of **endemic birds.**

◆ **www.birdingcolombia.com/ tour_operators.php**
You will find links to a host of companies specializing in **bird- watching tours** in Colombia, such as www.ecoturs.org (ProAves partner), Birding Colombia (www.birding-colombia.com), Birding Tropics (www.birding tropics.com) or Colombia Birding (www.colombiabirding.com).

◆ **www.proaves.org**
This is the site of **ProAves**, a non-profit foundation dedicated to protecting birdlife. It maintains two bird sanctuaries in the Andes (Cerulean Warbler and El Paujil) and one near Santa Marta (El Dorado).

◆ **www.rnoa.org**
Enthusiastic birders may find useful insider tips on bird sightings through the Red Nacional de Observadores de Aves de Colombia (RNOA).

OUTDOOR ACTIVITIES

With landscapes as varied as those of Colombia, the great outdoors is never far away, and there are many possible options for visitors in need of an energetic holiday or adrenaline sport.

◆ **www.colombiaextrema.com/ destinos.htm.** This website will give you a quick overview of what is available and where.

CANOPYING

Harnessing yourself to a cable and **ziplining** through the forest canopy or over river canyons is not for the weak-hearted. Landscape permitting, this kind of activity is becoming increasingly popular in Colombia.

◆ Some 152km/94mi east of Medellín, the Central Cordillera **Reserva Natural Cañon del Río Claro** offers great opportunities to glide over the Río Claro River and canyon. Visit **www.rioclaroelrefugio. com** for details.

◆ Other canopying options are possible at **Ecoparque Los Yarumos** near Manizales, in the Coffee Region. Browse **http://ecoparquelos yarumos.com.**

◆ You may also want to try **Las Ardillas'** 1,200m/3,900ft glide near Popayán. Their website is **www.colombiacontact.com/ en_Las-Ardillas-Canopy.html.**

◆ Arguably the most intense canopying adventure can be experienced in the **Amazon Basin,** with Leticia-based SelvAventura. Check **www. amazonascolombia.com** for further information.

CAVING

Various caves of easy to medium difficulty can be explored around **San Gil**, such as **Cueva del Indio**, entered by gliding down from the canopy and jumping into a well filled with water (*see SAN GIL*). For details, check **www.colombiarafting.com**. An interesting site to visit is the **Parque Natural Cueva de los Guácharos** near Florencia, in the southern department of Huila (*see NEIVA*). Colombia's oldest protected natural area, it consists of an intricate network of caves, resonating to the sounds of cascades and underground ponds and rivers; it is an important nesting site for the guácharo bird, a nocturnal oversize swallow.

Caving is allowed in two guácharo caves and two additional limestone caves. For more details, check **www.parquesnacionales.gov.co**. Additional caving opportunities also exist around **Villa de Leyva** (*see VILLA DE LEYVA*) and **Suesca** (*see AROUND BOGOTÁ*).

CYCLING

Biking is a favorite pastime in Colombia, and it is not unusual to see whole families out cycling together on weekends. The hills and mountains can require some challenging pedaling. Beware of the altitude before indulging in anything too strenuous. The nation's capital has joined in the cycling fever and is closing off large parts of the city to traffic every Sunday. Around 300km/180mi of bike paths run across **Bogotá** (*see sidebar p124*), which now encourages organized **cycling tours**. For more details, check **www.bogotabiketours.co.** Some 45km/27mi to the north of Bogotá, **Suesca** (*see AROUND BOGOTÁ*) attracts crowds of nature lovers, climbers and **mountain bikers** alike to its impressive clusters of rock blocks. One fact worth mentioning is that Suesca belongs to the restricted list of places where **bicycle renting** is possible.

♦ **www.colombiarafting.com**
Sites like this one provide you with information on **mountain-biking** options in San Gil, Colombia's adventure sports capital.

♦ **www.concesionesparques naturales.com/en**
Up to three-day mountain-biking trips may be arranged at **Parque Nacional Los Nevados**, near Manizales, in the heart of the Coffee Region (*see ZONA CAFETERA*).

DIVING

Colombia's **Caribbean islands** and **coast** offer a cornucopia of opportunities for dives, ranging from surface snorkeling to deep-sea diving. **San Andrés** and **Providencia** (*see SAN ANDRÉS Y PROVIDENCIA*) provide a great variety of **coral reef** diving options in crystal-clear waters. San Andrés alone has more than 40 diving sites. The beautiful coral reefs of **Old Providence McBean Lagoon**, on Providencia, are another hot spot for diving.

Within easy access of Cartagena, **Parque Natural Nacional Corales del Rosario** (*see CARTAGENA DE INDIAS*) consists of 43 coralline islands, where reefs reaching 30m/100ft deep host a wealth of marine life, from delicate shrimp to giant sea turtles. Lesser known **Islas San Bernardo**, just off Tolú, offers more pristine coral reef diving opportunities. Hidden jewels also lie just off the mainland cities of **Capurganá** and **Sapzurro**

Great Hammerhead sharks, Isla Malpelo

Yves Lefèvre/Fundación Malpelo

Colombia's ⌂ Beach Destinations

Colombia's lengthy coastline (3,000km/1,860mi) includes the popular, white-sand beaches of the Caribbean coast and islands, and beautiful stretches of gray sand along the Pacific Coast, framed by untrammeled rain forest.

CARIBBEAN COAST
Capurganá (☉ see p336). Undeveloped, unspoiled beaches a stone's throw from Panama.

La Guajira (☉ see p311). A land sparsely populated by Wayúus, with some large desert beaches.

Providencia (☉ see pp 13, 99 & 320). Idyllic setting of quiet beaches with calm, crystal-clear waters.

San Andrés (☉ see pp 13, 99 & 320). High-quality beaches that tend to get very busy in season.

San Bernardo, Rosario and Barú (☉ see pp 13 and 99). Little chunks of paradise, easily accessible from Cartagena.

Santa Marta (☉ see p13). Colombia's most popular beach resort, with fine beaches and developed hotel infrastructure.

Tayrona (☉ see pp 13 and 306). Spectacular, empty beaches backed by exotic rain forests.

PACIFIC COAST
Bahía Solano and El Valle (☉ see pp 331 and 335). Some great beaches nearby. Deep-sea fishing and scuba diving. Whale watching.

Gorgona (☉ see pp 99 and 344). A few unspoiled sandy beaches. One of Colombia's best spots for whale watching.

Ladrilleros (☉ see p342). Popular beach getaway for people from Cali. Whale watching.

Nuquí (☉ see p336). Some fantastic uncrowded beaches, great for surfing. Whale watching.

(☉ see sidebar p336), with coral pillars reaching depths of 45m/150ft and exuberant coralline deep-sea gardens.

- **www.diveandgreen.com**
  The Dive and Green dive center in Capurganá is recognized by PADI. It offers instruction, equipment rental and diving excursions.
- **www.bandadiveshop.com**
  On San Andrés, the Banda Dive Shop has 20 years of similar experience.

On the **Pacific** side, you'll be able to experience **wreck-diving**, exploring a scuttled navy boat off the coast of Bahía Solano (☉ see CHOCÓ REGION). Pacific volcanic islands may not be quite as idyllic as islands from the Caribbean, but marine life bubbles near their shores, with sharks by the thousand off remote **Isla Malpelo** or seasonal humpback whales (Jun–Nov) in the waters around **Isla Gorgona** (☉ see PACIFIC SOUTH COAST).

HIKING AND TREKKING
The country numbers quite a few hiking groups whose purpose is to guide visitors through Colombia's beautiful landscape.
Among these are:

- Bogotá-based Colombian Hiking Foundation **Sal Si Puedes**, a non-governmental, environment-minded association, offers a wide range of guided day hikes throughout the country. Their website is www.salsipuedes.org.

- The **Organizacion Caminera de Antioquia** also aims to help visitors discover various aspects of the local culture and way of life. Access www.organizacioncamineradeantioquia.org for more details.

- Another good source, full of useful links, is **http://camineriacolombia.blogspot.com**.

CLASSIC COLOMBIAN TREKS

Ciudad Perdida (&see p308)	*5-6 day trek round trip.* Buried deep in the jungle of the Sierra Nevada de Santa Marta, the ancient city of the Tayrona will require a 2-3 day demanding uphill trek , wrestling with the dense jungle and passing river crossings, before it can be reached. For details contact **Sierra Tours** (www.sierratours-trekking.com) or **Turcol** (www.buritaca2000.com).
Sierra Nevada del Cocuy (&see p171)	*5-6 day trek around the base of the Sierra.* A fine example of an altitude trail (around 4,000m/13,120ft on average), this trail will take you from the U'wa village of Güicán to the township of El Cocuy through a splendid landscape of glaciers and lakes dominated by some 20 snow-capped peaks. Visit **www.parquesnacionales.gov.co** for information.
Los Nevados (&see p257)	Breathtaking day or week treks, include climbing the slopes of ominous, glacier-capped volcano Nevado del Ruiz (5,300m/17,384ft) or ascending its steeper neighbor Nevado del Tolima (5,200m/17,056ft). Best trekking conditions from March to May. **www.parquesnacionales.gov.co** is a good source of general information.

HORSEBACK RIDING

Cattle country **Llanos lowlands** and **Andean highlands** are the traditional places to look for horse-riding activities in Colombia.

Rides through the vast expanses and impressive landscapes of **San Agustín** archaeological park can be readily organized from the city of San Agustín through various local *oficinas de turismo*. They may also be included in more general tourist packages (www.deunacolombia.com is a good example of these).

Neighboring **Popayán** offers horseback tours through its beautiful countryside, such as the **Circuito Ancestral**, a 15km/9mi trail. Inquiries can be made at **Aviatur** Popayán ✆+57 (2) 320 9332 or Popayán Tourist Office ✆+57 (2) 824 2251, http://popayantourism.com.

A few operators in the **Bogotá** and **Armenia** areas describe their programs and offer booking opportunities on www.colombiacontact.com. **Cabalgata Segura** (http://www.colombiacontact.com/es_Cabalgata-Segura.html) is a good example of those with circuits varying in length and difficulty. Horse riding opportunities may also be found near **San Gil** (www.colombiarafting.com).

PARAGLIDING

Wind, thermal and relief conditions all conspire to make the Santander department, particularly the region around **Bucaramanga**, the realm of paragliders; eight flying sites include **Barichara**, **Ruitoque** and various spots in the scenic **Chicamocha Canyon** (&see BUCARAMANGA). Flying conditions are excellent almost year-round, and 10-day trips, as well as **tandem** and **instruction flights,** can be easily arranged.

- **www.colombiaparagliding.com** Browse through this site for details on available options and bookings.
- **www.nativoxsangil.com** San-Gil based alternatives also exist.

Horseback riding in Valle de Cocora near Armenia

Proexport Colombia

23

ROCK CLIMBING AND RAPPELLING

Lying 45km/27mi north of Bogotá, **Suesca** (🔗 see AROUND BOGOTÁ) has nearly 400 known **climbing routes**. Suesca's **rappel site** is located some 8km/5mi farther, in the high basin of the Bogotá River. www.cundinamarca. gov.co/cundinamarca/turismo/frm_ turismoindex.asp.

Rappelling can be practiced at many locations in the Andean Cordilleras. **www.colombiaextrema.com**.

SURFING, WINDSURFING AND KITESURFING

Colombia's biggest waves build up on the **Pacific Coast**: the country's best **surfing** sites are also found there. Excellent spots such as **Pico de Loro** and **Juan Tornillo** are around the city of **Nuquí** (🔗 see CHOCÓ REGION). **Juanchaco**, near Buenaventura (🔗 see PACIFIC SOUTH COAST), is strictly for experienced surfers only. On the **Caribbean Coast,** surfing sites near **Barranquilla** and **Riohacha** offer smaller waves and are markedly seasonal; winter is best (Dec- Mar).

♦ **www.iguanamar.com**
This surfing community site is a hub directing to regional information such as weather forecasts (see section "Reporte"), surfing equipment online shops

and specialized tour operators, such as **Aquasalvaje Surf Travel** (www.aquasalvaje.com). Opportunities for offshore **kite-surfing** and **windsurfing** are best on the **Caribbean** shore, especially in the winter winds (Jan–Apr). **La Boquilla**, just off Cartagena, and **Cabo de la Vela**, in the Guajira Peninsula (🔗 see LA GUAJIRA), are the most spectacular of Colombia's surfing sites. **Lake Calima**, near Cali, and **El Peñol** lake region, near Medellín, are the hot spots for inland windsurfing and sailing.

♦ **www.colombiakite.com**
This website is a community hub for kite-surfers.

WHITE-WATER RAFTING AND KAYAKING

Powerful rivers and impressive rapids are part of the landscape around **San Gil** (🔗 see SAN GIL), the nation's self-declared capital of adventure sports. The **Río Fonce**, **Chicamocha** and **Suarez Rivers** offer white-water rafting within easy reach. Adrenaline junkies will appreciate riding the Chicamocha's class IV to V+ rapids.

♦ **www.colombiarafting.com**
Colombia Rafting Expeditions is a knowledgeable, San Gil-based operator who offers kayaking lessons.

♦ **www.magdalenarafting.com/ rafting_huila/**
San Agustín-based Magdalena Rafting knows the Lower Magdalena rapids. Week-long rafting expeditions and kayak classes are available.

♦ **www.amazonascolombia.com**
Calmer **river kayaking** experiences can be had in the Amazon Basin with Leticia-based SelvAventura.

♦ **www.bahiadelsolladrilleros.com**
Sea kayaking opportunities exist at some spots on the Pacific Coast, notably at **Ladrilleros**.

Rafting the canyons, Parque Nacional del Chicamocha

Parque Nacional Chicamocha-PANACHI/Proexport Colombia

BOOKS
HISTORY - POLITICS

The Search for El Dorado. John Hemming (1978). Former director of the Royal Geographical Society explores the facts and fiction of the mythical lost city of gold.

Simón Bolívar: A Life. John Lynch (2006). A recent biography of the man who was key to the Independence Movement in South America.

Colombia: A Brutal History. Geoff Simons (2004). An in-depth look at Colombia's history, from the succession of Panama onwards, in particular the country's relationship with the US.

Colombia: Fragmented Land, Divided Society. Frank Safford and Marco Palacios (2001). Examines Colombian history and politics from pre-Columbian times to modern day.

Walking Ghosts: Murder and Guerrilla Politics in Colombia. Steven Dudley (2006). Deals with Colombia's recent troubled past of guerrilla warfare, drug barons and corruption.

More Terrible than Death: Massacres, Drugs and America's War in Colombia. Robin Kirk (2004). A focus on the drug war in Colombia and its devastating consequences.

ECOTOURISM - CONSERVATION

Colombia Natural Parks. Benjamin Villegas (2007). A summary of Colombia's 51 natural parks with accompanying photography.

Primates of Colombia. Thomas Richard Defler (2005). Colombia is one of the most biodiverse countries in the world, and this illuminating book highlights 28 primate species.

Guide to the Birds of Colombia. Steven L. Hilty and William L. Brown (1986). The ultimate guide to Colombia's birds, this volume covers all 1,700 species, as well as Colombia's geography and climate, with handy maps.

ART - ARCHITECTURE

Colombia before Columbus: The People, Culture and Ceramic Art of Pre-Hispanic Colombia. Armand J. Labbe (1986). One of the few available books on the subject, this is a richly illustrated work on the traditions of early Colombian art.

Colombian Art: 3500 Years of History. Santiago Londoño Vélez (2001). Coffee table book covering the history of Colombian art.

The Art of Gold: The Legacy of Pre-Hispanic Colombia. Roberto Lleras, Clara Isabel Botero and Santiago Londoño Vélez (2007).

Casa de Hacienda: Architecture in the Colombian Countryside. Germán Téllez (2007). A colorful look at Colombia's ranches and country houses with good photography.

GENERAL

Colombia 360. Benjamin Villegas (2007). Colombia through 360-degree panoramic photos.

Secrets of Colombian Cooking. Patricia McCausland-Gallo (2004). Comprehensive guide to Colombian cuisine, with a wide selection of recipes from the Colombian-born author.

NOVELS

World-famous novelist Gabriel García Márquez (✆ see LITERATURE) features Colombia in most of his works, two of which are listed below:

Love in the Time of Cholera. Gabriel García Márquez (1985). This romantic story of thwarted love set in Cartagena was also turned into a film in 2007.

Strange Pilgrims. Gabriel García Márquez (1992). A collection of 12 short stories written by Márquez during the 1970s and 80s.

María. Jorge Isaacs (1867). This romantic novel is considered one of the most important works of Latin American 19C literature.

Calendar of Events

The list below is a selection of the many events that take place in Colombia. Note that these events may not fall on the same month each year. For information in English about Colombian festivals and fairs, check *www.colombia.travel/en/international-tourist/what-to-do/history-and-tradition/fairs-and-festivals.*

Barranquilla Carnival

Proexport Colombia

JANUARY
Carnival of Blacks and Whites in Pasto (Carnaval de Negros y Blancos en Pasto) – Recognized as part of Colombia's National Cultural Heritage, this carnival is celebrated in the Andean city of Pasto January 4-6 every year. www.carnavaldepasto.org.

Hay Festival – This festival of literature and culture takes place in Cartagena during four days at the end of January every year, bringing together **writers, artists, journalists, poets and musicians** from all over the world.

Manizales Fair (Feria de Manizales) – This fair takes place in the Coffee Zone the first week of January. Activities include bullfights, parades and fireworks, as well as the international coffee pageant.

Semana Santa procession, Mompox

© Richard McColl/MICHELIN

FEBRUARY
Barranquilla Carnival (Carnaval de Barranquilla) – One of the best in the world, Barranquilla's carnival is a part of UNESCO's Immaterial World Cultural Heritage. The celebrations take place during four entire days in the run-up to Lent. www.carnavaldebarranquilla.org.

MARCH
International Film Festival of Cartagena (Festival Internacional de Cine de Cartagena) – Week-long Ibero-American film festival. www.festicinecartagena.org.

MARCH-APRIL
Holy Week (Semana Santa):
 ♦ **Mompox**: among the oldest Easter celebrations in Colombia, held here since 1564.
 ♦ **Pamplona**: Easter religious parades and festival of international choral music.
 ♦ **Popayán**: traditional Easter celebrations with three main processions on Palm Sunday, Good Tuesday and Good Friday.
 ♦ **Sabanalarga**: Easter celebrations including the staging of the death of Jesus and the Holy Sepulcher procession.

APRIL

Festival of the Vallenato Legend in Valledupar (Festival de la Leyenda Vallenata en Valledupar) – Major music and folk festival held the last five days of April. Contests for best interpreter of accordion, caja vallenata, etc. www.festivalvallenato.com.

Green Moon Festival (Festival de la Luna Verda) – Held each year on Providencia Island, this is a 3-day celebration of the Afro Caribbean people. English language lyrics of calypso and reggae.

Ibero-American Theater Festival of Bogotá (Festival Iberoamericano de Teatro de Bogotá) – One of the largest, greatest performing arts festivals in the world. www.festivaldeteatro.com.co.

JUNE

Bambuco National Folk Festival and Beauty Pageant in Neiva (Festival Folclórico y Reinado Nacional del Bambuco) – Festivities and Bambuco dancing in conjunction with the Saint Peter and Paul holiday celebrations.

Ibagué Folk Festival (Festival Folclórico de Ibagué) – Held in the "Musical City" of Colombia. Traditional Andean rhythms. www.festivalfolclorico.com.

Joropo International Tournament (Torneo Internacional del Joropo de Villavicencio) – Traditional music of Los Llanos in a five-day tournament.

Wayúu Culture Festival in Uribia (Festival de la Cultura Wayúu) – Three-day festival celebrating the culture of the Wayúu people from the Guajira peninsula.

Yipao Parade and Contest in Calarcá (Desfile y Concurso del Yipao en Calarcá) – The Yipao, or Willy

Bambuco National Folk Festival, Neiva

Proexport Colombia

Jeep, takes center stage at these five-day celebrations in the Coffee Zone.

JULY

Medellín's Colombiamoda (Colombiamoda de Medellín) – The most important fashion trade show in Colombia.

Mono Núñez Festival (Festival del Mono Núñez) – Andean music festival in the town of Ginebra.

Ríosucio Carnival (Carnaval del Diablo en Ríosucio) – This is the longest feast in Colombia, beginning in July and ending in January. It's held on odd-numbered years, with the main celebrations taking place on January 5-10.

Rock in the Park Festival in Bogotá (Festival de Rock al Parque de Bogotá) – Biggest open-air rock festival in Latin America. Dates can vary (the festival has also been held in November).

AUGUST

Bandola de Sevilla Festival (Festival Bandola de Sevilla) – Colombian folk music festival in Valle del Cauca, presenting a mix of rhythms and musical expressions.

Bogotá International Book Fair (Feria Internacional del Libro de Bogotá) – The fair is particularly strong in Hispano-American literature and authors. www.feriadellibro.com.

Medellín Flower Fair (Feria de las Flores de Medellín) – Ten days with more than 140 events from trova singing to a chiva carnival, and a spectacular flower parade that includes orchids. www.feriadelasfloresmedellin. gov.co.

Petronio Álvarez Festival (Festival Petronio Álvarez de Cali) – Largest and most representative celebration of Afro-Colombian folklore from the Pacific coast, held in Cali.

Wind and Kite Festival in Villa de Leyva (Festival del Viento y de las Cometas de Villa de Leyva) – Two-day festival with numerous kite-flying competitions.

SEPTEMBER
Jazz in the Park Festival in Bogotá (Festival de Jazz al Parque de Bogotá) – Open-air jazz festival staged throughout Bogotá's parks, with top performers from Latin America and elsewhere.

Medellín Flower Fair

Proexport Colombia

Manizales Theater Festival (Festival de Teatro de Manizales) – International theater festival in the heart of the Coffee Zone.

San Pacho Feasts in Quibdó (Fiestas de San Pacho en Quibdó) – Saint Francis of Assisi celebrations on the Pacific coast. www.sanpacho.com.

OCTOBER
World Coleo Encounter in Villavicencio (Encuentro Mundial del Coleo en Villavicencio) – Cowboy festivities in Colombia's eastern plains. Traditional food, Joropo music and dancing, and rodeo-type competitions. www.mundialcoleo.com.co/site.

NOVEMBER
Independence of Cartagena and National Beauty Pageant (Independencia de Cartagena y el Reinado Nacional de Belleza) – Parades and festivities during the first two weeks of November.

International Festival of Amazonian Folk Music in Leticia: El Pirarucú de Oro (Festival Internacional de Música Popular Amazonense en Leticia: El Pirarucú de Oro). Three days honoring the music, culture and traditions of the Amazon region.

DECEMBER
Cali Fair (Feria de Cali) – Held immediately after Christmas, the Cali Fair features the best salsa dancing in Colombia, as well as horse-riding parades, orchestras and bullfights. www.feriadecali.com.

Festival of the Lights in Villa de Leyva (Festival de Luces en Villa de Leyva) – Dazzling festival of candles and fireworks on the evenings and nights of December 7-8.

Know Before You Go

USEFUL WEBSITES

www.colombia.travel/en
Colombia's official tourism portal explores tourist destinations and activities through articles, audios, videos, virtual tours and a photo gallery *(in English)*.

www.colombiaespasion.com/en
Colombia's official website. Contains rich information about the country, its culture, people, and a lot more *(in English)*.

www.parquesnacionales.gov.co
An outstanding source of information on Colombia's national parks and reserves, with details on ecosystems, access, permits and services *(in English)*.

www.colombianews.tv
Daily Colombian TV newscast *(in English)*.

http://colombiareports.com
Colombia's news, perspective, sports, culture, entertainment and travel *(in English)*.

www.eltiempo.com
Online version of Colombia's largest daily newspaper *(in Spanish)*.

www.elcolombiano.com
Online version of Medellín's main newspaper *(in Spanish)*.

www.colombiabogota.org
Bogotá news on business, foreign affairs, tourism, entertainment and nightlife *(in English)*.

www.colombiajournal.org
Analysis of Colombian political, social and economic issues *(in English)*.

http://en.equinoxio.org/
Independent Online Digital Magazine bringing together a wide range of points of view on Colombia *(in English)*.

www.nativeplanet.org/ indigenous/ethnicdiversity/ indigenous_data.shtml
Comprehensive database about indigenous communities from around the world, including Colombia, with all kinds of useful links *(in English)*.

Interested in...

... Cartography?
Discover Colombian official maps on the website of the Agustín Codazzi Geographic Institute at **www.igac.gov.co/ingles/ contenidos/home.jsp** *(in Spanish)*.

... the Arts?
You will learn everything there is to know about Colombian periods, styles, artists, collections and events on **http://www.colarte. com/colarte** *(in Spanish)*.

... History and Literature?
The Biblioteca Luis Ángel Arango, one of the finest libraries in Latin America, came up with a fantastic virtual library. Come and visit it at **www.lablaa.org/biblioteca virtual.htm** to have free online access to full-text Colombian books, journals and biographies, but also photographs, video and audio files *(in Spanish)*.

http://institucional.ideam.gov.co/ jsp/index.jsf
Official portal of Colombia's Institute of Hydrology, Meteorology and Environmental Studies (IDEAM). Daily weather forecast and alerts (fires, flooding, eruptions, earthquakes) for major cities and each geographical region of the country *(in Spanish)*.

TOURIST INFORMATION POINTS

Commonly referred to as **PITs,** Colombia's "Puntos de Información Turística" are part of a growing **national network** of tourist information areas with an easily recognizable red **logo** with the letter *i*. Located at strategic spots in some of the country's main tourist destinations, they are attended by **bilingual professionals** (Spanish-English) who will assist you with any inquiry you may have concerning **leisure** and **tourism**. They will provide you with **maps, brochures** and other appropriate **resource materials**.

Gobierno en Línea

The official government portal is a useful tool for finding information about any Colombian city: **www.gobiernoenlinea.gov.co** *(in Spanish)*.

– On the home page, click on **Directorio de Entidades**. In the search window, directly type the name of the Colombian city of your choice *or* click on the *Todos los departamentos* scroll-down menu, choose the appropriate department, then click on the *Todas la ciudades* scroll-down menu, choose your city and hit the *Buscar* button.

– This step brings you to a series of governmental links pertaining to the city you chose. It systematically includes the link to the **Alcadía** (the city's official website). Click on it and you'll find in-depth information about the city, including **maps**, **tourism highlights**, and more *(an English version is available for some major cities such as Bogotá and Medellín)*. Each Colombian municipality, regardless of its size, has a similar website, and all are linked to this main portal.

Here is only a selection of useful PITs across the country. For a complete listing of available PITs or other tourist sources, you may want to visit **www.colombia.travel** or check the official website for your destination:

◆ **Barranquilla**
Ernesto Cortissoz Airport
Arrivals Hall
Mon–Fri 7am–noon and
2pm–5pm, Sat 7am–1pm

◆ **Bogotá**
Palacio Liévano
Corner of Calle 10 and Carrera 8
✆+57 (1) 414 7935
Mon–Sat 8am–4pm, Sun
10am–4pm

◆ **Bucaramanga**
Palonegro Airport - Arrivals Hall,
Mon–Sat 8am–8pm

◆ **Cali**
Cali Cultural Centre
Carrera 5 # 6-05
Mon–Fri 8am–12:30pm and
2pm–5:30pm, Sat 8am–1pm.

◆ **Cartagena**
Plaza de la Aduana, Casa Márquez
de Premio Real # 30-53
✆+57 (5) 660 1583
Mon–Sat 9am–1pm and 3pm–
7pm, Sun 9am–5pm

◆ **Manizales**
Parque Benjamín López
Corner of Carrera 22 and Calle 31
✆+57 (6) 873 3901
Mon–Sun 8am–7pm

◆ **Medellín**
Convention Centre, Plaza Mayor
Calle 41 # 55-80
Mon–Sun 8am–6pm

◆ **Pereira**
Matecaña Airport, Arrivals Hall
Mon–Fri 8am–11am, 1pm–6pm

◆ **Popayán**
Cauca Chamber of Commerce
Carrera 7 # 4-36
✆+57 (2) 824 3625
Mon–Sun 8am–noon and
2pm–6pm

◆ **San Andrés**
Pedestrianized zone
Mon–Fri 10am–1pm and 3pm–
7pm, Sat–Sun 10am–5pm

◆ **Santa Marta**
Simón Bolívar Airport
Arrivals Hall
Mon–Sun 8:30am–7:30pm

◆ **Villa de Leyva**
Plaza Central, Casa de la Alcaldía
✆+57 (8) 370 4597
Mon–Sun 8am–12:30pm, and
2pm–6pm

INTERNATIONAL VISITORS
EMBASSIES AND CONSULATES

Colombian Embassies and Consulates Abroad

- **United Kingdom**
  3 Hans Crescent Flat 3A
  London SW1X
  ℘+44 (0) 20 7589 9177/5037
  www.colombianembassy.co.uk

- **Republic of Ireland**
  Calima Brighton Road
  Foxrock, Dublin 18
  ℘+353 (1) 289 3104

- **United States**
  2118 Leroy Place Northwest
  Washington, DC 20008-1847
  ℘+1 (202) 387 8338
  www.colombiaemb.org

- **Canada**
  360 Albert Street, Suite 1002
  Ottawa, Ontario K1R 7X7,
  ℘+1 (613) 230 3760
  www.embajadaencanada.gov.co

- **Australia**
  Level 2, 161 London CCT,
  CPA Building
  Canberra ACT 2601
  ℘+61 (2) 6230 4203/4206/4209
  www.embajadaenaustralia.gov.co

Foreign Embassies and Consulates in Colombia

- **United Kingdom
  (Embassy and Consulate)**
  Carrera 9 # 76-49, Bogotá
  ℘+57 (1) 326 8300

- **Republic of Ireland
  (Honorary Consulate)**
  De Las Americas # 56-41, Bogotá
  ℘+57 (1) 446 6114

- **United States
  (Embassy and Consulate)**
  Calle 22D Bis # 47-51, Bogotá
  ℘+57 (1) 315 0811 (Embassy)
  ℘+57 (1) 315 2264 (Consulate)

- **Canada (Embassy)**
  Carrera 7 # 115-33, Bogotá
  ℘+57 (1) 657 9800/9951

- **Australia and New Zealand**
  For both countries, Colombian
  affairs are handled by their
  respective embassies in
  Santiago de Chile.

  Australian Embassy
  ℘+56 (2) 550 3500
  consular.santiago@dfat.gov.au

  New Zealand Embassy
  ℘+56 (2) 290 9800
  embajada@nzembassy.cl

ENTRY REQUIREMENTS

- All visitors must present a
  valid passport upon arrival
  in Colombia.
- Visas are not required for a
  maximum stay of **90 days** for
  citizens of most countries in
  Western Europe, including the
  United Kingdom and Ireland, as
  well as the US, Canada, Australia
  and New Zealand.
- You may be asked to show a
  return ticket, as well as **proof
  of funds** to cover your stay.
- Should you wish to stay the full
  90 days, it's best to specify this
  upon entry, as 30- 60- or 90-day
  stays are issued at the point of
  entry. To extend your stay once
  in the country, visit the Office
  of Immigration in Bogotá (Calle
  100 # 11-27).
- An **exit tax** of US$66 is payable in
  cash at the airport upon leaving
  Colombia for any stay longer than
  two months. Insure that you have
  sufficient funds for this tax when
  departing.

CUSTOMS REGULATIONS

- **Duty free** items worth up to a
  maximum of US$1,500 may be
  purchased.
- Bringing **animal** and **vegetable**
  materials into the country is
  restricted.

Travel Advisories

The following sites provide updated travel advice on security risks for worldwide destinations, including Colombia:

- **www.fco.gov.uk/en** issued by the the British Foreign and Commonwealth Office.
- **http://travel.state.gov** issued by the US Dept. of State.
- **www.voyage.gc.ca** issued by the Dept. of Foreign Affairs and Int'l Trade Canada.
- **www.smartraveller.gov.au** issued by the Australian Dept. of Foreign Affairs and Trade.
- **www.safetravel.govt.nz** issued by New Zealand's Ministry of Foreign Affairs and Trade.

The overall security situation in Colombia has drastically improved in recent years. Travelers should still keep in mind that in parts of the country, the situation can change quickly, and that the more remote the area, the greater the potential threat to their safety.

- It is **illegal** to carry **drugs** or **fire arms** into Colombia.
- Travelers who enter the country with more than **US$10,000** or its equivalent in other currencies, including Colombian currency, in cash are required by law to declare it on the **Declaration of Baggage and Currency Form**.

HEALTH

Before departing for Colombia, it is recommended that you have up-to-date inoculations against **polio**, **tetanus** and **diphtheria**, as well as **hepatitis A** and **typhoid**. If traveling to remote areas, consider immunization against **rabies** and **hepatitis B**. In the Amazon there is a risk of **malaria** and **dengue fever**, and anti-malarials are recommended as well as bite prevention measures; also, a **yellow fever** certificate will be required at Leticia airport.

Three of the most frequent **ailments** suffered by visitors to Colombia are:

- **Mountain sickness**: Bogotá is the third highest capital in South America, so make sure to acclimatize yourself to the altitude by taking it easy and drinking plenty of water the first few days after your arrival.

- **Stomach problems**: although drinking water in Colombia is one of the safest in Latin America, contracting traveler's diarrhea from contaminated food or water is possible.

- **Heat exhaustion**: bear in mind that the sun can be strong, on the coast or at high altitudes. High-factor **sun screen** is recommended, as is drinking plenty of water to avoid **dehydration**, particularly in the Amazon region.

INSURANCE

Make sure you have adequate **travel insurance** for the duration of your stay. Be sure to check that your insurance covers all the areas of Colombia that you plan to visit, especially if your government advises against travel to certain zones, as such travel could **invalidate** your travel insurance policy.

If you plan to engage in any **adventure** or **extreme sports** while you are in Colombia, it is best to also check that such activities are covered under your insurance policy.

Getting There and Getting Around

GETTING THERE
BY AIR

Regular Airlines

A number of airlines serve Colombia's international airports, principally **Bogotá** and **Cartagena**, but also **Medellín**, **Cali** and **Barranquilla**. From **Europe**, there are direct flights from Paris with Air France *(www.airfrance.com)* and from Madrid with Avianca *(www.avianca.com)* and Iberia *(www.iberia.com)*. Flights from London go via Europe or the US.

From **North America**, these airlines have direct flights from respective hubs to Colombia: Continental *(www.continental.com)* from Houston, American Airlines *(www.aa.com)* from Dallas-Ft. Worth; Delta *(www.delta.com)* from Atlanta; Spirit Air *(www.spiritair.com)* from Detroit; Air Canada *(www.aircanada.com)* from Toronto. Lan Chile *(www.lan.com)* has connections via Santiago de Chile from **Sydney**, Australia and **Auckland**, New Zealand. Other airlines connecting Colombia with **Latin America** include Avianca *(www.avianca.com)* to/from Buenos Aires, Mexico City, Lima, Panama City, Quito, Santiago de Chile and San José; TACA *(www.taca.com)*; Copa *(www.copaair.com)*; and Aerolineas Argentinas *(www.aerolineas.com.ar)*.

Tours and Packages

◆ **Audley Latin America**
  ☎019 938 8000
  www.audleytravel.com

◆ **Colombia 57**
  ☎0800 078 9157 (toll free from the UK) ☎+57 (6) 886 8050
  www.colombia57.com

◆ **Cox and Kings**
  ☎ +44 (0) 20 7873 5000
  www.coxandkings.co.uk

Bargain Flights

To get the best deal on your international flight to Colombia, or on a domestic flight within Colombia, you may want to check the following websites:

www.justtheflight.co.uk
www.flightstocolombia.com
www.tripsworldwide.co.uk
www.dialaflight.com
www.despegar.com.co
www.vivirvolando.com

◆ **Eco Guías**
  ☎+57 (1) 347 5736 or 212 1423
  www.ecoguias.com

◆ **GAP Adventures**
  ☎0844 410 1030 (from the UK)
  ☎888 800 4100 (US and Canada)
  www.gapadventures.com

◆ **Journey Latin America**
  ☎+44 (0) 20 8747 8315 (London)
  www.journeylatinamerica.co.uk

◆ **Kuoni**
  ☎013 0674 7002
  www.kuoni.co.uk

◆ **Miller South America**
  ☎800 887 5686 (toll free from the US).
  www.miller.travel

◆ **STA Travel**
  ☎087 1230 0040
  www.statravel.co.uk

◆ **Trailfinders**
  ☎0845 058 5858 (worldwide flights, from the UK); ☎0845 054 6060 (tailor-made holidays, from the UK). www.trailfinders.com

◆ **Tucan Travel**
  ☎+44 (0) 20 8896 1600 (enquiries from UK/Europe); ☎+61 (02) 9326 6633 (from Australia, New Zealand, US and Canada).
  www.tucantravel.com

Colombian International Airports

- **Barranquilla – Ernesto Cortissoz Airport**. Located 7km/4mi from the city center. ☎+57 (5) 334 2110 or +57 (5) 334 8202. There are frequent buses to the city center from outside the airport *(traveling time approx. 30min)*. www.baq.aero

- **Bogotá – El Dorado International Airport**. Located 15km/8.3mi from the city center. Two passenger terminals: **El Dorado** ☎+57 (1) 425 1000 and **Puente Aéreo** ☎+57 (1) 425 1000 ext. 3218. Buses leave every 20min for the city center *(traveling time approx. 30min)*. www.bogota-dc. com/trans/aviones.htm and www.elnuevodorado.com

- **Cali – Alfonso Bonilla Aragón Airport**. Located 20km/13mi from the city center. ☎+57 (2) 280 1515. Mini-buses run every 10min to the city center *(traveling time approx. 25min)*. www.aerocali.com.co

- **Cartagena – Rafael Núñez International Airport**. Located only 1.5/km/.8mi from the city center. ☎+57 (5) 656 9200. Buses are available to the city center, but they can be crowded. Taxis are recommended because of the short distance and should not cost more than US$5 *(traveling time approx. 15min)*. www.sacsa.com.co

- **Medellín – Río Negro/José María Córdova International Airport**. Located in Río Negro, 29km/18mi from the city center. ☎+57 (4) 562 2828. Frequent *buseta* service into Medellín center throughout the day *(traveling time approx. 50min)*. www.airplan.aero/airplan.

BY ROAD

There are no roads at all between Colombia and northern neighbor **Panama**, and although it is, in theory, possible to cross on foot between the two countries, this crossing is not recommended due to safety risks in the **Darién Gap**.

There are two possible overland border crossings between **Venezuela** and Colombia at **Cúcuta-San Antonio** and **Maicao-Paraguachón**. International buses connect many main Colombian cities with Venezuela and the border crossing is relatively straightforward. Make sure you obtain an exit stamp from immigration officials in Colombia before attempting to enter Venezuela or you will be sent back and possibly also fined if attempting to re-enter Colombia at a later date.

If traveling independently, there are taxis from Cúcuta to the border and buses or *colectivos* from the Venezuelan side. At Maicao mini-buses and *busetas* also run to the border; the same entry and exit requirements apply.

The **Colombia-Ecuador** overland border crossing is located at **Ipiales-Rumichaca**, where it is possible to cross by bus, car or foot. Get your **exit stamp** from Colombia at the immigration office before entering Ecuador. There are *colectivos* and taxis that run from Ipiales to the border itself, if you are traveling independently.

José María Córdova International Airport, Rionegro

Proexport Colombia

Rescuro boat, Amazon River

© Gunther Michel/Bios/Tips Images

BY SEA AND RIVER

Tumaco in Colombia can be reached by sea from **Ecuador**, but it is necessary to travel to **Ipiales** to obtain your entry stamp upon arrival. Bear in mind that the sea can be rough and your belongings will need to be covered to avoid getting wet.
It is also possible to enter from **Panamá** via the **Carpuganá** route, with boats sometimes making a stop at the scenic San Blas Islands, but check the safety situation first.
Then, a classic entry route is to cross into both **Brazil** and **Peru** from Leticia, in the Amazonia region (*see LETICIA*). Exit stamps from Colombia are given only at the airport, so make sure you obtain one prior to departure, even if departing by boat. If arriving from Peru, make sure you have a Peruvian exit stamp, as well as a yellow fever certificate. All boats to and from Peru stop at Santa Rosa for immigration formalities. For Brazil, obtain exit/entry stamps in Tabatinga at the Policia Federal, near the docks. The **Fast Boat service** from Leticia to **Manaus** (Brazil) takes approx. 36 hours, or there are the slower, more popular **Recreo ships** (cargo and passengers) that stop in all towns and villages en route, taking approximately 4 days downstreavm (Leticia-Manaus) and over 6 days upstream (Manaus-Leticia). Check www.visitleticia.com for details. Boats also leave from Leticia and

Tabatinga for **Iquitos** (Peru) Tue–Sun, taking approx. 12 hours. For further information contact:

♦ **Transtur**
Hotel Cristina
Rua Marechal Mallet # 248
Tabatinga, Brazil
☎+55 (92) 412 3186
http://transturperu.vilabol.uol.com.br/transporte2.htm

GETTING AROUND
BY AIR

Domestic Airlines
Several domestic airlines, including Avianca, Aires, Satena and Aero República operate a fairly extensive network of national flights around the country, and prices have come down in recent years.
If you are pressed for time, flying between centers can be an excellent and safe option, particularly if crossing one of Colombia's three mountain ranges. The journey from Bogotá to Medellín takes some 9-10 hours by bus, but only 30min by plane.
These airlines offer domestic flights:

♦ **Avianca**
☎1 800 284 2622 (from the US and Canada)
☎+57 (1) 4013 434 (Bogotá)
☎+57 (4) 4443 434 (Medellín)
☎+57 (2) 3213 434 (Cali)
☎+57 (5) 3302 255 (Barranquilla)
www.avianca.com

Avianca

* **Aires**
  ☎ 1 888 950 2473 (from the US)
  ☎ (1) 294 0300 (Bogotá)
  ☎ 0 1900 331 9440 (rest of Colombia)
  www.aires.aero

* **Satena**
  ☎ (1) 605 2222 (from Bogotá)
  ☎ 01 8000 331 7100 (rest of Colombia)
  www.satena.com

* **Aero República**
  ☎ +57 (1) 320 9090
  www.aerorepublica.com

* **Aerolineas de Antioquia**
  ☎ 01 8000 514 232
  www.ada-aero.com

Domestic Airports
Some of the airports listed below are also open for international flights, but most are used for domestic purposes only.

* **Leticia – Alfredo Vázquez Cobo Airport.** ☎ +57 (8) 592 7771. Located 1.5km/.9mi. Taxis leave for the town center from outside the terminal. You may be asked to show a valid yellow fever certificate upon arrival, and there is also an obligatory environmental tax to be paid upon arrival.

* **Medellín – Enrique Olaya Herrera Airport**. Carrera 65A # 14-157, Medellín. ☎ +57 (4) 365 6100. Located within the city limits of Medellín, this airport can be reached by metro. www.aeropuertoolayaherrera.gov.co

* **Pereira – Matecaña International Airport.** ☎ +57 (6) 314 2765. Located 5km/3m from the city center. Taxis leave from outside the airport for the center. www.aeromate.gov.co

* **San Andrés – Gustavo Rojas Pinilla Airport** (also known as **Sesquicentenario**). Located a 15min walk from the main town. ☎ +57 (5) 512 0020 and +57 (5) 512 5386. Buses depart across the road and there are also taxis and *colectivos* from outside the airport.

BY BUS

Colombia's **extensive network** of buses covers most parts of the country, with the exception of Amazonia, where boats and planes are the best means of transport. Most buses tend to be **comfortable** and **reasonably priced**, but bear in mind that the distances covered are often great, and the roads can be slow with heavy traffic. In some parts of the country, there may be stops at **military check-points**, and although these are not too intimidating and usually brief, they add to the journey time. The number of times buses are stopped appears to be quite random, solely dependent upon who is in charge of a certain stretch of road.

A Colombian Institution

Also known as *escaleras*, **chivas** are rustic buses with a body made from wood or metal. They have become part of the Colombian folklore. Originally hailing from **Antioquia**, where they still run, they are frequently used in poorer, rural areas. *Chivas* are recognizable by their characteristic ladder at the back for passengers to reach the roof rack, traditionally used for carrying luggage, livestock and even people, if the bus is full. Brightly painted, often in the colors of the Colombian flag, they can be spotted from afar, and it is not unusual for the driver to have a nickname for his bus.

Since they were introduced in Medellín in the early 20C, *chivas* have enjoyed a long and loving relationship with Colombians in many parts of the country. Although these buses are gradually being replaced by faster, more modern ones, they are seemingly here to stay, not just as rural transport, but as party buses or bars-on-wheels in the bigger cities, or even as tour buses.

The majority of **long-distance buses** are equipped with **toilets** and **reclining seats**; they make stops for meals en route, usually for an hour at lunchtime and dinnertime. Do keep an eye on your driver or join his table at meal times to insure that you are not mistakenly left behind when the bus departs again.

Most buses tend to **leave on time**, at least from their starting point.

On long journeys, it is advisable to take **ear plugs** (since many buses often show loud and violent videos), an **eye mask** if you want to get some sleep, a bottle of water and some snacks, although vendors occasionally board buses or sell snacks through the windows.

If you are prone to **altitude sickness** or not acclimatized yet, it is worth keeping some medicine handy if crossing the Andes or arriving from the coast into Bogotá.

Beware that the larger the city, the more likely it is for the **bus station** to be **outside the city center**, and getting there may require an additional bus or taxi journey, as is the case with Bogotá. There are a variety of different bus services, offering various levels of comfort and facilities, as follows:

The **Ejecutivos** and **Servicio de Lujo** usually run long-distance, offering a high level of comfort and service. **Pullmans** and **Silencios** run shorter distances, but also usually offer excellent service.

Corrientes provide more of a local bus service; they stop everywhere and can be quite basic, with prices to match. These buses can usually be flagged down at any point, making them very handy off the beaten track.

APPROXIMATE JOURNEY TIMES BY BUS	
Bogotá–Barranquilla	20hrs
Bogotá–Cali	12hrs
Bogotá–Cartagena	23hrs
Bogotá–Ipiales	19hrs
Bogotá–Medellín	9hrs
Bogotá–Santa Marta	19hrs
Medellín–Cartagena	14hrs

Bus Operators

Their sheer number can seem daunting, but it keeps prices relatively competitive. Some of the better bus companies are included below, but there are numerous others. Most now have websites.

◆ **Berlinas** *(English)*
www.berlinasdelfonce.com/ingles/index.html

◆ **Bolivariano** *(Spanish)*
www.bolivariano.com.co

◆ **Coomotor** *(Spanish)*
www.coomotor.com.co

◆ **Copetran** *(Spanish)*
www.copetran.com.co

◆ **Expreso Brasilia** *(English)*
www.expresobrasilia.com

◆ **Expreso Palmira** *(Spanish)*
www.expresopalmira.com.co

◆ **Flota Magdalena** *(Spanish)*
www.flotamagdalena.com/inicio.html

◆ **Rapido Ochoa** *(Spanish)*
www.rapidoochoa.com

URBAN TRANSPORTATION

Urban Bus

Most Colombian cities and towns have good networks of buses such as **busetas** (often converted US school buses), or smaller **colectivos** (mini-vans or pick-ups). You pay the driver, either when getting on (for buses and *busetas*) or when getting off (for most *colectivos*).

In cities, there are designated **bus stops**, but in rural areas most transport can be hailed anywhere. Flagging down a bus is also usually true for *colectivos* in the cities. The less formal the mode of transport, the more flexible and patient you need to be. Although most tend to have a fixed route, *colectivos* usually leave only when full, but they offer the flexibility of getting on and off wherever you like, by alerting the driver. In **city centers**, *colectivos* are an inexpensive way to get around, but bear in mind that traffic can make such bus travel time consuming. *Colectivos* also operate **from town to town**, and although this option tends to be less economical than regular buses, it may be worth it if you're pressed for time or there are few regular buses in operation between destinations.

Mass Transit Systems

In the last decade or so, Colombia has started investing in more efficient transportation systems for its cities. **Medellín** is so far the only city to have an overground **metro system** that reaches most parts of the city. There are **lines A** and **B**, as well as two cable car lines, the **metro-cable lines J** and **K**, that reach the outlying areas of Santo Domingo Savio and San Javier. A number of other cities have also created their own mass transit systems. **Bogotá** has the TransMilenio, **Cali** has MÍO, **Bucaramanga** the Metrolínea, and **Pereira** the Megabús. There is usually a **set fare** for the rides, and tickets can be purchased in advance. Although rather clean and comfortable, metros can get quite crowded at times, but they are popular options for traveling through busy city centers. As always on public transportation, it's best to keep your wits and your belongings about you.

Useful Websites

◆ **Bogotá's TransMilenio**
(English) www.transmilenio.gov.co/WebSite/English_Default.aspx

◆ **Medellín's Metro and Metrocable** *(English)*
www.medellininfo.com/metro/index.html

◆ **Cali's MÍO** *(Spanish)*
www.metrocali.gov.co

◆ **Bucaramanga's Metrolínea** *(Spanish)*
www.metrolinea.gov.co

◆ **Pereira's Megabús** *(Spanish)*
www.megabus.gov.co

Taxis at Puerta del Reloj, Cartagena de Indias

Mauro A. Fuentes Alvarez/Proexport Colombia

TAXIS

Taxis are usually plentiful and reasonably priced in bigger cities. In all but small villages, they can be found and hailed in the street. For added security, get your **hotel** or **restaurant** to call one for you. Taxis are metered, so insure that the meter is used (and starting at 0) when you get in. Should the taxi not appear to have a meter, make sure you **agree upon the fare** in advance. Also check the **official badge** that should be displayed by every taxi on the dashboard.

If you arrive at Bogotá airport or at the main bus station, there are **taxi booths** where you pay for your trip in advance, and then get a taxi outside, presenting the **slip** stating the destination you've just pre-paid. *Never take a taxi if there is already someone in it other than the driver.* It's possible to **rent a taxi with a driver**, for longer distances or by the hour, for around town to different locations or for sightseeing.

CAR RENTALS

Renting a car in Colombia is relatively easy, provided that you have a valid driver's license from your country of origin. Multinational companies such as **Avis** *(www.avis.com)*, **Hertz** *(www.hertz.com)*, **Budget** *(www.budget.com)*, **National** *(www.nationalcar.com)* and others have offices in the country,

and you will find a variety of **local car rental** services as well.

However, with the high rate of accidents in Colombia, traffic safety is a real issue here. Aggressive **driving conditions** in urban areas can be very **stressful** (Bogotá alone has over one million cars using its roads on a daily basis). The quality of the roads varies widely across Colombia. Winding roads, rural roads and mountain passes, with the occasional livestock crossing, can be quite **intimidating**. For all these reasons, and for other risks for unsuspecting foreigners, the unaccompanied, first-time visitor should think twice before taking the wheel and randomly exploring the backcountry, since **public transportation** options are **safer** and often **cheaper**.

☺ Road Safety ☺

Although road safety in Colombia has dramatically improved since 2002, some areas are still deemed unsafe to travel through. Drivers should keep informed about recent regional news and ask someone about safety for their intended route before making definite plans. Doors should be kept locked at all times; cars should stop only for official military checkpoints, and driving after dark should always be avoided.

Where to Stay and Eat

WHERE TO STAY

As Colombia is gradually moving back into the spotlight as an exciting travel destination, its range of accommodations is significantly improving. Budget accommodations are often readily available, even in small towns, and although mid-range options can still be a bit thin, some pleasant places to stay can be found at very reasonable prices. International hotel chains and upscale luxury hotels tend to be present mainly in the major cities and resorts.

BUDGET ACCOMMODATIONS

Budget lodgings in Colombia come under many names, including *hostales, hosterías, posadas, ospedajes, residenciales, mesónes* and others. Although some places are well maintained, others are perhaps best avoided, as rooms in this category can be quite hit and miss. Prices vary according to standards and facilities offered, but generally speaking, expect to pay no more than **US$30** for **budget** accommodations.

Hostels and **backpacker lodgings** are on the increase, and these accommodations can often be booked online through the Internet. For other low-budget places to stay, the rule of thumb is to just turn up. If booking on the spot, don't be afraid to ask to see the room first, including the bathroom.

Youth hostels, where you can rent your own room or share dormitory style with other travelers, are often privately owned by expats who have settled in Colombia and usually offer good facilities such as free Wi-Fi, free use of the kitchen and other perks, attracting mostly younger travelers. For the latter, it is often possible to pay by credit card, but other smaller, locally-run establishments tend to take cash-only payments.

Pensiones or **residenciales** can be rooms in a private house, rented out to guests, rather like old-fashioned bed and breakfast accommodations in the US or UK. More often than not, they are cozy, friendly and may include a home-cooked meal. For such arrangements, a smattering of Spanish definitely comes in handy. There are also actual home stays available, particularly appropriate if you are trying to get a better grasp of the Spanish language.

Finally, budget accommodations that should be avoided are the so-called **acostaderos**, where Colombians, who either still live at home or don't want those at home to know, rent rooms by the hour.

- For information about **youth hostels** in Colombia, access www.hihostels.com/dba/country-CO.en.htm?hymap=Y and/or www.alberguesdejuventud.com/Colombia.htm

- For information about **Colombian hostels**, visit www.hostelworld.com/countries/colombiahostels.htm and/or www.colombianhostels.com

Useful Websites

- Check **www.colombia.travel/es/directorios** to get an idea of the types of accommodations available throughout the country.

- Browse through **www.cotelco.org/?q=afiliados/search** for a listing of the members of the Colombian Hotel Association (COTELCO). This listing is classified by region and city, and includes links to member hotels' websites (if any), addresses and phone numbers. A convenient central reservation service for these hotels is also available at: **www.reservashoteleras.com.co.**

MID-RANGE HOTELS

This category is one in which accommodations in Colombia tend to fall somewhat short, but the situation is starting to change as more options are opening up, particularly in the main cities and other areas of interest to visitors. Many of the names for budget accommodations (*hostales, hosterías, posadas*) could, perhaps somewhat confusingly, also apply to the mid-range category, so it is best to check the price (expect to pay no more than **US$65** for **mid-range** hotels) or ask to see a room, to get an idea of what to expect.

Although some of the mid-range options can be rather soulless and bland, they are often located in **town centers**, within easy reach of sights, shops, restaurants and bars. Some also have their own **restaurants** of varying quality, and **breakfast** is usually included in the rate. Most mid-range hotels offer at least a **private bathroom** with a toilet and shower, as well as **air-conditioning** in the rooms. Standards vary widely, but some excellent bargains can be found. It is usually possible to pay by credit card, and many mid-range hotels can be booked online directly with the hotel in question.

♦ For possible options, check
www.hotelstravel.com/
colombia.html

HIGH-END ACCOMMODATIONS

There are now excellent luxury accommodations in Colombia, offering all the amenities and facilities to be expected, including room service, Internet and business facilities, restaurants, bars, laundry service, safety deposit box and cable TV.

Most of these hotels can be found in the nicer areas of larger centers, such as **El Poblado** in Medellín and **Zona T** in Bogotá. While some are part of **international hotel chains**, there are also more individual and inspiring options, such as recently restored colonial buildings, particularly in

Cartagena. Several smaller, more intimate **boutique hotels** have opened up in both Cartagena and Bogotá. For **upscale** hotels, expect to pay up to **US$200**.

♦ For **boutique hotels**, check
www.colombia.travel/es/
directorios/Hoteles-Boutique
♦ For **luxury hotel options**, visit
www.luxurylatinamerica.com/
lux_colombia.html

RURAL TOURISM

Many of Colombia's coffee farms, or **fincas**, have been branching out into tourism in recent years. Nowadays it is not only possible to take a tour of a *finca* and sample the coffee, but also to stay there for one or more nights. Some *fincas* have been converted into cozy, first-class hotels, while others are still working coffee farms with a more rustic, authentic feel. It is possible to combine a *finca* stay with activities such as horseback riding or hiking in the Coffee Zone, or lending a hand on the coffee farm itself to get some real insight into the production of coffee.

♦ For information on **fincas**, visit
www.travelcolombia.org.
www.clubhaciendasdelcafe.com
www.paisatours.com/coffee_
country.htm
♦ For an overview of what the
country has to offer in terms of
rural accommodations, go

Posadas Turísticas

This government-sponsored program is aimed at creating a **tourism infrastructure** in regions of great natural beauty, with minimal impact on the environment. Do not expect five star hotels or shopping malls there. Lodgings are designed for travelers preferring authenticity over comfort, and willing to learn about the local culture while putting up with **basic amenities**. For more details, access www. posadasturisticasdecolombia.com

Quick Eats

Colombian snacks are usually fried and made of dough. Burgers and other fast food have yet to reach the popularity of local favorites such as **arepas** (flat cornbread, either plain or with many different fillings), **tamales** (steamed maize dough with meat fillings, wrapped either in corn husks or banana leaves), **empanadas** (oven-baked pastries with meat and/or vegetable fillings) or **pizza spreads** (allowing many toppings such as cheese, onions and mushrooms). Instead of looking for french fries, try **patacones**, their local savory substitute: fried, mashed green plantain (with or without topping).

online to www.colombia.travel/es/directorios/Alojamientos-Rurales

ECOTOURISM

With the rise in ecotourism in Colombia, top-end options are opening up, such as **jungle lodges** (*see p270*) and **ecolodges**.

♦ **www.ecotrotters.com**
is a community site dedicated to ecotourism worldwide.
It offers a listing of what to expect in terms of accommodations, and includes some information on **Colombian ecolodges** such as El Almejal (www.almejal.com.co) and Morromico (www.morromico.com), on the Pacific Coast.

♦ To know which Colombian national parks offer **ecolodge options**, you may want to visit www.parquesnacionales.gov.co (*look for the "Eco-tourism" section*).

WHERE TO EAT
COLOMBIAN CUISINE

Portions in Colombia tend to be **substantial**, and despite the abundance of gorgeous, unusual and colorful **fruits** and **vegetables**, there is a firm emphasis on **meat** in this country. **Rice** and **beans** accompany most main meals, along with **cornbread.**

The quality of **beef** is almost on the level with Argentina and Chile, so it is a bit surprising that **pork** reigns supreme, particularly in Antioquia, known as the Paisa region. It is here that you can savor La Bandeja Paisa, a vegetarian's worst nightmare (*see Menu Reader opposite*).

Blessed with two coastlines (Pacific and Caribbean) and plenty of rivers, Colombia boasts **fish** and **seafood** that tend to be excellent and fresh. Warming **stews** and soupy **broths** are popular in the Andean region and at higher altitude (Bogotá, for instance). In recent years, Colombia has seen somewhat of a culinary revolution, with a number of top chefs turning the home-grown **comida criolla** into unusual and tasty dishes, made from little-known local produce. The foodie event of the year is the **Otro Sabor Festival**, held in Medellín's botanical Garden, and Medellín is fast becoming the center for gastronomy in Colombia.

Be aware that it is not usual to have alcohol during the meal, and that the legal drinking age is 18. If you would like to have **wine** with your meal when eating out, bear in mind that all wines are **imported**, usually from **Chile** or **Argentina**, and prices can therefore be fairly high.

Instead, there are plenty of excellent local drink options, with or without alcohol. **Fruit juices**, **smoothies** or fruit **milkshakes** are widely available and usually delicious. Fresh blackberry, mangosteen or tree tomato are just some of the great number of fresh juices available. Colombia also has several excellent **rums**, as well as the potent **aguardiente**, made from sugarcane. It goes without saying that **coffee** is a national beverage in Colombia. If your plans permit, try to visit a coffee plantation where sampling is part of a tour. Or better yet, stay overnight in a *finca* in the Coffee Zone and see the production process firsthand.

RESTAURANTS

The major cities have a wide selection of restaurants to choose from in areas such as **El Poblado** in Medellín and **Zona Rosa** (or Zona T) in Bogotá. These dining spots offer not just Colombian fare *(comida criolla)*, but international dishes, with many cuisines represented, including Italian and Chinese, Peruvian and Mexican. Away from areas of interest to visitors, varied dishes can be harder to come by. Simple restaurants featuring local produce are usually the order of the day, but the meals are often home-cooked, inexpensive and tasty. Expect to pay less than **US$6** for a meal in a **budget** restaurant, up to **US$12** in a **mid-range** restaurant, and **more than US$12** in an **upscale** establishment.

😊 Tipping 😊

In restaurants, a **voluntary charge** is added to most patrons' bills. In smaller, inexpensive establishments, tipping is not always expected, but is much appreciated. In more upscale restaurants, tipping **10 percent to 15 percent** of the bill is expected.

Sobrebarriga—flank steak

Jorge Gamboa/Proexport Colombia

MENU READER

Dish	Ingredients
Ajiaco	Cundinamarca's chicken soup with three types of potato.
Arroz con coco	Rice boiled in coconut milk is a particularly popular dish along the Colombian coast, where it's often served with fish or seafood.
Bandeja Paisa	The Paisa dish from Antioquia, containing as much pork as you can eat, along with rice, beans, fried egg and other ingredients.
Charapa	Stewed tortoise meat from the Amazon region.
Cuy	Guinea pig, a traditional dish from the Andean region of southern Colombia.
Hormiga culona	Fat-bottomed fried ants from Santander in the north.
Lechona	Suckling pig stuffed with rice and peas, cooked in a clay oven.
Mazamorra	Cooked corn mixed with milk and water is a staple from Cundinamarca.
Posta cartagenera	A roasted meat dish hailing from Cartagena, with beef or veal. It's slow-cooked with onions, tomatoes, peppers, garlic, flour and wine, among other ingredients.
Puchero	A soup-with-stew from Cundinamarca, made with a variety of meats, manioc, plantain, boiled egg and hot sauce.
Sancocho	A soup of meat, manioc, yam and banana popular on both the Caribbean and the Pacific coasts, with regional variations.

Useful Words and Phrases

Basic Conversation

Hello/Goodbye/See you later
Hola/Adiós/Hasta Luego
How are you?/I'm fine
¿Cómo está?/ Muy bien
Please/Thank you/You're welcome
Por favor/Gracias/De nada
Nice to meet you/Likewise
Mucho gusto/El gusto es mío
Pardon me/Forgive me
Perdón/Disculpe
My name is … What's your name?
Me llamo… ¿Cómo se llama?
I don't understand
No entiendo

Orienting yourself

Right/left/ straight
A la derecha/a la izquierda/ derecho
In front/behind
En frente/atrás
I want to go to… Where is it?
Quiero ir a… ¿Dónde está/queda?
Is it near? Is it far?
¿Está cerca? ¿Está lejos?
I am lost. Can you help?
Estoy perdido/a. ¿Me puede ayudar?

TRANSPORTATION

Airport/train station/bus station
Aeropuerto/estación de trenes/ terminal de autobuses
Subway/tram/bus/boat/taxi
Metro/tranvía/autobús/barco/taxi
I need to go to…
Necesito ir a…
One-way/round trip ticket
Viaje ida/viaje ida y vuelta
At what time does the bus for… leave?
¿A qué horas sale el autobús a…?
How long does it take?
¿Cuánto tiempo dura?
Is this the bus for…?
¿Este es el autobús a…?
Where do I need to get off?
¿En qué parada tengo que bajar?

At the hotel

I would like to reserve a room
Me gustaría reservar una habitación
Single room/double/twin
Sencilla/doble/con dos camas
Room with a bathroom
Una habitación con baño
What does it cost per night?
¿Cuánto es por noche?
I will stay for … night(s)
Me quedaré … noches
I will be leaving tomorrow/the day after/on Monday…
Saldré mañana/el día siguiente/ el lunes…
Key/passport/reception desk
Llave/pasaporte/recepción

At The Restaurant

Breakfast/lunch/dinner
Desayuno/almuerzo/cena
I would like this dish, please.
Me gustaría este plato, por favor
Fork/knife/spoon
Tenedor/cuchillo/cuchara
Glass/plate/napkin
Vaso/plato/servieta
Water/sparkling water/wine
Agua/agua con gas/vino
Salt/pepper/butter
Sal/pimiento/mantequilla
Meat/vegetables/salad/fruits
Carne/verduras/ensalada/frutas
Cheese/dessert/coffee
Queso/postre/café
May I have the check please?
¿Me da la cuenta, por favor?

Money and Purchases

Bank/ATM
Banco/cajero automático
Could I change some money ?
¿Podría cambiar dinero?
How much is it?
¿Cuánto es?
Cheap/expensive
Barato/caro
Do you accept credit cards?
¿Aceptan tarjetas de crédito?
May I try this on?
¿Lo puedo probar?

Basic Information

BUSINESS HOURS

Banking hours vary, but are usually Monday–Friday 8am–11:30am or noon, and 2pm–4:30pm.

In bigger cities, many banks stay open during lunchtime. Foreign exchange *(casas de cambio)* may stay open until 6pm or later. Airmail **post offices** stay open Monday–Friday 7:30am–6pm, and 8am–noon on Saturdays. **Shopping hours** in Colombia are generally 9am–8pm Monday–Saturday, but in larger cities such as Bogotá, shops stay open later in the evenings. **Museum** opening times vary, but most museums are open Tuesday–Sunday, and closed Mondays.

DRINKING WATER

Drinking water from the **tap** is reasonably **safe** in Colombia, with only a few regional exceptions: San Andrés, Providencia, Guajira Peninsula and the Amazon. The Colombian mineral water **Agua Manantial** is very tasty, inexpensive and widely available for those not wanting to risk the tap water. If traveling to the Amazon, take water **purification tablets** with you.

ELECTRICITY

Most sockets accept both European and North American 2-pin plugs (round or flat). Depending on your country of residence, you may need an international **adapter/converter** to meet Colombian specifications of **110 volts AC**, 60 cycles per seconds.

EMERGENCY NUMBERS
(from a fixed line or a mobile phone)
Emergencies: ☎123 or 112
Police: ☎156
Fire Brigade: ☎119
Ambulances: ☎132

MAIL/POST

Adpostal and **4-72** are the main national postal services, both run by the government. There are also private national and international **courier services** operating in Colombia, such as **Deprisa**, **Servientrega, FedEx** and **DHL**, offering faster delivery, but at a higher cost.

STANDARD COST OF POSTAGE For letters and postcards		
Destination	**Weight**	**Price**
Within Colombia	Up to 500g	3,900 COP
North and South America	Up to 20g	4,800 COP
Rest of the world	Up to 20g	5,300 COP

MONEY
CURRENCY

The Colombian currency is the **peso**, abbreviated as **COP**. **Banknotes** circulate in the following denominations: 50,000, 20,000, 10,000, 5,000, 2,000 and 1,000 pesos, as well as the following **coins**: 500, 200, 100 and 50 pesos. Beware that larger bills can be difficult to use outside major centers, and change is sometimes in short supply. Smaller denomination Colombian bills or coins, as well as smaller US dollar bills are handy to have with you.

FOREIGN EXCHANGE

At the time of writing, these were the exchange rates for the UK, US, Canada, Australia and New Zealand currencies:

GBP 1 = 3,005 COP
USD 1 = 1,905 COP
CAD 1 = 1,885 COP
AUD 1 = 1,877 COP
NZD 1 = 1,428 COP

Prior to departure, you may want to check an online **currency converter** such as www.xe.com or www.exchange-rates.org/converter.aspx for an update on these rates, which fluctuate.

PUBLIC HOLIDAYS	
Jan 1	Año Nuevo (New Year's Day)
Jan 6	Día de los Reyes Magos (Epiphany)
Mar 19	Día de San José (Saint Joseph's Day)
Thurs and Fri before Easter Sun	Jueves Santo (Maundy Thurs) and Viernes Santo (Good Fri)
May 1	Primero de Mayo (Labour Day)
6 wks and a day after Easter Sun	Ascensión (Ascension of Jesus)
9 wks and a day after Easter Sun	Corpus Christi
10 wks and 1 day after Easter Sun	Sagrado Corazón (Sacred Heart)
Jul 3	San Pedro y San Pablo (Saint Peter and Saint Paul)
Jul 20	Independence Day
Aug 7	Battle of Boyacá
Aug. 15	La Asunción (Assumption of Mary)
Oct. 12	Día de la Raza (Columbus Day)
Nov. 1	All Saints' Day
Nov. 11	Independence of Cartagena
Dec 8	La Inmaculada Concepción (Immaculate Conception)
Dec 25	Navidad (Christmas Day)

CASH VERSUS CREDIT CARDS

When traveling around Colombia with cash or credit cards, in most towns of any size, changing money or finding an ATM will not be a problem. It is best, though, not to carry around large amounts of cash or higher denomination bills. US$ bills in smaller denominations always come in handy. Credit cards are also widely used and accepted, **VISA** and **MasterCard,** in particular.
Diners Club cards are accepted in some places, but American Express can be difficult to use.

There are plenty of **ATMs** for withdrawing cash in all main cities, making it easier not to carry around much cash with you.
ATMs in Colombia work slightly differently from those in Europe, and do not retain your card during the withdrawal. As in the US, you simply **swipe** your card and **remove** it, then enter your **pin** and the amount you wish to withdraw. If your card is retained during the transaction, do not enter your pin.
Make sure you alert your bank before you travel to Colombia, so it is aware of any card transactions while you are there. To report credit card loss or theft: VISA ✆0800 891725 or MasterCard ✆0800 964767.

TRAVELER'S CHECKS

It is becoming increasingly **difficult** to exchange traveler's checks in Colombia, and although possible in the main banks of larger cities or *casas de cambio*, the process can be very slow and even involve fingerprinting. You need to bring your **passport** and a **copy** of it. Proof of purchase of the checks may also be requested on occasion.
If using traveler's checks, **US dollar** checks are the best option. Sterling checks are almost impossible to change anywhere. Also note that hotels rarely change traveler's checks, and that the checks cannot be used as payment.

SMOKING

Colombia extended its existing tobacco control regulations in 2009, which now require all **indoor workplaces** and **public places** to be **smoke-free**, and prohibit tobacco advertising, promotions and sponsorship, and the use of terms such as "light" and "mild" on packaging. Packaging also requires large, pictorial health warnings.
The sale of tobacco products to **minors** is **prohibited**. Cigarettes or tobacco may be dispensed to persons only age 15 and older.

TELEPHONE
USING A FIXED LINE

Most towns have small **telephone shops** with *larga distancia* (long distance) signs, where you are assigned a booth and you either dial the number yourself or the receptionist dials it for you.

The cost of the call is displayed while the telephone is in use. These shops may be used for **local**, **national** or **international** calls.

There are also plenty of **phone booths** in the streets, as mobile phones are not as common as in Europe or North America. Some of these booths operate with **pre-paid cards**, but it is also handy to have **coins** of up to 500 pesos for calls.

USING A MOBILE PHONE

A popular option for travelers is the use of a Colombian mobile phone. Many local people simply rent out their own phone for you to make quick calls. You agree on the fee beforehand, and they dial the number for you. These entrepreneurial Colombians can be seen all around towns or along the road with little **rent-a-mobile** signs. It is an inexpensive and easy way to make calls, but a grasp of some Spanish comes in handy for these transactions. If planning to make many calls from a mobile, you may consider investing in a Colombian **SIM-card** or a **Colombian mobile**. A decent mobile with phone card costs on average about US$50 to purchase. Network coverage is usually good, except in mountainous areas or off the beaten track, of course.

MAKING A CALL

Directory Assistance: 113.
Making calls in Colombia, whether nationally or internationally, may seem somewhat complicated since the number you dial will depend on which operator you are using: the national provider, called **Telefónica Telecom** (9) or competing services **ETB** (7) or **Une-EPM** (5).

Colombia Mobile Info

The Colombian Tourist Board recently came up with an ingenious system that allows you to **download** all kinds of useful information about the country directly onto your **mobile phone**, either from a **computer** or from the **Internet**, if already available on your phone. If you do have a mobile Internet connection, you may proceed with the downloading by logging onto **http://m.colombia.travel**.

Country Codes

Colombia	📞 **57**
United Kingdom	📞 **44**
US and Canada	📞 **1**
Australia	📞 **61**
New Zealand	📞 **64**

From Land Line to Land Line

- **International call** : 00 + (9) or (7) or (5) + country code *(see above)* + area code + local number.
- **National call**: 0 + (9) or (7) or (5) + 1 or 2-digit Colombian city code + 7-digit local number.
- **Local call:** 7-digit local number only.

Making a call from or to a **mobile phone** is more complicated and will require initial assistance with prefixes.

TIME

Greenwich Mean Time minus 5hrs all year round throughout the country. Colombia uses a 12-hour clock am/pm format, example: 4pm is 16pm.

WHEN IT IS NOON IN BOGOTÁ, IT IS	
9am	in Los Angeles
11am	in Chicago
1pm	in New York
5pm	in London
1am+1	in Perth
4am+1	in Sydney
6am+1	in Auckland

Hacienda Guayabal, Chinchiná, Caldas
© Jane Sweeney/AWL Images

Colombia Today

Colombia is the third-largest country in Latin America after Brazil and Mexico. As the oldest democracy in South America, the nation has maintained a remarkably stable governance of its widely varied population and industrially diverse economy. In spite of major internal challenges, the Colombian people are fiercely committed to continued stability and prosperity.

POPULATION

With a total **population** of 45,483,650 (DANE's mid-2010 estimate), Colombia has a relatively moderate population **density** of 40 people per sq km or 120 per sq mi, spread over **four** regional **conurbations**, with a **major city** at its core. Principal centers are located in the Magdalena and Cauca river valleys and along the Caribbean coast. With a population of 6,778,691, the nation's capital, **Bogotá,** forms the heart of central Colombia. The hub of northwest Colombia is **Medellín**, the nation's "Second City," with a population of 2,219,861. Just slightly smaller is **Cali** in the southwest at 2,075,380. **Barranquilla**

DANE 2005 Census Report

Unless otherwise indicated, population figures used in this guide are based on the 2005 census carried out by **DANE,** the entity responsible for the planning, collection, processing, analysis and dissemination of Colombia's official statistics. See www.dane.gov.co/reloj/reloj_animado.php for its continually updated **population clock** *(reloj de población)*.

(Pop. 1,112,889) forms the nucleus of the Caribbean coastal region, seconded by the historical town of **Cartagena** at 895,400.

While Colombia's **eastern lowland** region composes half the country's landmass, it contains less than **3 percent** of its population.

THE URBAN FACTOR

Colombia's population is largely concentrated in its cities; almost 80 percent of its people reside in **urban areas**. Urban migration is due to lack of security, especially in rural areas, the center of paramilitary and guerrilla activity. In the past five decades, large numbers of pastoral communities have been displaced by conflict, prompting millions to flee to

Capitolio Nacional, Bogotá

Proexport Colombia

Ethnic Diversity

Colombia's ethnic mix draws from its border countries (Panama, Venezuela, Ecuador, Brazil and Peru), though most of its citizens hail from three main groups: its indigenous peoples and those of Spanish and African descent. This **multiculturalism** mirrors Colombia's colorful history, and today more than 58 percent of its population claims *mestizo* heritage (mixed **white and indigenous**). Though they retain power and clout, **whites** represent just 20 percent of the population. Some 14 percent are mixed **white and black**, 4 percent **black** and 3 percent mixed **black and indigenous**. Colombia's **indigenous groups** account for just 1 percent of the population. On the **Pacific Coast**, the black population dominates the Chocó region; in **Paisa country** (Antioquia), strong Basque roots remain. **La Guajira**, in the north is home to one of the largest indigenous populations (Wayúu) and to one of Colombia's biggest concentrations of Middle Eastern émigrés. **Immigration** began after WWI and the Cold War with a small, but influential stream of Italian, German, French, Swiss, British, Belgian, Dutch, Polish, Lithuanian, Asian and Croatian arrivals. Today immigration is largely from the Caribbean, the Middle East and Turkey.

Colombia's cities. As a result, the country has seen enormous societal change.

LANGUAGE

While **Spanish** is the **official language** of Colombia, the 80-plus indigenous languages and dialects of other ethnic groups are recognized under Article 10 of the Colombian Constitution, citing them as official in their territories and providing **bilingual education**.

COLOMBIAN SPANISH

Latin American Spanish is heavily peppered with American influences and mixed with Spain's formal European style. Colombia is no exception. This mixture is particularly apparent in greetings, taking the form of a lengthy elaborate exchange of pleasantries. Colombian slang is more colorful than its festivals and wholly different from other Latin American nations. To talk like a local, visitors should attempt to master a few of the hundreds of unique *Colombianismos*, words and phrases that liven up daily dialogue.

INDIGENOUS LANGUAGES

Belonging to over 20 linguistic families, the indigenous languages mainly derive from the **Chibchan**, **Arawakan**, **Carib** and **Quechuan** groups. Containing many more speech sounds than are found in European languages, these indigenous languages are almost impossible to write using a standard alphabet. As a result, few exist in any written form. For example, the Yuwe language has 37 consonants and 20 vowels (5 sets of 4: oral, nasal, glottalized, aspirated, and long), compared to the 20 consonants and 5 vowels of standard Spanish.

REGIONAL DIALECTS

As the second language, English is widely spoken by the educated classes, but is a scarcity away from Colombia's main cities. Therefore, visitors keen to explore the country should invest in learning a few carefully chosen Spanish phrases —the exception being those heading to the island of Providencia where an English patois is the primary language.

Generally, Colombians speak a clear, pure Spanish that is easy to understand. But across Colombia, there are 11 main dialects which, in turn, contain hundreds of unique words and phrases.

The **Pacific coastal dialect** is laced with a heavy drawl, while people from **Cundinamarca** and **Boyacá** are distinctive as they use the second-person pronoun *sumercé*.

Though it is hard to define, the **Paisa accent** common to the departments of Antioquia, Quindío, Risaralda and Caldas has a rhythmic, provincial quality and sing-songy charm.

Cuervo's Dictionary

Few linguistic works have had greater impact on the Spanish-speaking world as the *Diccionario de Construccion y Regimen de la Lengua Castellana* (Dictionary of Castilian language construction and regimen). Considered a South American Heritage since the early 2OC, it was created by **Rufino José Cuervo** (1844-1911), an illustrious Bogotá-born writer, grammarian, linguist and philologist who dedicated his life to the study of dialectal versions of Spanish in his homeland and promoted the unification of the different variants in the Spanish language. Today Cuervo's dictionary is maintained by scholars of the prestigious **Instituto Caro y Cuervo** in Bogotá as an ongoing project.

Costeños (those from the Caribbean coast) speak with a machine-gun directness and words mashed together, similar to Cuban Spanish. Spoken in the southwestern part of the country, the **Pastuso** (or Andean dialect) reveals some Quechuan influences. The people from **Popayán** speak with some southern influence too.

With a notable African linguistic style, the **Chocó dialect** on the Pacific Coast is highly distinctive. **Rolo,** considered the purest form of Spanish, is spoken by people in Bogotá with clear, chant-like diction, in sharp contrast to the **Criollo sanandresano** heard on San Andrés, Providencia and Santa Catalina—a sluggish linguistic lilt derived from English, Spanish and African languages.

GOVERNMENT

As Latin America's oldest and most stable official **democracy**, Colombia upholds a deep respect for political and civil rights—despite its checkered history. Few countries can claim a political arena as intriguing, contentious or dramatic as that of Colombia.

Led by an electorally elected presidential representative with a four-year ten-ure, Colombia is run in accordance with the **Constitution of 1991**, with fair and regulated voting (every citizen over the age of 18 having the right to vote). Apart from military intervention in 1830, 1854 and 1953, Colombia has enjoyed virtually uninterrupted constitutional and institutional stability, with only limited influence from the armed forces.

BASIC PRINCIPLES

The Colombian government consists of three branches, the **executive,** the **legislative** and the **judicial,** with the latter divided into a House of Representatives and a Senate. A strict **separation of powers** exists among the branches, as the legality of both executive and legislative measures may well be challenged by the Constitutional Court. Around 20 recognized political **parties** (plus a number of unofficial ones) make up Colombia's political landscape, although the main players are the Colombian Conservative Party (PC), Alternative Democratic Role (PDA), Liberal Party (PL), Radical Change (CR) and Social National Unity Party (U Party).

EXECUTIVE BRANCH

Headed by a president, the Executive branch comprises various government ministries, administrative departments and hundreds of semi-autonomous bodies.

Presidency of the Republic

Elected by popular vote for a four-year term, the Colombian president is supported in the function by a **vice-president**. The president is both the **head of state** and the **head of government** of the Republic of Colombia, overseeing a multi-party **representative democracy**. The president has the power to elect the members of the **Council of Ministers** who actually form a cabinet of advisors. The president is also responsible for appointing leaders to head the many administrative agencies under his control, without the approval of Congress.

In 2005 the four-year presidential tenure was amended in the Constitution by the

Colombian Congress, allowing future presidents to serve up to two consecutive four-year mandates.

Regional Affairs

The Republic of Colombia is made of a **capital district** (Bogotá) and 32 administrative divisions or **departments** (👆*see map p54),* each formed by a grouping of **municipalities** and enjoying a certain degree of autonomy. Only elected for a three-year term, and not immediately re-electable, department **governors, mayors** of cities and towns and other executive branch **officials** manage regional affairs. At the provincial level, executive power is also vested in local administrators for smaller administrative subdivisions, such as *corregidores* for **corregimiento**s (usually a remote rural settlement with a tiny population).

LEGISLATIVE BRANCH

Like the US, Colombia has a bicameral **Congress** *(Congreso de la República de Colombia)* that comprises a House of Representatives and a Senate. Congress convenes twice a year, unless the president summons a special session.

The **House of Representatives** *(Cámara de Representantes)* is made up of 166 seats. The **Senate** *(Senado)* totals 102 seats. Members of Congress serve four-year terms, and may be reelected indefinitely. Senators are elected on the basis of a **national ballot,** while representatives are elected by their **local constituents**. At a provincial level, the legislative branch is represented by **municipal councils** and **departmental bodies**, appointed 17 months after the presidential election.

JUDICIAL BRANCH

Colombia's legal system has its foundations in Spain. In the 1990s Colombian law underwent significant reforms that saw it move from an inquisitorial to an adversarial system. A new US-style criminal code modeled on American law was introduced in 2004.

The Colombian judicial system is divided into **four coequal organs** with powers

that extend to the review of legislative and executive acts.

Two **high courts** serve separate functions, judges for both serving an 8-year term. The first one, the **Supreme Court** (the highest legal court), consists of 23 judges appointed by the Legislature, and is divided into a Civil-agrarian chamber, a Labor chamber and a Penal chamber. The second one, the **Constitutional Court**, whose members are appointed by Congress from nominations made by the president and other high-ranking tribunals, interprets the Constitution and monitors observance of laws. It is responsible for amendments to the Constitution and international treaties.

The **Council of State** is the highest administrative law court; its judges are also chosen by the Superior Judicial Council and serve an 8-year term.

The **Superior Judicial Council** itself controls the civilian judiciary and resolves inter-court jurisdictional conflicts. Members are selected from among the three other courts and Congress and serve 8-year terms.

República de Colombia

Flag: Three horizontal bands of yellow (top, double-width), blue, and red.

The **yellow** represents the richness of Colombian gold.

The **blue** depicts the Pacific Ocean and Caribbean Sea.

The **red** represents the lives lost during the fight for independence and also represents the blood of Jesus, reflecting Colombia's Christian roots.

Coat of Arms: *Libertad y Orden* (Freedom and Order).

National Anthem: *¡Oh Gloria Inmarcesible!* (O Unfading Glory!).

ADMINISTRATIVE DIVISIONS
(DEPARTMENTS)

1	Amazonas	12	Chocó	23	Putumayo
2	Antioquia	13	Córdoba	24	Quindío
3	Arauca	14	Cundinamarca	25	Risaralda
4	Atlántico	15	Guainía	26	San Andrés & Providencia
5	Bolívar	16	Guaviare	27	Santander
6	Boyacá	17	Huila	28	Sucre
7	Caldas	18	La Guajira	29	Tolima
8	Caquetá	19	Magdalena	30	Valle del Cauca
9	Casanare	20	Meta	31	Vaupés
10	Cauca	21	Nariño	32	Vichada
11	Cesar	22	Norte de Santander	33	Bogotá, Distrito Capital

ECONOMY

As the most industrially diverse member of the five-nation Andean Community, Colombia has made major strides in expanding international trade. Former president Álvaro Uribe's pro-market policies and free-trade zones have bolstered one of the highest rates of growth in Latin America.

Today, shipments of Colombian coffee, textiles, coal, nickel, emeralds, **cotton, cut flowers, sugarcane, livestock, rice, corn, tobacco** and bananas are made daily to destinations worldwide.

However, after the accelerated growth of 2002-2007, which was powered by global confidence engendered as a result of Colombia's improved domestic security and rising commodity prices, economic growth slipped as the world's economic crisis took hold. Yet the economy managed to report growth at a respectable .4 percent in 2009.

Issues such as unemployment and narco-trafficking, and the overall infrastructure's need of updating remain significant challenges in this country that seeks further economic expansion.

AGRICULTURE

Since colonial times agriculture has been an important part of the Colombian economy, and although it has given way to secondary and tertiary sectors, it represents about 9 percent of GDP, providing a significant source of export revenue. Approximately a quarter of the work force is engaged in agriculture, and while the sector hasn't expanded significantly, it remains the foundation of the economy. A diverse range of **crops** thrive in Colombia's varied climatic zones, and improved farming methods reap impressive yields of wheat, maize, barley and potatoes together with **cattle** and **poultry**. Cacao, sugarcane, coconuts, bananas, plantains, rice, cotton, tobacco, cassava and most of the nation's beef cattle are produced at lower elevations with coffee, vegetables flowers and fruit in more temperate zones. **Timber** is harvested across the country, from eucalyptus and pine in highland areas to lowland tropical hardwoods.

Harvesting Colombian coffee beans

Proexport Colombia

Colombian Coffee

The Federación Nacional de Cafeteros de Colombia (Fedcafé) is the largest, most powerful Colombian agricultural organization, representing over 500,000 producers, mostly small, family-owned farms. As the world's second-largest producer of coffee, Colombia is responsible for approximately 10 percent of all the coffee produced on the planet. The Coffee Zone (Zona Cafetera), centered in three principal coffee-growing regions (Quindío, Caldas and Risaralda), provides more than half the country's 66 million-ton production, in a region that makes up 1 percent of the country's total landmass.

INDUSTRY

Colombia's industrial sector accounts for roughly 38 percent of GDP and 19 percent of the country's labor-force, though production across the board fell 5.9 percent in 2009 as a result of the global economic downturn, while employment in industrial production dropped by 6.3 percent. However, the situation is expected to reverse once the world global economy has fully recovered.

The nation's **industrial heartlands** are centered in the metropolitan areas of **Bogotá**, **Medellín**, **Barranquilla** and **Cali**. Today, a range of small and medium factories and large conglomerates are engaged in the production of oil, **food** and **beverages**, construction materials, **textiles** (lingerie being a

55

Tourism

Convulsed by internal violence just a few years ago, Colombia was an unlikely contender for international tourism. Today much has changed following President Uribe's crackdown on the biggest threats to national safety and security. Colombia now draws some 1.3-million tourists annually, primarily from South American neighbors and the US. A branding campaign called **Colombia is Passion** *(Colombian es Pasión)* was launched in 2005 to set the country apart in the global marketplace, accompanied by a red heart-shaped logo designed to represent the warmth and commitment of the Colombian people. In only four years, foreign visitation figures were boosted by up to 65 percent. In 2008 a slogan was added to soften the country's negative image on the international stage: **Colombia, the only risk is wanting to stay** *(Colombia, el riesgo es que te quieras quedar)*. Millions of Colombians, committed to becoming "ambassadors of tourism" for their country, display the heart logo with pride, spreading the message with a sense of national honor that reflects the hopes of a nation.

major component), machinery, ceramics, leather, automotive and automotive components, transformed steel and iron products and tools. **Chemical products** are also an extremely important industrial sector, from pure chemical products (acids and petrochemicals) to numerous derivatives (fertilizers, insecticides, detergents, etc.)

NATURAL RESOURCES

Given Colombia's wealth of natural resources, **mining** is an important commercial activity. World-renowned for its emeralds and gold, the country is also one of Latin America's major **nickel** producers and has the second largest **coal** reserves in Latin America after Brazil. It also has considerable energy resources and produces sizable amounts of **minerals**. Excavations for common clay, kaolin, dolomite, gypsum, limestone, hydrated lime and quicklime, magnesite, nitrogen, rock and marine salt, sand, gravel, marble, feldspar, phosphate rock, and sodium compounds, as well as small quantities of sulfur, asbestos, bauxite, bentonite, calcite, diatomite, fluorite, mercury, mica, talc, soapstone, prophyllite and zinc still take place across the country.

Colombia was once Latin America's only producer of **platinum**, and remains an important supplier of **cement**.

Colombian Emeralds

As the world's leader in emerald production, Colombia supplies approximately 60 percent of the earth's output. Renowned for their quality, Colombian emeralds are highly sought after due to their clarity. The nation's **emerald belt** is centered in the Andes Mountains.

Colombian Gold

Colombia ranks as Latin America's fifth-largest producer of gold after Peru, Brazil, Chile and Argentina. As the home of the **El Dorado legend** *(see sidebar p141)*, it once produced a third of all the gold mined by mankind. Much of its production stems from alluvial operations, including those along the **Nechi** and **Tigui rivers**.

Energy

Colombia's natural **gas reserves** totaled 3.7 trillion cubic feet in 2009, while its **crude oil reserves** amounted to 1.36 billion barrels, the fifth-largest in South America. Most of Colombia's crude oil production takes place in the Andes foothills and the eastern Amazonian jungles, within the Meta department in central Colombia, fast-emerging as an important production area.

Colombia has embraced the potential of **hydroelectricity** and ranks second to Brazil in Latin America, with hydropower accounting for roughly 65 percent of the nation's electricity generation.

SERVICE INDUSTRY

Colombia's service sector makes up 54 percent of its economy, and employs 59 percent of its work force. Key Colombian service industries include the country's extensive **banking sector,** headed by the Bank of the Republic, which functions as the central bank, and the modern **retail sector,** centered in urban areas. Services include **transportation**, **insurance**, **telecommunications** and **tourism** (☉ *see sidebar opposite*), an important sector earmarked for significant growth. Impacting virtually every area of business, services are a fundamental part of the economic infrastructure. Colombia is keen to demonstrate its recognition that efficient, high-quality services are essential to competitiveness in the global economy.

TRADE

In order of importance, Colombia's main **export goods** are oil, coffee, coal, nickel, emeralds, clothing, bananas and cut flowers. Its main **imports** include industrial and transportation equipment, consumer goods, chemicals, paper products, fuels and electricity.

A founding member of the **Andean Community**, Colombia is a long-standing supporter of free trade and a member of the **World Trade Organization** (WTO). It is also a member of two other trade associations: the **Group of Three** (Mexico, Venezuela and Colombia) and the **Association of Caribbean States** (ACS). The US is Colombia's largest trading partner, representing about 37 percent of Colombia's exports and 28 percent of its imports. Colombia is the US' fourth-largest trading partner in Latin America behind Mexico, Brazil and Venezuela and the largest agricultural export market in the hemisphere after the North American Free Trade Agreement (NAFTA) countries.

Relations with Colombia's second-biggest trading partner, **Venezuela**, were strained in 2009 when tensions rose over border incursions. Government-encouraged diversification led to **China's** becoming Colombia's number two export destination in late 2009.

RELIGION

The right of Colombian citizens to freely practice any faith is upheld by the Colombian Constitution of 1991, abolishing previous conditions applied by the Roman Catholic Church.

Religious liberty is celebrated each year in September at the **Festival of Religious Freedom** in Bogotá, the largest such gathering in Colombia.

CATHOLIC PREDOMINANCE

Despite a spiritual liberty that recognizes every faith, Colombia's religious demographics reveal that a thorough devotion to the Roman Catholic Church remains.

Often referred to as the most "Roman Catholic of all South American countries," Colombia is overwhelmingly Catholic (90 percent), with a ratio of priests to inhabitants of 1:4,000, one of the highest ratios in Latin America.

In 1991 the constitution outlined the diminished role of the Catholic Church, removing its status as State Church. The 1997 Public Agreement formed the foundation of the recognition of non-Catholic religions.

Non-Catholic Religions

Today, private faith schools of every type are permitted where there are no state-run counterparts. Colombia's immigrant **Lebanese**, **Turkish** and **Jewish** populations have places of worship in most large towns and cities. Small **Protestant** and **Evangelical Christian communities** can be found in the former English colonies of San Andrés and Providencia. **Seventh Day Adventists, Jehovah's Witnesses, Taoists, Hindus** and **Buddhists** all have a presence in Colombia. Yet it is the **Muslim** faith's many variants that form the basis of the fast-growing non-Catholic religious practices. In Maicao, the **Omar Ibn-al-Khattab Mosque** is the second-largest mosque in South America.

SPORTS

Although the national pastime is **tejo**, a thrilling throwing game, few things invoke greater passion in Colombia than **football** (soccer), be it local and regional league teams or national tournaments. Strong regional competition insures all matches between rivals are highly emotive. When the Colombian national squad (known as *Los Cafeteros)* failed to qualify for the 2010 World Cup, it was the topic of every street corner coffee bar. With local leagues and national competitions, **basketball** and **baseball** are also highly popular.

While government programs for **bike riding** aren't as robust as those in Europe, Bogotá is one of the world's most bicycle-friendly cities. The fiercest peaks in the area surrounding the Andean cordilleras have spawned some of the greatest climbing cyclists.

Much like the rest of the Americas, Colombia has a growing number of **golf** fans, especially since the meteoric success of home-grown talent Camilo Villegas. Colombia's amazingly diversified geography also lends itself to a wealth of **adventure sports**, from downhill mountain biking, white-water rafting, mountaineering, rappelling and caving to paragliding.

MEDIA
NEWSPAPERS

Colombia has maintained a deeply rooted tradition of **freedom of the press**, guaranteed under the Constitution of 1991. Its numerous, generally independent, high-quality newspapers include *El Tiempo* (highest circulation in the country) and *El Espectador* (one of the most influential newspapers in Colombia and Latin America). Despite improved security, Colombia remains one of the most dangerous countries for journalists in South America; some members of the press are benefiting from a protection program of the Ministry of Interior and Justice that seeks to safeguard their personal safety.

RADIO

Hundreds of commercial radio stations broadcast across Colombia, both as **licensed operations** and **pirated**. This type of media offers considerable diversity of listening material and holds a prime place in the daily life of Colombians. Board a bus and you'll be regaled with salsa music, jump into a taxi and you'll hear talk radio. The major national networks include state-run Radiodifusora Nacional de Colombia, RCN Radio and Caracol Radio, Colombia's main music radio station.

TELEVISION

The **National Television Commission** oversees the television programming of the five national and innumerable local and regional television channels that make up Colombia's TV broadcasting sector. Television stations include the three channels of RTVC (Radio Televisión Nacional de Colombia), Caracol TV, RCN TV and Canal Uno.

Colombian Telenovelas

At least four or five *telenovelas* (soap operas) are aired each night in Colombia, attracting large audiences across the country. Though storylines are renowned for melodrama, Colombian soaps are respected for their creativity. **Betty La Fea** (translated by more than 30 networks around the world) and **Café Con Aroma de Mujer** (set in the coffee-producing region of Colombia) are two classic examples of this popular television genre.

Once Caldas of Manizales vs. Nacional of Urguay, Libertadores Cup 2010

© Gal Schweizer/LatinContent/Getty Images

Bullfighting

Plaza de Toros, Manizales

Proexport Colombia

The Colombian tradition of bullfighting remains a legacy of the country's colonial past, with huge events that pull in mammoth crowds. Today the bullfighting sector stages events at some 80 permanent **bullrings**, the largest of which are located in Bogotá, Manizales, Cali, Medellín, Bucaramanga and Cartagena. More than 30 **breeding farms** produce fighting bulls, while 8 bullfighting schools tutor matadors in skills and protocol in Cali, Medellín, Manizales, Choachí, Sogamoso, Nobsa, Ubaté and Lenguazaque. A packed seasonal calendar runs from January to February each year, with an annual event in **Manizales** (arguably Colombia's "Bullfighting Capital") during the city's crowded *feria*. Despite attempts by animal protection groups to abolish bullfighting in Colombia, it remains a popular and legal pastime. In 2004 the bullfighting industry successfully secured one critical national law, the **Bullfighting Code**, which regulates the industry and declares bullfighting as "an artistic expression of human beings." However, Colombia is now the Latin American country with the most **anti-bullfighting** municipalities.

FOLKLORE AND TRADITIONS

Celebrating aspects of past and present culture and heritage is a popular Colombian pastime. Entire communities are often involved in planning large-scale **festive events** *(see Calendar of Events)* that can take months to set up, and that attract huge crowds. Given the mix of ethnicity, these events often center on folklore derived from **African** slave rituals, **Spanish** Catholic fiestas or **Caribbean** carnivals.

Like many of its South American counterparts, Colombia is rife with myths, taboos, proverbs, legends and folklore specific to individual communities, geographic location and ethnic origin.

Colombian society is peppered with numerous cultural oddities, from superstitions that retain a grip on every aspect of daily life—like hanging an aloe frond upside down on the front door to encourage wealth and love to come to the people within—to **rituals** that impact social conduct. Colombia's array of lore owes much to the heritage of its peoples. Many traditions focus on ghosts, monsters, urban myths, old wives' tales, occult practices and luck charms.

For instance, the African-influenced folkloric traditions that are strong in the San Andrés archipelago have their roots in the black-magic beliefs of the islanders' ancestors.

MYTHS AND LEGENDS

Oral tradition has played an important role in Colombia, particularly when it comes to myths and legends, as they are passed on from generation to generation by word of mouth.

Legendary creatures and mythical beings dominate the **Desfiles de Mitos y Leyendas**, "myths and legends parades" common to almost every Colombian municipality, large or small.

These imaginary figures are found in many aspects of popular culture; large numbers of Colombians believe in their existence, and many even claim to have encountered them.

Here is a selection of some of these folk tales, each story having several different regional variations.

El Hombre Caimán

This story takes place along the banks of the Magdalena River, where Chimila Indians once revered the caiman as their totem animal. One day a local fisherman and known philanderer asked a shaman to turn him into a caiman so he could spy on women bathing in the river. The fisherman could never fully return to human form. Today, the frightening half-man, half-caiman creature occasionally comes back to scare women away.

La Llorona

The legend has it that, once upon a full moon night, a flirtatious woman, fearing for her reputation, drowned her illegitimate son in the river. Consumed by remorse and grief, she returned to the river and disappeared in the water. Ever since, villagers can hear the heart-breaking cries of the "Weeping Lady,",a spirit who enters the houses, searching for children to take them away.

La Pastola

Some say this one-legged woman with a bovine hoof is the personification of a beautiful woman who was so cruel and perverted that she had her leg cut off with an axe and thrown into a bonfire made of corncobs. The angry creature has been endlessly roaming the mountains and forests ever since, looking for solace. To drive her away, some farmers have a special "prayer of the forest."

La Madremonte

This spirit manifests itself as a raging, putrid creature covered with moss, with fang-like teeth and fire emerging from her eyes. Protector of all living things in the jungles and mountains, she rules over the entire vegetal world as well, and has the power to produce floods, storms and drought. Fierce defender of the environment, she will punish farmers for their bad actions.

CUISINE

Colombian cuisine mixes **African** exotic spices with **Spanish** influences and the cooking styles of **Native Americans**, with many ingredients traceable back to pre-Columbian times, such as corn-breads and corn pastries, fried breads, and lima beans with tomatoes and corn. Huge regional variations are found across the country, with the food of the interior provinces wholly different from that of the coast. However, wherever you are, Colombian food is hearty, tasty and good value. As a national symbol and a pecuniary backbone, coffee is listed on every Colombian menu.

TYPICAL DISHES

While **la bandeja Paisa** doesn't quite have the status of Colombia's national dish, this man-size plate is generally recognized as one of the nation's great gastronomic delights. Loosen your belt before tackling this Colombian delicacy though, and don't attempt to eat it unless ravenous. This Colombian dish which, as its name suggests, hails from Paisa Country, is certainly not for delicate appetites. Typically it includes grilled steak (either ground or whole), *chicharrón* (fried pork rind), red beans, rice, chorizo, a fried egg and an *arepa*. It is usually accompanied by sweet fried plantains and a slice of avocado. Some versions include tomato or sauces like hogao, potato, or a slab of black pudding (blood sausage). Bandeja Paisa is typically followed by a bowl of **maz-amorra,** sweetened corn often served with ground **panela** (sugarcane) and **dulce de leche** (sweetened milk).

Another hearty traditional meal is **asado Bogotano**, the Colombian version of an American mixed grill that reads like a mouth-watering list of carnivorous delights. Expect a juicy pile of spicy chorizo, black pudding *(morcilla)*, chitterlings, sweetbreads, ribs, steak, chicken and even baby goat—rarely served with accompaniment, since the grill-fired flavors speak for themselves.

See also Menu Reader in Planning Your Trip, p43.

SOUPS

Colombia's many delicious soups are a meal on their own, often accompanied **rice** or boiled **potatoes**. Each region has its own specialties: for example, coastal soups will invariably contain seafood and Caribbean spices, while dishes in the interior provinces are more likely to be less spicy and wholly meat-based.

Ajiaco is a widely enjoyed soup made from a trio of native potatoes together with chunks of chicken, avocado and corn, perfumed with aromatic herbs *(guasca)*. Visitors to the capital should try the Bogotan version called **ajiaco santafereno**, a warming treat on a crisp, cool day in this high-altitude city.

Thick, robust **cuchuco**, prevalent in the Boyacá region, is made from wheat, beans, potatoes, peas and ribs.

While **sancocho** is found all over Colombia, no two places use the same recipe, so expect some delicious concoctions of yucca, maize and vegetables, often with poultry, fish or pork.

BREADS

Even the smallest community has a bakery *(panaderia)*, with freshly baked breads as a daily staple. Try delicious **almojabana**, a round-shaped maize bread roll. Or treat yourself to one of Colombia's many variations of **arepa**, a shaped cornbread cooked on a griddle: **arepa de choclo**, made with sweet corn and white *cheeseto;* sweet cheese-filled hard **arepa boyacense**, etc. **Bunuelos,** deep-fried ball-shaped cheese-dough fritters, are traditionally eaten at Christmas, though **pandebono**, a moist cheese bread found in the Cauca Valley region, is available year-round.

SAUCES AND SNACKS

All across Colombia, you'll see **hogao** on the menu: a rich sauce made with sautéed sliced onions, spring onions, chopped tomatoes, garlic, cumin and salt and pepper. Although **coconut rice** *(arroz con coco)* is a typical Caribbean accompaniment, it is sometimes found away from the coast, served with seafood. Delicious deep-fried pastries mpenadas and **carimanolas** are com-

Bandeja Paisa
© Richard McColl/MICHELIN

mon, with innumerable variations across the country. In the Bucamaranga region, **hormiga culona** is a seasonal local delicacy: roasted queen ant cooked in the same way as in pre-Columbian times and sold by roadside vendors.

BEVERAGES

For an alcoholic tipple with a kick, try **aguardiente**, Colombia's potent (up to 40 percent) national liquor, derived from sugarcane. **Rum** is served usually with ice and lime. Freshly squeezed **fruit juices** are often mixed with milk *(con leche)* or water *(con agua)*, while Colombian **coffee** (*tinto*: black coffee; *perico* or *pintado*: with milk; *café con leche*: with lots of milk) is served in every bar or by vendors on street corners.

Colombian Eating Habits

In general terms, the following eating habits apply:

◆ **Desayuno** (breakfast): usually eaten at 7am. Large-ish meal of fried *arepa* (maize pancake), scrambled eggs, coffee and natural fruit juice (orange, pineapple, watermelon or mango).

◆ **Almuerzo** (lunch): main meal of the day, eaten between noon and 2pm. Often a soup followed by grilled meat, fish or chicken and rice.

◆ **Cena** (dinner): eaten between 8pm-10pm. Tends to be lighter than lunch. Could be a filling soup with rice or fish.

History

From ancient civilizations rich with gold through exploitive Spanish rule, Bolívar's hard-fought liberation and a bloody civil war to a brief dictatorship and ruthless drug cartels, this land of emeralds and coffee beans has emerged to face the 21C with renewed hope and the promise of greater security.

PRE-HISPANIC PERIOD (PRIOR TO 1500)

Mystery surrounds the pre-Hispanic period of the region now called Colombia; biased, Spanish colonial accounts are not reliable sources. In recent years efforts have been made to unravel parts of this history, and scientists have made progress in attempting to undo some of the damages inflicted upon sacred areas by successive waves of marauders. The earliest evidence of human habitation in present-day Colombia is found at the **El Abra** site outside Bogotá, in the municipality of **Zipaquirá**. First excavated in 1969, the remains at El Abra were discovered in **rock shelters** around swamp areas, and date to about 12,400 years ago. Closely linked to the remains of hunted game found at the **Tibito** site near the current day town of Tocancipá, they are believed to be among the earliest in the Americas.

THE TAYRONA CIVILIZATION

On the Caribbean coast, more is known about the powerful Tayrona civilization because their direct ancestors, the **Arhuacos** and **Koguis**, still populate the area around the Sierra Nevada de Santa

Marta. Many studies have been made about **Ciudad Perdida**. Founded c. 800, some 650 years before Machu Picchu in Peru, the "Lost City," also known as **Buritaca**, is believed to have housed more than 2,000 people on its terraces. So advanced were the Tayrona that they knew all about **crop rotation**, methods to prevent soil erosion, and produced exceptional **gold** and **ceramic** works. At its height, prior to the arrival of the Spanish, their population could have numbered between 30,000 and 50,000 individuals. By the mid 16C, the Tayrona civilization was largely extinct.

THE MUISCA CULTURE

Inhabiting Colombia's central highlands for a period from about AD 1000 to AD 1550, the **Muisca** started out in small independent settlements, and as the 13C approached, evolved into a more centralized society. Linguistically related to the Chibcha family, the Muisca came south from Central America and settled on the savannas near Bogotá (or Bacatá) in the departments of Cundinamarca and Boyacá around 545 BC. With two organized Muisca communities, the **Zipa** and the **Zaque**, feuding over the land and the salt mines of the area of **Zipaquirá**, it was easy for the Spanish to conquer this already divided society. Remarkably expert in crop cultivation, hunting and goldsmithing, the Muisca are said to have been the source of the legend of **El Dorado**, based on ceremonies performed at the nearby sacred lake of **Guatavita**. The stone edifices that mark the burial mounds and rudimentary astrological site of **El Infiernito** are perhaps the best preserved Muisca ruins.

THE AGUSTINIAN CULTURE

The spectacular **anthropomorphic** sculptures of **San Agustín** make it the most interesting, visible pre-Hispanic culture today. Possibly it marks the northernmost outpost of the **Incan empire**, which reached its zenith between AD 100 and 800. There remain many unanswered question relating to the culture, but in recent years expert

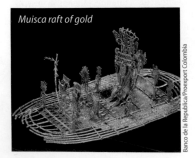
Muisca raft of gold

Banco de la Republica/Proexport Colombia

Key Dates and Events

12,400 BC – Oldest human settlement in Colombia recorded at El Abra.

545 BC – Early Muisca settlements.

1000-1400 – Golden Age of the Tayrona.

1509-1520 – Spain conquers the northern part of South America.

1549 – Creation of a Royal Audience in Bogotá, under authority of the vice-royalty of Peru.

1717 – New Granada becomes a vice-royalty.

1808-1810 – The Spanish Crown is overthrown by Napoleon, initiating independence efforts in South America.

1810 – Bogotá declares its independence from Spain.

1811-1813 – Nariño unites most of Colombia under Republican authority.

1816 – Spain reconquers New Granada.

1819 – Bolívar defeats Spanish forces at the Battle of Boyacá.

1821 – Congress of Cúcuta. Bolívar is officially sworn in as president of the Republic of Gran Colombia.

1830 – Ecuador and Venezuela leave Gran Colombia.

1899-1902 – Thousand Day Civil War.

1903 – Independence of Panama.

1948 – The murder of Jorge Eliécer Gaitán sparks a decade of political unrest known as "La Violencia."

1960s-1970s – Left-wing guerrillas and right-wing paramilitary forces emerge.

1980s – Powerful drug cartels assess their power in Medellín and Cali.

2000 – US financially-backed "Plan Colombia" is launched.

2002 – A new political era opens under the presidency of Álvaro Uribe.

2010 – Partido de la U candidate **Juan Manuel Santos** is elected president of Colombia.

have been able to divide the time line into three parts: the **formative period** (1000 BC-AD 300), defined by small agricultural villages; the **classic regional period** (AD 300-800), a time of population expansion; the **recent period** (AD 800-1600), when the people diversified their crops and cultivation. It is believed that this culture had all but disappeared before the arrival of the Spanish, and perhaps moved to the lowlands of the Amazon and Orinoco. Their remaining sculptures, blending deities and mythical animals, mark a vast cemetery.

Possibly linked to the Agustinian culture is **Tierradentro** (Cauca), known for its **necropolis** that may be 600 to 800 years old. Little is known about the people of Tierradentro, other than that they were master sculptors and painters, and probably shared roads and traded with their Agustinian neighbors.

OTHER CULTURES

Within the Cauca Valley, there are substantial signs of other pre-Hispanic communities, including the **Quimbayas** (AD 300-AD 1550), known for their gold work, and the hunter-gatherer **Calimas**, who arrived in the area around c.5000 BC and subsequently fell into decline around the 13C before dividing into various groups. Straddling the Colombian border with Ecuador, the **Nariño culture** (7C) was known for having significant contact with both the people of the Pacific and the Amazon; they were the last relatives of the Inca.

In the Pacific the **Tumaco** people, who lived between 600 BC and AD 400, were capable fishermen and farmers who inhabited the estuaries and inlets of the coast. They benefited from their access to the sea, and created irrigation channels for agriculture.

SPANISH CONQUEST (1500-1549)
THE BEGINNINGS

Alonso de Ojeda (1465-1515) was the first Spanish conquistador to set foot on Colombian soil and attempt a settlement there. Largely unknown, this key figure in the history of the New World was on **Christopher Columbus'** second voyage in 1493. He traveled, by his own account, with **Amerigo Vespucci** in 1499 to Trinidad, and embarked in 1509 with 300 men, among whom was **Francisco Pizarro**, on an expedition that charted the coast from **Panama** all the way to Lake Maracaibo in **Venezuela**. It is during this voyage that Ojeda founded **San Sebastián de Urabá**, the first European settlement on the South American mainland, located in the outskirts of what is known today as **Necoclí**. Nothing remains of the ill-fated settlement, as it was abandoned under duress from frequent attacks by local tribes and from lack of supplies.

Pedrarias Dávila founded **Panama City** In 1519. This event opened South America to European conquerors by providing them with a rear base from which they could launch expeditions to topple the Incan empire in Peru and settle Colombia.

STRUGGLE FOR POWER

Squabbling over what amounted to plundering rights and entitlement to the lands of **Nueva Granada**, three power-hungry conquistadors undertook most of Colombia's exploration and conquest. **Gonzalo Jiménez de Quesada** (1499-1579), the supposed model for Cervantès' *Don Quixote*, founded the city of **Santa Fé de Bogotá** in 1538 and ventured into the regions of **Guaviare** and **Orinoco** on ill-fated attempts to find and secure **El Dorado**. All the while, his rivals, the German **Nikolaus Federmann** (1501-1542), arriving from Venezuela, was attempting the same quest in the Llanos. Then governor of Quito, **Sebastián de Benalcázar** (1495-1551) was also afflicted with the desire for wealth and fortune, and moving north from Ecuador, founded the cities of **Cali** and **Popayán**. Benalcázar tried to ally with Federmann against Quesada, but ultimately his attempts fell short. These three remained in stiff competition with one another over the spoils to be found in these territories, and they ended up taking the argument to the court of **Carlos V**, King of Spain, in 1539, for resolution. In 1540 control of Bogotá was wrested from Quesada when Carlos V granted power to Benalcázar to rule from Popayán, overseen by the **Viceroyalty of Peru**.

EARLY SETTLEMENTS

Understandably, the Caribbean coast was the first region to be properly settled. In 1525 **Rodrigo de Bastidas** (1445-1527) founded the city of **Santa Marta,** the oldest permanently settled city in Colombia. In 1533 **Pedro de Heredia** (d.1555) established **Cartagena**, which soon overtook Santa Marta in importance and became the key port for the shipment of slaves and supplies. His brother, Alonso de Ojeda, founded the strategically important riverside town of **Mompox** in 1537. **Francisco de Orellana** (1490-1546) established the city of **Guayaquil** in Ecuador in 1537, but most importantly, navigated the length of the **Amazon River**, having entered via the River Napo. Against all odds, he and his men survived eight arduous months of attacks by hostile

Portrait of Gonzalo Jiménez de Quesada by unknown artist

© The Art Archive/Alamy

tribes, disease and scarcity of supplies. Orellana returned to the Amazon River in 1545, having been granted authority by the Crown to exploit the lands he had discovered, and succeeded in exploring 500km/310mi of the Amazon delta.

SPANISH RULE (1549-1808)

Until the middle of the 16C, the area that is now Colombia was administered in its entirety by the **Viceroy of Peru**, based in Lima, a centralized system of governance that would not prove to be effective for such vast territories.

ROYAL AUDIENCE

In 1549, in order to delegate some responsibilities to more autonomous and outlying regions, the **Royal Audiencia of Santa Fé de Bogotá** was created to oversee the key provinces of Popayán, Santa Marta and Guayana among others. The Royal Audience had its own president who, in turn, was answerable to the all-powerful Lima. However, given the enormity of the Viceroy's own task—he presided over a region stretching from Panama to Chile and east to Argentina, which led to a certain degree of lawlessness and opportunism—the northern territories were divided from the southern ones in the 18C.

VICEROYALTY

In 1717 the **Viceroyalty of New Granada** was created in Santa Fé de Bogotá to control territories that included Colombia, Ecuador, Venezuela, Panama, sections of western Brazil, northern Peru and as far east as Guayana.

This vast territory, while overseen from Santa Fé by a governor-president, was then divided into smaller provinces, the largest of which, **Popayán**, extended north to present day Antioquia, the Chocó and out to the Amazon Basin.

The idea behind the establishment of the viceroyalty had its roots not only in geographical and logistical difficulties. The new system was set up to more effectively administer the entry ports into the region, counter the industry of **contraband** and take stronger action

against **piracy** and **foreign designs** on Spanish colonial territory.

Again though, the geographical conundrum came into play, and despite being officially tied to Santa Fé, both the **Capitanía General** in **Caracas** and the **Royal Audiencia** in **Quito** gained some level of political and regional autonomy.

The Viceroyalty of New Granada endured until 1723, when it was suspended for financial reasons and returned to the authority of Lima. It was then re-established in 1739, lasting until the winds of independence blew through the colonies.

EMANCIPATION (1808-1819)
A FAVORABLE CONTEXT

Given the events that were taking place in Europe at the end of the 18C and the geographical difficulties encountered by the Viceroyalty of New Granada, it should come as no surprise that this land was fertile territory for the independence movement. The Spanish empire had reached its climax, and problems in the motherland were contributing to what could be described as imperial exhaustion.

When **Antonio Nariño** (1765-1823) translated the *Declaration of the Rights of Man* (1794), an act that landed him a stiff prison sentence, he brought fresh ideas of liberty and independence to the lands of New Granada. **Napoléon**'s invasion of Spain during the **Peninsular War** (1808-1813) was nothing short of catastrophic for any Spanish desire to hold on to their assets in New Granada.

Financially, the Spanish Crown was crippled, and news of the war in Spain ignited a more zealous independence fervor in South America, the colonies refusing to recognize Napoléon's brother as their new monarch.

INTERNAL CLASHES

When the news of the situation in Spain reached New Granada in 1810, the vacuum of power between this year and 1816 created what is commonly referred to as the **Patria Boba** (Foolish Fatherland). This period of fighting between provinces jostling for their slice of the pie culminated in civil war.

The province of **Santa Fé de Bogotá** was the first to set up an autonomous **governing junta**, declaring itself independent on July 20, 1810 (a national holiday in Colombia).

Other provinces followed suit and produced their own independent constitutions, including Cartagena, Antioquia, Tunja, Mariquita and Neiva, while provinces such as Pasto, Santa Marta and Popayán did not wish for independence and fought alongside the Royalists.

On November 27, 1811, several provinces held a congress in Tunja, where all but Chocó and Cundinamarca became the **United Provinces of New Granada**. The pro-Independence movement included both **traditionalists** and **liberals**. As a consequence, two ideologies emerged from the turmoil: **centralism** (around the state of Cundinamarca), and **federalism** (in the United Provinces). Both sides soon entered into armed conflict, attempting to rally the support of those provinces as yet undecided.

Following a successful campain (1812-1813), **Antonio Nariño,** commander of the centralist military forces, gained control over the United Provinces of New Granada. Subordinated to Cundinamarca, these provinces were merely joined for the purpose of common interest. They enjoyed a few years of *de facto* independence from Spain.

Nariño pursued forces loyal to the Crown in the south of the country. He captured Popayán in 1814, then moved on to Pasto. When reinforcements failed to arrive from Antioquia, he was defeated and captured in Pasto. Sentenced to prison for several years, he would not return to the political scene until 1821.

SPANISH RECONQUEST

With the Napoleonic wars over, Ferdinand VII was restored to the Spanish throne in 1814, and Spanish eyes were once again drawn to the Americas and their unruly outposts there. A veteran of the Battle of Trafalgar and the Peninsular War, General **Pablo Morillo** (1775-1837), referred to as "the Pacifier," was charged with bringing the colonies back to the fold. In 1815 he besieged and took control of **Cartagena**.

In 1816 the combined efforts of Royalist sympathizers and the Spanish army's marching south from Cartagena and Santa Marta and north from the strongholds of Pasto, Quito and Popayán, culminated in the reconquest of **Bogotá** and the fall of the independent New Granada.

A **military regime** was installed. Ruling with violent repression, it stripped of their property those accused of rebellion or treason against the Crown, and tried them in front of **tribunals**. The ensuing sentences varied from forced enrollment in the king's army to exile or death. Among those executed were patriots **Camilo Torres**, **Joaquín Camacho** and **Jorge Tadeo Lozano**.

INDEPENDENCE WARS

Leading a campaign of independence in his homeland, Venezuelan-born **Simón Bolívar** (1783-1830) had been forced to retreat to New Granada in 1813 after having failed to hold Caracas. Known as "El Libertador," he fought alongside Colombian independence forces before fleeing to the West Indies to escape the harsh reconquest carried out by General Morillo. Bolívar was well received by Haitian governing powers, newly independent from France. He raised money and forces, and was able to return to South America in 1816.

Based in southern Venezuela, and with the aid of **British mercenaries**, Bolívar started devising a plan to defeat Morillo. He decided to catch the Spanish forces off their guard and move his troops during rainy season.

Leaving the Venezuelan Llanos and heading through the Colombian lowlands, raising a further 400 men in Mompox, he moved on and then scaled the Andes at **Mérida**.

On July 25, 1819, Bolívar's ragged troops met the Spanish forces at **Pantano de Vargas** (Battle of Vargas' Swamp), and after surviving such an exhausting journey, escaped defeat through sheer determination.

The battle was a lesson to the Royalist forces. At the **Battle of Boyacá**, on August 7, Bolívar then defeated a Spanish force numbering 3,000. Most of the Royalist government in Bogotá at the time, including **Viceroy Juan José de Samáno**, fled the capital, leaving it clear for Bolívar's forces to enter on August 10.

FORMATION OF THE MODERN STATE
GRAN COLOMBIA (1819-1830)

Bolívar's victory at Boyacá and triumphant entry into Bogotá did not signal the end of the Spanish rule in New Granada. The wars of independence against the Spanish and those loyal to Spain fizzled out in the mid-1820s, and independence was not really achieved prior to 1824.

In 1819 Bolívar convened the **Congress of Angostura** (in present-day Venezuela), which actually met until 1821. It was during that time that its 26 delegates from Venezuela and New Granada laid the foundation for the new **Republic of Gran Colombia**.

Consisting of all territories composing New Granada—today's Colombia, Venezuela, Ecuador, Panama, parts of Brazil, Peru, Guayana, territories in the Caribbean including the Mosquito Coast in current day Nicaragua and up into Costa Rica—Gran Colombia was meant to be a cohesive, diverse and economically powerful state to compete with Europe.

In 1821 a formal **constitution** for the new republic was adopted at the **Congress of Cúcuta**. Bolívar was officially sworn in as president of Gran Colombia and **Francisco de Paula Santander** as vice president.

The republic quickly found its feet, and set aside regional differences to continue the armed struggle against imperial Spain. Bolívar dedicated himself to liberating the Royalist pockets remaining in Ecuador, the rest of Venezuela and achieving the independence of Peru.

On the strength of these victories, both Bolívar and Santander were re-elected in 1826. But the regionalist feeling that coursed through Gran Colombia

Portrait of Simón Bolívar (19C) by José Gil de Castro

© World Illustrated/Photoshot/Casa de la Libertad, Sucre, Bolivia

became too much for the new republic: the strong sentiments of federalism and centralism resurfaced, as thoughts of independence faded into the past.

The situation of **instability** was not aided by the public **ideological differences** about government between Bolívar and Santander.

Over the course of his vice presidency, Santander's full backing of the idea of a more federalist state placed him at odds with Bolívar, culminating in Bolívar's abolishment of that office in 1828, when he declared himself **dictator**.

Despite having largely run the country in Bolívar's long absences, Santander was forced into **exile** as a sort of pardon for having been implicated—yet unproven—in an assassination attempt on Bolívar.

SANTANDER PRESIDENCY

In 1830 Gran Colombia dissolved upon the secession of Venezuela and Ecuador, and with fissures in the republic all too apparent, **Bolívar** resigned from the presidency. In 1832 Santander returned to New Granada and was elected **president**, a post he held until 1837.

During this period, Santander proved himself to be an able administrator, carefully balancing the differences between the liberal and conservative Catholics, promoting trade with the **United States** and investing considerably in education. Overall, it can be

The Thousand Day War (1899-1902)

One of the country's major civil wars started at the end of the 19C when the fragile **Republic of Colombia** was still in its early stages of development. Known as the Thousand Day War *(Guerra de los Mil Días)*, this bloody conflict came about through the deep rifts created between the factions of **Liberals** and **Conservatives**. Violence broke out after the Conservatives were accused of holding onto the reins of power, following fraudulent elections in 1899. With notable battles in **Peralonso** and **Palonegro** and thousands of lives lost, the war spread over time to every corner of Colombia, furthering the economic ruin of a country already suffering from the collapse of the coffee market. The Conservatives claimed victory, but this win was nominal at best since the war had brought the country to its knees and never resolved the issues between the two factions. A **peace treaty** put an end to the bloody conflict in 1902.

said that Santander gave the new republic a steady hand. In 1840 Santander died, **Panama** declared its independence (not achieved until 1903), and Colombia plunged into the far-reaching unpleasantness of civil war.

CIVIL WARS (1849-1880)

The two opposing factions were divided thus: Centralists (or **Conservatives**) versus Federalists (or **Liberals**). The latter believed in a separation of Church and State and decentralized power. The former believed in a strong central government and stood opposed to the extension of voting rights. The Liberals were in power from 1849-1857 and 1861-1880, an era remembered for insurrections, civil wars and decentralization.

In 1856 the **Granadine Confederation** was formed. It consisted of

eight member states: Antioquía, Bolívar, Boyacá, Cauca, Cundinamarca, Panama, Magdalena and Santander. Being pro-federalist, the confederation gave greater autonomy to the supporting provinces, which was met with fervent disapproval from the Conservatives. Civil war raged on, and in 1863 the Granadine Confederation was replaced by the **United States of Colombia**, including the aforementioned states as well as Tolima.

Hostilities continued along the same vein, tit-for-tat retaliations between Liberals and Conservatives, until 1886, when the United States of Colombia became known, at long last, as the **Republic of Colombia** under the presidency of the Conservative **Rafael Núñez** (1825-94). Núñez governed the country from 1880 to 1894, his most famous accomplishment being that of the constitutional reform that created the **Republic of Colombia**.

INDEPENDENCE OF PANAMA

Colombia was broken, demoralized and humiliated when in 1903, in quick succession to the terrible events of the Thousand Day War, the region called **Istmo** or **Panama** received US backing to become independent.

This rapid turn of events came about after the Colombian Senate had failed to ratify the **Hay-Herran Treaty** to lease the zone to the US to create the **Panama Canal**.

The Republic of Panama was not officially recognized by Colombia until 1914, in return for rights to the canal.

In 1921 the **Thomson-Urrutia Treaty**, which was signed between the US and Colombia, awarded Colombia an indemnity of $25 million for the loss of Panama.

MODERN COLOMBIA: A DEMOCRACY ON THE EDGE

Seemingly reeling from interminable civil wars and the loss of national territory, Colombia tentatively stepped into the 20C in desperate search of an **identity**, yet the relentless switching between Conservatives and Liberals continued unabated. Conservative presidents held power between 1909 and 1930, and Liberals from 1930 to 1942.

NATIONALISM

Perhaps to insure no further loss of sovereign Colombian territory, the Colombian government reacted strongly when, in 1932, Peruvian civilians took control of the Colombian Amazonian port town of **Leticia**. A wave of nationalism spread through the nation, briefly sidelining the internal problems. A 1922 treaty had established the **Putumayo River** as the boundary between Colombia and Peru, aside from the small outpost of Leticia, in order to grant Colombia access to the **Amazon River**. The Colombian government sent a force to reclaim the territory in the **Leticia Conflict**, and despite being outnumbered and poorly equipped, the Colombians were victorious in the skirmishes. In 1934 a treaty was signed and Leticia was returned to Colombia.

LA VIOLENCIA (1948-1964)

After **World War II,** the violence and political divisions in Colombia intensified. The assassination of Liberal presidential candidate **Jorge Eliécer Gaitán** on April 9, 1948, was the spark that ignited the long running fuse to the eventual **La Violencia** that consumed Colombia from 1948 to 1964.

The killing of Gaitán kicked off the **Bogotázo**, a massive city-wide riot that left some 3,000 people dead in a day and essentially razed historical Bogotá to the ground.

The tense situation in Colombia had been primed for an explosion for some time, and La Violencia brought the misery in from the countryside to the cities, as **armed groups** rampaged through villages and towns, raping, pillaging and killing. There was sporadic guerrilla fighting between Conservatives and Liberals with no real political ideology, and in total more than 200,000 lives were claimed.

AUTHORITARIAN REGIME

Given all of the violence and bloodshed, it is no wonder that Colombia then flirted with a dictatorship, perhaps in a desperate attempt to give the rule of law some chance. In 1953 the army officer **Gustavo Rojas Pinilla** (1900-1975) led the coup that ousted **President Laureano Gómez**.

To try to rein in some of the violence in the countryside, one of Pinilla's first actions was to declare an amnesty for all those who had been fighting. It appeared to work initially, with battle-weary figures, eager to return to civilian life, turning in their arms. But, after a brief respite, heavy fighting broke out once more in the area of Tolima and Rojas Pinilla's popularity, already suffering, turned for the worse. He stepped down In 1957, handing over power to a **military junta.**

LEFTIST GUERRILLAS

With their roots deep in the times of La Violencia, Colombia's rural **rebel groups** did not disappear overnight. In fact, many strengthened. While politi-

The National Front

From 1958 Colombian politicians, determined to alter the damaging situation in the country, tried something different called the "National Front." This idea, conceived by politicians on both sides, was to create a political system that lasted 16 years and was defined by four presidential terms, two liberal and two conservative. In 1958 in free elections, the Liberal **Alberto Lleras Camargo** was elected president, and then in 1962, he was succeeded by the Conservative **Guillermo León Valencia.** In 1966 the Liberal **Carlos Lleras Restrepo** won, and then in 1970, the Conservative **Misael Pastrana Borrero**. Finally, in 1974, Colombia returned painlessly to the two-party system at the end of the National Front experiment with the election of the Liberal **Alfonso López Michelsen**.

cal experimentation was taking place in Bogotá, a new equally serious threat was developing: **communist-inspired guerrillas**. Government concerns in the early 1960s were subsequently directed at preventing a Cuban-style inspired revolution.

Contemporary Colombia has been plagued by various ills, not least the rise of leftist-inspired guerrillas such as the **ELN** (Ejercito de Liberación Nacional, founded in 1964), the **EPL** (Ejercito Popular de Liberación, 1967-1991),the **FARC** (Fuerzas Armadas Revolucionarias de Colombia, founded in 1964) and the **M19** (Movimiento 19 de Abril, 1970-1990), all aimed at toppling the Colombian state.

Both the EPL and M19 have now laid down their weapons, some of the former members having moved into formal politics. But there was a stage when both groups instilled a reign of terror in Colombia.

The M19 were responsible for the bloody siege of Bogotá's **Palace of Justice** in 1985. Many of the former combatants moved across into the rank and file of the ELN and FARC, both of which remain active to this day, but at greatly reduced numbers.

In addition to military losses, the FARC have lost support due to their policy of kidnapping and extortion. In 2008, the FARC took some severe hits, not only due to President Uribe's policies, but also due to the FARC second in command **Raul Reyes** being killed in a bombing raid by Colombian forces in Ecuadorian territory, and the death of the FARC leader and ideologist **Manuel "Tirofijo" Marulanda**. Add to this the daring rescue of former presidential candidate Ingrid Betancourt and three American contractors in **Operation Check Mate**.

RIGHT-WING PARAMILITARIES

The FARC guerrillas have seen their their influence wane somewhat with the rise of the right-wing paramilitary groups. Started initially by landowners intent on defending their property, these militias over time found that they could better finance themselves with a slice of the lucrative cocaine trade.

The **AAA** (American Anticommunist Alliance), founded in 1978 and disbanded in 1979, allegedly had its roots within the Colombian Armed Forces.

CONVIVIR, from 1994-1998, was a government-supported neighborhood watch program that moved into paramilitary activities before being disbanded. The **AUC** (United Self Defense Forces of Colombia), formed in 1997, became the umbrella group for all paramilitary actions before surrendering its arms in 2008. While the AUC supposedly started as a counterbalance to the left-wing guerrilla groups, it became a terrorist group in its own right, charging for protection and extorting from civilians.

In 2006 the bulk of the AUC laid down their weapons in an agreement reached with President Uribe and demobilized. This act by no means signaled the end of paramilitary activities, as smaller less-focused groups sprung up in the vacuum, such as the **Black Eagles**, implicated in drug trafficking, extortion, racketeering and kidnapping.

Plan Colombia

Conceived in 1998 by Colombian president **Andrés Pastrana Arango,** this ambitious blueprint originally aimed at finding a solution to the Colombian armed conflict, largely funded by the drug trade. In 1999, of the plan's projected $7.5 billion total cost, US president **Bill Clinton** pledged $1.3 billion to help the Colombian government and military in its war on drugs. In 2001 US president **George W. Bush** expanded the program to include further counter-narcotics initiatives and fumigation of the coca-growing regions. Critics of Plan Colombia argue that it proposes a military strategy, but fails to address major issues such as the institutional and social development in the coca-growing regions.

Democratic and Security Defense Policy (DSP)

This policy was launched in 2003, a year after President **Álvaro Uribe Vélez** took office, as a fundamental part of his pledge to make Colombia a safer place. He vowed to deny sanctuary to terrorists and to engage Colombian citizens in the destruction of the illegal drug trade. He also urged participation in improving security and safety, outlining the benefits to international trade and tourism. In a nutshell, the DSP's ambition to protect and strengthen the rule of law throughout Colombia is based on the assumption that the more citizens feel protected, the more they will be likely to participate. Transportation and access have significantly improved as Colombia has regained control over its roads and highways. Guerrilla groups and terrorist organizations have been weakened, and as confidence is gradually building and national spirit strengthening, so is security and safety.

COLLATERAL DAMAGE

The conflict that has spread through every level of Colombian society in every corner of the country, has led over four million Colombians to be **internally displaced**. Forcibly moved from their homes and land to the cities, these civilians form a massive underclass among poor urban populations.

The **cocaine trade** has also produced its share of victims and brought notoriety to the country. In the 1980s the most famous name in international narco-terrorism was that of **Pablo Escobar** (1949-1993) who ran the **Medellín cartel** before being gunned down in his native city. During his ruthless reign, he was directly responsible for the assassination of presidential candidate Luis Carlos Galan, car bombing campaigns against newspapers, the bombing of a commercial airliner, and the Palace of Justice siege orchestrated by the M19. Just as astonishing in its cruelty and violence, the rival **Cali cartel** was run by the **Orejuela brothers**.

Currently, there are still cartels in operation in Colombia, albeit less extravagant and less visible than those in the 1980s. Given the enormous financial gains associated with the cocaine trade, curbing drug trafficking may remain the ultimate challenge.

As one cartel head is assassinated, captured or extradited, another quickly springs up in his place.

A HEALING COUNTRY

Coming to power in 2002, President **Álvaro Uribe Vélez** signaled a change in Colombia, both domestically and internationally. During his two tenures, the country went through a period of history unlike any in its past, with major improvements in terms of domestic security and sustained economic growth.

The impact of his **Democratic and Security Defense Policy** (*see sidebar above)* helped the country shake off its lingering bad reputation and build a new image of Colombia as a place to invest in and visit.

After pushing through an amendment to the **Colombian Constitution** In 2004 allowing the president to run for a second term, Álvaro Uribe was re-elected in 2006. In spite of setbacks, he managed to maintain some of the highest approval ratings in Latin America.

Uribe attempted to push through a further resolution to enable him to run for a third term, but the Constitutional Court denied it in 2010, thus opening the way for **Juan Manuel Santos**, who was elected Colombia's new president in June 2010.

Art and Culture

Colombia's arts and architecture have evolved from imitation of European styles and traditions to experimentation with themes and settings that are unique to the country. Not only has Colombia forged an individual artistic identity, it is breaking new ground globally.

FINE ARTS AND CRAFTS
PAINTING
Pre-Columbian Period

Colombia's painting tradition extends all the way back to **Tierradentro** (Cauca), where geometric designs in shades of red, black and white (600-900 years ago) were found in huge underground burial caves. By no means are these the only examples of "primitive" art in Colombia, as new discoveries in **Chimita** (Santander) have revealed **petroglyphs** dating to 1300 BC. A spectacular piece of rock art known as the *Mural Guayabero* (300 BC) was discovered in the **Sierra de Chiribiquete**, a region at the confines of Caquetá and Guaviare, where the **Cerro Azul**, a large rock covered with layers of indigenous graffiti, was also found. Other remote parts of the country could reveal many other treasures like these.

Colonial Period
Early Religious Art 1530-1650

Most of the public art in the early Colonial period was brought from **Seville**. It displayed the two-dimensional religious style of Christian images that was in fashion at the time. But there was also artwork that caused ripples of devotion from the indigenous Muisca population, such as the *Virgen de Monguí* (Boyacá) which, as legend has it, was sent over to the New World by King Philip II. Examples of home-grown religious art are still visible in churches and fine houses today, particularly in Tunja and Villa de Leyva, and all through the regions of Cundinamarca and Boyacá. Created by **craftsmen** rather than artists, these pieces were **imitations** of original artwork from the motherland, with touches of medieval, Renaissance and indigenous symbolism added to them. Perhaps the first example of religious art truly native to New Granada came from **Alonso de Narváez** (?-1583) whose *Nuestra Señora de Chiquinquirá* is seen by fervent Catholics as a piece of art that miraculously restored itself without human intervention.

Baroque Religious Art 1650-1750

One of the most prominent figures of the Latin American Baroque movement, **Gregorio Vásquez de Arce y Ceballos** (1638-1711) is considered by many as the best painter of the Spanish Colonial period. His highly controversial representation of the *Holy Trinity* as a three-faced head can be seen as an elaborate Creole interpretation of European masters, influenced by the artistic tradition from the **Quito** and **Cuzco** schools of painting. Another Creole artist, a contemporary of Gregorio Vásquez, was **Baltasar de Figueroa** (1629-67), the inventor of Colombian Baroque. In 1658 he was commissioned to do a series of 20 paintings for the **Convento de la Concepción** in Bogotá, a contract he did not honor. In 1660 he signed on to paint all the images for the **Iglesia de Nuestra Señora de Chiquinquirá**. He did not complete this work either, but he did leave behind many notable works, including the *Coronación de la Virgen* (1663), with delicate facial features.

Detail of Símbolo de la Trinidad by Gregorio Vásquez de Arce y Ceballos

Santiago Martínez Delgado (1906-1954)

Born of a wealthy family, Martínez studied at the Art Institute of Chicago and spent some time at **Frank Lloyd Wright**'s Taliesin studio in Wisconsin. Strongly influenced by Art Deco, he produced over a hundred paintings, murals, book illustrations, sculptures, stained glass works and lithographs. In 1947 he was commissioned to do a **mural** for the elliptic room of the **Colombian National Congress.** Spared by the fires that raged through Bogotá during the Bogotazo riots of 1948, the resulting work, *Bolívar and Santander in the Cúcuta Congress*, is a staggering feat. Martínez was not only a distinguished artist, but also a **writer** and **art historian**. His discovery, in 1948, of a *Madonna and Child* by Raphael, now referred to as the *Madonna of Bogotá*, created quite a stir in the art world. Gazing at his oil paintings in Cúcuta's Cathedral or at the beautiful *Interludio* on display at the Museo Nacional in Bogotá makes one wonder what else Martínez could have achieved, had he lived longer.

Possibly painted by Figueroa or Ecuadorian artist **Miguel de Santiago**, the famous series of 12 archangels known as *Arcángeles de Sopó* that decorate the **Iglesia Divino Salvador** in **Sopó** (Cundinamarca) stake the claim of being the most representative example of Colombian Baroque art. This exceptional work in oil is indicative of the **emotionalism** that appealed to a more humanitarian viewer in the wake of the **Counter Reformation**.

With the **Spanish Enlightenment** of the 18C came political change, which in turn affected artistic output, and there emerged a warmer, more colorful style. In addition to painting aristocratic portraits, **Joaquín Gutiérrez** produced a series of 26 paintings entitled *La Vida de San Juan de Dios* (1750). Many of his works can be seen at Bogotá's **Museo de Arte Colonial** (see Bogotá).

Republican Period

Upon the advent of independence and the struggle for it, Colombian art took on a **romantic** quality in order to display and justify the **heroism** of its leaders and the battles fought. Works of this nature are no better illustrated than by **José María Espinosa Prieto** (1796-1883) who painted portraits of Simón Bolívar. However, his most famous work may be his memoirs in the painted word, *Memorias de un Abanderado* (1876).

Ramón Torres Méndez (1809-85), a self-taught artist famed for his *Señora Desconocida* and *Cristo se aparece a la Magdalena,* gained further renown by saving religious artworks from destruction.

A faithful witness to an inhospitable time in Colombia's history, **Ricardo Acevedo Bernal** (1867-1930) found inspiration in topics of a patriotic nature. He also painted landscapes and religious subjects, and was a fine portraitist, although his work was criticized by some as being somewhat paternalistic and classist.

The Republican period was not only one of searching for a national identity, it was also a great age for **scientific missions** such as those led by Italian geographer **Agustín Codazzi,** who elaborated the first map of the Colombian territory. Artists were often contracted for such missions, as was the case with **Manuel María Paz** (1820-1902), one of Codazzi's traveling companions, who focused on landscapes and portraits, and charted all levels of society in New Granada.

Modern Painting

Straddling the Republican styles, but not quite fully embracing the modern period, is **Fidolo González Camargo** (1883-1941) whose portraits and landscapes ably reflect a French romanticism. His drawings, particularly his charcoals of *Tipo Callejero* and the *Sirvienta Bogotana,* can be seen at the **Museo Nacional de Bogotá** (see BOGOTÁ).

Carlos Jacanamijoy
"Antes que pintor indígena"

Born in 1964 in the Amazon region of the **Putumayo** department in southern Colombia, this son of a shaman from the **Inga** tribe is considered one of the shining talents on the current South American art scene. The originality of his work derives from his willingness to celebrate the heritage of his forefathers and express his knowledge, experience, beliefs and values through a highly spirited artistic statement where **nature** is seemingly the center of attraction. The jungles near the valley of Sidunboy provide the basis for his vibrant, **abstract landcapes** that tend to form images of vertigo and poetic hallucination.

Muralism 1920-1940

There is no dearth of Colombian muralists, but **Pedro Nel Gómez** (1899-1984) was undoubtedly one of the greatest artists of his kind, his name referenced alongside that of Mexican legend **Diego Rivera**. The **Museo de Antioquia** (☝see *MEDELLÍN*) has a large collection of Gómez's works, including an impressive tryptic called *Triptico del Trabajo*.

The Road to Colombian Art

In the 20C, art in Colombia gradually turned from the **academic tradition** and the parameters of **European realism**, and shifted to **national** and **social concerns**. Artists started to consider questions of identity and, searching for a uniquely Colombian style, they used the geometrically abstract forms of **cubism**, among others, to define the new era of the nation's art. With a certain "Colombianization" of art, the shackles of the Colonial and Republican legacies of religious artwork from Spain were finally removed. A new generaton of artists emerged, and these talented figures went on to define the routes that have led to Colombian Art of today.

As the founding father of modern Colombian painting, **Alejandro Obregón** (1920-92) earned his place on the list of Colombia's Top Five artists, along with **Enrique Grau** *(see below)*, **Eduardo Ramírez Villamizar**, **Edgar Negret** *(see Sculpture)* and **Fernando Botero**. Obregón's painting was clearly influenced by Picasso, but he incorporated a whole repertoire of Colombian themes in his works, including the vio-

Detail of Flor de mangle *(c. 1965) by Alejandro Obregón*

Photography

Colombian interest in historical photographs is fairly recent. It all started with an impressive exhibition entitled *100 Years of Photography,* which took place in Medellín in 1981, and awoke a national interest in the subject. Since then, efforts towards rescuing, cataloging and preserving Colombia's photographic heritage has really taken hold.

This important task is being led for the most part by the **Biblioteca Pública Piloto de Medellín para América Latina.** Founded in 1952 by UNESCO, this library houses the largest photo archives in Latin America, with a collection of about 1,500,000 frames, including some dating back to 1849.

Alberto Urdaneta (1845-87) was the first Colombian to really promote the new art form of photography. With his colleague **Demetrio Paredes** (c.1830-c.1898), he created the journalistic publication *Papel Periódico Ilustrado* in 1881.

Julio Racines Bernal (1848-1913) was a major contributor as well, and together they compiled images and portraits of some of the most important characters of the time. With Urdaneta's passing, the *Papel Periódico Ilustrado* folded, and with it, one of the golden eras of Colombian photography. But in the 20C came a new and different take on the art form.

Luis Benito Ramos (1899-1955), who studied in France, was greatly influenced by the work of Henri Cartier-Bresson. Back in Colombia, he set up an exhibition entitled *50 aspectos fotográficos de Colombia* for Bogotá's 400th anniversary in 1938. His photos got the public's attention, as they appealed to the national sentiment of the time. Ramos also documented the human condition in the countryside, and was critically acclaimed for capturing the essence of the period with compassion and dignity. Another great photographer was **Melitón Rodríguez** (1875-1942), particularly famous for his artistic portraits that recorded the growth of a new urban society in his native Medellin.

Perhaps some of the photos that most impacted Colombia were shot by a contemporary artist named **Juan Manuel Echavarría Olano**, born in Medellín in 1947. The color studio shots and haunting black-and-white compositions of this novelist-turned-photographer evoke images of death and destruction in a country wounded by years of violence and internal conflict. Exhibited worldwide, his emotionally charged photos consistently engender an overwhelming feeling of empathy in viewers.

lent period of social unrest in the late 1940s, featured in his harrowing *Estudiante Muerto.*

Enrique Grau (1920-2004) is a surrealist and tropical artist, whose studies were mainly of *mulatas,* flowers and his beloved **Cartagena**. In Cartagena's **Teatro Heredia**, the stage backdrop Grau painted is profoundly Colombian in its symbolism. Another artist affected by the political turmoil of the 1940s was **Marco Ospina** (1912-83), Colombia's first abstract painter. His watercolors embody a picturesque, provincial reality. As Colombia approaches its bicentenary, attitudes towards art have changed greatly, and an acceptance of modernity blended with the *métissage* of indigenous, European and African backgrounds has paved the way for a diversification of **Colombian Art**.

Juan Cárdenas, Raúl Restrepo, David Manzur, Carlos Rojas, Alvaro Barrios, Beatriz González, Sara Modiano—these are just a few of the artists who have contributed to Colombian Art's distinctive syle and essence. By exploring and embracing various genres—from Neo-Realism to Neo-Expressionism, Hyperrealism, Minimalism and Performance Art—they have developed their own identity as Colombians as well as artists.

SCULPTURE

Pre-Columbian Period

Also see Crafts.

The wealth of archaeological vestiges left by the cultures found in Colombia prior to the arrival of the Spanish attests to the importance for pre-Columbians of sculpture as an art form.

Outstanding examples can be found in the departments of Huila and Cauca, where two UNESCO World Heritage sites are located: **San Agustín** and **Tierradentro** (*see SAN AGUSTÍN and POPAYÁN*). These spectacular necropolises are famous for their **anthropomorphic** and **zoomorphic statuary**.

The **La Tolita-Tumaco** culture (500 BC-AD 300) extended from Ecuador to the Colombian Pacific. It produced some of the most beautiful examples of pre-Columbian art—compared by some to early Greek sculpture—including funerary and erotic ceramic figures, and many representations of disease and medical disorders.

The **Nariño** culture (600 BC-AD 1500) is known for its *coqueros*, or small seated ceramic figures traditionally depicted as chewing coca leaves.

Statue, Parque Arqueológico de San Agustín

© Richard McColl/MICHELIN

In the regions around Bogotá, the **Muisca** (1000-1550) left impressive rows of phallic **standing stones** at the **El Infiernito** site (*see VILLA DE LEYVA*).

Republican Realism

By the 19C Colombian sculpture took on a more realistic, academic edge, but following the same lines as the Colonial period. **Bernabé Martínez** and his son **Toribio Martínez** (dates unknown)

Colonial Period (16C-18C)

Much like paintings, **early religious sculptures** in Colombia during the Colonial period were either imported from the homeland, or were imitations of originals done by Spanish settlers. For example, in the early colonial days, when Tunja (*see TUNJA*) was a major city, the **Capilla de los Mancipes**, in the cathedral, received imported sculptures by **Juan Bautista Vázquez the Older** (1510-1588), a founding member of the Sevillian School, who had worked on both Seville's and Toledo's cathedrals. Also in Tunja's cathedral, anthropomorphic figures visible near the altar are, without doubt, **imitations** of work done by the Dutch Renaissance artist **Vredeman de Vries** (1527-1607).

Perhaps the most celebrated Colombian sculptor of the 17C was **Pedro de Lugo Albarracín**, who worked on the *Cristo Caído*, better known as *El Señor de Monserrate*, located at the highest point in Bogotá and a destination in its own right for many pilgrims (*see BOGOTÁ*).

Later, as the **Baroque** movement swept through the colonies, it was again the city of Tunja that would arguably benefit most from religious sculptures. Part of the **Iglesia Santo Domingo**, the **Capilla del Rosario** is often referred to as the "Sistine Chapel" of Latin American Baroque art, in particular due to the eight polychrome wooden reliefs done by **Lorenzo de Lugo.**

As for the **Rococo** movement in Colombia, the best examples—done by **Pedro Laboria** (1700-1784)—can be seen in Tunja's cathedral and **Templo de San Ignacio,** as well as in Bogotá's Cathedral.

created what can only be described as a small dynasty of religious sculptors.

Modern Sculpture

Santiago Martínez Delgado (1906-1954) and **Pedro Nel Gómez** (1899-1984), mentioned extensively herein in the introduction to Colombian painting, have a place in an overview of sculpture since their legacy in the art world is considerable. Martínez worked on the carving on the façade of the **National Palace** in **Cúcuta**. Gómez used several materials for his creations: wood for *Mujeres Emigrantes*, bronze for the *Cacique Nutibara Fountain* in Medellín, and marble for *Barequera melancólica*.

One notable **academic** sculptor was **Gustavo Arcila Uribe** (1895-1963). Any visit to the capital city includes seeing his work, such as the illuminated *Virgen Milagrosa* (1946), visible by day and night on top of the **Cerro de Guadalupe**, above the colonial Candelaria district.

In the **abstract** field, look no further than **Hugo Martínez González** (b. 1923), whose smooth lines and careful movement are somehow transposed on works such as *Cabeza de Mulata* and *La Huida*.

Considered one of Colombia's finest living sculptors, **Edgar Negret** (b. 1920) started out in stone **modernism** before moving into metal **constructivism**. Using doubled-up aluminum such as in the *Cabeza de Bautista*, he is able to create a feeling of space, all the while using colors of bright red, blue and yellow inspired by pre-Columbian art.

Recognized alongside Negret as one of the masters of Colombian sculpture, **Eduardo Ramírez Villamizar** (b. 1923) can be regarded as traditional, in spite of the abstraction and the breadth which traverse the constructivism of his work.

With regards to **nationalist** sculpture, a fine example is the *Monumento a la Raza* by **Rodrigo Arenas Betancur** (1919-1995) in Medellín. Made from bronze and concrete, this piece rises to a height of 38m/125ft. The artist also made the striking bronze, concrete and steel **Memorial to the Vargas Swamp Battle** *(Monumento conmemorativo de la batalla del Pantano de Vargas)* in Paipa (Boyacá).

A great deal is understandably made of multi-talented **Fernando Botero** (◯ *see sidebar p78),* whose works portray his signature adipose human and animal figures, in **bronze** as well as on canvas. But many other Colombian sculptors are worthy of recognition, and have played a decisive role in opening up the international stage to a new generation of Latin America artists.

Profoundly affected by the problems of violence in her country and their devastating impact on the social fabric, **Doris Salcedo** (b. 1958) tends to use reconfigured pieces of furniture in her work as a way of mourning the loss of their former occupants. In creating a 167m/548ft-long crack in the floor of the Tate Modern's Turbine Hall, her striking installation entitled *Shibboleth* (2007) seems to expose a fracture in modernity.

Taking a controversial look at contemporary consumerism, **Nadín Ospina** (1960) has gained significant international recognition for his pre-Columbian totem sculptures of popular cartoon characters. His combining ancient artistic traditions with products of mass-culture upbringing is a clever way of engaging a reflection on authenticity and falsity in art.

Monumento a la Raza
by Rodrigo Arenas Betancur,
Centro Administrativo La Alpujarra José
María Córdova, Medellín

Proexport Colombia

Museo Donación Botero, Bogotá

Proexport Colombia

The Big Picture

An accomplished **sculptor** and a talented **painter** with the dexterity of an Old Master, **Fernando Botero** (b. 1932) is Colombia's most famous artist. His rotund world, peopled with the **corpulent** humans and animals who have become his trademark, has brought him universal recognition.

Clearly influenced by his upbringing, Botero constantly refers to his **native Colombia** in his work. For instance, as a young man, he was sent off to train as a bullfighter, an experience reflected in his famous series on the *corrida*. In painting or sculpture, he fuses the **folklore** of his homeland with **Western artistic traditions**, deforming figures from famous artists such as Velázquez, Dürer and their like so as to create elaborate **parodies** that some critics have compared to **satires**. Botero focuses mainly on **everyday life**, his preferred subjects including family portraits, nudes, still life, food, music and religion, but beneath his cheerfully whimsical depictions, the strains of the artist's reach for the Colombian **national identity** can be perceived. His religious composition *Our Lady of Colombia* includes a tiny national flag, and even a piece like *Marie-Antoinette and Louis XVI* seems to be set in a Colombian village street.

A visit to Botero's home city of **Medellín** will provide close encounters with a large number of his works. In front of the **Museo de Antioquia**, for example, and in the **Parque Berrío** stand 14 of his fleshy bronze figures, including *La Mano*, *Cabeza* and *Adam and Eve*.

Quirky in tone, most Botero **paintings** seem lighthearted, with a love for simple joys. Yet Botero has a knack for shaking up the viewer with the occasional piece that embodies cutting **social commentary** or is a sober reflection of the dark side of Colombian life. Just as you are getting accustomed to smiling at his carefree women preening in the mirror, or a young couple holding hands in the park, a Botero painting like *Carrobomba* or *Secuestro* shakes your notion of the artist as naive or simplistic. Nowhere is this upheaval more impactful than his highly stylized portrayal of notorious drug kingpin, *Pablo Escobar,* being gunned down by government troops. But it is the *Bird of Peace* sculpture in the **Parque San Antonio** in Medellín that really brings the Colombian situation up close. In 1995 a bomb was placed at the feet of this sculpture, and 23 people lost their lives. When asked if he wished to replace the sculpture, Botero declined, deciding instead to create an identical statue and place it alongside the destroyed one to show the futility of the action.

GOLDSMITHING

Pre-Columbian Period

Colombia's wealth of pre-Columbian cultures as well as archeological accounts from expeditions and finds by grave robbers, indicate the range and extent of gold craftsmanship in the country. The Spanish would undoubtedly have spent far less time here had there been neither precious metals, nor the legend of **El Dorado**.

Most of the best preserved and interesting pieces of gold can be found in the **Museo del Oro** in Bogotá (👆 *see BOGOTÁ*), such as those of the **Calima** culture (AD 200-AD 1200), in particular the pectoral ornaments and breastplates made from hammered gold sheets.

For the **Tolima** culture (1200 BC-AD 1500), gold was a symbol of power and hierarchy, and their ornaments such as the human-headed bird, the avian pendant and the ornamental **Tumi** knife are some of the most representative of pre-Columbian gold craftsmanship from the region.

The **Quimbaya** (300 BC-AD 1550) placed a strong importance on fertility. Digs in the region of Cauca have yielded **zoomorphic** figurines, nose rings and assorted jewelry, and the intriguing ceremonial **poporos**, containers holding the lime used in coca-leaf chewing.

Clearly an important trading route, given its geographical location and

Tumbaga

Tumbaga was the name given by the Spaniards to the **gold** and **copper alloy** widely used by pre-Columbian cultures to make religious objects. With a melting point lower than that of pure gold, tumbaga was easier to work with, making it more desirable to the goldsmiths. It was versatile and could be hammered into whatever form or design they desired. The conquistadors frequently melted their New World plunders into bars of tumbaga to facilitate its transport back to Spain.

Filigrana Momposina

Mompox (Bolívar), a beautiful town along the banks of the River Magdalena, gave its name to this particular **filigree technique**, which produces some of the most intricate and sought-after jewelry in Colombia. Delicately coiled **gold** or **silver** is painstaking melted and manipulated into shapes to create earrings, pendants, necklaces and bracelets. In recent years, with the influx of tourists, the styles have become slightly more contemporary and international, but on the whole, the jewels are created with traditional designs in mind. These designs, a subtle blend of Hispanic, indigenous, African and Arabic influences, reflect Mompox' own multi-ethnic heritage.

calm waters, **Urabá** was chosen by the conquistador **Alonso de Ojeda** to create the first Spanish settlement on the South American mainland. The Urabá people, using this area as a route to **Panama**, left behind gold ornaments portraying female figures as well as pendants and flasks.

Finds from the **Sierra Nevada**, ancestral territory of the **Tayrona** culture (AD 900-AD 1600), have produced hammered nose plates and breastplates as well as gold figurines of animals.

In the **Chocó**, on the Pacific side, the pre-Columbian tribes had access to greater gold deposits and created masks with feathers, as worn by **shamans**.

In the highlands of **Cundinamarca** and **Boyacá**, where the **Muisca** people (545 BC-AD 1550) were in power, comes the legend of El Dorado (👆 *see sidebar p141*). Gold offerings were made to the goddess Guatavita and were tossed into **Lake Guatavita,** creating the famous legend. Typically, Muisca gold featured **anthropomorphic**, as well as bird-man, figures.

CRAFTS

Textiles

Crossing Colombia from east to west could lead you to believe that you have actually left one nation and entered another. The variations in cultural habits are quite strong, and the country's textile heritage is no exception.

In the chillier highlands of the **Andes**, and in particular throughout the rural departments of Boyacá and Antioquia, the **ruana** is a traditional and frequently worn type of sleeveless poncho used to ward off the cold and dampness. It is a symbol of pride to many, and has become a national heritage symbol. Former president Álvaro Uribe was seen on many occasions making a gift of a *ruana* to a visiting head of state .

Recently voted as a symbol of Colombia, the **vueltiao** is a wide-brimmed hat made from the woven fibers of the arrow cane palm tree. The weaving tradition comes from the **Zenú** Indians of the Caribbean coast, supposedly having some significance in their cosmology. The finer the weave and ability to fold or roll up the hat, the higher the quality and the more it will cost.

On the **Caribbean coast**, bordering Venezuela, the **Wayúu** people of the **Guajira** peninsula have become known for their **knitwear**, in particular their **chinchorros** (hammocks) and their **mochilas** (shoulder bags). Tightly woven and brightly colored, these products are long lasting and have become incredibly fashionable, both nationally and internationally.

The Gulf of **Urabá,** which extends south from the autonomous Panamanian territory of the Kuna Yala and San Blas islands, is home to the **Kuna** or **Tule** people. Their brightly colored **molas** are hand-made patchworks with animal and cosmological references.

The city of **Cartago** (Valle del Cauca) is famous for its **hand embroidery**, an Hispano-Arabic legacy brought over from Andalusia. Floral and geometric motifs are particularly representative of the technique.

In the town of **San Jacinto**, on the road from Cartagena to Mompox, you will find every shape, color and size of cotton **hammock**.

Basketry

In the village of **Guacamayas** (Boyacá), in the ancestral homelands of **Lache** and **Tunebo** Indians, local people perpetuate the indigenous practices of basket weaving and making products from **straw** and **fique**, a natural plant fiber.

The tradition of **spiral basketwork** uses rolls of straw created and fastened by fique threads. Once the desired shape is made, the fibers are dyed in a natural process. Baskets, dishes, place mats and bowls are made from straw and fique.

On the **Pacific coast**, in **Pichimá** (Chocó), the **Waunana** Indians weave handsome, unique **werregue** baskets. This technique, which probably origi-

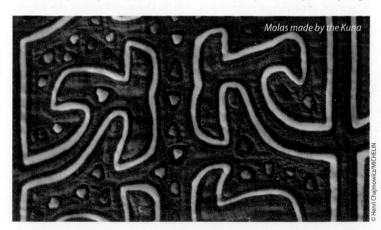

Molas made by the Kuna

© Henri Chajmowicz/MICHELIN

nated in Africa, uses flexible werregue fibers rolled up in a spiral fashion and attached to a wooden base. Depending on its size, each basket can take between 30 and 60 days to make.

Ceramics

Also see Sculpture. Pre-Columbians made all kinds of offerings to their deities, including **ceramic offerings**. These offerings reflected their beliefs and illustrated some aspects of their **daily lives**, which were largely controlled by the elements and the seasons.

Some **recurring themes** such as fertility and maternity can be found all across Colombia, for example in the ceramics of the **Calima** culture (BC 1500-AD 100), or those of the **Quimbaya** people (300 BC-AD 1550), in Cauca, with some pieces curiously in the shape of pregnant women.

Of course, death was of major significance to the indigenous people, a topic that features heavily in their symbolism. The **Tolima** culture (1200 BC-AD 1500) from the Magdalena Valley, around the current site of **Ibagué**, has provided some spectacular funerary urns.

The **Tumaco** culture (500 BC-AD 300) stood apart from the other cultures in that they used a system of **molds** in the pottery-making process, evidently designed for mass production.

When viewing pre-Columbian ceramics, notice the **painting** and **artwork**, since there are several **styles**. In the **Tierradentro** culture, funerary urns were decorated with images of snakes and lizards, and plates, pots and tripods were usually painted black, coffee brown and dark red.

The **Nariño** culture (600 BC-AD 1500) used the technique of negative painting: leaving a part of the surface blank and applying color around the blank space to give it emphasis. They used black as the negative on cups and red for the background; creamy colored cups with red and white designs were a variation.

Clearly another key facet to pre-Columbian pottery is the abundance of **anthropomorphic** shapes and designs. By no means was this habit restricted

Pottery from the Andean Region

Proexport Colombia

Colombian Pottery Today

The epicenter of ceramic pot-making in contemporary Colombia is the town of **Ráquira** ("city of pots" in the Chibcha language). Largely exported, its production includes various styles, from traditional cooking pots and water jugs to mass-produced platters and other ware. The basic clay colors are black (with high levels of charcoal), white, yellow or red.

In the Andean region of **Tolima** and in the town of **La Chamba**, local artisans create a black pottery in keeping with indigenous traditions. The clay is pulverized and molded into shape, then left to dry for 30 days before being baked. Later, it is buffed to give it its shiny finish. All the ceramic pieces are handmade from local micaceous clay. Some archaeologists have reported that the immediate region of La Chamba is home to the oldest pottery produced in the Americas.

to any one indigenous group. In fact, it was practiced by most, including the **Muisca** (545 BC-AD1550) who created bowls held by human figures. Yet, they were mostly recognized for the prevalence of **zoomorphic** references such as frogs and snakes.

The **Zenú** (200 BC-AD 1600), on the Caribbean coast, would also paint various representations of the local fauna, such as waterfowl and crocodiles.

PERFORMING ARTS
MUSIC AND DANCE

Colombia's music and dance traditions comprise a rhythmic mix of different genres that fuse influences from **America**, **Europe** and the **Caribbean**. Often commemorative in character, many songs honor certain times of year, specific people or momentous events. Broadly speaking, key Colombian music and dance genres fall into four geographic zones, each with a distinct sound and a unique heritage that reflects the peoples, characteristics, traditions, rituals and history of the region.

Music of the Andes

Instantly recognizable because of the bright sound of Colombia's 12-string **tiple guitar**, this music is loaded with influences from the music of the Arabic-Spanish genre, and often features a cacophony of string sounds courtesy of strummed and plucked **mandolins**, **guitars** and **bandolas** (small guitars inherited from Moorish Spain). Expect to hear an occasional burst of a flute, harmonica or lyre peppered with the sound of a shaking maracas or beating drum. In some forms, the *guacharaca* picks up the strong Spanish pulse, often with a tinkling piano. Genres such as the **bambuco** (Colombia's national dance that boasts a beat structure similar to the European waltz), **pasillo guabina** and **torbellino** provide lively interpretations.

Music of the Atlantic Coast

On the Caribbean coast, a complex mix of African rhythms was popularized as a primal communication method of the slaves using **drums**, simple **vocals** and tit-for-tat-style dance moves. Tales of slavery were set to **pounding rhythms**, with shuffling footwork used to portray the shackles of ropes and ankle chains. In the 1940s and 1950s, the sounds of the coastline evolved from a rural form to a more refined style.

Rhythmic **cumbia** is danced with gusto, often in large groups of male and female couples, with women swirling long skirts while holding a candle, and men dancing behind with one hand on their back. The urbanization of *cumbia* helped it gain respectability. Yet at least spiritually, it remains a stalwart of Colombia's working classes. Today several modern artists fuse elements of *cumbia* with other genres, such as **vallenato**, pop and rock. Synonymous with songwriter **Rafael Escalona**, *vallenato* is a celebrated genre from the northern tip of Colombia that combines European-style accordion riffs with traditional folkloric themes. Former soap star **Carlos Vives** has become a national hero for his championing of *vallenato, cumbia* and *porró* before a new, young audience. In Cartagena, **champeta** is the street music of "dirty dancers" with gutsy rhythms and scandalously risqué lyrics.

Music of the Pacific Coast

The Pacific Coast probably retains the closest musical links with Africa, using heavy **drumbeats** tinged with telltale Spanish inflections. Rhythms are protec-

Colombian Salsa

In the 1960s salsa joined Colombia's many variants of its older musical styles to dominate the nation's music scene. With its origins in Puerto Rico and Cuba and its catchy sensuality, this music-and-dance mainstay soon became a key part of Latino culture. Salsa was embraced with particular gusto in Cali and Barranquilla, where snappy interpretations and unforgettable classics became a fixture in every club, bar and studio. Today **Cali** is dubbed the country's undisputed **Capital de la Salsa** with hundreds of clubs, festivals, dance schools and concerts. Each year, the city hosts an annual weeklong **Summer Salsa Festival** that lures many of the world's greatest salsa bands and devotees to dance shows and competitions. The event includes the **World Salsa Championship** and **World Salsa** Congress.

tively monitored by the descendants of slaves who safeguard their ancestral heritage, staying true to the traditions of the genre. Using an instrument known as a **marimba de chanota** (the equivalent of a West African xylophone made from bamboo and chonto wood), drums (*redoblante*), bass, clarinet and **guasa** (a seed-filled percussive bamboo tube), Pacific Coast musicians compose captivating Afro-Colombian **currulao songs** laced with tales of love, deity and family. Younger artists have developed a hip-hop mainstream style that has exploded across the region. Favorite bands include **ChocQuibTown**, with hit song *Somos Pacifico*, infused with the rich tones of the marimba for a stunning effect.

Music of the Plains

In the rolling cattle-strewn savannas of Los Llanos, the music of the region tends to be accompanied by a **harp**, **cuatro** (a small, four-string guitar) and **maracas**, though dozens of variations insure that no music and dance rhythm is quite the same. As the sound of the plainsman and cowboy, lyrical styles focus on heart-felt sentiment with proclamations of love and regional pride sung at top-of-the-lung volume. Llanera's harp-led melodies in traditional **joropo style** (together with regional variants) blend machismo desires with big-hearted passion. Often the distinctive staccato **flamenco** beats can be heard together with the tum-tum-tum of the European **waltz**. Poetic prose captures the essence of the isolation of these vast, sprawling flatlands while joyous, rhythmic, string-and-percussion-based choruses gather momentum at a syncopated pace. Some of the famous *musica llanera* artists include such greats as Alma Llanera, Cimarron, Luis Ariel Rey, Carlos Rojas, Sabor Llanero, Arnulfo Briceño and Orlando Valdemarra.

Music of the Amazon

The geographic range of Amazonian music is vast, covering a large part of northern Brazil, southeastern Colombia, Ecuador, Peru and southcentral Venezuela. With over 100 native tribes,

Modern Trends

Pop music in Colombia is dominated by several headline-grabbing, home-grown musical icons. **Shakira**, a two-time Latin Grammy Award-winner, remains Colombia's biggest musical celebrity, selling 50 million albums and establishing herself in history as the only Colombian artist to reach number-one on the Billboard Hot 100 and UK Singles Chart. Bogotá-born heartthrob **Fonseca**'s acclaimed double-platinum album *Corazon* blends hints of *vallenato*, *bullerengue* and *tambora* with boy-band vocals. Since launching his solo career in 1998, triple-Grammy Award-winner Medellín-born **Juanes** has taken the Spanish-speaking world by storm. At grassroots level, hip hop and reggae continue to sell well with **La Etnnia** and **Gotas de Rap,** considered the trailblazers in Colombian rap music.

Colombia's remote Amazonian region is still home to indigenous languages and music. However, little has been documented, given its small scale compared to other bigger regions of the Amazon. **Cumbia andina** (a Peruvian rhythm) is often mixed with the Brazilian rhythms of samba, *forro* and *lambad*a in Amazonian towns, with similarities to Andean musical traditions and sparse use of instrumental accompaniment (often just a carved wooden **flute**) to haunting, mesmerizing acoustic voice.

Cumbia dancers

Mauro Fuentes/Proexport Colombia

THEATER

Using Colombia's diverse landscape, array of cultures, and political and social instability as a creative template, numerous Colombian artists have developed a colorful theatrical tradition. It combines intellectual reflection on the nation's history with new and exciting formats that have influenced the arts in general across Latin America. Today a plethora of regional, national and international festivals celebrate and promote Colombian theater and its highly-progressive and inventive arts scene.

Colonial Period

Before the arrival of the Spanish, **poetry**, **theatrical skits**, **mime** and **comic shows** were vehicles for indigenous communities to connect with their spiritual world. **Zarzuela**, a style of theater brought from Spain, dominated the colonial era and became a strong influence on Colombia's theatrical tradition, with musical performances that fused comedy with tragedy.

Festival Iberoamericano de Teatro de Bogotá

The largest theatrical event of its kind in all of South America, this two-week event was founded in 1988 under the the slogan "un acto de fe por Colombia" (an act of faith for Colombia). Its success shows no sign of abating as an enormous event on Colombia's cultural calendar. Held every two years in the capital, it is staged in numerous theaters, squares, shopping centers, and even the city's bullring, and hosts a multitude of performances, premieres, seminars, workshops and concerts. The festival attracts hundreds of established international repertories from all over the world, such as Britain's Royal Shakespeare Company. Large crowds of spectators attend some 600 shows featuring as many as 3,000 artists and performers.

Republican Period

The Republican era brought with it significant investment in architecture. Elaborate buildings were erected—several for Colombia's burgeoning theatrical scene, including **Teatro Cristóbal Colón** (1885) and **Teatro de La Candelaria** (1890), both in Bogotá.

Modern Period

Colombian theater truly came into its own in the early part of the 20C, largely due to the efforts of playwrights **Antonio Álvarez Lleras** and **Luis Enríque Osorio**, who penned scripts based on politically themed subjects. The intellectual, thought-provoking plays of the **theater of the absurd** and **avant-garde theater**, which both emerged in the 1950s, tackled increasingly contentious themes; they would prove to strike a chord with audiences in need of an expressive outlet during Colombia's rapidly escalating domestic conflicts.
The late 1970s and early 1980s saw a resurgence of more conventionally scripted drama. With growing levels of paramilitary and cartel violence terrifying the nation, activist theater suffered a decline as audiences turned away from reality in search of escapist themes.
Alternative theater has strengthened its hold on Colombian audiences, largely due to the efforts of pioneers **Henry Díaz** and **Victor Viviescas**, and with the work of playwrights such as **Santiago Garcia**. Other talented modern playwrights include Medellín's **José Manuel Freydell**, a prolific creator murdered in 1990 after an illustrious career.
In the last decade or so, Colombia has experienced a revival of **street theater**, with groups performing a variety of music, mime and drama for public consumption in shopping malls and plazas.
Dedicated to fomenting the arts, hundreds of well-organized **theater groups** and **drama schools** are now installed in both urban and rural areas of the country, including the Cali Theatre School (TEC), the Medellín University Theatre, the Bogotá Popular Theatre and Manizales University Theatre.

CINEMA

Despite a long history dating back over 110 years, the Colombian movie industry has been slow to evolve as a thriving entity. Lack of funding and disruption of filming schedules in a country torn by internal conflict frustrated cinematographic efforts and jeopardized the future of this fledgling industry. Today Colombia is finally gaining in recognition and producing films that are receiving critical acclaim in several festivals around the world.

A History of Struggle

Cinema arrived in Colombia in **1897**, but failed to break through to popular culture because of domestic issues. The di Domenico brothers' **Salon Olympia** in Bogotá became a major force in Colombian cinema, airing documentaries such as *El drama del 15 de Octubre*. In the **1920s** short documentaries and landscape films continued to dominate the movie industry. Under severe financial strain from **1928 to 1940**, film production came to a halt, missing the transition from silent movies to talking picture technology, but reestablishing itself in the **1940s**. The sector soon collapsed again due to lack of financial support, and restarted in the **1950s** under the impulse of Gabriel García Márquez and Enrique Grau. In the **1970s** "miserabilist films" hit the screen, depicting the reality of everyday Colombian life in a grim way. Created in **1978** to help the movie industry, state-run agency **FOCINE** was dismantled 15 years later, after inspiring a new generation of creative filmmakers. The Colombian congress passed **Law 397** In 1997 to better support the movie industry, and in 2003 approved the **Law of Cinema** to boost national film production. Colombia has since generated numerous box office hits with government sponsorship.

International Recognition

Released in 2000, the internationally acclaimed **La virgen de los sicarios** (*Our Lady of the Assassins*), directed by Frenchman Barbet Schroeder, was based on Colombian Fernando Vallejo's semi-

Colombian Movie Festivals

Colombia's biggest film festivals now attract a truly international field of notables from the movie industry. The **Festival de Cine de Bogotá**, inaugurated in 1984, takes place in October and is organized by the Corporación Internacional de Cine. However, it is the Caribbean city Cartagena that plays host to the oldest film festival in Latin America. The **Festival Internacional de Cine de Cartagena** was launched in 1960 by Victor Nieto, who remained its director for 48 years before handing over the mantle, prior to his death in 2008 at age 92, to Lina Paola Rodriguez.

autobiographical novel. After 30 years away from his hometown of Medellín, the main character returns to discover a culture of drug-related violence and homicide. The film received an array of international accolades, including the "Best Latin American Film" at the Venice Film Festival and "Nuevo Cine" at La Habana International Festival in 2000. Release of the US-Colombian production **Maria, llena eres de gracia** (*Maria Full of Grace*) in 2004, filmed by Joshua Marston, won considerable acclaim for dealing with drug-trafficking and social issues in Colombia. Catalina Sandino was awarded the 2004 Berlin Golden Bear for Best Actress for her performance in the principal role in the film.

Two Colombian movies, **1989** and **Los Viajes del Viento** (*Wind Journeys*), were selected to compete at the 2009 Cannes Film Festival, the first Colombian films to do so in 11 years.

In 2010 Colombian director Oscar Ruiz de Navia was awarded an international critics' prize at the Berlin International Film Festival for his debut work **El vuelco del cangrejo** (Crab Trap); he dedicated it "to the whole community of La Barra," a village on Colombia's northern coast where the movie was filmed.

85

ARCHITECTURE

Colombia's cities and towns are a melting pot of architectural styles that range from humble to opulent, and that ideally can reflect the political ideologies and intellectual desires of the time. One may be wandering through a typical town only to spot an Art Deco theater or some of the best preserved Colonial architecture in the Western Hemisphere. Colombia is a country of regions, evident in the architectural variations from wooden Caribbean structures to the Paisa-style buildings of the Coffee Zone.

In some places it seems that every style of architecture has descended upon the nation in a hurry, with Neoclassical and Gothic Revival styles thrown together in no particular order.

*Malocas in a Kogui village
in Sierra Nevada de Santa Marta*

Colombia's rapid urbanization—due to population displacement from the countryside—has only added to this chaotic environment, a complexity that is being addressed in several cities, with positive results.

Ciudad Perdida, Sierra Nevada de Santa Marta

Henri Choimet/MICHELIN

Burial chamber, Alto de Segovia, Parque Arqueológico de Tierradentro

MAIN TRADITIONAL STYLES

Pre-Columbian Style

Generally speaking, this term not only refers to the architecture during that period, but also applies to structures inspired by it and constructed in such a fashion as to evoke the indigenous habitat from pre-Hispanic times (prior to 16C).

It would be ill-informed to judge this architecture as primitive since indigenous practices such as the use of **bahareque** (*see sidebar p260*) and **guadua bamboo** were widely adopted in Spanish construction in the New World. While most indigenous dwellings consisted of oval or rectangular **malocas**, the **Muisca** people, located in the regions of Bogotá and thereabouts, never employed the use of stone despite the prevalence of this building material. Most pre-Columbian dwellings incorporated products such as **palm fronds** for roofing and ran straight to the ground. Today this building style can be seen when trekking to the **Ciudad Perdida** or visiting **Parque Nacional Tayrona** (*see SANTA MARTA*).

Colonial Style

The Colonial period (16C–18C) left an impressive architectural legacy perhaps best seen in the towns of **Mompox**,

Popayán and **Barichara**, and in the cities of **Bogotá** and **Cartagena**. Colonial architecture is notable for thick walls, clay-baked roof tiles and internal patios situated around low, cloister-style buildings. A fine example of a religious building in this style is the church of the **Convento de Santo Domingo** (1578) in Cartagena, with its austere façade and high ceilings. In order to see preserved versions of Colonial dwellings, there is no better place than the town of Mompox, found farther inland, and the **Calle Real del Medio**, where one can view unaltered Colonial houses with ironwork windows and skilled carpentry on the roofs. A further place of interest is **Plaza de Bolívar** (1539) in **Tunja**, with its cathedral, official buildings and Casa de la Cultura (*see TUNJA*).

Neoclassical Style

With its Doric façade, carved stone and cornices, the late 19C **Teatro Colón** in Bogotá's Candelaria district is definitely in the Neoclassical style, as is the **Palacio de Nariño** (damaged during the Bogotazo riots of 1948 and restored in the 1970s) in the Plaza de Bolívar, just downhill. Its columns, stonework and Louis XV salon help make it an impressive seat of government. In towns throughout Colombia, inclu-

87

Henri Choimet/MICHELIN

Neoclassical: Teatro de Cristóbal Colón, Bogotá

ding **Bucaramanga** with its **Club del Comercio** and **Cartagena** with the **Edificio Banco Bolívar**, one can see other versions of Neoclassical design. Formerly, perhaps they were ornate and played a central commercial role; now they have been incorporated into the sprawl of urban centers.

Republican Style

With the industrial revolution already under way, the Republican style came to a Colombia anxious to break out of the mold of the colonial regime. In **Cartagena**, the Republican architecture was more or less placed on top of the old Colonial buildings, particularly in the sought-after **barrio San Diego**, increasing their size from single story to three stories and opening spaces in order to proclaim an architectural independence, not only a political one.

The desire of the city of **Manizales** to step up from its image as a provincial town to that of a wealthy coffee elite is evident in such architectural examples as the Republican-style edifices of the **Palacio de la Gobernación de Caldas** and the **Edificio Manuel Sanz**.

Gothic Revival Style

A whole host of churches in Colombia are designed in the Gothic Revival style. They range from the **Iglesia del Señor de las Misericordias** (1921) in downtown Medellín to the most striking

and well recognized **Santuario de Las Lajas** (fifth and final stage completed in 1949), close to Ipiales in the south of the country. With huge flying buttresses and ornate windows, this sanctuary is a popular site for pilgrims from all over Colombia. What is even more amazing is that the church is built on a twin-arched bridge over a river *(see sidebar p397)*.

Mudéjar Revival

Inspired by an elaborate form of medieval Spanish-Muslim architecture, this style became fashionable in Europe in the late 19C-early 20C. There are a few versions of Mudéjar Revival architecture in Colombia, such as the tower to **Iglesia**

Republican: Edificio Manuel Sanz, Manizales

Henri Choimet/MICHELIN

de San Francisco (1751) in the center of Cali. Its unmistakable blend of Hispano-Arabic styles is employed in both the tower section of the church and the lateral doorway. The most remarkable example of this architecture could well be Bogotá's **Santa Maria Bullring** (1931). Even the city of Cartagena, better known for its Colonial and Republican architecture, is not exempt from Mudéjar edifices; a fine example of this style, with its smooth curves and high entrances, is the Casa Covo (1931), in the well-heeled **barrio** Manga.

Art Deco

While perhaps not striking visitors as the most scenic place to visit, the Caribbean port city of Barranquilla houses more than its share of Art Deco buildings, including the imposing **Estadio** Romelio Martínez Stadium (1934), the handsome **Edificio García** (1938) and the colorful **Teatro Colón** (1940s). But it is not just in

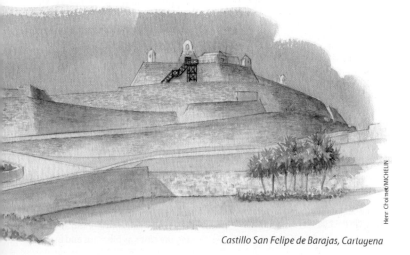

Henri Choimet/MICHELIN

Castillo San Felipe de Barajas, Cartagena

89

Henri Choimet/MICHELIN

Iglesia Santa Barbara, Mompox

Calles and Carreras

At first glance, addresses in Colombia can seem a complete soup of numbers suitably organised to ensure an ambiguous final location. In actual fact, the **grid system** that is employed in most towns and major cities consisting of *Carreras* and *Calles* is quite straightforward. In Bogotá for example, Carreras run North to South and Calles perpendicular to these from East to West. So, should the address you are looking for be Calle 16 No 1-05, then you can locate it by heading first to Calle 16, and then heading to the block or *cuadra* between Carreras 1 and 2, the 05 refering to the building number. Cartagena's old town is, of course, an exception to the rule since the nomenclature has been handed down by the Spanish, and streets and avenues have names just like in Europe, such as the Calle del Cuartel of Media Luna.

Barranquilla that one can see structures representative of this style, since they can be found all over the country, from the smallest towns to major cities.

URBAN CONTEXT

Urban Planning

Colombia's urban structure has undergone a transformation of almost biblical proportions in the last 50 years. Much of this change can be attributed to the rising **rural-urban migration** due to violence raging in the countryside. Between the late 1930s and early 1970s, Colombia's urban population increased from 30 percent of the national total to nearly 60 percent. Faced with such a **population explosion**, the cities were placed under immeasurable pressures that produced uncontrolled and somewhat chaotic construction.

The ensuing shambles of roads and poorly constructed buildings can still be seen today, but these undesirable conditions are improving since Colombian politicians have been taking a more active role in urban planning and remaking the cities as pleasant and inclusive

Santa Fé de Antioquia

© Peter M. Wilson/Corbis

Paisa Architecture

With strong influences from Spain, Paisa architecture has been put in place and developed in the areas around Medellín and the Coffee Zone from 16C colonial times until well into the 20C. Using a method known as **bahareque**, which employs the materials of **cane** and **mud** in the construction, Paisa architecture owes its structure in no small part to the practices of the indigenous communities of Colombia that were using this method long before the arrival of the Spanish. Over time, the materials have evolved, but the overall form of the house remains the same. Traditional Paisa houses, which can be seen in the towns of **Santa Fé de Antioquia** and **Jericó**, with their elegantly **painted trim**, have a large independent and self-contained entrance hallway or **zaguán**, tall **windows** and baked **clay tiles**; all of the rooms and bedrooms surround an **interior courtyard**, emphasizing the Paisa belief in large families.

Employing the same theories of design as a Paisa home, the **pueblo Paisa** is a village modeled on a Spanish design, with the **church** at the center, situated by the **main plaza** or park. In this same area is the **town hall**. All streets extend outward from the park, making it consistently the most important place in town. In the rural parts of Antioquia, this design can be seen over and over again, but if pressed for time, visit the **Pueblito Paisa** in Medellín, which should give you some idea of the layout (*see BOGOTÁ).

places in which to live. The former mayor of Bogotá **Antanas Mockus** and the former mayor of Medellín **Sergio Fajardo** deserve special recognition for their work in their respective cities. **Bogotá**, the capital, has been plagued with increasingly hazardous **traffic,** especially the uncontrolled number of buses and taxis endangering motorcyclists and pedestrians. Gradually and steadily, city officials have been tackling this problem, and since 2001 the **TransMilenio** bus system has been taking additional vehicles off the roads as commuters opt for public transport. Colombian politicians and urban planners are betting heavily on this system being integrated into the surrounding areas. Similar transportation is now being implemented in cities such as **Barranquilla**, **Cali** and **Bucaramanga**, albeit under different names.

Truly the jewel in Colombia's crown of integrated and inclusive public transport is the city of **Medellín**. With a **metro system** that is air conditioned and maintained in pristine condition, as well as a grateful, supportive citizenry,

Parque Biblioteca La Ladera León de Greiff, Medellín

Medellín is the envy of every Colombian city. Given the city's extreme geography, sitting deep in the Aburrá Valley, urban planners came up with the novel idea of connecting the metro and integrating it with a **cable car service** that rides up and over the hills to the poorer *barrios* located beyond the actual city limits. Not surprisingly, the cable car system itself has become a tourist attraction. But not all plaudits go to Medellín. In 2006 Bogotá was awarded the **Golden**

Cable car, Medellín

Samara Croci/Proexport Colombia

Lion Award for Architecture, in recognition for having addressed "the problems of social inclusion, housing, education and public space, especially through innovations in transport," and for having "applied Mies Van der Rohe's dictum 'less is more' to the automobile: less cars means more civic space and more civic resources for people," as well as providing "a model for streets which are pleasing to the eye as well as economically viable and socially inclusive."

Modern Architecture
Colombia has more than its fair share of skyscrapers and modern buildings, and talented architects are making a name for themselves by creating original and sustainable buildings in all corners of the country. Built in 1978, the tallest building in Colombia, Bogotá's 50-story **Torre Colpatria**, was to be dethroned by Cartagena's Torre de la Escollera, but construction of this 58-story tower, begun in 2005, was suspended due to foundational flaws, and the project was halted in 2007. The title of Colombia's tallest building will now go to the **Faro-Monarca** in Medellín or Bogotá's **Edificio BD Bacatá**, due for completion in 2013 and 2014 respectively.
Colombia's infatuation with the **brick** deserves special mention, since build-

Henri Choimet/MICHELIN

ings from Bogotá to Cali have been constructed in this material to great effect. The Torres del Parque (1970), in Bogotá's Macarena district above the Plaza de Toros, is such an example. His masterful command of the use of brick allowed **Rogelio Salmona** (1927-2007), the designer of this famous residential complex, to conceive amazing soaring towers with exposed brick and subtle undulating walls. A real break from Salmona's much-imitated, yet never-equalled creations, the futuristic **Maloka Interactive Science Museum** (1998) is a Colombian version of the world-famous Epcot Center. The three rock-buildings that make up the boulder-like **Biblioteca España** (2007) in Medellín are truly a sight and have generated optimism in this city about the future.

Henri Choimet/MICHELIN

Guaducto—a bridge made of bamboo, Universidad Tecnológica de Pereira

LITERATURE

With its heterogeneous racial backdrop of **Spanish**, **Indian** and **African** influences, Colombian literature is perhaps the perfect example of a continual and lively struggle to forge an identity out of the heritages and conditions inherent in this country.

Obviously, such conflicting yet colorful history has enabled Colombia to inspire a nation of writers and poets who seek to escape the realities of contemporary Colombia or express vitriolic discontent with the political situation.

There is no doubting **Gabriel García Márquez**'s strong influence on current Colombian literature which, in many cases, strives to step out of his long shadow. But this is not to say that there is no vast reservoir of other authors and poets to craft further imagery to hasten visitors to Colombia's doors.

PRE-COLUMBIAN PERIOD

Proving that the literary tradition in Colombia dates back significantly, one can reference the **oral traditions** of the **Kogui** of the Atlantic coast and their beliefs in *Creación*, or indeed the *Chiminiguagua*: *Creación del mundo*, of the **Chibcha** or **Muisca** people from the country's central highlands. *El Diluvio* from the Chocó, Colombia's lush Pacific coast that stretches up to the borders with Panama, re-creates life as the **Embera** people know it in the tangle of jungle found there.

CHRONICLES AND POETRY OF THE SPANISH DOMINION

Gonzalo Jiménez de Quesada (1495-1579), the founder of Bogotá, discoverer and conqueror of all but small parts of Nueva Granada, was also a noted chronicler. While neither copies of his *Relación de la Conquista del Nuevo Reino de Granada* nor *Compendio Historial de las Conquistas del Nuevo Reino* exist, we have been left with his insightful take on, and refutation of, the Italian archbishop of Nochera Paolo Jovio's anti-Hispanic writings of the era in his recognized tome *Antijovio* (1567).

19C NATIONAL EMANCIPATION

Correctly, much has been made of **Antonio Nariño** (1765-1823), whose works of journalism embrace an honest desire for liberty, justice and equality. A native of Bogotá, Nariño dedicated himself to improving the quality of life of his compatriots, and in turn translated from French into Spanish the *Declaración universal de los derechos del hombre y ciudadano* (1794).

Remembered as a distinguished writer, politician and soldier, **Jorge Isaacs** (1837-1895) led the editorial team, from 1867, in the recently formed Conservative newspaper *La Republica*.

However, It is his masterful work *Maria* (1867) that epitomizes the Romantic literary movement in Colombia at the time known as *Costumbrismo*. It is this single work of Isaacs' that has become one of the cornerstones of Latin American Romanticism.

The poet **Candelario Obeso** (1849-1884) differs somewhat from the previous two authors since he is of a mixed race background and is considered the forefather of Black Latin American poetry. Born in the wetland area of the Depresion Momposina, a place known for its heat, Colonial architecture and mestizo roots, Obeso enshrines the struggle of the local mestizo class in their voice in his most striking poem, *Cantos Populares de mi tierra*. This work gained him posthumous fame after his brief life ended in suicide.

MODERN LITERATURE AND POETRY

The new wave of Colombian literature found itself between two literary fashions, **Costumbrismo** (nostalgic depiction of customs in a changing society) and **Romanticism** which ran parallel to political events such as civil wars and the independence from Spain still fresh in the memory. Known for such works as *En la diestra de Dios padre* (1897) and *La Marquesa de Yolombó* (1928), **Tomas Carrasquilla** (1858-1940) was particularly affected by the goings on around him in Colombia at the time and gained fame for his writing only later in his life. His historical novels often blurred the line between *Costumbrismo* and Romanticism, causing his writing to fall into both categories, but specializing in neither.

José Eustasio Rivera (1888-1928), after traveling and witnessing with his own eyes the atrocious treatment and life which the rubber plantation workers barely survived in Casanare, bordering Venezuela, wrote **La Vorágine** (1924), one the most important Colombian novels of all times.

His literary efforts, in particular *One Hundred Years of Solitude* (1967), which won him the Nobel Prize in 1982, have made **Gabriel García Márquez** (1927) an international household name. Known as the master of **Magic Realism**, which acknowledges the magic inherent in the ordinary, Colombia's most recognized author has addressed almost every era dating from the period of independence with *The General in his Labyrinth* (1989) to the sinister themes of the current day in *News of Kidnapping* (1996). In the middle of the 20C, Márquez joined the **Grupo de Barranquilla**, a circle that consisted of a number of writers, philosophers and journalists who nurtured one another's writings in a bohemian haunt of *La Cueva*. During the 1940s and 50s, they produced and edited the magazine *Cronica*, and cemented their fame as hawkish purveyors of culture throughout the region. Barranquilla and the Colombian coast remain constant as key influences in Márquez's writing. *Memorias de mis putas tristes* (2004) recalls a Barranquilla of the 1930s, and his autobiography *Vivir para contarla* (2002) is thick with memories of his hometown of Aracataca and his travels in the Colombian Caribbean.

Having criticized Gabriel García Márquez for his use of Magic Realism, **Laura Restrepo** (1950) blends tough realities with fiction, pushing readers to read between the lines in her novels, in particular *El Leopardo al Sol* (1993), a wretched tale of two families killing one another and their links to the drugs trade, while never actually mentioning the word "drugs" in the text.

The Athens of South America

Known for its well-educated citizenry, Bogotá was named by UNESCO as **World Book Capital** in 2007.

Colombians do not take lightly this honor bestowed upon their capital. Examples of this seriousness can be seen in the annual **Bogotá Book Fair** that attracts thousands, and on any given day in the **Luis Angel Arango Library** in Central Bogotá that, statistically anyway, is better attended than the New York Public Library.

But Colombia's love affair with the written word runs much deeper. The former mayor of Medellín, Sergio Fajardo, enjoyed significant success in bringing literacy to the most at risk in his city by placing libraries in seriously downtrodden and overlooked *barrios*. And of course, there is the enchanting and widely publicized tale of the **Biblioburro**, a traveling library in the nether regions of Colombia via two donkeys, Alfa and Beto.

Restrepo was politically charged as a one-time member of the Socialist Workers Party in Spain, as part of an underground resistance movement opposing the dictatorship in Argentina and as a mediator in the Colombian peace talks. Her writing often includes, as one would imagine, political themes and struggles, making Colombia an ideal backdrop for this writer.

Fernando Vallejo (b. 1942) presents a far bloodier and far less glamorous image of Colombia. He goes to great lengths to debunk the myths and misplaced style of the narco-culture that is embedded in Colombia's psyche. Reading the *La Virgen de los sicarios* (1994), adapted to the big screen in 2000, leaves one in no doubt of the damage wrought upon Colombia by the drug trade.

Nature

Colombia sits atop the South American continent, benefiting from both Pacific and Caribbean coasts and covering a total of 1,138,914sq km/707,691sq mi. Marking the beginning of the Andes, its high cordilleras run the length of the country, drawing together the tectonic plates and making way for vast savannas, depressions, topographical anomalies, and coursing rivers that include the mighty Amazon. Given Colombia's great variety of landscapes and shared borders with Panama, Ecuador, Venezuela, Peru and Brazil, it takes no stretch of the imagination to realize that just about every microclimate on earth is represented within its boundaries—which is why Colombia belongs to that restricted circle of the world's "megadiverse" countries.

With such natural riches comes a great responsibility: that of protecting the wealth of fragile ecosystems. A large network of national parks and natural reserves exists in Colombia, allowing humanity to observe rare birdlife, unique flora and fauna and amazing landscapes. Drawn by the opportunity for high-altitude adventures, visitors will be just as pleased as those seeking the country's coralline islands, white sand Caribbean beaches or verdant settings of the Coffee Zone.

Orinoco Basin, La Primavera, Vichada Department

Willy Angulo Gómez/Proexport Colombia

GEOLOGY AND HYDROGRAPHY
ORINOCO BASIN

The westernmost portion of the **Guiana Shield,** an ancient, stable part of the South American continental plate, falls within the country's borders. The largest expanse of tropical rain forest in the world disassembles here, offering a topography of broken rocks, streams, and mountainous terraces.

One of the richest parts of Colombia in terms of sheer biodiversity, this region was shaped by the vast fluvial plains of the **Orinoco Basin**, dominated by tabletop mountains. These include **Serranía de Macarena**, a narrow mountain range 30km/19mi wide and 120km/74mi long that blends the convergence of Andean, Amazonian and Orinoquian fauna and landscapes. Algae and mosses enflame the **Caño Cristales River** in the Parque Nacional Natural Sierra de la Macarena in otherworldly colors of yellow, blue, green, black and red, leading to claims that this is one of the world's most beautiful rivers.

AMAZON BASIN

Bordered to the west by the eastern slopes of the Cordillera Oriental, the area is crisscrossed by half a dozen big rivers, all of them well over 1,000km/555mi in length. Most of them belong to the **black rivers** category, referring to the color of organic sediment carried by these lowland waterways. The **Guaviare River** marks the geographical boundary between the humid savannas of the Orinoco Basin and the **Amazon rain forest**. Heading back from the Guaviare River, one can trace the blue line snaking on the map as it extends to the **Vaupés River** and then the **Guainía River**, known outside Colombia as the **Río Negro**. Forming part of the border between Venezuela and Colombia, the Río Negro then flows east, connecting with the **Solimoes** in Brazil and forming the mightiest river of all, the **Amazon River**. The Guaviare, Vaupés and Caquetá rivers flow within Colombian territory, whereas the **Putumayo River** is shared with Ecuador and Peru. But

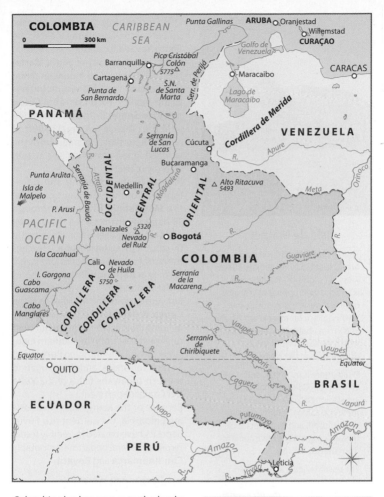

COLOMBIA

CARIBBEAN SEA

0   300 km

Punta Gallinas   ARUBA   Oranjestad
Willemstad
CURAÇAO
Golfo de Venezuela

Pico Cristóbal
Colón
5775 △

Barranquilla

Maracaibo

CARACAS

Cartagena

S.N.
de Santa
Marta

Lago de
Maracaibo

Punta de
San Bernardo

PANAMÁ

Serranía
de San
Lucas

Cúcuta

Cordillera de Merida

VENEZUELA

Punta Ardita

ATRATO R.

OCCIDENTAL

Serranía de Baudó

Medellín

CENTRAL

Bucaramanga

Magdalena R.

ORIENTAL

△ Alto Ritacuva
5493

Apure R.

Orinoco

Isla de
Malpelo

P. Arusi

PACIFIC
OCEAN

Manizales   ○5320
△
Nevado
del Ruiz

○ Bogotá

Meta R.

Isla Cacahual

Cali   Nevado
de Huila
△
5750 ○

I. Gorgona

Cabo
Guascama

COLOMBIA

CORDILLERA

Serranía
de la
Macarena

Guaviare R.

Cabo
Manglares

CORDILLERA

CORDILLERA

R.

Equator

Serranía
de
Chiribiquete

Vaupés R.

Apaporis R.

Uaupés

Equator

○ QUITO

Caquetá R.

BRASIL

ECUADOR

Napo R.

Putumayo R.

Japurá R.

Amazon

PERÚ

Amazo R.

R.

N

Yavarí

Leticia

Colombia also has access to the banks of the Amazon, which flows 116km/64mi along Colombia's border with Peru. The level of all those rivers depends on the prevalent rainfall at their respective sources, which is highly seasonal, depending on the movements of the Intertropical Convergence Wind Zone. These restless winds rarely stay quiet for long, causing frequent flooding.

THE ANDES

The northern section of the **Andes**, the world's longest mountain range, runs north to south through Colombia in three cordilleras, the **Occidental**, **Central** and **Oriental**. Often rising above 5,000m/16,400ft, these impressive

Tatacoa Desert, Andean Region

Proexport Colombia

97

Fundación Malpelo/Proexport Colombia

Isla de Malpelo

This **UNESCO World Heritage Site** is located some 490km/304mi west of Colombia's Pacific coast. It is a rocky outcropping of volcanic origins that serves as both a busy nesting place for **migratory birds**, and an incubator for **marine life,** which makes it one of the top **diving** sites in the world.

While there is no official settlement on Malpelo, Colombian vessels are stationed there to insure that the huge colony of birds remains undisturbed, and to protect the surrounding marine environment from **illegal fishing**.

These cold waters are home to eagle rays, green Murray eels, red-lipped batfish, the occasional sailfish, baitballs, dolphins and a large population of **sharks** that includes hammerheads and the extremely rare smalltooth sand tiger (*Odontaspis ferox*).

mountains were created by the subduction of the **Nazca plate** beneath the **South American** continental plate. **Volcanoes** are a common sight in the Colombian Andes, and they have wrought considerable havoc over time and permanently altered the terrain. As a consequence, east-west transportation and communication between isolated valleys are some of the long-standing challenges to Colombia's economy.

Often erroneously considered to make up part of the Cordillera Oriental, the **Sierra Nevada**, located on the Caribbean coast close to the city of **Santa Marta**, is actually an isolated mountain range that hosts the two highest mountains in the country, **Pico Cristóbal Colón** and **Pico Simón Bolívar**, culminating at approximately 5,700m/18,700ft. It is from here that snowmelt from the world's highest coastal range runs into an array of rivers.

Pivotal to the founding and development of modern-day Colombia, the **Magdalena River** runs through 18 departments between the Oriental and Central cordilleras from its source in the southern region of **Huila**. It reaches the northernmost point of its formidable journey at **Barranquilla**, on the shores of the Caribbean.

Converging with the Magdalena is the **Cauca River**, another key waterway in Colombian history. This major river runs northeast from the southern highlands, passing the imposing **Puracé** and **Sotará** volcanoes, and then irrigating the lush sugarcane fields of the **Valle del Cauca** department.

Because of the many rivers crisscrossing Colombia, the nutrient rich fluvial deposits have created incredibly fertile terrain in several departments, notably **Cundinamarca** and **Boyacá**.

COASTAL COLOMBIA

Colombians proudly state that theirs is the only country in South America with coastlines on both the Pacific and the Caribbean, a staggering 3,208km/ 1,925mi in total—1,760km/1056mi on the Caribbean and 1,448km/869mi on the Pacific. These two coastlines have marked differences.

Caribbean lowlands extend from the swamps of Panama into the arid semi-desert bordering Venezuela. To the west the **Río Atrato** ends in a swampy delta in the **Gulf of Urabá**, one of the rainiest points of the continent. Farther east lie the alluvial plains of the Magdalena and Cauca rivers, followed farther north by a wealth of sandy beaches. Beyond Barranquilla, the **Sierra Nevada de Santa**

Marta come abruptly into the sea, bringing tropical rain and snowmelt to the very shore. The eastward coast then flattens, the landscape changing again to become scrub and desert in the **Guajira** Peninsula, northernmost point of the continent, sitting at the end of the Cordillera Oriental.

An extension of the Isthmus of Panama, the **Serranía de Baudó** flanks the Colombian **Pacific Coast**.This narrow mountain range is separated from the Cordillera Occidental by a densely forested **tropical piedmont**. The **Atrato** and **San Juan rivers** are the main waterways of this area of outstanding natural beauty and endemic birdlife, where the thick jungle seemingly tumbles directly into the sea. South to Buenaventura, **alluvial plains** run toward the coast, frequently covered with mangrove swamps.

INSULAR COLOMBIA

As a further addition to Colombia's already exuberant geographical offerings, there are the islands of the **Caribbean** and the **Pacific**.

The **Islas del Rosario** lie 46km/28.5mi southeast from the coastal city of Cartagena, and form a chain of 43 **coral islands** that make up part of a protected marine area.

The former pirate islands of the archipelago of **San Andrés**, **Providencia** and **Santa Catalina** are located some 775km/480mi to the northwest of the Colombian mainland. They lie next to an important undersea ridge, the **Jamaica Ridge**, and are supposed to be evidence of ancient **volcanic activity**. This indication is particularly clear for the island of Providencia, reaching 363m/1,190ft at its highest point, whereas small San Andrés may be the tip of an ancient **undersea mount**, now ringed by white coralline sandy beaches.

Just 35km/22mi off the Pacific coastline, the former prison island of **Isla Gorgona** is likely to be an ancient eruptive site. Now turned into a national park and encircled by coral reefs and meager mangrove swamps, the **volcanic** island (9km/5.6mi by 2.5km/1.5mi) hosts a small number of tourists that come to glimpse endemic species and the annual humpback whale rituals that take place within view from the shore.

Lying west of the Colombian mainland, the far away island of **Malpelo** (☙ *see sidebar opposite*) exhibits steep cliffs of rock, reaching more than 4,000m/13,000ft under sea level, that betray its **volcanic past** (the island sits on one of the main volcanic ridges of the Eastern Pacific).

CLIMATE

The country's weather pattern consists of a dry and a wet season. For the most part, the **rainy season** extends from April to November, the wettest months being May and June. The **dry season** lasts from December to March. This general pattern of rainfall is subject to **local variations**, depending on proximity to the cordilleras, but also on seasonal changes in winds from the north and southeast. The latter account for the **Eastern Llanos** experiencing a real rain slack in the dry season, while the **Amazon Basin** sees regular rainfall reaching an average high of well over 300cm/118in per year.

There is no real respite in the central **Pacific Coast** lowlands, where rainfall may reach a record high of 1,000cm/393in a year.

Pacific **El Niño** perturbations occasionally bring unexpected rainfall far inland. Geological quirks may cause desert patches to appear in otherwise luxuriant or temperate surrounds, notably in the Andes or the Caribbean Coast.

City of Eternal Spring

It may seem that Colombia's temperatures are either too hot or too cold, but there are some happy mediums. Located deep in the Aburrá Valley, the city of **Medellín** maintains a year-round balmy 20°C/68°F, and is therefore referred to as the "City of Eternal Spring" for its enviable climate.

ALTITUDINAL ZONES

Colombia exhibits six altitudinal climatic zones. The first one, covering more than 80 percent of the country, is called **Tierra Caliente** (hot land). Found below 1,000m/3,280ft, it has an annual average temperature of 24°C/75°F. This is also the land of the heaviest rainfall.

Tierra Templada (temperate land) lies between 1,000m/3,280ft and 2,000m/6,560ft and covers 10 percent of the country. Its temperature oscillates between 17°C/62°F and 24°C/75°F.

Tierra Fria (cold land) occurs between 2,000m/6,560ft and 3,000m/9,842ft. Bogotá falls within that zone. Covering 8 percent of the country, Tierra Fria maintains temperatures between 12°C/53°F and 17°C/62°F.

Above Tierra Fria marks the end of most cultivated land and the beginning of the **Zona Forestada** (forested zone). This is indeed an altitude forest, growing beyond the 3,000m/9,842ft limit, with temperatures below 15°C/59°F.

Beyond the Zona Forestada come the **Páramo** plateaus, extending from 3,500m/1,148ft to the snow limit. Bleak and chilly, the mean temperature here is below 12°C/53°F. Highest of all, the **Tierra Nevada** (snow zone) covers all land above 4,500m/1,4764ft, with temperatures always cold enough to maintain a frozen and barren environment.

A Megadiverse Country

Owing to its enviable range of microclimates and impressive diversity of species, Colombia was identified as "megadiverse" by the United Nations' **World Conservation Monitoring Center**. This title was bestowed upon 17 countries which, among them, account for less than 10 percent of the world's total surface, but hold 60 to 70 percent of all biodiversity on earth. Brazil, Ecuador, Mexico, Peru and Venezuela are the other Latin American countries to appear on the UN's prestigious list.

NATURAL REGIONS AND LANDSCAPES
CARIBBEAN COAST

Best known for its crystalline turquoise sea and white sandy beaches, the Colombian Caribbean coast is actually an intricate mesh of varied landscapes and ecosystems.

Tracing the coastline northward from the **swamps** of the Gulf of Urabá, near the Panamanian border, one finds the remaining **wetlands** of the Sinú River Valley, now largely set aside for cattle grazing, especially around Monteria and Sincelejo. Close by, in the resort destinations of Tolú and Covenas and farther west, near to Cartagena, thick and protected **mangrove swamps** replete with birdlife act as barriers for the land against the sea.

Moving northeast from Cartagena towards Barranquilla, passing the mouth of the Magdalena River, one comes across the remnants of vast **coastal savannas**. By the town of Ciénaga, an ancient arm of the Magdalena delta has turned into a gigantic **coastal marsh** ringed with mangrove, called **Ciénaga de Santa Marta**. It is a now recovering reservoir of fish, protected from the sea by a narrow strip of land.

Nearby snow-capped Sierra Nevada de Santa Marta is a very different place. Rooted in the coastline, this mountain harbors fragile **montane woodlands**, a lush **cloud forest** reaching 25m/80ft in average height, and even South America's northernmost Páramo grassland.

To the northeast of Santa Marta, arid desert-like conditions become prevalent. Merciless **Guajira Peninsula,** near the Venezuelan border, is a 150,000sq km/57,000sq mi-wide **xeric scrubland** whose meager rainfall—the lowest in Colombia—averages a scant 30cm/12in per year. The landscape is barren, with **cactus** and contorted **divi-divi trees** providing little shade.

Well suited to life in this harsh environment, herds of goats bred by the local **Wayúu** people can be seen grazing under scorching temperatures.

Páramo,
Parque Nacional
Natural Los Nevados

Jorge Sanabria/Proexport Colombia

PACIFIC COAST

From the northern border with Panama to the southern border with Ecuador, the Colombian Pacific coast alters only slightly and bears many similarities with the landscapes of the Caribbean coast to its north. Both coastlines share the **Darien Gap**, an almost impenetrable cornucopia of jungle known for its lawlessness. The **Atrato Swamp** is a muddy deluge measuring 65km/40mi that has prevented engineers from developing any effective ground transport through the region from the Chocó into Panama. The **Serranía del Baudó** coastal range gives an aspect of steep cliffs to the northern coastline, with small cobble beaches occurring here and there. Along with the western edge of **Andean Cordillera Occidental**, it marks the wettest part of the region. The **tropical rain forest** that extends through the departments of the **Chocó**, **Valle**, **Cauca** and **Nariño**, is one of the wettest, most biodiverse places on earth. Shrouded in mists and drenched with heavy rains, these forests are laden with parasitic albeit exquisite flora: **bromeliads** and a mind-boggling wealth of **orchids**. **Mangrove forests** occur in and around the municipalities of **Guapi**, **Tumaco** and **Buenaventura** and harbor **piangua** mollusks, a staple food for locals. Fertile **alluvial forests** have been created in the flood plains of several rivers, including the **Atrato**, **San Juan** and **Baudó**.

ANDEAN REGION

A total of 22 different landscapes, or ecosystems, are represented in the Colombian Andes, of which two are unique to the country.

Oak forests still occur in the northwestern lowlands of the Cordillera Occidental. The dominant tree species there is the Humboldt oak, and epiphytes such as bromeliads are quite common.

The **coffee-growing zone** occurs higher up the slopes. An internationally renowned national treasure, this crop has had a big impact on native altitude mountain forests, leaving "green patches" isolated by areas clear-cut for crops. However, some types of coffee crops, like shade crops, are believed to help preserve the local fauna by bridging patches of remaining forest.

Still higher up lie Colombia's **cloud forests**. The vegetation here is mainly determined by exposure to the hot seasonal winds blowing inland from the ocean. Upon encountering the Andes, those winds move upward, getting colder and releasing their humidity, thus creating lingering rain and clouds on the slopes. Understandably, suspended valleys enclosed by secondary mountain ranges, or eastern mountain slopes, receive less rainfall than average. The variations in temperature, altitude and rainfall all concur to create an extremely diversified landscape, with a few common characteristics. Moss and lichens thrive here, whereas epiphytes, especially **orchids**, occur in the wildest variety of colors and shapes.

Beyond the tree limit—a narrow belt of epiphytes, contorted dwarf trees and shrubland—is a zone of high-altitude humid grassland, better known as **páramos**. High grass, streams and peat bogs compose the landscape of this otherwise dreary and cold environment. Espeletia plants, locally known as **frailejónes**, thrive here and come in all sizes, including giant ones more than 2m/6.5ft high. With an area of 178,000 ha/439,660 acres, Bogotan Sumapaz páramo is believed to be the largest páramo in the world.

Beyond the snowline, a discrete, deep-rooted flora manages to survive the daily frost-defrost cycle of the **altitude desert**.

The Andean landscape also contains oddities like the **Tatacoa Desert**, a semi-arid region lying in the department of Huila, surrounded by fertile valleys. Home to many species of cactus, this 330 sq km/125 sq mi area is renowned for its erosive relief and reddish soils.

EASTERN ALLUVIAL PLAINS

Open grasslands, along with patches of **gallery forests**, concentrated around the numerous waterways, are the main feature of the landscape in the Llanos, or eastern plains. Making up almost 30 percent of the country's territory, this nearly uninhabited area is a region of great seasonal contrasts: torrential floods roll almost unhindered over the land during the wet season, whereas the winter brings drought and great fires to the plains.

All the sizable rivers of the region drain into the **Orinoco Basin**. Between the Guaviare and Vaupés rivers, a **transitional savanna** is found, whose vegetation links the open grasslands with the neighboring Amazonian tropical forest.

The **Serranía de Macarena** is a noteworthy landmark of the southern Llanos. This mountainous range bears a close resemblance to the Guiana Shield **tepui tabletop mountains**, just over the

nearby Venezuelan border. Unparalleled in terms of avian biodiversity, these **dry forest rocky highlands** resonate with the sound of many crystal-clear streams and torrents.

AMAZON FORESTS

The Amazon region accounts for a staggering 42 percent of the country's territory, occupying an area of 480,000 sq km/187,200 sq mi. Hardly hospitable to man, it understandably exhibits the lowest population density of all Colombian regions, a scant 2 inhabitants per sq km. Amazonian **tropical rain forest** obviously comes to mind as the main landscape type; this sprawling, immense snarl of foliage and vegetation occupies two-thirds of the Amazonian territory. But the region's array of landcsapes is actually a lot broader.

Eastern **rocky tabletop outcrops**, such as the Serranía de Chiribiquete support specific low-altitude vegetation, with a prevalence of broadleaved and fern-like herbaceous communities. Tree species have adapted to the exuberant hydrography, creating a unique ecosystem of seasonally **inundated forest** in the alluvial plains.

Savannas, such as the Yarí, western Andean piedmont **cloud forests** and lowland forests make up the rest of the Amazonian landscape.

ECOLOGY
BIODIVERSITY – ENDEMISM

Due to its wealth of **ecosystems**, Colombia is one of the most biologically **diverse** countries in Latin America and the Caribbean, and second only to Brazil. The country hosts about 10 percent of the **world**'s species of **fauna** and **flora**. The highest rates of **endemism** (both animal and vegetal) are found in the **Amazon Basin**, the **Pacific** coastal region (especially in the Baudó range), the **Cocora Valley** (home to the unique Quindío Wax Palm) and on **Isla Gorgona**.

Colombia is home to about 1,800 species of **birds** (20 percent of the world's total), more than 600 types of **amphibians** (10 percent), about 400 species

Three National Symbols

Emblazoned on Colombia's coat of arms, the **Andean Condor** is the world's largest land-flying bird. Found in the Andean highlands, it is a huge creature that can fly impressive distances in the same day. A symbol of strength and power, this ruler of the Upper World in native Andean mythology is a fitting emblem for the Colombian nation.

Andean Condor

With its amazing diversity of climates and environments, ranging from cloud forests to mountain grasslands, Colombia is blessed with an exuberant variety of endemic **orchids**. It comes as no surprise that the national flower is one of them: *Cattleya trianae*, a graceful epiphytic cloud forest species, locally known as *Flor de Mayo*.

Cattleya trianae

Found in the Valle de Cocora, in the northern part of Quindío, the **Quindío Wax Palm** *(Ceroxylon quindiuense)* grows up to 60m/197ft in height and is Colombia's national tree, since 1985. This now-rare, endemic, high-altitude palm tree was chopped down for Palm Sunday celebrations and used in the candle-making process, actions that pushed it to the brink of extinction.

Wax palms, Valle de Corcora

© Tomaz Kunst/Fotolia.com

© Carlos Ortega/epa/Corbis

Proexport Colombia

of **mammals** (7 percent), more than 500 species of **reptiles** (6 percent) and some 3,200 species of **fish**. About 20 percent of all these exist nowhere else on earth: they are endemic to Colombia. Birds, notably **hummingbirds** or **tanagers**, provide a good insight into the wealth of Colombian animal endemism. The best example of all vertebrates is found in **frogs**, of which nine new species were discovered as late as 2009 during a quick assessment program in a mountain range bordering Panama; they are remote cousins of the already known Pacific Coast endemic **Golden Dart Frog** and the **Black-legged Dart Frog**, both considered as the most poisonous vertebrates on earth.

More than 50,000 species of plants have been reported in the country, of which about 16,000 exist only in Colombia. A special mention must be given to **orchids**, numbering more than 3,000 species in Colombia, a staggering 15 percent of the world's total, which is not surprising, since nearly 90 percent of Colombia's forests are **primary forests**, the most biodiverse of all.

One must keep in mind that Colombia's biodiversity is a highly **threatened** one, as deforestation, pollution and human pressure have already brought 1,000 species of plants (mostly orchids), 89 species of mammals, 133 species of birds, 20 species of reptiles and 8 fish species to near extinction.

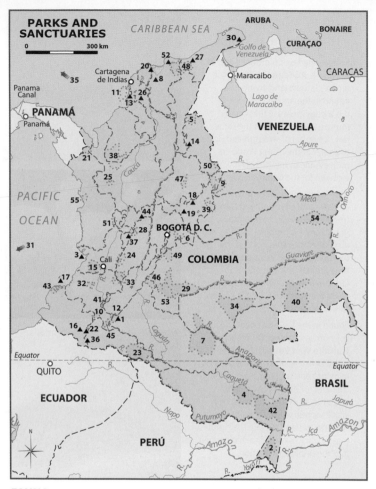

PARKS AND SANCTUARIES

0   300 km

CARIBBEAN SEA

ARUBA

BONAIRE

CURAÇAO

Golfo de Venezuela

CARACAS

Cartagena de Indias

Maracaibo

Panama Canal

PANAMÁ

Panamá

Lago de Maracaibo

VENEZUELA

Apure R.

PACIFIC OCEAN

Cauca

Meta R.

Orinoco R.

BOGOTÁ D. C.

Cali

COLOMBIA

Guaviare R.

Equator

QUITO

Caquetá R.

Anaporis R.

Caquetá R.

Equator

BRASIL

ECUADOR

Napo R.

Putumayo R.

Japurá R.

Amazon

PERÚ

Amazo R.

Içá R.

Yaí R.

FAUNA

Along the Caribbean coast, the mangrove swamps play an important role in protecting some curious fauna native to Colombia's coastline, namely the ungainly yet communicative **manatee** (*Trichechus manatus*). Just a bit farther inland, one can find the dainty **American flamingo** (*Phoenicopterus ruber*). In addition to the ubiquitous **egrets**, **ibis**, **pelicans** and **iguanas**, perhaps the most interesting creature is the **Crab-eating raccoon** (*Procyon cancrivorus*), if only for its voracious appetite for crab, lobster, crustaceans, small amphibians, turtle eggs and fruits.

In the cloud forests of the Andes, the timid **White-tipped Quetzal** (*Pha-romachrus fulgidus*) and the brightly colored **Andean Cock of the Rock** (*Rupicola peruvianus*) are the birdlife stars, albeit hardest to spot.

At higher altitudes, the lucky viewers may catch a glimpse of the reclusive **Spectacled Bear** (*Tremarctos ornatus*) or of the endangered woolly **Mountain Tapir** (*Tapirus pinchaque*). Sharing this ground in the páramos are plentiful species of hummingbird, the scarce **Andean Duck** (*Oxyura jamaicensis*) and the **Andean Condor** (*Vultur gryphus*). On their annual migration south, the breaching of the **humpback whales** (*Megaptera novaeangliae*) attracts many visitors to the Pacific coast. But it is the checkered variety of highly venomous

National Parks

1　Alto Fragua Indi Wasi PNN
2　Amacayacu PNN
3　Bahía Málaga PNN
4　Cahuinarí PNN
5　Catatumbo PNN
6　Chingaza PNN
7　Chiribiquete PNN
8　Ciénaga Grande de Santa Marta SFF
9　Cocuy PNN
10　Complejo Volcanico Doña Juana - Cascabel PNN
11　Corales del Rosario y de San Bernardo PNN
12　Cueva de los Guácharos PNN
13　El Corchal ¨El Mono Hernández¨ SFF
14　Estoraques ANU
15　Farallones de Cali PNN
16　Galeras SFF
17　Gorgona PNN
18　Guanentá Alto Río Fonce SFF
19　Iguaque SFF
20　Isla de Salamanca VP
21　Katíos PNN
22　La Corota SFF
23　La Paya PNN
24　Las Hermosas PNN
25　Las Orquídeas PNN
26　Los Colorados SFF
27　Los Flamencos SFF
28　Los Nevados PNN
29　Macarena PNN
30　Macuira PNN
31　Malpelo SFF
32　Munchique PNN
33　Nevado del Huila PNN
34　Nukak RNN
35　Old Providence McBean Lagoon PNN
36　Orito Ingi Ande SF
37　Otún Quimbaya SFF
38　Paramillo PNN
39　Pisba PNN
40　Puinawai RNN
41　Puracé PNN
42　Río Puré PNN
43　Sanquianga PNN
44　Selva de Florencia PNN
45　Serranía de los Churumbelos PNN
46　Serranía de Los Picachos PNN
47　Serranía de Los Yariguíes PNN
48　Sierra Nevada de Santa Marta PNN
49　Sumapaz PNN
50　Tamá PNN
51　Tatamá PNN
52　Tayrona PNN
53　Tinigua PNN
54　Tuparro PNN
55　Utría PNN

Legend

PNN　Parque Nacional Natural
SFF　Santuario de Fauna y Flora
SF　Santuario de Fauna
RNN　Reserva Nacional Natural
VP　Via Parque
ANU　Area Natural Unica

and delightfully colored frogs that may be the main attraction. In addition to the **Golden Dart Frog** *(Phyllobates terribilis),* there are the **Harlequin Poison Frog** *(Dendrobates histrionicus)* and the brilliant blue **Pangan Poison Arrow Frog**.

Bordering Ecuador, the **Parque Nacional Natural Sanquianga** is a preferred nesting place for varieties of marine turtles, including the **Olive Ridley** *(Lepidochelys olivacea)* and the **Leatherback Turtle** *(Dermochelys coriacea).*

Perhaps less graceful than its marine cousins, the carnivorous **Mata Mata Turtle** *(Chelus fimbriatus),* of the Llanos and the Orinoco Basin region, has a

Pelican

Proexport Colombia

Jabiru Stork

© Richard McColl/MICHELIN

of *Moby Dick,* **sperm whales** *(Physeter macrocephalus)* were spotted along the Colombian island chains. Sightings of deep-diving **Pigmy-beaked Whales** *(Mesoplodon peruvianus)* were also recorded, but our understanding of these enigmatic marine mammals remains very limited. Throngs of birds, including the elegant **Red-Tailed Tropic Bird** *(Phaethon rubricauda)* with its streaming central tail feathers and satiny plumage, make their homes on cliffs and in island colonies. **Gannets** *(Morus bassanus),* **cormorants** *(Phalacrocorax carbo)* and marauding **frigatebirds** *(Fregata magnificens),* with their inflating red gullets, nest by the thousands and fill the skies with their cries.

head shaped as if entwined by thorns and resembling fallen leaves. Also in this region, the huge **Jabiru Stork** *(Jabiru mycteria)* patrols the nearby rivers and ponds in search of mollusks, fish and small reptiles. At risk from **Anaconda** snakes *(Eunectes murinus),* the **Orinoco Crocodile** *(Crocodylus intermedius),* differing from like species by its yellowish hide and brown bands, is a critically endangered species now found almost exclusively in the Meta River Basin.

The biologically unrivalled **Amazonian Basin** harbors the **Kinkajou** *(Potos flavus),* often associated with the closely related **Olingo** *(Bassaricyon gabbii),* a raccoon-like animal with superb climbing skills owing to its prehensile tail. Another curious creature of the region is the poor-sighted, pinkish River Dolphin *(Inia geoffrensis),* with its low dorsal fin resembling a hump, the subject of many native legends. Dwarfing all other South American freshwater fish, the giant **Arapaima** *(Arapaima gigas)* can weigh at times up to 100kg/220 pounds. The male of this occasional air-breather nurses its young in its mouth until they are old enough to fend for themselves. Fiercely territorial **Giant River Otters** *(Pteronura brasiliensis)* glide sleekly between the roots of inundated parts and have been known to reach a length of 1.8m/5.9ft.

The Pacific coast is not alone in being an ideal habitat for whales. Straight out

FLORA

With Colombia's diversity of landscapes comes a large variety of plant species, covering the whole of the vegetal reign, from tiny mosses to giant trees and from drenched cloud-forest bromeliads to high-altitude cactus.

The **divi-divi tree** *(Cæsalpinia coriaria)* manages to survive in the arid scrubland of the Guajira Peninsula by reducing its height and twisting its shape. Threatened **mangroves** occur in estuarine patches along the Atlantic Coast, forming mixed forests of **red** *(Rhizophora mangle),* **black** *(Avicennia germinans)* and **white** *(Laguncularia racemosa)* mangrove trees.

The Colombian Andes harbor the world's highest palm tree, the endemic **Quindío Wax Palm** *(Ceroxylon quindiuense).* Altitude grasslands are home to the *Espeletia* shrub family, relatives of the common daisy. Locally known as **frailejón,** this genus includes giant *Espeletia grandiflora,* reaching 2m/6.5ft in height, whose thick trunk, covered with dead leaves, is the very emblem of the páramos landscape.

No account of the Colombian flora would be complete without mentioning the amazing array (some 3,000 species) of often endemic **orchids** that occur in all shapes and sizes, ranging from miniature 5cm/2in epiphytic *Restrepia Antennifera* to giant 33cm/13in *Odon-*

toglossum grande (known as the "Tiger Orchid").

In 2008 the Colombian government established the **Amazonian Orito Ingi-Ande Sanctuary**, set up to create a protected area for the local **medicinal plants** and **trees**. Examples of these fauna include the **Cinchona** tree (*Rubiaceae*), a natural source of malaria-treating **quinine**, the **coca** plant (*Erythroxylum coca*), a natural local anesthetic, and the **Yoco liana** (*Paullinia yoco*), known by jungle healers for time immemorial for its curative properties.

ENVIRONMENTAL ISSUES

Colombia's environment is under constant threat from **natural** disasters—be they related to the country's proximity to dangerous tectonic fault lines or to drastic climatic shifts—and **man-made** misuse and hazards.

NATURAL HAZARDS

Owing to its geographic position, Colombia's territory is constantly threatened by **seismic movements**. Reaching over six on the Richter scale, a catastrophic earthquake followed by landslides hit the Coffee Zone in 1999, wreaking havoc in the city of Armenia and leaving over 1,000 people dead and 200,000 homeless.

Eruptive events in deforested volcanic highlands with large concentrations of population often have dramatic consequences. The entire town of **Armero** was wiped out, and some 23,000 lives were lost in **mudslides** following the 1985 eruption of Nevado del Ruiz, a volcano that had been dormant for more than a century.

In 2005 the eruption of the **Galeras volcano**, now considered Colombia's most active volcanic threat, caused the evacuation of 9,000 people living on its slopes.

In 2010 a particularly intense episode of **El Niño** put Colombia on alert for **water shortages** and **risk of fires**. As a result of severely dry weather conditions, the Carribean and Andean regions reported significant losses in agricultural production.

During El Niño-affected years, while the Caribbean coast is generally hit by drought, the Pacific coast suffers from terrible **floods**. These dramatic swings in the normal climate patterns bring with them further problems such as **malaria** and **dengue**, caused by disease-carrying mosquitoes.

HUMAN EFFECT

Colombia is one of the countries where there is a growing interest in finding possible ways to protect natural resources and achieve sustainable development. Great challenges lay ahead though, as an estimated 1.5 to 2.2 million acres (600,000 to 900,000ha) are deforested in Colombia each year, mainly in the **Amazon** and the **Chocó**. At this pace, **deforestation** may deplete the nation's reserves within 40 years, in addition to severely upsetting the social dynamic of many indigenous groups and destroying unique flora and fauna.

Numerous factors are contributing to this situation, incuding legal and illegal logging, reckless farmland expansion, mining projects carried out with no regard to environmental consequences, and **cocaine production**. The latter has led to chemical contaminants being released into water systems and into the atmosphere from the fumigation and eradication flights.

Also poor **drainage** has had disastrous consequences for the people near the cities of Cartagena and Ciénaga, where **water purity** has been affected.

In Bogotá **gas emissions** from vehicles using low-grade fossil fuels stifle the high-altitude air, and in spite of a recycling campaign launched in the late 2000s by the local government, the **waste habits** of its residents remain a challenge in the nation's capital.

Colombia has set aside 55 protected natural areas in an effort to preserve its natural resources: national natural parks, sanctuaries, and other places where the public is welcome. They are repositories of great beauty or uniqueness to be enjoyed, but tacitly to serve as reminders of the importance of conservation for future generations.

Roofs of La Candelaria, Bogotá
IDT Cortesía Germán Montes/Proexport Colombia

BOGOTÁ AND SURROUNDINGS

Located on the eastern portion of the Andean plateau of the Altiplano Cundiboyacense, Bogotá is the nation's capital and the country's largest city, a metropolis of nearly seven million people. The lofty altitude of 2,640m/8,661ft did not dissuade the Muisca people—the original inhabitants of this altiplano—nor the Spanish conquistadors from settling here. "Bacatá" was a thriving region, principally due to its key geographical location, a fact not lost on Gonzalo Jiménez de Quesada who, in 1538, founded what became known as Santa Fé de Bogotá. The city boasts years of tradition and history that can be viewed and experienced by wandering the colonial center as well as making day outings into the surrounding rural communities. With clear, crisp mornings that give way to drizzly and gray afternoons, Bogotá and the surrounding areas lend themselves to strolling picturesque streets, investigating museums and enjoying a hearty broth of traditional *ajiaco* after a day of cultural and historical excesses.

Highlights

1 Wander idly through history in Bogotá's colonial **Candelaria** district (p116)

2 Visit Bogotá's **Museo del Oro** for its outstanding collection of pre-Columbian gold relics (p129)

3 Take a trip to see the feat of engineering that is the **Salt Cathedral** at **Zipaquirá** (p139)

4 Try your rock-climbing skills at **Suesca**, an hour from the capital (p140)

5 Ride a horse or hike a trail in the oasis not far from the city that is **Parque Natural Chicaque** (p144)

Athens of South America

Colombia's capital may not have the visible sophistication of Buenos Aires or the order of Santiago, but beyond the chaos and mayhem of the traffic and seeming lack of regard for any building code is an incredibly cultured and diverse urban development.

Often referred to as the "Athens of South America" for its well educated and polite citizenry, Bogotá is a historical center that has been home to pre-Columbian indigenous tribes, Spanish settlers, Creoles and successive waves of immigrants.

Aside from the region's historical importance, the geographical area astounds visitors with its prevalence of protected zones, national parks and destinations for outdoor pursuits. Mere short drives from the capital can lead to the delicate high-altitude ecosystems of the **Parque Nacional Natural Sumapaz,** the **Parque Nacional Natural Chingaza** and the town of **Guasca** where you can enjoy walking trails and sighting endemic flora and fauna. The rocky mountain vistas populated by deer, high in rainfall and an abundance of *espeletia* plants are also an ideal destination for climbing and camping.

Out in the **Sábana of Bogotá** lies the pilgrimage center of **Zipaquirá** and its famed Salt Cathedral. To get there, leaving through the capital's northern suburbs shows the cross section of this altiplano, from the colonial center via business hubs, luxury high-rise apartment complexes and more residential neighborhoods before arriving in the vast open highland plains, with greenhouses scattered along the route. The mysticism and pre-Columbian legends of the areas around Zipaquirá become apparent since the salt mines where the cathedral is located were controlled by Muisca overlords.

With this indigenous background, **Bogotá** and the regions of **Cundinamarca** and **Boyacá** house a healthy blend of people with Indian features. But there is more to this **cultural mixing,** since various waves of European settlers have made their home here. There are *mestizos*, those of European and indigenous descent, white

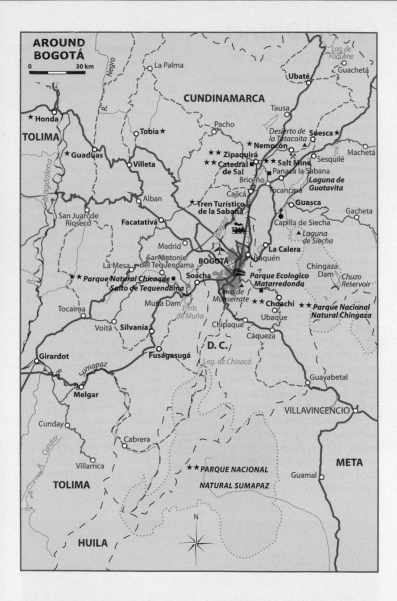

AROUND BOGOTÁ

0   30 km

CUNDINAMARCA

Europeans from Germany, Italy and Spain all fleeing persecution and wars, and a large contingent of people of Middle Eastern ancestry, as well as a small contingent of people of African descent who have moved inland from Cartagena. Some of these immigrants have taken to the norm of cooler weather better than others. With its subtropical highland climate, the average temperature here is 14°C (57°F).

A good place to start your tour and get a physical overview of Bogotá and the surrounding area is from the top of the **Cerro de Monserrate** that rises up to 3,152m/10,340ft. From here an unobstructed view is permitted of this city of nearly 7 million people as well as the entire region. The urban sprawl appears as if poured onto the eastern cordillera, and spreading without obstruction to the west.

Capital District of Bogotá★★★

Cundinamarca

A good set of walking shoes and a healthy pair of lungs are the order of the day for your trip to Bogotá, located high up on the Andean plateau. Colombia's largest city, and the third-highest capital city in the world at 2,640m/8,660ft (after La Paz and Quito), is a busy cultural and business center, with people from all walks of life making their homes here. In Bogotá the old is mixed with the new, and Colonial architecture sits alongside sleek 21C buildings. By equal measure, the chaos of disorderly diesel-spewing buses, lawless taxis and clogged rush-hour traffic is balanced by quiet residential barrios and verdant parks and mountainsides. In recent years, the metropolis has been winning accolades for urban design, as city planners and politicians look to change Bogotá's negative image. They seek to make it an inclusive center of learning, open spaces and desirable housing, and to confront the problems that have arisen by rapid mass migration from the countryside to the urban area, including transportation challenges.

▶ **Population:** 6,778,691.

◔ **Michelin Maps:** p111, p115 and p122.

▤ **Info:** Several official tourist information points include the **PIT Centro Historico** (corner of Carrera 8 and Calle 10, Palacio Liévano, 1st floor, ℘(1) 283 7115. www.bogotaturismo. gov.co/puntos-de-informacion-turistica-pit.

▶ **Location:** Bogota has two principal sections: Zona Centro, which includes the compact La Candelaria, the historic core, centered on Plaza Bolívar and having the most attractions of interest to visitors, and farther uptown, Centro Internacional, the main business and financial sector. Zona Norte, north of the central zone, is the posh residential area, with upscale shops and fine restaurants.

◕ **Timing:** Allow 4-5 days to appreciate Bogota's assets.

⊙ **Don't Miss:** A walk through the colonial Candelaria district and the gold pieces in the Museo del Oro.

Bogotá and Cerro de Monserrate

Proexport Colombia

GETTING THERE

BY AIR - **El Dorado Aeropuerto Internacional** (BOG), 15km/8mi northwest of the city; its main passenger terminal **El Dorado** (*℘+57 1 425 1000; www.bogota-dc.com/ trans/aviones.htm*), handling most of the international and domestic flights, lies 1km/.6mi west of the other, **Puente Aéreo** (*℘+57 1 425 1000 ext. 3218;. www. elnuevodorado.com*). Both terminals are accessible from the city center by *busetas* and *colectivos* (*see p38*) marked "Aeropuerto'"; the best are Calle 9 and Carrera 10, which stop running about 8pm. **Taxis** cost about 15,000 COP with a surcharge *(sobrecargo)* of 3,100 COP. At the **taxi booth** at El Dorado's baggage claim area exit, look for a special taxi service operating protected fares; pay for your trip in advance and show the pre-paid slip to the taxi driver (*see p39*). **Buses** leave every 20min for the city center (approx. 30min ride).

BY BUS - Located 5km/3mi west of the city center, the **bus terminal** Diagonal 23 (69-60 off Ave. de La Constitution) serves domestic and international departures from its building that is divided into five color-coded parts. All arrivals come into No. 5 at the eastern end. *Colectivos* (*see p38*) leave for nearby towns from No 4., north- and east-bound buses depart from red No. 3, south-bound from yellow No. 1 and both international and west-bound buses from blue No 2.

GETTING AROUND

BY BUS - Buses remain the **most economic** form of transportation in the city. Each destination is written clearly on a signboard in the front window. Bogotá's transit and transport system is chaotic. Be warned that pickpockets are commonplace. Also, drivers routinely swerve across lanes to pick up a client, and slam on the brakes to miss the ubiquitous potholes. On the **TransMilenio**

TransMilenio bus

Luis Fernando Jaramillo/Proexport Colombia

(*see p38 for website*) articulated bus system (buses on exclusive lanes), be prepared to spend 1,600 COP for a single trip. TransMilenio connects to small operators that can take you from the northernmost TransMilenio station, **Portal del Norte**, to places such as Guatavita and Villa de Leyva.

BY TAXI - Bogota's cabs are an easy and reasonably priced way to get around. Have your hotel call a reliable company for you rather than hail a cab. For security, **never share a ride** with anyone. Meters should start at 25 COP (check when you step into the taxi); Sundays, holidays or after dark have a 1,500 COP surcharge. Taxi Express *℘411 1111*, Taxi Real *℘333 3333* and Radio Taxi *℘288 8888*.

BY CAR - Renting a car is **not recommended** since taxis (legitimate yellow cabs) are inexpensive and reliable.

ON FOOT - Generally, all **avenidas** and **carreras** run north to south; all **calles** run east to west accordingly. Almost everything of interest can be found near or relatively near **Carrera 7**, an easy thoroughfare to negotiate. Keep in mind that few drivers obey the traffic signals, and so be very **cautious** when **crossing the street** (*see sidebar on Safety p116*).

A BIT OF HISTORY

The Muisca People

Because of its strategic location in the cordilleras, the area of and around today's Bogotá has long been settled. Archaeological finds have shown that the Muisca people inhabited the region from about AD 700. Early Spanish records state that theirs was one of the most sophisticated communities that the conquistadors had encountered.

The Muisca, of the **Chibcha** linguistic family, were an agricultural people organized into **centralized villages**. They excelled in working with **gold**, and had rituals involving **emeralds** and other **precious metals** that attracted the Spanish in their quest for wealth and desire to find **El Dorado**. Muisca remains, and other vestiges of their communities are frequently being unearthed in the southern barrio of **Usme** in Bogotá.

Colonial Days

The arrival of the conquistador **Gonzalo Jiménez de Quesada** on August 6, 1538, and his "founding" of the city at the present spot of the **Chorro de Quevedo,** in the sector of what is today's colonial Candelaria, did not spell the end for the Muisca. While conflicts occurred over the years, the Muisca still exist in Bogotá today, as many people bare the obvious indigenous physical traits. While there was a spat between Gonzalo Jiménez de Quesada, **Sebastián de Belalcázar** and **Nikolaus Federmann** over to whom the territory of Nueva Granada belonged, the city of Bogotá prevailed. Construction and development all took place (for instance, the Plaza de Bolívar, formerly Plaza Mayor, dates back to 1553), and during the colonial period, the city became the seat of government for the **Viceroyalty of New Granada**.

A Capital in the Making

By the 19C, and with the first mutterings of independence in 1810, Bogotá had grown to a city with a population of 30,000. In 1814 the liberator of Northern South America **Simón Bolívar** marched triumphantly into Bogotá for the United Provinces of New Granada. The Span-

ish reconquest put on hold any ideas of independence until 1819, when Bolívar's triumph at the **Battle of Boyacá** truly sealed freedom for the country. Bogotá became the capital of the newly declared **Gran Colombia**, which covered mainly the territories of modern-day Colombia, Ecuador, Venezuela and Panama.

After the breakup of Gran Colombia until the Republic of Colombia was formally created, Bogotá remained the capital of a country in tatters, split by conflict and continual civil war. By the turn of the 19C, Bogotá had reached a population topping 100,000.

The city entered a period of sophistication and urban growth, placing an emphasis on education and the arts. The era put in place some of the most stunning buildings and museums, and fostered the talent that was drawn here.

Bogotazo Riots

Yet, the aggression that had been simmering nationally did not skirt Bogotá. The ill feelings between Conservatives and Liberals spilled over into the Bogotazo riots following the assassination of the liberal presidential candidate **Jorge Eliécer Gaitán** on April 9, 1948. The old city center was largely destroyed in the looting and destruction that left 3,000 people dead and 136 buildings ablaze, including the **Palacio San Carlos** and the **Palacio de Justicia**.

The Urban Context

After the Bogotazo of 1948, part of city was irreversibly altered in that the wealthy, who owned the large stately houses in and around the center of Bogotá, decided to move to the north of the city to places such as **Suba** and **Usaquén**. This move became justified when the ruling political party started work on a **highway** to the north of the country, and placed these inhabitants at the center of their plans.

The colonial center, known as the **Candelaria**, fell into decay and disrepair, and became a no-go zone, until subsequent city administrations in the past decade or so saw its educational and touristic potential.

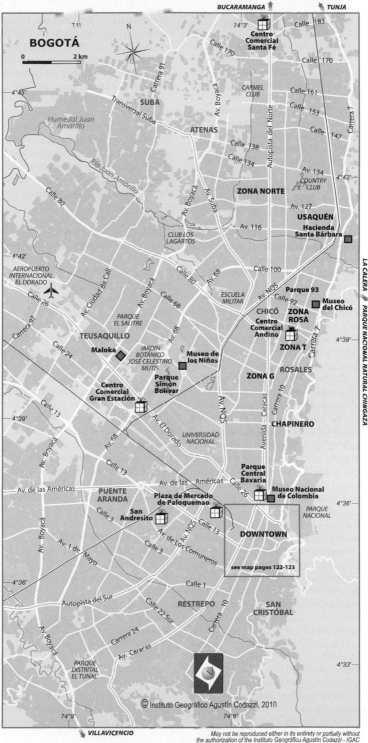

BUCARAMANGA TUNJA

BOGOTÁ

0   2 km

N

SUBA

Humedal Juan
Amarillo

Transversal Suba

ATENAS

Río Juan Amarillo

Calle 80

Av. Boyacá

Av. Suba

Carrera 91

74°3'

Centro
Comercial
Santa Fé

Calle 170

Calle 170

Calle 183

CARMEL
CLUB

Calle 161

Calle 153

Calle 147

Autopista del Norte

Carrera 7

Calle 138

Calle 134

Av. 134

COUNTRY
CLUB

4°45'

4°42'

4°42'

ZONA NORTE

USAQUÉN

Hacienda
Santa Bárbara

Av. 127

Av. 116

CLUB LOS
LAGARTOS

Calle 100

AEROPUERTO
INTERNACIONAL
EL DORADO

Calle 26

Carrera 97

Calle 80

Av. Ciudad de Cali

Av. Boyacá

Calle 68

Av. 68

Calle 80

ESCUELA
MILITAR

Av. NQS

Calle 92

Parque 93

CHICÓ

ZONA
ROSA

Museo
del Chicó

LA CALERA

PARQUE NACIONAL NATURAL CHINGAZA

PARQUE
EL SALITRE

TEUSAQUILLO

Calle 24

Maloka

Av. 68

JARDÍN
BOTÁNICO
JOSÉ CELESTINO
MUTIS

Museo de
los Niños

Centro
Comercial
Andino

ZONA T

ROSALES

4°39'

Centro
Comercial
Gran Estación

Parque
Simón
Bolívar

ZONA G

Carrera 7

Calle 13

Av. 68

Av. El Dorado

Av. NQS

UNIVERSIDAD
NACIONAL

Avenida Caracas

Carrera 10

CHAPINERO

4°39'

Av. Boyacá

Calle 13

Av. de las Américas

PUENTE
ARANDA

Av. de las Américas

Calle 26

Parque
Central
Bavaria

Museo Nacional
de Colombia

4°36'

San
Andresito

Calle 3

Plaza de Mercado
de Paloquemao

Av. de Los Comuneros

Calle 13

Av. NQS

PARQUE
NACIONAL

DOWNTOWN

see map pages 122-123

Calle 3

Autopista del Sur

Av. 1 de Mayo

Calle 1

Calle 22 Sur

RESTREPO

Carrera 10

SAN
CRISTÓBAL

4°36'

Av. Boyacá

Carrera 24

Av. Caracas

PARQUE
DISTRITAL
EL TUNAL

4°33'

© Instituto Geográfico Agustín Codazzi, 2010

74°9'

74°6'

VILLAVICENCIO

😊 Personal Safety Tips 😊

Bogotá suffers from chaotic transport and **petty** and **violent crime**. Use **common sense** and be aware that, especially In the Candelaria and the Centro Internacional, **purse snatching** is common. Do not advertise your wealth. Keep cameras and personal belongings hidden on your person. Stay on main streets with plenty of other people. Wandering dark and empty streets of the Candelaria after nightfall is asking for trouble.

There has been a notable betterment in **public transport**, sites of interest have been **restored** and **security** has been improved not only Downtown but in many areas.

Given Colombia's high level of **internal displacement** from the countryside to the cities, Bogotá has found itself under severe pressure. **Invasiones** or illegally-built homes and communities have sprung up in outlying areas such as **Ciudad Bolívar**. Through projects of social interest housing and a better network of public transport systems, Bogotá is addressing this problem and making the city more inclusive.

Lauded by city planners, the new **Trans-Milenio** articulated bus system was, at the time of its creation in 2000, the solution to the city's transportation ills. Ten years later, without a greater passenger capacity in relation to Bogotá's growth, the city seems to be crying out for a more comprehensive system to alleviate the pressures of urban circulation.

Yet, the city has been somewhat returned to its inhabitants, in particular under the former mayor **Antanas Mockus**, who actually managed to get drivers to stop at red lights, using an ingenious idea of mime artists in position at key intersections, and created an extensive network of bicycle lanes (🕯 see sidebars p124).

Often depicted in various media as a polluted, congested, crime-ridden capital, Bogotá, the nation's largest city, is a major financial, political and cultural center, with a host of universities, museums and cosmopolitan attractions. While at times completely lawless and chaotic, the city does hold interest for everyone, be it attending the biannual **Festival Iberoamericano de Teatro** or the **Feria del Libro**, enjoying a hot chocolate with cheese in a small nook of a cafe in the Candelaria, shopping for **haute couture** in the well-heeled northern barrios, participating in some spirited **tejo** game in a southern suburb, or enjoying exquisite pre-Columbian pieces at the outstanding Museo del Oro.

ZONA CENTRO★★★

Downtown Bogotá, loosely comprising the areas between Carreras 1 to 14 and Calles 5 to 34, is the busiest, most congested sector of the city, as well as the most interesting. The roots of the city run deep in this area, with the colonial **Candelaria** district, governmental and related offices, museums and historic churches. Many businesses remain in this quarter, specifically in the cement edifices of the **Centro Internacional**; at first glance, seemingly a business wasteland, it is also a gastronomical center catering to a lunchtime clientele of politicians, financiers and businessmen. Unless you are here on a whistle-stop layover, or solely for a business meeting, make time to visit central Bogotá's cultural and historical attractions that make this South American city so special.

👣 WALKING TOURS
1 LA CANDELARIA★★★

Allow a full morning for strolling the Candelaria, and save time for lunch here.

▷ *Start your walking tour at Plaza de Bolívar, between Calles 10 and 11 and Carreras 7 and 8.*

The Candelaria is the most important zone in the city for any visitor, and time must be allowed to explore its grid pattern of streets that climb from the **Plaza de Bolívar** up the eastern mountains to

The Candelaria's Graffiti

With the seemingly incessant demonstrations, protests and marches that descend upon the **Plaza de Bolívar**, it is no wonder that the area is covered with some fairly vitriolic graffiti, and let's not forget the presence of some eight universities in this area as well. After May Day demonstrations, the Carrera 7 looks as if a multicolored paint bomb has been detonated along its course, from the Centro Internacional to the heart of the Candelaria. This defacement of public property is all run of the mill and routine backlash, of course. But, as you wander the streets of the Candelaria, keep an eye out for far more interesting and creatively done graffiti that is becoming a favorite attraction for the hipsters that visit Bogotá. Clever prints made out to be something inoffensive often shield a double meaning and have a strong resonance as a protest to the violence taking place in Colombia's countryside. What looks, at first glance, like a dandelion has machine guns for branches; same goes for the dragonfly with armored wings and the hand grenade that, from afar, resembles a pineapple. These small, quiet messages of protest show another side to the conditions plaguing Colombia, and are an interesting side detail in the mix. Much of this protest artwork can be seen along the **Parque de los Periodistas** and on the **Carreras 3** and **4** in the Candelaria.

Carrera 3, and from bustling **Avenida Jiménez de Quesada** at its northern end south to **Calle 6**. It is within this loose frame that one can find some of the most interesting Baroque and colonial-era churches, palaces, museums, cultural centers and popular restaurants. There is just so much packed into this relatively small area, and it is no exaggeration to say that every nook and corner have a tale to tell or have played some historical role in the formation of this city, if not the country.

La Candelaria

Proexport Colombia

Plaza de Bolívar★★★

Originally, this plaza was called the Plaza de la Constitución and was surrounded by market stalls, but since then, this austere location has lost the market, the traffic and trams to its current pedestrians-only zone status. The bronze statue of **Simón Bolívar**, In the center of the plaza, is a focus for all demonstrations that take place in Colombia, and it would almost be miraculous if, on the day of your visit, there was no protest or demonstration. Public healthcare workers, teachers, families of loved ones lost to the "troubles" or just particularly zealous students are almost always present here. Whatever the cause or fight being fought, you will find these protestors polite and eager to explain their qualms to you, making for a truly Colombian experience.

This plaza is framed by imposing buildings of different architectural styles on all four sides, such as the **Capitolio Nacional**★ (1876-1926), at the southern end, which houses the Colombian Congress, with a spectacular **mural** by Santiago Martínez Delgado (*Calle 10 # 7-50, between Carreras 7 and 8; ⊘open for public debates; ✆(1) 212-6315*).

Other notable buildings around the plaza include the **Alcaldía Mayor** *(Palacio Liévano, Carrera 8 # 10-65; ⊘open*

Catedral Primada de Colombia, Plaza de Bolívar

© Florian Kopp/Imagebrokers/Photoshot

Mon–Sat 8am–6pm, Sun & public holidays 10am–4pm; ℘(1) 283 7115), the **Palacio de Justicia** *(Calle 11, between Carreras 7 and 8; ☛ closed to the public)* and Bogotá's cathedral.

Catedral Primada de Colombia★★

Carrera 7 # 10-80.
www.catedraldebogota.org.
Located on the northeastern corner of Plaza de Bolívar, this cathedral is the resting place of **Gregorio Vásquez de Arce y Ceballos** (1638–1711), Colombia's most famous painter of the colonial era. Built between 1807 and 1823, this Neoclassical structure occupies an enormous area of 5,300sq m/6,338sq yds housing no less than 14 different chapels.

Take special note of the towers that collapsed during the 1827 earthquake, and the façade that was restored in 1943 by the Spaniard **Alfredo Rodríguez Orgaz** (1907-1994).

▷ *Walk south, next door to the cathedral.*

Capilla del Sagrario de la Catedral de Bogotá★

Carrera 7 # 10-40.
Seemingly attached to the cathedral, this example of Neo-Grenadine architecture (1660-1700) shows off an ornate and excessive Baroque façade.
Inside, you can view more works of art with scenes from the Old and New Testament by the aforementioned Gregorio Vásquez de Arce y Ceballos. In 1819 **Bolívar** was received here for a mass of thanks after the **Battle of Boyacá**. Unfortunately, little remains of the original altar, made from ivory and ebony, after being repeatedly damaged in the earthquakes of 1827 and 1917.

Palacio Arzobispal [E *on map*]

Carrera 7 # 10. ☛ *Closed to the public.*
This is a site that witnessed some of the most turbulent times in Colombia's history. The present structure was buit between 1952 and 1959 to replace the old Archbishop's Palace, almost completely destroyed in the **Bogotazo** of 1948. It used to be the **Royal Customs House** where the Viceroy **Antonio José Amar y Borbón Arguedas** (1742-1826) was imprisoned after the first motions of independence in the capital.

▷ *Walk up Calle 10, the most scenic in the Candelaria.*

Colegio de San Bartolomé de Bogotá [B *on map*]

Carrera 7 # 9-96.
☛ *Closed to the public. ℘(1) 444 2530. www.sanbartolome.edu.co.*
Founded in 1604 by the Jesuits, this functioning high school is the oldest educational establishment in Colombia. It has turned out no less than 26 presidents and various notables, including **San Pedro Claver**.

The small, enclosed plaza on this corner is now called the **Plazuela Camilo Torres**, in honor of independence martyr **Camilo Torres Tenorio** (1766-1816). It was the site of Spanish executions of revolutionaries during the **Reconquista** of 1816.

▶ *Continue less than half a block up a gentle gradient on Calle 10.*

Museo de Trajes Regionales de Colombia★ [D *on map*]
Calle 10 # 6-20. 🕐*Open Mon–Fri 10am–4:30pm, Sat 10am–4pm.* 💰*2,000 COP.* 🎧*Guided tour available.* 💰*4,000 COP* 📞*(1) 282 6531. www.museodetrajes regionales.com.*

This two-storey Colonial house contains a permanent exhibit of more than a thousand **costumes** from all over Colombia, including pre-Hispanic and indigenous examples.

In 1828, the dwelling belonged to Bolívar's mistress **Manuela Sáenz** (1795-1856), due to its proximity to the Palacio San Carlos, where the Great Liberator was residing.

Opposite *(Calle 10 # 6-35),* one can see the **Iglesia de San Ignacio** (1610-43), inspired by the **Church of the Gesù** in Rome. Terribly damaged in the earthquake of 1763, San Ignacio was rebuilt with Renaissance, Mannerist, Baroque and Neoclassical touches. If you go in, be sure to check out the lavish 17C and 18C artwork.

▶ *Reaching the next corner heading up the hill, turn right to the entrance of the Museo de Arte Colonial.*

Museo de Arte Colonial★★
[C *on map*] *Carrera 6 # 9-77.* 🕐*Open Tue–Fri 9am–5pm, Sat–Sun 10am–4pm.* 💰*2,000 COP, no charge last Sun of month.* 📞*(1) 341 6017.*

Originally founded as the **Colegio Máximo de la Compañíade Jesús en la Nueva Granada** in the 17C, and then known as the **Casa de las Aulas**, this former Jesuit school now houses a museum that any visitor interested in colonial art should see. It boasts an impressive collection of silverware, glassware, furniture and paintings from the era. Within these austere brick walls, one can view yet more astonishing works by **Gregorio Vásquez de Arce y Ceballos**.

▶ *Return to Calle 10 and continue to the following block uphill.*

Palacio San Carlos
Calle 10 # 5-51. 🚫*Closed to the public.* On the right hand side, you will notice this palace dating back to 1580. Do not expect to gain entry here since security is tight at the Ministry of Foreign Affairs, but keep in mind that this used to be the residence of **Simón Bolívar**, who actually escaped an assassination attempt here.

Teatro de Cristóbal Colón★
Calle 10 # 5-32.
🚫*Closed for renovation until February 2012.* 📞*(1) 284-7420.*
Directly opposite is the unmistakable national theater of Colombia (1885-92), with its Tuscan Doric and Neoclassical façade. If you make arrangements to watch opera or ballet here, you will not be disappointed, as the interior is decorated lavishly in a Florentine style.

The theater also hosts countless shows during the biennial **Iboamerican Theater Festival**.

▶ *Continue up the hill to the Museo Militar.*

Museo Militar de Colombia
Calle 10a # 4-92. 🕐*Open Mon–Fri 8am–3:30pm, Sat–Sun 8am–12:30pm.* 📞*(1) 281 2548.*
Housed in a building that belonged to the family of a hero of Bolívar's independence movement, Capt. **Antonio Ricaurte**, this museum is home to an array of Colombian military uniforms. Its forecourt is filled with various tanks and rockets.

One exhibit room contains a replica of the **Battle of Vargas' Swamp**, complete with light and sound effects.

◯ *Turn south and walk along Carrera 5, crossing Calle 9.*

Teatro Camarín del Carmen★

Calle 9 # 4-93. ℘(1) 283 1772. www.tucomedia.com.

This old **Carmelite convent** (1655) served as a barracks and military hospital in the late 19C. Faithfully restored, with ornate overhanging balconies, it can seat up to 500 in its auditorium.

◯ *Continue on the same block.*

Santuario Nuestra Señora del Carmen★★

Carrera 5 # 8-36.

Designed by **Giovanni Buscaglione** (1874-1941), the santuary embodies a Florentine Gothic style with influences of Byzantine art and an Arabic finish that make it Bogotá's most striking church (1926-38).

◯ *Turn right on Calle 8 and head down the hill for one block.*

Museo Arqueológico Casa del Marqués de San Jorge★

Carrera 6 # 7-43. ◷Open Tue–Fri 8:30am–5pm, Sat 9:30am–5pm, Sun 10am–4pm. ◷Closed public holidays. ⚑3,000 COP. ℘(1) 243 1048. www.musarq.org.co/colecciones/ceramica.htm.

Santuario Nuestra Señora del Carmen

© Ethel Davies/ImageState/Alamy

This fine example of a 17C Colonial residence hosts the best and most important collection of **pre-Columbian ceramics** from groups such as the Tayrona, Muisca, Guane, Quimbaya, Calima, Nariño, Sinú, Tumaco and Cauca.

This is an excellent second opportunity, after the Museo del Oro, to learn about the pre-Hispanic cultures in Colombia.

◯ *Head downhill one full block.*

Palacio de Nariño★★

Carrera 8 # 7-26. ⚷Closed to international visitors. http://web. presidencia.gov.co/narino.

You should now be in the shadow of this regal and Neoclassical palace (1908), the official residence of the **president of Colombia**, located on the very site where the patriot and hero **Antonio Nariño** (1765-1823) was born.

Watching from the east side, you will get the best view of the **Changing of the Guard★** (◷Wed, Fri & Sun 4pm) in the **Plaza de Armas**.

☺Beware, this changing of the guard is a serious event here in Bogotá; visitors should not try make the professionals soldiers laugh, as at London's Buckingham Palace.

Observatorio Astronómico

On the grounds of the presidential garden. ⚷Closed to the public.

☀Solar viewings take place with prior reservations Thu 6pm–8pm. ℘(1) 541 4680. www.observatorio.unal.edu.co.

Best seen from Carrera 8 is the first observatory in Latin America (1803), which had the legendary botanist and mathematician **José Celestino Mutis** (1732-1808) as its first director.

◯ *Continue south along Carrera 7 to Calle 7, and cross the road.*

Iglesia San Agustín

Carrera 7A # 6-25.

Crossing the Calle 7 which was, at one point, the **River Manzanares**, brings you to this old church (1637-68).

San Agustín is notable for its ornamentally carved **altar** and interesting de◄

The Ghosts of the Candelaria

It will not escape your notice, as you take the Candelaria walking tour or if you stray a little from the suggested walk, that there are further curiosities in this barrio. Worth a mention are the so-called "ghosts of the Candelaria." Often in a state of anguish, they may "appear" on rooftops and on balconies. These blue-painted **papier maché creations** made in the likeness of actual human beings are part of the living history of the Candelaria. Placed in the actual location where someone who was executed used to live, or more sinisterly someone who was murdered in that very spot, the ghosts of the Candelaria add to the macabre, yet fascinating Republic and Independence eras of history here in the Zona Colonial. There is a "ghost" on the rooftop of the tourist information building, in the southwest corner of the Plaza de Bolívar, and numerous others on Calle 10 and along Carrera 3, including a representation of a lawyer who supposedly murdered his wife and was later hung. Unfortunately, these representations are not protected, and no historical value has been placed upon them, so they are at the mercy of the severe elements of Bogotá's climate, and many are in poor condition.

including some paintings by **Gregorio Vásquez de Arce y Ceballos**.

▶ *Take Calle 7 to the corner of Carrera 8, and head north.*

Claustro de San Agustín

Carrera 8 # 7-21. 🕐*Open Mon–Sat 10am–4pm.* ✆*(1) 342 2340. www.divulgacion.unal.edu.co.*
This former monastery (c.1733) is a unique example of Colonial religious architecture in that it does not have a church of its own. Part of this huge complex is used as an **art exhibition** space, while the rest is being gradually restored by the Universidad Nacional de Colombia.

Museo del Siglo XIX

Carrera 8 # 7-93. 🕐*Open Mon–Fri 8:30am–5:30pm, Sat 9am–1pm.* 💲*3,000 COP.* ✆*(1) 281 9948.*
Here you will find an interesting collection of Colombian paintings, drawings, etchings and furniture from the Republican period, with works from artists such as Ricardo Acevedo Bernal, Ricardo Alvarez Borrero and José María Espinos. Do not miss the reconstruction of a 19C pharmacy (La Botica de los Pobres).

▶ *Move north a few doors.*

Palacio Echeverri

Carrera 8 # 8-43.
This palace, which now houses the Ministry of Culture, was built between 1900 and 1906 by French architect **Gaston Lelarge** (1861-1934) on grounds belonging to the old Santa Clara Convent, at the behest of Gabriel Echeverri, a wealthy socialite from Medellin.

Museo Iglesia de Santa Clara★★

Carrera 8 # 8-91. 🕐*Open Tue–Fri 9am–5pm, Sat–Sun 10am–4pm.* 💲*2,000 COP, no charge last Sun of month.* ✆*(1) 337 6762.*
Originally a **convent** of the Clarissas, this building (1647) gives you the opportunity to immerse yourself in the architecture, decoration, imagery and artwork of the 17C and 18C. Mostly destroyed in the 20C, it still houses the breathtaking temple **vault** built in a barrel form and coated with golden floral motifs.

▶ *Turn the corner and walk down Calle 9.*

Museo Histórico de la Policía Nacional

Calle 9 # 9-27. 🕐*Open Tue–Sun 8am–5pm.* ✆*(1) 281 3284.*
To learn about the history of the Colombian police forces, visit this museum, housed in a remarkably restored Repu-

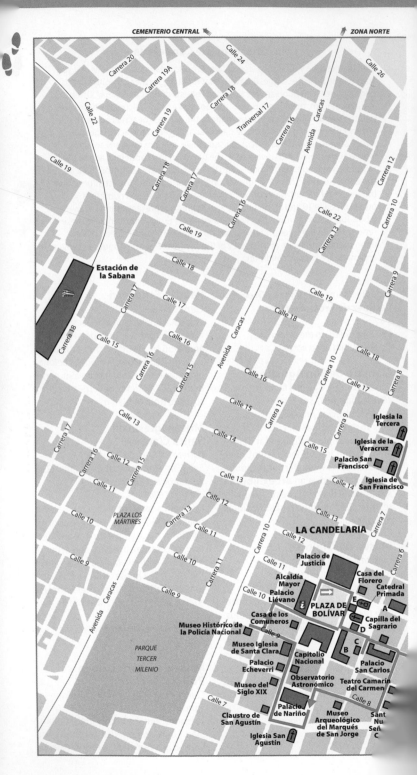

CEMENTERIO CENTRAL

ZONA NORTE

Calle 24

Calle 26

Carrera 20

Carrera 19A

Carrera 19

Carrera 18

Transversal 17

Avenida Caracas

Carrera 16

Carrera 12

Calle 22

Carrera 18

Carrera 17

Carrera 16

Calle 19

Carrera 10

Carrera 13

Carrera 9

Calle 22

Estación de la Sabana

Calle 18

Calle 19

Calle 18

Carrera 18

Carrera 17

Calle 17

Calle 16

Avenida Caracas

Calle 18

Carrera 10

Calle 18

Calle 17

Carrera 8

Calle 15

Carrera 16

Carrera 15

Calle 16

Calle 16

Carrera 12

Iglesia la Tercera

Calle 13

Calle 15

Carrera 9

Iglesia de la Veracruz

Carrera 17

Calle 14

Carrera 15

Calle 15

Palacio San Francisco

Carrera 16

Calle 12

Calle 13

Carrera 10

Iglesia de San Francisco

Carrera 15

Calle 11

Calle 12

Calle 14

Carrera 7

Calle 10

PLAZA LOS MÁRTIRES

Carrera 13

Calle 11

Calle 13

Calle 12

LA CANDELARIA

Calle 9

Calle 10

Carrera 11

Calle 11

Carrera 10

Calle 12

Carrera 6

Palacio de Justicia

Avenida Caracas

Calle 10

Calle 11

Alcaldía Mayor Palacio Liévano

Casa del Florero

Catedral Primada

PLAZA DE BOLÍVAR

E

A

Casa de los Comuneros

Capilla del Sagrario

PARQUE TERCER MILENIO

Museo Histórico de la Policía Nacional

Calle 9

D

Museo Iglesia de Santa Clara

Capitolio Nacional

C

B

Palacio Echeverri

Palacio San Carlos

Observatorio Astronómico

Museo del Siglo XIX

Teatro Camarín del Carmen

Calle 7

Calle 8

Claustro de San Agustín

Palacio de Nariño

Museo Arqueológico del Marqués de San Jorge

Sant Nu Señ C

Iglesia San Agustín

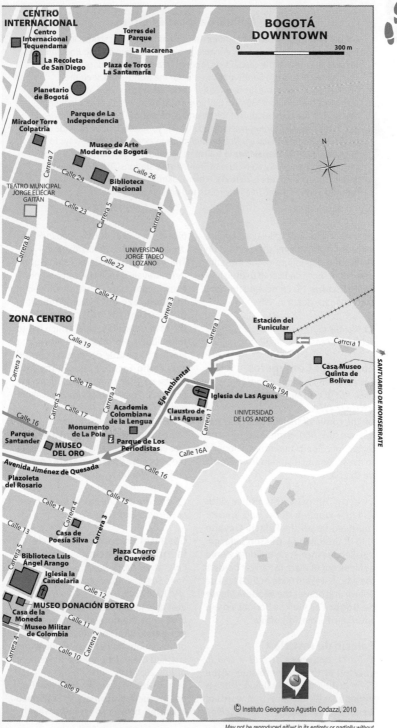

CENTRO INTERNACIONAL

Centro Internacional Tequendama

Torres del Parque

La Macarena

La Recoleta de San Diego

Plaza de Toros La Santamaría

Planetario de Bogotá

BOGOTÁ DOWNTOWN

0   300 m

Mirador Torre Colpatria

Parque de La Independencia

Museo de Arte Moderno de Bogotá

Carrera 7

Calle 24

Calle 26

Biblioteca Nacional

TEATRO MUNICIPAL JORGE ELIÉCAR GAITÁN

Calle 23

Carrera 5

Carrera 4

Carrera 8

UNIVERSIDAD JORGE TADEO LOZANO

Calle 22

Calle 21

Carrera 3

N

ZONA CENTRO

Calle 19

Carrera 1

Estación del Funicular

Carrera 1

SANTUARIO DE MONSERRATE

Carrera 7

Calle 18

Eje Ambiental

Casa Museo Quinta de Bolívar

Carrera 5

Calle 17

Calle 19A

Carrera 4

Academia Colombiana de la Lengua

Iglesia de Las Aguas

Calle 16

Carrera 1

Claustro de Las Aguas

UNIVERSIDAD DE LOS ANDES

Monumento de La Pola

Parque Santander

MUSEO DEL ORO

Parque de Los Periodistas

Calle 16A

Avenida Jiménez de Quesada

Calle 16

Plazoleta del Rosario

Calle 15

Calle 14

Carrera 4

Calle 13

Casa de Poesía Silva

Carrera 3

Plaza Chorro de Quevedo

Carrera 5

Biblioteca Luis Ángel Arango

Iglesia la Candelaria

Calle 12

MUSEO DONACIÓN BOTERO

Casa de la Moneda

Calle 11

Museo Militar de Colombia

Carrera 2

Carrera 4

Calle 10

Calle 9

ᘛ Building a Bicycle Culture

Bogotá's eco-progressive city administration has made great strides in reducing harmful emissions by encouraging some 3 million cycling *Bogotános* to make the most of the capital's cycle paths created by a visionary initiative. This model program in South America—if not the world—has seen the installation of one of the most extensive **cycle-ways** *(ciclorutas)* on the planet, with more than 300km/186mi of paths reserved exclusively for people riding bikes. Since the construction of the *ciclorutas*, bicycle use has increased five-fold in the city, and today an estimated 300,000 to 400,000 trips are made daily by cycle in Bogotá. Plans are already underway to extend the cycle-ways to fully link up to the **TransMilenio** transport system. Free and convenient cycle storage facilities are located close to TransMilenio stations. Another big part of Bogotá's bicycle culture is **ciclovia**, when 120km/74mi of roads are closed to cars and opened traffic-free for cyclists and walkers to enjoy.

blican era building. A collection of police uniforms from all over the world is on view, but the highlight of the museum is an entire room dedicated to drug lord **Pablo Escobar**, his crimes and the hunt that led to his death in 1993.

◗ *Go one block along Carrera 9, and head uphill east on Calle 10.*

Casa de los Comuneros
Carrera 8 # 8-83, on the corner of Calle 10. ◷*Open Mon–Fri 8am–5pm.* ℘*(1) 327 4900.*
On the corner of the Plaza de Bolívar is this rare surviving example of civil architecture of colonial times that belonged to the scribe and historian **Juan Flórez de Ocáriz**.

Directly opposite this house with its large wooden doors and interior courtyard stands the **Palacio Liévano** (1907). Designed by **Gaston Lelarge**, this Renaissance-style building would not look out of place in Paris. It borders the whole western side of the Plaza de Bolívar and houses the **Alcaldía Mayor de Bogotá** as well as Bogotá's main **tourist information office**.

Palacio de Justicia★
Calle 11, between Carreras 7 and 8.
Located at the northern side of the Plaza de Bolívar, this building (1989) is inscribed with the immortal words of **General Santander** (1792-1840): *Colom-*

bianos; las armas os han dado independencia las leyes os darán libertad.
The Palace of Justice has undergone much travail, hence the contemporary construction date. It was destroyed in the **Bogotazo** of 1948, and rebuilt in the 1960s. In 1985 it was taken over by the **M19** guerrilla group, which led to the military's storming the building and leaving 55 people dead. It is believed that Pablo Escobar backed the M19 attack so that they could incinerate extradition papers that would have sent him to the US.
In 1998 architect Roberto Londoño did some major work on the structure.
The emblematic building now houses the **Supreme Court** and **State Council** and is under heavy guard.

◗ *End the walking tour at the corner of Carrera 7 and Calle 11.*

Casa del Florero – Museo de la Independencia★
Calle 11 # 6-94. ◷*Open Tue–Fri 9am–5pm, Sat–Sun 10am–4pm.* ⊜*3,000 COP.* ℘*(1) 336 0349.*
Visit this 16C house to see some of the best kept memorabilia of the **Independence War**. The house was the site of the famous **flower vase** incident that sparked the independence movement of July 20, 1810.
Step inside to discover how two Creole brothers, **Antonio** and **Francisco Morales**, broke the vase of a wealthy

Casa del Florero – Museo de la Independencia

collection of some 85 works by great international artists such as Renoir, Dalí, Chagall, Picasso, Miró and Pollock, to name a few.

Casa de la Moneda★
Calle 11 # 4-93. ◑*Open Mon, Wed–Sat 9am–7pm, Sun and public holidays 10am–5pm.* ☞*Guided tours Mon, Wed–Fri 11am & 4pm, Sat 10am, noon, 2pm & 4pm.* ✆*(1) 343 1212. www.lablaa.org.*

This pleasant colonial building, complete with an inner courtyard, housed the former **Mint**, founded by order of King Phillip II in 1621. The first gold coins in South America were originally minted here. The Mint was expanded in the 17C to meet burgeoning demand.

The exhibits here illustrate an interesting journey through history, showing the techniques involved in the production of coins and bills. The Banco de la República has major art collections throughout the country (particularily pre-Columbian gold pieces). Their numismatic collection is not exhibited in the headquarters of the bank, but here, in the old Mint (an appropriate choice for such an exhibit. The **numismatic collection** is a must see of course, but also take time to admire the richly adorned 18C religious artifacts here.

Spaniard named **José Gonzalez-Llorente**, thereby symbolically breaking the colonial yolk of Imperial Spain.

AROUND LA CANDELARIA
Biblioteca Luis Ángel Arango★
Calle 11 # 4-14. ◑*Open Mon–Sat 8am–8pm, Sun 8am–4pm.* ◑*Closed public holidays.* ✆*(1) 343 1212. www.lablaa.org.*

Built in 1958, and embodying the Brutalist architecture of the era, Colombia's most important library is also one of the most visited in the world. More than 10,000 people use it daily (more than the New York Public Library), probably due to the high prevalence of universities in the area. In addition to housing some two million books, the library puts on interesting exhibits and concerts.

Museo Donación Botero★★★
Calle 11 # 4-41. ◑*Open Mon, Wed–Sat 9am–7pm, Sun and public holidays 10am–5pm. Last entry 30min before closing.* ☞*Guided tours Mon, Wed–Fri 11am & 4pm, Sat 10am, noon, 2pm & 4pm.* ✆*(1) 343 1212; www.lablaa.org/ museobotero.htm.*

Located in front of the Biblioteca Luis Ángel Arango, this museum exhibits no less than 123 drawings, paintings and sculptures by Colombian artist **Fernando Botero** (& *see sidebar*). It also houses the artist's stunning private art

Centro Cultural Gabriel García Márquez [A *on map*]
Calle 11 # 5-60. www.fce.com.co.

With its smooth circular lines and ample use of brick, this modern building definitely stands out among its colonial neighbors on Calle 11. The cultural center bears the signature hallmarks of **Rogelio Salmona** (1929-2007), most renowned for his work on the Eje Ambiental and the Torres del Parque (& *see below*). it makes for a nice place to take a break, with its excellent **bookstore**, restaurants and coffee shops.

Plaza Chorro de Quevedo★
Calle 13 and Carrera 2.

Marked by a small fountain, this spot is supposedly where, in 1538, the conquistador **Gonzalo Jiménez de Que-**

125

sada stopped to water his horses and founded the city of Bogotá.

Today it is a bohemian hang out, with some eclectic **bars** situated nearby offering conventional drinks as well as the local *chicha*, a very potent Andean alcoholic homebrew. In the early evening, **storytellers** *(cuenteros)* take up residence in front of the small chapel here and regale the crowd with often humorous tales.

😮*Caution is strongly advised after dark in this area.*

Casa de Poesía Silva

Calle 14 # 3-41. 🕐*Open Mon–Fri 9am–1pm, 2pm–6pm.* 🔎*Guided tour available with prior reservations.* 📞*(1) 286 5710. www.casadepoesiasilva.com.* Possibly built around 1715, this house has been set up as the national museum of poetry, with an extensive library. There are frequent poetry readings here.

It is named after the poet **José Asunción Silva** (1865-96), who lived here, and later took his own life.

Iglesia la Candelaria

Carrera 4 # 11-62.
Started in 1686 and completed in 1703, this church—one of the oldest in the Candelaria—shows off obvious Colonial details.

Inside, It houses important religious artwork by **Pedro Alcántara Quijano** (1878-1953), and its **roof painting** in

the central nave is considered the most evocative example of Baroque period art in all of Bogotá.

② EJE AMBIENTAL DE LA AVENIDA JIMÉNEZ

▷ *Start at the Estación del Funicular. on Carrera 2 Este.*

Since 2002 this snaking main thoroughfare has been closed to cars and adapted for sole use of the **TransMilenio** bus system. There are many points of interest all along this route, made more accessible with the amplification of **pedestrianized** sections in the Eje Ambiental in 1997, from the **Estación del Funicular** continuing west to the **Estación de la Sabana**. Walk this tour on a **weekday**, when there are plenty of students frequenting the area.

🚫*Best to avoid Sundays or public holidays when there is often a flea market in the Parque de los Periodistas that attracts the city's ne'er-do-well residents.*

Estación del Funicular

Carrera 2 Este # 21-48 Paseo Bolívar.
🕐*Funicular operates Mon–Sat 7:45am –11:45am, Sun and public holidays 6am –6:30pm.* 🕐*Cable car operates Mon–Sat noon–midnight, Sun 9am–5pm.* 🎫*14,000 COP Mon–Sat & public holidays,* 🎫*17,000 COP Mon–Sat from*

TransMilenio bus, Eje Ambiental de la Avenida Jiménez

© Luis Gomez/Flickr

Cerro de Monserrate★★

The **Santuario de Monserrate** is visible from just about every corner of the city, as it sits atop the highest point at 3,152m/10,340ft on the eastern ridge, blindingly white in the glare of a sunny day. Accessible by either **cable car** or **funicular** (☙*see opposite page for details*), it offers breathtaking **views**★★★ from the top. From this vantage point, you will be able to understand the layout of Bogotá and its continuing sprawl across the altiplano. You may even see as far as the Parque Nacional Natural Los Nevados

Santuario de Monserrate

Proexport Colombia

(☙ *see ZONA CAFETERA*), some 300km/186mi away. The **Basílica del Señor de Monserrate** (1925) is a destination for pilgrims, and on religious holidays it gets quite crowded. ☙*After a spate of violent robberies on the often empty trail, walking up to the top of Monserrate through the Andean forest was no longer advised. However, at the time of writing, improvements were being made to the path, and by early 2011, hiking up to the sanctuary might be safe again; check beforehand.*

5:30pm, ☙8,000 COP Sun. ☎(1) 284 5700. www.cerromonserrate.com.
Located at the foot of the Cerro de Monserrate (☙ *see sidebar above*), this funicular and cable car station is the perfect place to start your walking tour of Eje Ambiental de La Avenida Jiménez because of its convenient relation to the rest of the sights.

Casa Museo Quinta de Bolívar★

Calle 20 # 2-91 Este. ☙*Open Tue–Fri 9am–5pm, Sat–Sun 10am–4pm.*
☙*Guided tour in English Wed 11am.*
☙*3,000 COP.* ☎*(1) 336 6419.*
www.quintadebolivar.gov.co.
This 19C villa was a gift from the new government to **Simón Bolívar**, right after independence was achieved. Over the years the building was used as a school, a brewery and a political center. It has now been converted into a museum celebrating the life of the Great Liberator.
Bolívar first inhabited the house in 1821, and later in 1826, before making it his home in 1827, when he returned with his mistress, **Manuelita Sáenz**.
On display are various objects that belonged to Bolívar, including his

notably short bed, and various pieces of furniture and objects from the era. One artifact that is painfully missing is **Bolívar's sword**, which was stolen from the museum in 1975 by the M19 guerrilla group, notorious for its high-profile actions.

▶ *Walk down past Los Andes University and along Eje Ambiental.*

Iglesia de Las Aguas★

Carrera 3 # 18-66.
Built in 1644 this simple yet elegant church sits back from the street; if you're not actually looking for it, you may miss it. This is one of the oldest churches in the capital, as attested by its Colonial façade.
The Gothic Revival **San Antonio Chapel**, on the northern side, was added in 1901, and the whole building was restored in in 2004.
Visitors can now enjoy the artwork within, done by notables such as **Gregorio Vázquez**, **Antonio Acero de la Cruz** and **Baltasar de Figueroa**.

Claustro de Las Aguas

Carrera 2 # 18A-58. ☎*(1) 286 1766.*
www.artesaniasdecolombia.com.co.

Monumento de la Pola★

Carrera 3 and Calle 18. There are many statues of male martyrs of the Colombian independence movement, but very few of women. This makes the statue of **Policarpa Salavarrieta Ríos** (c.1791-1817), erected in 1968, of special interest. During the **Spanish Reconquista**, Policarpa spied for the revolutionary forces and was executed by the Viceroyalty of New Granada for high treason. Originally created by **Dionisio Cortés** (1863-1934), this moving monument was then sculpted in bronze by the Peruvian sculptor **Gerardo Benítez**. The statue shows this young heroine with her hands bound behind her back, awaiting her fate.

© Richard McColl/MICHELIN

Right next door, this old convent, which was also used as a hospital and orphanage, now houses the head offices of **Artesanías de Colombia**, known for its high-quality handicrafts and clothing from all over the country. If you have no budgetary restraints, then this store is definitely the place to pick up some crafts and souvenirs.

▶ *Continue along Eje Ambiental. Cross the road.*

Academia Colombiana de la Lengua

Carrera 3 # 17-34. ⚊*Closed to the public.* ℘*(1) 334 1190.*
Designed by the Spaniard **Alfredo Rodríguez Ordaz** toward the end of the 1950s, this Neoclassical building is a replica of the Royal Spanish Academy. It is the seat of the **Colombian Academy of Language** founded in 1871, which makes it the oldest of its kind in the Americas. Inside, a mural by **Luis Alberto Acuña Tapias** (1904-1994) depicts Colombian and Hispanic authors.

Parque de los Periodistas

Avenida Jiménez and Carrera 3.
This large, brick-paved space feels at times like a traffic island between careening TransMilenio buses, but

it actually offers a breather of sorts under the gaze of Simón Bolívar. Created in 1883 by Italian sculptor and Colombian resident **Pietro Cantini** (1847-1929) for the centenary of Bolívar's birth, the **Templete del Libertador** now resides here.
On Sundays and public holidays, there is a very basic **flea market** where Bogotá's down-on-their-luck sell just about anything. *⊘If you search here for curiosities, please be most vigilant about your personal belongings.*

▶ *Walk down Avenida Jiménez two long blocks.*

Plazoleta del Rosario★

Calle 14 and Carrera 6.
Lined with traditional cafes from the 1930s that have changed little since then and still exude the same ambience, this pleasant plaza has a statue of **Gonzalo Jiménez de Quesada**, the founder of Bogotá, right in its center. Impress a local with your knowledge by recounting that here, in the **Café Pasaje,** one of the big football (soccer) teams in the city, **Santa Fé**, was created. On the south side of the plaza sits part of the **Universidad del Rosario**, founded in 1653. Frequently local artisans and book vendors are invited to set up stalls here in the plaza, and some good deals can

be found, especially if you are looking for Spanish language literature.

▷ *Head west toward Carrera 7, and cross diagonally.*

Iglesia de San Francisco★
Calle 16 # 7-35.
www.templodesanfrancisco.com.
Bogotá's oldest church (1550-67) should be visited, if only to see the restoration work done on the building, which was repeatedly damaged in earthquakes. The only remaining original sections are the façade, the tabernacle and the tower. Inside, do not miss the fabulous Baroque **wood carvings**.

Iglesia de San Francisco

Proexport Colombia

Palacio San Francisco
Avenida Jiménez # 7-50.
There used to be a Franciscan monastery next to the San Francisco church, but it was razed in the 20C to make way for this palace (1933).
Originally, it housed the headquarters of the **governor of Cundinamarca** behind its Neoclassical façade, but it now makes up part of the Universidad del Rosario. The building was burned down in the **Bogotazo** of 1948, but rebuilt entirely according to the original blueprints.

▷ *Walk along Carrera 7, heading north.*

Iglesia de la Veracruz★
Calle 16 # 7-19.
Situated between the **Iglesias San Francisco** and **La Tercera**, this church was built in 1546. Its façade is quite modest and its interior rather sober. However, its historical importance is undiminished, as prisoners prayed to the crucifix of the *Cristo de los Agonizantes* the night before their execution.
The *Cristo de los Martires* is a canvas that accompanied those prisoners on their way to execution. Many heroes and martyrs of the independence movement killed during the Spanish reign of terror around 1815 are buried in the **National Pantheon** here.
Note also the fine altar decorated in fine Mudéjar style.

Iglesia la Tercera★
Calle 16 # 7-35.
Continuing the religious theme and making up the third part of the most important set of religious architecture in Bogotá (the others being the San Francisco and La Veracruz), La Tercera (1761-1774) has a beautiful colonial **façade**, but lacks the extravagance of its neighboring churches. It does boast superb **wood carvings** from the 18C. Be sure to look for its Rococo style altars and pulpits.

▷ *Cross the road heading East.*

Parque de Santander★
Between Avenida Carrera 7 to Carrera 5 and Calle 16.
Usually filled with book vendors and shoe shiners, this park, complete with a bronze statue of **Francisco de Santander** in its center, makes a good place from which to observe the bustle of Downtown Bogotá. There are some tourist-oriented galleries and shops at the eastern end, but the principal point of interest around the park is undeniably Bogotá's outstanding Gold Museum.

Museo del Oro★★★
On the corner of Carrera 5A and Calle 16.
🕐*Open Tue–Sat 9am–7pm, Sun and public holidays 10am–5pm. Last entry*

129

Gold winged fish from San Agustín, Museo del Oro

Proexport Colombia

1hr before closing. ✍Guided tours in English Tue–Sat 11am & 4pm. ⊚3,000 COP, no charge Sun. ✆(1) 343 2222. www.banrep.gov.co/museo.

✍To get a good overview of pre-Hispanic Colombia, be sure to rent one of the audio sets and allow yourself to be led around the key items.

Enough cannot be said about this museum. It is simply the most impressive museum of its type in the world, and one that no visitor to Colombia should miss, as it houses exquisite artifacts from the Calima, Quimbaya, Muisca, Tayrona, Sinu, Tolima and Magdalena, to name a only few.

Completely overhauled in 2008, the museum celebrates the talents and mysteries of the **pre-Columbian cultures**. There are some 34,000 pieces to gaze at, and just like the Met in New York or the British Museum in London, you could spend days here taking in the exhibits. Its permanent exhibits are conveniently divided into four major themes—Mining and Metalwork; People and Gold in pre-Hispanic Colombia; Cosmology and Symbolism; and Offerings—showcasing everything from body adornments to sacrificial vessels.

The final room alone is worth the visit, as you are asked to pause slightly; then the lights come up, revealing a circular room completely covered in **gold artifacts**. The museum's creators claim that this grand finale will remain etched in your memory, perhaps forever.

CENTRO INTERNACIONAL

This area is located slightly farther uptown from the Candelaria district, and is, for the most part, an architectural jumble of styles between **Calles 24** and **32** and **Carreras 5** and **14**. This is the main business and financial sector, as the name suggests, but there are plenty of sights here such as museums, parks and architectural curiosities to interest the visitor to Bogotá, not to mention some of the city's finest dining options for lunch, given the proximity of so many offices.

La Recoleta de San Diego
Calle 26 # 7-30.
Little remains of the original structure of the Recoleta de San Diego built in 1608 by the **Franciscans**. The development of the area to allow for major road systems and skyscrapers has taken its toll.
There is a plain church with a chapel devoted to the *Nuestra Senora del Campo*, still worshipped today by local farmers and indigenous people.

Parque de la Independencia★
Calle 26 and Carrera 5 to Carrera 7.
✆(1) 282 7937. www.idrd.gov.co.
Built in 1910 to celebrate the first 100 year anniversary of Colombia's independence in 1810, this green area is welcome amid an otherwise cement and glass jungle.
Filled with pine and acacia trees, it is the most traditional park in the city. Its small

kiosks and architectural elements were designed by the Italian **Pietro Cantini** (1847-1929).

Within the park are several points of interest.

Planetario de Bogotá

Carrera 6 # 26-07. Open Tue–Sun *and public holidays 10:30am–4pm.* 3,500 COP for projections. Call for *other events.* (1) 334 4546. *www.planetariodebogota.gov.co.* This is Bogotá's largest planetarium (1969). With Latin America's biggest cupola (diameter: 25m/82ft), it offers much in the way of light shows, laser projections and astronomy work- shops.

Biblioteca Nacional

Calle 24 # 5-60, between Carreras 5 and 6. Open Mon–Fri 8am–6pm, Sat *9am–2pm. Check website for temporary exhibitions.* (1) 341 3061. *www.bibliotecanacional.gov.co.*

Founded in 1777 Colombia's National Library occupies, since 1938, an Art Deco building designed by **Alberto Wills Ferro** (1906), which was remodelled in 1977.

It is a testament to the country's biblio- graphic wealth, with countless editions, including some 30,000 books published before 1800.

Museo de Arte Moderno de Bogotá (MamBo)★★

Calle 24 # 6-00. Open Tue–Sat 10am– *6pm, Sun noon–5pm.* 4,000 COP. (1) 286 0466; www.mambogota.com. Designed by **Rogelio Salmona** (1929- 2007), Bogotá's Museum of Modern Art was inaugurated in 1979. Its compre- hensive collection of modern artwork consists of paintings, drawings and sculptures by Colombian and interna- tional artists.

Among the 2,000 works on exhibit, you will find a truly inspiring number of works by Colombian maestros such

---

Down Memory Lane

Just west of the Centro Internacional, crossing the Carrera 26 that leads from the Centro Internacional Tequendama to the airport, is Bogotá's most historic cemetery. Clearly, this is not the city's oldest cemetery, if you think from the perspective that all hillsides and barrios of the capital served as an enormous burial ground for the Muisca people and various other pre-Columbian peoples. A visit to the **Cementerio Central** *(Carrera 20 # 24-80, open Mon–Sun 8am–4:30pm)* is an opportunity to study the past catalog of historic figures who have helped create modern Colombia. Its alleyways running alongside large family mausoleums of the country's wealthy rival anything seen in Buenos Aires' La Recoleta, and are enshrouded with intrigue and lore. You can easily spot references to the Masons, historical personalities and the country's forebears.

It is strongly recommended that you arrive and leave here by taxi, as the cemetery backs onto Santa Fé, one of Bogotá's less salubrious barrios.

Little known and largely unvisited *(permission to visit is needed from the British Embassy,* see p31, United Kingdom), the **Cementerio Britanico** is a reminder of the historical solidarity that the Great Liberator Simón Bolívar received from overseas in his push for independence from the Spanish regime.

Located next door to the Cementerio Central, behind a nondescript doorway, is the final resting place of many of the British Legion who fought for Bolívar. In a solemn thanks to these brave souls, Bolívar made a gift of this plot of land to those British who fell in battle here in Colombia. This resting place is possibly the only Protestant burial ground in Bogotá, a real discovery for history enthusiasts and genealogists looking to trace gentlemen from small towns in the UK such as **Kirkbride** and **Woking**, from where these soldiers hailed. Well- maintained, the cemetery also has spaces set aside for British expatriates.

Illuminated Mirador Torre Colpatria viewed from La Macarena

© Gunther Beck/iStockphoto.com

as **Botero**, **Negret**, **Grau** and **Obregón**, along with art by Manzur, Villamizar, Alvaro Barrios, Ana Mercedes Hoyos and María de la Paz Jaramillo, to name a few.

Mirador Torre Colpatria★

48th floor, Torre Colpatria, Carrera 7 # 24, at the intersection of Calle 26 and Carrera 7. Open Sat–Sun and public *holidays 9:30am–6pm.* 2,500 COP. *(1) 283-6665.*

As one of the tallest buildings in Colombia and a major financial center in its own right, the Torre Colpatria (1978) is nothing less than an iconic piece in Bogotá's jigsaw skyline.

On weekends, the **viewing platform** opens to the public for unrivaled **views** over the city from the 48th floor, extending from the Cerros Monserrate and Guadalupe in the east to Ciudad Bolívar in the south, and the Sabana Cundiboyacense to the west.

Exterior lighting panels illuminate the tower in various colors at night.

Torres del Parque

Carrera 5 and Calle 27 by the Plaza de Toros. Art exhibitions are organized in the Galería Mundo, Carrera 5 # 26A-19. Open Mon–Fri 10am–6pm, Sat 10am *–2pm.* Guided tours available with *prior booking.* (1) 232 2408. *www.galeria-mundo.com.*

Yet another creation of **Rogelio Salmona** (1929-2007), this imposing trio of brick towers was designed between 1965 and 1970. They are difficult to ignore since they back onto the eastern *cerros* of the city, and are perhaps the most striking elements of the Bogotá cityscape.

The 300 apartments in this **residential complex** follow the curve of the Plaza de Toros in front. An emphasis was placed by Salmona in creating covered and external spaces for each unit. Iconic and unmistakable, Salmona's style has been imitated by Colombian architects ever since.

La Macarena★★

The barrio of La Macarena, located around the base of the Torres del Parque, loosely between Carreras 3 and 5 and Calles 26 and 30, is Bogotá's hippest foodie destination.

In the 1930s La Macarena was a wealthy neighborhood, but time took its toll, and the socioeconomic breakdown changed. The evolution of this zone has been favorable; it has become a chic bohemian hangout filled with restaurants offering cuisine from Colombian to Arabic and Yugoslavian.

Frequented by actors and beat poet look-alikes, La Macarena is a fascinating place to spend an evening sipping wine in moody bars or exploring new and unknown galleries that support up and coming Colombian artists.

Plaza de Toros La Santamaría
Carrera 6 # 26-50.
Bullfighting in Bogotá is a serious pastime, and in bullfighting season *(Jan and Feb)*, this plaza (1931) is filled to its 14,500 person capacity.
The cattle baron **Ignacio Sanz de Santamaría** plunged a great part of his fortune into this project, undertaken by the architects **Adonaí Martínez** and **Eduardo Lazcano**. In the 1940s the Spaniard **Santiago Mora** added its Moorish façade.

Plaza de Toros La Santamaría surrounded by Torres del Parque
© Tijs Zwinkels/Dreamstime.com

Museo Taurino
Plaza de Toros La Santa María, Puerta 6. 🕐*Open Mon–Fri 2pm–4pm, prior reservations neccessary.* ✆*(1) 282 2792. www.ctaurina.com.*
This museum has a good exhibition on the history of bullfighting in Colombia, and a variety of matadors' clothes and bullfighting equipment.

Museo Nacional de Colombia★★
Carrera 7 # 28-66. 🕐*Open Tue–Sat 10am–6pm, Sun 10am–5pm. Last entry 30min before closing.* 📷*3,000 COP.* ✆*(1) 334 8366. www.museonacional. gov.co .*

Founded in 1823 Colombia's oldest museum is housed in a building that was used as a **penitentiary** until 1946. One glance at the building, and you can see the history worn on its hard brick and fortress-like exterior. Way back then, this was the country's most important and impenetrable prison.
The first floor of the museum is dedicated to pre-hispanic Colombia and the Spanish Conquest; the second floor is devoted to the period of the Republic and subsequent history up until 1886; and the third floor is reserved for arts industries and a look at modern Colombian life. The museum also hosts excellent traveling exhibitions.

Centro Internacional Tequendama
Carrera 10 # 27-51.
The construction of the Centro Internacional Tequendama was a watershed in Colombian architectural history as well as city planning.
In the 1950s, with all businesses moving north due to the social decay of the core of the city following the Bogotazo of 1948, urban planners decided to build a hotel and business office complex here to bring about a **regeneration** of the area. This project coincided with the construction of the **El Dorado airport** and the renovation of the **highway** that connected the terminal directly to this center, making it geographically pivotal to business. **Gabriel Serrano Camargo** (1909-82), a pioneer of modern Colombian architecture, was the brains behind it, and his work achieved many firsts in new methods of employing concrete.

Parque Central Bavaria
Carrera 13A # 28-18. ✆*(1) 287 6948. www.parquecentralbavaria.com.*
Almost as if tacked onto the Tequendama complex, this **residential area**, with its open spaces and parks, won the **National Prize of Architecture** in 1998. It is built from brick, continuing Bogotá's love affair with this material, or perhaps as homage to the works of Rogelio Salmona.

ZONA NORTE★

As you leave the Candelaria and the Centro Internacional and move uptown, the residential neighborhood of **Chapinero** appears and the change becomes evident as Colonial architecture makes way for tall **apartment blocks** and student **residences**.

You soon enter the Zona Norte, residential and chic, with tree-lined barrios brimming with **boutiques**, expensive **hotels**, first-class **restaurants**, **bars**, **clubs** and several enormous **shopping centers**.

Here, you will find the embassies, foreign language bookstores and eating places with any cuisine you desire, making parts of Uptown indistinguishable from parts of New York or Madrid. In areas such as the Zona Rosa (◷ *see below*), you can wander around as carefree as you would in a European capital city.

ZONA G★★

Located in the desirable barrio of **Rosales**, the Zona G is loosely defined by Carrera Septima to the west, Carrera 4 to the east and Calles 67 to 79. In this small area, the Zona G or **Zona Gourmet** is filled with fine eateries from all corners of the globe. Some of these exclusive restaurants are owned by renowned chefs such as Harry Sasson, with his self-named restaurant, and Jorge and Mark Rausch, who preside over the Criterion restaurant.

ZONA T AND ZONA ROSA★★

The **Zona T** is so called since it is a **pedestrianized** area on Calle 82 and Carrera 13 in the shape of a T.

The center of Bogotá's Uptown **nightlife district**, but not as exclusive as the Zona G, it caters to a student-age crowd. Its selection of restaurants is great, attracting diplomats and politicians. At Christmas time, the area is lit up in spectacular fashion. At other times there are street-side photographic exhibitions.

The **Zona Rosa** is the umbrella name for the whole **nightlife district** in this section of the Zona Norte, including the Zona T. The streets are lined with **bars** and **clubs** and **fancy shops**.

A little more sophisticated than the Zona T is the **Parque 96**. This space consists of a leafy plaza with a park in the center ringed by high-end restaurants and bars.

Museo del Chicó

Carrera 7 # 93-01. ◷*Open Mon–Fri 10am–5pm, Sat 8am–noon, last Sun of month 10am–4pm.* ◷*2,500 COP.* ℘*(1) 622 2183. www.museodelchico.com.*

This museum is located in one of the grand old colonial *estancias* that was out in the Sabana de Bogotá when it was built, and now sits firmly in the heart of the urban center. Here, you will see a remarkable, eclectic collection of antiquities and art: works by religious masters, furniture, pre-Columbian ceramics and even coins from the time of Nueva Granada.

While the exhibits are fun, the house and its **gardens** are the real treat, since this structure and its grounds are examples of colonial country grandeur, with touches of the Republican era.

Hacienda Santa Bárbara★

Carrera 7 # 115-60. ◷*Open Mon–Fri 10am–10pm, Sat–Sun 10am–midnight, public holidays 9:30am–10pm.* ℘*(1) 612 0388. www.haciendasanta barbara.com.co.*

This hacienda is a fine example of a sprawling colonial country estate (1847) that has been restored and converted into a shopping center. Most importantly, the architects kept the original structure and line of the building, so when you are visiting the 300 odd shops contained herein, you can still feel the ambience of a historic country home.

Parque Simón Bolívar★

Calle 63 and 53 between Carreras 48 and 68. ◷*Open daily 6am–6pm.* ℘*(1) 660 0288.*

With 16km/10mi of pathways, a large lake and a running track, this open 113ha/279-acre space—actually larger than New York City's Central Park—helps Bogotá breathe. Large-scale events take place here, from Metallica and Coldplay concerts to the yearly free

Usaquén★★

Once a farming community, this residential and commercial neighborhood in northern Bogotá was incorporated into the city in 1954. Its colonial square is bordered by the Colonial-style **Santa Barbara Church** (1665), now ringed by chic restaurants. The atmosphere here is different from the rest of Bogotá. Its narrow grid-pattern streets hold bakeries and small independent boutiques. A Sunday **designer flea market** in the car park up the hill from the plaza has prices for an upper middle-classe clientele. Enjoy a Colombian brew, a meal in a sushi restaurant or a faux English pub. The village-like feel has made this vicinity popular with international and expat crowds.

Rock al Parque Festival or the open-air mass given by Pope Paul VI in 1968 and Pope John Paul II in 1986.

Museo de los Niños

Carrera 60 # 63-27. Guided tour *(1hr 30min) Tue–Fri 8:30am, 10:30am, 1:30pm, 3:30pm; Sat–Sun, public and school holidays hourly 9:30am–3:30pm.* Closed Good Friday. *9,000 COP.* (1) 225 7587. www.museodelos ninos.org.co.

This museum is designed to educate children in the topics of science, technology, culture and the arts. It is split into seven color-coded zones dealing with everything from how coal is extracted to dental hygiene.

Maloka – Centro Interactivo de Ciencia y Tecnología★

Carrera 68D # 24-51. Open Mon–Fri *8am–5pm, Sat–Sun and public holidays 10am–7pm.* 9,000 COP. Imax Theater *10,500 COP.* (1) 427 2707; www.maloka.org.

The Maloka is an interactive museum spread out underground. It covers a variety of science and technology-related topics such as the universe, the human body, telecommunications, bio-diversity and others. Children will love the **hands-on approach** that makes physics, biology, geology, mechanics and all kinds of other disciplines easy to understand. They will also have fun watching 3D movies on the giant screen in the Maloka's futuristic **dome**.

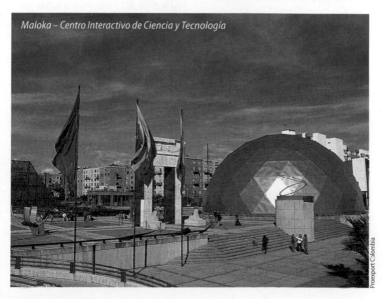

Maloka – Centro Interactivo de Ciencia y Tecnología

Proexport Colombia

ADDRESSES

For price categories, &see the Legend on the front cover flap.

STAY

$ Platypus Hostel – *Calle 16 # 2-43, Bogotá. &(1) 341 3104. http://platypus bogota.com. 23 rooms.* A good choice if you're on a budget, the Platypus gives you value for your money. It's located in the historic La Candelaria district. Spread over three houses, it offers simple dorms or private double rooms, a small kitchen area and a friendly staff—and it fills up fast. Morning coffee and Wi-Fi Internet are complimentary.

$$ Hotel Amabala – *Carrera 5 # 13-46, Bogotá. ✕&(1) 342 6384. www. hotelamabala.net. 22 rooms.* A good choice for those looking for reasonably priced accommodations, the Amabala boasts a friendly and helpful staff. Relatively small rooms have a private bathroom, AC, Internet access and TV.

$$$$ Bogotá Plaza Summit Hotel – *Bogotá Plaza. Calle 100 # 18A-30, Bogotá. P✕Spa &(1) 632 2200. www.bogotaplazahotel.com. 190 rooms.* Bogotá Plaza borders many of the tourist areas in the north part of the city. Good service comes at a price here, but rooms are non-smoking and cater to comfort with memory-foam mattresses and custom pillow menus. A gym, spa services and a business center complete the amenities.

$$$$ Hotel Casa De La Botica – *Calle 9 # 6-45, La Candelaria, Bogotá. ✕Spa &(1) 281 0811. www.hotelcasade labotica.com. 10 rooms.* This restored Republican-style house has a fascinating history, details of which are displayed on-site for guests to read. The city's libertarian and literary movers and shakers once met here, and it's still surrounded by many key political and cultural institutions. Rooms face an open interior courtyard decorated with a small fountain.

$$$$ Hotel De La Opera – *Calle 10 # 5-72, Bogotá. ✕⌂Spa &(1) 336 2066. www.hotelopera.com.co. 15 rooms.* Over the years, the two restored historic buildings that today make up this grand property housed several noteworthy residents, including some of the city's first settlers and later, the personal guard of Latin American liberator Simón Bolívar. Locals love dining at **La Scala** restaurant and taking in the waters at Thermaé Spa.

$$$$ Hotel La Bohème Royal – *Calle 82 # 12-35, Bogotá. ✕&(1) 618 0168. www.hotelesroyal.com. 66 rooms.* In the Zona Rosa, La Bohème Royal serves as a good base for experiencing the city's theaters and nightclubs. An on-site business center makes the hotel a solid choice for business travelers as well as tourists. Guest rooms are equipped with modern comforts; business rooms have added amenities such as CD players, coffeemakers and bathrobes.

$$$$ Hotel La Fontana Estelar – *Av. 127 # 15A-10, Bogotá. P✕&(1) 615 4400. www.hotelesestelar.com. 218 rooms.* Located in one of Bogotá's most exclusive areas and near one of the city's largest shopping centers, this luxury chain hotel offers a good range of comfortable rooms along with efficient service. A Jacuzzi, sauna and beauty salon are on-site, and the staff is multi-lingual.

$$$$ Hotel Tequendama Crowne Plaza – *Carrera 10 # 26-21, Bogotá. P✕&(1) 382 0300. www.ichotels group.com/h/d/cp/1/en/hotel/bogha. 578 rooms.* Combining elegance, comfort and modern technology with the highest standards of service, this hotel lies in the heart of Bogotá. Off the lobby you'll find shops, a tour operator and an English-style pub. Ask for a room at the back of the hotel to avoid traffic noise. A complimentary buffet breakfast is included in the rate.

$$$$ Morrison Hotel – *Calle 84 Bis # 13-54, Bogotá. ✕&(1) 622-3111. www.morrisonhotel.com. 62 rooms.* Located next door to Leon de Greiff Park, Hotel Morrison sits in Bogotá's commercial center. Neutral tones and mountain views facilitate a restful stay in the well-appointed rooms. If it's recreation you're after, there's a gym on the property, and La Cima golf course lies nearby.

$$$$$ Hotel Charleston Casa Medina – *Carrera 7 # 69 A-22, Bogotá.* ✕ Spa *(1) 217 0288. www.hotelcharleston casamedina.com. Closed 17 Dec–10 Jan. 58 rooms.* Set inside a Colonial-style building, now a National Historical Conservation Monument, Casa Medina enjoys a location close to shopping. Hand-carved wooden wall panels and ceiling beams, wrought-iron railings, and stone walls accent the rooms; suites have fireplaces. Dine on international cuisine at the hotel's restaurant.

ⴵ EAT

$$ Candela Café – *Calle 9 # 4-93, La Candelaria, Bogotá. (1) 283 1780. Closed Sun.* This cafe is both a popular lunch venue and a fine place for dinner (dimming the lights changes the atmosphere considerably). Expect heaping helpings of tasty, reasonably priced food, with an emphasis on dishes such as pasta, gratins and meatballs. **International**.

$$ Sopas de Mama y Postres de la Abuela – *Carrera 9 # 10-50. Lunch only. (1) 243 4432. www.sopasy postres.com.co.* A great value, this restaurant delivers what its name promises: "Mother's soups and Grandmother's desserts." Traditional, home-style Colombian staples are served in generous portions. There are a number of branches throughout the city. **Colombian**.

$$$ Astrid y Gastón – *Carrera 7 # 67-64 (enter on Calle 68), Bogotá. Closed Sun. (1) 211 1400. www.astridygaston. com/web/index.php. Dinner only.* Located in the "gourmet zone" of the city, this restaurant is one of a family-owned chain. Its decor is elegantly modern, and the menu offerings range from *aji de gallina* (a piquant chicken stew) to *tiradito* (tuna and snapper in a chili ponzu sauce). **Peruvian**.

$$$ Leo Cocina y Cava – *Calle 27B # 6-75, Barrio La Macarena, Bogotá. (1) 286 7091. www.leonorespinosa.com. Closed Sun.* This place owes its local popularity and world-wide renown to chef/owner Leonor Espinosa. Decorated in white with red and pink accents, the artsy dining room sets the stage for regional Colombian fare such as

snail carpaccio with lemon and olive oil, and fish wrapped in banana leaves. **Colombian**.

🛒 SHOPPING

While areas such as the **Zona T** and the **Zona Rosa** in Bogotá boast designer boutiques as well as mainstream chain stores, Colombians love their **shopping malls**. More interesting for visitors are the Sunday flea markets, the antique shops along Carrera 9 *(south of Calle 60)*, and the wholesale market at **Plaza de Mercado de Paloquemao** *(Av. 19 # 25-04)*.

Centro Comercial Andino – *Carrera 11 # 82-71. (1) 621 3111. www.centroandino.com.co.*

Centro Comercial Gran Estación – *Calle 26 # 62-47. (1) 579 0906. www.geimpresionante.com.*

Centro Comercial Santa Fé – *Calle 185 # 45-03. 605 0707. http://centrocomercialsantafe.com.*

Hacienda Santa Bárbara – *Carrera 7 # 115-60. (1) 612 0388. www.haciendasantabarbara.com.co.*

San Andresito – *Carrera 38, between Calle 8 and 9.*

🎭 ENTERTAINMENT

Andrés DC – *Calle 82 # 12-15. El Retiro, Zona Rosa, Bogotá. (1) 863 7880. www.andrescarnederes.com.* Meat fills the menu and rumba packs in the crowds in this four-level club.

The Bogotá Beer Company – *www.bogotabeercompany.com.* This Bogotá microbrewery has branches throughout the city. Try the one at Usaquén *(Carrera 6 # 119-24)* or on Avenida 19 *(# 120-74).*

Cachao – *Carrera 11A # 93 -18, Bogotá. (1) 623 3003. www.tocatusentidos.com.* Mojitos and salsa music preside at this Cuban club in the Zona Rosa.

Cha Cha – *Carrera 7 # 32-26, Bogotá. (1) 350 5074.* There's always a party at Cha Cha, on the 41st floor of the Hilton.

Salome Pagana – *Carrera 14A # 82-1, Bogotá. (1) 221 1895. www.salomepaganaclubsocial.com.* This Zona Rosa salsateca is popular with savvy locals.

Around Bogotá★★

Cundinamarca, Tolima

Since Bogotá sits at a high altitude, upon leaving the thin air of the capital, you are transported for the most part into lower-lying regions that offer a kinder climate, rivers full of Andean precipitation and rolling foothills that ease you down from the Sabana Cundiboyacense. Small villages and farming communities spread out, underpinned by indigenous and pre-Columbian history and myth that add to their mystique. The clear air and outdoor activities available in the national parks and open spaces beyond the rough and tumble of Bogotá are a welcome release and make for pleasant and rewarding rural distractions.

A BIT OF HISTORY

The regions around Bogotá have long been inhabited by the **Muisca** people and their Chibcha-speaking relatives, and to some extent, the traditions have remained the same ever since.

The Spanish came rampaging through in the 16C, conquering all before them. **Gonzalo Jiménez de Quesada** allied himself with the Muiscas to defeat the rival **Panche** tribe at the **Battle of Tocarema** in 1538, and brought the territory under Spanish control. The indigenous population gradually became absorbed into Spanish society and *mestizo* communities.

Over time, the inequalities of land distribution between the peasant class and the hacienda-owning fiefs created an atmosphere of violence and aggression that raged through the regions and led to politically charged divisions between the Liberals and Conservatives.

In the 1980s and 90s, confrontations between the military and the guerrillas took place in some rural areas around here, but more recently, the strong tactics of President Uribe have pushed these threats back.

- ⚓ **Michelin Map:** p111.
- 🅰 **Info:** Before leaving Bogotá to explore its surroundings, your best bet is to stop by one of its tourist information points such as **PIT Centro Historico** (corner of Carrera 8 and Calle 10, Palacio Liévano, 1st floor, ℘ (1) 283 7115) to gather up information. Check www.bogotaturismo.gov.co/puntos-de-informacion-turistica-pit for more details.
- 🕐 **Timing:** For any trip outside Bogotá, allow a full day and plan on lunching in the countryside. Traffic is usually snarled heading out from or into the city in any direction.
- 🚫 **Don't Miss:** There are all sorts of activities to be enjoyed, but if your time is limited, be sure to visit the Salt Cathedral in Zipaquirá. Perhaps do some rock climbing in Suesca, and stop by the lake that inspired the myth of El Dorado at Guatavita.

A BIT OF FOLKLORE

As the indigenous blood and traditions run deep through the highland plains and valleys of Cundinamarca, there are countless tales and myths that have been unearthed and shared, not least the **legend of El Dorado** (⚓ *see sidebar*), containing its immeasurable quantity of gold as well as tales of shamans and rituals, and witches that metamorphose into night-flying birds.

The musical folklore from Cundinamarca retains a melancholy edge due to the history of conquest of the highland people by the Spanish. Traditional Cundiboyacense dance is heavily influenced by the Spanish, but the romances and legends shield a greater sense of the **superstitions** inherent in the region.

NORTH FROM BOGOTÁ
Zipaquirá★★
▶ *49km/30mi N of Bogotá via Carretera 45, and then via the road north of Cajicá. Bus from Portal del Norte (45min).*

Known as the "Land of the Zipa" in the Muisca language, Zipaquirá (Pop. 100,038) is a pleasant rural town that falls within the boundaries of greater Bogotá, and can be reached by train. Here in the **Abra Valley** where Zipaquirá is located, archaeologists have found some of the most **ancient human remains** in all of Colombia, dating back 12,400 years. Subsequent explorations and studies have shown that this was largely the center of the **Muisca empire**. The **salt mines** that brought wealth to the town were first established by the Muiscas, and then later taken over by the Spanish who settled here and built elegant Colonial buildings around a main square.

Museo de la Salmuera
Calle 3 # 7-64. 🕐*Open Tue–Sun 10am–4pm.* ≈*2,000 COP.* ✆*(1) 852 2366. www.catedraldesal.gov.co.*

Here at this museum, located in the town of Zipaquirá, visitors will find all kinds of information and exhibits about the salt-mining process, environmental education and the history of salt mining in the region.

Parque del Sal
▶ *SW of Zipaquirá.* 🕐*Open daily 9am–6pm.* ☚*Guided tour (1hr).* ≈*17,000 COP.* ✆*(1) 852 3010. www.catedraldesal.gov.co.*

Zipaquirá's most striking attraction is its world-famous **Catedral de Sal**★★, a true feat of engineering that turned the former salt mine into an amazing **underground salt cathedral**.
The present structure (1995) was built 60m/200ft below a former cathedral completed in 1951. The floor surface area in the cathedral extends to a staggering 8,500sq m/91,493sq ft.
Visitors are guided past a series of 14 small chapels representing the various Stations of the Cross. This work is truly an awe-inspiring sight. The columns and

Catedral de Sal

Proexport Colombia

pillars are high reaching and the illuminated cross is enormous in size.

Nemocón★
▶ *65km/40mi NE of Bogotá along Carretera 45, or 15km/9mi NE of Zipaquirá by way of Vía Zipaquirá-Nemocón.*

Known for its salt mine, this small colonial town has a population of 11,093. Around 1537 the first Spanish expeditions began arriving in the area. The Spaniards who first came here found the area to be an attractive place to settle. The **salt mines** and plentiful maize production of the Muisca were influencing factors.

Salt Mine★★
▶ *SE part of Nemocón.* 🕐*Open daily 9am–6pm.* ≈*15,000 COP, child* ≈*8,000 COP.* ✆*(1) 854 4120.*

Visitors to Nemocón should take a tour around the town's salt mine, which encompasses a 2.5km/1.5mi circuit. The mine reaches depths of 60m/197ft and offers visitors a look at **stalagmites,** and **salt waterfalls** deep beneath the earth. Astoundingly, nine million tons of salt have been extracted from the mine in Nemocón.

Additional Sights
Close to town, it is a comfortable stroll to the **Cerro de la Virgen del Carmen** *(SW of Nemocón; access via paved road).*

"Tren Turístico de la Sabana" Bogotá - Colombia

Tren Turístico de la Sabana★

Built by the English architect **William Lidstone**, the Neoclassical **Estación de la Sabana** (1917) would be an attraction for train spotters and curious tourists in Downtown Bogotá, were it not located in such an unruly section of the city.

As it is, you can organize your trip out to Zipaquirá via the touristic train that runs from this station, making a day trip that departs early from the city. Pulled by a classic steam engine, the train takes passengers through the chic, residential *bogotáno* neighborhood of **Usaquén** and then on through **Cajicá** to Zipaquirá. You will be regaled with live **papayera** music on your way to the **Salt Cathedral.**

Estación de la Sabana (in Bogotá), Calle 13 # 18-24. ○*Departs Sat–Sun & public holidays 8:30am.* ◎*35,000 COP,* ◎*5,000 COP return transportation to the Salt Cathedral of Zipaquirá or the Salt Mine of Nemocón.* ☏*(1) 375 0557.* *www.turistren.com.co.*

Just 6km/4mi from here *(N along Vía Nemocón-Suesca)*, at a small desert called the **Desierto de la Tatacoita**, you can enjoy ecotourism activities *(cycling tours organized by Cicloaventureros in Bogotá;* ◎*70,000 COP;* ☏*(1) 605 7400; www.cicloaventureros.com).*

Suesca★
▶ *10km/6mi NE of Nemocón via the Nemocón-Suesca road.*
An ideal place for a day trip or a weekend getaway, Suesca (Pop. 13,985) has everything to offer the outdoor enthusiast. With the **Rocas de Suesca** just outside the town *(1km S of Suesca on the Nemocón-Suesca road)*, visitors can enjoy **rock climbing** at every level of ability on a **cliff** face that extends 4km/2.5mi.
Adventure-seekers can also enjoy mountain-biking, trekking, rappelling and caving in Suesca, since the upper basin of the Bogotá River is becoming an **extreme sports** capital of the region.

Laguna de Guatavita
▶ *63km/39mi N of Bogotá via Sesquilé along Carretera 45.*
This is a favored destination for *bogotáno* students embarking on camping trips. Located near the community of **Sesquilé**, Guatavita resembles a meteor crater. It is one of the sacred lakes of the **Muisca**, and the basis for much of the **El Dorado** myth *(↻see sidebar opposite).*
From the dock at **Tominé**, people launch into an array of **water sports**. The place may feel a bit sanitary, but the surroundings are charming.

Parque Jaime Duque
▶ *34km/21mi NE of Bogotá via Tocancipá on Carretera 45. Call for hours.* ◎*7,500 COP entry,* ◎*27,000 COP all attractions (Sat–Sun & public holidays).* ☏*(1) 857 4233. www. parquejaimeduque.com.*
Located in the town of **Tocancipá**, this park was opened in 1983. It has become

a dated testament to family entertainment, with its kitschy replicas of the Taj Mahal and the Seven Wonders of the Ancient World. The huge **relief map** of the entire country is worth a look, and children might enjoy the **zoo** with its birds, primates and reptiles.

Panaca la Sabana

45km/28mi NE of Bogotá via Briceño along Carretera 45 (or 4km/2mi N of Briceño on the way to Zipaquirá).
Open Fri–Sun & public holidays 9am–6pm. 25,000 COP. (1) 307 7002. www.panacasabana.com/jos.
This is an agro-tourism theme park aimed at educating children about the countryside and animals.
Housing more than 2,400 animals, the park offers hours of fun for young ones, and countryside themed activities such as **horse-riding**, **petting zoos** and even a **zip wire** for older children.

Ubaté

97km/60mi NE of Bogotá via Zipaquirá.
This small rural town is the "Milk Capital of Colombia" (Pop. 32,781). Building on this title, it created the **biggest cheese** ever made in the Americas, weighing in at over one ton.
In the town itself, a bustling marketplace heavy on dairy products, and a Gothic-style cathedral, home to *El Milagroso Santo Cristo de Ubaté* are two popular attractions.
Nearby hikes to the top of the **Cerro de la Teta,** at 3,000m/9,840ft, offer a **view** of the whole of the Ubaté Valley. Farther hikes will lead to **Los Chorros de Soagá** and the various rivers that flow from that point.

Guasca

51km/32mi NE of Bogotá via La Calera along the Avenida Circunvalar.
Like so many of the towns around Bogotá, Guasca (Pop. 12,208) is steeped in pre-Columbian history and had a thriving Muisca population prior to the arrival of the Spanish. **Fishermen** enjoy Guasca for the opportunities offered along the banks of the **Siecha** and **Chipatá** rivers. In the southeastern section of the páramo is the sacred **Laguna de Siecha**, where you can camp nearby and enjoy the thermal **hot springs**.

Capilla de Siecha

Turn right 29km/18mi along the Via a Guasca, before the Río Siecha. Open daily 8am–5pm. 1,000 COP. http://capilladesiecha.blogspot.com.
Beside this small colonial church with three naves are the ruins of an old Dominican convent.

The Legend of El Dorado

Born out of the New World in the early 16C, the story of El Dorado remains one of the most prevalent myths that influenced Spanish exploration. In the 1530s conquistador **Gonzalo Jiménez de Quesada** brought back tales of a gilded man and untold riches after discovering the **Muisca Indians** in what are the modern day highlands of Boyacá. Rumors soon became laced with exaggeration about a gilded man offering gold to the gods, a myth spawned by a Muisca ritual involving the naked body of the chief being covered in gold dust.

Quesada told of ceremonies held around Lake Guatavita, where subjects threw jewels and gold into the water as gifts to the gods. As the story was retold, the legendary "El Dorado" was soon imagined as an empire with a king of gold. Numerous explorers have since sought to locate this realm of riches, including doomed searches undertaken by **Francisco de Orellana** in 1541, **Phillip von Hutten** the same year, and **Sir Walter Raleigh** in 1595.

Today, El Dorado has become a byword for a place where wealth can be accumulated quickly. Several films and books have helped immortalize the story, including Milton's *Paradise Lost*, Voltaire's *Candide* and two Walt Disney comic books, *The Gilded Man* and *The Last Lord of Eldorado*.

EAST FROM BOGOTÁ
La Calera
▶ *9km/6mi NE of Bogotá along the Avenida Circunvalar.*

Just a 15min steep drive out of the city leads to this rural suburb of Bogotá, and a weekend destination for *Bogotános* eager to enjoy a big Sunday meal with views of the city. La Calera (Pop. 23,308) is also a **nightlife hub**, as bars and clubs have sprung up, taking advantage of their proximity to Bogotá to entice rumba seekers out here.

La Calera is on the route to the Parque Nacional Natural Chingaza (*see below*), On weekends, driving the stretch of road to La Calera is not for the fainthearted, as it is jammed with Colombian families heading out for lunch, as well as dozens of cyclists testing their athletic abilities and stamina in this extreme setting with its thin air.

Parque Nacional Natural Chingaza★★
▶ *55km/34mi NE of Bogotá via La Calera and Piedras Gordas.*
🕐 *Open Sat–Sun 9am–4pm.*
💰*20,000 COP.* ✈ *Guided tours organized by Clorofila* ✆*(1) 616 8711. www.viajesclorofila.com.* ✆*(1) 243 1634 www.parquesnacionales.gov.co.*

The **páramo** of Chingaza, on the eastern side of the Andes, links the highlands of Cundinamarca with the sultry lowlands of the department of **Meta**. It could be considered Bogotá's water factory. Here swamp mosses absorb the mountain precipitation and provide the capital with 80 percent of its high quality **potable water**. The water that flows down from the waterfalls and Andean jungles found here in the Chingaza park, goes into the **Chingaza dam** and then the **Chuzo reservoir** to provide Bogotá with its drinking water. In 2002 the dam was damaged slightly in a FARC bomb attack.

Frailejones spatter the landscape, making it seem otherworldly. The 76,600ha/187,800 acre park is home to species such as the **spectacled bear**, the **páramo tapir**, the **cock of the rock** and the **Andean condor**. Three glacially created lakes can be visited, namely the **Buitrago**, **Teusaca** and **Siecha**, the latter containing **Muisca** archaeological remains and gold offerings nearby.

Choachí★★
▶ *38km/24mi SE of Bogotá via the hills of Monserrate and Guadalupe.*

A nail-biting Andean highway with hairpin turns frequented by less than cautious bus drivers is encountered on any trip to Choachí (Pop. 10,874).

This pleasant town sits lower than Bogotá, but at one point along the trip, **views** of the **Cerro de Monserrate** are possible from above.

Look for ancient **rock paintings** and **petroglyphs**, admire **La Chor-**

Laguna de Siecha, Parque Nacional Natural Chingaza

Carlos E. Porras/Proexport Colombia

rera waterfall, with its impressive 590m/1,935ft drop, or while away the hours in the **Santa Monica hot springs** *(3km/2mi N of Choachí off the road to Bogotá;* 🕐 *public baths open daily 7am–6pm;* 🎫 *16,000 COP Mon–Sat,* 🎫 *20,000 COP Sun & public holidays;* ✆ *(1) 8486571; www.termalessantamonica.com).*

Parque Ecologico Matarredonda
▶ *20km/12mi SE of Bogotá on the road between Bogotá and Choachí by the Cerro de Guadalupe.* 🎫 *20,000 COP.* ✆ *(1) 209 6384. www.choachi-cundinamarca.gov.co.*
For ecotourism and **hiking**, head to the spot where water that flows into the source of the **Orinoco** originates.

SOUTH FROM BOGOTÁ
Fusagasugá
▶ *64km/40mi SW of Bogotá along Carretera 45.*
The capital of the province of Sumapaz (Pop. 107,259) is often referred to as the "City of Flowers." It is reputed for its fine woolen carpets and leather goods.

Fusagasugá was an obligatory passage in pre-Columbian times for the **Mulsca**, **Panche** and **Pijao** peoples, given its relatively level terrain between the southwestern highlands and the **Cundiboyacense altiplano**. Today it still is a key connection point to reach the cities of Ibagué, Neiva and Cali.

Highlights in town include the **Coloma Coffee Ranch** *(*🚶*guided tours available from Nueva Lengua Tours;* ✆ *(1) 813 8674; www.nuevalenguatours.com),* the **Casona Tulipana** *(Transversal 9 # 16-92;* 🕐 *open Mon–Fri 3pm–8pm, Sat 8am–noon;* ✆ *(1) 886 8304),* which hosts art exhibts, and the **Quinta Coburgo**, declared a National Monument in 1996 *(*🔒 *closed to the public).*

The **Casona la Palmal** *(*🔒 *closed for restoration)* hosted interesting guests over the years, such as **Simón Bolívar** and Manuelita Saenz, José Celestino Mutis and Alejandro Humboldt. The hacienda became a center for botanical research and for efforts to seek a cure for malaria.

Silvania
▶ *65km/40mi SW of Bogotá along Carretera 45.*
Originally populated by the **Sutagaos**, Silvania (Pop. 20,872) is principally known for its **wicker work**, in addition to products made from wool, leather and bamboo. There are **trails** nearby for hiking in an ecological reserve.

Melgar and Girardot
These two towns are both **holiday resort** destinations for those seeking to escape the chillier climes of Bogotá for the comfortable temperatures here, averaging 28°C /82°F.

Known as the "City of Acacias," **Girardot** (Pop. 95,496) *(134km/83mi SW of Bogotá along Carretera 45)* was an important port on the **Magdalena River** in the era when passenger transport still moved fluvially. The city was a major link to Bogotá, as attested by its old **railway bridge**. Today the town has many hotels, bars and clubs, as well as options for **paragliding**.

Very similar to Girardot, **Melgar** *(98km/61mi SW of Bogotá along Carretera 45)* is located in the neighboring department of **Tolima**. The city (Pop. 32,636) boasts some 5,000 pools, hence its name "City of Swimming Pools."

Horse riding, **hiking**, and swimming or **rafting** in the **Sumapaz River**★ are popular activities in the area.

For spelunking enthusiasts, the **Cueva del Tigre**★ provides an adventure. This network of huge caves with stalagmites and stalactites can be found 6km/4mi along the Melgar-Cannan road *(*🚶*guided tours organized by Andarríos;* ✆ *(1) 606 4557; www.andarrios.com.co).*

Soacha
▶ *1km/0.5mi W of Bogotá along Carretera 45.*
Soacha (Pop. 398,295) may look like any other industrial suburb bordering Bogotá, yet it is incredibly important: first, for the presence of the **Muña Dam** that provides hydroelectric power to the capital, and second, for its archaeological and environmental significance.

Horse riding, Parque Natural Chicaque

Parque Natural Chicaque

Salto de Tequendama

▷ *30km/19mi W of Bogotá by San Antonio del Tequendama, off the road to La Mesa via Calle 17.*

Passing through the Sabana de Bogotá, the **Funza River**, at altitudes above 2,300m/7,546ft, leads to this waterfall, with a drop of some 165m/541ft.

In the 1970s, a group of **rock shelters** here revealed traces of ancient camps and burials, and produced abundant evidence of a **human presence** carbon-dated to about 12,460 years ago.

Unfortunately, the pollution of the Bogotá River and the extremes in climatic variations attributed to the **El Niño** phenomenon have ravaged this wonderland of nature and long-time tourist attraction. The building alongside the falls, the 1928 **Hotel El Salto**, was connected to the outside world by a small railway line; the abandoned hotel has now been left to the elements.

Parque Natural Chicaque★★

▷ *10km/6mi W of Soacha on the Soacha-Indumil road.* ◐*Open Mon–Fri 8am–4pm.* ◑*10,000 COP.* ↞*Guided tours available in English* ◑*120,000 COP.* ℰ*(1) 368 3114. www.chicaque.com.*

This privately-run natural reserve, dedicated to ecotourism and environmental education, has been open since 1990. It is a well-organized set up with many attractions that appeal to all ages, such as gentle **hikes** along well-maintained trails, **horse riding** and guided **bird watching** tours. Even though it's close to Bogotá, this oasis of nature is home to 300 species of birds and 20 species of mammals that can often be spotted from several viewpoints.

Parque Nacional Natural Sumapaz★★

▷ *Laguna de Chisacá, 31km/19mi S of Usme in Bogotá after the Vía a Nazareth. www.parquesnacionales. gov.co.* ↞*Guided tours organized by De Una Colombia Tours* ℰ*(1) 368 1915; www.deunacolombia.com.*

⊛*This park was used as a transit point for FARC guerrillas in the past, and although a military base has been set up nearby that has largely ended the problem, you should check the park's security prior to any visit.*

Bordering Bogotá and the departments of **Huila**, **Meta** and **Cundinamarca**, Sumapaz is the most important and fragile ecosystem in the area surrounding the nation's capital. Within its 154,000ha/380,542 acres is contained the world's largest **páramo**; 14 types of **frailejon plant**; mountainous landscapes that are interrupted only by frigid, yet scenic lakes; countless river sources; and pre-Columbian **archaeological sites**.

You can hike to the following **lakes**: Laguna de Chisacá, Laguna Negra, Laguna Bocagrande and the Pantano de Andabobos, and marvel at this central point in the country that provides Colombia's principal water networks such as the **Magdalena River**, the **Guaviare River** and the **Meta River**.

WEST FROM BOGOTÁ
Facatativá
▶ *42km/28mi NW of Bogotá along the highway to Villeta.*

As you can tell by its name, Facatativá (Pop. 106,067) was a Muisca settlement. It was visited by **Gonzalo Jiménez de Quesada** in his pursuit of the Muisca leader **Cacique Tisquesusa** in 1537. Today **flower cultivation** is the town's main industry, given its favorable climate and altitude (2,640m/8,661ft). The **Catedral de Facatativá** *(Plaza Simón Bolívar)* is the most striking local example of Spanish architecture (1787), but it is the pre-Hispanic history that provides Facatativá with its main attraction.

Parque Arqueológico de Facatativá
🕑 *Open Tue–Sun & public holidays 9am 5pm.* 🎟6,000 COP. 📞(1) 561 9700. www.icanh.gov.co.

This park features a spectacular collection of rocks with indigenous painting thought to date back some 10,000 years. The pictographs are found on rock formations that were formerly part of a flood area of a lake that would rise onto the **Sabana de Bogotá**.

Unfortunately, the paintings have not been well protected from the elements or vandalism, but there are projects under way to restore this important archaeological heritage.

Villeta
▶ *91km/56mi NW of Bogotá via Facatativá.*

Villeta (Pop. 23,620) is another weekend retreat for *Bogotános,* based on its proximity to the city and its climate and lower altitude of 800m/2,625ft.

Watered by the **Cune River**, Villeta is known for its sugarcane production and cattle ranching. The town even hosts the beauty pageant of **Reinado Nacional de La Panela** every January.

Water from the river provides bathing spots as well as the **Saltos de los Micos** waterfalls. Near the waterfalls lies part of the old **Camino Real**—the route used by the Spaniards to reach the interior after the Magdalena River became unnavigable—that connects to the town of **Honda**.

Tobia★
▶ *74km/46mi NW of Bogotá off the Autopista Medellín before it turns south to Villeta. www.lostobianos.com.*

Not to be confused with Tabio (a town that has fallen into disrepair in recent years), Tobia is a capital of **extreme sports** since its varied natural landscapes lend perfectly to activities such as rappelling, camping, hiking, rafting and canoeing in the **Río Negro**.

LOWER MAGDALENA RIVER VALLEY
Many towns in this part of the country have conserved their colonial charm and ambience. Here is a sampling of those just a stone's throw from the capital.

Guaduas★
▶ *114km/71mi NW of Bogotá via the western exit of Villeta.*

Surrounded by a great variety of ecosystems, the town of Guaduas (Pop. 31,250) was chosen by **José Celestino Mutis** (1732-1808) as one of the locations for his botanical expedition. Interesting points include the well-preserved colonial **Calle Real** and the **Alcaldia**, where Bolívar is believed to have stayed.

Casa de la Pola
Calle 2 # 4-40. 🕑*Open Tue–Sat 8:30am –noon & 2pm–6pm, Sun & public holidays 8:30am–noon & 2pm–5pm.* 📞*(1) 846 6052.*

Guaduas was the birthplace of **Policarpa Salavarrieta** (c.1791-1817), a heroine and martyr of the independence movement who was executed by the Spanish for spying on behalf of the revolutionary forces. Her former home is now a museum in memory of her life.

Festival de la Subienda

If you happen to be passing through Honda in February, you are strongly advised to stay long enough to witness the craziness of the Subienda Festival. Countless fishermen descend upon the Magdalena River in an attempt to catch the biggest and the greatest number of fish. Taking full advantage of this event, the town's organizers have created affiliated activities such as concerts, rodeos and even the ubiquitous beauty pageant.

Salto de Versalles

▶ *A 20min walk along the Carretera that leads to Guaduero.*

This impressive 20m/66ft waterfall is worth a visit.

Honda★

▶ *142km/88mi NW of Bogotá or 82mi via Guaduas.*

Sometimes referred to as the "Cartagena of the Interior," given its Colonial and Republican architecture and narrow streets from the era, Honda (Pop. 26,873) is also known as the "City of Bridges," for its total of 29.

Honda experienced its golden age between 1850 and 1910 when it was the last navigable point on the **Río Magdalena**, if coming in from the Caribbean coast.

There were three major ports during colonial times: **Cartagena, Mompox** and Honda. From here, the boats would stop, and the journey would then continue on horseback, or later by railroad. The architecture here in the old town is worth seeing, and the current efforts of restoration and recovery have made it all the more scenic.

Honda's quality of life dipped in recent years, as a main highway was placed in the center of the town, but corrective measures will soon divert traffic around the historic center, once again making it a pleasant place to visit. There are many attractions to see, including museums.

Museo del Río Magdalena

Calle 10 # 9-01, Equina Cuartel de la Ceiba. ◯*Open Tue–Thu 9am–noon, Fri–Sun & public holidays 9am–noon, 2pm–6pm.* ◉*2,000 COP.* ✆*(1) 251 0129.*

This museum charts the history of explorations along the river in past eras.

Museo Alfonso Lopez Pumarejo

Calle 13 #11-75 Esquina Plaza de América. ◯*Open Tue–Sat 9am–noon & 2pm–6pm, Sun & public holidays 9am–noon.* ◉*2000 COP.* ✆*(1) 251 3484.*

Located in the former home of twice president **Alfonso Lopez Pumarejo** (1886-1959), exhibits give a good overview of the politician's life and the history of his political activity.

Street in Honda

© Jeremy Horner/Corbis

ADDRESSES

🚶 *See Bogotá's ADDRESSES for a greater selection of accommodations and restaurants.*

🏠STAY

$ El Vivac Hostal – *Vereda de Casicazgo, Suesca (67km/42mi northeast of Bogotá via Carretera 45. ☎311 284 5313. http:// elvivachostal.com. 4 rooms.* A prime setting for climbing the sheer rock walls that surround the Valle de los Halcones, this little farmhouse is located in front of the bridge in the village of Suesca. El Vivac is run by a local rock-climber who arranges climbs and rent bikes and tents to her guests. It's just a 15-minute walk from the hostel to the nearest climbing cliffs.

$ Hotel Colonial – *Calle 3 # 6-57, Zipaquirá. ☎(1) 852 2690. 50 rooms.* You'll find the bright yellow façade of the Hotel Colonial right in the center of town, less than two blocks southwest of the main square. This hacienda-style hotel offers 50 basic, clean rooms overlooking well-kept courtyards. Private rooms have a private bathroom with hot water and cable TV; linens and towels are included for the dormitory accommodations.

$$ Hacienda Betania – *Vereda Trinidad, Sector Betania (50 minutes northeast of Bogotá via El Salitre along the right, turning on the road to Guasca).* ✖ *☎(1) 850 4987. www.hotelhacienda betania.com. 5 rooms.* Located very close to Guasca, this imposing pink stucco family-run hacienda-style hotel has a pleasant interior and lovely terraces for taking in views of the countryside. It also has a restaurant, a bar, landscaped gardens, and a volleyball court. You can even rent a horse on-site and explore the forest that adjoins the hacienda's property.

$$$ El Refugio – *2km/1mi before reaching Sasaima; 80km/50mi north-west of Bogotá via Calle 13 and Madrid, along the Pan-American Highway.* ✖ 🛏 Spa *☎(1) 243 3564. www.elrefugio hotelspa.com. 13 rooms.* True to its name, El Refugio is indeed a lovely oasis just outside the village of Sasaima. Rooms, four of which are set in a separate house on the grounds, have hardwood floors, garden views, and are beautifully furnished with bright, cheery colors.

🍽/EAT

$$$ Andrés Carne De Res – *Calle 3 # 11A-56, Chía. ☎(1) 863 7880. www. andrescarnederes.com.* Bigger seems to be better at this bar and grill on the outskirts of Bogotá. Mojitos come in glasses of soupbowl-like proportions, and food servings are generous. The seating area is comfortable and offers a good view. If you're eating late, expect the ambience to slowly change from peaceful eatery to big, boisterous party. The dining space is decorated with Colombian artifacts, bric-a-brac and historic photographs. **Colombian**.

$$$ El Humero – *Variante a Cota road, 2km/1mi from Chía (to the left of the traffic lights). ☎(1) 863 6662.* If you're looking for good local, no-frills food in a pleasant atmosphere, try El Humero. The food here tends to be a little greasy at times, but the service is efficient and friendly, the portion sizes are just right, and the restaurant itself is located in an agreeable setting. **Colombian**.

$$$ El Pórtico – *Autopista Norte, KM 19, between Carretera 45 and Carrera 7; north of Bogotá on the road to Chía. ☎(1) 676 0752 . www.elportico.com.co.* Located about 30 minutes north of Bogotá, this tile-roofed hacienda serves as a convention center during the week and as an informal restaurant on weekends. The large restaurant is open all day, and is known for its excellent breakfasts. The house speciality is *ajiaco*, a traditional Bogotano soup made with three kinds of potatoes, chicken, corn-on-the-cob, and a variety of local herbs and spices. **International**.

NORTHEASTERN COLOMBIA

Head north from Bogotá toward Venezuela or the Atlantic coast, and you take a journey into the beating heart of historic Colombia through picturesque valleys, canyons and spectacular mountain passes. Still known as the "Land of Freedom," Boyacá has a history that runs deep since Simón Bolívar's army fought a decisive battle against the Spanish there. Set high on a plateau, Tunja, the ancient Muisca capital, stands apart due to its splendid colonial heritage. Gorgeous green valleys and ornate villages such as Villa de Leyva litter the core of the pre-Columbian Muisca empire, whose gold the Spanish greatly coveted. Hot springs at Iza and Paipa and the rich culture and fresh mountain air of Monguí act as therapy for both body and soul. In the region's northeast lies the Sierra Nevada del Cocuy, a range of jagged ice peaks and breathtaking lakes that rival any in South America. In all, through the departments of Boyacá, Santander and Norte de Santander, there exists an enormous diversity of topography and geography, from Colombia's largest glacier mass to the sweltering lowlands of the border city of Cúcuta.

Highlights

1 Retrace Bolívar's footsteps to the very point where independence was secured, a few miles south of **Tunja** (p152)

2 Admire the amazing 120 year-old fossil of a baby kronosaur near colonial **Villa de Leyva** (p166)

3 Hike the glacial valleys and highland pastures of the **Sierra Nevada del Cocuy** (p170).

4 Conquer your fear of heights by paragliding over the spectacular Chicamocha Canyon, a short drive from **Bucaramanga** (p183).

5 Explore the caves and pre-Columbian underground tombs in Curití near **San Gil** (p185), extreme sports capital of Colombia.

Geographical Wonderland

The climate in this part of the country varies dramatically with altitude. At an elevation of 2,960m/9,710ft and with an average temperature of 12°C/53°F, Güicán is one of the highest and coldest towns in the region. Tunja, with two rainy seasons (spring and autumn) manages a year-round average temperature of 13°C/55°F while lowlying Cúcuta, on the border, flounders with a close and humid average of 27°C/80°F. Lower-

lying Bucaramanga is warmer still, while Barichara has a perfect year-round average of 22°C/71°F. At Norte de Santander the Cordillera Oriental meets the hot lowland plains that stretch across into Venezuela. The east side of the mountains offers cool retreats.

This whole region is becoming a favored destination for both ecotourists and enthusiasts of outdoor pursuits. Extreme- and adventure-sports fans can have their fill of white-water rafting, paragliding, caving, rappelling, hiking or mountain biking in the San Gil area, or trekking amid the spectacular glacial scenery of El Cocuy. There is also an abundance of hot springs and renowned lagoons, of which the largest is Tota in Boyacá.

Cultural tourists won't find the region lacking either, since it is dotted with archaeological sites dating back to pre-Hispanic civilizations, preserved colonial villages, historic landmarks and monuments intimately linked with the liberation of the country. They will enjoy the rustic charms of colonial Barichara, and perhaps also shopping in nearby Girón or clubbing in Bucaramanga.

In Norte de Santander, beyond the high Cordillera, colonial-era towns like Pamplona make for a pleasant stopover on the overland trail. Cúcuta is a market town better known for its contraband than its sights, despite being a key historical city in the quest for independence from Spain, but you may need to stop here if planning to cross the border.

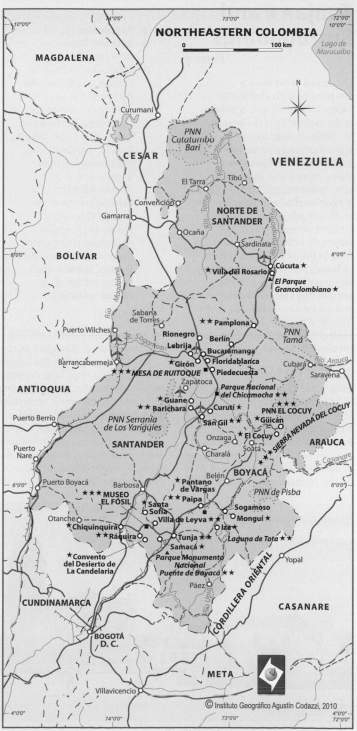

NORTHEASTERN COLOMBIA

0 100 km

MAGDALENA

Lago de Maracaibo

VENEZUELA

Curumaní

PNN Catatumbo Bari

CESAR

El Tarra
Tibú

Convención
NORTE DE SANTANDER

Gamarra

Ocaña

Sardinata

BOLÍVAR

Cúcuta ★
★ Villa del Rosario
▲ El Parque Grancolombiano ★

Sabana de Torres

★ ★ Pamplona

Puerto Wilches

PNN Tamá

Rionegro
Berlín ★
Lebrija ★
Bucaramanga
Barrancabermeja
★ Girón ★ Floridablanca
Cubará
Rio Arauca
Saravena
★ ★ ★ **MESA DE RUITOQUE** ■ Piedecuesta

Zapatoca
■ *Parque Nacional del Chicamocha* ★ ★

ANTIOQUIA

★ Guane
★ ★ Barichara
★ Curutí ★ ★
PNN EL COCUY
★ ★ ★
Güicán ★
SIERRA NEVADA DEL COCUY

Puerto Berrío
San Gil ★ ★ ★
PNN Serrania de Los Yariguies
El Cocuy ★
ARAUCA

Puerto Nare
SANTANDER
Onzaga
Soatá ★ ★ ★
R. Casanare

Charalá
★ ★ ★ **SIERRA NEVADA DEL COCUY**

Puerto Boyacá
Belén
BOYACÁ
PNN de Pisba

Barbosa
★ Pantano de Vargas
★ Paipa

★ ★ ★ **MUSEO EL FÓSIL**
Santa Sofía ★
Sogamoso
Monguí

Otanche
★ Villa de Leyva ★ ★
★ Iza ★

★ Chiquinquirá
★ ★ Ráquira
Tunja ★ ★
Laguna de Tota ★ ★

Samacá
Yopal

★ Convento del Desierto de La Candelaria
Parque Monumento Nacional Puente de Boyacá

Páez

CUNDINAMARCA
CASANARE

BOGOTÁ D.C.

CORDILLERA ORIENTAL

META

Villavicencio

© *Instituto Geográfico Agustín Codazzi, 2010*

Tunja★★ and Surroundings
Boyacá

The capital of the Boyacá department is situated some 140km/87mi northeast of Bogotá in the high valley of the Boyacá (or Teatinos) River. Being the highest city in Colombia (elevation 2,820m/9,200ft), it has a cool alpine climate with an average temperature of 13°C/55°F. Tunja is a commercial, agricultural and communications hub as well as a bustling university town, well-known for hosting several festivals. Despite the ungainliness of some of Tunja's modern buildings, many visitors come here to enjoy its outstanding Colonial architecture and ornate Baroque details. Given its central location, Tunja is the perfect base from which to explore the sights of Boyacá.

A BIT OF HISTORY

Tunja is one of very few colonial cities to have been established on a native settlement, in this case, an important **Muisca** tribal village. Its original name may have been **Hunza**, a name associated with a tribal chief of the **Muisca** nation. The city was founded in 1539 by the conquistador **Gonzalo Suá-**

▶ **Population:** 152,419.
👤 **Michelin Maps:**
p149 and p154.
ℹ **Info:** Culture & Tourism Office, Casa del Fundador, Carrera 9A #19-56. ℘(8) 742 3272. www.tunja.gov.co.
👁 **Don't Miss:** The stunning Capilla de la Virgen del Rosario, considered the jewel of American Baroque architecture in New Granada; the Casa del Escribano Don Juan de Vargas, for its murals and delightful Andalusian-style gardens; the pre-Columbian Muisca carvings known as the Cojines del Zaques on Alto de San Lázaro.

rez Rendón (early 16C-1589), and to this day proudly displays edifices constructed back in the 16C. The Spanish king Charles V granted Tunja city status within two years of its colonial founding, and it became the capital of the **New Kingdom of Granada**. The coat of arms of Charles V can still be seen carved above the entrances to many buildings in the city. Such was the religious zeal of the early colonists that many important convents were established here over the

Plaza Bolívar, Tunja

© Omar Bechara Baruque/Eye Ubiquitous/Corbis

GETTING THERE

BY BUS - Tunja can be reached by bus from several cities. The **bus terminal** is located on Avenida Oriental, east of Carrara 7; it is a short but steep walk to Plaza de Bolívar to the northwest. Buses arrive from Bogotá (3hrs; 18,000 COP), Bucaramanga (7hrs; 35,000 COP), Ráquira (45min; 3,000 COP) and San Gil (4.5hrs; 20,000 COP). Minibuses service Tunja from Villa de Leyva (45min; 5,000 COP), which sits to the west.

BY CAR - Tunja is accessible by driving 140km/87mi along the Pan-American Highway linking Bogotá and Cúcuta.

GETTING AROUND

BY BUS - City buses and minibuses are plentiful and inexpensive.

BY TAXI - Somewhat expensive, taxis are available throughout Tunja, but it's best to have your hotel call a cab for you, rather than hail one in the street.

ON FOOT - Since the majority of Tunja's main sights are clustered in and around Plaza de Bolívar, walking is a definite option. Just avoid the heat of midday, and take a break at one of the many cafes or street vendors around the plaza. Always be alert.

GENERAL INFORMATION

ACCOMMODATIONS - Given Tunja's central location, you may want to make it your base for touring outlying areas. Several clean, modern hotels, some with Wi-Fi, are available in the city's center. *For a selection, see ADDRESSES at the end of this chapter.*

INTERNET - To cater to Tunja's large student population, Internet cafes abound here, with hourly rates.

---

following centuries. The architecture of the day displays the traditional form of colonial houses which consists of two or three stories rising up around a central courtyard giving access onto a corral. By the beginning of the 17C Tunja boasted 300 houses located around its central plaza as well as many civic and religious buildings. The plaza supposedly occupies the site of the original Muisca village, giving the whole area an almost mystical or otherworldly feel. Tunja declared its independence from Spain in 1811. Shortly thereafter, in 1819, it was the focus of **Simón Bolívar**'s successful campaign to liberate Colombia, which culminated in the **Battle of Boyacá** (*see sidebar p156*)—a victory which Bolívar credited to the involvement of a legion of British soldiers. During the conflict between the Liberals and Conservatives in the **Thousand Day War** (1899-1902), parts of the city were destroyed. As this turbulent period came to a close, a decade of reconstruction from 1910 to 1919 celebrated the centenary of the liberation from Spain that also fostered the urban recovery of Tunja. Education has always been at the center of Tunja's identity, and it was

here in 1822 that the first public school in Colombia was founded.

Today, the city is routinely referred to as the "Ciudad Universitaria de Colombia" for the almost disproportionate number of universities found in such a small urban center.

Alto de San Lázaro

NW of Tunja (road to Villa de Leyva). This hill just outside Tunja is also known as the **Loma de los Ahorcados** (which translates loosely as the "Hill of the Hanged"). It was here that the Muisca Indians would hang lawbreakers within their community. The San Lázaro Chapel (1587) was built to commemorate a terrible plague that almost wiped out the town. **Views**★ of Tunja from up here at 2,940m/9,645ft are spectacular.

It is from this vantage point that **Simón Bolívar** was able to watch the maneuvers of the Spanish troops under Colonel José María Barreiro, before engaging him at the **Battle of Boyacá**.

151

🔊 WALKING TOUR
AROUND PLAZA DE BOLÍVAR★★

The main focal point of Tunja's historical center, and a logical place to start your discovery of its architectural heritage, is **Plaza de Bolívar**, a vast square that highlights the city's important status in colonial times.

Catedral Santiago de Tunja★★
Plaza de Bolívar and Carrera 9.

The oldest Catholic church in Colombia, officially named Basílica Metropolitana de Santiago el Mayor de España, was built roughly between 1565 and 1598. This extraordinary example of the Renaissance Revival-Mudéjar style miraculously survived all of the natural disasters that beset it, including the earthquake of 1928.

Upon entering the Renaissance-style **doorway**, completed in 1600, a stunning interior of delicately carved gold-studded ornaments on a mercurial red background appears. Highlights include the dazzling **main altar★★** by Agustín Chinchilla Cañizares (1637), some artwork by Gregorio Vásquez de Arce y Ceballos and Alonso Fernández de Heredia, and a **mural★** by Ricardo Acevedo Bernal. Tunja's founder, Gonzalo Suárez Rendón, rests in peace in the Domínguez Camargo Chapel, attached to one side of the cathedral, in an ornate **marble tomb★** carved by the sculptor Olinto Marcucci.

La Casa del Fundador Capitan Gonzalo Suárez Rendón★★
Carrera 9A # 19-56. 🕐*Open daily 8am–noon, 2pm–6pm.* 🔊*Guided tours available.* ☎*(8) 742-3272.*

Now the seat of Tunja's Academy of History, this fine Colonial mansion (1540) was home to conquistador Gonzalo Suárez Rendón, the founder of the city. Much of Tunjana history can be seen in the documents and objects on display, since the house was a key meeting point in the period leading up to independence from Spain. From the second story of the building, an unequaled **view** of the cloister-style architecture around the carefully maintained **Andalusian gardens** is obtained.

Iglesia de Santo Domingo★★
Carrera 11 between Calle 19 and Calle 20. 🔊*Guided tours available upon request daily 8am–noon, 2pm–5:30pm.*

A true masterpiece of the colonial period, this church, dating back to 1568, is ensconced on a narrow, busy street just one block from the main plaza.

Inside, admire the ornate and exquisitely carved **gold-washed altar★** framed by an archway decorated with floral carvings as well as representations of animals. The naves are divided by sedan-like confessionals and marked by smaller golden altarpieces.

In spite of flickering candles that light the temple, making it all the more atmospheric, everything pales in com-

Capilla de la Virgen del Rosario, Iglesia de Santo Domingo

Proexport Colombia

Muisca Sites Around Tunja

Today little remains of the Muisca culture that thrived in the region around Tunja prior to the arrival of the Spanish. So do not miss the opportunity to see the **Cojines del Zaque**★★ right outside Tunja *(at the base of the Alto de San Lázaro hill, close to the road to Villa de Leyva)*. Dubbed the "Cojines de Diablo" by the Spanish, these two large carved **stone disks** bear witness to the importance of the worship of the sun god in pre-Columbian times. It was here that the Muisca performed dances and occasional human sacrifices. In a particularly sanguine ritual, 12-year-old boys known as **los moxas** had their hearts cut out and their blood poured over the Cojines del Zaque in hopes of a plentiful harvest and fertility.

Another interesting site is the **Pozo de Hunzahúa** (sometimes referred to as the Pozo de Donato), a small lagoon located north of Tunja *(on the campus of the Universidad Pedagógica y Tecnológica de Colombia, Avenida Central del Norte)*. Fed by groundwater, it had strong religious connotations for the Muisca people. It was into this sacred lagoon that the **Zaque Quemuenchatocha**, under pursuit from the Spanish, threw his treasures. Later, in the 17C, a Spaniard called Jerónimo Donato de Rojas attempted to drain the pond at great personal expense, in order to rescue these promising riches. Similar to many tales along this vein, he was unsuccessful and the treasures supposedly remain there.

parison to the **Capilla de la Virgen del Rosario**★★★ attached to the south side of the central nave and representing the jewel of American Baroque architecture in New Granada. For its outstanding murals, artwork and carved wooden boards, the chapel is known fondly as Latin America's Sistine Chapel.

A series of 15 wooden carvings represent the mysteries of the Rosario and are divided into themes of Joy, Suffering and Glory. The 16C carved image of *Nuestra Señora del Rosario* was created by Roque Amador in Spain, then sent to the New World.

Capilla Museo Santa Clara La Real★

Carrera 7 #19-58. ⏱*Open Mon–Sat 8am –noon, 2pm–6pm, Sun 8am–2pm.* 💬*Guided tours available.* 📞*(8) 742 3032.*

The first convent in New Granada was built under the patronage of Francisco Salguero and his wife, Juana Macías de Figueroa. The construction of its chapel began in 1571.

Inside is a truly impressive **collection**★★ of religious art by Gregorio Vásquez de Arce y Ceballos. The floors of the chapel are unremarkable, but the **Mudéjar walls** and **ceiling** are decorated in

tones of red, with carved-wood motifs that range from a two-headed eagle of the coat of arms of Tunja to a brilliant **sun**★ on the roof. This sun, being of such importance to the local indigenous people despite its Christian significance, drew in indigenous worshippers from the surrounding villages. Author of *Afectos Espirituales* (published 1896) in which she grapples with her alienation and spirituality, the polemic **Madre Francisca Josefa de la Concepción del Castillo y Guevara** (1671-1742) had her cell here in this chapel.

Iglesia Santa Bárbara★★

Carrera 11 between Calle 16 and Calle 17.

Built in 1623, this church is perhaps the most unusual of Tunja's churches, unfortunately hemmed in by neighboring buildings.

Upon entering the atrium and immediately to the right, a room is full of niche tombs. In the sanctuary, the **golden altar**★, at the far end of the sloping nave, is accented with giltwood orchid flowers. The blue-gray walls are rather unassuming when compared to the intricate Mudéjar decoration. Mainly concentrated on the various altars, the decoration is not

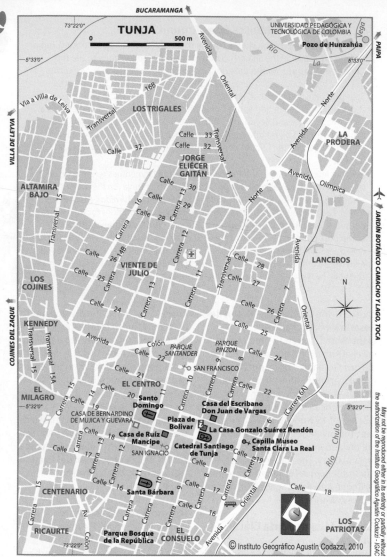

© Instituto Geográfico Agustín Codazzi, 2010

PARQUE MONUMENTO NACIONAL PUENTE DE BOYACÁ ⚓ BOGOTÁ, SAMACÁ

so much stunning in size, but superbly crafted and exquisitely detailed, with ample use of gold patina. The ceiling is adorned with flowering-vine **murals**★★. Some red silk vestments that were embroidered in gold and silver thread by Queen Joanna of Castile, the mother of Charles V, are exhibited on the transept to the left. Note the small statue of **La Pilarica**, a miniature version of the Nuestra Señora del Pilar in Zaragoza, Spain.

Casa del Escribano Don Juan de Vargas★★

Calle 20 # 8-52. ⏰*Open Tue–Fri 9am–noon, 2pm–5pm, Sat–Sun & public holidays 9am–noon, 2pm–4pm.* 🎫*2,000 COP.* ☎*(8) 742 6611.*

Don Juan de Vargas became scribe of Tunja in 1585, an important post he kept until his death in 1620. Along with the chronicler **Don Juan de Castellanos** (👉*see sidebar p160*), he had a profound influence on the development of the city and its culture at the end of the 16C and beginning of the 17C. Vargas' home is considered one of Tunja's most beautiful Colonial mansions.

Andalusian gardens surround a cloistered courtyard, but the best feature may well be inside, where a fanciful **painted ceiling**★★ manifests a strange juxtaposition of images of hippopotami, elephants and mythical figures mixed with Christian symbols. Because of its uniqueness, this composition constitutes an outstanding artistic heritage.

Casa de Ruíz Mancipe★

Calle 19 # 11-13.
Captain Antonio Ruiz Mancipe was Mayor of Tunja in 1591, 1601 and 1606. Inscribed above the front door of his former house is the year of completion (1597) of this traditional Baroque Latin American building. The colonial mansion, with an elegant patio, features some interesting **plateresque details** such as columns topped with Corinthian capitals decorated with animals, ornamental foliage and other motifs.

Parque Bosque de la República

Carrera 11 and Calle 15.
In this 147ha/363 acre park, the **Paredón de los Mártires** (Wall of the Martyrs) still bears visible evidence of the bullet holes that resulted from the execution, in 1816, of soldiers of the independence movement. These tragic events occurred during the **Spanish Reconquest** and the ensuing regime of terror that was renewed by General **Pablo Morillo**.

SURROUNDINGS
Jardín Botánico José Joaquín Camacho y Lago★

◐ *Vía Circunvalar, E of Tunja.*
•‿•*Guided tours available.*
0✆(8) 742 3272 *(tourist office).*
Walk through this 33ha/81 acre garden and learn about the ecosystems in the **Colombian Andes**. Designed and maintained as a center for the study and preservation of endangered Andean flora, the garden makes an excellent introduction to the region's ecology. Given the

chillier climate here, high up near Tunja, this is a good place to test your stamina if planning further high-altitude treks.

Parque Monumento Nacional Puente de Boyacá★★

◐ *16km/10mi SW of Tunja via Carretera 45 towards Bogotá.*
Blink and you'll miss this park as you pass by on the road between Bogotá and Tunja. Here, on an immaculately tended hillside, are monuments that hark back to the struggle for **independence** from the **Spanish empire**. It was here that one of the most important military events relating to the Spanish colonies was played out. The significant defeat at the Battle of Boyacá *(◔see sidebar p156)* of the Spanish and Royalist forces by Republican soldiers under **Simón Bolívar** on August 7, 1819, paved the way for the capture of **Bogotá** and sent tremors of independence down the length of the Andes.

On the park's grounds, the famous **Puente de Boyacá** was the epicenter of the fighting; its crossing by **Santander** and Bolívar was of profound historical importance. The 18C stone bridge over the **Teatinos River** was rebuilt in 1939. A few interesting monuments commemorate the event, including an 18m/60ft tall **Monumento a la Gloria de Simón Bolívar** by Ferdinand Von Miller (1940), decorated with allegoric figures symbolizing Colombia, Venezuela, Ecuador, Bolivia and Peru. A **triumphal arch** by

Puente de Boyacá

Proexport Colombia

155

The Battle of Boyacá

On August 7, 1819, the Republican forces pushing for independence against the Spanish Crown achieved a significant and decisive victory that led, in turn, to the creation of **Gran Colombia**. South American patriots, Creole fighters and a British legion led by **Simón Bolívar** and brigadier generals **Francisco de Paula Santander** and **José Antonio Anzoátegui** met the Spanish on the field of battle at a location known as the **Casa de Teja** by the Teatinos River, 150km/93mi from Bogotá and close to the city of Tunja.

The two armies met at this point since the Spanish were looking to defend the strategically important city of Bogotá, which was clearly coveted by the Republican forces. Given that the revolutionaries had split their army in two after the grueling **Battle of the Pantano de Vargas** (July 25, 1819) so that they could rest, the Spanish mistakenly took the reduced force to be nothing more than a reconnaissance party. Simón Bolívar's troops flanked the Spanish rearguard and forced them to surrender. Other Republican forces crossed the river near the **Casa de Piedra**, dividing the Spanish forces and causing them to panic and flee. The Republicans captured some 1,600 enemy troops and started a chain reaction of military events that arguably destabilized the Spanish yolk in South America irreparably. After the Battle of Boyacá, the route to Bogotá was open for the Republican forces to march upon the city. This victory weakened the Spanish and ignited the independence fervor in Ecuador, Peru and Bolivia that culminated in the Battle of Ayacucho (Peru, 1824).

Luis Alberto Acuña (1954) pays tribute to the soldiers of all origins who fought in this decisive battle and whose mixed backgrounds (Indian, African and Hispanic) represent the essence of the Colombian people.

EXCURSIONS
Samacá★
▷ *32km/20mi SW of Tunja via Carretera 45 and then via the road to El Desaguadero from Puente de Boyacá.*

En route to Villa de Leyva, this quaint town (Pop. 17,352) has some interesting archaeological sites nearby, such **El Santuario** (a pre-Columbian sacred cave) and the burial ground of **El Venado**, a former Muisca village. Outdoor lovers will be able to do some hiking, fishing, mountain biking and bridge swinging in the nearby vicinity.

Paipa★★
▷ *40km/25mi NE of Tunja via Carretera 55.*

The Muiscas inhabited this area prior to the arrival of the Spanish, but over time the occupying forces took control. Today, this 16C colonial town (Pop. 27,274) has retained its charm of yesteryear, with well-preserved streets lined by whitewashed houses with green trims.

Hacienda del Salitre
▷ *3km/2mi S of Paipa on the road to Toca. ℘(8) 785 1508. www.hacienda delsalitre.com.*

Built in 1736 and now converted into a hotel, this picturesque colonial estate received in its time **Simón Bolívar** for a night or two.

Centro de Hidroterapia
▷ *Vereda La Esmeralda, 4km/2mi S of Paipa, on the road to the Pantano de Vargas.* ◷*Open Mon–Fri 7am–9pm.* ✍*Check website for hydrotherapy courses available. ℘(8) 785 0585. www.termalespaipa.com),*

Paipa is known for its curative **hot springs**, making it a key tourist destination in Boyacá.

Pantano de Vargas★
▷ *9km/6mi S of Paipa on the Paipa to Pantano de Vargas road.*

A short drive from Paipa leads to the site of the famous **Battle of the Pantano de Vargas** (Vargas Swamp), which took place on July 25, 1819, laying the foundation for the decisive **Battle of Boyacá** (⚅ *see sidebar opposite),* just 12 days later. While history books establish this battle as a victory for Bolívar and the Republican forces, it resulted in heavy casualties on both sides.

To celebrate 150 years of independence, Rodrigo Arenas Betancur (1919-95) created Colombia's largest sculpture: the **Lanceros del Pantano de Vargas**★★. Framed by a concrete structure, this bronze sculpture sits imposingly over the battlefield and rises to 33m/108ft. It features 14 Llanero lancers and their horses seemingly charging upwards. It serves as a poignant memorial to the men who fought for the Republican cause under the guidance of **Juan José Rondón**, who led the cavalry charge. It was this bold maneuver on the battlefield that supposedly changed the course of the battle and put the rebels in control.

Sogamoso
▶ *80km/50mi NE of Tunja via Duitama, and then SE along Carretera 62.*
Some 15km/9mi beyond Paipa, at Duitama, a road to the right following the Chicamocha river valley reaches Sogamoso (Pop. 114,486). Appropriately known as the "City of the Sun and Steel," Sogamoso was a religious center of great importance to the **Muiscas**.

It is now an industrial city largely relying on coal mining and steelwork, yet it offers a few noteworthy tourist attractions.

Parque y Museo Arqueológico★
Calle 9A # 6-45. ⏰*Open Tue–Sat 9am–noon, 2pm–5pm, Sun & public holidays 9am–3pm.* ☛*Guided tours available.* ✆*3,500 COP.* ✆ *(8) 770-3122).*
For more background information on the Muisca art and culture, you are well advised to make a side trip here. The museum's extensive collections include pieces of pottery, basketry, jewelry, all kinds of weapons, utensils, conch shells used in healing ceremonies, musical instruments and sacred objects associated with phallic worship. You will also

learn about the mummification process, as Muiscas preserved the dead and ornamented their skeletons.

In the park, built on the old Muisca **necropolis**, stands a replica of the **Temple of the Sun** that was burned by the Spanish at the time of the Conquest.

Iza★
▶ *13km/8mi SW of Sogamoso via the road to Pesca.*
Make a trip here midweek, and you'll feel as if you are the first people to discover Iza (Pop. 2,081). Founded in 1595, the town is picturesque, with pretty colonial streets and whitewashed walls wrapped with bougainvillea.

Like so much of the region, Iza is blessed with thermal **hot springs**. The most popular one with the locals is called **Piscina Erika** *(Vereda Aguacaliente, 500m/1,640ft from Plaza Principal;* ✆*4,000 COP;* ✆*310 881 0731),* but there is also a nearby natural spring called the **Pozo Natural** *(1.2km/0.7mi from Iza).*

Monguí★
▶ *93km/58mi NE of Tunja via Duitama and Belencito.*
Founded in 1555 by Gonzalo Dominguez Medellín and Fray José Camero de los Reyes, Monguí (Pop. 4,901) was originally populated by the Tutasá, Tirem, Teguas and Sanoas tribes. In all, it is a charming highland town with cobblestone streets and a deep history. One look at the stone-built **Puente del Calicanto** (1692-1715) reveals the fine craftsmanship that was required to construct it.

Nowadays, Monguí is still renown for its production of ornate and colonial-style **balconies**, but it is most famous for its **Basilica y Convento de Nuestra Señora de Monguí**★ (1694-1760), an outstanding Franciscan basilica with notable works by **Gregorio Vázquez de Arce y Ceballos** *(1638-1711),* one of the most important painters of the Spanish colonial era in Colombia.

From Monguí, you can explore nearby **Páramo de Ocetá,** with springs and waterfalls, a colorful flora and a rich fauna that includes white-tailed deer

An Ancient Game

Declared the Colombian national sport in 2000, **tejo** is the modern version of a pre-Columbian Muisca game born in **Turmequé**, a tiny town located some 45km/28mi southwest of Tunja *(via Villa Pinzón, Nuevo Colón and Ventaquemada)*. Widely played across the country, but mainly in the highlands of **Boyacá** and **Cundinamarca**, tejo consists of throwing a small circular metal disk the distance of nearly 20m/66ft down an area that is 2.5m/8.2ft wide. At the far end, there is a plasticine or clay trough tilted at an angle to meet the tejo disk, and in the center of this trough is a metal ring upon which are placed several small triangles *(mechas)* of gunpowder. If the tejo disk successfully strikes the *mecha* and the metal ring, there will be an explosion and inevitably some smoke. Over time, certain things have changed, in particular the metal tejo disk which in pre-Hispanic times was called the *zepguagoscua* and was made from gold.

Traditionally, a team comprises three people taking turns to throw the tejo disk. Scoring applies to the proximity of the thrown disk to the *mechas* in the clay target. The sport is taken very seriously, and there are leagues and large boisterous tournaments throughout the region. However, many people just choose to play socially, buying rounds of beers for each match.

and condors. **Ciudad de Piedra** (City of Stone) is a stunning collection of natural monoliths that should not be missed.

Laguna de Tota★★

▶ *45km/28mi E of Tunja via Tota on the road to Sogamoso.* ℘*(8) 779 4118. www.aquitania.gov.co.*

Local tales of a terrifying black fish with an oxen head and a giant caiman with teeth of gold have been told about this sacred placeof the Muiscas. The largest freshwater lake in Colombia (12km/7.5mi long by 47km/29mi wide) boasts waters

that are an exquisite aqua blue in color. Its banks are dotted with picturesque settlements including Tota, Cuítiva and **Aquitania** (the largest one, on the eastern shore).

If you are undeterred by the frigid temperature, the lake is a great place for **water sports**. The white sandy beach at **Playa Blanca** would not seem out of place in the Caribbean, were it not for the lung-taxing altitude.

Dine out on **trout** and wash it down with a local *refajo* drink, a mixture of beer, apple soda and malt.

Laguna de Tota

Proexport Colombia

ADDRESSES

STAY

$ Hosteria San Carlos – *Carrera 11 # 20-12, Tunja. ☎(8) 742 3716. 11 rooms.* The San Carlos may just well be the best budget option in downtown Tunja. The hosteria is run by a friendly grandmother and it occupies an old colonial house that has loads of character, comfortable guest quarters and period furnishings. There's also a room with five beds that accommodates families or small groups. The rooms vary in size, so ask to see them before you commit.

$ Hotel Conquistador de America – *Calle 20 # 8-92, Tunja. ☎(8) 742 3534. 20 rooms.* This colonial building at the corner of the Plaza de Bolívar offers large rooms—each non-smoking—with a TV, a safe deposit box, and a private bathroom with shower. Rooms that face the street are large, but can be quite noisy; the small rooms tend to be dark and not fit for people who are claustrophobic. Ask to see what's available.

$$ Hotel Casa Real – *Calle 19 # 7-65, Tunja. ☎(8) 743-1764. 11 rooms.* Located in the historic section of the city, between the bus station and the main plaza, the Casa Real is a modest single-story hotel. Pastel-painted rooms are sparsely but adequately furnished and come with private baths, cable TV and hot water. Ask to see a room as far removed from the noise of the streets as possible.

$$ Hotel Boyacá Plaza – *Calle 18 # 11-22, Tunja.* ▣ ☎(8) 740 1116. *40 rooms.* This small and efficient non-smoking hotel boasts air-conditioning and brisk and attentive service appropriate for its business-oriented clientele. Hotel Boyaca Plaza is located two blocks away from the Plaza de Bolívar, and on-site parking makes it a safe and easy option for those who are traveling by car. Wi-Fi Internet access is available.

☕/EAT

$ Pizza Nostra – *Calle 19 # 10-36, Tunja. ☎(8) 740 2040.* Set just off the Plaza de Bolívar and in Tunja's pedestrian zone, this restaurant is popular with locals, students and business people alike. The menu offers a wide variety of large and tasty pizzas, accompanied by a reasonably priced selection of beverages. **Italian**.

$ Santo Domingo de Guzman – *Carrera 11 # 19-66, Tunja. ☎(8) 742 2619.* This family-friendly restaurant is one of the most popular places to eat in this part of Tunja. Traditional dishes are featured in a comfortable, friendly and homey atmosphere. The smell of the on-site bakery will make your mouth water, and the fresh fruit stand is always tempting. **Regional Colombian**.

$$ El Maizal – *Carrera 9 # 20-30, Tunja. ☎(8) 742 5876.* Packed tables bear witness to the popularity of the delicious cuisine at El Maizal. The place may not look like much from the outside, but once inside, you'll discover excellent regional fare. Try one of the generous portions of good, simple chicken-and-rice dishes at incredibly reasonable prices—or go for the daily set-price meal specials. **Regional Colombian**.

$$ Restaurante Mamá Grande – *Av. Oriental # 9-67, Tunja. ☎(8) 742 3372.* Three separate dining rooms decorated with paintings by local artists provide a comfortable and spacious environment in which to sample the best of traditional Boyacán cuisine. The varied menu includes classic dishes such as *mazamorra chiquita* and *cuchuco* (both hearty soups). The rainbow trout also comes well-recommended. For breakfast, nothing beats the *changua* and the *tamal*. **Regional Colombian**.

Villa de Leyva★★
and Surroundings
Boyacá

One of Colombia's most scenic colonial towns lies just 37km/23mi northwest of Tunja. Declared a National Monument in 1954, Villa de Leyva has taken great pride in preserving its architectural legacy—its ancient streets and period buildings being protected by stringent heritage laws. There is somehow the feeling that the hills rising to one side, that offer stunning mountain scenery, are watching protectively over this precious enclave and its main square, a sprawling cobblestone affair. Villa de Leyva is a preferred weekend destination for many Bogotanos, given that the trip from the capital takes about four hours. Around town, numerous archaeological sites and quaint villages will entice you to explore these mystical pre-Columbian lands.

▶ **Population:** 9,645.
◔ **Michelin Maps:** p149 and p163.
▤ **Info:** Oficina de Cultura y Turismo, Casa del Primer Congreso de las Provincias Unidas, Corner of Carrera 9 and Calle 13. ℘(8) 732 0232. www.villadeley vatur.com.
◉ **Don't Miss:** Monasterio de las Carmelitas Descalzas and its outstanding collection of religious art, one of Colombia's best; the alignment of phallic stones at El Infiernito, the site of an important Muisca astronomical observatory; a hike in the fresh air along the trails in the Santuario de Flora y Fauna Iguaque; the Sunday market in Ráquira, "the City of Pots," for deals on exquisite black pottery.

A BIT OF HISTORY

Named after the president of New Granada, **Don Andrés Díaz Venero de Leyva**, the city was originally founded in 1572 by Captain **Hernán Suárez de Villalobos** near the Muisca settlement of **Zaquencipá**, where an important sacred observatory was located. Because of strong protests by the local Caciques, the settlement was moved 12 years later to its present location.

In the colonial era, Villa de Leyva became the summer retreat of choice for the governing classes and aristocracy, including the viceroys. Over time, the little colony grew famous for its **olive oil** and **wheat**, both of which brought a certain prosperity to the town.

Don Juan de Castellanos (1522–1607)

Part of the first wave of conquistadors who undertook Colombia's exploration and conquest, Juan de Castellanos personally knew some of the most powerful figures of the time, such as **Gonzalo Jiménez de Quesada** (future founder of Santa Fé de Bogotá) and **Gonzalo Fernández de Oviedo y Valdés** (the royal chronicler who participated in the Spanish colonization of the Caribbean).

A soldier-turned-priest, Castellanos was also a poet and an excellent chronicler. His **Elegías de Varones Ilustres de Indias** *(available on http://books.google. com)* is a fascinating account, interspersed with personal observations, of what transpired in this early chapter of South America's colonial history.

Also called **Los Portales**, the **Casa de Juan de Castellanos** *(Carrera 9 # 13-11)*, where Don Juan de Castellanos wrote some of his stories about the conquest, is one of the finest Colonial-style mansions (1585-1607) in town.

Plaza Mayor

Proexport Colombia

One of the heroes of the independence movement and a captain in Bolívar's army, General **Antonio Ricaurte** (1786-1814) was born in Villa de Leyva and perhaps because of his exploits, the town became a key political seat in the fledging post-independence period. It was here that was held, in 1812, the first meeting of the **United Provinces of New Granada**, during which Camilo Torres was elected president of the federal republic.

The politician, journalist and soldier General **Antonio Nariño** (1765-1824) died in Villa de Leyva, lending even more importance to the town as an intellectual and political center.

With Tunja as the departmental capital a short distance away and Bogotá within a few hours travel, Villa de Leyva has been overshadowed in its contemporary significance by its neighbors. Yet its whitewashed walls, bougainvillea and delicately restored plazas make it a great historical town par excellence, and certainly a sight not to be missed.

⚒ WALKING TOUR
AROUND PLAZA MAYOR★★

Centered on a huge square surrounded by whitewashed Colonial mansions and other fine examples of 16C Spanish-style architecture, Villa de Leyva's historic core looks like it was transported in its entirety from Andalucía. Begin your walking tour here.

Plaza Mayor★★
Carrera 9 and Carrera 10 with Calle 12 and Calle 13.
At 14,000sq m/46,000sq ft, this square is one of the largest cobblestone plazas in the Americas. Uneven yet beautiful, it can be quite a struggle to cross it. At its center the plaza features a tiny **Mudéjar fountain** which, for centuries, was the village's sole water source. During the **Spanish Reconquest** of the 1810s, gallows were constructed here from which many rebels were hanged.

Today, the plaza is home to all kinds of festivals and celebrations, including the **Festival del Viento y de las Cometas** (a kite festival held in August), the **Festival de Luces** (a dazzling festival of lights that occurs in early December), and even an astronomical festival, the **Festival Astronómico**, in late January.

Iglesia Parroquial
Carrera 9 between Calle 12 and Calle 13.
Located on the east side of the square, this lovely parish church (1608) looks directly onto it. Inside, you will notice the three-tiered gilded **altarpiece** of its chapel, an elaborate piece of work that contrasts with the whitewashed simplicity of the rest of the church.

Casa del Primer Congreso de la Provincias Unidas★
Corner of Carrera 9 and Calle 13.
Houses the tourist office.

GETTING THERE

BY BUS - Villa de Leyva is accessible by bus from points north and south. A few direct buses service the town from Bogotá (4hrs; 14,000 COP), but the best way to get here is to take a bus from Bogotá to Tunja and change there for Villa de Leyva (45min; 5,000 COP). Minibuses also run regularly between Villa de Leyva and Tunja (45min; 4,500 COP). The town's **bus terminal** sits three blocks southwest of Plaza Mayor on the road to Tunja.

GETTING AROUND

BY BUS - Buses service the town and run to Chiquinquira (1hr, 7,000 COP) and Ráquira (45min, 3,000 COP).
BY TAXI - Area tours are offered by some taxis. Check with the tourism office for a listing of reputable ones.

ON FOOT - Walking is your best option since the town is small and road traffic is usually light.
BY BIKE - Bicycles can be rented in town; check with the tourism office.
BY ORGANIZED TOUR - A few local companies offer area tours that may include hikes and horseback rides; check with the tourism office.

GENERAL INFORMATION

ACCOMMODATIONS - Villa de Leyva has a wide selection of hotels and camping sites in all price ranges. On weekends and holidays, prices rise, and it can be hard to find a room, given the town's popularity with tourists. In high season prices can be double those charged in low season, so best to reserve ahead. *See ADDRESSES at end of the chapter.*

Open Tue–Fri 8am–12:30pm, 2pm–6pm, Sat 8am–3pm. (8) 732 0232.
It was here, in this corner house, that the first Congress of the **United Provinces of New Granada** met from 1812 to 1816, holding historic elections.

Real Fábrica de Licores★

Calle 13 between Carrera 8 & Carrera 9. The building is run by a branch of Telecom. Open Mon–Fri 10am–noon, 2pm–6pm, Sat–Sun 2pm–8pm. (8) 732-0232 (tourist office).
Now turned into a museum with sporadic exhibitions, the former **Royal Liquor Factory** was founded in 1736. It was the first official, but by no means the first, distillery in New Granada.
Don't miss the ostentatious, yet authentic, 16C Spanish **coat of arms★** above the Baroque doorway.

Casa Museo de Antonio Ricaurte★★

Calle 15 # 8-17, Parque Ricaurte. Open Wed–Fri 9am–noon, 2pm–5pm, Sat–Sun & public holidays 9am–1pm, 2pm–6pm. 1,500 COP. (8) 732 0876.
A hero of the independence movement, **Antonio Ricaurte** (1786-1814) was born in this very house. Rooms contain weaponry that Ricaurte used or may have used, an inner **courtyard** and an interesting kitchen with implements dating back to the era.

Monasterio de las Carmelitas Descalzas★

Calle 14 # 10-04.
Set along the small, peaceful **Plazoleta del Carmen★**, this whole complex was founded by order of Philip IV in 1645. It includes the convent itself (1648) and the typically Andalusian **Iglesia del Carmen** *(open during mass)* comprising two chapels: the older one (1645) is dedicated to the Virgen del Carmen; the second one (1848) to the Virgin of Chiquinquirá.
Enjoy the well-tended gardens and ample colonial corridors that offer a peaceful respite from the rigors of pounding the streets of Villa de Leyva.

Museo del Carmen★★

Open Sat-Sun & public holidays 10am–1pm, 2pm–5pm. 2,000 COP. (8) 732 0214.
The hundreds of works exhibited here make up one of the best religious art

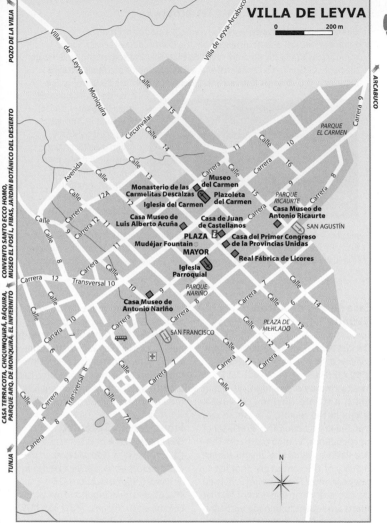

ARCABUCO, MUSEO PALEONTOLÓGICO DE VILLA DE LEYVA ✦ SANTUARIO DE FLORA Y FAUNA IGUAQUE

VILLA DE LEYVA

0   200 m

POZO DE LA VIEJA

ARCABUCO

CONVENTO SANTO ECCO HOMO,
MUSEO EL FOSIL, FIBAS, JARDIN BOTÁNICO DEL DESIERTO

CASA TERRACOTA, CHICUINQUIRÁ, RÁQUIRA,
PARQUE ARQ. DE MONQUIRÁ. EL INFIERNITO

TUNJA

PARQUE EL CARMEN

PARQUE RICAURTE

Monasterio de las Carmelitas Descalzas
Museo del Carmen
Plazoleta del Carmen
Iglesia del Carmen
Casa Museo de Luis Alberto Acuña
Casa de Juan de Castellanos
Casa Museo de Antonio Ricaurte
SAN AGUSTÍN
PLAZA MAYOR
Mudéjar Fountain
Casa del Primer Congreso de la Provincias Unidas
Iglesia Parroquial
Real Fábrica de Licores
PARQUE NARIÑO
Casa Museo de Antonio Narlño
PLAZA DE MERCADO
SAN FRANCISCO

N

collections in the country. Dating from the 17C-20C, they include fine pieces by **Gregorio Vásquez de Arce y Ceballos**, and a variety of paintings, carvings, altarpieces and other religious objects by known or anonymous artists.

Casa Museo de Luis Alberto Acuña★★

Carrera 10 # 12-83. ⏱*Open daily 10am –1pm, 2pm–6pm.* 💵*2,000 COP.* 📞*(8) 732 0422. www.gratisweb.com/ museoacuna.*

Colombian painter and sculptor **Luis Alberto Acuña** (1904-94) was strongly influenced by Picasso and also by **pre-Columbian art**.

Housed in an elegant mansion that is worth the visit alone, the museum exhibits a great deal of his work, but also fossils and archaeological artifacts that Acuña and his friends collected. The patio, filled with his murals and sculptures, reflects the artist's fascination with mythology and indigenous storytelling.

Casa Terracota★★

On the outskirts of Villa de Leyva *(on a little dirt road off the road to Sutamarchán)*, just a short distance from the town's colonial center, you will come across a radically different dwelling that looks like something pulled from the pages of Grimm's *Fairy Tales*. Designed by Colombian architect **Octavio Mendoza,** this **ceramic house**—locally known as "La Casa de Barro" or "La

Casa Terracota

Casa de los Picapiedras" (the Flintstones House)—was built in 2007 with the argillaceous soil found directly on the construction site, then baked to a high heat to give it durability. The result is an eco-sustainable, low-cost house with antiseismic properties that is impervious to water and comfortably cool in hot climates. Made from the very land that was trod by dinosaurs, the 500sq m/5,382sq ft structure is actually the **world's largest ceramic piece.** See www.casaterracota.com.

Casa Museo de Antonio Nariño★

Carrera 9 # 10-25. Open Mon–Tue, Thu–Sat 9am–6pm, Sun & public holidays 8:30am–5pm. 3,000 COP. (8) 732 0342.

As a testimony of the high esteem in which **Antonio Nariño** (1765-1824) is held in the region, a museum was founded in his honor. The "Precursor of Independence," Nariño translated Thomas Paine's *Rights of Man* and fought in many of the campaigns that led to independence. The museum is housed in a two-story mansion (early 17C) that boasts an elegant colonnade bordering the courtyard and a balustrade overlooking it from the first floor.

At the foot of the **statue** in his memory is a quote attributed to him: "I have loved my country; only History will say what this love has been."

EXCURSIONS
Pozo de la Vieja★

6km/4mi W from Villa de Leyva on the road to Gachantivá. Guided tours organized by Cascadas de Aventura; (8) 744 8640.

Associated with the legend of **Bachué,** the mother of Mankind (see sidebar p168), this pond just outside Villa de Leyva was sacred to the Muiscas.

Fed by the **Río Cane** and framed by bulky rocks, its clear blue waters, tinged with a sulfurous yellow, seem almost otherworldly. Some people come here to bathe, while others are content hiking the scenic countryside nearby.

Fibas, Jardín Botánico del Desierto★

7km/4mi W of Villa de Leyva on the road to Santa Sofía. Open Wed–Sun 8:30am–5:30pm. 2,000 COP. Guided tours organized by Colombian Highlands. 311 308 3739. www.colombianhighlands.com.

This once-completely wind-eroded patch of land has been rescued and transformed into a **xeric garden** of **cacti** and other desert plants, as well as a place of **meditation** and peace. It has been constructed as a **maze** in an attempt to express mankind's position in relation to the universe.

Museo El Fósil★★★

See sidebar p166.

Parque Arqueológico de Monquirá, El Infiernito★★

◉ *5km/3mi W of Villa de Leyva on the road to Santa Sofía.* ◷ *Open Tue–Sat 9am–noon, 2pm–5pm, Sun & public holidays 9am–3pm.* ⊜*3,000 COP.* ☞*Guided tours available.* ☎*310 286 6161.*

Dubbed "El Infiernito" (Little Hell) by the Spaniards, this Muisca sacred site was dedicated to the worship of the sun and associated fertility and purification rituals.

Its twin lines of 54 to 55 **stone columns** each (1.80m/6ft high by 40cm/16in wide)—many of them with a **phallic shape**—were most likely used as a rudimentary **solar observatory**. The monoliths are arranged in such a way as to allow the formation and movement of shadows, which would have helped Muisca astronomers predict the culmination of the sun at its zenith, equinoxes, solstices, eclipses and other significant occurrences that affected the crops. Most monoliths in the park were carbon dated to around 900 BC, but fairly recent archaeological excavations have uncovered a 4,000 year-old early Muisca burial site.

Convento Santo Ecce Homo★

◉ *Vereda Valle del Santo Ecce Homo, Municipio de Sutamarchán, 11km/7mi W from Villa de Leyva, off the road to Santa Sofía.* ◷*Open Mon–Fri 9am–5pm.*

Colombian Wine

The Colombian wine industry is still a nascent one. The country's main vineyards are located in the upper reaches of the Cauca River Valley. Other wine-producing areas can be found around Santa Marta, and in the departments of Cundinamarca, Tolima and **Boyacá**, where one of the most famous local wineries, called **Viñedo Aim Karin** *(10km/6mi W from Villa de Leyva, off the road to Santa Sofía, between Sutamarchán and the Convento Santo Ecce Homo)*, is open to tourists. Since 1998 this vineyard, which sits at an altitude of 2,100m/6,890ft, has been supplying national supermarket chains with **Cabernet Sauvignon** and **Chardonnay**. *Open daily 10am–5pm.* ☞*Guided tours Mon–Fri & Sat (except Sat before bank holidays).* ⊜*8,000 COP (20min),* ⊜*45,000 COP (2hrs).* ☎*317 518 2746.* *www.marquesvl.com.*

☞*Guided tours available,* ⊜*2,000 COP.* ☎*(8) 732 0217.*

The buildings of this monastery, established in 1620 by Dominican monks, are dotted with **fossils** embedded in the stones. The original chapel has an impressive gilded **altarpiece** and apse arch decorated with **sun** and **moon**

Stone column, Parque Arqueológico de Monquirá, El Infiernito

the city paper/Proexport Colombia

Fossil of Kronosaur, Museo El Fósil

the city paper/Proexport Colombia

In the Land of Dinosaurs

Covered by an ancient sea some 250 million years ago, the area around Villa de Leyva is literally studded with **fossils** and has yielded some important finds over the years:

◆ The most complete specimen to date of a 120-million-old **kronosaur**, a short-necked plesiosaur from the lower Cretaceous Period, that was unearthed in 1977. It measures 7m/23ft from snout to tail, with a skull more than 2m/5.6ft wide.

◆ The well-preserved fossil of a **plesiosaur**, a carnivorous marine creature that lived from the early Jurassic Period until the end of the Cretaceous Period. This specimen, found in 1945, measures an astonishing 13m/43ft long.

◆ An **ichthyosaur** measuring about 8m/26ft without its tail. This dolphin-like marine reptile, with an age dating from between 110 and 115 million years, was discovered in 1977.

Anyone interested in what the earth around Villa de Leyva has yielded in the way of fossils should take time to visit these two museums:

Museo Paleontológico de Villa de Leyva★

▶ *1km/0.6mi NE of Villa de Leyva via the road to Arcabuco.* ◷*Open Tue–Sat 9am–noon, 2pm–5pm, Sun & public holidays 9am–3pm.* ✆*2,000 COP.* *Guided tours available.* ✆*(8) 732 0466. www.unal.edu.co/museopale.*

Housed in an old **mill** dating to the 17C, this museum makes an excellent introduction to the region's paleontological riches. The vast majority of the fossils exhibited here—ammonites, gastropods, echinoderms, bivalves, vertebrates such as marine and reptilian creatures, and plant fossils—are from the lower Cretaceous Period, with older pieces from the Mesozoic Period.

Museo El Fósil★★★

▶ *Vereda de Monquirá. 4km/2mi W of Villa de Leyva on the road to Chiquinquirá and off the road to Santa Sofía.* ◷*Open Fri–Wed 9am–noon, 1pm–6pm.* ✆*2,500 COP.* *Guided tours available.* ✆*310 884 9666.*

There are only two specimens of **kronosaurus** on display in the world: this one, and another one in Australia. So do not miss the opportunity to see such a prehistoric marvel. When farmers stumbled over this amazing fossil, there were calls to move the petrified remains to a specialized museum. The local residents created an uproar over "their fossil," and a happy medium was reached, with the creation of this museum, to house the fossil and put other examples on display.

motifs. The columns of the cloister's arcade represent the 33 years of Christ. A collection of religious art and artifacts includes paintings, sculptures, vestments, liturgical pieces and books from 16C-19C. Traditional Muisca tools and clothing are also on display, a most fitting setting since the monastery was built on an important pre-Columbian site known as as **pavachoque**.

Run by a community of Dominicans, the monastery has been partly converted to a hotel; its silence is broken by only buffeting desert winds.

Santa Sofía★
20km/12mi NE of Villa de Leyva.
This quaint agricultural community (Pop. 3,012) is centered on a **main square** with a picturesque **church** (1771).

Natural features in Santa Sofia's surroundings include **Cascada del Hayal**, a 25m/82ft high waterfall, and a 50m/164ft deep cave called **Hoyo de la Romera**, in which indigenous tribes used to throw adulterous women.

The **Paso del Angel** is a vertiginous trail only 20cm/8in wide at some points, with a vertical drop of 160m/525ft at a 70-degree angle on one side, and a 30m/98ft deep drop at 90 degrees on the other.

Museo Paleontológico de Villa de Leyva★
See sidebar p166.

Santuario de Flora y Fauna Iguaque★
15km/9mi NE of Villa de Leyva, toward Arcabuco. Access from the Carrizal Zone. 34,000 COP entry fee. Guided tours organized by the Organización Comunitaria Naturar Iguaque del Municipio de Arcabuco. 312 585 9892. www.parques nacionales.gov.co.

From the Furachioga Visitors Center, a winding trail leads up to **Laguna de Iguaque**★, the park's main attraction. This sacred place in the Muisca mythology (*see sidebar p168*) is located high on a misty highland plateau. All around are vast numbers of *frailejones,* bromeliads, lichens and orchids. For birders, this high Andean forest is ideal for sighting hummingbirds, green toucans and grassland yellow finches. You may also glimpse white-eared opossums, foxes, deer and ocelots. In 2010 a devastating **forest fire** swept through the park, burning more than 1,200ha/2,965 acres. At its most furious moment, the fire threatened the outskirts of Villa de Leyva. Today the park is on its way to recovery.

Santuario de Flora y Fauna Iguaque

Proexport Colombia

167

The Bachué Legend

The Muisca believed that **Bachué** (Mother Earth) rose up from the waters of **Laguna de Iguaque** with a baby in her arms. This baby grew up and later became her husband. Together, they populated the Earth. After giving birth to Mankind, **Bachué** and the **parrot god** (her husband, now an adult) became snakes and returned to the sacred pond of **Pozo de la Vieja**. The Spanish chronicler **Fray Pedro Simón** (1574-c.1628) wrote that the indigenous people also referred to Bachué as **Fuzachogua**, and they believed she returned from the Underworld to guide her people when they needed her.

Ráquira★★

▶ *25km/16mi SW of Villa de Leyva via Tinjacá, off the road to Chiquinquirá.*
Founded in 1580 the "City of Pots" (in the ancient Muisca tongue) is a town (Pop. 12,299) crowded with handicrafts shops. Brightly painted and dissimilar to any other Colombian town in this region, it is a pleasant place to while away a few hours. Ráquira needs no special introduction to Colombians, as they flock here in the high season from Villa de Leyva on day trips to snap up deals on pottery at the colorful **Sunday**

Ráquira street

Proexport Colombia

market. The local clay is special here in that it comes in various colors, including an obscure black stained by coal.
The town is surrounded by the **Desierto de la Candelaria** that sits at an altitude of 2,000m/6,562ft.

Convento del Desierto de la Candelaria★

▶ *6km/4mi SE of Raquirá.* ◷*Open daily 9am–noon, 1pm–5pm.* ✆*(8) 732 0232 (tourist office, Villa de Leyva).*
The first Augustinian community in America settled here in 1604, within the confines of the Desierto de la Candelaria, its members living in caves until the monastery itself was built in 1661. Visitors will get to see the chapel, the library and the cloister. They will also enjoy a notable collection of artwork dating from the 17C, with several pieces attributed to **Gregorio Vásquez de Arce y Ceballos** and the **Figueroa brothers**. The monastery's **gardens** and ornate **courtyard** are a real treat to visit.

Chiquinquirá★

▶ *Approx. 36km/22mi E of Villa de Leyva via the road to Chiquinquirá.*
Known as one of Colombia's major religious capitals, this town (Pop. 54,949) sits at a high altitude (up to 3,200m/10,499ft) and is almost always shrouded in mist, hence its indigenous name **Xequenquirá** (covered in clouds). Its most famous landmark attracts pilgrims from all over the country.

Basílica Nuestra Señora del Rosario de Chiquinquirá★

Carrera 13 # 17-48. ◷*Open daily 6am–noon, 2pm–8pm.* ✆*(8) 726 2435.*
Built between 1796 and 1812, the basilica is visited by great numbers of believers who come here to honor the much-revered image of **Our Lady of Chiquinquirá,** the patroness of Colombia.
Painted by **Alonso de Narváez** in 1555, the portrait of the Virgin was damaged over time, but self-healed without human intervention, inspiring great veneration from the faithful.

ADDRESSES

🛏STAY

$ Renacer Hostel and Campsite – *1km/.6mi northeast of Villa de Leyva off Via la Colorada.* 🅿 ✆(8) 732 1201. *www. colombianhighlands.com. 7 rooms.* Created, managed and maintained by the biologist and ecotour guide Oscar Gilede of Colombian Highlands tours, this lovely guesthouse exudes a real feeling of comfort. Hammocks surround a well-maintained garden, where you can relax when you're not using the communal alfresco kitchen and brick oven. The four dormitories and three private rooms are spotless; there's even a luxury suite. The guesthouse is tricky to find, so stop by Colombian Highlands for directions.

$ Zona de Camping San Jorge – *Vereda Roble, along the Via Arcabuco (in front of the fire station), Villa de Leyva.* ✆(8) 732 0328. *http://villaleyvanos.com/ pardo.* This campground consists of a huge grassy field with space for 120 tents, an apartment for 6 people, clean bathrooms with hot water, a big shared kitchen, and great mountain views. There's also a small restaurant and shop on-site. It's about a 25-minute walk from here to the town plaza.

$$$ Hotel and Spa Getsemaní – *Av. Perimetral # 10-35, Villa de Leyva.* ✖ 🆂🅿🅰 ✆(8) 732 0326. *www.hotel getsemani.com. 29 rooms.* An easy walk from the main plaza, this 15-year-old hotel combines the town's Colonial style with a Mediterranean interior design. Inside, the contemporary decor fashions a relaxing atmosphere using natural materials. Each room has a private Jacuzzi and a terrific view. In-room coffeemakers, Wi-Fi access and an umbrella-shaded terrace round out the amenities. Enjoy Mediterranean cuisine in **El Manantial** restaurant.

$$$ Hotel Plaza Mayor – *Carrera 10 # 12-31, Villa de Leyva.* 🅿✖🍽 ✆(8) 732 0425. *www.hotelplazamayor.com.co. 31 rooms.* Although this hotel is expensive, it provides good value for the money. Your every whim is attended to, and rooms are decked out with light woods and tile floors. On the rooftop, El Meson restaurant overlooks the main square. Friendly service, an excellent location, and many thoughtful extras make this hotel a wise choice.

🍴EAT

$ Pizzeria Al Horno – *Carrera 10 # 11-23, Villa de Leyva. No lunch Mon–Wed.* ✆311 354 5006. This bistro focuses on the oven for which it is named. Pink walls and local artwork create an energizing atmosphere here, while the menu boasts 12 different types of pizza, a good range of pasta dishes, great burgers and a variety of sandwiches. Crêpes and *arepas* are also served. **Italian**.

$$ Antique Café y Vinos – *Centro Comercial Casona La Guaca, Villa de Leyva. Closed Mon & Tue.* ✆311 808 6494. *www.villadeleyva.com.co/antique.* This romantic rooftop restaurant goes all out to impress its patrons with candlelight, Spanish love songs, excellent service and a delectable contemporary menu (think trout with mango, coconut and prawn sauce) complimented by an extensive wine list. **Colombian**.

$$ Restaurante Savia – *Casa Quintero, Local 20, Villa de Leyva. No dinner Mon. Closed Tue–Thu.* ✆312 435 4602. *http://villaleyvanos.com/savia.* Savia dishes up inventive vegetarian, vegan and organic cuisine (there's also an on-site shop that sells organic products). So carnivores don't feel left out, it also offers organic poultry dishes and fresh seafood. A plaque outside the restaurant commemorates the last concert performed by Elvis Presley's drummer, Bill Lynn, who died here in 2006. **Colombian**.

$$ Sazon y Sabor – *Carrerra 10 #12-13, Plaza Principal, Villa de Leyva. No dinner Mon.* ✆310 285 3278. Popular with local students, this venerable cafe also appeals to travelers on a budget. An array of delicious and reasonably priced dishes made from fresh, high-quality ingredients fills the menu, which changes every day. **Colombian**.

Sierra Nevada del Cocuy★★★

Boyacá

One of the most awe-inspiring and dramatic mountain ranges in all of South America, the Sierra Nevada del Cocuy straddles the departments of Boyacá, Arauca and Casanare. This region of extreme beauty, with waterfalls and clear blue glacier-fed lakes, is still relatively unknown. However, the trickle of Colombian trekkers and international visitors who come all the way up here is steadily growing due to increased security and the development of a tourist infrastructure that is now allowing for greater access into this mountainous landscape. With the highest peak of Ritacuba Blanco at an impressive altitude of 5,330m/17,490ft, the mountain range of the Sierra Nevada extends only 30km/19mi and in this short distance boasts an impressive 21 peaks. Within the confines of the Parque Nacional Natural El Cocuy, there is an abundance of plant life with figures suggesting that nearly 700 species are present here. Starting points for treks are the two villages El Cocuy and Güicán, where one can obtain the necessary permits from the park's authorities.

⌖ **Michelin Maps:** p149 and p177.

▤ **Info:** Casa de la cultura, Calle 8 # 4-15, El Cocuy; ℘(8) 789-0024; http://elcocuy-boyaca.gov.co/index.shtml. Asociación ASEGÜICOC de los municipios de Güicán y Cocuy, Calle 8 # 4-74, El Cocuy. Guided tours available from private outfitters upon request in the towns of Güicán and El Cocuy. ℘311 557 7893. www.parquesnacionales.gov.co.

⊚ **Don't Miss:** A light walk through Andean forests to hot springs along the Camino Desecho, which passes ancient petroglyphs; and for a real challenge, the five-day mythical trek along the base of the Sierra.

A BIT OF GEOGRAPHY

Three branches of the **Andean Mountains** rise dramatically, as if studded onto the map of Colombia, and the easternmost of these, where the **Sierra Nevada del Cocuy Güicán y Chita** is located, crosses into each of the departments of Boyacá, Arauca and Casanare,

Parque Nacional Natural El Cocuy

GETTING THERE

BY BUS - In **El Cocuy** buses arrive at the plaza on Carrera 5 from Bogotá (11hrs; 35,000 COP) and Güican (40min; 2,500; COP). The Concorde bus (Carrera 5 # 7-16) from/to Bogotá Is the more luxurious of the companies; Libertadores and Gacela (Carrera 5 # 7-34) also offer services from Bogotá. In **Güicán**, buses arrive at the town plaza from Bogotá (12hrs; 40,000 COP) and El Cocuy (40min; 2,500 COP).

HIKING INFORMATION

ACCESS - Entry to the park can be purchased in Güicán or El Cocuy. From Güicán, the **northern circuit** trails start at Cabanas Kanwara, reachable by 5hr hike, private car hire (about 100,000 COP) or a morning ride on the daily milk truck, La Lechero (5,000 COP), which drops you at the nearest available point to your destination.

OPTIONAL ROUTES - in Sierra Nevada

♦ **Route 1** (south) Lagunillas – Púlpito del Diablo – Pan de Azúcar.

♦ **Route 2** (center) Laguna Grande de la Sierra – Los Cóncavos.

♦ **Route 3** (north) Güicán – Cabañas Kanwara – Ritacuba Blanco (highest peak on the Sierra).

♦ **Route 4** (south – north direction) from El Cocuy, or in opposite direction from Güicán. The most popular route is the clockwise circuit from here ending at El Cocuy (5-6 days). Routes 1, 2, and 3 allow the possibility of returning on the same day to park cabins or to the towns.

PARK SECURITY - The areas of Parque Nacional Natural El Cocuy described in this section are within the safe zone of Boyacá (army units patrolling the park may ask for your ID). The dense wilderness of the park's Llano side in the Arauca and Casanare departments falls within a zone of civil war activity, and should be considered **off limits**. Always ask for local advice on safety status and political climate. Stay on marked trails. You must **register your itinerary** with park officials: a search-and-rescue mission will commence if you fail to exit the park by the date you specified. Using the **services of a guide** is strongly recommended. The northeastern sectors, in U'wa territory, need a **separate permit**, obtainable from their office in Bogotá. Check in advance with the park's office to make sure your destinations are covered by your permits.

TREKKING TIPS - Carry **water-proof warm clothing**, including thermal base-layers. Sleeping bags should be rated to at least –10°C/14°F. Bring camping equipment, as you won't find any on sale nearby. Wear **sunglasses** with a strong UV filter. Keep water bottles full (4 liters/0.88 gallons per person per day); consult a guide to know where to safely refill them during your trip. Use a minimum SPF 30 sun block. Have high-energy chocolate bars, nuts, whole cereal and cookies or crackers. Stick to official trails. Age restrictions apply, so unless you are under 60 and over 12, it's unlikely you'll be allowed in. Do not bring non-biodegradable plastic bags or aerosols, which are understandably prohibited.

ALTITUDE SICKNESS - El Cocuy is a high-altitude park, and it is likely that you will have ascended quickly on the way from Bogotá. Acclimatize gradually before trekking in the park to avoid acute mountain sickness, high-altitude pulmonary edema (also known as HAPE), which hits the lungs, or high-altitude cerebral edema (or HACE), which affects the brain. These illnesses can be fatal.

Do not push yourself to begin hiking early. Most travelers visit the villages of El Cocuy or Güicán first, then acclimatize by staying overnight at one of several cabanas located just outside the park boundaries (Cabañas Kanwara, Hacienda Pena Blanca or Posada Sierra Nevada, deeper in the park). Always try to sleep at a lower altitude than your day's trek, and drink lots of water early and often.

Disappearing Glaciers

Most likely affected by global warming, five major glaciers in the Parque Nacional Natural El Cocuy, that were expected in 1983 to last at least 300 years, are now under serious threat. They have been retreating at unprecedented speeds over the last few years.

As well as having a direct impact on wildlife due to radical alterations and changing ecosystems, losing the glaciers could have a huge impact on energy supplies if the current climatic trend continues. In 2009 the head of Colombia's Environmental Studies Institute stated a 90 percent probability that Colombia would lose its glaciers within 25 years.

Disappearing glaciers could have a serious effect on Colombia's ability to generate power, as 73 percent of the country's electricity is generated by hydro power and much of this from glacial meltwater.

spanning an area of 306,000ha/75,6139 acres. With **glaciers**, glacier-fed **lakes**, countless **streams** and **waterfalls** and **snow-capped mountains**, this mountain range is a key part of the **hydrological cycle** in Colombia, if not one of the most important in northern South America.

From here, the meltwaters flow down from the snow-capped peaks through high plateaus, Andean forests and through further microclimates, until they feed and irrigate the savannas of the **Llanos** in the east of the country. More than 90 percent of all freshwater produced here flows east into the **Casanare** and **Arauca Rivers**, while a small percentage drains to the west into the famous **Chicamocha River**.

Fifteen of the mountains found here stand higher than 5,000m/16,400ft, the tallest of which is the **Ritacuba Blanco** at 5,330m/17,490ft. A quantity of ecosystems can be found in this area that begins at an altitude of 600m/1,968ft and climbs more than 5,000m/ 16,400ft, supporting an extraordinarily diverse collection of flora and fauna.

A BIT OF HISTORY

The Parque Natural Nacional El Cocuy was created in 1977 and is now the fifth-largest in Colombia.

For the most part, prior to the arrival of the Spanish, the area was settled by an indigenous tribe known as the **U'wa**, but there were also representatives of the **Tunebos**, **Laches** and **Muiscas** in

the area. These indigenous groups were masters of the terrain, and according to the altitude, were able to cultivate various crops including **maize**, **coca**, **potatoes** and **beans**.

Some records seem to indicate that the German **Georg von Speyer** (1500-40) passed through these lands in 1533, coming from Venezuela en route to the eastern savannas. He was followed in 1542 by the Spaniard **Hernán Pérez de Quesada** (d. 1544)—brother of conquistador Gonzalo Jiménez de Quesada, who founded the city of Bogotá. Following quickly in their wake were the Dominicans and Augustinians, looking to evangelize and convert the indigenous tribes.

The villages of El Cocuy and Güicán as we know them today sprung up between 1754 and 1822. Over the years, the region was passed back and forth while Colombia came to grips with its territories and how best to structure them and administer them as departments.

From the late 1970s into the 80s, the Sierra Nevada del Cocuy was an off-limits area, with various fronts of the **FARC** and **ELN** moving their forces in and effectively controlling vast swaths of the land. Since former **President Uribe**'s no-nonsense approach to battling the guerrillas, the land has once more been brought under the jurisdiction of the state, and the tourists are coming back, attracted by a relatively unknown climbing and hiking destination.

Cathedral, El Cocuy

© Roberto Orrú/Alamy

EL COCUY★

▶ *253km/157mi NE of Tunja via the road to Boavita off Carretera 55.*

Sittng at an altitude of 2,794m/9,167ft, this photogenic village (Pop. 5,383) strongly depends on tourism. As the most commonly used **entry point** to Parque Nacional Natural El Cocuy, it boasts a dozen **hotels**, several **restaurants** and **bars**, and a number of **outfitters** offering guide services and providing visitors with any necessary equipment required to hike and climb in the park.

Voted Boyacá's most beautiful village on more than one occasion, El Cocuy has worked hard to preserve its original character, and the locals are justly proud of the pleasant Andean ambience preserved here. You will see a good number of **Colonial-** and **Republican-style buildings** painted white with green trim, with traditional Spanish-style red tiled roofs.

Major highlights besides the breathtaking scenery include the **Iglesia de Nuestra Señora de la Paz** *(Carrera 3 and Calle 7)*, a salmon-pink church that is located on the flower-filled **Parque Principal**, the town's main square with fine mountain views, where residents congregate to chat, play basketball and eat kebabs and *arepas* from local vendors.

West of the village, a high bluff called **Mahoma** lends itself to **paragliding**.

GÜICÁN★

▶ *10km/6mi N of El Cocuy via the Cocuy-Güicán road. Regular bus service links the two villages.*

Güicán (elevation 2,963m/9,721ft), the other gateway to Parque Nacional Natural El Cocuy, has strong ties to the **U'was**, whose reservations overlap the park, their ancestral territory.

Although much of the village's original Colonial architecture was destroyed during the **Thousand Day War** (1899-1902), it is a well-maintained community (Pop. 5,920) with quite a few interesting highlights.

Parque Principal★

Carrera 4 and Calle 3.

This pleasant park has a combination of local and exotic vegetation under tall trees that contrast with the ornate **church**, the clear blue Andean skies and the mountains that circle the village.

Shrine to the Virgen Morenita de Güicán★

Templo Parroquial, Plaza Principal.

Upon first arriving in the vicinity of Güicán in 1736, the missionary **Father Miguel Blasco** used a small picture of the Virgin Mary in order to preach Christianity to the indigenous tribes. He was surprised when he was told by the local people that they had a far more impressive image. They took him to the nearby mountains, and in an area named **El**

El Peñón de los Muertos★★

Vereda El Tabor, 2km/1mi E of Güicán via Carrera 4 toward the Parque Nacional.
This imposing rock formation, which looks as if the earth's crust had been thrust upwards and skywards, is the place from which the **U'was**, led by **Cacique Güaicaní**, jumped to their deaths upon the arrival of the conquistadors in the mid-18C, rather than live under Spanish rule. Expansive **views**★★ over the valleys and the surrounding region unfold from the top of this tragedy-marked cliff (*approx. 2hr hike uphill*).

Cóncavo, they showed him a cave called **La Cuchumba**, with a painted image of the Virgin Mary, dressed as an indigenous princess. He was told that many years before the Spaniards arrived, the Indians prayed to the heavens for relief from famine. This princess had come to them and returned the rain to their lands. She went away, leaving behind this large image of her. Father Miguel convinced their leader, **Cacique Güaicaní**, to bring the image to town, where it has been venerated ever since.

Monumento a la Dignidad de la Raza U'wa★

On the roundabout by Parque Principal.
Created in 2007 by Delfín Ibáñez, a native of Güicán, this poignant monument commemorates the fate of the **U'was** at the **Peñón de los Muertos** (*see sidebar below*). Note the symbolic features and U'wa proverb at its base.

Camino Desecho★

Trail begins after the Hotel La Sierra, Calle 5 # 6-20.
This charming downhill trek along a worn, stone-paved trail (which translates as "the undone road") leads to a boulder covered in ancient **rock art**, and

continues to local **hot springs** *(Vereda de San Luis, 5km/3mi W of Güicán via the road to Bogotá; small entrance fee).*

PARQUE NACIONAL NATURAL EL COCUY★★★

For information, contact the Asociación ASEGÜICOC de los municipios de Güicán y Cocuy, Calle 8 # 4-74, El Cocuy.
34,000 COP park entry fee.
Guided tours available from private companies upon request in the towns of Güicán and El Cocuy. 311 557 7893. www.parquesnacionales.gov.co.
Established in 1977, this vast park covers approximately 306,000ha/756,142 acres, of which about 92,000ha/227,336 acres were set aside as **U'wa reservations**. Most of the park consists of a unique high-plateau ecosystem: a páramo with a remarkable rate of endemism. This neo-tropical system of valleys, plains and mountain lakes was formed by **glaciers**, and actually includes the largest perpetual snow mass north of the equator. Sadly, due to rising temperatures, the glacier fields are rapidly melting (*see sidebar p172*).

Plant Life

Still relatively unknown outside of Colombia, the Sierra Nevada del Cocuy ecosystem contains an exuberant flora. Its eastern slopes harbor humid **Andean rain forests**, while its western slopes exhibit **low forests** and even **desert scrubland**. The most remarkable among some 700 different species of plants are the rare **frailejones**, **cardón cacti** and **sietecueros trees**. Numerous varieties of **mosses** and **lichens** have also colonized the land, and the dazzling orange, blue and white colors of the Valle de los Cojines, carpeted with alpine **cushion plants**, is a definite must see.
More than 200 species of **vascular plants** have been identified on the Cocuy plateau, many of which cannot be seen anywhere else on earth. The park is also home to a number of **medicinal plants** that are used regionally, such as the *lítamo real*, *granizo* and *árnica*.

Fauna

Despite the harsh environments found here, the park is home to a wide variety of animal life, including **spectacled bears**, **pumas**, mountain tapirs, ocelots, white-lipped peccaries, woolly monkeys, not to mention dozens of bird species. You might catch a glimpse of the black-chested buzzard-eagle, the torrent duck, the scarlet-bellied mountain tanager or the famous **Andean condor**, powerful symbol of Colombia.

Climate

Given the great variety of terrains within the boundaries of the park—from the tropical rain forests of the piedmont to high-altitude plateaus and zones of perpetual snows—the climate here varies considerably, year-round averages ranging from 20°C/68°F to −10°C /14°F. The best time to trek in El Cocuy is December-February, as this time of year is fairly free of heavy rain, snowfall and chilling winds.

Environmental Issues

El Cocuy is considered a priority conservation area due to its high levels of endemism and biodiversity. Yet the presence of **haciendas** in and around the park has placed a significant strain on its fragile ecosystems. Studies show that terrains below an altitude of 3,500m/11,483ft have been considerably affected by severe **overgrazing** of cattle and sheep. Deforestation and slash-and-burn practices are some other causes of concern.

Southern Sector

Access to the park's southern sector via the town of El Cocuy - Alto de la Cueva, where a meteorological station is located.

Most visitors usually enter via this point since it offers the most straightforward access and a great variety of hiking and sightseeing options.

You will discover an impressive series of peaks such as **El Concavito** (5,100m/ 16,732ft), **El Cóncavo★** (5,200m/ 17,060ft), **El Portales** (4,850m/ 15,912ft), **El Toti** (4,900m/16,076ft), **El Pan de Azúcar** (5,100m/16,732ft) and the emblematic "Devil's Pulpit" (*see below*). Stand back and take in this sight, as all of the aforementioned summits together form a spectacular **horseshoe cirque** around part of **Laguna Grande de la Sierra★** (4,450m/14,600ft), a perfect spot to set up a base camp for access to any of these peaks.

Púlpito del Diablo★★

The park's most famous landmark is this unusual, massive square rock formation, at 5,070m/16,633ft. Its ascent takes more lung capacity, but after a brisk hike through the snow and then up the vertical walls of this promontory—an Andean version of the Devil's Tower in

El Pan de Azúcar

The Three Worlds

Genetically and culturally related to the now-vanished **Muisca** civilization, the **U'wa People** are the original inhabitants of the Sierra Nevada del Cocuy. Deeply connected with nature and strongly attached to their ancestral land, they have a profound respect for Mother Earth that is reflected in their three-dimensional vision of the world.

At the core of their culture is the strong spiritual belief that the physical world in which they live, the **Middle World**, is delicately balanced between the **Upper World** (masculine, pure, white, sustaining spiritual life) and the **Lower World** (feminine, impure, red). Should this balance be upset, the Universe would come to an end. U'was believe it is their duty to maintain that balance and protect life by living in harmony with nature.

Wyoming, USA—you will encounter spectacular **views**★★ of the Laguna Grande de la Sierra.

🐾Be warned though, that the sheer cliff faces rise to 1,000m/3,280ft in some places and require a high level of proficiency in alpine climbing.

El Cóncavo★

This hike is an incredibly popular trek, in particular with first-timers to the park, due to its proximity to the entrance and the Laguna Grande de la Sierra. From here, in addition to ascending the 5,200m/17,060ft peak, enthusiasts can strike out in other directions as well, for example to the Pico Toti.

Laguna Grande de La Plaza★★

Located southeast of the Laguna Grande de la Sierra, this lake (4,300m/14,108ft) is possibly the most beautiful in El Cocuy. It is surrounded by many peaks, all of which seem to be reflected in its icy, shimmering waters. **El Diamante** (4,800m/15,748ft), to the west, is known for the range of colors it exhibits with the changing angles of daylight.

Additional Sights

Other highlights in the southern sector include the sweeping **Valle de Lagunillas** with a chain of charming small lakes, all distinct with their varied colors: La Pintada, La Cuadrada, La Atravesada, La Parada.

Northern Sector

Access vía Güicán and Cabañas Kanwara (4,050m/13,287ft).

This sector offers experienced climbers the opportunity to attempt the two highest peaks in the Sierra.

Ritacuba Blanco★★

At 5,330m/17,486ft, this massif is indeed the highest peak in the region. The challenging climb over ice and rock consists of a roughly five-hour ascent of the gentler face, but take into account that you should be acclimatized to the altitude beforehand.🐾The peak is usually clouded by noon, so an early start is required for security.

Ritacuba Negro★★

This 5,300m/17,388ft peak is less visited because its ascent requires traversing a glacier, the narrow trip to the top leaving you exposed to the elements. If you make it all the way to the summit though, you will enjoy spectacular **views**★★, with the towering **Pico Aguja**★ (5,000m/16,404ft) and **Picos Sin Nombre** (5,000m/16,404ft) to the northeast.

Additional Sights

Other highlights farther north in the sector include **Laguna Grande de los Verdes** (3,900m/12,795ft), accessible from the Parada de Romero via paths that run by the Río Cardenillo.

If you have the time, try the 7-8hr walk between Laguna Grande de los Verdes and tiny **Laguna del Avel-**

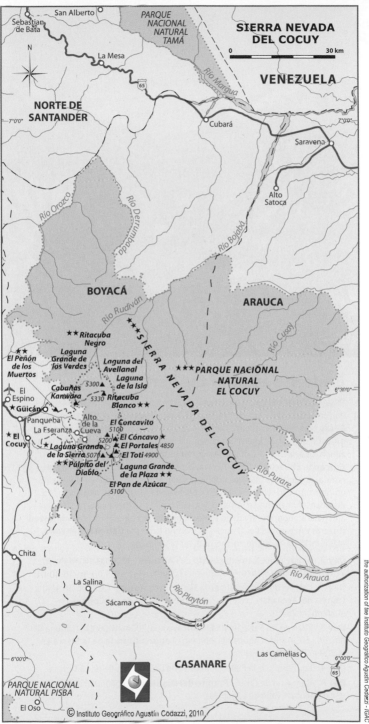

Valle de los Cojines

Archivo Parques Nacionales Naturales de Colombia

Eastern Sector of the Park

The **Vuelta al Cocuy** may some day become as famous as the Inca Trail in Peru or the Ciudad Perdida in northern Colombia, as this demanding **5-day trek** *(walking about 8 hours per day)* inspires and continues to entice a growing number of international visitors every year to this region. The route, which follows the base of the Sierra, can be done either north-south from **Güicán** to **El Cocuy** or the other way around, and unveils most of the park's natural attractions. During a goodly portion of the trek, you will enjoy almost uninterrupted **views**★★★ of snowy peaks and icy summits, and given the distances that are being covered, you will traverse a great variety of terrain and have an opportunity to do some mountain climbing. Here is a **suggested itinerary** *(variations being possible)*, starting from the **Cabañas Kanwara** (4,050m/13,287ft) in the northern sector of the park.

Day 1 Boquerón de Cardenillo - Alto de los Frailes - Laguna Grande de los Verdes - **Ritacuba Negro**★★ (5,300m/17,388ft).

Day 2 Laguna de la Isla - Alto de la Sierra - **Pico Aguja**★ (5,000m/16,404ft) - Laguna del Avellanal - Los Picos Sin Nombre - **Valle de los Cojines**★★ (4,300m/13,780ft).

Day 3 Picos de los San Pablín - **El Cóncavo**★ (5,200m/17,060ft) - Laguna del Rincón - El Castillo - Laguna del Pañuelo - **Laguna Grande de la Sierra**★★ (4,300m/14,108ft).

Day 4 Los Cerros de la Plaza - Alto de Patio Bolas - Laguna de La Tigresa.

Day 5 Boquerón de Cusirí - **Púlpito del Diablo**★★ (5,070m/16,633ft) - Pan de Azúcar - Valle de Lagunillas.

lanal (4,300m/14,108ft). Passing en route **Laguna de la Isla**, which sits at 4,400m/14,436ft, this path is well worth considering since it is dominated eastward and westward by some of the most majestic peaks of the El Cocuy Park.

ADDRESSES

🏨 STAY / 🍴 EAT

$ Brisas del Nevado – *Carrera 5 # 4-59, Güicán.* ✕ ☎*(8) 789 7028. 14 rooms.* Housing both the most comfortable inn and one of the area's best **restaurants ($$)**, Brisas del Nevado claims natural-light-filled rooms, many of which share baths. The best accommodations are in the cabañas in the garden behind the entrance to the main building, but they cater to larger groups. The town's main plaza is just half a block away.

$ Cabañas Kanwara – *Vereda el Tabor, 2km/1mi east of Güicán via Carrera 4.* 🅿✕☎*311 231 6004. 15 rooms.* You'll need an off-road vehicle to reach these lofty cabins, located in the north end of the park near Güicán. At 4,050m (13,287ft), this place is a good stop to adjust to the altitude as you climb. Each of the three comfy A-frame cabins has five bedrooms, a kitchen and a bath.

$ Fundación Casa Museo la Posada del Molin – *Carrera 3A # 7-51, El Cocuy.* ✕☎*(8) 789 0377. http://elcocuycasa museo.blogspot.com. 8 rooms.* More than 200 years old, this renovated Colonial mansion with its vividly painted balcony is said to be haunted. Staying in one of the six well-appointed rooms—each with a private bath—is a treat. Accommodations surround a courtyard covered with fossil-laden rocks (a local tradition) and punctuated by a small brook. One of the best **restaurants ($)** in the area resides here, serving satisfying regional cuisine.

$ Hotel El Eden – *Transversal 2 # 9-58, Güicán.* ✕☎*(8) 789 7093. 5 rooms.* About a 10-minute walk north of the plaza, along a dirt road, this family-run guesthouse exudes a rustic charm with its fragrant wood-lined rooms and its garden filled with turkeys, ducks and other animals. Fresh regional specialties are served in the on-site **restaurant**

($$). Most rooms have private baths, and some sport lofts as well.

Hotel La Sierra – *Calle 5 # 6-20, Güicán.* 🅿✕☎*(8) 789 7074. 12 rooms.* A hostel rather than a hotel, this place is not marked by a sign, but has been around for so long that locals can easily give directions. The knowledgeable owner is a fount of information for those guests interested in the national park. Rooms have both TV and private hot-water baths; ask for an airier room on one of the upper floors.

$ Hotel Restaurant Casa Vieja – *Carrera 6 between Calle 7 and Calle 8, Parque Olimpo Gallo, El Cocuy.* ☎*313 876 8783. 6 rooms.* Celebrated local artist Roberto Arango owns this little hotel, which, despite its name, no longer has a restaurant. Rooms could use some perking up, though those at the back have been renovated with shared hot-water baths. Overflowing with flowers, the courtyard is a lovely spot to relax, while the portico serves as a gallery for Arango's paintings.

🏃 RECREATION

Parque Nacional Natural El Cocuy – *Southeast of Bucaramanga, accessible via the towns of Güicán and El Cocuy. Park office is in El Cocuy, at Calle 8 # 4-74, Güicán.* ☎*311 557 7893. www.parquesnacionales.gov.co.* From its temperate rain-forest floor to its 21 snow-capped peaks, the park displays an impressive variety of ecosystems. Visitors must pay the admission fee (34,000 COP) at the park office and register their itinerary.

Refugios in the Park
Ideal for acclimatization or resting between hikes, cabaña-style accommodations can be found in Alto de la Cueva, La Esperanza and Ritaku'wa. Be sure to reserve ahead.

$ Cabañas del Pulpito – *Vereda la Cueva.* 🅿✕☎*314 272 9524. 9 rooms.*

$ Cabañas Herrera – *Vereda Cañaveral.* ☎*318 416 9920. 3 rooms.*

$ La Capilla Hospedaje – *Vereda la Cueva.* 🅿✕☎*313 419 2258. 4 rooms.*

$ Posada Sierra Nevada – *Vereda el Tabor.* ✕☎*311 237 8619. www.posada sierranevada.com. 7 rooms.*

San Gil★★ and Surroundings

Santander

Colombia's adventure-sports capital is a picturesque colonial town with a typical 18C plaza, balconied buildings and quiet winding streets. Located in the deep valley of the Río Fonce, it sits in a part of Santander where the rivers and gorges lend themselves to some of the best white-water rafting and canoeing in the country. Yet San Gil not only offers a wide range of outdoor pursuits, it also makes an excellent base for exploration, since it is conveniently located on the road from Bucaramanga to Bogotá. Various cultural and historical interests such as Guane or the charming colonial settlement of Barichara are easily reached from San Gil. The town is also a great place to divide the journey from the interior of Colombia to the Caribbean coast or vice versa.

▶ **Population:** 19,448.
◔ **Michelin Maps:** p149 and p180.
🈳 **Info:** Casa de la Cultura Luis Roncancio, Calle 12 #10-31. There are also two tourist information points, located at Carrera 10 #11-85 and at Malecón Turístico Cacique Guanentá. 𝒫(7) 724 4617. www.sangil. gov.co/sangilturistica.
🕸 **Don't Miss:** Test your nerves and take a splash as you enjoy some world-class white-water rafting on the Río Fonce; for extraordinary views of the Chicamocha Canyon, ride the cable car that traverses 6km/4mi of stunning landscape; wander the cobblestone streets of Barichara, one of Colombia's most beautiful colonial towns.

A BIT OF HISTORY

The history of the department of Santander is intimately linked to that of the **Guanes**, an ancient native culture related to the Muiscas. Known for their fair complexion that set them apart from other native peoples, Guanes were mostly farmers and skilled artisans who also engaged in fishing and hunting. The arrival of the Spanish and the ensuing conquest brought them on the verge of extinction. By 1586 Guanes were

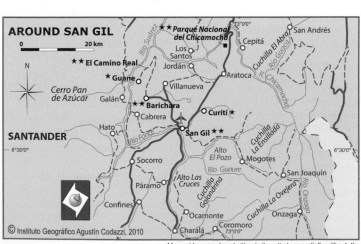

GETTING THERE

BY BUS - San Gil has three bus stations (🔊 *see also Getting Around below*). **Direct buses** arrive at the station 3km/1.8mi west of central San Gil on the road to Bogotá from Baranquilla (15hrs; 70,000 COP), Bogotá (7hrs; 35,000 COP), Bucaramanga (2.5hrs; 15,000 COP), Cúcuta (9hrs; 40,000 COP), Medellín (11hrs; 65,000 COP), Santa Marta (13hrs; 60,000 COP). From this station, **busetas** leave for town (to the corner of Carrera 10 and Calle 15). A **taxi** ride to town costs 2,800 COP.

GETTING AROUND

BY BUS - From the Cotrasangil **bus terminal** (Carrera 11, No. 8-10), buses depart for Bucaramanga via Parque Nacional de Chicamocha (2.5 hrs; 15,000 COP). The **local bus terminal** (Calle 15 & Carrera 10) has buses to Barichara (20-45min; 3,300 COP). Every 45min buses leave Barichara from Cotrasangil bus office (Carrera 6 No. 5-74 📞*736 7132*) to San Gil; you can also travel to Guane (15min; 2,000 COP). Most intercity buses operate from the station 3km/1.8mi west of central San Gil.

GENERAL INFORMATION

ACCOMMODATIONS - Low budget lodgings are plentiful around Calle 10 in San Gil; luxurious and all-inclusive options tend to be on the outskirts. Barichara is far more expensive, especially in high season when hotels are usually full. Locals often rent out rooms in both places; ask around in their centers about affordable options. 🔊 *See ADDRESSES at the chapter's end*.

reduced to just a few hundred who most likely mixed with the Spanish population. Today, many local place names such as **Guanentá** ("plantation" or "grove") or **Monchuelo** (the original Guane name for the Río Fonce, meaning "place of the young man's bath") keep their memory alive and extend their heritage. Pottery shards and ancient stone-laid bridle paths along the river are further reminders of times long gone when San Gil was indeed the heart of the Guane territory.

San Gil actually owes its name to a certain **Don Gil Cabrera y Dávalos**. Back in the colonial days, Don Gil was the president of the Royal Audience (which had a legislative role in the administration of the territory) and as such, he authorized a few farmers, led by **Don Leonardo Betancur Currea**, to found a town under the name of "Santa Cruz y San Gil de la Nueva Baeza" in 1689.

San Gil itself and more generally, the whole Santander area, played an important role in the **independence** movement, which is a source of great pride to *Sangileños*. In 1781 *mestizo* **José Antonio Golán** led the **Revolt of the Comuneros** (🔊 *see sidebar p188*) in Charalá, while similar uprisings occurred in Mogotes, Onzaga and **Socorro**. The region is now part of the **Ruta de Los Comuneros** (🔊 *see p16*), a historical route that is a celebration of all of the key places that expressed the idea of self-government for the first time, foreshadowing the fight for independence from Spain.

In the late 19C-20C, San Gil and the surrounding villages were flashpoints for **civil wars**, in particular the tragic **Thousand Day War** (1899-1902), and the scene of violent events that followed the assassination of liberal presidential candidate **Jorge Eliécer Gaitan** in Bogotá in 1948.

Today, as the capital of the **Guanentá Province** and a town with great potential for **tourism**, San Gil provides a significant contribution to the regional economy.

A BIT OF GEOGRAPHY

San Gil and the surrounding countryside benefit from an almost permanent **spring-like climate**, ranging between 16°C/60°F and 30°C/86°F. Just one look at the terrain and the quantity of **rainfall** here will tell you all you need to

Giant Toasted Leafcutter Ants

The **Guane People** of the Santander region believed that *atta laevigata*, a large type of ant called **hormiga culona** in Spanish, had aphrodisiac properties. They harvested the ants when they surfaced after heavy rains and roasted them—a practice that did not meet with the approval of early Spanish colonists.

Today, served toasted and salted and eaten like nuts, "fat-ass ants" have become a favorite snack in the Santander region, particularly around areas like San Gil, Barichara, Socorro, Zapatoca or Suárez, where the Guane culture has left a strong imprint.

Bite into their crunchy exterior to get a taste of their redolent, slightly acidic juices. You may actually grow to like the taste.

know: this part of Santander is fertile and ideal for the cultivation of **vegetables** and **fruits**.

The region being located mostly along the western branch of the **Andes** that runs through central Colombia, it is the **runoff** from these mountains that feeds the **rivers**, **gorges** and **canyons**, making this location blessed for adventure sports. Due to the movements of the **Nazca**, **Cocos** and **Pacific plates**, there is a great deal of **seismic activity** around the area, and all cities, towns and villages are at risk. Bucaramanga, the capital of Santander, just 96km/60mi north of San Gil, is no exception, and records an average 85 small tremors per day, being so close to the epicenter.

TOWN

San Gil is a lot more than just a place for thrill seekers. The town's streetscape of long-standing **colonial buildings** is indeed worthy of interest. Many visitors spend time strolling through its 18C plaza, surrounded by handsome buildings with balconies, all seemingly untroubled by the passing of time.

Two blocks south of the central plaza, the **Río Fonce** divides the town into northern and southern halves. The waterfront **malecón** promenade runs parallel along the north bank of the river, beginning at Calle 10 near the bridge, and ending east at the front gates of Parque El Gallineral.

Parque La Libertad★

Carrera 9 and Carrera 10 with Calle 12 and Calle 13.

This quaint 300-year-old square, also called Parque Principal, is really the city's historic center. Here, a central **fountain** is surrounded by large **ceiba** and **heliconia trees**. The atmosphere

Rafting on Río Fonce

Proexport Colombia

The Great Outdoors Around San Gil

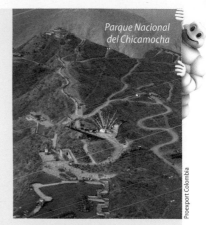

Parque Nacional del Chicamocha

Proexport Colombia

San Gil is increasingly recognized as a center for Colombia's burgeoning adventure-sports industry, and is receiving adrenalin junkies from far and wide. The whole region lends itself to a range of outdoor pursuits, and along with them, attracts many adventure vacation companies, each with varying competence and equipment. It is essential that you do your research to find the most credible outfitters.

Caving Along the road to Barichara, a series of caves known as **La Antigua** features caverns full of spiders and bats, and a guided crawl through small tunnels of mud and water that reach underground waterfalls. Close to the town of El Páramo, just 10km/6.2mi from San Gil, the **Cueva del Indio**★ makes an ideal destination for avid spelunkers and thrill seekers. Visitors will have to harness up and zip-line down an 80m/262ft cable into the cave. They will explore the depths of this beautiful cavernous underworld, complete with stalactites and stalagmites, and then swim out an exit farther along. Other caving opportunities include the **Cueva de la Vaca** and **Cueva del Yeso** in Curití, both considered the best in the department of Santander.

Hiking and Trekking A network of old **indigenous trails**, known as the Lenguake or **Camino Real**★★, runs through the countryside around San Gil and links many lovely villages such as Barichara and Guane. Hardcore adventurers will prefer more extreme options in and around the stunning **Cañón del Chicamocha**.

Kayaking Three-day beginners' courses on the **Río Fonce** include eskimo-roll training in a local swimming pool. More experienced kayakers can make runs with experienced guides on the region's different rivers, and are rarely disappointed since there are a variety of challenges for all skill levels.

Paragliding The two best locations for paragliding around San Gil are **Curiti** and the **Cañón del Chicamocha**. You will fly over tobacco farms and thrill to plunging views of Colombia's largest canyon.

Rafting Blessed with three rivers in close proximity to one other, San Gil offers excellent rafting opportunities for people of all levels of experience. The main river running through town, **Río Fonce**★★ is the best choice for beginners, with Class II-III rapids. The trip begins 11km/7mi outside San Gil and winds up downtown, opposite Parque Gallinera. The **Río Chicamocha**★★ has rapids that range from Class I to IV, and travels through the spectacular Cañón del Chicamocha. For a more extreme experience, the **Río Suárez**★ has Class IV+ rapids.

Rappelling Daredevils will enjoy rappelling down the sheer face of the **Cascadas de Juan Curi**★★, a spectacular three-tier 180m/590ft waterfall *(22km/13.6mi from San Gil on the road to Charalá; you can book this activity with one of a number of tour companies)*. Also a popular hiking destination, it features an attractive swimming spot at the base of one of the cascades. You can climb to the second of the three tiers using a number of ladders and ropes.

here, when illuminated in the evening, is one of tranquillity. Overlooking the square, the **Catedral de la Santa Cruz** has interesting octagonal towers and dates back to 1791. Inside, note a fine altarpiece by Jacinto García (1965).

There is a good **view** of the square from **El Cerro La Gruta**, the shrine overlooking the town from the north—look for the cross. Up here, the pilgrims come to pay their respects to the Virgin, and a mass is held every Saturday.
Another local landmark, also signaled by a cross, is the **Cerro de La Cruz**, on the banks of the Río Fonce.

Casa de la Cultura Luis Roncancio★

Calle 12 # 10-31. Open daily 8am–6pm. (7) 724 4617.
The **Fundación Museo Guane**, a small museum exploring the history and culture of the Guane people of Santander, should provide an understanding of the culture and forbears of the region. Situated in an 18C Colonial house, it also has temporary art exhibits and a cafe.

Parque El Gallineral★★

Carrera 7 & Calle 6. Open daily 8am–6pm. 4,000 COP. (7) 724 0000. www.planetaazulcolombia.com.
This enchanting 4ha/10 acre island park is ideally located near the center of San

Chiminango tree with Spanish moss

Gil, right where the **Quebrada Curití** runs through a delta to the **Río Fonce**. "Gallineral" is another name for the ornamental **chiminango** *(Phitecellobium dulce)*, a species of tree that dominates the park. Many trees are covered with a **Spanish moss** known here as *barbas de Viejo* (old man's beard) that hangs from the branches forming translucent curtains of foliage and filtered sunlight. Numerous small streams help create a lush **botanical garden** full of **butterflies** and **birds**. Look for heliconias and the huge ceiba near the playa

Parque El Gallineral

Kayaking in Parque Nacional del Chicamocha

Proexport Colombia

where canoes end their trip down the Río Fonce. There's a restaurant, and a natural public **swimming pool** that uses water siphoned from the Quebrada Curití.

EXCURSIONS
Curití★
▶ *7km/4mi NE of San Gil via Carretera 45.*

With its narrow streets lined with whitewashed homes, this typical Santanderean town (Pop. 11,343) makes a pleasant day trip from San Gil or Bucaramanga. Curití is particularly famous for the locals' artistry in weaving bags, sandals and espadrilles with the natural fiber of the **fique** plant. This traditional material, used by pre-Columbian cultures to make ropes, clothes and other utilitarian objects, is now being turned into sustainable, eco-friendly fashion accessories.

The most famous **caves** to visit in Santander— **Cueva del Yeso** and **Cueva de la Vaca**—are located nearby Curití. A large number of fossils and evidence of early human occupation have been ~~f~~ound in the Cueva del Yeso, a totally **dry** ~~lim~~estone cavern full of interesting rock ~~form~~ations, and accessible by rappelling ~~down~~ a line.

Quite different, the Cueva de la Vaca is a **wet** cave, and access is restricted, depending on the water levels.

Parque Nacional del Chicamocha★★
▶ *39km/24mi NE of San Gil via Carretera 45. The park's office is located at Calle 44 # 35-27, Bucaramanga.* ⏱*Open Tue–Thu 9am–6pm, Fri–Sun & public holidays 9am–7pm.* ⏱*Cable cars operate from 9am–4:30pm.* ⏱*Closed first day of month.* 🎫*12,000 COP (*🎫*36,000 COP including cable-car ride),* 🎫*6,000 child (*🎫*18,000 COP including cable-car ride).* ☎*(7) 657 4400. www. parquenacionaldelchicamocha.com.*

Deeper than Arizona's Grand Canyon in the US (2km/1.24mi versus 1.6km/1mi), this natural wonder was formed some 4.6 billion years ago.

The **Chicamocha River** runs the course of the canyon, later joining the Fonce, Suárez and Sogamoso rivers, which all flow in the region and provide an invaluable water source for activities such as canoeing and kayaking. This harsh, desert-like environment is home to iguanas, foxes and snakes, and the temperatures here drop to around 11°C/52°F at night, but in the day can hit highs of up to 32°C/90°F.

185

Barichara

Proexport Colombia

To protect the northern rim of the canyon, a 264ha/652 acre park—also called **Panachi**—was created in the vicinity of the municipality of Aratoca. Entirely dedicated to **ecotourism**, it is gradually being primed to become one of Santander's, if not Colombia's, most-visited tourist attractions.

The park has a little something for everyone. Perhaps the most exciting activity, in particular for those with no wish or precious little time to enjoy a **hike** along the well-tended and marked pathways, is the option of taking one of the longest **cable car**★★ rides in the world.

Covering a distance of some 6.3km/4mi, during which the cable car descends from one rim to the bottom of the canyon and up again on the other side, this ride affords amazing **views**★★★ out over the Chicamocha River as it winds its way from Soatá to Lebrija. Other activities include **zip lining**★, canoeing, rafting, paragliding, and for little ones, having fun in a playground and enjoying the animals in a petting zoo.

A traditional Santanderean village celebrates all things from the department. Take a look at the **Monumento a la Santandereanidad**, which commemo-

rates the Revolt of the Comuneros (◖*see opposite sidebar*) and visit the museum dedicated to the Guane Culture.

BARICHARA★★

▶ *24km/15mi NW of San Gil via the road to Canta Rana.*

Sitting on a bluff overlooking **Suárez River Valley**, Barichara (Pop. 7,063) is considered as one of the most beautiful towns in Santander. Founded in 1705 by **Francisco Pradilla y Ayerbe**, it was declared a National Heritage Monument in 1975 for its remarkable Colonial architecture.

☙ WALKING TOUR

After some adrenalin-pumping activities in nearby San Gil, you will no doubt appreciate the quiet and peace of this charming town, which was the setting for many Colombian soap operas.

Dotted with the usual benches, pretty trees and tropical plants and a water fountain, the main square in town, the **Plaza Principal**, is a good starting point to explore the city. The best way to soak up Barichara's artsy, bohemian ambience is to wander its cobbled streets at your leisure.

🐾 El Camino Real from Barichara to Guane★★

Linking Barichara to Guane is El Camino Real, an ancient stone-paved road which, prior to the Spanish arrival, was a **key pathway** for the indigenous **Guane People**. Built and rebuilt continuously over the centuries, it was declared a National Monument in 1988. From Barichara *(starting at the intersection of Called 4 and Carrera 10),* this 9km/5.6mi easy hike will take only about two hours to complete. The trail is mostly downhill if you start from Barichara, and occasionally crosses the modern highway that leads to Guane. Start by climbing down the rim of a canyon, then traverse a valley full of cacti and trees. Apart from a few grazing goats and cows here and there, you should be on your own. As you walk, note the **fossils** embedded throughout the stone road. 😊*Don't forget to bring water and sunscreen with you, and wear appropriate shoes.*

A longer, more difficult three-day option takes you through Barichara, Guane, Villanueva, Los Santos and the ghost town of **Jericó**, heading down and then up the **Chicamocha Canyon**. You will come across various hostels and places to sample local food and drink en route.

Catedral de la Inmaculada Concepción

Carrera 7 between Calle 5 and Calle 6.
Looming over the Plaza Principal, the imposing **Catedral de la Inmaculada Concepción** is a fine 18C Colonial building framed by twin towers. Its yellowish stonework—which appears as a rich, deep orange at sunset—contrasts with the whitewashed houses surrounding it. This ornate building features a **clerestory**, which is quite unusual for a Spanish Colonial church.

The interior, supported by ten 5m/16ft-high fluted columns, features a main altar with gold-leaf details, a carved wooden ceiling, and a chapel dedicated to the *Virgen de la Piedra.*

Casa Natal de Aquileo Parra

Calle 6 and Carrera 2. 🕐*Open Mon–Sun by appointment only.* ✆*(7) 691 3279.*
The birthplace of **Aquileo Parra** (1825-1900), who served as Colombia's 11th president from 1876 to 1878, houses a small historical museum, though most of the building is now a cooperative for elderly **weavers**.

Museo Casa de la Cultura Emilio Pradilla González

Calle 5 # 6-23. 🕐*Open Mon–Sat 8am–⌐on, 2pm–6pm, Sun 9am–1pm.* ✆*Call ⌐rices for temporary exhibitions. ⌐uided tours available.* ✆*(7) 726*

7002. http://casaculturabarichara. blogspot.com.
Named after a high-profile former governor of Santander, who was also a writer and poet, born in Barichara in 1881, this building features temporary exhibits promoting the town's cultural, artistic and historical heritage.

Additional Sights

Three other churches, all of them with simple, even stark, interiors, can be found in Barichara.

The **Capilla de San Antonio** *(Carrera 4 and Calle 5)* dates from 1831. It boasts an unusual adobe-and-stone façade.

Built in 1797 with crudely carved blocks of stones, which adds to its charm, the **Capilla de Jesús Resucitado** *(Carrera 7 and Calle 3)* was damaged by lightning, and unfortunately lost a part of its bell tower. Be sure to visit the **cemetery** next to the chapel, as its stonework and wrought-iron details are quite extraordinary.

On the north end of town, the **Capilla de Santa Bárbara** *(Carrera 11 and Calle 6),* built about 1800, was carefully reconstructed in the 1990s.

Up the hill behind the chapel is the **Parque de las Artes Jorge Delgado Sierra★,** a lovely little park decorated with 22 stone carvings by local and international sculptors, and an outdoor amphitheater that occasionally hosts

The Revolución de Los Comuneros

In the 18C, tied up in a costly war with England, Spain decided to increase **taxes** in New Granada to strengthen its war chest. Led by **Manuela Beltrán** (b. 1750-death date unknown), a civilian resistance movement started in the early 1780s in the Santanderean town of **Socorro** *(SW of San Gil via Carretera 45)* and spread across the country. More than just a popular uprising against abusive taxes, the revolt soon took pro-independence undertones; people started demanding further changes such as the protection of **indigenous lands** and the election of **Creoles** to public office. Later on, in 1810, Socorro was among the very first towns in Colombia to declare its independence from Spain.

live music concerts. From the park, one can enjoy a breathtaking **view**★ of Barichara and the neighboring valley.

From the **Mirador** *(at the top of Carrera 10)*, there is a superb wide-ranging **view**★ across the **Río Suárez** to the **Cordillera de los Cobardes**, the last section of the Cordillera Oriental before the Magdalena River Valley.

GUANE★

▶ *9km/6mi NW of Barichara.*

Seemingly caught in time, this tiny, peaceful village was once the **capital** of the indigenous **Guane culture**.

Like many other villages in the region, it is dominated by a pleasant **central square** featuring bright orange acacia trees and a monument studded with fossils that was erected in memory of **Guanetá**, the last Guane cacique. Overlooking the square, the charming **Iglesia de Santa Lucía,** with a balcony, was built In 1720.

Colonial period houses abound in this sleepy village, uneventful enough that everyone seems to stop and stare when a horse carriage trundles by or when a tourist happens to walk through town.

Museo Paleontológico y Arqueológico de Guane

Carrera 6 # 7-24. ⏱*Open daily 8am–noon, 1pm–5pm.* 🎫*2,500 COP.* ✆*(7) 724 7522*

This museum is stocked with a huge collection of about 10,000 fossils, all of which are more than 60 million years old. Naturally focusing on the Guane culture, the archaeology section exhibits some skulls and a 700-year-old mummy, a large number of ceramic pieces (pots and bowls, jugs and other items), grinding stones, woven textiles and other indigenous artifacts.

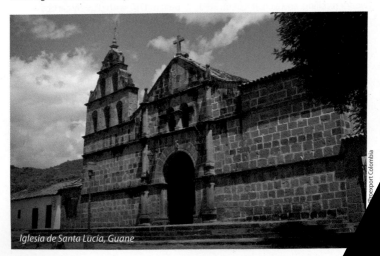

Iglesia de Santa Lucía, Guane

Proexport Colombia

ADDRESSES

🛏 STAY

$ Hotel El Carambolo de Barichara – *Calle 5 # 3-27, Barrio de San Antonio, Barichara. ☎(7) 726 7082. 5 rooms.* Close to the main square, this small hotel occupies a converted colonial house. Five comfortable rooms with spacious baths face an interior courtyard. The Spanish owner is a trained chef and will cook an evening meal if asked; many of his meals are Colombian with a Mediterranean influence. The helpful staff is happy to arrange transfers, confirm flights and facilitate adventure trips.

$ Macondo Guesthouse – *Calle 12 # 7-26, San Gil. ☎(7) 724 4463. www.macondohostel.com. 5 rooms.* This colonial house has been converted to serve as a laid-back hostel. Rooms are basic but clean, and baths are shared. The helpful Australian owner is knowledgeable and can book adventure activities and tours for you. The lovely communal areas include hammocks, cooking and laundry facilities and Wi-Fi. Be sure to book in advance.

$$ Hotel La Cascada – *8km/5mi southwest of San Gil on the road to Socorro.* ⓟ✕🛏 *☎(7) 723 6700. www.hotella cascadasangil.com. 10 rooms.* Comprised of a series of bungalows nestled in a wooded area, this hotel also offers a campsite. Rooms are comfortable but fairly basic, with tiled floors, private baths and TV. **Restaurant Iris** has a large covered outdoor dining area where guests can enjoy international fare. Facilities for ballo, tejo, basketball, volleyball and soccer are also available.

$$ Hotel Posada Campestre – *2km/ 1mi southwest of San Gil on the road to Charalá.* ⓟ✕🛏 Spa *☎(7) 723 8000. www.hotelposadacampestre.com. 720 rooms.* Rooms here fall into two categories: a standard room, with TV, private baths, balconies with sea views; and the Gold rooms, which are all air-conditioned. There's a disco and a popular bar on-site, but if it's outdoor fun you seek, the staff can organize local adventure sports such as rafting, boating, rappelling, paragliding, caving, hiking, horseback riding and paintball.

$$ Mesón del Cuchicute – *1km/.6mi southwest of San Gil on the road to Socorro.* ✕🛏 *☎(7) 724 2041. www.comfenalcosantander.com.co. 78 rooms.* An exceptional value for one's money, this all-inclusive, environmentally conscious resort lodge lies on the outskirts of western San Gil. Family-run, its clean, brick-floored, air-conditioned rooms are amply sized and equipped with TV, mini bar and private balconies. On-site recreation includes a children's playground, Jacuzzi, sauna, gym and game room.

$$$ Hotel Boutique Wassiki Campestre – *Pinchote, 3km/2mi from San Gil toward Socorro.* ⓟ✕🛏 *☎(7) 724 8386. www.hotelwassiki campestre.com. 13 rooms.* Located about a five-minute drive from central San Gil, this nicely appointed boutique-style hotel offers complimentary coffee, a game room, a campsite, and a small pool tucked amid lush gardens with mountain vistas in the distance. Each brightly colored room has a private bathroom, TV and minibar, while the deluxe suite has its own Jacuzzi.

$$$ Hostal Misión Santa Bárbara – *Calle 5 # 9-12, Barichara.* ⓟ Spa *☎(7) 726 7163. www.hostalmisionsanta barbara.info. 31 rooms.* This beautifully renovated Colonial mansion fosters relaxation in its grapevine-covered patio, small pool, and colorful gardens punctuated by artfully hung hammocks. Large, individually decorated rooms are comfortable and clean, but not air-conditioned (the weather here is mild, so air-conditioning is not necessary).

🍴 EAT

$ Cafetería Donde Betty – *Corner Carrera 9 and Calle 12, San Gil. ☎(7) 724 6297.* This pleasant local cafe serves huge breakfasts with great *huevos revueltos* (scrambled eggs); it also offers fruit juices, sandwiches, *arepas* and thirst-quenching fruit shakes and teas throughout the day. It's a great spot for people-watching. **Colombian**.

$ El Maná– *Calle 10 # 9-10, San Gil. No dinner Sun & Mon.* ☎(7) 724 7130. Expect set meals, large portions and excellent quality food in this charming restaurant. Reasonably priced, El Maná is a local favorite for its friendly atmosphere. The chicken stuffed with ham and cheese, and chicken in plum sauce come highly recommended. **Regional Colombian**.

$ Rogelia – *Carrera 10 # 8-09, San Gil.* ☎(7) 724 0823. Favored by backpackers, this little eatery is open only during the daytime. Rogelia is located in a beautiful Colonial building decorated wtih large wooden beams. Local specialties such as *cabrito con pepitorio* (goat) and *carne oreada* (equivalent of beef jerky) abound, and the breakfast is generous. **Regional Colombian**.

$$ Color de Hormiga – *Calle 8 # 8-44, Barichara. Closed Tue.* ☎(7) 726 7156. Arguably the best of Barichara's excellent eateries, Color de Hormiga specializes, as its name suggests, in serving fat-bottomed ants. The food is beautifully presented and varied. The restaurant also offers a number of traditional dishes that contain no insects, along with an extensive wine list and great desserts. **Regional Colombian**.

$$ Restaurante Carnes y Carnes – *Carrera 12 # 8-09, San Gil.* ☎(7) 724 6246. Difficult to find, because the only sign of this restaurant is a hanging banner on the gate, Carnes y Carnes is one of San Gil's most popular, expensive and upscale restaurants. Locals love this place for its large roofed garden with a huge grill at its center. Carefully prepared meats come with rice and potatoes and represent an excellent value. **Colombian**.

$$ Restaurante Vegetariano Saludable Delicia – *Calle 11 # 8-40, San Gil. Closed Sat.* ☎(7) 724 3539. At this vegetarian restaurant, you'll find a set lunch menu available until 2pm and à la carte only thereafter. Healthy, natural and delicious meals are served in a peaceful atmosphere by a helpful and soft-spoken staff. Massage services are also offered here. **Vegetarian**.

$$$ Restaurante Algarabia– *Calle 6 # 10-96, Barichara.* ☎(7) 726 7417. Specializing in traditional Spanish recipes that have been passed down through generations, this new high-end eatery is run by a Spanish man and his Colombian wife. Although it focuses on paella and seafood, the menu includes *tortilla española, pavo de castilla* and *calamares romana*. While the food is great, the service is inconsistent. **Spanish**.

☆RECREATION

San Gil is a fantastic place for rafting, and you can find many tour operators at the entrance to Parque El Gallineral. Tour prices are government controlled, so don't bother shopping around.

Aventura Total – *Calle 7 # 10-27 in front of the Malecón, San Gil.* ☎(7) 723 8888. www.aventuratotal.com.co. This company offers a wide range of adventures and is perhaps best known for its paragliding tours.

Brujula Promotora Turistica – *Carrera 11 # 6-60, in front of Parque El Gallineral.* ☎(7) 723 7000. Good prices and a willingness to do almost anything you want mark this family-run operation.

Colombia Rafting – *Carrera 10 # 7-83, San Gil.* ☎311 283 8647. www.colombiarafting.com. With a focus on safety, this 10-year-old tour operator is one of the better ones in the area. Experienced guides speak English as well as Spanish.

Tierra a la Vista – *Calle 11 # 9-39, interior 4, San Gil.* ☎(7) 724 7347. www.tierraalavista.com.co. Part of the Living Earth Foundation, this non-governmental organization promotes projects that preserve Barichara's cultural heritage.

Planeta Azul – *First floor, Parque El Gallineral center, San Gil.* ☎(7) 724 0000. www.planetaazulcolombia.com. One of the larger organizations of its kind, Planeta Azul offers a variety of activities, from rafting to paintball.

Bucaramanga and Surroundings

Santander

Set in the scenic valley of the Río de Oro, the capital of the Santander department is blessed with a pleasant year-round climate and fresh mountain air that blows in from the Andes. Along with its immediate suburbs, the city forms one of the largest metropolitan areas in the country. Locally known as "Buca," it is both an important commercial hub and a major university town. As most fast-growing cities, it suffers severe peak-hour traffic congestion, which should start easing now that the planned massive public transport system has opened. Packed with all kinds of restaurants, bars and clubs, Bucaramanga is renowned for its active nightlife. It also offers great shopping and a few tourist attractions, its main draw being sights that lie near the city, such as colonial Girón, and farther south, the stunning Chicamocha Canyon.

- ▶ **Population:** 509,918.
- ⚲ **Michelin Maps:** p149 and pp 194–195.
- 🛈 **Info:** Instituto Municipal de Cultura y Turismo, Calle 30 # 26-117, Parque de los Niños. ✆(7) 634 1132. www.bucaramanga turistica.com.
- ⊗ **Don't Miss:** Taking a leisurely walk around Parque García Rovira, at the heart of Bucaramanga's colonial district, then shopping for some great bargains on shoes, one of the local specialties; soaring high as you paraglide above the outskirts of "Buca" in the region of Ruitoque; taking time to enjoy the intact colonial architecture of Girón; savoring a traditional *oblea* wafer with *arequipe* caramel sauce in Floridablanca.

A BIT OF HISTORY

The **Guane People**, who were prevalent all through the eastern part of Santander, inhabited the area around Bucaramanga prior to the arrival of the Spanish. The first Europeans moved into the area in 1622 because of its strategic location at the confluence of two rivers, **Río Oro** and **Río Frío**, but mostly because **gold** had been found around here. In early colonial records, the city

Bucaramanga

© Joel Carillet/iStockphoto.com

191

GETTING THERE

BY AIR - **Palonegro International Airport** (BGA) is located 30km/18mi west of Bucaramanga. Flights are available from Bogatá, Medellín, Cúcuta. A **taxi** (about 5,000 COP) is faster than a local bus into town.

BY BUS - La Teminal de Transportes de Bucaramanga **bus station** lies southwest of town. Buses arrive from Barrancabermeja, Cúcuta, Bogatá, San Gil, Santa Marta and Yopal on paved roads and from Venezuela, Ecuador and Peru as well.

GETTING AROUND

BY PUBLIC TRANSPORTATION - In early 2010 **Metrolínea**, a mass transportation system, began serving Bucaramanga and Floridablanca; it will eventually also serve Piedecuesta and Girón. Consisting of articulated dual carriage buses, the Metrolínea has a standard cost of 1,400 COP per ride, and operates daily 5am–10pm.
📞 7 643 9090; www.metrolinea.gov.co.

BY TAXI - Taxis are metered; minimum fare is about 5,000 COP, which covers most of the city center.

BY BUS - Local buses, other than Metrolínea, cost about 2,000 COP. Outlying towns of Girón and Piedecuesta can be reached by bus.

GENERAL INFORMATION

PERSONAL SAFETY - With a half a million residents, Bucaramanga has its share of dangers. Avoid being out after dark, or keep to well-lit main streets with plenty of people. Guard your personal belongings, and in general be alert to your surroundings.

La Ciudad de Los Parques

Bucaramanga is known as the "City of Parks" for its abundance of green spaces, mostly pleasant little squares or plazas shaded with trees and frequented by various and sundry people, making a nice break from exploring the city. Here is just a small selection of them.

◆ **Parque Centenario**
Between Carrera 18 and Carrera 19 with Calle 31 and Calle 33.

◆ **Parque de los Niños**
Between Carrera 26 and Carrera 27 with Calle 30 and Calle 31.

◆ **Parque de Mejoras Públicas**
Corner of Calle 36 and Avenida Quebrada la Rosita.

◆ **Parque Las Palmas**
Carrera 29 and Calle 44.

◆ **Parque San Pío**
Calle 45 and Carrera 35.

◆ **Parque La Flora**
Calle 57, between Carreras 33 and 36.

was appropriately referred to as **Real de Minas de Bucaramanga**.

Gold mining gradually declined, but Bucaramanga continued to grow and played a significant role in the pre-independence period. One of the town's illustrious sons, General **García Rovira**, became president of the **United Provinces of New Granada** before being executed in 1816 by order of Pablo Morillo (the "Pacifier") during the **Spanish Reconquest**. After independence, some German colonists arrived in the region, led by an engineer named **Geo von Lengerke** (1827-82) who, local legend dictates, is responsible for many European-looking offspring for which Santander is known.

Bucaramanga became the capital of Santander in 1857. The **Thousand Day War** (1899-1902) brought the city to its knees, but it did recover. Today Bucaramanga—an important trading partner with neighboring **Venezuela**—has evolved into a major commercial hub in northeastern Colombia. It is also regarded as a fine academic town, many **universities** having a signific cultural impact on the region.

Parque García Rovira

© Juan Antonio Alonso/Robert Harding

🐾 WALKING TOURS
AROUND PARQUE GARCÍA ROVIRA★

A bustling focal point in Bucaramanga, the old colonial quarter contains several interesting highlights.

Parque García Rovira★

Between Calle 35 and Calle 37 with Carrera 10 and Carrera 11.

Inaugurated in 1897 the park is the ideal place to begin an exploratory walk in this part of town. Its tall palms and plentiful benches scattered around a grassy center are a welcome break from the city's hustle and bustle.

Erected in the middle of the park, the **statue** (1907) of General García Rovira stands as a tribute to this Neogranadine statesman and fervent supporter of independence who was born in Bucaramanga in 1780.

Casa de la Cultura Custodio García Rovira★

Calle 37 # 12-46. ◷*Open Mon–Sat 8am –6pm.* 🐾*Guided tours available.* ✆*(7) 630 2046.*

Cultural events are routinely performed in this character-packed old building. It houses the **Museo Artesanal e Santander** with its collections of ntings and crafts by local artists and erous exhibitions on indigenous e history and Colombian art.

Capilla Nuestra Señora de los Dolores★★

Carrera 10 and Calle 35, on the corner of Parque García Rovira.

A National Heritage Monument, and one of Bucaramanga's key points of interest, this church is the oldest surviving church in town (1750) and the final resting place of the famous Santanderean poet **Aurelio Martínez Mutis** (1885-1954).

Small and unassuming, with its whitewashed walls and exposed rough stones, the church really strikes a different chord for the simplicity of its architecture.

Back in the 19C, during his stay in Bucaramanga (🐾*see below*), Simón Bolívar came here for a private moment of prayer. Today the church no longer serves as place of worship.

Museo Casa de Bolívar★

Calle 37 # 12-15. ◷*Open Mon–Fri 8am– noon, 2pm–6pm.* 🎟*1,000 COP.* ✆*(7) 630 4258.*

History buffs will love the **Museo de Arqueología e Historia de Santander**, fittingly housed in this elegant colonial mansion where **Simón Bolívar** stayed for eight weeks in 1828. On his way to Venezuela, Bolívar had stopped in Bucaramanga to replenish supplies, and from this house, he planned the strategy of his campaigns.

Do not miss the exhibit detailing the history of Bolívar's stay in Bucaramanga.

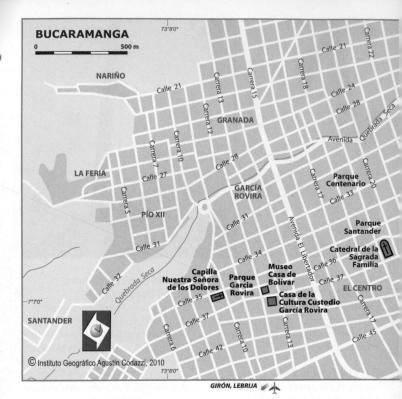

The extensive collection of **Guane arti-facts** and the section devoted to the **Thousand Day War** are of interest.

AROUND PARQUE SANTANDER

Equally as busy as the environs of the Parque García Rovira, this neighborhood is dominated by Bucaramanga's impos-ing cathedral that seems to tower over every other building. If you are in search of great bargains, be sure to duck into the plentiful bric-a-brac stores that can be found around the area.

Parque Santander★

Between Calle 35 and Calle 36 with Carrera 19 and Carrera 20.

Located at the heart of this modern part of town, Parque Santander is a tree-shaded square with a large statue of **Francisco de Paula Santander** (&*see sidebar p205*) right in the middle of it. This emblematic figure of the Colombian independence movement was carved by **Raoul Verlet** (1857-1923), a notable French sculptor, and the elegant **street lamps** (1925) were imported from Paris, giving the park a European feel.

Catedral de la Sagrada Familia★

Calle 36 between Carrera 19 and Carrera 20. &*(7) 642 7708.*
http://arquidiocesisbucaramanga.org.
Overlooking Parque Santander, this Romanesque Revival-style cathedral (1887) is by far the largest and most impressive church in the neighborhood, and one of the principal grand works of the 19C in Bucaramanga.

Placed under the patronage of the **Sacred Family**, whose statues greet visitors as they come in, the building is particularly beautiful at night when the lights enhance the graceful architectur with its sober central façade framed two elegant twin towers.

The interior, which consists of t naves, features fine **stained-

194

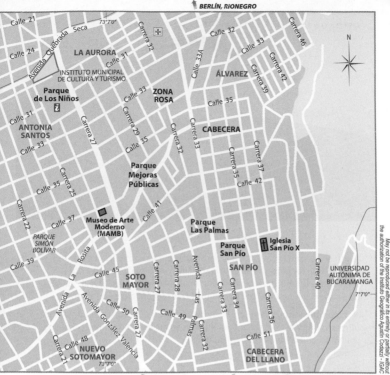

BERLÍN, RIONEGRO

FLORIDABLANCA · PIEDECUESTA · BARICHARA · PARQUE NACIONAL DEL CHICAMOCHA, PARQUE LA FLORA

windows, a collection of pictorial works made by famous local artists such as **Luis Alberto Acuña** and **Oscar Rodríguez Naranjo**, and an exquisite Italian marble **altar**. The ceramic **cupola** was brought directly from Mexico.

ADDITIONAL SIGHTS
Museo de Arte Moderno (MAMB)

Calle 37 # 26-16. ◷*Open Mon–Sat 9am –noon, 3pm–6pm.* ◉*2,000 COP.* ☛*Guided tours available.* ☏*(7) 645 0483.*

Housed in a Neo-Republican building dating from the 1940s, this museum features **temporary exhibits** of works by national artists, with a strong focus on sculpture.

The permanent collection includes *Terrazas de Machu Picchu* by **Eduardo Ramírez Villamizar** (b. 1923), *Observatorio* by Eduardo Estupiñán, and pieces by artists such as Ricardo Gómez Vanegas y Guillermo Espinoza.

Nightlife Scene

Bucaramanga's nightlife is an active, living organism. Besides the **Barrio Cabecera** (◷*see next page*), some of the most popular bars and clubs can be found on the east side of town in the **Zona Rosa** and along the road to the **airport**. These venues include **Babilonia** (*13km/8mi W of Bucaramanga via the road to Palonegro airport;* ☏*7 684 1176*), **Mi País** (*Carrera 34 # 52-07;* ☏*7 647 8021*) and **La Salsa All Star** (*Calle 33 #31-35;* ☏*7 634 8927*). Most clubs start after 11pm and are open until dawn.

Iglesia San Pío X
Carrera 36 # 45-51.

The main attraction of this church, built in 1955, is its paintings by **Oscar Rodríguez Naranjo**, a Santanderean artist born in 1907 in nearby Socorro and best known for his oil paintings on canvas.

Paragliding at Mesa de Ruitoque

Proexport Colombia

Mesa de Ruitoque★★★

South of Floridablanca, this long windward mesa has not only become the regional hub for **paragliding**, but is actually considered Colombia's best training site for this sport. It possesses top launching and landing areas, lots of alternative landing sites, and optimum and consistent flight conditions.

◆ **Colombia Paragliding** (*℘312 432 6266; http://colombiaparagliding.com*) offers everything, from tester tandem rides to the complete course, enabling you to become a licensed paragliding pilot.

Barrio Cabecera
E zone of Bucaramanga, along Carrera 30.
This neighborhood, replete with bars, cafes and nightclubs, has displaced the **Zona Rosa** *(between Calle 33 and Calle 34 with Carrera 31 and Carrera 33)* as a hub for the nightlife of Bucaramanga.

Calle de los Mariachis
Carrera 33 between Calle 37 and Calle 39
Nightclubs with mariachis include El Guitarrón (Carrera 33 # 37-34) and El Sombrero (Carrera 33 #37-15).
This part of the Cabecera district has a distinctly Mexican flavor. If you head here after a certain hour, you will see all of Bucaramanga's **mariachis**, dressed in traditional costumes, coming out to drum up business. A few play on the street, but most perform at nearby clubs and nightclubs every night.

SURROUNDINGS
Bucaramanga's metropolitan area, which is now spreading to Ruitoque *(see sidebar above)* and Palonegro, includes several unexpected highlights.

Floridablanca
◗ *8km/5mi SE of Bucaramanga via Carretera 45.*
Archaeology lovers should know that Floridablanca (Pop. 252,472) is not just another suburb of Bucaramanga.
Just a few blocks from its main plaza stands a piece of great historical significance: a massive boulder known as the **Piedra del Sol**★, decorated with spiral and circlular designs carved by **Guane People** more than 1000 years ago.

Museo Arqueológico Regional Guane★
1st floor, Casa de la Cultura, Carrera 7 # 4-35. ○*Open Mon–Fri 8am–noon, 2pm–6pm.* ▭*1,000 COP.* ⟍*Guided tours available.* ℘*(7) 649 7864.*
This museum is known for its impressive collection of artifacts from the Guane Culture. Founded in 1994 it currently contains some 850 archaeological pieces that include gold objects, skull and skeletal remains, shell ceramics, te tiles, stones, spears, and *pintaderas* (r art) dating from the 8C to the 16C.

Jardín Botánico Eloy Valenzuela★★
○ *1km/.6mi from the main plaza.*
◐ *Open daily 8am–5pm.* ◎ *500 COP.*
℘ *(7) 634 6100.*
Located along the banks of the **Río Frio**, these 7.5ha/18.5 acre gardens feature hundreds of different plant species that are representative of the wet and dry forests of the Santander department. The collections include **orchids, heliconias**, epiphytes and ferns, medicinal plants, bamboos rising skyward, palms, and many others. Close to the river, the gardens are also home to squirrels, tortoises, butterflies, birds, ducks, iguanas, chameleons and armadillos.

Piedecuesta
○ *17km/11mi SE of Bucaramanga via Carretera 45.*
Particularly famous for its **hand-rolled cigars** (◐ *see sidebar below*), furniture carving and jute-weaving, Piedecuesta (Pop. 116,914) numbered only some 500 indigenous people and 50 Spaniards back in 1573. It has now been swallowed up by urban sprawl.

Girón★
○ *9km/6mi SW of Bucaramanga via Carretera 66.*
In this well-preserved colonial suburb (Pop. 135,531) of Bucaramanga, the cobbled streets, horse carts and unhurried atmosphere are solid memories of a time gone by.
Founded in 1631 on the banks of the **Río de Oro**, the sleepy colonial outpost was declared a National Monument in 1963. it is now popular with weekending urbanites, and is a magnet for artists, with an established avant-garde arts scene.
On the town's main plaza, you can't help notice the **Basílica Menor San Juan Bautista**★, whose construction, begun in 1646, was not finished until 1876. Don't miss the **Mansion del Fraile**★ *(Calle 30 # 25-27)*, where Colombia's independence was authorized by the actual signing. The **Parque las Nieves**★ *(Carrera 28)* is a majestic ode to the past, with al architecture; many young Bumanas plan to have their wedding here **chapel** before the *Virgen de las*

Nieves. Head down to the **Malecón** (the riverfront promenade), in particular on a Friday or Saturday evening, to enjoy one of the orchestras usually playing.

EXCURSIONS
Parque Nacional del Cañón del Chicamocha★★ (◐ *see p185*)
○ *54km/34mi SE of Bucaramanga.*

Rionegro
○ *20km/12mi NW of Bucaramanga via Carretera 45.*
A picturesque **coffee town**, Rionegro lies near the **Laguna de Galago** and a lively waterfall. Hiking is good along the old **railway** that once ran between Bucaramanga and Rionegro.

Lebrija
○ *22km/14mi W of Bucaramanga via Carretera 66.*
This town (Pop. 30,984) is famous for its **pineapples**, the source of the annual **Feria de la Piña** in July.

Berlín
○ *35km/22mi NE of Bucaramanga via Carretera 66.*
Nestled in a 3,100m/10,170ft high valley, surrounded by peaks 4,000m/13,123ft tall, this village is a great place to appreciate the dramatic landscapes of the **Eastern Cordillera**.

Tobacco Growing in Santander

You can visit cigar factory shops in the areas of **Piedecuesta** *(Cigarros Chicamocha; Carrera 7 # 5-49;* ℘*7 654 4941; www.cigarroschicamocha. com)* and **Barichara** *(Fabrica de Tabacos Gordelia; Carrera 5 # 0-84;* ℘*7 726 7684; http://gordelia.com).* Every year in mid-August, **Girón** holds a tobacco festival, the Feria Tabacalera *(for more information, contact the tourist office, Calle 25 # 26-64, Girón;* ℘*7 646 1337),* with concerts, a beauty pageant and competitions among the regional growers to show off their best tobacco produce.

ADDRESSES

STAY

$ Kasa Guane – *Calle 49 # 28-21, Bucaramanga. ℰ(7) 657 6960. www.kasaguane.com. 5 rooms.* Called KGB by those in the know, this backpackers hostel was opened by local paragliding fans. Good service and a location in a nice neighborhood make it a wise choice. Dormitories and private rooms, a kitchen and laundry facilities and an Internet cafe add value. Guests also have free access to the gym, pool and tennis courts at a local country club.

$$ Finca Buenos Aires – *1km/.6mi after El Chorro in the direction of Villanueva. ℰ313 262 9664. www.fincabuenos aires.com. 8 rooms.* Built with local Barichara stone, beautiful wood and clay, this traditional century-old property was renovated in 2010. Many rooms have views that include the neighboring towns, and breakfast is included in the rate. Coffee trees, guamos, pomarrosas and fruit trees fill the grounds, while a pool table, complimentary bicycles and a bar provide guests with things to do.

$$$ Hotel Chicamocha – *Calle 34 # 31-24, Bucaramanga.* ⊡✕⊿ℰ(7) 634 3000. www.hotelchicamocha.com. 162 rooms. One of the best hotels in town, Chicamocha is just 30 minutes from the international airport in the middle of a residential area. The 10-floor hotel, part of a Colombian chain, features clean, comfortable rooms that vary in size and style. A steam bath, sauna and gym add to the amenities.

$$$$ Hotel Ciudad Bonita – *Calle 35 # 22-01, Bucaramanga.* ⊡✕ℰ(7) 635 0101. www.hotelciudadbonita.com.co. 65 rooms. Affordable and centrally located, the hotel is convenient to both the airport and the Exhibition and Conference Center. It is also near Parque Santander. Most rooms are small and cooled by fans, but for a small surcharge, bigger rooms with fridges and AC are available. The hotel's **Restaurante Doña Petrona** serves seafood with good views.

$$$$$ Hotel Dann Carlton Bucaramanga – *Calle 47 # 28-83, Bucaramanga.* ✕⊿ℰ(7) 643 1139. *www.dannbucaramanga.com.co. 133 rooms.* This exclusive hotel has a well-maintained air of grandeur. With a rooftop terrace, gorgeous suites and extras like a gym, Jacuzzi and sauna, this place books up fast.

EAT

$$ El Viejo Chiflas – *Carrera 33 # 34-10, Bucaramanga. Closed Sun. ℰ(7) 632 0640.* El Viejo Chiflas focuses on grilled meat, and locals consider the food here to be a gold standard. Be sure to try the *cabrito* (young goat), a speciality in this region. The kitchen uses locally grown fruits and vegetables. **Colombian**.

$$ Restaurante La Carreta – *Carrera 27, # 42-27, Barrio Sotomayor, Bucaramanga. ℰ(7) 643 6680. www.lacarreta.com.co.* Gourmet food at a good value distinguishes this upscale restaurant, which has been going strong for 45 years. **International**.

$$$ Radha Govinda's – *Carrera 34 # 51-95, Cabecera, Bucaramanga. Lunch only. Closed Sun. ℰ(7) 6430 3382.* Healthy vegetarian food in a serene atmosphere holds sway here from 9:30am to 6:30pm. Next door, a shop sells vegetarian ingredients. **Vegetarian**.

$$$ Restaurante Le Bulli Mediterraneo – *Carrera 32 # 48-45, Bucaramanga. ℰ(7) 643 4266. www.lebullicolombia.com.* Avant-garde art and innovative Mediterranean cuisine rule at this casual restaurant, which even has a children's club. **Mediterranean.**

PLAY

Parque Nacional Del Chicamocha – *54km/34mi south of Bucaramanga off Carretera 45 (the road to San Gil). ℰ(7) 657 4400. www.parquenacional delchicamocha.com.* Any bus between San Gil and Bucaramanga goes to this national park in spectacular Chicamocha Canyon. To return, flag down a bus from the road or catch of the minibuses that leave freque from the parking lot.

Norte de Santander

Norte de Santander

Named for one of the key figures in the independence of New Granada from Spain, the Norte de Santander department of northeastern Colombia comprises three distinct geographical regions. The eastern area contains sections of the Andes Mountains. The Catatumbo and Zulia river plains lie to the northwest, and in the south is the Magdalena River Valley. Norte de Santander is also home to the Maracaibo Basin, some desert terrain, and the hottest location in all of South America. The proximity to Venezuela is evident in the local cultural traditions and cuisine, and the department capital of Cúcuta is home to many Venezuelan expatriates. Like most border towns, Cúcuta has a reputation for contraband and smuggling, but is also the location of many important events that helped shape contemporary Colombia. The few tourists who make the journey here are usually en route to or coming from Venezuela, but those who take time to explore the region will discover some real gems, such as colonial Pamplona.

Michelin Maps: p149 and p177.

Info: Corporación Mixta de Promoción de Norte de Santander, Calle 10 # 0-30, Edificio Rosetal, Cúcuta. (7) 571 3395. www.nortedesantander. gov.co. Instituto de Cultura y Turismo de Pamplona, Calle 6 #2-56, Museo Casa Colonial. (7) 568 2043. www.ictp.gov.co.

Don't Miss: A visit to Pamplona's Casa Anzoátegui for a slice of the history of Colombia's independence from Spain; head to Villa del Rosario to wander through the ruins of the Templo Histórico de Cúcuta, where the founding fathers drew up the Constitution; take in the sunset and spend the evening along the Malecón that runs by the Pamplonita River in Cúcuta.

A BIT OF GEOGRAPHY

Norte de Santander is bordered by **Venezuela** to the east, and by the Colombian departments of **Cesar** to the north, and **Santander** and **Boyacá**

Pamplona

Aviatur/Proexport Colombia

199

GETTING THERE

BY AIR - **Camilo Daza International Airport** (CUC) lies on Cúcuta's north side and serves most major Colombian cities, including Bogotá (1hr; 113,000 COP), Cali (3hrs; 231,000 COP), Cartagena (3hrs; 290,000 COP) and Medellín (4hrs; 261,000 COP).

Minibuses marked *El Trigal Molinos* go to Avenida 1 or Avenida 3 in the city center. A **taxi** costs about 10,000 COP. Flights to Venezuela depart from the nearby Venezuelan airport in **San Antonio del Tachira**, southeast of Cúcuta.

BY BUS - Buses run frequently to and from Bogotá (16hrs; 80,000 COP), Bucaramanga (6hrs; 40,000 COP) and Pamplona (2hrs; 12,000 COP). Pamplona's **bus terminal** is half a mile southwest of the main square.

BORDER CROSSINGS

A border town, Cúcuta has crime. Confine outdoor activities to daylight hours. If crossing the border here, be aware of the political situation between Colombia and Venezuela. The border can close suddenly. Check guidelines of your country's foreign travel advisory service (*see sidebar p32*) prior to crossing. The international bridge between Colombia and Venezuela is southeast of Cúcuta. Buses connect many main Colombian cities with Venezuela, and the border crossing is relatively straightforward. Be sure to obtain an **exit stamp** from immigration officials in Colombia before attempting to enter Venezuela, or you will be sent back, and possibly also fined if attempting to re-enter Colombia at a later date.

---

to the south. Within its small territory, Norte de Santander enjoys a huge range of **climates** and variety of **landscapes,** from the rugged peaks of the Cordillera Oriental to wide swaths and smaller patches of desert, cool plateaus, muggy sub-tropical plains and gently sloping verdant hills. The whole region is strongly influenced by neighboring **Venezuela**, as can be seen from its dialects, culture, traditions and food.

A BIT OF HISTORY

Prior to the arrival of the Spanish, Norte de Santander was inhabited by the **Chitareros** (related to the Chibcha-speaking peoples near current day Bogotá) and the **Motilones** (linked to the Carib People). Today the ethnic breakdown of the department includes descendants of the Motilones, the rest of the population being either of white European or mixed descent.

The first conquistadors to explore the region encountered fierce resistance from the indigenous population, as illustrated by the German **Ambrosius Ehinger** (1500-33) who met his end in Chinácota, between Pamplona and Cúcuta, at the hands of the Chitareros.

Both **Hernán Pérez de Quesada** (d. 1544) and **Alfonso Pérez de Tolosa**, brother of the governor of Venezuela, suffered heavy casualties in the 1540s when they led expeditions through the zone. Such retaliatory violence continued over several decades, but the Spanish somehow managed to gradually wear down the indigenous resistance. Cúcuta grew into an important city, along with Pamplona, and as the **independence movement** bore fruit in the 19C, the city played a central role, since it was here that **Gran Colombia** was created during what is known as the **Congress of Cúcuta**, which ran from August to October in 1821.

Today the whole region has grown in importance due to vital commerce with neighboring Venezuela. It also gained notoriety in the 1980s for contraband **smuggling** and **armed groups**. Smuggling is still an issue along this border, and while overall security has improved, the area remains very volatile.

As previously mentioned, checking the political situation with Venezuela before making any plans is strongly advised, since the border may close a *a moment's notice.*

PAMPLONA★★

▶ *74km/46mi SW of Cúcuta and 460km/286mi NE of Bogotá via Carretera 55.*

A delightful town of old churches, narrow streets and bustling commerce, "La Ciudad Patriota" is a worthwhile stopover between Bucaramanga and Cúcuta. Set in the lush **Valle del Espiritu Santo**, at an altitude of 2,200m/7,217ft, it enjoys a cool, average temperature of 16°C/61°F, a pleasant contrast to the oppressive heat in nearby Cúcuta.

A BIT OF HISTORY

Pamplona was originally founded in 1549 by **Pedro de Ursúa** (◐ *see sidebar*) and **Ortún Velasco de Velázquez**. During the colonial era, its importance was equaled only by Bogotá. The independence movement was begun here in 1810 by **Águeda Gallardo**, one of Colombia's proudly fierce female patriots.

In the early days, Pamplona was an important **mining town**, but it has always been best known as a seat of **learning**. Five convents were established here soon after its foundation, and the town swiftly developed into an important religious and political center. The resulting population boom led to construction of churches and homes for the wealthy. Today students and faculty of the **Universidad de Pamplona** make up a significant part of the population. In 1875 a severe **earthquake** destroyed much of Pamplona's original architecture, some of which has been restored and the rest replaced with structures of more modern design.

Today, with more museums than Cúcuta and Bucaramanga combined, Pamplona is a great place to visit for those interested in learning about the history of Norte de Santander.

⬫ WALKING TOUR
AROUND PARQUE ÁGUEDA GALLARDO

Pamplona is eminently walkable. With many of the town's key sights located nearby, there is no better starting point to discover its colonial wonders than the centrally located park, from which colonial Pamplona grew.

Pedro de Ursúa (1526–1561)

In 1560 **Francisco Pizarro** sent a group of explorers into the impenetrable jungles of Peru's upper Amazon to confirm Francisco de Orellana's discoveries and search for the legendary city of El Dorado.

A classic movie directed by Werner Herzog (1972), **Aguirre, the Wrath of God**, features the tragic death of Don Pedro de Ursúa—one of the original founders of Pamplona and the leader of this ill-fated expedition—who was murdered by Lope de Aguirre, his second in command.

◐ To learn more about Ursúa's life and read a fascinating account of the New World in the 1550s, you may want to get a copy of William Ospina's novel **Ursúa**.

Parque Águeda Gallardo★

Between Calle 5 and Calle 6 with Carrera 5 and Carrera 6.

One of the most emblematic highlights of Pamplona, this park was named in honor of **Doña Águeda Gallardo**, whose courageous act of civil disobedience eventually led to Pamplona's independence from Spain—an event re-enacted every year during the **Conmemoración del Grito de Independencia** (◐ *see sidebar opposite page*).

The park sits at the very heart of the original settlement of Pamplona, where once, as legend has it, 38 apple trees grew. Much neglected for a while, this public space is now being renovated by volunteers.

Catedral Santa Clara★★

Calle 6 between Carrera 5 & Carrera 6.

The most important cathedral in Norte de Santander, this austere, massive building with five naves dates from the 16C. Damaged by earthquakes, it had to be rebuilt over the years. Santa Clara was originally constructed in 1584 as the church of the **Convento de Santa**

Museo Casa Anzoátegui

Museo Casa Anzoátegui

Clara de la Concepción, which was founded by Doña María Velasco de Montalvo, the daughter of conquistador **Ortún Velasco**, co-founder of Pamplona. When the **Iglesia Nuestra Señora de las Nieves** was destroyed in the earthquake of 1875, the diocese of Pamplona decided that the convent's church should become the town's new cathedral, a role it still fills today.

Museo Casa Anzoátegui★★

Carrera 6 # 7-48. ⏰*Open Mon–Sat 9am –noon, 2pm–5:30pm.* 💰*1,000 COP.* 📞*(7) 568 0960. www.museoanzoategui. blogspot.com.*

In 1819 one of Bolívar's most famous generals, **José Antonio Anzoátegui**, died in this house at the age of 30, three months after the Battle of Boyacá. This illustrious soldier is credited for having played a major role in the victory, and a state in northeast Venezuela is named after him.

Turned into a museum, the restored mansion exhibits various objects relating to this important chapter of Colombia's history, and houses the city's archives, covering the colonial and Republican periods from 1574 until 1900.

Plazuela Almeyda

Calle 9 and Carrera 5.

This elegant square was named post-humously to honor two brothers, **Ambrosio** and **Vicente Almeyda**, who created a guerrilla army to confront **Pablo Morillo**'s Spanish forces during the **Spanish Reconquest** in 1817. A striking obelisk was erected in their memory in 1910.

Casa del Mercado★★

Calle 6 between Carrera 4 and Carrera 5.

This market house was constructed in the southeast corner of Parque Águeda Gallardo in 1920 to provide a much needed meeting place where daily produce could be sold. It was built on the site of an old Jesuit school dating to 1622, giving this spot a wealth of history.

Associated with the Declaration of Independence of Pamplona, **Francisco Soto Montes de Oca** held a meeting here on July 31, 1810, in which he shared the news of the Revolution of July 20 in Bogotá.

The **Independence Act of Pamplona** was signed here, a document of which the city is justly proud.

Convento Santa Clara

Calle 6 between Carrera 3 & Carrera 4.

Located on the site of the former 16C Clarissas convent, the **Capilla del Niño Huerfanito** houses the much-revere statue of the infant Jesus called *El H fanito,* which miraculously surviv 17C earthquake.

Museo Casa Colonial★

Calle 6 # 2-56. ⏲Open Tue–Sun 8am–noon, 2pm–6pm. ⬛1,000 COP. ☁Guided tours available. ☏(7) 568 2043.

This picturesque 17C adobe house—one of the oldest in Pamplona—was turned into a museum. Its rich, eclectic collection includes fossils, coins, some colonial art, weapons and various objects from the Thousand Day War and the independence period. Don't miss the section dedicated to the indigenous people of Norte de Santander, with some **pre-Columbian pottery** and artifacts from the **Motilones** and **Tunebos**.

Ermita de las Nieves

Carrera 3 and Calle 5.

Pamplona's first church (1550) is a humble place of worship, which has kept its original **adobe altar**.

Museo Arquidiocesano de Arte Religioso★

Carrera 5 # 4-87 Centro. ⏲Open Wed–Mon 10am–noon, 3pm–5pm. ⬛1,000 COP. ☁Guided tours available. ☏(7) 568 1814. http://arquipamplona.org.

A must see while in town, this museum contains all kinds of religious artifacts made of gold and silver, sculptures, vestments, woodcarvings and paintings by renowned artists such as Antonio Acero de la Cruz, Bartolomé de Figueroa, Alonso Hernández de Heredia and the greatest painter of the colonial period, maestro **Gregorio Vásquez de Arce y Ceballos**.

Museo de Arte Moderno Ramírez Villamizar★★

Calle 5 # 5-75, Casa de las Marías. ⏲Open Tue–Sun 9am–noon, 2pm–6pm. ⬛2,000 COP. ☁Guided tours available. ☏(7) 568 2999. http://mamramirezvillamizar.com.

Declared a National Monument in 1975, this 450-year-old mansion is definitely one of the best examples of civil Colonial architecture in Pamplona.

Conmemoración del Grito de Independencia

Commemorating the day when Pamplona rebels declared their independence from Spain in 1810, this festival is held during the two weeks prior to **July 4** every year. While such celebrations take place all over the country, Pamplona is known for hosting some of the best ones, and for year-round planning to live up to this reputation. During the festivities celebrating of the "Cry of Independence," which include various processions, bullfighting, and music and dancing, the town is literally awash with revolutionary spirit.

Courtyard, Museo de Arte Moderno Ramírez Villamizar

Aviatur/Proexport Colombia

The museum features an extensive collection of paintings and sculptures by **Eduardo Ramírez Villamizar** (1922-2004), regarded as one of Colombia's major artists. The exhibit offers considerable insight into his development from Expressionism to geometric abstract sculpture. Villamizar's work has often been described as an artistic response to the agitated political situation in Colombia.

Casa de Doña Águeda Gallardo★

Carrera 6 and Calle 5.
No visit to Pamplona is complete without a stop here, at the former house of **Doña María Águeda Gallardo Guerrero de Villamizar** (1751-1840).
In the 19C this intelligent, well-educated and strong-willed woman of almost 60 years of age became the leader of Pamplona's **independence movement**.
On June 29, 1819, defying the local Spanish governor's ban on celebrating San Pedro Day, she incited the townsfolk to overthrow him. Threatened with arrest, Doña María was smuggled out of town for her own safety. However, her removal was not the end of the matter. Doña María's act of disobedience set in motion the uprising that occurred on July 4 of the same year, when the townsfolk arrested the governor, called a town meeting and formed a **revolutionary junta** that took control of the city. These events actually occurred before the historical uprising in Bogotá of July 20, so Pamplonans are eager to remind visitors that their city was indeed first in the important series of uprisings against the colonial rule of Spain.

Iglesia Nuestra Señora de las Nieves★

Carrera 7 and Calle 5.
Built in 1557, the original church was largely destroyed in the earthquake of 1875. Some elements salvaged from the former **Convento de Santo Domingo** have been incorporated into the present structure. Inside, a statue of *Señor Caído* and a side altar are reminders of the colonial times.

Ermita del Señor del Humilladero ★★

Calle 2 between Carrera 7 and Carrera 8.
In New Granada it was common to find small roadside oratories at the entrance and exit of each town, so that travelers could stop there and pray. In Pamplona, one of these oratories was built on the left side of the road that led to Chopo, also known as Pamplonita. Around 1605, it was replaced by a larger structure. Today, this picturesque, whitewashed church, sitting at the entrance of a **cemetery**, is regarded by the locals as one of their most beautiful sanctuaries. It offers a fine **view**★ of the city.
Inside, a realistic depiction of Christ is known as **Cristo del Humilladero**★. This Spanish sculpture dates from the first half of the 16C. Also note another fine piece of art by Juan Bautista de Guzman (1595) featuring two thieves.

CÚCUTA★

⊙ *585km/364mi NE of Bogotá. 75km/47mi NE of Pamplona via Carretera 55.*
Cúcuta (Pop. 585,543) is the most populous city in the region, and an undeniable center of trade. Known as "the Pearl of the North," it lies only 16km/10mi west of the border with Venezuela.

A BIT OF HISTORY

Founded in 1733 by **Juana Rangel de Cuellar**, the capital of the department of Norte de Santander was the scene of major historical events that eventually led to the creation of Colombia as it is known today.
While many border towns tend to lack charm, Cúcuta has a number of pleasant **parks** and makes good use of trees to moderate the otherwise oppressive heat, the average temperature here being about 29°C/84°F.
A Venezuelan engineer named **Francisco de Paula Andrade Troconis** (1840-1915) actually designed most of the green spaces after the **earthquake** of 1875, which did plenty of damage here, but evidence of it is now hard to detect.
Rapid growth since the 1960s has se the city develop urban sprawl. Today

"City without Borders" has a mix of Venezuelan and Colombian inhabitants.

SIGHTS
Catedral de San José★★

Avenida 5 between Calle 10 and 11.
In spite of the cathedral's almost total destruction in the earthquake of 1875, the **Capilla de San José,** on one of its sides, survived and served as a refuge for the Liberals against the Conservative threat during the troubles of the early period of the Republic.

The cathedral is largely Romanesque in style and contains a wealth of historical and ecclesiastical artifacts of interest, such as **oil paintings**★★ by **Salvador Moreno** (1874-1953). The cathedral, located on the **Parque Santander,** is curious in that it has three doors at the front, supposed to represent the various phases of the building's existence.

Torre del Reloj

Calle 13 # 3-67. ○*Open Mon–Fri 7:30am –noon, 2pm–6pm.* ●*Guided tours available.* ℘*(7) 571 6689.*
This example of Republican architecture (early 20C) with its distinctive **clock tower** that plays the national anthem on the hour, houses art exhibits.

Battle of Cúcuta
February 28, 1813

At a time when the **Cúcuta Valley** was under **Royalist control,** Bolívar and his 400 men launched their offensive from the left bank of the **Magdalena River**. After a few hours of fierce fighting, they subdued the troops of Spanish general **Ramon Correa,** killing 20 Spanish soldiers and injuring 40.

More than a great strategic achievement, the Battle of Cúcuta was a highly symbolic victory in that it boosted the morale of **Simón Bolívar**'s troops en route to Caracas, and paved the way for his **liberation campaign of Venezuela** from the Spaniards.

SURROUNDINGS
Villa del Rosario★

▶*5km/3mi SE of Cúcuta via Autopista Internacional Vía San Antonio.*
Founded in 1750 by **Don Asencio Rod-riguez** on the **Río Táchira**, this town (Pop. 69,991) is located on the road to the border with Venezuela. Here, the **Congress of Cúcuta** met on August

Francisco de Paula Santander (1792-1840)

Santander was born in an upper-class **Creole** family, whose money came from cacao, sugarcane and coffee plantations. He was a law student in 1810 when the independence movement in South America commenced. He eagerly joined the fight against the Spanish, and by 1812, had risen in rank to captain. In 1813, Bolívar promoted him to major and gave him responsibility for defense of the **Cúcuta Valley**. Defeated by Royalist forces, he fled to Venezuela. He was promoted to colonel in 1816, and served on Bolívar's staff in the Casanare region. Bolívar then promoted him to general. Crossing the Andes with Bolívar, he played a key role in the **Battle of Boyacá**, and was rewarded with a promotion to division general.

As Bolívar traveled to fight for independence, Santander was left in charge as effective vice-president. He encouraged free trade and sent missions abroad, resulting in the recognition of **Gran Colombia** by the US (1822) and Great Britain (1825). Santander found the large Republic of Gran Colombia unwieldy, and his first loyalty was always to New Granada (Colombia), believing that Ecuador and Venezuela would eventually split off from Gran Colombia. He found himself increasingly at odds with Bolívar, who wanted to unify most or all of South America, using Colombian troops and funds to do so. He is remembered for his long and bitter disputes with Bolívar after independence.

Templo Histórico de Villa del Rosario, El Parque Grancolombiano

Aviatur/Proexport Colombia

30, 1820, to draft the **Constitution** of **Gran Colombia**.

El Parque Grancolombiano★
8km/5mi along the Autopista Internacional Vía San Antonio.
This historic complex encompasses the ruins of **Templo Histórico de Villa del Rosario**, a church destroyed by the 1875 earthquake. The founding fathers held sessions here to agree on the final version of the bill. Only the dome has been reconstructed. The park includes other important historical landmarks.

Casa de la Bagatela
Open Mon–Fri 7:30am–noon, 2pm–6pm, Sat 7:30am–2pm. 3,000 COP. (7) 570 6396.
Also known as the **Casa de Gobierno**, the building served as a base for the executive power in 1821. Originally two stories, it was mostly destroyed in the earthquake of 1875.

The **Tamarindo Histórico** is a tamarind tree where the editors of the constitution liked to rest in the shade after their long meetings. This tree is still standing today. For inspiration, take a rest here, just as Colombia's forbears did.

Casa Natal del General Santander
Open daily 8am–noon, 2pm–6pm. Guided tours available. (7) 570 0265.
Dedicated to the period of the independence campaigns and the contribution made then and later by **Francisco de Paula Santander** (see sidebar p205), his reconstructed birthplace became a National Monument in 1959 and museum in 1971. It includes some Santander's personal belongings, as his sword and uniform.

Some of Cúcuta's Monuments

- **Monumento Cristo Rey**
Avenida 4 with Calle 19. The best **views**★ of Cúcuta can be obtained from this hill, topped by a 12m/40ft high statue of Christ. Artist: Marco León Mariño (1946).

- **Columna Bolívar**
Barrio Loma de Bolívar. A 6m/20ft-high column crowned by a bronze sphere, commemorating the Battle of Cúcuta. Artist: Pedro Tobías Vega (1923).

- **Columna de Padilla**
Barrio El Contento. A tribute to Colombian admiral José Padilla's 1823 victory in the Battle of Lake Macaraibo. Artist: unknown (1923).

- **Monumento Al Indio Motilon**
Across from the bus station. An homage to the indigenous Motilones People. Artist: Hugo Martínez (1968).

ADDRESSES

STAY

If you stay in Cúcuta overnight, pick a hotel at least five blocks (preferably more) away from the Terminal de Transportes. Many of the lodgings in this red-light district are either brothels or rooms rented by the hour, and are not safe.

$ Hotel Amaruc – *Av. 5 # 9-73, Cúcuta. (7) 571 7625. 40 rooms.* A mid-range hotel overlooking the city's central square, the Amaruc is also close to Parque Santander and the cathedral. All rooms have a TV, desk and phone; some have fans, while others offer air-conditioning.

$ Hotel El Alamo – *Calle 5 # 6-68, Pamplona.* (7) 568 2137. 30 rooms. If you're watching your pennies, the El Alamo is one of the better low-budget options in town. Closet-size yet clean rooms all have TV and private bathrooms. You'll have to plan your showers here; hot water is available only at certain times of the day (between 9am and 6pm at the time this was written).

$$ Cariongo Plaza Hotel – *Corner of Carrera 5 and Calle 9, Plazuela Almeyda, Pamplona.* (7) 568 1515. http://cariongoplazahotel.com. 81 rooms. Housing one of the town's few nightclubs, this property could do with a facelift; the decor in the club is far brighter than that of the hotel. Nonetheless, this is a good, reliable hotel with 24-hour room service and a heated pool. All rooms have TV, but the bathrooms are mostly cold water only.

$$ Hotel Bolivar – *Av. Demetrio Mendoza, in the direction of San Luis, Cúcuta.* (7) 576 0764. www.hotel-bolivar.com. 83 rooms. Though the Bolivar is located close to the airport and within an easy walk of restaurants, stores and a small shopping mall, you'll have everything you need—including three pools and two restaurants—right on the property. Standard hacienda-style rooms come with Wi Fi and two

twins or one king bed; refurbished superior rooms have two double beds and upgrade with a work desk and LCD TV.

EAT

$ La Mazorca – *Av. 4 # 9-67, Cúcuta.* (7) 571 1800. This lovely little budget restaurant offers traditional *comida criolla* (Creole food) and a good choice of wines. Dine in a sunny, serene courtyard bedecked with hanging baskets of flowers, saddles and the kind of vessels that Antioquians once used to transport their goods to and from the market. **Colombian**.

$$ El Palacio Chino – *Calle 6 # 7-32, Pamplona. Closes 8pm.* (7) 568 1666. While the spartan interior could hardly be compared to a palace, this restaurant nonetheless dishes up creative Colombian interpretations of Chinese food at reasonable prices. Noodle dishes, steamed vegetables, sweet-and-sour options and rice dishes prevail, along with some intriguing fusions of Chinese and Colombian cuisine. **Chinese**.

$$ Piero's Pizza – *Calle 5A # 8B-67, Pamplona. No lunch Sun.* (7) 568 1964. http://domains-40.com/amhoiu4fikmium/pieros_ie.htm. A mid-priced pizzeria, Pierro's has been run by an Italian family for more than 20 years and enjoys a large following among the local student population. Generous portions of pizza are served here with your choice of a selection of 150 different toppings. There is also a branch in Cúcuta *(Avenida 3E # 7-38B)*. **Italian**.

$$ Punto Cero – *Av. 0 # 15-60, Cúcuta. Open 24 hours.* (7) 573 0153. This restaurant, which is named for its address, provides typical Colombian food such as *bandeja paisa* (a complex and time-consuming Antioquian dish made with beef, beans, chorizo, plantains, fried eggs and chicharrones) and *sancocho* (a traditional stew). In this friendly place, the attentive staff do their best to make you feel comfortable and at home. **Colombian.**

Tierra Paisa—the lands that encompass Medellín, its surrounding rural areas and the Zona Cafetera—is blessed with fertile, sweeping terrain characterized by banana plantations, coffee fields, dramatic valleys and soaring volcanoes. Sleepy colonial villages seemingly stuck in time provide a stark contrast to the sophisticated urban chic and ultra-sleek modernity of Medellín, the prosperous capital of Antioquia. As the center of Paisa Country's cultural scene, Medellín boasts a long-standing patrimony of the arts, finding expression in innumerable theaters, orchestras, operatic companies, ballets and comedy clubs. Having emerged from darker years of conflict, Medellín has been reborn as one of the nation's most progressive and safest cities, and has taken its place again in the global community.

Highlights

1 Marvel at **Medellín**'s spectacular array of urban outdoor art, iconic landmark buildings and space-age structures, all symbols of the city's rebirth (p213)

2 Order a famous specialty called **La Bandeja Paisa**—a stomach-busting plate of grilled steak, fried pork rind, rice, red beans, avocado, fried plantains, fried egg, *arepa* and chorizo—in the town of **Santa Fé de Antioquia** (p239)

3 Ride a horse through scenic trails lined with coffee fields, banana palms and macadamia trees in the bird-rich rural idyll of the **Zona Cafetera** (p251)

4 Explore the snow-capped peaks, glacial lakes and misty forests of the magnificent **Parque Nacional Natural Los Nevados** (p257), home of the páramo hummingbird.

5 Visit the **Museo del Oro Quimbaya** (p263) in the coffee-production hub of Armenia, and learn about this fascinating pre-Columbian culture that produced exquisite gold artifacts and anthropomorphic pottery.

Paisa Country

Sixteen Colombian departments enjoy the best weather conditions for growing coffee plants. The most representative are Antioquia, Valle del Cauca, Caldas, Risaralda and Quindío. The last three form a triangle within Paisa terrain that makes up what is referred to simply as the "Coffee Region." Known by the locals as **Eje Cafetero** and by Colombian tourists as **Zona Cafetera**, this particular area is characterized by folds of tufted coffee fields dotted with *fincas* (small holdings of land) around the main coffee-producing towns of **Manizales** (Caldas), **Pereira** (Risaralda) and **Armenia** (Quindío).

Unknown even to native Colombians until the mid-2000s, the "Coffee Region" is now one of the country's fastest up-coming tourist destinations. It is wholly dedicated to Colombia's beloved bean, with a myriad of attractions designed to entertain and inform. Visitors can learn about crop yields, pick coffee plants and sample an array of coffee varieties at a host of traditionally-run working coffee farms or at the Parque Nacional del Café, a theme park with a coffee focus.

Paisa Country is rich in **outdoor** pursuits, from hiking, birding, river fishing and kayaking to zip-lining through rainforest canopies and mountain biking. It makes an excellent base from which to explore one of Colombia's most exceptional national parks, the resplendent **Parque Nacional Natural Los Nevados**, and discover the wax-palm-studded terrain of scenic Valle de Cocora, home of Colombia's majestic national tree.

The region is also known for its traditional **architecture**, particularly its *bahareque* houses made from simple bamboo (*guadua*) and mud, an ancestral technique adopted by the first Spanish settlers, inspired by pre-Columbian building practices.

MEDELLÍN AND THE INNER NORTHWEST

Because of its unique cultural, natural, urban and architectural characteristics, Colombia's "coffee cultural landscape" is presently on the **UNESCO** World Heritage Site **tentative list**, with hopes for ratification by 2011.

Paisa People

By the 18C almost all of the Paisa Country's indigenous peoples had disappeared. They had fought hard, but were no match for the conquistadors who first claimed the territory, and then enforced slavery. Today, perhaps more than in any other part of Colombia, the cultural identity and ethnic makeup of Spanish settlers left a powerful legacy.

Arriving from the Basque region of Northern Spain during the 17C and 18C, the colonizers set about establishing small homesteads in what is now eastern Antioquia—a mountainous area similar to that of their homeland. These pioneers began to shape the character of the region, introducing a robust work ethic and developing close-knit, conservative communities with a formidable settler's drive.

Today, Paisa people are the so-called "Texans of Colombia" (the Spanish *paisano* means "countryman"). Proud, resolute, resourceful and self-sufficient, they have become synonymous with strong family values and hard work.

Medellín★★★ and Surroundings

Antioquia

Nestled in a valley surrounded by the majestic ranges of the Cordillera Central, the "City of Eternal Spring" is the pride of Paisa Country. Capital of the department of Antioquia and second-most populated city in Colombia, Medellín has undergone a dramatic transformation that has helped consign a lingering reputation for drug cartels and violence firmly to the past. Today this clean, green and prosperous town is a cosmopolitan center of culture, buzzing with potential and a stellar example of social urbanism. Part of Medellín's mammoth regeneration, its spectacular integrated transportation system was a major factor in reshaping entire districts. It was an important dynamo that powered sweeping societal changes and made this beautiful, intriguing city a desirable tourist destination, at long last.

▶ **Population:** 2,219,861.

Michelin Maps: p209, p217 and p225.

Info: Tourist information points (PITs) at the Convention Center on Plaza Mayor, Calle 41 # 55-80; at the Arrivals Hall of Aeropuerto José María Córdova and Aeropuerto Olaya Herrera; at Cerro Nutibara, Calle 30A # 55-64. ℰ (4) 232 4022. www.medellin.travel and www.guiaturisticade medellin.com.

Don't Miss: A stroll along the Paseo Peatonal Carabobo, a cobblestone pedestrian walkway with the historical charm; marvel at homespun artist Fernando Botero's rounded sculptures in the Plaza de Las Esculturas; browse the trendy boutiques and upscale cafes in Poblado, Medellín's uber-swank address.

A BIT OF HISTORY
The Beginnings
The **Aburrá Valley**, then peopled by Yamesíes, Niquías, Nutabes and Aburraes, was discovered by Spanish explorer **Jerónimo Luis Téjelo** in 1541, but the first actual settlement, named **San Lorenzo de Aburrá**, was established by **Francisco Herrera y Campuzano** in 1616 on the site of present-day Parque El Poblado. In 1675, by order of the

Medellín's urban train and Palacio de la Cultura Rafael Uribe Uribe

Proexport Colombia

GETTING THERE

BY AIR - **José María Córdova** (MDE), Medellín's international airport (4 562 2828), lies 35km/22mi southeast of the city center, near Rionegro. Avianca has regularly scheduled shuttle flights from **Bogotá**. Serving destinations within Colombia, the smaller **Aeropuerto Olaya Herrera** (EOH) (4 365 6100) is situated next to the southern bus terminal (see BY BUS, below).

Buses depart the international airport and stop behind Hotel Nutibara (6,000 COP). **Taxis** to the city center take about 30min (48,000 COP).

BY BUS - Medellín has two bus terminals. Buses serving the country's north, east and southeast arrive at the **Terminal de Norte** (4 230 8514) 3km/1.8mi north of the city center: Baranquilla (14hrs; 65,000 COP), Bogota (9hrs; 50,000 COP), Cartagena (13hrs; 65,000 COP), Santa Fe de Antioquia (2hrs; 9,000 COP) and Santa Marta (16hrs; 75,000 COP). Buses from the west and south come into **Terminal del Sur** (4 361 1499), 4km/2.5mi southwest of the city center, and require a short taxi ride (4,000 COP): Armenia (6hrs; 18,000 COP), Cali (9hrs; 45,000 COP) and Manizales (5hrs; 85,000 COP).

GETTING AROUND

BY PUBLIC TRANSPORTATION - Clean, easy and efficient, Medellín's **integrated transportation system** consists of **diesel buses**, and modern commuter **trains** (metro) running mostly on ground level but also on elevated tracks through the city center operating Mon–Sat 4:30am–11pm and Sun 5am–10pm, and 10-person **cable cars** (metrocable) running Mon–Sat 4:30am–11pm and Sun 9am–10pm. 1,550 COP basic ticket price (includes one metrocable ride). (4) 510 9030. www.metrodemedellin.org.co (see online map). The 25 metro stations launched in 1995 will number 34 by the end of 2010. **Line A** departs from

Medellín's modern metro

Proexport Colombia

Itagüí to Niquía, while **Line B** goes from San Antonio to San Javíer. **Line K** begins on Acevedo Station on Metro Line A, and continues uphill, with a cable-car service ending in Santo Domingo Savio. **Line J** starts in the San Javíer Station and goes through Juan XXIII and Vallejuelos to the La Aurora district, and is also a cable car. **Line L** operates from Santo Domingo Savio and continues farther uphill to El Tambo in Arví Park near Guarne (serving tourists desiring to travel to the lake, again by cable car). In 2010, expansion works began on Line A to add an intermediate station near Calle 67 Sur, with the final station close to Calle 77 Sur. Santo Domingo Savio— now one of the metro's busiest stations—was once considered to be a dangerous no-go area. Today, due entirely to the transport network, it is well-traveled and fully integrated with the rest of the city.

BY BUS - The city is well served by buses, with most routes starting on Avenida Oriental and Parque Berrio (see opposite for hours).

BY TAXI - If you must take a taxi, have your hotel call the cab and get the taxi number in advance; take only the taxi called. Taxis charge based on a **meter** (look at the meter for the standard minimum fare when you get in).

USEFUL NUMBERS
Metropolitan Police: 112

Queen of Austria, it was renamed **Villa de Nuestra Señora de la Candelaria de Medellín**. As the town established itself as a major player at the regional level, it finally became the departmental seat of Antioquia in 1826, a status that Santa Fé de Antioquia had maintained since 1813.

Industrial Expansion

In the 19C Medellín was already a dynamic town, exporting gold, then coffee. After the Thousand Day War (1899-1902), it was the first Colombian city to fully embrace the **Industrial Revolution**. **Railways** were built, which helped the export business to expand, and the creation of **universities** and institutions of higher learning set the frame for a city oriented toward the arts and culture. This period saw the **textile sector** flourish. Medellín soon was acclaimed as the fashion capital of South America.

Out of Darkness

Yet, despite the hard-working ethics and values of its Paisa people, Medellín's industrial growth was severely hampered by drug cartels. By the 1980s **Pablo Escobar** (1949-93), the son of a peasant farmer in the rural suburbs of Medellín, controlled roughly 80 percent of all cocaine shipments entering the US. He was responsible for the killing of three Colombian presidential candidates. Bombings and shoot-outs were commonplace. After brief imprisonment, escape and 16 months on the run, Escobar was killed in a gun battle in 1993. His death marked the end of a violent era, and signified a turning point for the city of Medellín.

Plaza Mayor Medellín
Proexport Colombia

EL CENTRO★★★

There is no better way to see **Downtown Medellín** than on foot, given that the city can be dissected into neat, manageable walkable sections, each with plenty to see and explore.

🔊WALKING TOURS

1 LA ALPUJARRA★

Start in Downtown's **financial and administration district** to get a feel for Medellín's modern-day renaissance. This area is testament to the city's successful urban transformation and push for international tourism and business. Around Medellín's Convention Center, where you will begin your walk, you'll see a succession of **corporate headquarters**, **municipal offices**, departmental **government buildings** and original **urban spaces**. These architectural gems form an important part of the city's new character. They aren't just works of art, they are symbols of Medellín's bright new era. Many are part of the **Empresas Publicas de Medellín** (EPM Group), an integrated utilities company providing electricity, gas and water services for the city.

Plaza Mayor Medellín

Calle 41 # 55-80. ℘(4) 261 7200. www.plazamayor.com.co.
Both a **Convention Center** and **Exhibition Hall**, this huge state-of-the-art complex is at the heart of the cutting-edge Alpujarra district. Inaugurated in 2005, it was built in a bid to attract major national and international fairs, conventions and exhibits, an unthinkable concept not so long ago when Medellín had the sad designation as Colombia's "homicide capital." Today Plaza Mayor houses major events such as **Colombiamoda**, the country's most important annual fashion trade show.

Teatro Metropolitano de Medellín José Gutiérrez Gómez

Calle 41 # 57-30. ℘(4) 232 2858. www.teatrometropolitano.com.
Home to the prestigious **Medellín Philharmonic Orchestra**, the city's main

Sergio Poroger/Proexport Colombia

Parque Biblioteca España

A City Reborn

In recent years Medellín has effected a dramatic turnaround, restoring hope and pride in its people. The city owes much to former Colombian president **Alvaro Uribe**, himself a Paisa, whose pledge to crack down on crime during his two consecutive mandates was instrumental in freeing Medellín from the legacy of Pablo Escobar. It also owes much to the vision of former mayor **Sergio Fajardo Valderrama**, a US-educated math professor and son of an architect with an evangelical enthusiasm for his hometown. During his 2004-2007 tenure, he invested in civil commitment through integrative urban development and spearheaded Medellín's rebirth under the inspirational banner "From Fear to Hope."

Less than two decades after Escobar's death, Medellín is a city transformed. With its state-of-the-art transportation system and architectural splendor, the city is enjoying a new era of relative safety and security. It still faces some very real challenges, as hidden dark forces remain and serve as a powerful reminder of the evils of the past. Yet Medellín is indeed a thriving metropolis and a flourishing center of academic and medical excellence, home to more than 30 universities and numerous pioneering hospitals and clinics. The city boasts considerable sophistication, with its luxury hotels and classy restaurants, snazzy bars, high-end boutiques, street art, plush galleries and antique dealers. In typical Paisa style, Medellín's inhabitants are fiercely proud of their new improved metropolis and its regeneration ongoing. As of April 2010, there were 124 sleek high rises under construction in Medellín, including 42 at the blueprint stage, outpacing all other major Colombian cities. A large number of international conglomerates have a presence in or around Medellín, among them Phillip Morris, Levi Strauss, Renault, Toyota, Kimberly Clark and Mitsubishi.

Among the star features of Medellín's urban rebirth are five enormous **library parks** *(two additional ones are currently under construction: San Cristóbal and 12 de Octubre)* that were designed by Colombia's best architects. They are strategically located in some of the most disadvantaged sectors where educational, cultural and public spaces as well as basic services are lacking. Perhaps the most iconic example is **Parque Biblioteca España**★★ *(Carrera 33B # 107A-101;* ⏱*open Mon–Sat 9am–8pm, Sun & holidays 10am–4pm; ☎4 385 7598; www.reddebibliotecas.org.co),* an eye-catching trio of buildings (Giancarlo Mazzanti, 2007) that look like giant black boulders jutting out from a hillside slope in the **Santo Domingo Savio** neighborhood. This structure of exemplary architecture houses a library, an auditorium, an art gallery, computer rooms and a day care center.

1,634-seat theater is a striking redbrick building with exposed girder work and wide, central steps.

Since it opened in 1987, it has played an active role in developing local talent through its work with schools and colleges, while offering a first-class, wide-ranging schedule of events.

Edificio Inteligente de Empresas Públicas★★

Carrera 58 # 42-125.

A model of smart technology, with futuristic, high-tech features and six distinctive towers, this palm-flanked building sits on an expansive green plot and is renowned for its multi-colored lighting after dark.

An advanced architectural design, the building's **Auditorio Himerio Pérez López** (*4 380 6960; www.fundacionepm.org.co*) is housed in a giant standalone cube to the side of the building.

Parque de los Pies Descalzos★★

Carrera 58 and Calle 42A.

This "barefoot park" is yet another striking urban space. The public plaza was designed to offer visitors a number of atmospheric texture zones.

Slip off your shoes to stroll through sandbars to a peaceful **Zen garden**, gently cascading **pools**, **bamboo forest** and water **fountains**. Several cafes overlook this fine city landmark—a popular venue for orchestral performances and events year-round.

Puerta Urbana★

In the corner of the park, look out for this quirky "urban door," a 9m/30ft cascading water sculpture adorned with lights at night that symbolizes the "door being always open" to visitors.

Museo Interactivo Empresas Públicas de Medellín

Carrera 57 # 42-139. Guided tours (2hr) Tue–Fri 8am–1pm, 3pm–6pm, Sat noon–6pm, Sun & public holidays 10am–5:30pm. 6,000 COP, child 4,000 COP. (4) 380 6950. *www.museointeractivoepm.org.co.*

With 200 interactive gadgets and exhibits spread across four distinct zones, this highly entertaining museum has managed to transform electricity and water treatment—a potentially dull topic—into a fun, educational field trip centered on scientific, technological and environmental themes.

Centro Administrativo La Alpujarra José María Córdova★

Between Calle 42 and Calle 44 with Carrera 52.

Home to both provincial and city governments, this impressive complex occupies two identical buildings separated by a huge, open plaza in which

Water fountains, Parque de los Pies Descalzos

ner/Proexport Colombia

Plaza de Cisneros
© Sarah Woods/Michelin

an attractive sculpture by legendary Colombian artist Rodrigo Arenas Betancur entitled **Monumento a la Raza** curves upward to the sun.

Estación Antiguo Ferrocarril de Antioquia

Carrera 52 # 43-31. ✕ 🕐 *Open Mon–Fri 8am–5:30pm.* ✆ *(4) 380 0733.*

After such a succession of contemporary architectural statements in clean, concrete design, the completely restored railway station of the **Ferrocarril de Antioquia** is a pleasant anachronism in the urban landscape.

Started in 1870 the construction of this now defunct railway signaled a new era of industrial growth for Medellín and the department of Antioquia.

The station's traditional central courtyard contains an antique **steam locomotive** as a reminder of the building's former function. Today the station houses public agencies and private businesses, together with a cafe.

Plaza de Cisneros★★

Carrera 54 # 44-48.

Also known as the **Parque de la Luz**, this public space is definitely one of Medellín's most stunning. Built on the site of its old marketplace, it features an **urban forest**, with a smooth concrete pavement symbolizing the "mud," the 300 light-topped needle-thin concrete columns being the "trees." Real bamboo plants, benches and fountains complete this unique setting. At night, the lighting effect is quite dramatic.

Biblioteca Empresas Públicas de Medellín★

Carrera 54 # 44-48, Plaza de Cisneros. 🕐 *Open Mon–Sat 8:30am–5:30pm.* ✆ *(4) 380 7500. www.2.epm.com.co/ bibliotecaepm.*

The amazing forest of light poles described above is overlooked by this oddly shaped building (2005) representing the **pyramid** of knowledge in design terms.

It houses the EPM's library collections on science, industry, technology and the environment.

② AROUND PASEO PEATONAL CARABOBO★★

To discover Medellín's architectural charm of yesteryear, stroll along the **Carabobo Pedestrian Walkway**. The district extends to about eight blocks in length *(along Carrera 51A between Avenida San Juan and Calle 53)*, and boasts some particularly fine examples of heritage restoration of award-winning architectural merit. Quaint cobblestone walkways pay homage to a bygone age, while stately buildings have been fully-restored to their former grandeur. Entirely **traffic-free**, the Old Quarter is now home to an eclectic array of trendy boutiques, art galleries, book stores and cafes, and provides a pleasant journey back through time. The following are some prime landmarks along and around the Carabobo walkway.

Edificio Carré★ and Edificio Vásquez★

Carrera 52 # 44B-17 and # 44-31.
An important part of Medellín's architectural heritage, these two faithfully renovated redbrick buildings overlook Plaza de Cisneros, which works brilliantly as a dividing line between the modern Alpujarra district and this older part of town. Dating back to the late-19C, both structures were constructed in the style of the coffee-bean drying buildings found in traditional *fincas* throughout Paisa Country. Dwarfed by the city's modern skyline, the Edificio Carré once had the distinction of being the tallest building in town. It was designed by French architect **Charles Émile Carré** (1863-1909) who also drew the plans for Medellín's cathedral.

It is now home to the office of the Secretary of Education of Medellín, while the Vásquez Building, designed under Carré's mentorship, houses the headquarters of a social agency.

Palacio Nacional★★

Carrera 52 # 48-45. ⏱*Open Mon–Sat 8am–7pm.* ☏*(4) 513 4422.*

Palacio Nacional

Designed by Belgian architect **Agustín Goovaerts** (1885-1939), this former government building is a grand Modern-Romantic construction (1925) that was completely revamped and turned into a bustling shopping mall, jam-packed with hundreds of stores, restaurants and bars.

An escalator will whisk you all the way to the top floor, where you can enjoy a nice **view** of the opulent interior architecture with its countless arches.

Parque Berrío

Carrera 50 and Calle 50.
This neatly paved park dating back to 1680 is the geographical heart of the city. It is distinctive for its towering palms and for its statue of **Pedro Justo Berrío**, a local leading political figure in the 19C.

Benches crammed with people, scuttling shoppers laden with bags and street vendors crowd every far-flung corner of this popular meeting place, flanked by several important buildings.

Banco de la República

Calle 50 # 50-21, floors 3 & 4.
The main interest of this building may not reside inside, where you can see the fine **Colección Filatélica** and its 300,000 stamps from all over the world (⏱*open Mon–Fri 8am–11:30am, 2pm–5:30pm;* ☏*4 576 7402; www.lablaa.org*), but outside. Right in front of the edifice, notice the rounded exaggerated curves of one of Fernando Botero's signature bronze sculptures **Torso Femenino★★**, nicknamed *La Gorda* (The Fat One).

Basílica Nuestra Señora de la Candelaria★★

Carrera 49A # 50-85.
The original church built on this site (1649) was replaced by this Neoclassical edifice (1767) that served as Medellín's cathedral from 1868 until 1931. The basilica is particularly famous for its **coffered ceiling**.

Do not miss its much-acclaimed figure of the *Señor Caído* (Fallen Christ), its Spanish Colonial-style *Virgen de la Candelaria* painting and its fine main retable.

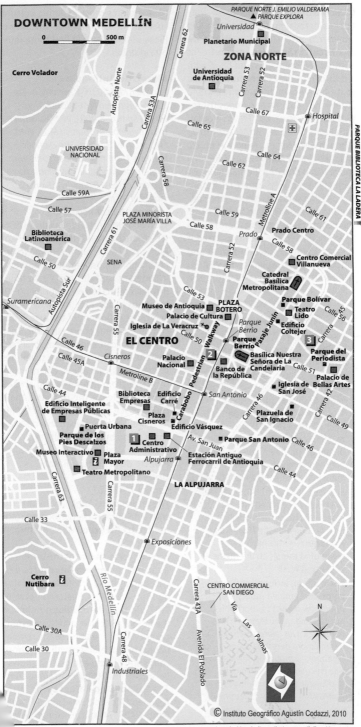

DOWNTOWN MEDELLÍN

0   500 m

Cerro Volador

Autopista Norte

Carrera 62

PARQUE NORTE J. EMILIO VALDERAMA
▲ PARQUE EXPLORA

Universidad

Planetario Municipal

ZONA NORTE

Universidad
de Antioquia

Carrera 53A

Carrera 53

Carrera 52

Calle 67

Hospital

UNIVERSIDAD
NACIONAL

Carrera 58

Calle 65

Calle 64

Calle 62

Calle 59A

Calle 57

Calle 59

Metroline A

Calle 61

PLAZA MINORISTA
JOSÉ MARÍA VILLA

Calle 58

Prado

Prado Centro

Calle 58

Biblioteca
Latinoamérica

Carrera 61

SENA

Carrera 52

Centro Comercial
Villanueva

Calle 50

Calle 53

Catedral
Basílica
Metropolitana

Autopista Sur

Carrera 55

Museo de Antioquia

PLAZA
BOTERO

Parque Bolívar

Teatro
Lido

Calle 55
56

Suramericana

Palacio de Cultura

Iglesia de La Veracruz

Walkway

Calle 50

*Parque
Berrío*

Pasaje Junín

Edificio
Coltejer

EL CENTRO

2

Parque
Berrío

Basílica Nuestra
Señora de La
Candelaria

3

Parque del
Periodista

Calle 46

Calle 45A

Cisneros

Palacio
Nacional

Pedestrian

Carabobo

Banco de
la República

Calle 51

Iglesia de
San José

Palacio de
Bellas Artes

Metroline B

Calle 44

Biblioteca
Empresas

Edificio
Carré

San Antonio

Carrera 46

Carrera 42

Calle 49

Edificio Inteligente
de Empresas Públicas

Plaza
Cisneros

Edificio Vásquez

Plazuela de
San Ignacio

Puerta Urbana

Parque de los
Pies Descalzos

1

Centro
Administrativo

Av. San Juan

Parque San Antonio

Calle 46

Museo Interactivo

Plaza
Mayor

Alpujarra

Estación Antiguo
Ferrocarril de Antioquia

Calle 44

Teatro Metropolitano

LA ALPUJARRA

Carrera 63

Carrera 55

Calle 33

Exposiciones

Cerro
Nutibara

Río Medellín

Carrera 43A

CENTRO COMMERCIAL
SAN DIEGO

Vía Las Palmas

N

Calle 30A

Calle 30

Carrera 48

Avenida El Poblado

Industriales

© Instituto Geográfico Agustín Codazzi, 2010

PARQUE BIBLIOTECA LA LADERA

Plaza Botero★★★

The major focal point of the city's Old Quarter is also known as **Plaza de Las Esculturas**. It is a magnificent outdoor sculpture museum filled with works donated by **Fernando Botero** to his hometown, including *La Mano* (The Hand), *Caballo con Bridas* (Horse With Bridal), *Mujer con Fruta* (Woman with Fruit), *Eva* (Eve), *Mujer con Espejo* (Woman with Mirror), *Hombre y Caballo* (Man and Horse), *Maternidad* (Maternity) and *Soldado Romano* (Roman Soldier). Each piece is now part of the "Botero legend" that suggests rubbing the statues brings love and good fortune.

This delightful paved area, dotted with a variety of tree species, two cascading water features, seating areas and curious pathways, spans some 7,500sq m/80,729sq ft and represents one of Medellín's most dynamic cultural spaces. In the immediate vincinity of Plaza Botero, you will find some interesting sights.

Museo de Antioquia★★

Carrera 52 # 52-43. ⏱*Open Mon–Sat 10am–6pm, Sun & public holidays 10am–5pm.* 🎟*8,000 COP.* 👥*Guided tours available in Spanish Mon, Wed, Fri 2pm, Tue, Thu, Sat–Sun & public holidays 11am.* 👥*Guided tours with English speaking guide available by booking at least 8 days in advance.* ☏*(4) 251 3636. www.museodeantioquia.org.co.*

This handsome Art Deco building (1936), which once housed the City Hall and Municipal Council, is now home to one of Colombia's most important museums, founded in 1881. It boasts a stunning **Botero collection★★** comprising 108 paintings in different media by Medellín's great exponent of the arts. It also contains an array of pre-Hispanic, Colonial, Republican, and contemporary collections, including paintings, sculptures, photographs, caricatures, and drawings by artists from Colombia and abroad. Before you leave the museum, make sure you see Pedro Nel Gómez's colorful murals (⏱ *see sidebar*) that decorate some of the building's walls.

Palacio de la Cultura Rafael Uribe Uribe

Carrera 51 # 52-03.
This resplendent Gothic landmark (1936) with a distinctive checkerboard façade used to be the seat of the government of Antioquia.

It was a great source of frustration for its architect, **Agustín Goovaerts**, who encountered many obstacles and delays during the project. Restored between 1987 and 1998, the building now houses the historical archives and features temporary exhibits relating to the region's unique heritage, along with artist workshops and theater and cinema shows. Be sure to visit its two small museums. The **Sala museo Rafael Uribe Uribe** (⏱*open Mon–Fri 8am–5pm, Sat 9am 3pm;* ☏*4 251 1444; http://cultura.sedu*

A Prolific Muralist

A real pioneer in Colombian public art, **Pedro Nel Gómez** (1899-1984) became famous for his socially conscious, yet controversial, murals that radically broke from mainstream styles. Throughout his career, the artist painted more than 2,000sq m/21,528sq ft of frescos in public buildings, portraying the life of hard-working Paisa folk and the industrialization of the region.

Between 1935 and 1938, Pedro Nel Gómez decorated the Palacio Municipal de Medellín, now occupied by the **Museo de Antioquia**, with a spectacular series of 11 murals on the theme of Life and Work.

These murals include a striking **tryptic★★** entitled *Tríptico del trabajo* (Homage to Labor). This outstanding fresco features *De la bordadora a los telares eléctricos* (From Embroideress to Loom Operator), *El problema del petróleo y La energía* (The Problem of Oil and Energy) and *El trabajo y la maternidad* (Work and Maternity).

Plaza Botero

IM - Editores/Proexport Colombia

gov.co) is dedicated to Rafael Uribe Uribe (1859-1914), an Antioquian lawyer, writer and politician.

The **Sala de Patrimonio Artístico** (🕒*same hours)* features fine pieces by famous artists such as Rafael Sáenz, Melitón Rodríguez, Ignacio Gómez Jaramillo and Débora Arango.

Iglesia de La Veracruz★
Calle 51 # 52-58.

Medellín's only Colonial-style church was built in 1682 and is renowned for its original main altar, brought from Spain. The church was declared Cultural Heritage of the Nation in 1982, along with its Colonial-style courtyard.

Don't be fooled by the building's plain white masonry exterior. The interior provides visitors with dignified splendor, albeit in simple style.

③ PARQUE BOLÍVAR TO PARQUE SAN ANTONIO

Heading southwest from Parque Bolívar towards Parque San Antonio provides the opportunity to discover another side of the Downtown: the neighborhood of Villanueva, including a stroll along a popular shopping walkway and a detour by one of Medellín's oldest parks, the Plazuela de San Ignacio, framed by vesti-ges of the colonial and Republican eras. ▪he walk ends in Parque San Antonio, a ▪▪ly public place with a strong artistic ▪ but a painful past.

Parque Bolívar★
49 Junín and Calle 54.

Located on land donated by Englishman Tyrrel Stuart Moore in 1844, the area was provisionally called **New London** until the community renamed it **Villanueva**. In 1871 the park was also renamed, in honor of Simón Bolívar whose equestrian statue was added in 1923. Streets that lead from the park are actually all named in memory of Bolívar, with Calle 54 (Caracas), Calle 55 (Peru), Carrera 28 (Ecuador) and Carrera 49 (Venezuela) evoking his home town and three of the countries he freed from Spanish rule.

👁If you visit Parque Bolívar on the first Saturday of the month, you'll find a colorful market called **Mercado artesanal de San Alejo**.

As part of the weekend events held in the park, a Sunday morning concert is usually performed by the University of Antioquia's Symphony Orchestra—a truly atmospheric use of this imposing space. As one of the city's great landmarks, Parque Bolívar is surrounded by grand buildings such as the following.

Catedral Basílica Metropolitana★
Carrera 48 # 56-81.

Located on the north side of the park, this Romanesque Revival edifice was designed by **Charles Émile Carré** and built between 1875 and 1930. It claims to be the largest church on earth made entirely of brick (an estimated one mil-

Ballet Folklórico de Antioquia building

Ballet Folklórico de Antioquia

Prado Centro★★

This Heritage Conservation neighborhood *(between Carrera 45 and Carrera 51D with Calle 67 and Calle 59)* makes a pleasant diversion on a sunny afternoon. It is a picturesque enclave with stunning good looks and a peaceful ambience that dates back to the 1930s-50s, when it was Medellín's most exclusive neigbourhood. Born out of a businessman's vision to create an upscale district to mirror that of the same name in the Caribbean city of Barranquilla, Prado Centro surpassed all expectations. Striking architectural features combine Republican-style houses, with European, Mediterranean, Colonial, Belle Epoque, Neoclassical and even kitschy designs that range from sprawling aristocratic villas and mansions to Art Deco town houses. Wide, tree-lined streets and pavements trimmed with flowering cadmium and guayacan trees are ideal for exploration on foot, with the district's many art houses and theaters installed in handsome old mansions. As you stroll around the area, you may want to take a look at a few of these special places:

Santiago Vélez/Casa Tres Patios

Installation by Jessica Sanchez, Casa Tres Patios

Teatro Prado El Águila Descalza *(Carrera 45D # 59-01)*, with its permanent schedule of year-round events and inviting coffee bar.

Palacio Egipcio *(Carrera 47 # 59-54)*, a curious architectural oddity of ostentatiously etched columns built to palatial proportions.

Teatro El Tablado *(Carrera 50 # 59-06)*, renowned for its workshops, concerts, art exhibits, poetry readings and cultural events.

Sede Ballet Folklórico de Antioquia *(Carrera 50 # 59-71)*, a bastion of Colombian and Paisa dance traditions housed in a colorful building.

Casa del Teatro *(Calle 59 # 50A-25)*, Medellín's most popular alternative art space, with extensive archives on Colombia's theatrical history.

Casa Tres Patios *(Carrera 50A # 63-31)*, famous for staging some of the most experimental contemporary art in the city.

lion bricks were used in the construction).

Highlights of this vast building include dazzling Spanish stained-glass windows, altar canopy, pulpit, marble fonts and organ, together with **El Cristo del perdón**★—a much-viewed piece of religious art by Antioquian painter **Francisco Antonio Cano Cardona** (1865-1935).

Centro Comercial Villanueva
Calle 57 # 49-44. 🕐*Open Mon–Sat 8am–7pm.* 🚫*Closed public holidays.* 📞*(4) 251 0366.*
Close to the cathedral, this shopping mall is well worth visiting as it is housed in the **Seminario Mayor de Medellín** (1928), a genuine architectural gem by **Giovanni Buscaglione** (1874-1941). This architect designed many religious buildings in Colombia, including Bogotá's **Santuario Nuestra Señora del Carmen**, considered his masterpiece.

Teatro Lido
Carrera 48 # 54-20. 🎧*Guided tours Thu–Sat 4pm, Sun 9am.* 📞*(4) 514 2376.*
Located on the southeastern side of the park, this restored building (1945) has recaptured its former splendor.
It is famous for its small-scale artistic performances, from comedy shows and musical acts to alternative theater.

Pasaje Junín
One of Medellín's most famous streets is this bustling major **pedestrian walkway** notable for its varicolored flower stalls and ice-cream vendors. Very much a hub of everyday life, the street extends from the southern end of Arque Bolívar to La Playa, and contains a mix of discount shops, bookstores, restaurants and coffee shops.

Edificio Coltejer
Calle 52 # 47-42. 📞*(4) 251 4977.*
Completed in 1972, this needle-shaped tower block is Medellín's highest structure (175m/574ft). It was erected as a corporate symbol by a major Colombian textile company anxious to pay homage

Edificio Coltejer

Proexport Colombia

to the city's traditions in the **textile** and **clothing** industries.
Today the landmark spire is home to financial, commercial and media companies, with each office boasting spectacular city vistas.

Iglesia de San José
Carrera 46 # 49-90.
A paved courtyard with a **fountain** created by artist Francisco Antonio Cano Cardona signals this Baroque style church (1847-1902). It was built on the site of a former chapel dedicated to San Lorenzo that had fallen into disrepair and was later demolished.
Interior highlights include several notable pieces of fine religious art, such as a resplendent gilded San José high altarpiece, the acclaimed *Bautismo de Jesús* by Cano, and a painting of San Lorenzo, the city's first patron saint.

Plazuela de San Ignacio★
Carrera 44 between Calle 48 and Calle 49.
As one of Medellín's oldest squares, this plaza has been central to city life for generations, with shoeshine vendors and snack stalls flanked by an impressive display of towering 100-year-old ceiba trees. A fine statue of General **Francisco de Paula Santander** and a bust of **Marceliano Vélez** draw attention to the newly paved center of the plaza.

Plazuela de San Ignacio with Edificio de San Ignacio and Iglesia de San Ignacio

Proexport Colombia

On its eastern side, a trio of historic buildings vie for position.

Edificio de San Ignacio★

This structure is the birthplace of the **Universidad de Antioquia**, one of Colombia's finest institutions of higher learning, founded in 1803. Its campuses and buildings are scattered around the city, but this splendidly restored building is special.

It boasts **interior patios** decorated with flower-filled gardens and fountains, and affords plenty of places in which to read, think and study. Also here are several library collections, various student institutions, and the **history section** of the **university museum** (Carrera 44 # 48-72; ☿open Mon–Thu 8am–6pm, Fri 8am–4pm, Sat 9am–1pm; ✆(4) 219 5180; http://museo.udea.edu.co/sitio).

Iglesia y Claustro de San Ignacio

Carrera 44 # 48-18.

⊶The cloister is closed to the public, now being the seat of Comfama; www.comfama.com.

In 1812 the Franciscan community that had built a cloister and a church on the Plazuela left Medellín for good.

During civil wars in 1885, the buildings were occupied by troops as an army barracks and severely damaged as a result. They ended up under the care of the Jesuits, who had them remodelled in the early part of the 20C by prominent architects such as **Agustin Goovaerts** and **Félix Mejía**. Take a look at the early 19C church, whose Spanish Baroque façade hides a truly Colonial interior.

Parque San Antonio★★

Between Calle 46 and Calle 44 with Carrera 46 and Carrera 49.

If you enter this huge plaza (33,000sq m/355,209sq ft) through its northeast side, you will be greeted by the *Puerta de San Antonio,* a fine piece by Colombian artist **Ronny Vayda** (b. 1954), the author of several other outdoor sculptures with clean, sharp lines gracing the city.

This wide urban space is also home to **Fernando Botero**'s much photographed *El Torso Masculino* (Masculine Torso), *La Venus Durmiente* (Sleeping Venus) and two versions of **El Pájaro de Paz** (Bird of Peace). In 1995 the original statue was blown up by a terrorist bomb, killing and wounding innocent passersby.

After sculpting an identical copy, Botero placed it alongside the mangled remains of the damaged original sculpture, thus sending a strong message of hope and resilience in the face of adversity.

Bulevar Artesanal San Antonio★

Some 50 permanent wooden stalls house a variety of craftspeople and vendors at this bazaar-style marketplace where artisans can showcase a range of traditional Paisa handicrafts ma of wood, bamboo, clay, leather, seeds, fabric and macramé.

ADDITIONAL SIGHTS
Parque del Periodista★
Carrera 43 and Calle 53.
An oasis of daytime calm, this small paved square at the heart of the **Zona Fucsia** is Downtown's answer to the Zona Rosa in **El Poblado**. The park is a popular meeting place largely because of the plethora of well-known bars and restaurants in and around it. A memorial to Cuban **Manuel del Socorro Rodríguez** (1758-1819), a pioneer in journalism in Colombia, serves as a reminder of the journalists who lost their lives to violence.

Palacio de Bellas Artes
Carrera 42 # 52-33. ✆ (4) 229 1400. www.bellasartesmed.edu.co.
Medellín's Fine Arts Academy is a grand Republican-style building (1936) that was designed by Nel Rodríguez. It is popular not only for its concerts, "Art Film Fridays" and other free events, but also for some great works of art.
The Sala Beethoven—Medellín's oldest concert hall—is decorated with eight landscapes by **Eladio Vélez** (1897-1967), while the Sala de exposiciones Eladio Vélez exhibits the artwork of past and present students. In the main lobby, note the fine mural by Antioquian artist **Ramón Vásquez** (b. 1922).

Parque Biblioteca La Ladera León de Greiff★
Calle 59A # 36-30. ◷ Open Mon–Sat 9am–8pm, Sun & public holidays 10am–4pm. ✆ (4) 385 7331. www.reddebibliotecas.org.co.
This pioneering "library park" was named in honor of Colombian poet **León de Greiff** (1895-1976), a native of Medellín. The architect for this daring project was **Giancarlo Mazzanti**, who also designed the outstanding **Parque Biblioteca España** (◷ see sidebar p213). Built on the site of a former prison and seemingly wedged into the hillside, three block-style units with bright red accents—housing a community center,

a library and a cultural center—have been arranged in such a way that they open to the **city view**. Linked by paths, green spaces and inclined plazas, these "modules" make an interesting urban landscape with multiple meeting points.

ZONA NORTE
The city's northern portion doesn't offer a cohesive string of attractions that would lend itself to a walking tour. Yet, the number of cultural, entertainment and natural sights is significant—and likely to grow. In this part of town is a surprising mix of architectural styles, from large, old mansion houses to quirky avant-garde structures.

Casa Museo Maestro Pedro Nel Gómez★
Carrera 51B # 85-24. ◷ Open Mon–Sat 9am–5pm, Sun & public holidays 10am–4pm. ✆ Guided tours available by prior reservation. ✆ (4) 233 2633.
The former house and studio of **Pedro Nel Gómez** (◷ see sidebar) features 1,500 of his drawings, watercolors, oils, sculptures, and some of his murals, most of them having been painted on public spaces all over town. Documents and archives provide details on the life of the man behind Colombia's great **muralist movement**.

Jardín Botánico de Medellín Joaquín Antonio Uribe★★
Carrera 52 # 73-298. ◷ Open daily 9am–6pm, last entry 5pm. ✆ (4) 444 5500. www.jbmed.org.
Since its opening in 1978, Medellín's botanical garden has grown in size and stature.
A walk down the garden's meandering wooden path through verdant undergrowth encourages a feeling of total immersion into Colombia's **jungle**. The outstanding feature is the **Orquideorama José Jerónimo Triana★★**, an award-winning organic structure designed by Felipe Mesa and Alejandro Bernal (2006). Protected by a honeycomb-like roof covered with translucent slats of pinewood that provide indirect

Orquideorama José Jerónimo Triana

Proexport Colombia

light, this intricate wooden meshwork of modular giant "flowers" serves many functions: temporary gardens, butterfly breeding place and bird feeding facility, with a special space reserved for **orchids** and other exotic and tropical flower displays.

Acuario Parque Explora★

Entrance by the University Metro station between Carrera 52 and Carrera 53.
⏰Open Tue–Fri 8:30am–6pm (ticket office closes 4pm), Sat–Sun & public holidays 10am–6:30pm (ticket office closes 5pm). ⊚9,000 COP, ⊚13,000 COP with 3D show, ⊚16,000 COP with aquarium. ℰ(4) 516 8349. www.parqueexplora.org.

Dedicated to science and technology, the huge Explora theme park is home not only to some 300 interactive experiments and educational activities, but also to the only aquatic attraction in town.

The aquarium itself is a vast 25,000sq m/269,098sq ft watery world. It contains 25 freshwater and saltwater tanks that give visitors the opportunity to get close to some 4,000 specimens of 400 species of fish, amphibians, reptiles, and arthropods from Colombia's oceans and rivers (Río Magdalena, Orinoco, and others). One of the highlights is the re-creation of the **Selva Inundada**★ (flooded jungle plain), containing species from the Amazon such as the world's largest freshwater fish called pirarucú *(Arapaima gigas)*, and the extraordinary lungfish *(Lepidosiren paradoxa)*, which can survive long periods of drought by burrowing into the mud (it uses its fins as legs to crawl across the river bottom). Do not miss the eye-catching electric fish, jellyfish and a host of colorful marine settings, including coral gardens packed with a rainbow of sponges and lesser-seen oceanic species.

Parque Norte J. Emilio Valderrama

Carrera 53 # 76-115, one block from the University Metro station.
⏰Open Tue–Thu 9:30am–5pm, Fri 10am–7pm, Sat 11am–7pm, Sun & public holidays 10:30am–6pm. ⊚5,000 COP entry fee; ⊚23,500 COP Tue–Fri, ⊚24,500 COP Sat–Sun with unlimited entry to attractions, other packages available. ℰ(4) 210 0300. www.parquenorte.gov.co.

Hugely popular with the Medellínese, this city-run amusement park is a sprawling attraction centered on a large **lake** dotted with rowing boats and motorboats.

Thrill rides and kiddie rides, water slides, a ferris wheel, tricycle tracks, bumper cars and others vie for attention with the visiting crowds.

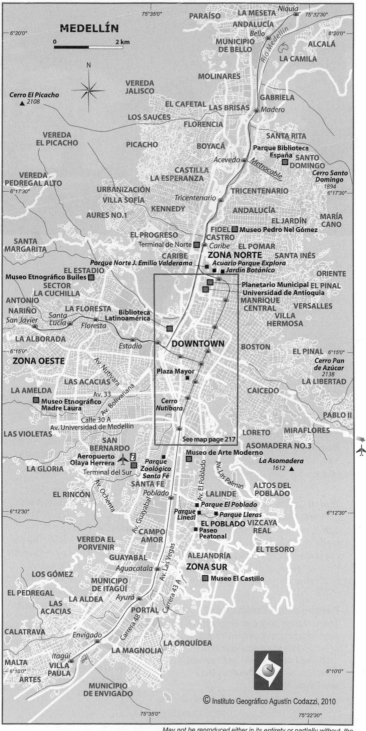

MEDELLÍN

0   2 km

N

PARAÍSO   LA MESETA   Niquía
ANDALUCÍA
Bello
MUNICIPIO   ALCALÁ
DE BELLO
LA CAMILA
Río Medellín
Cerro El Picacho
▲ 2108
VEREDA
JALISCO
MOLINARES
EL CAFETAL   LAS BRISAS   GABRIELA
LOS SAUCES   Madero
FLORENCIA
VEREDA   SANTA RITA
EL PICACHO   PICACHO   BOYACÁ   Parque Biblioteca
España   SANTO
Acevedo   DOMINGO
VEREDA   CASTILLA   Cerro Santo
PEDREGAL ALTO   LA ESPERANZA   Metrocable   Domingo
URBANIZACIÓN   TRICENTENARIO   1894
VILLA SOFÍA   Tricentenario
AURES NO.1   KENNEDY   ANDALUCÍA   MARÍA
EL JARDÍN   CANO
SANTA   EL PROGRESO   FIDEL   Museo Pedro Nel Gómez
MARGARITA   CASTRO   EL POMAR
Terminal de Norte   Caribe   SANTA INÉS
CARIBE   ZONA NORTE
Parque Norte J. Emilio Valderama   Acuario Parque Explora   ORIENTE
EL ESTADIO   Jardín Botánico
Museo Etnográfico Builes   Planetario Municipal   EL PINAL
SECTOR   Universidad de Antioquia
LA CUCHILLA   MANRIQUE   VERSALLES
ANTONIO   LA FLORESTA   CENTRAL
NARIÑO   Santa   Biblioteca   VILLA
San Javier   Lucía   Latinoamérica   HERMOSA
Floresta
LA ALBORADA   Estadio   DOWNTOWN   EL PINAL
BOSTON   Cerro Pan
ZONA OESTE   de Azúcar
Plaza Mayor   2138
LA AMELDA   LA LIBERTAD
LAS ACACIAS   CAICEDO
Av. 33   Cerro
Museo Etnográfico   Nutibara   PABLO II
Madre Laura   Calle 30 A   LORETO   MIRAFLORES
Av. Universidad de Medellín
LAS VIOLETAS   See map page 217   ASOMADERA NO.3
SAN   Museo de Arte Moderno
BERNARDO   La Asomadera
Aeropuerto   1612 ▲
Olaya Herrera   Parque   ALTOS DEL
Terminal del Sur   Zoológico   POBLADO
Santa Fé   LALINDE
LA GLORIA   SANTA FE   Parque El Poblado
EL RINCÓN   Poblado   Parque   Parque Lleras
Lineal   EL POBLADO   VIZCAYA
VEREDA EL   CAMPO   Paseo   REAL
PORVENIR   AMOR   Peatonal   EL TESORO
GUAYABAL   ALEJANDRÍA
Aguacatala   ZONA SUR
LOS GÓMEZ   MUNICIPIO   Museo El Castillo
EL PEDREGAL   DE ITAGÜÍ
LA ALDEA   Ayurá
LAS   PORTAL
ACACIAS
CALATRAVA   Envigado   LA ORQUÍDEA
MALTA   Itagüí   LA MAGNOLIA
VILLA
PAULA
ARTES   MUNICIPIO
DE ENVIGADO

Av. Nutivara   Av. Bolivariana   Av. Guayabal   Av. Ochenta   Av. Las Vegas   Av. El Poblado   Av. Las Palmas   Carrera 43 A   Carrera 48

75°35'0"   75°32'30"
6°20'0"
6°17'30"
6°15'0"
6°12'30"
6°10'0"

© Instituto Geográfico Agustín Codazzi, 2010

Pueblito Paisa

Proexport Colombia

Hills of Medellín★

Seven hills, collectively called **Cerros Tutelares de Medellín**, surround the city. With the exception of El Salvador *(east of town),* which hasn't been promoted for tourism, each of them offer **recreational opportunities**, from adventure sports to ecotourism and ethnotourism.

Cerro Nutibara★

Comuna 16, S of town. Accessible via Calle 30A # 55-64, or from Carrera 32 and Carrera 63A, by the Samé Clinic. **Elevation:** 1,562m/5,125ft. This 33ha/82 acre park provides a **panorama** of the Valle de Aburrá.

Teatro Carlos Vieco Ortiz

Calle 32D # 63A-153. ✆ (4) 235 8370. A number of tentacle-like **nature trails**, rich in lush, bloom-rich tropical vegetation, surround this 3,800-seat theater, the setting for outdoor plays, musicals and concerts.

Parque de las Esculturas★

This sculpture park is another permanent fixture, containing an exhibit of striking abstract **sculptures** from renowned national and international artists, including **Carlos Cruz Diez** and **Edgar Negret**.

Pueblito Paisa

✗🕐*Open daily 6am–midnight.* Perched atop the summit, guarded by the statue of Cacique Nutibara by José Horacio Betancur, this popular sight—one of Medellín's prime touristic landmarks—offers visitors a replica of a typical Antioquian Paisa pueblo from the colonial era, complete with a cobbled plaza, church, fountain, city hall, shops and houses.
A handful of nice bars and a typical Paisa restaurant serve good, hearty regional dishes year-round.
At Christmas, the whole place is illuminated by fairy **lights and lanterns**—a truly delightful sight.

Cerro Volador★

Comuna 9, W of town. Accessible via Carrera 65 by the Universidad Nacional or by Calle 70 with Carrera 79. **Elevation:** 1,628m/5,341ft. The hill was once inhabited by indigenous people, and today **trails** weave through these ancient ancestral lands. Particulary popular with **bird watchers**, Cerro Volador is developing a growing reputation for ecotourism. Weekending urbanites escape the city to fly **kites**, **cycle** downhill tracks and **exercise** in natural open spaces where **barbecue areas** give family and friends a chance to relax and enjoy the stunning **views**.

Cerro El Picacho★

Comuna 6, NW of town. Accessible via Carrera 86 with Calle 104 in Barrio El Triunfo or by acceso Los Rieles at Carrera 85 with Calle 97; by the Universidad Nacional or by Calle 70 with Carrera 79.
Elevation: 2,108m/6,916ft. Cerro de Picacho overlooks the city and the Valle de Aburrá. It is dubbed the "Protector of Medellín" for its hilltop image of **Cristo Rey**, an iconic landmark that has stood for three decades and is often visited by pilgrims. **Bird watching** is a popular activity along the elevated leafy trails. The steep paths are used for **cross-country running** competitions.

Cerro Santo Domingo

Comuna 1, NE of town.
Accessible via cable car from estación Santo Domingo del Metro Cable at Calle 107 with Carrera 31.
Elevation: 1,894m/6,214ft. The Cerro Santo Domingo is enjoyed by visitors from all corners of the city, especially its **picnic areas**, which are popular with large family groups.
The cerro's foothills are located in **Santo Domingo Savio**, which used to be Medellín's most notorious neighborhood. Now served by the metro cable and redefined by pleasant public spaces, the community boasts one the most iconic examples of Medellín's remarkable urban regeneration: the

Parque Biblioteca España★★
(see sidebar p213).

Cerro Pan de Azúcar★

Comuna 8, E of town. Accessible via Carrera 23 with Calle 53EH, or by Calle 55 with Carreras 15 or 5A.
Elevation: 2,138m/7,014ft. Located on the north side of a gorge, "Sugarloaf Hill" is the site of an ancient pre-Hispanic route, the **Camino de Cieza de León**, which connects to **Parque Arvi**. Affording **views**★ across Medellín from the hill's pilgrim sites, the cerro is visited by hundreds of Catholics during May's "Day of the Holy Cross" —a ritual in which the devoted speak the name of Jesus one thousand times, believing this will protect them in the coming year.

La Asomadera

Comuna 9, E of town.
Accessible via Carrera 36A with Calle 38A or by Calle 34 with Carrera 48A. ℘(4) 434 0392. www.medellin.gov.co.
Elevation: 1,612m/5,289ft. This hill is home to native trees that contain a variety of **birds**, butterflies and squirrels. With a sports area, **swimming pools**, volleyball nets and **bicycle paths**, La Asomadera has the ambience of a neighborhood park, complete with **barbecue areas**. Several trails lead up to **La Cueva del Indio** (a cave).

Hills of Medellín

Proexport Colombia

227

Planetario Municipal Jesús Emilio Ramírez González

Carrera 52 # 71-117. ⏰*Open Tue–Fri 9am–noon, 2pm–5pm, Sat–Sun & public holidays 1pm–6pm. Approximately ⊜3,500 COP (fee varies with exhibits).* ✆*(4) 527 2222. http://200.58.204.195/planetario/el_ planetario.php.*

Medellín was the first South American city to be equipped with a computer-controlled planetarium.

Today, this interactive science learning center houses powerful telescopes, all kinds of thematic exhibits, as well as earth and space shows under a 17.5m/57ft diameter dome.

Children especially will have fun while learning about the universe and solar system.

Universidad de Antioquia

Calle 67.

The main campus of "U de A" is a mammoth complex of interconnecting buildings set among a great variety of trees and grassy green space.

Several other university structures are spread around the city, such as the venerable Edificio de San Ignacio.

Walking around the campus, you will note some outstanding works of art, including Rodrigo Arenas Betancur's *Hombre creador de energía,* Germán Botero's *Fuente ceremonial,* and one of Pedro Nel Gómez's murals entitled *El hombre ante los grandes descubrimientos de la física.*

On-site buildings of note include the **Museo Universitario** and its varied collections of anthropology, history, natural science and visual arts *(Calle 67 # 53-108 block 15;* ⏰*open Mon–Thu 8am–6pm, Fri 8am–4pm, Sat 9am–1pm;* ✆*(4) 219 5180; http://museo.udea.edu.co/sitio).*

ZONA SUR
EL POBLADO★★

For many Medellínese, the city's South *is* El Poblado, such is the eclipsing allure of this upscale **residential neighborhood**. It is also home to the city's official money hub—Medellín's financial center. Nestled in the southeastern corner of

town, on the edge of a steep valley, El Poblado stretches to Envigado (south), Santa Elena (east) and La Candelaria (north), and boasts great **views** of the city, with property prices to match.

El Poblado marks the site of the original founding of Medellín in 1616. By the early 20C, the district had become a desirable address for affluent families to build rural mansions. Once a road was built to connect it to Medellín, land increased dramatically in value. El Poblado became a suburb of the city itself through growth in the early 1950s. In the 1970s it established itself as an exclusive neighborhood, with a particular stretch of luxury villas that earned it the nickname **Milla de Oro** (Golden Mile).

El Poblado is not just about elegant hotels, fine restaurants and high-end shopping. It was part of an enviable urban planning model that won widespread applause. The neighborhood's development involved introducing striking modern architecture in synergy with the district's **historic heritage** and the nearby **Andean forest**.

Several highlights are worthy of discovery, with the following just a selection.

Parque El Poblado

Between Carrera 43A and Carrera 43B with Calle 9 and Calle 10.

The area where the first settlement in the Aburrá Valley was built in the early 17C today serves as a backdrop for the **Iglesia San José del Poblado** *(Carrera 43A between Calle 9 and Calle 10).* As you'd expect from the wealthiest part of town, the grass is manicured and well-tended. Neat pathways set among the trees and paved areas are a popular meeting place for office workers, shoppers and delivery drivers grabbing a cup of coffee on the run.

Paseo Peatonal El Poblado

Stretching 8 blocks from the Parque El Poblado to the Loma de Los Balsos in the south.

This scenic, pedestrianized modern mall is blessed with aromatic trees and plants. Shop amid abundant vegetation

Zona Oeste

This sector of Medellín offers some isolated sights of interest hidden among the office blocks and major intersections.

Museo Etnográfico Madre Laura★

Carrera 92 # 34D-21, Barrio Belencito. ○*Open Tue–Fri 9am–noon, 2pm–5pm, Sat–Sun 2pm–5pm.* 🎟*3,000 COP.* 💬*Guided visits upon request.* ✆*(4) 252 3017.*

Named in honor of Mother Laura, a nun who brought attention to the plight of the indigenous peoples, this museum showcases a fine array of pieces from Central and South America as well as Africa: clothing, baskets, archaeological artifacts, necklaces, jewelry, building tools, musical instruments, ritual objects.

Museo Etnográfico Miguel Ángel Builes

Carrera 81 # 52B-120. ○*Open Mon–Fri 8am–noon, 2pm–5pm, Sat–Sun by previous appointment.* ✆*4) 421 6259. www.yarumal.org.*

Well off the beaten track, this museum is similarly dedicated to the cause of the indigenous peoples, with a strong focus on Colombian ethnicity. The collections contain an impressive number of ritual artifacts, together with a **Maloca** dwelling from the Amazon Basin.

Biblioteca Pública Piloto para Latinoamérica★

Carrera 64 # 50-32. ○*Open Mon–Fri 8:30am–6:45pm, Sat 9am–5:45pm.* ✆*(4) 230 2482. www.bibliotecapiloto.gov.co.*

Ranked among Colombia's top cultural institutions, this prestigious library contains one of the largest collections of original **photographic records** in Latin America, with some glass plates dating back to 1849.

and greenery characterized by soaring ceiba trees, yellow acacias, and pink and yellow guayacan trees that are home to squawking multi-colored parrots and iguanas. Few purposed-designed urban walkways are so pleasant, with some particularly fine black olive trees and baskets of fragrant blooms, herbs and vines along the way.

Parque Lineal La Presidenta

Carrera 43A opposite Calle 7.

A testament to the city's ongoing commitment to creating public green space, this park provides a picturesque walkway to Parque Lleras. It includes a trio of bridges crossing a stream. Benches, tables and viewing decks are set within 46 species of trees, with

Parque Lineal La Presidenta

© Holger Mette/iStockphoto.com

Museo El Castillo

© Fernando Bengoechea/Beateworks/Corbis

recreation zones for children and tranquil areas created to maximize peace and quiet.

Parque Lleras★★

Known as the city's **Zona Rosa** *(between Calles 9-10 and Carreras 36-42)*, the lively area around this fashionable tree-lined park has become the hub for nightlife, trendy bars and great restaurants in Medellín. It is a vibrant scene for after-work drinks and the setting for weekend partying on a grand scale.

Museo El Castillo★

Calle 9 Sur # 32-269, Loma de los Balsos. ⏱*Open Mon–Fri 8:30am–noon, 2pm–6pm, Sat 9am–noon.* ✆*(4) 266 0900.* Inspired by the castles of the French Loire Valley, this Medieval-style turreted mansion (1930) is considered the jewel in the crown of El Poblado. Designed by architect Nel Rodríguez and set in lovely French gardens, it now houses a museum with a collection of European fine art, decorative art and furniture displayed within nine period rooms.

ADDITIONAL SIGHTS

Besides El Poblado, Medellín's Zona Sur contains a few interesting highlights.

Museo de Arte Moderno de Medellín (MAMM)★

Carrera 44 # 19A-100. ⏱*Open Tue–Fri 9am–5:30pm, Sat 10am–5:30pm, Sun 10am–3:30pm.* 💰*9,000 COP.* ✆*(4) 444 2622. www.elmamm.org.* Medellín's Modern Art Museum was recently moved to a derelict smelting plant in an area in need of regeneration—a suitably edgy industrial space for some of Latin America's bravest examples of modern and contemporary art. The facility provides a grand space for the exhibits, offering cavernous climate-controlled rooms that can now attract international collections.

You will enjoy works of significant artistic and historical value, including an important sampling of works by Antioquian **Débora Arango**.

Yet, it is the future of modern art in Medellín that remains the focus of this forward-thinking institution.

Parque Zoológico Santa Fé★

Carrera 52 # 20-63. ⏱*Open daily 9am–5pm.* 💰*8,000 COP, child 💰4,000 COP.* ✆*(4) 235 1326. www.zoologico santafe.com.* Since it was founded in 1960, Medellín's zoo has shifted its stance toward conservation, and now partners with institutions across the world on breeding and protection projects. The 4ha/9 acre facility is presently home to a thousand residents representing some 238 different species, mostly from Central and South America. The aviary, the vivarium and butterfly house are of particular interest. You will also enjoy more than 500 species of trees and shrubs, including an impressive range of indigenous plants and palms.

Museo Casa Santa Fé
Entry included with the zoo fee.
Located on the zoo's grounds, this finely restored Republican-style hacienda, complete with its central courtyard decorated in Arabic ceramic tiles, houses a collection of 19C furniture from Egypt and Persia, inlaid with mother of pearl and ivory. Some resplendent pieces of religious art include a representation of Christ dating back to the 13C.
Visitors can also see a collection of tools used in the construction of the old Antioquia Railroad.

EL VALLE DE ABURRÁ★

The Aburrá Valley sits in a natural basin formed by the **Medellín River**. It is a 60km/37mi long lush corridor cradling the metropolitan area of Medellín. Located in the **Cordillera Central**, the valley stretches from south to north, with the southern tip higher than the northern end. Dramatic **variations** in **climate** characterize the region, with the **nine municipalities** of the Aburrá Valley also offering a variety of Paisa cultures, from modern to traditional.
The valley's attractions can be divided into two sections: south and north.

SOUTHERN PART
Envigado★

◐ *10km/6mi S of Medellín via Carrera 50 or Carrera 42. Envigado metro station is on Line A.*
Best known in Colombia for its **First Division Soccer Club**, this Paisa town (Pop. 175,337) was founded in 1775 and declared a municipality in 1814. It preserves several fine old buildings.

Iglesia de Santa Gertrudis
© moonrat42/Flickr

Iglesia de Santa Gertrudis★
Carrera 42 # 37 Sur-20.
This Renaissance Revival church (1897) is elaborately decorated with a stunning portico entrance and grand façade.
Its interior is filled with precious artifacts and features a much-admired altar, tabernacle and pulpit. Expansive areas of inlaid marble flooring and elegant stucco are highlighted by crystal chandeliers with a canopied central nave serving as the dramatic centerpiece.

Casa Museo Otraparte
Carrera 43A # 27A Sur-1. ◐Open Mon–Fri 8am–8pm, Sat–Sun 9am–5pm.
℘(4) 276 1415. Check website for special events. www.otraparte.org.
The former house of Antioquian writer and philosopher **Fernando González Ochoa** (1895-1964), a defender of Latin American identity, is dedicated to his life and work.

Other attractions worthy of note include the Gothic Revival **Iglesia de San José** *(Calle 49 Sur # 24A-25)*, the Neo-Colonial **Iglesia de Santa Bárbara de Ayura** *(Carrera 47 # 39 Sur-82, barrio Las Flores)* and the town's main park, **Parque Marceliano Vélez** *(Carrera 42 and Carrera 43)*, which boasts a particularly nice central fountain and is adorned with twinkling lights in the run-up to Christmas each year.

Itagüí

11km/7mi S of Medellín via Carrera 42. Itagüí metro station is on Line A.

Renowned as the most industrialized city in Colombia, Itagüí (Pop. 235,567) thrives on wholesale trading, particulary in the **design** and **fashion** sectors. Unfortunately no longer opened to the public, the handsome estate of **Mariano Ospina Pérez** (1891-1976), Colombia's president from 1946 until 1950, is famous for its impressive array of **orchids**.

Sabaneta★

14km S of Medellín off Avenida la Poblado.

For most domestic tourists, Sabaneta (Pop. 44,874) is a party playground for weekend carousing in and around its many **bars** and **clubs**. Yet the town, which dates back to 1896, also offers plenty of local arts and crafts, and some charming old buildings as well.

Casa de la Cultura La Barquereña

Calle 68 Sur 42-40. ⏰*Call for details about temporary exhibitions.* ℘*(4) 288 5933.*

Set around a large green lawn, this cultural center is housed in a fine building that blends Colonial and Roman architectural styles. It stages regular artistic shows and events including exhibits of **local art**.

La Estrella★

16km/10mi SW of Medellín off Carrera 64.

Dubbed "The Green City," La Estrella (Pop. 52,763) is conveniently located near a nature reserve.

Laguna del Alto del Romeral★

5km/3mi SW of La Estrella via the pathway that leads to Angelópolis.

Part of the 5,171ha/12,751 acre **Reserva Ecológica y Forestal El Romeral**, this sparkling lagoon is notable for its **trails** dating back to the pre-Columbian era. Popular with weekending families, the lake is surrounded by scenic **picnic areas** rich in unspoiled fauna and flora.

Caldas

22km/14mi S of Medellín via Carretera 25.

This town is yet another typical Paisa community (Pop. 68,157) with some interesting natural sights on its outskirts.

Outdoor dining, Sabaneta

© Lionela Rob/Alamy

Alto de San Miguel★

◐ *E of Caldas at el Yolombo.*
✏ *Guided tours provided by Ecoturismo Estrategico ☎(4) 302 3500; www.ecoturismoestrategico.com.*

A local **birding** hot spot complete with observation huts wedged among the trees, this ecological reserve comprises a variety of Andean terrain, from wetland floodplains and forests to flattened summits. It forms a splendid recreation space, popular with downhill **mountain bikers**.

The reserve was named after the the mountain peak that forms part of the gruelling Colombian **cycle race** called **Vuelta Ciclista al Pais Vasco**.

NORTHERN PART

Bello★

◐ *10km/6mi N of Medellín, to the north of Carrera 50 and Carrera 49.*

Founded in 1679, the "Beautiful," as its name translates, is the second-most populated municipality (Pop. 373,013) in the valley after Medellín.

Due to its flourishing artistic traditions, this pretty settlement is also known as Colombia's "City of Artists," with plenty of scenic surrounding countryside to inspire painters, poets and photographers alike.

Sitio Arqueológico Indios Niquías

✏ *Information available from the Casa de la Cultura Cerro del Ángel, Calle 53A # 52-23. ☎(4) 272 5756.*

Visitors with a couple of hours to spare should walk three magical historical trails: the **Tierradentro**, the **Camino Corrales** and the **Sendero de Piedra**, believed to have been hand-cut by the indigenous **Niquia People**. All are signed out of town and are considered an important part of Bello's heritage.

Copacabana

◐ *18km/11mi NE of Medellín via Carretera 25.*

Located in the narrowest part of the valley, this small surburban town (Pop. 61,421) is one of many jumping-off

points for the nearby **Parque Ecológico de Piedras Blancas**, a forested expanse about 8km/5mi away.

Named after some large white **rocks** believed to have had sacred significance to ancient indigenous tribes, this natural setting is popular with **mountain bike** enthusiasts.

Girardota

◐ *26km/16mi NE of Medellín via Carretera 62.*

The area around Girardota was originally inhabited by **Yamesíes** and **Nutabes**. It was settled by Europeans in 1620, with **African slaves** brought in to work the sugarcane fields.

Today the town (Pop. 42,818) is distinctive for its **plantain farms** and **sugarcane distilleries** *(trapiches)*, some of them open to the public such as **Trapiche en San Diego** and **Trapiche de las Finca Caimitos** *(information can be obtained from la oficina de Planeación, Palacio Municipal de Girardota, Carrera 15 # 6-35; ☎4 405 4200 ext. 126).*

Also worth seeking out is Calle 13, a block behind the main park, where Girardota's string of **Colonial buildings** can be seen, many now beautifully restored.

Barbosa

◐ *38km/24mi NE of Medellín via Carretera 62.*

Nestled in the lowest part of the valley, Barbosa (Pop. 42,547) is famous for its traditional **Fiesta de la Piña** (Pineapple Festival), a rowdy affair that draws crowds from all over Antioquia.

The **Barbosa pineapple** is said to be especially plump and juicy, with the fruit held in such esteem by the locals that it has been celebrated with gusto every two years since 1961.

Numerous religious blessings honor the "Tierra de la Piña" (Land of the Pineapple) before a song contest centers on music and lyrics dedicated to the fruit. Other events include a beauty pageant at which the Pineapple Queen is crowned, held in December in the central **Parque Diego Echavarría Misas**.

Medellín's Corregimientos★

Conveniently located close to town, Medellín's five **annexed villages** are pleasant places to escape the city bustle and experience the rural charm of Medellín's surroundings. These peaceful, picturesque villages make a welcome change of pace.

Altavista★
4km/2mi SW of Medellín, W of Carrera 83 and Calle 20.
Bordered by San Cristóbal and Medellín to the north, San Antonio de Prado to the west, Itagüí to the south and Medellín to the east, **Altavista** barely spans 9.4km/5.8mi, but is a relaxing place in which to while away the hours.
Altavista is famous for its collection of unusual **stone walls** built by ancient indigenous groups. You will also discover some old Nutibara Indian **trails**, trodden later by **Spanish colonists**, that are today explored by adventurers on horseback, ready to discover the heritage of the region.
Key festivals in Altavista include the 9-day **Fiestas Patronales Nuestra Señora del Rosario de la Piedra**—a response to an 1857 apparition of the Virgin in a rock in an outlying area of town. A kite festival called **Festival de Cometas** also takes place in June each year, attracting quite a crowd.

San Antonio de Prado★
11km/7mi SW of Medellín via Carrera 50A and then Calle 36.
Bordered by Palmitas and San Cristóbal to the north, Altavista to the east, Itagüí and La Estrella to the south and Heliconia and Angelopolis to the west, this village shares with Altavista the **Reserva Altavista Alto de Manzanillo**, an important biological corridor of Antioquia.
The region is a popular place to **hike** and **bird-watch**.
The town's Gothic Revival church, in front of the main park, is distinctive for its castle-like machicolations, and contains some fine works by the Spanish painter José Claro.

San Cristóbal★
8km/5mi NW of Medellín via Carretera 62.
A charming **flower-growing town** with fields and greenhouses evident on its outskirts, San Cristóbal is also renowned for less tranquil pursuits. Surrounding lakes, streams, waterfalls and rugged terrain attract visitors seeking to partake in extreme **outdoors adventures**, from rappelling and canyoning to trekking, mountain biking and fishing. Once used by hunters, settlers and mules, an old trail, the **Camino Viejo**★, connects Santa Fé de Antioquia with Medellín and areas farther south. Local caves such as the Cueva del Indio are the subject of many legends. Not only are they believed to have been created by wild animals, but they are also thought to contain buried treasures.
Cultural events take place monthly in San Cristóbal, creating an opportunity to meet artisans, poets, musicians and folk dancers, and also buy local **crafts**.

San Sebastián de Palmitas
17km/11mi NW of Medellín via the Túnel de Occidente.
Known to have been settled by indigenous groups in 1745, San Sebastián de Palmitas sits at an altitude of between 1,400m/4,593ft and 3,100m/10,171ft and is cool and crisp. Known for its old **path** stretching to the coast—an important ancient trade route—the town is wholly based on agriculture, with **coffee**,

Parque Ecoturístico Arví★

Metro Cable Line L connects Santo Domingo Savio with Parque Arví. ⏴⏴Guided walks organized by the Corporación Parque Regional Ecoturístico Arví, 18km/11mi E of Santa Elena on the road to Piedras Blancas. ☎*(4) 414 2979. www.parquearvi.org.* This brand new natural reserve (16,000ha/39,536 acres) is still in its early stages of development, but it already offers a number of promising tourist attractions such as horseback riding, visits to traditional flower growers and of course, the possibility of **guided hikes** through native forests and pine groves. The park conceals other unexpected treasures, including some pre-Hispanic ruins and the **Camino Cieza de León**, a stone path that may be as old as 1,500 years.

plantains, **onions** and sugarcane the major crops. It shares its most exhilarating, rugged slopes with San Cristóbal and San Antonio de Prado. Under a full moon, on a Saturday, the town's artistic community stages an evening of **storytelling**, poetry, art, music and food. In January each year, the **Fiestas de San Sebastián** honor the patron saint of the district, with street processions, music, religious services and folk dances.

Santa Elena★★
▶ *8km/5mi E of Medellín via Calle 49.*
Comprised of 17 **hamlets** or *veredas*, this rural farming community nestles in the mountain folds east of Medellín, in a setting praised for its pure, fresh air. Local farmers grow mainly potatoes, blackberries and strawberries, and produce milk. Each *vereda* has its own distinct culture and character; to discover them, follow one of the tiny side roads that lead to settlements like **El Plan**. From here, a road heads to **El Chispero**, and a path ascends to one of the best viewpoints in Santa Elena—a must for truly mesmerizing **vistas**★ of the valley and Medellín.

The region's **silleteros** (farmers) play a key role in Medellín's annuala, the famous flower parade that takes place in August each year. It's a time when the farmers leave their villages for the big city, and stride through Medellín, carrying huge arrangements of colorful fresh flowers, greeted by the enthusiastic cheers of thousands of onlookers.

The scenery around Santa Elena is truly breathtaking, with rolling hills, gushing streams, forests and the nearby **Parque Ecoturístico Arví** (⏺ *see sidebar above*), a vast nature reserve recently linked to Medellín by cable car.

Silletero in Feria de las Flores

Froeeport Colombia

235

ADDRESSES

☆STAY

$ Casa Kiwi – *Carrera 36 # 7-10, Barrio El Poblado, Medellín.* ✆ *(4) 268 2668. www.casakiwi.net. 19 rooms.*
An American-owned hostel in the center of Medellín's Zona Rosa, Casa Kiwi added some new double rooms, so it's more attractive to couples. With free Wi-Fi, kitchen, bike rental, a DVD library and a pool table, this hostel has some terrific amenities for the price.

$ Hotel Capitolio – *Carrera 49 # 57-21, Medellín.* ✗ ⊥ ✆ *(4) 512 0012. 39 rooms.*
Large standard rooms here have their own bathrooms, TVs and stocked mini-bars. Surprisingly quiet for this area of the city, the Capitolio features an open-air bar by the swimming pool and a reasonably priced **restaurant ($$)**.

$$ Hotel Conquistadores – *Carrera 54 # 49-31, Medellín.* ✗ ✆ *(4) 512 3232. www.webteam.com.co/hconquist. 38 rooms.*
Located downtown near the museums, this small family-run lodging is ideal for a quiet boutique-style stay away from all the backpackers. The Conquistadores caters to budget business travelers; the staff are proud that it doesn't accept hourly room rates *(por rato)*, so it's surprising that guests have reported police raids here. Rooms have cable TV and private baths with hot water; there's a small budget restaurant on-site.

$$ Hotel Nutibara – *Calle 52A # 50-46, Medellín.* ✗ ⊥ ✆ *(4) 511 5111. www.hotelnutibara.com. 140 rooms.* Situated next to the Museum of Antioquia, this hotel once housed the presidents of Colombia, before the city's more luxurious hotels were built. Although the Nutibara has since faded in places, it oozes style and character, and still displays original Art Deco accents.

$$$ Hotel Park 10 – *Carrera 36B # 11-12, Barrio El Poblado, Medellín.* ℙ✗ ✆ *(4) 266 8811. http://hotelpark10.com.co. 55 rooms.* From its marble and wood-paneled lobby to its well-appointed suites, this glitzy post-Modern hotel focuses on mid-week business clients—and consequent weekend discounts. Guests consistently rave about the service and staff. Earth tones and dark woods furnish the spacious rooms, while suites have Jacuzzi tubs. The fitness facility is just average, but the location a few blocks from the Parque Lleras is unbeatable.

$$$$ Hotel Dann Carlton – *Av. El Poblado, Carrera 43A # 7-50, Medellín.* ℙ✗⊥ Spa ✆ *(4) 444 5151. www.danncarlton.com. 200 rooms.* Adjacent to Parque Linear, this hotel offers top-notch service, including fresh flowers in your room. Room service and the front desk staff are available 24/7. Modern conveniences include hairdryers, phones and mini-bars; suites add walk-in-wardrobes. For the best views, request a room facing the park. Dine at the revolving 19th-floor restaurant.

$$$$ Hotel Poblado Plaza – *Carrera 43A # 4 Sur-75, Barrio El Poblado, Medellín.* ℙ✗ ✆ *(4) 268 5555. www.hotelpobladoplaza.com. 84 rooms.* This well-situated hotel attracts a high-end business clientele as well as wealthy local tourists. Freshly cut flowers adorn the lobby; elsewhere on the property you'll find a gym and sauna, and free Wi-Fi on every floor. Comfort abounds in spacious rooms done in warm brown tones. For the best Wi-Fi access, ask for a central room on any floor; for peace and quiet, request a room at the end of the building.

☆/EAT

$$ Il Forno – *Calle 37 # 8-9, Medellín.* ✆ *(4) 268 9402.* One of seven locations in Medellín, this satellite of Il Forno is set in the middle of the Zona Rosa. The open-air restaurant with its wood-burning oven serves consistently good and inexpensive thin-crust pizza, lasagna, ravioli, tomato soup and more. The staff could be more attentive, but for this price you can put up with some flaws. **Italian**.

$$ Mango Maduro – *Calle 54, # 46-5, Medellín.* ✆ *(4) 512 3671. Lunch only. Closed Sun.* This tiny bohemian restaurant was once one of Medellín's best-kept gastronomic secrets. With nine small tables, a friendly waitstaff and a single set menu, Mango Maduro is worth seeking out. Arrive early to get a seat to sample traditional Colombian cuisine. **Colombian**.

$$ Restaurante La Vera – *Carrera 43B # 8-65, Medellín.* 🖉*(4) 311 5877. Lunch only.* A favorite place downtown for the 9-to-5 set, this restaurant takes its name from a famous Spanish tango song. Set meals revolve around regional dishes, and are always moderately priced. Specials might include pumpkin soup, and traditional dishes such as *ajiaco* (Bogotano stew). **Colombian**.

$$ Thaico – *Calle 9A # 37-40, Medellín.* 🖉*(4) 352 2166.* Laid-back by day, this little charmer puts on a party atmosphere later in the evening. One of the few Thai restaurants in Colombia, Thaico doesn't go overboard on the spiciness of a cuisine that is known for being fiery. Go before 7pm for half-price entrées and 3-for-1 cocktails. **Thai**.

$$ Tramezzini – *Calle 9A # 37-56, Parque Lleras, Medellín.* 🖉*(4) 311 5617. Closed Sun.* Named for the little crustless sandwiches served in Italy, this trattoria is lauded by Medellín's food press and foreign visitors. With first-rate service and cuisine, Tramezzini regularly hosts a local A-list of personalities, who dress the part. **Italian**.

$$$ El Cielo Cocina Creativa – *Carrera 40 # 10A-22, El Poblado, Medellín.* 🖉*(4) 268 3002. http://elcielococinacreativa. com. Closed Sun.* Located in the El Poblado area, El Cielo offers a chic and artful dining experience. Chef Juan Manuel Barrientos' elaborate tasting menus range from 11 (**$$$**) to 20 courses (**$$$$**). The menu changes every six weeks, but past creations have included sirloin steak with chocolate sauce, blue cheese and a parmesan crisp. **Contemporary.**

🏃🏻 RECREATION

Jardín Botánico – *Calle 73 # 1D-14, Medellín.* 🍽 🖉*(4) 444 5500. www.botanicomedellin.org.* Newly refurbished with a trendy cafe serving light fare, these gardens are easily accessed by metro (the nearest stop is Universidad). The lovely grounds comprise several distinct areas, including a tropical forest and a desert garden. The Orquideorama houses a collection of orchids, and an herb garden supplies the on-site restaurant.

Pueblito Paisa – *2km/1.2mi southwest of the city center.* 🍽🖉*385 5555.* A 20-minute walk uphill from the Industriales metro brings you to Pueblito Paisa, a re-creation of a typical Antioquian village. Along with an art gallery and open-air theater, the Pueblito atop Cerro Nutibara affords stunning views over the city. 🔍*See p226.*

Zona de Vuelo – *6km/4mi north of Medellín in Bello, on the road to San Pedro de los Milagros.* 🖉*(4) 388 1556. www.zonadevuelo.com.* Given Medellín's thermal winds, the area is an ideal place for paragliding. Zona de Vuelo is a well-established paragliding school that offers tandem flights and 10-day courses. It can also arrange paragliding and non-paragliding trips.

🎭 NIGHTLIFE

La 33 – Jam-packed with bars, discos and restaurants, this long avenue from Barrio San Deigo to Laurenels is a bit less posh than the Zona Rosa. La 33 isn't serviced by the metro, but it is easily accessible by taxi or bus.

El Patio del Tango – *Calle 23 # 58-38, Medellín.* 🍽 🖉*(4) 351 2856.* Off the main drag, this little club is the place to get a good Argentine steak, listen to live tango music and on some nights, even dance. The owner often sings here and regales guests with tales of Medellín's rich tango history.

Theater – *www.medellinenescena.com.* Medellín boasts a vibrant theater scene with more than 10 venues staging a variety of productions. Here are some:

Teatro Pablo Tobon Uribe (*Carrera 40 # 51-24; www.teatropablotobon.com*) is the city's largest performance space, while **Casa del Teatro Medellín** (*Calle 59 # 50A-25, Barrio Prado Centro; www. casadelteatro.org.co*) hosts different local theater groups and has a good library devoted to Colombian theater.

Teatro Metropolitano (*Calle 41 # 57-30; www.teatrometropolitano.com*) offers opera, ballet and performances by a philharmonic orchestra.

Tierra Paisa★ around Medellín

Antioquia, Caldas

A subcultural rather than a natural region, the area referred to as "Paisa Country" not only encompasses the department of Antioquia, but also Caldas, Risaralda and Quindío, which form the greater part of Colombia's famous Zona Cafetera. The Paisa culture extends even to the northern part of Valle del Cauca and northwestern Tolima.

With huge areas once off-limits because of guerrilla violence, Tierra Paisa is now much more accessible to visitors. Here a great variety of vivid landscapes are waiting to be discovered by travelers to Colombia, as well as picturesque villages held together by a strong sense of identity and tradition.

PAISA IDENTITY

Unlike the rest of Colombia, where residents use their local demonym (Bogotano, Medellínese, etc.), the Paisa folk simply refer to themselves as **Paisa**. Named after the Spanish apocope of *paisano* (one from the same country), the Paisa are sometimes considered a distinct ethnic group (Raza Paisa) in Colombia—so unique is their cultural identity.

Michelin Maps: p209 and p245.

Info: Before departing Medellín to explore its surroundings, your best bet is to stop by one of its **tourist information points** (PITs) such as the one at the **Centro de Convenciones**, Plaza Mayor, Calle 41 # 55-80 to gather information. Also check www.medellin.travel/en/ and www.antioquiaturistica.com for practical information on the department of Antioquia.

Don't Miss: People-watching from an open-air cafe found in any of the Pueblitos Paisas around Medellín; Santa Fé de Antioquia, with its pretty whitewashed Colonial buildings and narrow streets; the spectacular views of Antioquia's countryside from El Peñol.

In the minds of many Colombians nationwide, the fictional **Juan Valdez**—Colombia's most famous name and personage in coffee advertisements—is the quintessential Paisa: a hard-working mustached coffee worker, clad in a

Guatapé's colorful houses

Andrés Marquine/Proexport Colombia

poncho and sombrero with a rawhide shoulder bag, standing alongside his faithful mule with the mountains in view. A stereotype? Certainly, yet not without foundation, as almost every Paisa person will readily bear out.

Paisa Roots

The Paisa identity owes much to the Antioquian colonizers who settled here from **rural Spain**, bringing their enterprising qualities with them. Desiring to own land and be economically independent, these **farmers** from Spain's mountainous **northern regions** were wholly different from their counterparts from the Spanish South.

Their descendants placed great importance on ancestry, and old **Basque** surnames are still commonplace throughout society. Known for their deep-rooted pragmatism, adventurous spirit and business acumen, they form strong interfamilial bonds, love the land and enjoy the challenge of forging new paths. Fervent Catholic beliefs structure much of their everyday activities, with heartfelt values passed down through the generations.

The Paisa speak in a particular way, sometimes referred to as **Español Antioqueño**—a fast-uttered, soft dialect that uses *vos* for the second person singular pronoun with a stress on the *s*, much like the distinct Castilian sound.

Paisa Architecture

Paisa towns were established along different lines than other colonial settlements, with adaptations to suit the undulating, steep slopes and high altitude. Built from **tapia** (or cob) and **bahareque** (plaited cane and mud) with mud roof tiles, the Antioquian houses were decorated with woodcarvings, fretwork and appliqué. Motifs of birds, animals and flowers adorned these rural dwellings. Their layout was designed to integrate the structure with the surroundings—allowing residents to enjoy the landscape from any part of the house. Stables, granaries, henhouses, storage rooms, and a *helda* (a covered area where coffee growers could leave

Paisa musician

Andrés Marquine/Proexport Colombia

the parchment coffee to dry in the sun, protected from the rain) were annexed to the living quarters—a design that reflects the inextricable link between a Paisa at home and work.

Paisa Food

The Paisa people are also distinctive for their culinary traditions, with food in the region famous for **heartiness**, large portions, careful preparation and taste. Almost every recipe relies on locally-grown Paisa produce, either freshly harvested or preserved using unique storage methods typical of the region. Many of these dishes have their origins in **Northern Spain**, such as robust Basque-style **stews** and wholesome **soups**. Home-cooking is highly regarded, typical delicacies being *sopa de mondongo, empanada antioqueña, frijoles, mazamorra* and *arepa antioqueña*. However, it is a stomach-churning dish called **La Bandeja Paisa** that most Colombians associate with Antioquia. Old-style **cafes** remain important to the Paisa male (much like they do in Spain) as a place to talk business and set the world straight.

Paisa Folklore

Paisa people are proud of their fiercely upheld folk music, with **musica de carrilera** (rail music) the region's much-loved country sound, born of the Antioquian Railway. Festivals continue to play an important role in Paisa culture, with Aguadas' **Festival del Pasillo**—a Colombian folk dance festival—one of the biggest annual events.

WEST OF MEDELLÍN★

Also called Túnel de Occidente, the **Túnel Fernando Gómez Martínez**—the largest tunnel of its kind in Latin America—connects Medellín to the western region and its traditional **Antioquian pueblos**. Blessed by pleasant weather, this pleasing expanse of verdant hills, banana palms and **fruit trees** nourished by **scenic rivers** is developing its own brand of regional tourism, based on its unique **history** and cultural treasures.

San Jerónimo★

◐ *41km/25mi NW of Medellín via Carretera 62.*

The newly improved road to San Jerónimo skirts the Río Cauca, passing through fruit fields before entering this 17C town (Pop. 11,603), located on the eastern foothills of the Cordillera Central. Visitors can fish around here, enjoy a refreshing swim in river pools and waterfalls, or walk to the **Quebrada Guaracú**★, a creek where gushing waters over a gorge form dramatic rock-carved shapes in a scenic spot bounded by trees. A day trip out to a park on the outskirts of town is also possible.

Parque Los Tamarindos

Accessible from the via Guillermo Gaviria Correa. ◐*Open Tue–Fri 9am–5pm, Sat–Sun & public holidays 9am–6pm.* ◐*Closed Tue after Mon public holiday.* ◈*8,400 COP.* ✆*(4) 858 0475. www.comfenalcoantioquia.com.*

This all-purpose recreation zone contains swimming pools, artificial sandy beaches, ecological trails, whirlpools and picnic areas.

Sopetrán

◐ *40km/25mi NW of Medellín (off Carretera 62, the turn after San Jerónimo).*

The "Fruit Capital of Antioquia" (Pop. 13,352) is a mango-growing town, worthy of a visit on the basis of its scenic farming terrain. As part of Antioquia's **Ruta de Sol**—a trio of towns that includes San Jerónimo and Santa Fé de Antioquia—it shares a history as one of the region's oldest settlements, dating back to the early 17C.

Tourists passing through may want to check the Colonial-style **Ermita de San Nicolás** *(corregimiento de San Nicolás, SW of Sopetrán),* one of the oldest churches in the department of Antioquia (1662), or visit the **Vivero Municipal Andrés Posada Arango** *(4 blocks from the Parque Principal; information available from the Palacio Municipal of Sopetrán;* ✆*4 854 1560),* which ranks as the first **nursery** of its kind in Latin America, with 38 varieties of mangos, 26 varieties of citrus and other fruits such as sapodilla and papaya.

NORTH OF MEDELLÍN★

Steeply sloping terrain and flatter grassy meadows characterize this farming area where **cattle raising**, dairy herds, **vegetable crops** and, to a lesser extent, **mining** are the bedrock of the local economy. Lands rich in **indigenous heritage** are honored in some particularly well-stocked local museums, while regional handicrafts range from ceramics to woven bags.

Puente de Occidente★

6km/4mi E of Santa Fé de Antioquia, on the road to Sopetrán (between Olaya and Santa Fé de Antioquia).

A true gem of 19C engineering, this Colombian National Monument is one of the world's first suspension bridges. The metal-and-wood construction, which straddles the Río Cauca and links Olaya and Santa Fé de Antioquia, was designed by **José Maria Villa** (1850-1913), a Colombian architect who trained in New Jersey and contributed to New York's Brooklyn Bridge.

Villa built four bridges on the Cauca River, but this one, with its distinctive twin turrets on either end, took eight years to complete (1887-1895). Stretching 291m/955ft, it carried traffic until 1978. It is now used only by light vehicles, but is best walked for a disorienting wobbly effect.

Santa Fé de Antioquia★★

▶ *67km/42mi NW of Medellín via Carretera 62.*

Antioquia (Pop. 22,613) is set in a low-lying, steamy valley watered by the Cauca and Tonusco rivers. Dubbed "Ciudad Madre" (the Mother City), the town—the oldest settlement in the region—has handsome streets virtually unchanged from the early 18C.

A BIT OF HISTORY

Founded in 1541 by **Jorge Robledo**, the original settlement received the title of City of Antioquia from **King Phillip II of Spain** in 1545. The town prospered and was beautified under Spanish colonial rule, fulfilling the role of **Capital of Antioquia** from 1584 to 1826. Today it preserves its Colonial buildings in grand style.

🐾 WALKING TOUR

To discover Santa Fé de Antioquia, simply walk its narrow, cobblestone streets, lined by single-story pastel-colored buildings set around flower-filled courtyards and plazas.

Begin at the **Plaza Mayor**★ to get an appreciation for one of the lovely streetscapes and the carvings that decorate each wooden doorway. Pause to marvel at the 450-year-old **fountain** close to a fine bronze statue of **Juan del Corral**, an early 19C local political figure.

Facing the plaza, the **Catedral Basílica Metropolitana de la Inmaculada Concepción**★ (1797-1837) is notable for its white and colored stone and brick façade, typical of the *calicanto* style. Peer inside to view its 17C Christ figure.

Don't miss the impressive mid-18C Baroque **Iglesia de Santa Bárbara**★ *(Calle 11 and Carrera 8)* and the **Iglesia de Jesús Nazareno**★ *(Calle 10 and Carrera 5)*, an elegant example of 19C classical style.

Street in Santa Fé de Antioquia

© Lionela Rob/Alamy

Pieces of sacred art can be found at the **Museo de Arte Religioso Francisco Cristóbal Toro**★ *(Calle de la Amargura, Calle 11 # 8-12;* ⏱ *open Sat–Sun & public holidays 10am -5pm;* 💰 *2,000 COP;* 📞 *4 853 1031)*, including paintings by Gregorio Vásquez de Arce y Ceballos.

The **Museo Juan del Corral** nearby *(Calle 11 # 9-77;* ⏱ *open Mon–Tue, Thu–Fri 9am–noon, 2pm–5pm, Sat–Sun & public holidays 10am–5pm;* 💰 *1,000 COP;* 🐾 *guided visits available;* 📞 *4 853 4605)* has artifacts from all historical periods.

Built on the site of a 17C Franciscan temple, the 19C **Nuestra Señora de Chiquinquirá**★ *(Carrera 13 and Calle 10)* was used as a prison for a time. It adjoins the **Palacio Arzobispal** *(Carrera 12 and Calle 10)*. Renovated in the Republican style, this building (1902) boasts a patio and handsome exterior windows—a stunning contrast to the church's Baroque detail.

👃 Sample the local **pulpa de tamarindo**, a super-sweet candy with a touch of sour made from tamarind grown in the surrounding valley; vendors on Plaza Mayor sell it from battered wooden stalls.

La Sixtina de Antioquia★

The **Basílica Menor del Señor de los Milagros** *(in San Pedro de los Milagros, 42km/26mi N of Medellín via the road from San Cristobal; ℘4 882 3456; www. parroquiasanpedro.org)* has been dubbed "the Sistine Chapel of Antioquia," such is its quality. Dedicated to the Lord of Miracles, this fine building (1895) attracts large numbers of pilgrims from across the Antioquia region, its image of Señor de los Milagros being considered miraculous.

Decorated with elaborate gold and silver flourishes and delicate gilded work, a replica of Michelangelo's masterpiece in the domed ceiling forms a stunning centerpiece. In recent years, the building has been lavished with new, magnificent stained-glass panels and ornate columns. The 14 stations of the Cross were also reinstated, using extensive golf leaf.

Entrerríos

◗ *60km/37mi NE of Medellín via Carretera 25 and then W via the road from Don Matías.*

This traditional agricultural town (Pop. 8,452) is set among the steep slopes that characterize the terrain between the Río Grande and Río Chico. The main focus here is dairy farming and growing tomatoes, potatoes, beans and maize. Entrerríos' **Casa de la Cultura y Unidad Cultural** *(Calle 10 # 13-149; ◷open Mon–Fri 8am–noon, 1pm–noon, Sat 8am–noon; ℘4 867 0253)* contains a collection of pieces used in the tanning of leather, together with ceramics from the Catío and Nutabe cultures.

The town of Entrerríos also has its own 75m/246ft high **Piedra del Peñol de Entrerríos**, a modest version of the **El Peñol** monolith located near Guatapé, east of Medellín.

Santa Rosa de Osos

◗ *72 km/45mi NE of Medellín, along Carretera 25.*

This town (Pop. 31,028) is famous for its delicious *pandequesos* (cheese biscuits) and dairy products (pudding, cream and yogurt). It is also renowned as the birthplace of **Porfirio Barba Jacob** (1883-1942), one of the most important Antioquian and Colombian poets, commemorated with a museum dedicated to his craft, the **Museo Cultural Porfirio Barba Jacob** *(Calle Caldas; ◷open Mon–Fri 8am–5pm, Sat–Sun by appointment; ⌁guided tours available; ℘4 860 8016).*

Overlooking the central plaza, the imposing twin-domed **Catedral Principal** *(Parque Principal)* presents a formidable landmark and is the focal point for all of Santa Rosa de Osos's religious festivals. The town is also the seat of Fundación Universitaria Católica del Norte (FUCN), Colombia's first **virtual learning e-academy,** with all studies and lectures conducted online.

San José de la Montaña★

◗ *128km/80mi NW of Medellín via Carretera 25 and then from los Llanos de Cuivá on the road to Ituango.*

This village (Pop. 3,077) of white-washed houses sits at an altitude of 2,550m/8,366ft in a landscape of verdant meadows, dairy farms, oak forests and rivers. It boasts some well-preserved historical buildings, including the **Casa Cural** *(corner of Parque Principal),* with its ceramic tiles, color-washed walls and a large courtyard full of blooms, birds and trees. Some pleasing natural attractions are located on the town's outskirts, such as the **Alto del Cristo**★, a high-point reached via a nature trail offering fine views of the surrounding villages. Other treks lead across the **Valle de Frailejones** through rolling fields covered in the region's distinct grasslands *(frailejones).* Once a hive of mining activity, the **Cavernas de Santa Bárbara** were abandoned 50 years ago, but one of the largest **mule paths** in the history of the northern and western Antioquia department is still visible.

Yarumal★
▶ *123km/76mi NE of Medellín, along Carretera 25.*

The author of the lyrics of the Antioquian anthem, **Epifanio Mejía**, was born in this highland town (Pop. 31,816) where banana, yucca, corn, coffee and sugarcane are the mainstay of the local economy.

Yarumal is best known for the **Vereda Chorros Blancos**★, a trail leading to the famous battleground of Chorros Blancos where, in 1820, Royalists loyal to the Spanish Crown attempted to regain control of New Granada. Occuring six months after the Battle of Boyacá, the upsurge was defeated by **José María Córdova** (✎ *see sidebar p244*), the governor of Antioquia province who was in charge of some of Bolívar's troops. Today an **obelisk** serves as a memorial to this important event in the fight for independence.

EAST OF MEDELLÍN
Rolling fertile farmland, bountiful crops and plentiful livestock characterize the landscapes of this **breadbasket region**. Multi-colored patchwork fields of coffee, beans, maize and tomatoes form a resplendent checkerboard terrain dotted with traditional red-roofed **Paisa fincas** (small holdings) and **greenhouses** filled with blooms. Machete-wielding **campesinos** (farmers) slash away at fast-sprouting roadside vegetation on steep grassy banks where tethered horses graze. Small communities engaged in proud agricultural traditions typify this farming heartland where a burgeoning ecotourism sector centers on its many **walking** and **cycling trails** with steep uphill spurs and exhilarating descents.

El Retiro★
▶ *32km/20mi SE of Medellín via Envigado, off the road to La Ceja.*

"The Retreat" is a sleepy colonial, cattle-ranching settlement (Pop. 16,974), famous for its wooden **furniture-making** tradition. Most of its residents are engaged in vegetable farming and dairy production. Built in 1825 the **Hacienda**

Fizebad★ is a lovely old mansion with a dazzling collection of **orchids** from all over the region; part country club, the estate also houses a replica of a typical **Pueblito Paisa** and a **Museo de la Antioqueñidad** (✎ *open Sat–Sun and holidays 9am–5pm; ℰ4 542 1313; www.haciendafizebad.com*) dedicated to the Antioquian culture.

From El Retiro you can hike out to a fine array of natural pools and **waterfalls** in the surrounding countryside, including the **Salto del Tequendamita**, a stunning 20m/66ft high cascade on the road to La Ceja.

La Ceja★
▶ *41km/25mi SE of Medellín via Envigado. This flower-growing town (Pop. 46,366) is home to the glorious* **Fiesta del Toldo y las Flores** *in December. Inhabited by peaceful maize-farming Tahamies in pre-Columbian times, La Ceja was settled by the Spanish in 1541. Some 15 local* **flower producers** *are engaged in the export of lilies, tulips, carnations, hydrangeas and chrysanthemums.*

While in town, visitors should sample some of La Ceja's homemade candy, puddings, toffee apples, jams, caramel and chocolate, available for sale in and around the central **Plaza de Bolívar**.

Land of Flowers

Colombia boasts an impressive portfolio of 1,600 different varieties of flowers. It is the world's second-largest exporter of cut flowers after the Netherlands, and the main provider to the US—77 percent of all flowers sold there being imported from Colombia. The flower industry has really taken hold in the high, sunny plateaus around Medellín, where excellent light levels produce long-lasting blooms.

Some popular flowers used in festivals and on various occasions in Colombia are gerberas, gingers, roses, sunflowers and orchids.

José María Córdova (1799-1829)

The equestian statue of this great Antioquian hero, found in Rionegro's **Parque de la Libertad**, honors the memory of the most prominent general in the region during the period of independence. Vehemently defending democracy, Córdova fought the Spanish Royalists and actually defeated them in January 1820, at the famous battle of **Chorros Blancos**, putting an end to the Spanish military presence in Antioquia. Córdova then rebelled against **Simón Bolívar** for his "dictator pretensions" and was under investigation for the conspiracy of the **Noche Septembrina**, a failed assassination attempt on Bolívar's life by mutinous officers.

Rionegro★

45km/28mi SE of Medellín (via Carretera 60 from the NE of Medellín, and then the right turn before Marinilla).
Rionegro (Pop. 101,046) is home to Medellín's **Aeropuerto Internacional José María Córdova**. It is also known for the role it played during Colombia's struggle for independence. The **Constitution of 1863** (also called "Consti-

tution of Rionegro") was promulgated here, which gave birth to the **United States of Colombia**. Years later, this Constitution was repealed by **Rafael Núñez** and replaced with the **Constitution of 1886**. From then on, the nation was officially called **Republic of Colombia**.

A small museum, the **Museo Histórico Casa de la Convención** (Calle 51 # 47-67; open Mon–Fri 9am–5pm, Sat 9am–1pm; 4 561 0710) pays tribute to these defining moments in Colombian history, and the town's large, whitewashed Colonial-style **cathedral** should be seen.

El Carmen de Viboral★★

54km/34mi SE of Medellín (via Carretera 60 from the NE of Medellín, and then the right turn before Marinilla).
This town (Pop. 40,968) is famous all over Colombia for its fine Vajillas del Carmen, or **painted ceramics**, most of which are still made using **handcrafted methods**.

Typically, delicate **floral designs** trim the base or neck of vases, bowls, jugs or cups, which are plain white or cream in color. Numerous outlets around town offer the opportunity to snap up some local pottery, including **Ceramicas Esmaltarte** (Carrera 31 # 37-05; 4 543 0890), which has a kiln in a small courtyard, containing pieces ready to be fired for a second time.

Catedral, Rionegro

© Jan Csernoch/Alamy

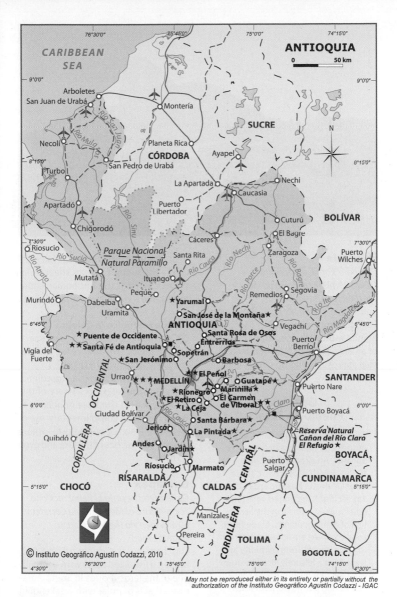

Marinilla★

▶ *47km/29mi SE of Medellín (via Carretera 60 from the NE of Medellín).*

Known as "La Ciudad con Alma Musical," Marinilla (Pop. 45,658) hosts a thriving home-grown music scene.

As host of the annual **Festival de Música Andina Colombiana** *(Nov)*, it attracts its fair share of melody-loving tourists. Its **Festival de Música Religiosa**, which takes place during Holy Week, is another well-attended musical event.

Fabrica de Guitarras Ensueño

Calle 22 # 31-18. ☎*(4) 548 4076.*

Renowned throughout the region and beyond, this guitar factory has been in the Arbeláez family since the 19C. It specializes in wood-crafted, handmade stringed instruments, and welcomes tourists with a passion for music.

El Peñol and the reservoir of Guatapé

Proexport Colombia

El Peñol★★

▶ 62km/39mi E of Medellín (30km/19mi NE of Marinilla via the road to Guatapé).

Somewhat reminiscent of Rio's Sugar Loaf, this impressive 200m/656ft-high granite **monolith** rises from the banks of an artificial lake. Reached by a 650-step staircase built into one side of the rock, the **lookout platform** (⬡5,000 COP) at its summit reveals spectacular **views**★★ across the Antioquian countryside, and is well worth the uphill climb.

Parque Ecológico la Culebra

⏱Open Mon–Sat 8am–5pm, Sun 9am–6pm. ⬡2,000 COP entrance fee, pedalos complimentary. ✆(4) 851 5488.

Pack a picnic or barbecue ingredients and enjoy the relaxing scenery of this small park near the base of hulking El Peñol rock. The complimentary use of *pedalos* offers an opportunity to explore the farthest reaches of the lake and even go fishing.

Guatapé★

▶ 3km/2mi beyond El Peñol rock and 75km/47mi E of Medellín (via Carretera 60 and then via the Marinilla to Guatapé road).

This charming lakeside town (Pop. 5,800) borders a fish-filled **reservoir**—actually one of the largest ones in South America—that is popular with weekending boaters. In the 1960s, the creation of this artificial lake and construction of its **dam** involved flooding the village of **El Peñol** and actually relocating it. Guatapé is one of the major electric production centers in the country and as such was a target during the early 1990s. Today, patrolled by government forces, the area is safe again, and Guatapé has reverted to a quiet little town blessed by nature.

Guatapé "Pueblo de Zócalos"

Guatapé is famous for its Colonial houses and their distinctive **zócalos**. An exported Spanish tradition with a local twist, these bright, colorful **baseboards** (about 1m/3ft high), decorated with high-relief friezes, embellish the lower half of many buildings. Made from concrete, they are actually meant to protect walls from humidity and wear. Take a leisurely stroll through Guatapé to fully appreciate these fascinating public works of art, a real insight into local life, as they sometimes feature satirical figures and political humor. *Zócalos* have become such an integral part of Guatapé's identity that they are now protected by city ordinance.

🔊Some of the most traditional *zócalos* are to be found along the **Calle del Recuerdo**, just a couple blocks from the main plaza.

Beside the multiple nautical attractions derived from the reservoir, a few interesting highlights in town include its famous *zócalos* (& *see sidebar below*), its pleasant **malecón** (a walkway running parallel to the lake, lined with restaurants) and its white and red Greco-Roman **Iglesia Nuestra Señora del Carmen** *(Parque Principal)* with a curious clock face erroneously featuring the wrong Roman numeral for 4.

Reserva Natural Cañon del Río Claro El Refugio★

152km/94mi E of Medellín close to La Mesa Norte, via Carretera 60 toward Bogotá. (4) 268 8855. www.rioclaro elrefugio.com. Visitors should pack a flashlight (for caves), rubber-soled shoes (for climbing over rocks) and swimsuit.

For unforgettable views of one of Colombia's most beautiful rivers, head to this private nature reserve.

More than 250ha/618 acres of gorgeous tropical terrain on the southeastern slopes of the **Cordillera Central** offer visitors an extravaganza of flora and fauna characterized by lush **rain forest** on a rugged bed of **limestone** rock.

Boasting rich biodiversity, the reserve centers on a spectacular river-carved **marble canyon**, and is popular with outdoor enthusiasts wanting to hike, raft, kayak, bird-watch, swim, snorkel or experience the rain forest from a canopy zip line.

Small sandy coves bounded by rocky outcroppings offer idyllic natural **pools**. Marked **trails** lead upriver for a scenic 4hr hike, with **caving** excursions along ant-riddled paths to caves along a thrilling 500m/1,640ft descent.

Class II rapids along the **Río Claro** offer a relatively tranquil 2hr paddle within beautiful rain forest by raft, unless you opt for a kayak to dodge and weave through the massive boulders, all along a riverbank animated with birds.

SOUTH OF MEDELLÍN★★

Shaggy carpets of coffee bushes herald the early beginnings of Colombia's **Zona Cafetera** (& *see ZONA CAFETERA*), although here, in this introductory part, the terrain is devoted principally to growing vegetables.

Expect to see chickens picking at corn by the roadside, and machete-wielding farmers tending to crops in the fields. Stalls piled high with bunches of plump bananas line leafy country lanes in front of a backdrop of pretty Paisa towns and well-preserved colonial-era settlements.

Santa Bárbara★

53km/33mi S of Medellín via Carretera 25.

A growing number of camping zones and cabins have sprung up in and around this town (Pop. 23,442). These accommodations cater mainly to **cyclists** attracted by the steep routes

Reserva Natural Cañon del Río Claro El Refugio

Aviatur/Proexport Colombia

Marmato Gold District

◐ *120km/75mi S of Medellín via Carretera 25.*

This small town of the Caldas department (Pop. 8,175) claims a 500-year-old gold-mining tradition. Defying gravity, it clings tightly to the slopes of **El Burro**, a gold-laden Andean mountain that made the town one of Colombia's most important gold districts. The first Spaniards to discover the area were soldiers under the command of **Sebastián de Belalcázar** in 1536. By the mid-16C, the mines were fully operating under Spanish control. Marmato was first mined by the indigenous **Cartama people**, then by **black slaves** brought by the Spanish from Cartagena. In 1825 **Simón Bolívar** conceded the mines to England as collateral to fund the war of independence from Spain, and as a result, some skilled **Cornish miners** abandoned the ailing mining industry of their homeland for a new start and better life in Marmato.

Once a center for numerous individually owned mining concessions, the little community is now facing an uncertain future. Its small teams of subsistence miners using traditional techniques were gradually replaced by a single mining entity over the last few years, and large-scale gold-mining operations could lead to the displacement of *Marmateños* to a new location.

A native of Marmato, writer and poet **Ivan Cocherín** (1909-82), a pseudonym for Jesús González Barahona, talks about the *Marmateño* condition and the tragic saga of miners in two of his works *Túnel* and *Derrumbes*.

along the mountain spine, with dramatic drops on both sides to the valleys and the Río Cauca below.

Santa Bárbara affords stunning **views**★★ of surrounding banana, sugar and coffee plantations.

La Pintada★

◐ *74km/46mi S of Medellín via Carretera 25*

This village (Pop. 6,997) is dominated by the rocky peaks of **Cerro Amarillo**★ (1,453m/4,767ft), rising imposingly in the middle of the Cauca Valley. The gushing waters of the Río Cauca, Río Poblanco and numerous creeks riddle the landscape where evidence of a great prehistoric past has been found in pottery remains and **petroglyphs**.

Much like Santa Bárbara, La Pintada has geared itself up for ecotourism, with camp sites and hostels aimed squarely at **paragliders**, **cyclists**, **birders** and hikers Cerro Amarillo is served by local tour guides, many of whom offer ecological walks through areas rich in avifauna and botanical interest.

Jericó

Aviatur/Proexport Colombiaa

Jericó

▶*104km/65mi SW of Medellín via Carretera 60 to Bombolo, and then via Peñalisa on the Marginal del Cauca road.*

Famous for its handmade Antioquian cow-hide **carrieles** (shoulder bags) and for its fine examples of **Republican architecture,** the town of Jericó (Pop. 12,761) boasts plenty of charm on account of its staunch support for regional traditions. It makes a good base for exploring the surrounding hills that provide the venue for the annual **Festival de la Cometa**, an August extravaganza that sees the skies fill with thousands of multicolored **kites** of every conceivable shape and size.

Parque Ecológico Las Nubes

▶*3km/2mi W of Jericó. Accessible from the cable car station at El Morro del Salvador, 10 blocks from el Parque Principal.* ↖*Guided tours organized by Jericó Turistico;* ⊗*40,000 COP;* ☏*(4) 852 3634; www.jericoturistico.com.*

Situated at 2,050m/6,726ft, this park offers rocky streams, tiny paths and a great diversity of plant and bird life. Conservation zones of protected plants have been created, featuring threatened species from all over Antioquia.

Andes

▶*117km/72mi SW of Medellín via Carretera 60 to Alfonso López, and then the southern road via San José and Buenos Aires.*

This bustling coffee-trading town (Pop. 41,491) is home to **Carlos Castañeda**, a *Cafetero* who was selected by the National Federation of Coffee Growers of Colombia as the new face of national icon **Juan Valdez** (ⓒ*see p238*). Perched high on lush mountain slopes and intersected by the Río Taparto and Río San Juan, the town delineates the very edge of Colombia's Coffee Region. A number of sloping trails lead out to the surrounding high spots of Alto de Caramanta, Alto San Fernando, Alto La Venada, Alto Lanas and Alto Bocato, all of which offer memorable **views**★ of coffee fields and beyond.

Jardín★

▶*138km/86mi SW of Medellín via Carretera 60 to Alfonso López and then the southern road via San José and Andes.*

This small town (Pop. 14,32) sits within countryside characterized by cattle pastures, forests, trout farms, coffee plants and banana palms. It contains typical whitewashed Paisa buildings, with balconies and doorways painted in bold red, blue and yellow. Jardín's shining jewel is undoubtedly its Gothic Revival **Basílica Menor de la Inmaculada Concepción** (*Carrera 3 # 10-71*, a statuesque edifice containing a resplendent Italian marble altar, now listed as a National Monument, as is the town's flower-filled **Plaza Principal.**

Out-of-town attractions centre on **ecological trails** and ancient **stone paths** that spread like tentacles into the coun-

---

Carnaval del Diablo

Since 1847, on odd years, the people of Riosucio have celebrated the Carnival of the Devil, a spirited fiesta of Spanish and African origins—totally devoid of any evil significance—for which the town is famous. This fiesta is the perfect example of how reality can be transformed by the magic of dance, costume, poetry and music. Designed as a succession of rituals geared to the devil, the carnival has five parts: **mocking oratory pieces** that begin several months before the festival; dramatized **calls to the devil** a few days before the carnival; the **entrance of the devil** and a **crowning ceremony**; a **procession** that features colorful costumes, merriment and humor; and a **burial** that symbolizes the demonic power of drink and the end of the devil's reign. A series of parades involve lanterns, music and dancing, with bullfighting, folkloric events and shows. **http://carnavalriosucio.org**

tryside. These include the **Camino de la Herrera**, a crumbling old road dating back to 1858, and the **Camindo de la Herradura** (leading to Jericó), built across stretches of boulder-strewn river once used by mules and traders.

Ríosucio

▶ *150km/93mi S of Medellín via Carretera 25.*

Located in the Caldas department, Ríosucio (Pop. 35,843) is wedged at the foot of the **Cerro Ingrumá**, an impressive granite formation. The town's main claim to fame is its very peculiar **Carnaval del Diablo** (◔ *see sidebar)*, a true example of **syncretism** and Colombia's longest event, initiated in July and ending six months later in January.

ADDRESSES

◔ *See Medellín for a further selection of accommodations and restaurants.*

🛏 STAY

$ El Meson de la Abuela – *Carrera 11 # 9-31, Santa Fé.* ✕ ☎*(4) 853 1053. 6 rooms.* The six rooms in this welcoming little hostel include a six-bed dormitory. Each room, while fairly basic, comes with a TV, a private bathroom and a fan. You can catch a decent bite to eat in the outdoor dining room downstairs, then take to the porch, where you'll find hammocks for napping. Breakfast here provides a lot of value for a few bucks.

$$ Hotel Caserón Plaza – *Calle 9 # 9-41, Parque Principal, Santa Fé.* 🄿✕🛁 ☎*(4) 853 2040. www.hotelcaseronplaza. com.co. 30 rooms.* This historic Colonial building on the town's main square was once home to local gentry. Ample, sunny-colored rooms are arranged hacienda-style around an attractive central courtyard. Just ask the attentive staff, and they'll be glad to help you with most any request; guests here come to feel like friends or family members by the time they leave. As amenities go, besides the refreshing pool, pretty garden and small gym, the restaurant serves a set menu as well as à la carte entrées from the grill. Breakfast is not included in the room rate.

$$ Hotel Guatatur – *Calle 31 # 31-04, Parque Principal, Guatapé.* ✕☎*(4) 861 1212. www.hotelguatatur.com. 16 rooms.* Medellíno couples favor this little resort in Guatapé's central park as a romantic getaway, and weekend packages oblige. The staff can organize a variety of activities such as boat trips, horseback riding, jet-skiing and visits to the monastery. The restaurant serves meals on the hotel terrace, which boasts a stunning view of the lake. Several of the rooms alsooverlook lake; reserve a suite for even better views as well as a Jacuzzi tub.

🍽 EAT

$ Restaurante Plaza Mayor – *Parque Principal # 4-59, Santa Fé.* ☎*(4) 853 3448.* Set within the Hostal Plaza Mayor, this restaurant offers consistently tasty dishes at good value. Those on a tight budget will appreciate the generous portions. Note the suggested meal on the menu, as this is often the best value. If the weather is fine, the staff will move tables out onto the Plaza Mayor for alfresco dining. **Colombian**.

$$ La Fogata – *Calle 30 # 31-34, Guatapé.* ☎*(4) 861 1040.* Directly across from the lake, this restaurant affords a great view of the boats floating on the tranquil water. Cuisine from the region is the mainstay here. If you're hungry or have friends in tow, go for the *bandeja paisa*, a crowd-pleasing Colombian dish that includes 13 varied ingredients and is served on a large platter. For a lighter meal, the *trucha* (trout) is always a sure bet. La Fogata also offers several **rooms** above the restaurant at reasonable rates. If you do decide to stay, a good breakfast is available for those who overnight here. **Colombian**.

$$ Restaurante Portón del Parque – *Calle 10 # 11-03, Santa Fé.* ☎*(4) 853 3207.* Considered by many to be one of the best restaurants in town, Portón del Parque resides in an elegant Colonial house with high ceilings. The kitchen here uses top-quality ingredients to craft traditional dishes including *ajiaco*, a Colombian potato soup, and *arequipe con leche* (a sweet dessert of boiled milk and sugar, similar to *dulce de leche*). When the weather permits, grab a table in the lovely courtyard. **Colombian**.

Zona Cafetera★★

Caldas, Quindío , Risaralda

A hotbed of seismic activity at a triple junction where the Nazca, Cocos, and Pacific plates converge, the rugged and verdant Zona Cafetera is the country's largest coffee-growing region. Located in the Andean highlands of western Colombia, it features rolling plantations and quilted slopes that produce half of all Colombian coffee in a landscape that accounts for barely one percent of the national landmass. Discover the tri-city coffee-growing axis formed by Manizales, Pereira and Armenia, where some 10 percent of the world's coffee supply is grown between the magical altitudes of 800m/2,625ft and 1,800m/5,906ft. It is a unique slice of Paisa Country, with emerald valleys nourished by frequent rainfall and Andean snow-capped peaks you won't forget.

COFFEE IN ITS VEINS

Parts of the Zona Cafetera were settled by **Antioquians** in the 1850s, at a time of civil disturbances farther north. A significant number of immigrants from **Valle del Cauca**, **Bogotá** and other major Colombian cities also contributed to the development of the Coffe Zone.

⌖ **Michelin Maps:** p209 and p259.

▤ **Info:** You'll find several **tourist information points** (PITs) in the Zona Cafetera's tri-city axis. **Manizales:** PIT Parque Benjamín López, Carrera 22 and Calle 31, Mon–Sun 8am –7pm, ✆(6) 873 3901. www.manizales.gov.co. **Pereira**: PIT Aeropuerto Matecaña, Arrivals Hall, Mon–Fri 8am–11am, 1pm– 6pm. www.pereira.gov.co. **Armenia** : PIT Aeropuerto El Edén, Arrivals Hall, Mon–Sat 7:30am–7:30pm. www.armenia.gov.co. www.ciudadeje.com.

☺ **Don't Miss:** Salento, with its fine examples of Bahareque architecture; the Valle de Corcora and its majestic wax palms; the five snow-covered peaks of Los Nevados, home of glacier parakeets.

In 1879 the Colombian Congress passed the **Coffee Act** (Law 29), a pledge by the government to sponsor, support and promote the growing of coffee in suitable regions. Between 1880 and 1920, the production of coffee in Colombia

Hacienda El Caney near Manizales and the Andes Mountains

251

GETTING THERE

BY AIR - There are several daily flights to **Manizales' Aeropuerto La Nubia** (MZL) (℘6 874 5451), located about 8km/5mi southeast of the city center and just off the road to Bogotá. Take the bus to La Enea, then walk 5min, or take a taxi (10min; 10,000 COP). A new international airport is being built an hour west of Manizales expected to open in a few years. **Airlines:** Avianca www.avianca.com, ADA www.ada-aero.com, Aires www.aires.aero.

Pereira has a new international airport 5km/3mi west of the city center: **Aeropuerto Matecana** (PEI) (℘6 326 0021 or 314 2765), a 20min ride by urban bus or taxi (8,000 COP) to the city center.

Airlines: Avianca www.avianca.com, Aires www.aires.aero, AeroRepublica www.aerorepublica.com, Satena www.satena.com.

Armenia's El Edén Airport (AXM) (℘6 747 9400 or 747 5707) lies 20km/12mi outside the city, on the road to Calcan and is reached easily by taxi (15,000 COP). **Airlines:** Avianca, Easyfly (www.easyfly.com.co) and Aires offer daily flights from Bogotá.

BY BUS - **Manizales'** main bus station, (Avenida 19, northeast of Plaza Bolívar), scheduled to be replaced, is served by buses and minibuses. The new terminal will be on the highway outside Manizales. From Bogotá (8 hrs; 25,000 COP), Cali (5hrs; 11,000 COP), Medellín (5hrs; 8,500 COP).

Armenia's bus terminal (corner of Carrera 19 and Calle 35) lies about 1.5km/1mi southwest of the city center and can be reached either by taxi (4,000 COP) or by bus. Buses arrive from Bogotá (8hrs; 33,000 COP) and Cali (4hrs; 18,000 COP).

GETTING AROUND

BY BUS - In **Manizales** minibuses depart from the main bus station to Armenia (2.5hrs; 7,000 COP), Pereira (1.5hrs; 7,000 COP), Salamina (2.5hrs; 9,000 COP). For tours to **Nevado del Ruiz**, find a recommended local guide or go with the city's tour operators, such as Bioturismo Arte y Café ℘6 884 4037, Centro Comerical Parque Caldas, Tesoro Tours Manizales Hotel Escorial, Calle 21 # 21-11, ℘6 883 7040, Ecoturismo Calle 11 # 63-05, ℘6 880 8300, www.aventurascolombia.com. From **Pereira's** central bus terminal, take minibuses for Armenia (1hr; 5,000 COP) and Manizales (1.5hrs; 5,000 COP). **Megabuses** serve the city and environs. www.megabus.gov.co.

Armenia's main bus terminal (Calle 35 # 20-68, ℘6 747 3355 or 747 5705), 1.5km/1mi southwest of the city center, is served by minibuses that run to Pereira (1hr; 6,000 COP), Manizales (2.5hrs; 11,000 COP) and Parque Nacional del Café (30min; 2,500 COP).

COFFEE-FARM TOURISM

Many growers open their **fincas** to visitors, offering B&B services. ranging from **rustic rooms** on a shoestring in a primitive, rural setting to **luxurious suites** in stately country estates. Almost every *finca* offers homemade **regional food**, local knowledge (coffee history and tours) and free-flowing Colombian coffee. Stay during **harvest**—two per year, each four to eight weeks—to experience the back-breaking process done entirely by hand. Some tour operators offer **packages** including transport. *Finca* owners often offer to drive visitors to nearby towns to see the local sights. Activities can include horseback rides and white-water rafting. Sites for rural accommodations in the Caldas, Quindío and Risaralda departments:

◆ www.clubhaciendasdelcafe.com
◆ www.turiscafe.net
◆ www.turiscolombia.com/eje_cafetero.htm
◆ www.paisatours.com/coffee_country.htm
◆ www.travelcolombia.org

Finca El Rosario near Manizales

Proexport Colombia

surged from 107,000 to 2.4 million bags per year (60kg/132 pounds per bag). **Small growers** were driving this rapid growth—planting, processing and selling their coffee virtually unaided by state support. Bamboo forests and wetlands were soon transformed into coffee plantations in what is now known as the Coffee Region. Ideal **growing conditions** in the cool **highlands** at between 1,000m/3,281ft and 2,000m/6,562ft were further enriched by the region's fertile **volcanic soils.**

In 1927, the **Federación Nacional de Cafeteros de Colombia** or **Fedecafé** (FNC) was founded to represent the growing number of coffee growers, most of them small family-run producers. Membership grew as these smallscale *cafeteros* began selling their coffee to the FNC, which then channeled profits back to the growers. The organization also helped to provide a buffer against the **volatile** and unpredictable international **coffee market**, which routinely saw prices rise and fall. However, Colombian *cafeteros* are under no obligation to sell to the FNC, as there is no commercial monopoly. Indeed, a number of private shippers and co-operatives in the Coffee Region operate independently within the trade.

The Coffee Region extends to about 870,000ha/2,149,817 acres, a reduction of nearly 200,000ha/494,211 acres since 1970, but is now experiencing **intensified production**. In 2010 the harvest rose to between 10 and 11 million bags, from 7.8 million bags in 2009, a year in which production slumped.

MANIZALES

> *180km/112mi SE of Medellín along Carretera 25 and then, turn left before Valparaíso via La Merced.*

Part of the tri-city coffee-growing axis, Manizales (Pop. 368,433) is the capital of the **Caldas department**. It is a gritty, commercial hub set on mountainous terrain riddled by seismic instability.

Famous throughout the country for its high number of private and public **universities**, Manizales has a sizable **student population**. This population lends a laid-back, arty character to a city almost devoid of original architecture, due to **earthquake** damage and **fires** that virtually destroyed it in the 1920s. The ensuing reconstruction left the city with some fine buildings such as its statuesque cathedral and several notable Republican-style buildings, mostly concentrated in the historic center, which was declared a National Monument in 1999.

Within driving distance of great nature reserves, traditional coffee farms and the spectacular Los Nevados National Park, Manizales provides an excellent base from which to explore the region.

CITY CENTER★

As the main city square, the **Plaza de Bolívar★** is the undisputed heart of Manizales, with the unusual statue of the Great Liberator by Rodrigo Arenas Betancur occupying center stage. Known as **Bolívar-Cóndor★**, this daring bird in bronze is one of Colombia's most quirky homages to Simón Bolívar. Also note the **ceramic murals** by Guillermo Botero.

Most of the fine **Republican-style buildings** erected after the fires of the 1920s are concentrated around Calle 22 and Calle 23. They include the **Palacio de la Gobernación★** *(Carrera 21 between Calle 22 and Calle 23)*, to the north of the square, and the elegant **Edificio Manuel Sanz★** *(Calle 22 # 23-17)*, designed by Italian architects Gian Carlo Bonarda and Angello Papio.

South of the plaza, the imposing Gothic Revival **Catedral Basílica de Nuestra Señora del Rosario★** *(Carrera 22 # 22-12)* dominates the view. Built in 1929, it is the third church to occupy this site. With an impressive 106m/348ft-high **spire**, the cathedral (1928-1939) sits atop a terrace of steps.

Sightseers visit for a glimpse of the church's elaborate **gold canopy**, beautiful **stained-glass windows** and four towers dedicated to Saint Inés, Saint Mark, Saint Paul and Saint Francis. A simple, yet elegant **marble font** to the left of the west door provides a sharp contrast to the dismal reinforced concrete of the edifice itself. It should be noted that this is the largest religious monument in Latin America to be built of this particular material.

Museo el Oro Quimbaya★

Carrera 23 # 23-6. ◷*Open Mon–Fri 9am –noon, 2pm–6pm.* ✆*(6) 884 5534. www.banrep.gov.co/museo.*

A block south, this museum is notable for its small collection of **Quimbaya** gold and ceramics.

ADDITIONAL SIGHTS
Parque Caldas★

Calle 29 between Carrera 22 and Carrera 23.

Set beneath leafy trees, the city's second plaza is a gathering point for city-dwellers of all ages, from old men playing chess on park benches to teens swapping text messages, gossiping housewives, students pouring over books and grandmothers knitting.

Overlooking the park, the **Iglesia de la Inmaculada Concepción** *(Calle 31 # 22-27)* is a 20C Gothic Revival church with fine wood carvings and an interior in the shape of a ship's hull.

Palacio de la Gobernación

Proexport Colombia

Centro de Museos

Universidad de Caldas, Palogrande Campus, Carrera 23 # 58-65. ©*Open Mon–Fri 8am–noon, 2pm–6pm.* ℘*(6) 885 1374. http://museos.ucaldas.edu.co.*
Offering a range of permanent and temporary exhibits, the University of Caldas' collections of archaeology, geology, natural history and art are all housed in the old seminary building of the city of Manizales.

Inside, admire a selection of ceramics and gold artifacts from the **Quimbaya** culture. There are specimens of **minerals** and **fossils** from various parts of Colombia, including the Sierra Nevada de Santa Marta and the Desierto de La Tatacoa. The museum boasts the fourth-largest naturalist collection in the country, particularly renowned for its **butterflies**.

Lastly, a dozen paintings by **Andrés Manzur**, from a series entitled *El Martirio de San Sebastián* are on view.

Estación del Cable y Torre de Herveo

School of Architecture of the Universidad Nacional de Colombia, Manizales Campus. Avenida Santander and Calle 65. www.unal.edu.co.
Farther out on the road to Bogotá, notice the tower hovering over Manizales' old terminal of the **aerial cableway** that went 75km/46m to Mariquita from 1922 till the 1960s.

The cableway was used to ferry coffee up to the Alto de Las Letras pass (3,700m/12,139ft) and down the other side, rather than transport it by road, a long and difficult journey. From Mariquita, the coffee was then taken by road and rail to the Río Magdalena for shipment and export.

The cableway system was supported by **376 towers**. The one you see today, the highest of all, was actually located near the town of Herveo (in the Tolima department). Rescued in the 1970s, it was moved to its present location and now appropriately stands by the old cable station.

🙂 Photo Tips 🙂

For panoramic **views** of the city and surrounding valleys, take a stroll in **Los Colonializadores★**— a beautiful hilltop public park overlooking Manizales and the coffee-rich basins below out to the Río Cauca *(accessible via the west side of Avenida 12 de Octubre in Chipre, a suburb of Manizales, NE of downtown).*

While you are in the neighborhood, take a look at **Iglesia Nuestra Señora del Rosario** *(Calle 10 # 12-48)*, a replica of Manizales Cathedral, and the **Monumento a los Colonizadores** *(Avenida 12 de Octubre)*, a gigantic bronze statue by Luis Guillermo Arias, paying tribute to the Paisa founders of Manizales.

Plaza de Toros

Avenida Centenario. ℘*(6) 883 7629. www.cormanizales.com.*
The most popular bullring in Colombia was inspired by the arena in Cordoba, Spain. It is a monumental Moorish-style complex where the fiercest bullfights take place in late January and early February, with another season in June and July (this time with younger bulls).

SURROUNDINGS
Ecoparque de Selva Húmeda Tropical Yarumos★

▶ *NW of Manizales, in Barrio Minitas.* ©*Open daily 9am–6pm.* ⬗*3,200 COP basic entry,* ⬗*23,000 COP including all activities.* ℘*(6) 875 5511.*
Named after the Yarumo tree, this 70ha/173 acre state-funded nature park is located in a cloud forest. It contains 60 plant species, over a dozen species of trees and a wealth of migratory and native birds, together with butterflies, monkeys, frogs, snakes and iguanas.

A couple of well-maintained manmade **trails** offer pleasant walks to several **waterfalls** and **bird-heavy forests**. There is also a large ice rink, a kids playhouse, and the possibility of doing some rappelling, though it is the **canopy ride** that is the real highlight of the park. Slung across a spectacular stretch of forest, the zip-line allows stunning **views**★ right in the thick of the park.

El Recinto del Pensamiento
◯ *11km/7mi E of Manizales on the road to Magdalena.* ✆*(6) 874 7494. www.recintodelpensamiento.com.*
A pleasant **chairlift ride** gives you an aerial view of this 179ha/442 acre park run by the Caldas branch of the Federación Nacional de Cafeteros de Colombia.
Follow the 2.5km/1.5mi **interpretative path** through native landscapes, which leads to a **butterfly garden** and a striking 14m/46ft high **bamboo pavillion** built with native *guadua*. Some 280 different species of **orchids** thrive in the park's own cloud forest in all colors. The **aromatic garden** features 80 different varieties of plants used to flavor food and drinks.

EXCURSIONS
Chinchiná
◯ *23km/14mi SW of Manizales via the road to Pereira.*
Wedged snugly in a valley clad in coffee bushes, Chinchiná (Pop. 51,301) is known as the "Heart of Colombian Coffee." It is home to two notable names in Colombian coffee: **Buendia Coffee Factory** *(Carrera 4 and Calle 16 Vía Palestina;* ✆*6 850 4040; www.buendiacoffee.com)* and **Cenicafé**, a coffee research center *(Sede Planalto, 4km/2mi NE of Chinchiná on the road to Manizales;* ◯*library open Mon–Fri 8am–noon, 1pm–5:30pm;* ✆*6 850 6550; www.cenicafe.org).*
Chinchiná's **Colina del Sol**, a small hillside producer in a *finca* overlooking the mountains, welcomes visitors for tours and tastings *(Carrera 8 # 8-63, 30min uphill climb from Chinchiná;* ◄▪*guided tours available for a small fee, call before visiting;* ✆*300 362 9578).*

Salamina★★
◯ *75km/47mi N of Manizales via Neira and Aranzazu.*
A popular day-trip destination from Manizales, Salamina (Pop. 18,281)

ranks among the oldest settlements of the Zona Cafetera, dating back to 1825. It was declared a National Monument in 1982 on account of its finely preserved traditional **Caldanese architecture**. Most visitors take a gentle stroll around the streets, marveling at the fine collection of **Bahareque** (◯*see sidebar p260)* and adobe houses, buildings adorned with plant-filled balconies and Baroque detailing.
The town's **Templo de la Inmaculada Concepción**★ (1865) is worth a look, with its unusual single-nave design, a ceiling decorated in carved wood, some stunning stained-glass windows and a bell made from melted-down jewelry donated by members of the congregation. The local **cemetery** is also interesting from a social perspective, as it was once divided into areas for the rich and the poor. However, in 1976 Archbishop Luis Enrique Hoyos broke down the barriers of class and put an end to all discrimination in the graveyard.

Aguadas★
◯ *126km/78mi N of Manizales via Salamina.*
Founded in 1808 by Antioquian muleteers, Aguadas (Pop. 22,307) is home to charming **coffee fincas** (◯*see p252),* many of which have thrown open their doors to tourism.
The town is known for a fine woven hat: the **sombrero aguadeño**. Using fiber from the iraca palm, this typical Paisa headwear forms an important part of local culture.
Like Salamina, Aguadas has its own **Templo de la Inmaculada Concepción**★ (1883), a striking Renaissance Revival building, whose statue of *Señor Caído*, carved in an orange tree trunk, is the object of much devotion.

Santuario de San Antonio de Arma★
◯ *Villa Serrana de Santiago de Arma, a corregimiento of Aguadas, 15km/9mi NW of Aguadas.*
This redbrick church (1930s) contains fine historical relics and pieces of art that include the image of San Antonio,

Nevado del Ruiz

Proexport Colombia

Parque Nacional Natural Los Nevados★★

This magnificent park is not technically troublesome, yet few tourists should consider visiting it without a **guide**, as relatively small distances are difficult to gauge, and constant uphill walking in difficult conditions can make progress slow. The effects of altitude have troubled numerous visitors. Freezing temperatures can also be a hazard. By using a guide, you'll be trekking along the best trails, in the safest manner, via the easiest access routes.

Los Nevados is a dramatic 58,000ha/143,321 acre stretch of the Andes, topped by five extraordinarily beautiful **snow-covered peaks**, running from **El Ruiz** (5,300m/17,388ft)—a still-active volcano at the northern end of the park, which last erupted in 1985, wrecking havoc on its path—to **El Cisne** (4,800m/15,748ft), **Santa Isabel** (4,950m/16,240ft), **El Quindío** (4,800m/15,748ft), and **El Tolima** (5,200m/17,060ft), the park's southernmost mountain. This spectacular terrain is home to spectacled bears, mountain tapirs, white-eared opossums, elusive pumas, squirrels, bats and birds such as the Andean condor, the páramo hummingbird and the glacier parakeet. It is also notable for its various species of bromeliads, fern and moss, and *frailejones* up to 12m/39ft high.

Most visitors enter the park at **Las Brisas** (⊙ *14km/9mi SW of La Esperanza, which is 27km/17mi SE along the road to Bogotá from Manizales;* ⏣ *56,000 COP entry fee;* ⛐ *tour packages and accommodations available through Aviatur; www.concesionesparquesnaturales.com).* From this entry point, one can explore the easily accessible **northern sector** of the park, roughly around Chalet Arenales *(3km/2mi from Las Brisas),* Refugio del Ruiz and **Centro de Visitantes El Cisne** *(24km/15mi from Las Brisas).* The road actually goes as far as **Laguna del Otún** *(a 4hr trip).* Other access to the more remote western and southern reaches of the park are also possible.

From Las Brisas, the road stretches 10km/6mi to the edge of slumbering **Nevado del Ruiz**, a classic day trip from Manizales for anyone short on time, but far from ideal with so much to see and explore *(the best alternative being to stay overnight).* Trails run through cloud forests to the summit of El Ruiz *(about 2hrs),* climbing up through varying altitudes across diverse terrains.

El Ruiz actually has a trio of craters: **Arenas**, **Olleta** and **Piraña**. Like the other glaciers in the park, dramatically affected by **global warming**, El Ruiz has been receding at an alarming rate over the last few years.

believed to have been brought to Quito by the wife of conquistador **Jorge Robledo** in 1549. On the 13th of each month, hundreds of local pilgrims come here to honor Our Lady of the Rosary.

PEREIRA★

▶ *56km/35mi SW of Manizales via the road to Chinchiná and 225km/140mi S of Medellín via Carretera 25.*

Nicknamed "The Pearl of the Otún River," Pereira (Pop. 428,397) is the capital of the **Risaralda department** and the largest city of the Zona Cafetera's trio. Like Manizales, it is a jigsaw of architectural treasures, having been rebuilt several times after devastating earthquakes. Few original buildings remain other than some telltale historic structures in Pereira's center.

Today the local mass-transit system, called **Megabús**, has dramatically improved the infrastructure of the city, which makes a convenient base for exploring the region's fertile valleys and coffee plantations.

✿ CITY CENTER★

Much like Manizales, Pereira has its own **Plaza de Bolívar**★, with yet another unusual monument to Simón Bolívar in the form of Arenas Betancur's **Bolívar Desnudo**★. The 8.5m/28ft high bronze sculpture (1963) features a naked El Libertador on horseback.

The Plaza forms a paved carpet at the feet of the once-fine **Catedral de Nuestra Señora de la Pobreza** (*Carrera*

Catedral de Nuestra Señora de la Pobreza

7 between Calle 20 and Calle 21), a much-repaired building dating back to 1875. Excavation work done after the 1999 earthquake revealed that the cathedral was built on the foundations of a much older church (c.1540). The cathedral's elegant interior boasts some chandelier-adorned inlaid ceilings. Its distinctive dome is supported by a complex structure made of 13,000 pieces of wood.

ADDITIONAL SIGHTS
Pereira's Parks

Besides the central Plaza de Bolívar, there are three other public spaces worth seeing.

Parque Jorge Eliécer Gaitán★ *(Carrera 4 between Calle 25 and Calle 26)*, with its

---

Pereira's Public Art

Art lovers who enjoy **Arenas Betancur**'s work will find three other interesting sculptures by him in town:

◆ **El Monumento a los Fundadores** *(Carrera 13 and Calle 12)*.
◆ **El Cristo Sin Cruz** *(in the Capilla de la Fátima, Avenida 30 de Agosto between Calle 49 and Calle 50)*.
◆ **El Prometeo** *(in the Universidad Tecnológica de Pereira, on Calle 14)*.

Notable pieces by other artists include:

◆ **Jorge Eliécer Gaitán** by Alexandra Ariza (*Parque Jorge Eliécer Gaitán)*.
◆ **General Rafael Uribe Uribe** by Franco A. Cano *(Parque El Lago)*.
◆ **El Viajero** by Antonio Segui *(Avenida 30 de Agosto)*.

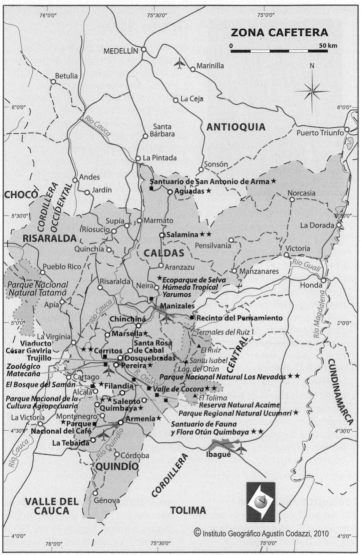

ZONA CAFETERA

0   50 km

N

© Instituto Geográfico Agustín Codazzi, 2010

shoeshine stands, kiosks and food vendors, is a popular meeting point.

Parque La Libertad★ *(Carrera 7A and Carrera 8A with Calle 13 and Calle 14)* is decorated with a handsome mosaic by artist Lucy Tejada.

The scenic **Parque del Lago Uribe Uribe**★ *(Carrera 7A and Carrera 8A with Calle 24 and Calle 25)* features an illuminated fountain and manmade lake that attract visitors.

Viaducto César Gaviria Trujillo

Built in 1998 to stretch over the mighty Río Otún, this viaduct links Pereira to the industrial town of **Dosquebradas** (Pop. 173,452). Ranking among the longest cable-stayed bridges in South America, the structure was named in a tribute to the 40th president of Colombia, Pereira-born **César Gaviria**, who served from 1990 to 1994.

Richard Emblin/Proexport Colombia

Green Steel

Known in Colombia as **guadua** *(Guadua angustifolia)*, the bamboo that grows here is used extensively in building practices, particularly in Tierra Paisa, where it is used to construct inexpensive, yet surprisingly durable houses. This highly desirable and sustainable product is increasingly gaining international fame for its **antiseismic properties**, and is sometimes referred to as "environmental steel" for its **strength** and **durability**.

Bamboo grows to its full height (20-25m/66-82ft) in less than a year at rates of up to 12cm/5in daily. Most bamboo can be harvested after five years if used for construction purposes. Once cut, bamboo regenerates itself quickly, sprouting from the ground at full width. It is **economical** to use due to the ease in which it is cultivated, maintained and harvested. It also costs little to transport because of its relatively light weight.

Unlike other parts of South America, bamboo is used in a sophisticated way in structural Colombian construction. In the Coffee Region, many houses made from simple bamboo and mud can look like they've been constructed with brick. Inspired from pre-Columbian practices, the **bahareque technique** was adopted early on by the Spanish colonists. It consists of structural bamboo used as **studs** in walls, then covered with **bamboo laths**. The roughest part faces outwards (exterior) to provide a good base of adherence for the **mud plaster** (which, for reinforcement and better resistance to seismic events, can be replaced with cement plaster).

In addition to dwellings built in bamboo, locals have fashioned furniture, but it is the amazing **bridges** constructed from guadua—with tensile strength higher than many alloys of steel—that perhaps win the greatest plaudits. Located on the grounds of the **Universidad Tecnológica de Pereira** *(on the outskirts of Pereira via La Julita)*, the **Guaducto**★ is an amazing example of engineering and craftsmanship that should not be missed.

Zoológico Matecaña

W of Pereira along the Vía al Aeropuerto Matecaña. ◷*Open daily 9am–5pm.* ✺*12,500 COP, child* ✺*5,500 COP.* ✎*Guided tours in English available with advance reservation.* ☏*(6) 314 2639. www.zoopereira.org.*

This 10ha/25 acre zoo is home to some 1,200 birds, mammals and reptiles from the Americas (including Colombia), Asia and Africa. It also has an interesting taxidermy display featuring all kinds of animals. With a clear focus on conservation, it hosts guided tours, seminars and lectures.

In 1993 the zoo received on loan some of the animals from Pablo Escobar's pri-

vate collection at **Hacienda Napoles** near Puerto Triunfo (Antioquia). During his criminal heyday in the 1980s, Escobar had imported rare animals from all over the world and established a private zoo in his country estate. With an impressive array of giraffes, ostriches, elephants, ponies, antelopes, hippopotamuses, zebras, buffalos, camels, lions and an ocelot, together with exotic birds, Escobar's collection was considered one of the best in Latin America. After his death, the estate was seized by the authorities, but proved expensive to maintain, and the abandoned animal population began dwindling rapidly. Some of the animals were fortunately placed under the care of institutions like this one.

SURROUNDINGS
Cerritos★★

◐ *5km/3mi W from central Pereira, on the Pereira to Cartago road.*
This pretty rural stretch is characterized by rounded grassy verges behind which are a succession of gateways and turns that lead to a large number of tastefully converted **fincas** (◔ *see p252*). This concentration of old farmhouses now forms the basis of the city's agricultural tourism. Careful renovation (or in some cases, just some simple care) has transformed these farm buildings into stylish hotels, bars and restaurants. Good-sized rooms often retain considerable character with furniture from the early 19C, overlooking gardens and courtyards against a backdrop of coffee fields.

EXCURSIONS
Termales de Santa Rosa★

◐ *9km/6mi E of Santa Rosa de Cabal, 15km/9mi NE of Pereira.* ◔ *For times and charges, check packages on website.* ℘*(6) 364 5500. www.hoteltermales.com.*
Blessed with a stunning location and gorgeous views, the forest-ringed rural town of **Santa Rosa de Cabal** (Pop 67,410) is famous for its **hot springs**. Visitors flock to a trio of naturally-heated mineral-rich waters reaching up to 70°C/158°F. The resort boasts a 170m/558ft **waterfall** as a backdrop,

Waterfall, Termales de Santa Rosa
Richard Emblin/Proexport Colombia

quite a spectacular sight. You may want to stay overnight in a lodge, hotel or cabin, or enter as a day guest to use the restaurant, bar and pools.

Santuario de Fauna y Flora Otún Quimbaya★★

◐ *Vereda La Suiza, 14km/9mi SE of Pereira via La Florida.* ◉*5,000 COP entry fee.* ◔*Guided tours available from the Asociación Comunitaria Yarumo Blanco del Municipio de Pereira.* ℘*(6) 314 4162. www.parquesnacionales.gov.co.*
This tiny 5sq km/1.9sq mi stretch of **Andean forest** is used extensively for conservation studies. Its rolling slopes, rivers and cascades are home to a great variety of butterflies, **birds** and mammals (including mountain tapirs and spectacled bears), but also rare plant species such as the emblematic **wax palm** and all kinds of bromeliads and orchids. **Nature paths** at altitudes of between 1,800m/5,906ft and 2,400m/7,875ft, lead to nearby Parque Ucumari (*3 to 4hr hike*).

Parque Regional Natural Ucumarí★

◐ *30km/19mi SE of Pereira via El Cedral. The main entrance point is at Refugio La Pastora, 6km/4mi walk from El Cedral.* ℘*(6) 325 4781. http://pereira ecoturismo.blogspot.com.*
Nicknamed the "Land of Birds" for the 185 different species that have been recorded here, this 4,200ha/10,378 acre natural reserve in the middle of the **Otún River Basin** is relatively unexplored (and unmapped), though it boasts an array of wildlife, including spectacled bears. Hiking paths weave through hillsides to cloud-cloaked summits and **waterfalls** such as Peña Bonita, La Vereda y El Bosque.
From El Cedral, a trail along the Río Otún heads to the park's visitor center, called **Refugio La Pastora** (◔*guided ecotours organized by Fecomar;* ℘*(6) 314 4162; www.fecomar.com.co*), and continues to the western part of **Parque Nacional Natural Los Nevados**, leading to its lake, **Laguna del Otún** (*6 to 7hr hike one-way*).

Marsella★

▶ 30km/19mi NW of Pereira.

Lying within the 604ha/1,493 acre **Parque Natural Municipal de La Nona**★, declared a reserve in 1979, this typical Paisa village (Pop. 20,683) is known as the "Cuidad Verde" for its surrounding emerald hills and coffee fields that define its character.

Jardín Botánico Alejandro Humboldt★

Avenida Villa Rica de Segovia, between Carrera 9 and Carrera 10. ◷*Open daily 8am–6pm.* ☞*2,500 COP.* ☏*(6) 368 5233.*

A fine celebration of the Zona Cafetera's ecosystems, these botanical gardens were named after German naturalist and explorer **Alexander von Humboldt** (1769-1859), renowned for his expedition to Central and South America and Cuba. His journeys formed the basis of the sciences of physical geography and meteorology. Numerous species of grasses, palms, trees, plants and orchids are here, as well as many native birds and migratory species in the gardens.

Located on the premises, the **Museo de la Cauchera**★ *(same hours and admission)* is dedicated to the protection of the 482 species of local **avifauna**. It was instrumental in numerous educational initiatives, including a **slingshot** amnesty in schools, encouraging kids to give up their bird-killing catapults.

El Monumento al Esfuerzo by Rodrigo Arenas Betancur

Jorge Eliécer Junca/Proexport Colombia

Cementerio Jesús María Estrada

▶ 1km/0.6mi NE of Marsella, next to Urbanización La Carmela.

Boasting a mix of Gothic, Baroque, Romantic and Corinthian styles, this cemetery was built on a slope, with distinctive vaults laid out on a terrace.

ARMENIA★

▶ 42km/26mi S of Pereira via the road from Cartago, and 266km/165mi S of Medellín via Carretera 25.

Capital of the **Quindío department**, the city of Armenia (Pop. 272,574) has an impressive history of rebirth against the odds. After suffering the devastating effects of an **earthquake** in 1999, in which a third of the city was razed to the ground, Armenia was rebuilt with stoic grit and determination.

Today the city continues to rely on the production of coffee, plantains and bananas, although **ecotourism** is playing an increasing role, with visitors keen to traverse Armenia's spectacular surrounding mountainous terrain.

♥•ᴗ CITY CENTER

Like Pereira and Manizales, Armenia has its own **Plaza de Bolívar**★, with a classic bronze statue (1930) of El Libertador in full uniform by Roberto Henao Buriticá. On the same plaza, the monumental bronze and concrete sculpture (1978) **El Monumento al Esfuerzo**★by Rodrigo Arenas Betancur depicts a couple of Paisa *campesinos* pointing forward in pioneering spirit, as a tribute to the hardworking, strong-willed people of Armenia.

An imposing piece of post-Modern architecture (1966), the **Catedral La Inmaculada Concepción**★ *(Avenida Bolívar and Calle 40)* is located on the southeastern side of the plaza. It really stands out, with its separate bell tower and its peculiar **triangular design** symbolizing the Holy Trinity.

Inside, some mammoth stained-glass windows depict a series of great historical moments in the life and death of Jesus.

Quimbaya Metalwork

True masters at working gold and *tumbaga*, Quimbaya goldsmiths became renowned for their innovative **lost-wax method** of casting. Using this simple technique, they could produce complex figures on a large scale. The process consisted of:

- Creating a core made of charcoal and clay
- Covering the core with a layer of beeswax used as a sculpting material
- Carving the beeswax into the desired shape and cooling it in water to harden it
- Coating the beeswax with a layer of clay
- Heating the object so as to harden the clay and liquify the wax
- Pouring out the wax and pouring in molten gold or *tumbaga* into the clay mold
- Letting the metal cool down and solidify
- Breaking the mold and removing the gold object

ADDITIONAL SIGHTS
Museo del Oro Quimbaya★★

Avenida Bolívar # 40N-80. ⊙*Open Tue–Sun 10am–5pm.* ℘*(6) 749 8433. www.banrep.gov.co/museo.*
This outstanding collection is housed in an award-winning building that earned **Rogelio Salmona** (1927-2007) the National Prize of Architecture in 1986. You will discover an exquisite selection of gold objects (including *poporos*, traditional receptacles holding the lime used for chewing coca leaves), pieces of anthropomorphic pottery, stone sculptures and carvings mainly from the **Quimbaya** people, who inhabited the mid-Cauca region, in today's departments of Caldas, Risaralda and Quindío, prior to the arrival of the Spanish.
Known for their remarkably sophisticated goldwork, the Quimbaya produced some of their finest, most emblematic pieces between AD 300 and AD 600.

Parque de la Vida

Avenida Bolívar and Calle 6 Norte. ⊛*1,000 COP.* ℘*(6) 744 2817.*
This 8ha/22 acre park is a pleasant oasis of nature in the bustle of the city. It offers extensive trails and rustic bridges, waterfalls, a lake with ducks and geese, and lush flora. Inspired by the regional architecture, a structure made of bamboo and clay tiles houses exhibits of arts and crafts.

Parque de la Vida
Aviatur/Proexport Colombia

Estación del Ferrocarril

Calle 26 between Carrera 18 and Carrera 19. ⊶ *Closed for restoration (at time of writing, it was in the process of being converted into an art museum).*
Declared a National Monument in 1989, this old 1927 Republican-style railway station has retained its original colors, wrought-iron details and even some gargoyles. It is surrounded by gardens of lush vegetation, representative of the regional flora.

SURROUNDINGS
Jardín Botánico del Quindío

◗ *Avenida Centenario # 15-190, Calarcá, 3km/2mi SE of Armenia via the road to El Valle.* ⊙*Open daily 9am-4:30pm.* ⊛*14,000 COP.* ℘*(6) 742 7254. www.jardinbotanicoquindio.org.*
These well-stocked gardens contain a large **butterfly house** regarded as the Zona Cafetera's finest. Built in the shape of a giant butterfly, it houses more than 1,500 specimens from all over Colombia and other nations. Walks through

leafy gardens rich in towering ferns and **palms** lead to secondary forest and orchids, with a 22m/72ft-high **lookout tower** that is great for spotting numerous species of birds.

La Tebaida

◗ *13km/8mi SW of Armenia along the Pan-American Highway.*

Set in a pretty rural area, this town (Pop. 32,748) is actually home to Armenia's **Aeropuerto Internacional El Edén**, but don't let this put you off. Situated among expansive fields with fruit stands along the road side, La Tebaida's numerous stalls sell milk, bags of oranges, sacks of bananas, local foods and many different crafts.

EXCURSIONS
Quimbaya★

◗ *21km/13mi NW of Armenia along the road to Cartago.*

Bounded to the north and west by the department of Valle del Cauca, with the Roble River to the south and Filandia to the east, Quimbaya (Pop. 32,928) was founded in 1914. The city was named after the Pre-Columbian culture that inhabited the area prior to the arrival of the Spanish. These particularly proud, well-organized and fierce-fighting indigenous tribes (AD 300-1550) were excellent **goldsmiths**, valuing gold not for its material worth, but for its usability, much like iron. The Quimbayan craftsmen, who employed metalworking techniques such as the lost-wax method of casting *(see sidebar p263)*, favored *tumbaga*—an alloy composed mostly of copper—and created exquisite pieces featuring anthropomorphic and fruit designs. They battled the Spanish and were acclaimed warriors, although their vast riches insured their days were numbered.

Evidence suggests that the Quimbaya people had disappeared by the end of the 16C, following a slow process of eradication.

Today the town of Quimbaya is known throughout Colombia for its paper lanterns and flickering candles during the wonderful **Festival de Velas y Faroles**,

held annually on December 7 and 8. The fiesta prompts each neighborhood to compete to produce the most spectacular lighting arrangements that attract visitors from all over the country.

Parque Nacional de la Cultura Agropecuaria (PANACA)

◗ *26km/16mi NW of Armenia and 7km/4mi from Quimbaya via Montenegro, then left at Quimbaya, before following the signpost left again.*
◷ *Open 9am–6pm daily (Tue–Sun in low season).* ⊙ *20,000 for 8 attractions, 54,000 COP all attractions.* ✆ *018000 123 999. www.panaca.com.co.*

Aimed at Colombian families from the city, this part fun, part educational agro-tourism theme park showcases the nation's agricultural sector. The rural setting lies among rolling pasture, bamboo thickets and woodlands. The livestock, crop-growing and dairy exhibits are reached by an old jalopy.

The park spans some 103ha/266 acres across eight distinct farming zones devoted to cows, sheep and goats, poultry, pigs, dogs, horses and mules. Silkworms are raised here and medicinal and aromatic plants are cultivated.

Interactive exhibits, horse-riding, bull-roping, feeding and animal shows take place throughout the day, and there are scenic picnic areas and lookout points. PANACA produces its own eggs, milk, meat and fruit for the restaurants on-site. A large proportion of the park's fuel needs are met by manure, with an emphasis on organic farming methods and recycling.

El Bosque del Samán

◗ *15km/9mi N of PANACA at Alcalá Vereda La Caña, via the road to Cartago. Approx.* ⊙ *40,000 COP.* ✆ *(6) 336 5589. www.bosquesdelsaman.com.*

Set around a *finca,* this woodland reserve is dedicated to high-energy nature pursuits. Located at an elevation of 2,000m/6,562ft, the setting is truly picturesque, with stunning views over surrounding villages and undulating countryside.

Parque Nacional del Café

Proexport Colombia

Parque Nacional del Café★

▶ *15km/9mi W of Armenia, near the small town of Pueblo Tapao (6km/4mi from Pueblo Tapao on the road to Montenegro).* ⏱ *Open 9:30am–6pm, check website for opening days as they vary.* ☞*19,000 COP basic entry,* ☞*49,5000 COP with all attractions included.* ✆*(6) 741 7417. www.parquenacional delcafe.com.*

The Federación Nacional de Cafeteros de Colombia (FNC) is the driving force behind this 48ha/118 acre **theme park**. An homage to Colombian coffee, it is an unexpected blend of **informative exhibits** about the heritage and history of Colombian coffee and **family entertainment** (roller coaster, bumper cars and boats, splash ride, panoramic gondola lift, train ride, horse rides and even a musical extravaganza centering on the life of Paisa coffee pickers).

Processing Coffee

♦ The average coffee plant takes about four years to grow to full size and blossom.
♦ Ripe, deep red coffee cherries are harvested by hand and placed in fique sacks.
♦ They are taken to a de-pulping machine to separate the seed from the outer layer of flesh.
♦ The beans are fermented in containers for 24 hours before being carefully washed and removed of any excess material.
♦ They are then spread out to dry in the sun on open-air terraces.
♦ They are finally roasted, which changes the starches into aromatic oils, and gives the coffee its distinctive flavor.

One of the highlights of the park is the **Sendero del Café**, a pleasant trail through spectacular coffee bush terrain that allows visitors to touch and learn about all varieties of coffee, while discovering the coffee-making process from fruit-picking to drying and roasting the bean. In the **Muséo del Café**, inaugurated in 2009, a 3D video shows the daily life of a Colombian coffee grower. Do not miss the **Torre Mirador**, a striking 18m/59ft high lookout tower that has become the symbol of the park and affords fine **views** of Armenia, Montenegro and La Tebaida. This imposing structure was made of *guadua*, a type of native bamboo known for its strength and flexibility, that is honored in the **bambusario**, a pretty bamboo forest. Don't leave the park without taking a look at the **Pueblo Quindiano**, a replica of a typical coffee town, and needless to say, without having sampled coffee in one of the many stands scattered around the place.

For Telenovela Fans

Filandia★ *(23km/14mi NE of Armenia via Salento)* is a pretty Paisa village (Pop. 12,510) with an abundance of colorful painted doorways and windows together with balconies filled with blooms. As the legendary setting of popular *telenovela* **Café Con Aroma de Mujer** (Coffee with the Scent of a Woman)—a TV series made by **Fernando Gaitán Salom** of *Ugly Betty* fame—it attracts TV-loving tourists anxious to check off the sights. While in Filandia, soak up magnificent **views**★★ of the distant peaks of Los Nevados National Park, and marvel at the gray and white three-domed **Iglesia de la Inmaculada Concepción**★ *(Calle 7A # 3-29, on the Plaza Municipal)*, built in 1892. A **mirador** near to the cemetery also affords great **vistas** of Pereira, Armenia, Cartago and Quimbaya.

Rappelling, rope-bridging, hiking and horse riding are highly popular. Yet the reserve is most famous for its **zip-line canopy**, with routes that run from 100m/328ft to 400m/1,312ft at heights of up to 70m/230ft, with speeds reaching about 70km/43mi per hour.

Salento★★

◗ *25km/16mi NE of Armenia via the Doble Calzada del Café, which runs between Quindío and Risaralda.*

This traditional Antioquian settlement (Pop. 7,001) is the oldest in Quindío, dating back to 1850. The town sits around a pleasant **plaza**★★ trimmed by fine old houses converted to hotels, restaurants and shops. Salento is renowned for having some of the best examples of **bahareque architecture**★★ (◖*see sidebar p260*) in the Zona Cafetera.

At the heart of the community rises the imposing gray and white **Iglesia de**

Nuestra Señora del Carmen *(Calle 5 # 6-15, on the Plaza de Bolívar)* set on an old-world riddle of backstreets lined with color-washed houses, cafes and ceramic and crafts shops.

Follow a trail from Calle Real up a 250-step climb to the **Mirador de Salento**, where extraordinary **views**★★ unfold across the wax-palm-studded terrain of the Valle de Cocora, with the impressive peaks of the Cordillera Occidental to the west.

Valle de Cocora★★

◗ *12km/7mi N of Salento.*

⬥*Guided tours can easily be arranged in Salento. If you prefer to hike on your own, the best option is to hire a jeep and its driver in Salento to take you to the nearby village of Cocora, where the trail starts. Rubber boots are highly recommended as it can get quite muddy.*

Street in Salento

Proexport Colombia

Wax palms, Valle de Cocora

Proexport Colombia

Framed by sharp peaks and edged by the crystal-clear waters of the Río Quindío, this enchanting green valley stretches east of Salento into the southwestern reaches of **Parque Nacional Natural Los Nevados** *(main entry to the park is via the north side).*

It is a striking terrain characterized by splendid landscapes, with pine and eucalyptus trees eclipsed by gigantic, towering **wax palms** *(Palma de Cera)*— Colombia's majestic National Tree.

Endemic to the Andean highlands, the *Palma de Cera* grows on fertile, deep, well-drained mountainous terrain, at altitudes higher than 1,000m/3,281ft. It is the tallest palm species on earth, reaching up to 60m/197ft in height. Highly protected, it boasts imposing beauty, extraordinary strength and longevity, as it can live up to 120 years. Its cylindrical, smooth, light-colored trunk and dark green leaves with a grayish tinge provide a habitat for many unique life forms, including the bright **yellow-eared parrot**—an endangered species.

Reserva Natural Acaime

From the village of Cocora, walk past the trout farm. The trail head is clearly signposted. 5hrs round-trip. Small fee required in Acaime.

Walking to this natural reserve and back is a popular way of discovering the Cocora Valley. A reasonably strenuous hike leads you down and across the **Río Quindío**, through grassland and **wax palms**, then through a pristine **cloud forest**. At some point, you will come to a fork in the trail. Going right leads you to Acaime (elevation 2,770m/9,088ft), where you will be able to get something to eat and drink.

Enjoy the sight of **hummingbirds** that gather around the feeders hanging here before heading back to Cocora.

Ibagué

103km/64mi E of Armenia via the road to Cajamarca.

Dubbed the "Musical City of Colombia" due to its musical heritage, renowned music academies and calendar of prestigious musical events, Ibagué (Pop. 495,246) is the capital of the **Tolima department**.

Technically located outside the Zona Cafetera, it is, however, one of the access points to the **Parque Nacional Natural Los Nevados** and its southernmost peak, the **Nevado del Tolima** (5,200m/17,060ft).

Jardín Botánico San Jorge

Antigua Granja San Jorge, along the road to Calambeo. Open Mon–Fri 8am–5pm with minimum 24hr previous appointment, Sat–Sun & public holidays 8am–4pm. 6,000 COP for a walk around el Mirador Sindamanoy or Los Arrayanes, 7,000 COP for a walk around Mirador Los Fiques. 🕿 *(8) 263 8334. www.jardinbotanicosanjorge.org.* The town's botanical garden is worth a visit for its leafy, bird-rich nature trails not to mention its collections of **orchids**, bromeliads, heliconias and araceas.

ADDRESSES

🛏 STAY

$ Hacienda Venecia – *Vareda el Rozario, 20min by jeep west of Manizales off the road to Chinchiná.* 🅿✕🛁 🕿*(6) 870 2990. www.hacienda venecia.com. 7 rooms.* This well-preserved farmhouse-turned-boutique-hotel sits on an award-winning single-origin coffee plantation. Guest rooms display old photographs, while the house itself is decorated in an equestrian theme. Relax in the hammocks or rocking chairs on the wrap-around veranda, or unwind in the lush gardens or by the swimming pool. Ask the staff in advance to arrange a visit to the hacienda's coffee operation.

$ Hotel Mi Casita – *Calle 25 # 6-20 Pereira.* ✕ 🕿*(6) 333 9995. 18 rooms.* The staff are happy to oblige at this quaint mid-range hotel. It's a great deal for the price, with private hot-water bathrooms, cable TV and free Wi-Fi. In the small cafe, natural light flows in from the skylight overhead.

$ La Suiza Visitor Center – *Santuario de Fauna y Flora Otún Quimbaya, 14km/ 9mi east of Pereira via La Florida. Santuario Otún Quimbaya.* ✕ 🕿*(1) 382 1616. www.parquesnacionales.gov.co. 22 rooms.* The visitor center in this nature reserve 18km/11mi southeast of Pereira also offers dorms that come with or without bath and budget meals. There is warm water but no central heating; fires are not permitted. Rooms on the second floor have small balconies facing the Andean forest.

$$ Hotel Bolívar Plaza – *Calle 21 # 14-17, Armenia.* ✕ 🕿*(6) 741 0083. www.bolivarplaza.com. 19 rooms.* This new boutique hotel with its sleek façade is named for its proximity to Plaza Bolívar. While standard rooms are on the small side, they are sparklingly clean, and have tile-lined baths. Many include small balconies overlooking the Cordillera Central, good views of which are also visible from the hotel's restaurant.

$$$ Hacienda Bambusa – *9km/6mi from El Caimo toward Portugalito.* ✕🛁 🕿*676 2645. www.haciendabambusa.com. 8 rooms.* An exclusive country retreat outside Armenia, Bambusa used to be a coffee farm (now the surrounding land contains banana plantations and cattle pastures). The owner's son is an artist who speaks excellent English and is happy to act as host and guide. Modern artwork decorates the airy rooms, many of which have balconies. Though this lodging is not accessible by public transport, the staff can transport you here from Armenia.

$$$ Hotel Termales – *5km/3mi southeast of Santa Rosa de Cabal.* 🅿✕ Spa 🕿*(6) 364 6500. www.hotel termales.com. 28 rooms.* Luxury lodgings in the sprawling three-story mansion include three meals a day and access to the resort's thermal springs, at the foot of three adjacent waterfalls. A full-service spa also takes advantage of the healing properties of the thermal waters. The older Casa Finca portion of the hotel has shared baths. Rates here are lower during the week.

$$$ Varuna Hotel – *Calle 62 # 23C-18, Manizales.* 🅿✕ 🕿*(6) 881 1122. www. varunahotel.com. 38 rooms.* A popular lodging for business travelers, this new hotel has tasteful accommodations done in minimalist style with polished wood floors. Its central location on Avenida Santander is just a short walk from Cable Plaza. Additional benefits include free Wi-Fi, cable TV and an on-site restaurant. For the best views, request a room on an upper floor.

🍴 EAT

$ Los Geranios – *Carrera 23 # 71-67 Milan, Manizales.* 🕿*(6) 886 8400. No dinner Sun & Mon.* This restaurant is famous for its huge portions of traditional Colombian food. The extensive menu includes *bandeja paisa*, *ajiaco* (Colombian potato soup) and five kinds of *sancocho*. Each entrée can be accompanied by one of five different types of sauce. Not a place for quiet conversation, Los Geranios is constantly abuzz. **Colombian**.

$$ Club Manizales – *Carrera 23 # 25-60C, Manizales.* ☎*(6) 884 1611. www.clubmanizales.com.co. Closed Sun.* The dining room at this private club is open to the public (reservations required) and lauded as one of the best places to eat in Manizales. You won't go wrong with *langostinos al whisky* (king prawns in whisky), *jaibas* (crab) Thermidor, and *trucha mediterraneo* (trout with mushroom and shrimp sauce). Prices on the wine list will make your wallet smile. **Colombian**.

$$ El Mirador – *Av. Circunvalar and Calle 4, Pereira.* ☎*(6) 331 2141. www.elmiradorparrillashow.com. Dinner only. Closed Sun.* A stunning place outside the city atop a mountain, this hotel restaurant provides panoramic views of the twinkling lights of Pereira. Meat lovers will appreciate the churrasco Argentina (an assortment of grilled meats) paired with a fine Argentine wine. Come for live tango shows Friday and Saturday night, and be sure to book in advance. **Argentinian**.

$$ Mama Flor – *Calle 11 # 15-12, Los Alpes, Pereira.* ☎*(6) 335 4793.* Perched on a hill in a quiet residential area, this old-fashioned eatery is deservedly famous for Colombian cooking. Try *parrila de carnes* (mixed meat grill)—a carnivore's delight—or order the *robalo* (sea bass) if you prefer fish. **Colombian**.

$$ Restaurante Bakkho – *Calle 41 # 27-56, Calarcá, 5km/3mi E of Armenia via Carretera 40.* ☎*(6) 743 3331. http://bakkho.com.* Decorated with bright murals and modern decor, this newcomer touts its extensive wine selection (Bakkho refers to the ancient Greek translation of the wine god Dionysus). To pair with the wine, a themed menu fuses global flavors in its dishes. **International**.

$$ Restaurante Don Juaco – *Calle 65 # 23A-44, El Cable, Manizales.* ☎*(6) 885 0610.* Main dishes such as lasagna and *casuela* come in clay bowls here, while the complete meal option comes with salad, chips and a dessert. Wash it all down with *mazamorra con panela*, a regional drink made from crushed corn and typically served with a candy made from sugarcane juice. No alcohol is served. **Colombian**.

$$ Restaurante El Solar – *2km/1mi northeast of Armenia, along the road to Circasia.* ☎*(6) 749 3990.* Near Armenia's Zona Rosa, this grill's quirky decor includes children's bicycles, umbrellas and wine bottles. It's jammed on Friday night, when live music plays. If the crowd's too much for you, walk down the hill to one of the nearby discos. **International**.

⚞ RECREATION

Hacienda Guayabal – *Quebrada Guayabal, 3km/2mi south of Chinciná, off the road to Pereira.* ☎*(6) 850 7831. www.haciendaguayabal.com.* Tour this working coffee farm near Chinchiná; guides speak Spanish only.

Mango Biche – *La Badea, 1km/.6mi north of Pereira, in Dosquebradas.* ☎*(6) 330 4242.* Salsa music with a touch of merengue entertains inside this club within a large farm-like structure.

Panaca – *26km/16mi northwest of Armenia or 7km/4mi from Quimbaya.* ☎*01 800 012 3999. www.panaca.com.co.* A short bus ride from Armenia, this farm-themed park features animal shows and pig races.

Kumanday Adventures – *Carrera 23 #60-13, Manizales.* ☎*(6) 885 4980. www.kumanday.com.* Adjacent to the Universidad Catolicia, Kumanday specializes in mountaineering and mountain-biking tours.

Ecoparque Los Yarumos – *Calle 61B # 15A-01, Manizales.* ☎*(6) 875 5621. http://ecoparquelosyarumos.com.* Overlooking Manizales, this hilltop nature park offers a host of activities.

Parque Nacional Natural Los Nevados – *Entrance at Las Brisas, 14km/9mi south of La Esperanze (or 27km/17mi east of Manizales). Park office (34,000 COP entrance fee) is at 64A # 24-30 in Manzinales.* ☎*(1) 607 1597.* This Andean mountain park centers on the 5,300m/ 17,388ft high volcano for which it is named. Snow glare can be blinding, so be sure to wear sunglasses and sunscreen.

Along its 1,600km/995mi Caribbean coastline, Colombia possesses a lifetime of travel opportunities, from elegant colonial cities to pre-Columbian ruins nestled deep in rain forests. Rivers and plains bless these lands, adding an untamed, yet pastoral feel. Culturally diverse, the Colombian Caribbean is an inspiration for artists, writers, historians and musicians with its blend of indigenous, African, Spanish and other heritages. The indigenous communities of the area further offer venues for ethno-tourism, while the deserts, mountains and jungles, teeming with flora and fauna, provide innumerable options for ecotourism. This melange all contributes to making the Caribbean coastline a unique tourist destination, marked by sharp contrasts and variations. It is a perfect place to escape the contingencies of everyday life and get an education in the process.

Geo-Cultural Diversity

Most of the Caribbean region is made up of **lowland wetlands** and **jungles**. The geographical anomaly is the snow-capped **Sierra Nevada Mountains**, which fill the region's rivers with cooling runoff. The nation's highest peaks, these mountains reach lofty altitudes of close to 6,000m/19,000ft.

A few hours drive toward Venezuela, the stark, yet intriguing, scrub and dunes of the **Guajira Peninsula** appear, their drabness contrasted with the colorful dress of the **Wayúu** people.

Of great interest and universally captivating is the Caribbean coast's social blend of the distinct cultures and backgrounds of Colombia's Caribbean population. Beside the banana plantations and beautiful bays of the **Gulf of Urabá** near Panama are found the **Tule**, or **Kuna,** Indians. The ethno-racial mix is further diversified by the descendants of **African slaves**, **Spanish Creoles**,

and the **Arhuacos** and **Koguis**. Even in more contemporary times, there have been additional migrations of people of other descent so that one can enjoy a fine Arabic platter, for example, in the city of **Barranquilla**.

Given the variety of backgrounds of the people of the region, it is natural that one can find any type of music to fit the occasion, from the **salsa** of the Caribbean, **cumbia** of the banks of the Magdalena River, and **vallenato** in the department of Cesar, all of which aurally define the region and embody Colombia's roots in Africa, Europe and the Americas.

In terms of **ecotouristic** pursuits, the Caribbean offers a bounty of choices. For beach lovers, birders, scuba divers and all-round nature enthusiasts, the region is awash with an array of sites and sounds to explore and appreciate. Here can be found national parks such as **Tayrona**, the coral reefs of the **Islas del Rosario**, the cloud forests of the **Sierra**

Highlights

1 For a step back in history, walk around the colonial walled city of **Cartagena** (p274)

2 Whet your literary taste buds in the town of **Mompox**, an inspiration for Colombian author Gabriel García Márquez (p283)

3 Test your stamina for festive partying at the **Barranquilla** Carnival (p293)

4 Relax among the Wayúu in the extreme settings of the **Guajira** desert (p314)

5 Celebrate Henry Morgan's pirate legacy with a *coco loco* on the beaches of **Providencia** (p327)

Nevada, the **Santuario de los Flamencos**, and the **wetlands** and curiosities of the **Depresión Mompósina**.

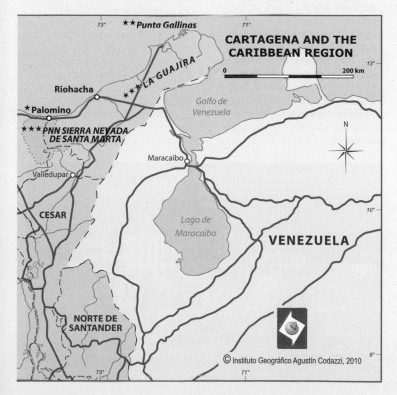

Cartagena de Indias★★★and Surroundings

Bolívar

Enough cannot be written about this Caribbean colonial jewel. A UNESCO World Heritage Site, the first Spanish city on the South American mainland was founded in the 16C. The historic port boasts the most extensive fortifications on the entire continent; its incredible castillo has survived as the impregnable stronghold it was meant to be, when construction began in the 17C. Regularly attacked by hordes of European pirates keen on stealing gold and silver from the Spanish empire, Cartagena courageously defended its walls, earning it the name "La Ciudad Heroica." Discover this fortified city's handsome cathedrals, grand palaces, interesting museums, eclectic restaurants, and brightly painted houses made from hard coral and stone with hidden inner courtyards and high colonial roofs. Walk the narrow calles and carreras that wind around breezy plazas, shaded cafes, and ornate churches, and gain an appreciation for this city's long and rich history.

▷ **Population:** 895,400.
◔ **Michelin Maps:** pp 270–271 and p275.
▯ **Info:** There are several official tourist information points or **PITs** in Cartagena, such as the ones on Plaza de la Aduana, Plaza de los Coches and Plaza San Pedro Claver. Call ✆(5) 660 1583 or access www.colombia.travel/es/turista-internacional/informacion-practica/puntos-de-informacion-turistica for details.
◖ **Location:** The city has three main districts: the walled Old Town, the residential San Diego, and Getsemani barrio.
◕ **Don't Miss:** To make the most of your time, take a guided tour of the Old City organized by your hotel, a horse-drawn carriage tour along the water, or a city tour in an open-sided *chiva*. Visit the Castillo San Felipe de Barajas for a good idea of Cartagena's layout from on high.

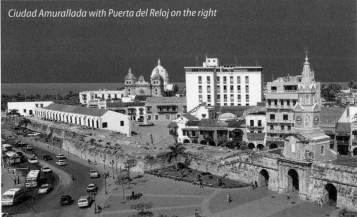

Ciudad Amurallada with Puerta del Reloj on the right

Proexport Colombia

GETTING THERE

BY AIR - International Airport Rafael Núñez (CTG), www.sasca.com.co, 1.5km/.8mi north of the old city, serves major Colombian carriers; Bogotá flights are frequent. *Colectivos* and shuttles called **metrocars** depart the airport for Monumento a la India Catalina. **Taxis** (9,000 COP) to city center are available from the taxi station outside national arrivals.

BY BOAT - Cartagena can be reached by traveling overland to Buenaventura from Medellín and catching a slow boat (normally Thu & Fri, 30 hrs). Boat travel is not advised due to irregular schedules.

BY BUS - Buses arrive from Bogotá (23hrs) and Medellín (13hrs). The **bus terminal** is about 40min east of the city center. Reputable bus companies include Expresso Almerlujo, Rapido Ochoa, Torcorama (all 5 663 2119) and Unitransco 5 663 2067.

GETTING AROUND

BY BUS - *Colectivos* and crowded **Intercity buses** vary in price if they are air conditioned, but usually cost under $1 and service Bocagrande. **Long-distance buses** depart for Barranquilla (2.5hrs), Mompox (6hrs), Riohacha (8hrs), Santa Marta (7hrs).

BY TAXI - Unmetered, rides are priced by zones: most parts of the city 6000 COP. www.cartagenainfo.com/taxis.

GENERAL INFORMATION

ACCOMMODATIONS - The Getsemani area has hostels and budget hotels, especially in Calle de la Media Luna; upscale hotels are concentrated in Bocagrande. *See ADDRESSES below.*

A BIT OF HISTORY

Just a few kilometers from the actual city of Cartagena is **Puerto Hormiga**. Located on the department lines of Sucre and Bolívar, it is the first recorded pre-Columbian settlement, dating to 7,000BC.

Upon the arrival of the Spanish in the 16C, indigenous tribes related to the **Karibs** were present in the area. **Pedro de Heredia** founded Cartagena in 1533 on the site of the indigenous **Calamari** village, naming it after the famous city in Spain, since many of his sailors hailed from there. Cartagena soon became a key port for the empire, and the tales of its new found wealth attracted corsairs and pirates including **Jean-François Roberval**, **John Hawkins** and **Francis Drake** who destroyed a large portion of the city in 1586.

Given the constant threat to the city, the Spanish Crown poured money into its defense, and in 1536, construction began on the formidable **Castillo San Felipe de Barajas**. Due to its slanted and astoundingly thick construction, Cartagena became a stronghold once more. In the years it took to complete the castle (1756), the **Inquisition** was installed, and the city changed from being the seat of movement of **Incan gold** and **silver** from New Granada to Spain to a **slave** trading city. This is not to say that there were no slaves beforehand, but the focus changed.

In 1741 the city faced its greatest threat at the **Battle of Cartagena**, when Admiral **Edward Vernon** led a combined force of American and British soldiers and ships against the city. While the massive invading forces made a good beginning, the rainy season was upon them.

After a 67-day battle, the Anglo-American fleet had to withdraw, succumbing from massive battle losses, yellow fever, dysentery and starvation.

In 1811, after 275 years of Spanish rule and several years of prosperity and expansion, the city declared its independence from Spain. Cartagena suffered some serious crises in the mid-19C like major outbreaks of **cholera** .

By the turn of the 19C, waves of immigration by people of Arabic descent and from the interior of the country helped put Cartagena back on its feet.

CIUDAD AMURALLADA★★★

The **Inner Walled Town** has been drawing visitors for some 40 years, making it Colombia's eternal tourist destination, and rightly so, as this unrivaled setting overlooking the blustery Caribbean Sea is steeped in history and exudes romance, and is now filled with contemporary fashion.

Within the humid confines of 30-odd square blocks of the **San Diego** and **San Pedro** districts is Cartagena's most beautiful and scenic place to visit. The country's rich history courses almost visibly through these streets, just as the flame-colored bougainvillea cascade from the ornate wooden balconies of the nation's best boutique hotels, restaurants and shops. The Ciudad Amurallada is not to be missed at any cost.

⚜ WALKING TOUR
Allow a half day.

▷ *Begin at the large archway just west of Parque del Centenario.*

Puerta del Reloj★

This imposing aged archway trimmed with white borders was Cartagena's principal entrance. It offers a small amount of shade for book vendors and other salespeople peddling tourist curiosities. This might just be the most striking symbol of the city, since you are following in the footsteps of dignitaries, rebels and brigands who have passed through this ancient archway.

Once through, you are greeted by the sight of the **statue**★ of Cartagena's founder Pedro de Heredia, and finely polished **horse-drawn carriages** waiting to give visitors a guided tour in the **Plaza de los Coches**★, with its tall and imposing buildings.

Portal de los Dulces★

In this corridor of archways, test your dietary constitution by trying some extremely sweet Caribbean candies, and recall that it is here that in Gabriel García Márquez's *Love in the Time of the Cholera*, the letter writers would sit to compose the text for the illiterate.

Portal de los Dulces

©Richard McColl/MICHELIN

▷ *Continue walking to your left through the Plaza de la Aduana and up Calle San Juan de Dios to Plaza San Pedro Claver.*

San Pedro Claver Church and Monastery

A jesuit missionary and a true pioneer of human rights, **San Pedro Claver Corberó** (1581-1654) arrived in Cartagena at the age of 20, and devoted the 40 years of his ministry to the service of the **slaves**. Many people are content to enter only the imposing **Iglesia de San Pedro Claver**★★ (1580, rebuilt 1654) named after him, gaze at the ornate architecture and take shelter from the sun. But to get beneath the surface of Cartagena's history, it's recommended that you make a side trip here to fully explore the sprawling San Pedro compound.

It includes a **plaza,** shaded by elegant broad-leaf trees, the **trough** in which San Pedro baptized the slaves, and a religious art museum.

Museo Santuario de San Pedro Claver

Carrera 4 # 30-01, Plaza de San Pedro Claver. ⏱*Open Mon–Fri 8am–5pm, Sat–Sun 8am–4pm.* 🎟*6,000 COP.* ☎*(5) 664 4991.*

Housed in a building whose stone façade is a true example of American Baroque style, this museum exhibits personal effects that belonged to San

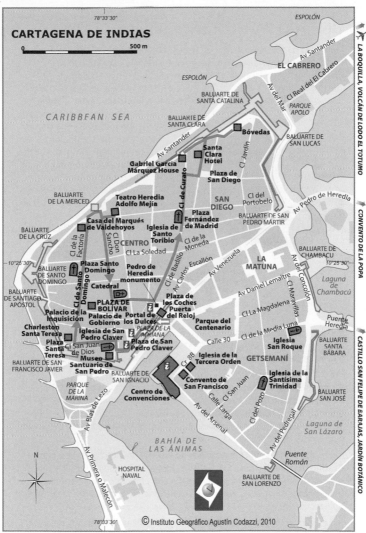

CARTAGENA DE INDIAS

0   500 m

78°33'30"

ESPOLÓN

LA BOQUILLA, VOLCÁN DE LODO EL TOTUMO

Av. Santander

EL CABRERO

Cl Real del El Cabrero

ESPOLÓN

Av. del Mar

PARQUE APOLO

BALUARTE DE SANTA CATALINA

CARIBBEAN SEA

BALUARTE DE SANTA CLARA

Bóvedas

BALUARTE DE SAN LUCAS

Av. Santander

Santa Clara Hotel

Cl Jardín

CONVENTO DE LA POPA

Gabriel García Márquez House

Plaza de San Diego

Cl de Curato

SAN DIEGO

Cl del Portobelo

Av. Pedro de Heredia

BALUARTE DE LA MERCED

Teatro Heredia Adolfo Mejía

Plaza Fernández de Madrid

Casa del Marqués de Valdehoyos

Cl Don Sancho

Iglesia de Santo Toribio

BALUARTE DE SAN PEDRO MÁRTIR

BALUARTE DE LA CRUZ

Cl de la Factoría

CENTRO

Cl La Soledad

Cl de la Moneda

Cl de Badillo

Cl de Carlos Escallón

Av. Venezuela

LA MATUNA

BALUARTE DE CHAMBACÚ

Laguna de Chambacú

10°25'30"

BALUARTE DE SANTO DOMINGO

Plaza Santo Domingo

Cl de Santo Domingo

Pedro de Heredia monumento

10°25'30"

BALUARTE DE SANTIAGO APÓSTOL

Catedral

PLAZA DE BOLÍVAR

Plaza de los Coches

Av. Daniel Lemaitre

Cl Maravillas

Av. del Corzón

Palacio de la Inquisición

Palacio de Gobierno

Portal de los Dulces

Puerta del Reloj

Parque del Centenario

Cl La Magdalena

Puente Heredia

Charleston Santa Teresa

PLAZA DE LA ADUANA

Cl de la Media Luna

Iglesia San Roque

BALUARTE SANTA BÁBARA

Plaza Santa Teresa

Cl San Juan de Dios

Iglesia de San Pedro Claver

Plaza de San Pedro Claver

Calle 30

Cl 88

GETSEMANÍ

CASTILLO SAN FELIPE DE BARAJAS, JARDÍN BOTÁNICO

BALUARTE DE SAN FRANCISCO JAVIER

Museo

Santuario de San Pedro

BALUARTE DE SAN IGNACIO

Iglesia de la Tercera Orden

Cl San Juan

Iglesia de la Santísima Trinidad

PARQUE DE LA MARINA

Convento de San Francisco

BALUARTE SAN JOSÉ

Av. Blas de Lezo

Centro de Convenciones

Calle Larga

Cl del Pozo

Laguna de San Lázaro

N

BAHÍA DE LAS ÁNIMAS

Puente Román

Av. Primera o Malecón

HOSPITAL NAVAL

Av. del Arsenal

Av. del Pedregal

BALUARTE DE SAN LORENZO

78°33'30"

© Instituto Geográfico Agustín Codazzi, 2010

BOCAGRANDE

Pedro Claver, but mainly artwork and sculptures honoring his life and deeds.

As you leave this complex and are finding your bearings in the **Plaza San Pedro Claver,** you will, no doubt, be approached by countless vendors who are hawking emeralds, artwork, Cuban cigars, ethnic jewelry and other wares. You may want to politely decline and continue your walk.

Move on up Calle San Juan de Dios.

Plaza Santa Teresa
Dominating the Plaza Santa Teresa is a stylish Cartagena institution that has catered to the world's rich and famous over the years.

Charleston Santa Teresa
Carrera 3A # 31-23. Guided tours available upon request. *(5) 664 9494. www.hotelcharlestonsantateresa.com.* Formerly the **Santa Teresa Convent★** (17C), this colorful hotel is much favored by visiting dignitaries such as US

275

UNESCO World Heritage Site

Cartagena was declared a UNESCO World Heritage Site in 1984 due to its **fortifications,** the most extensive in South America, in addition to its Andalusian-style palaces, and colonial- and Republican-era buildings. The fortifications of the protecting wall are free to visit and make a fascinating hour-and-a-half walk from the **Baluarte de San Francisco Javier**, passing the commercial districts near to the **India Catalina** statue, and then continuing on to the **Puente Roman** and the **Playa de Barahuana**. Start this walk mid-afternoon, and make sure to be back in the more secure **San Diego district** for a sun-downer, when you can reflect on what it must have taken to build these bastions ordered by **Felipe II**.

Cannons at the fortifications

© Maura Reap/Dreamstime.com

To fully understand these pockmarked, salt-deteriorated walls, make a further visit to the **Museo de las Fortificaciones**★ *(Castillo San Felipe de Barajas CAVI;* ⏲*open daily 8am–6pm;* 🎫*6,000 COP;* ☏*(5) 664 4790; www.fortificacionesdecartagena.com),* and while away some time in the old 18C garrison known as the **Bóvedas**, now home to several artisans shops.

Sixteen of the 21 original bastions still exist on the fortifications, and these played a key part in Cartagena's survival against the continuing attacks by foreign pirates. The **Baluarte de San José** *(Avenida Playa del Pedregal;* ⏲*free access),* begun in 1631 and completed in 1776, protected the area of Getsemaní with its impressive artillery of 12 cannons.

Key in repelling Admiral **Edward Vernon** in 1741 were the fortifications in **Castillo Grande de Santa Cruz** *(Carrera 15 and Calle 6, Barrio Castillo Grande;* 🔒*closed to the public)* which guarded the entry into the city's interior bay, now frequented by enormous cruise ships. Unfortunately, access to these ramparts is restricted since they are situated in the Naval Officer's Private Club.

Almost directly opposite Castillo Grande, on the Manzanillo Island, is the **Fuerte de San Juan de Manzanillo** *(*🔒*closed to the public),* created to attack invading ships from the other side should they attempt to enter the inner bay. Back in Manga is the **Castillo San Sebastián del Pastelillo** *(Club de Pesca Restaurant and Marina;* ☏*(5) 660 4594; www.clubdepesca.com).*

Overshadowing all of these impressive fortifications is the **Castillo San Felipe de Barajas**★★★. Designed by **Antonio de Arévalo**, it was mainly constructed between 1639 and 1657, but then expanded in 1762. Built with African slave labor on **San Lázaro** hill, it dominates the Cartagena skyline and must have been a deterring sight to possible invaders. Its tunnels, store rooms, turrets and slanted walls made it near indestructible, and for this reason, it is considered one of the most formidable defense structures ever built by the Spanish military. **Don Blas de Lezo**, the castle's commander at the time of the **Battle of Cartagena**, stands on in statue form, reminding all of the might of this stronghold.

president Bill Clinton for its attention to detail and mix of contemporary and Colonial style.

Little of the original design remains, but there is a great restaurant on the roof from which you can see ominous storm fronts rolling in and enjoy rooftop **views** of all of Cartagena.

▷ *If your plan is to shop, turn left out of the Charleston hotel.*

Calle de Santo Domingo★

This street is the place to find a traditional **guayabera** shirt, the formal attire on the coast. The various boutiques on this fashionable but pricey stretch are both international and Colombian, including designer togs by local favorite and native of Mompox, Hernan Zahar.

Wander along the Calle de Santo Domingo, taking a peek into large and opulent houses such as the **Casa de Pestagua**★ *(Calle de Santo Domingo # 33-63; guided tours available upon request Mon–Fri 9am–4pm; ℘5 664 9510; www.casapestagua.com).*

This former aristocrat's mansion, with its Moorish-palace style of the 16C-17C, is now a hotel and a popular setting for wedding ceremonies and receptions. More often than not, as you will notice, these high-walled mansions have been converted into boutique hotels or fancy restaurants.

▷ *Continue three blocks until you reach Plaza Santo Domingo.*

Plaza Santo Domingo★

Here, in the shadow of the church and convent of the same name (16C), **street performers** and **musicians** entertain the public in the evening.

Local legend has it that the twisted appearance of the bell tower of the Iglesia Santo Domingo was, in fact, the work of the devil in a failed attempt to destroy it.

▷ *Continue on Calle de la Factoría.*

Casa del Marqués de Valdehoyos★★

Calle de la Factoría # 36-57.
🕐*Open Mon–Fri 8:30am–noon, 2pm–6pm. ℘(5) 664 0904.*

History remembers him as a remarkably cruel taskmaster, but the **Marques de Valdehoyos** definitely had an eye for property. His opulent two-floor residence and enormous internal courtyard are now a testament to the wealth that flowed through Cartagena during the height of the **slave trade**.

Inside are the slave quarters, storage rooms and ornate double balconies. Apparently, **Simón Bolívar** is believed to have bedded down in one of these rooms during his stay in the city.

▷ *Walk until you reach the Old City wall, turn right and go two blocks.*

Teatro Heredia Adolfo Mejía★

Plaza de la Merced # 38-10.
Guided tours Mon–Fri 8am–11:30am, 2pm–5:30pm. 11,000 COP. ℘(5) 664 6023.

Constructed on the ruins of the former **Iglesia de la Merced** (1625), this handsome theater was named in honor of the city's founder. Inaugurated in 1911, it was restored in 1998.

Though its façade is subdued, its interior, with a 650-person capacity, presents a staggering display of style and theatrical extravagance. Often used to

Teatro Heredia Adolfo Mejía

Corporación Turismo Cartagena de Indias

Plaza de Bolívar

Richard Emblin/Proexport Colombia

host literary symposiums during the **Hay Festival Cartagena** *(www.hay-festival.com/Cartagena)*, it is the ideal location for all kinds of cultural and festive events.

▷ *Double back along Calle Don Sancho to reach Plaza de Bolívar.*

Plaza de Bolívar★★★

It is well worth spending some time in this attractive and shaded square (1896) since there are a number of interesting sights around it. Put your feet up in front of the statue of the Great Liberator; and enjoy a cold drink offered by strolling street vendors before moving on.

Catedral de Santa Catalina de Alejandría

Corner of Calle Santos de Piedra and Plaza de la Proclamación.

Towering over the walled city, the cathedral's illuminated **bellfry** of pastel colors and 20C **dome** light up the night skyline, leaving an unforgettable impression. This structure is one of the oldest cathedrals in the Americas. Its construction started in 1575, in place of a humble structure made of straw and reeds. As the cathedral was nearing completion, the edifice had to be overhauled after the cannonball strikes of 1586 and **Sir Francis Drake**'s attack upon the city. The cathedral was rebuilt between 1598

and 1612. Fabulously restored in recent years, it no longer seems to recall the slings and arrows of misfortune thrust its way in the past.

Do not miss its **altar**, completely made of wood and richly adorned with gold.

▷ *Remain around Plaza de Bolívar.*

Palacio de la Inquisición★★

Calle 34 # 3-11, Plaza de Bolívar.
🕒*Open Mon–Sat 9am–7pm, Sun and public holidays 10am–4pm.* 🎫*11,000 COP.* 📞*(5) 664 4570.*

Having arrived in 1610, the **Inquisition** was expelled in 1810 and reinstalled in 1815 before being finally pushed out of Cartagena in 1821. The inquisitioners left behind a grim legacy of intolerance and brutality that can be viewed in this museum in which heinous devices of torture are on display.

Under the arches of the **Palacio de Gobierno**, in stark contrast to the austere remnants of history all around, are street plaques alongside the Plaza de **Bolívar** denoting all of the **Miss Colombia** winners. Pageants are truly a megabucks business here in Colombia. The contest is held each December in Cartagena, and this event is routinely the most-watched televised program in the country. In fact, Colombia comes to a complete standstill when the pageant is being broadcast. In the building, beside the plaques that are placed as a sort of Hollywood-esque style homage to the beauty queens, are the offices that create the vast mechanism of the pageant.

> *Leave Plaza de Bolívar and head down Calle de Badillo.*

Barrio San Diego★★★

Leaving the area of the Old Town or "Ciudad Vieja," you move on to the colonial neighborhood known as San Diego, which is far calmer and even more scenic. Often, this area's quiet and picturesque streets seem devoid of visitors.

Plaza Fernández de Madrid★

This peaceful and scenic plaza looks ideal for a movie set, a fact not lost on some film producers and directors as parts of the film adaptation of Gabriel García Márquez's *Love in the Time of the Cholera* were filmed here.

Just up from here if following the **Calle del Curato**, passing the squat and colorful colonial buildings of the Barrio San Diego leads to the **Plaza de San Diego★**. Lined by expensive, but fantastic restaurants, the Plaza's main draw is a red-painted hotel.

Santa Clara Hotel★★

Calle Del Torno # 39-29.
Guided tours available upon request.
(5) 650-4700. www.sofitel.com.
Just like the Santa Teresa across town, the **Santa Clara** was built as a **convent** (1621), and has since been restored and converted into a hotel.
Owned by the Sofitel Group, it is a sight to see since the communal areas, which can be visited upon request, are kept intact as they must have been in the 17C. Tall rooms with high beam-heavy ceilings and walls painted red only add to the atmosphere. The central **cloister** is dense with tropical plants, and has its own resident mischievous **toucans**, ably equipped at stealing the fruit from guests' breakfast. Along the

☺ Don't Miss ☺

Since Cartagena's history has been so influenced by attacks and piracy, no trip is complete without a stroll around the main **ramparts of the wall★★★**, that extend a total distance of 11km/7mi. This walk may be too much to do in one go, given the heat, distances and sheer quantity of sights, so it's best to split it up into sections. You can walk for hours along the walls and over the ramparts, looking out to sea and back at this architecturally precious city.

passageways are original colonial furnishings, and beneath the decadent **El Coro Bar** (try their mojitos) is the old **crypt chapel**.

> *Step out from the peaceful confines of the Santa Clara, and turn left towards the Caribbean and the city wall.*

A few short blocks from the Santa Clara stands the **Bóvedas**, part of the old 18C garrison. Handily located in one corner of the city, it is a good place to start a stroll around the ramparts of the wall. As you pass the ocean side of the Santa Clara, walking south, looking

Shops in the Bóvedas

Proexport Colombia

279

Bocagrande

Bocagrande is the antithesis of the Ciudad Amurallada. From the top of **La Popa** (♨ *see opposite*), or just about any high point in the city, you can clearly make out this area, with its tellingly **modern skyline** littered with high-rise condominiums and fancy apartments. At one stage, there were some fortifications here to guard the entry to the bay, but over time, Bocagrande's role changed, and it became a playground for the wealthy. **Art Deco houses** soon sprang up. However, these masterpieces of architecture have long been bulldozed and given way to multi-story **apartment buildings** and **timeshares** as well as Gaudí 1980s-era **hotels** and **casinos** aimed at package tours.

out towards the spit of land and the unsightly high rises of **Bocagrande**, check out the next house, painted in a terra-cotta color. Without being intrusive, take a look, for here resides one of literature's *maestros*, **Gabriel García Márquez**, whose literary contributions have put Colombia on the map for all the right reasons and seem to embody the Colombian Caribbean spirit.

ADDITIONAL SIGHTS
Castillo San Felipe de Barajas★★★

Avenida Arévalo, Cerro San Lázaro. ⏱*Open daily 8am–6pm.* ⏲*6,000 COP.* ☎*(5) 656 0590. www.fortificaciones decartagena.com.*
♨*See sidebar p276.* Not to be missed, this formidable **fortress** was begun in 1536 to effectively protect the city from marauders. The massive stronghold was worked on in earnest from 1639 to 1657 and enlarged in 1762. As the most extensive fortifications in South America, the complex was designated a UNESCO Heritage Site in 1984. *To see the tunnels, be sure to take a flashlight.*

Convento de la Popa★

Calle Nueva del Toril # 21, Cerro de la Popa. ⏱*Open daily 9am–5pm.* ⏲*6,000 COP.* ☎*(5) 666 2331. www.conventodelapopa.com.*
Located a little farther from the Old Town, this **monastery**, built in 1607, was used at times as a fortress because of its strategic location. It houses a lovely interior **patio**, a colonial **museum** and a **chapel** dedicated to the Virgen de la Candelaria. But it is mostly famous for offering by unparalleled **views**★★ of the city from the top of its 150m/492ft high hill. There is no better point to be at **sunset**, as these views extend out far and wide, and show the real lay of the land.

Courtyard, Convento de la Popa

Richard Emblin/Proexport Colombia

GETSEMANÍ★

Just a short walk from the upscale and gracefully restored Republican era buildings of the San Diego neighborhood lies the more down-at-the-heels, yet no less interesting, **Outer Walled Town** barrio of Getsemaní, with a clutch of Spanish castles nearby.

Originally, when Cartagena was growing under Spanish rule, this area of the city was populated with the **working classes**, and to some extent, that is still true today, although there have been significant efforts to gentrify the area and embrace it as another fashionable destination. The jury remains out on whether this upgrade will completely alter the ambience of the area, or whether it will benefit the locals.

Centro de Convenciones Centro Cartagena de Indias

Proexport Colombia

Convento de San Francisco

Calle Larga # 10-27.

In the beginning, Getsemaní was the seat of Franciscans who put their cloisters here in 1555. Over time, the area served as headquarters for the Inquisition. This old monastery now houses tourist shops, art galleries and private offices, but visitors are welcome to come and browse during office hours.

Parque del Centenario

Alongside this welcome oasis of green in the visible chaos of book vendors and street hawkers sits Cartagena's Convention Center.

Centro de Convenciones Centro Cartagena de Indias

www.corpocentros.com.

This imposing, ultra-modern convention center creates quite a striking juxtaposition with the Colonial architecture hereabouts. It has hosted just about every type of event or seminar, including the annual **Miss Colombia Pageant**.

In the off-season, these conventions keep Cartagena's hotels and tourist industry afloat. Conventions are now a huge business in Cartagena, and due to this state-of-the-art focal point, restaurants and more economical lodgings have sprung up in the immediate vicinity. Directly in front, the **Camellón de**

los Mártires, a wide and spacious walkway, leads back to the **Torre de Reloj** *(Avenida Blas de Lezo)*.

Iglesia de la Tercera Orden

Carrera 8B and Calle 25.

This colonial church faces the **Bahia de las Animas**, along the **Calle del Arsenal**, which now is home to a collection of bars and restaurants, making it one of the city's nightlife districts.

According to some accounts, General **Don Blas** is buried in this church, beneath its imposing beams. A military strategist with one eye, one leg and one arm, Blas was able to quell the attacks by Admiral **Edward Vernon** in 1741.

Iglesia de la Santísima Trinidad★

Carrera 10, Calle San Antonio # 25-174.

Other churches here in Getsemaní include this decaying cathedral-like structure, completed in the second half of the 17C.

Iglesia San Roque★

Carrera 10C and Calle Espíritu Santo # 29-222.

Standing near the backpacker haven of the **Calle Media Luna**, with its budget hostels, this church was built in 1674 after a particularly prevalent outbreak of yellow fever in Cartagena.

SURROUNDINGS

La Boquilla

▷ *7km/4.5mi N of Cartagena via Carrera 28 and Anillo Via.*

This fishing village, which has always been home to Afro-Colombian inhabitants, is a great place to take a **bird-watching** canoe trip into the **mangrove swamps** and enjoy Afro-Colombian cuisine.

The original ambience of La Boquilla has been lost somewhat with the increase in Cartagena's popularity. Many of the original inhabitants have been pushed out to make way for mega-constructions of **condos** and **resorts**. In some corners of La Boquilla, you can still find locals dancing in the street to rhythmic and traditional drumbeats in the evening.

Jardín Botánico Guillermo Piñeres

▷ *18km/11mi SE of Cartagena, in Turbaco (Sector Matute Apartado 5456, off Carretera 90).* ◷ *Open daily 8am –4:30pm.* ⬤ *5,000 COP.* ℘ *(5) 673 1474.*

These botanical gardens were created in 1978 for the study and conservation of the flora and fauna of the Colombian Caribbean.

Visitors can enjoy some 12,600 species of plants here, including the remarkable **sabals** (fan palms), while following pathways through the gardens amid desert, rain forest and tropical forest.

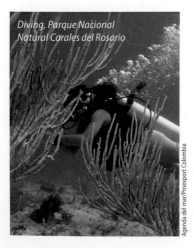

Diving, Parque Nacional Natural Corales del Rosario

Agenda del mar/Proexport Colombia

EXCURSIONS

Parque Nacional Natural Corales del Rosario y San Bernardo★

▷ *45km/28mi SW of Cartagena.* ◷ *Call for opening times.* ⬤ *3,800 COP.* ℘ *(5) 665 5655.*

This 120,000ha/296,526 acre park of roughly 30 islands was created to protect fragile underwater ecosystems of fish, invertebrates and **coral** as well as extensive seagrass beds, algae prairies and mangroves forests. Each outcrop is a habitat for a wide variety of **marine life** and **birdlife**.

Its shallow, clear waters and coral reef are ideal for **diving** and **snorkeling**.

Playa Blanca★

▷ *20km/12.5mi from Cartagena.*

Escape the humidity of the city and head out to the white-sand beaches of Islas del Rosario, in particular Playa Blanca on **Isla Barú**. As part of the Parque Nacional Natural Corales del Rosario, this 3.5km/2mi beach and its turquoise waters are protected. They are pretty much free of currents, and therefore safe for **swimming**.

For complete relaxation Playa Blanca is best enjoyed midweek, when there are few crowds and you get to experience the true feeling of being in a picture postcard setting, sharing the beach with only your companions and diving sea birds.

Volcán de Lodo El Totumo★

▷ *52km/32mi NE of Cartagena. Calle el Totumo, close to Galerazamba.*

Resembling a giant anthill, this **mud volcano** can make a fun half-day outing. Clamber up the wooden steps to the bubbling mud **cauldron,** and bathe hippo-like in the sulphurous discharge, a thick dark mud that oozes up out of the cone into the nearby lake and is believed to have restorative properties.

Don't feel that you have to accept the massages offered by local "experts." Later, head down to the lake where the spouses of the aforementioned "experts" will offer to help you wash off the mud for a tip.

Iglesia Santa Barbara, Mompox

Proexport Colombia

SANTA CRUZ DE MOMPOX★★

248km/154mi SE of Cartagena, via bus or taxi to Magangué and then a ferry ride across the Magdalena River.
Edging the **Magdalena River**, inland and southeast of Cartagena, is a fairy-tale, elegantly decaying colonial won-derland. Mompox (Pop. 41,326), also spelled "Mompós," is a town founded as a safe port along the river in 1540 by **Alonso de Heredia**, brother of Pedro, the founder of Cartagena.

After Cartagena, Mompox is the second **UNESCO World Heritage Site** in Colombia, and rightly so, as its six ornate churches, all positioned along the three streets that run parallel to the river, are awesome sights to see.

While the probable inspiration for the **Macondo** of Gabriel García Már-quez's *100 Years of Solitude* is the author's own hometown of Aracataca, Mompox has been said by many to be the actual representation of this fabled place, the last fully colonial town in the Colombian Caribbean.

A Bit of History

Known for its **cumbia** music, which traces its roots down to the drumbeat right back to Africa, Mompox is also a land of legends, ghost stories and tales of times past.

It was key in **Simón Bolívar**'s missions to free this region of New Granada, for it was here that the Great Liberator raised

an army of 400 *Mompósinos* to march on Caracas.

The support from Mompox for Bolívar led him to state, *If to Caracas I owe my life, to Mompox I owe my glory.* His words are a source of much pride to the locals here; they are imprinted on the **statue** of Bolívar in the plaza of the same name. As always, there is a story behind the story, and it is believed that the majo-rity of the 400 *Mompósinos* riding with Bolívar, upon reaching the chillier climes of the Andes near Merida in Venezuela, turned around and headed for home.

A key port on the Río Magdalena for ships transporting the **gold** and **silver** from Ecuador up to Cartagena, Mompox grew exponentially in the colonial era, but its importance gradually waned when the river started to silt up with mud, and the town fell into oblivion. It is its relative isolation that has enabled Mompox to remain intact as a colonial relic. If the town feels mired in decay and neglect to you, know that it is at the top of the Colombian government's list of heritage sites to protect, and restoration projects are in the making.

☛ WALKING TOUR
WALKING MOMPOX

Allow 2hrs. Begin at the riverfront.
Explore the town on foot, since every-thing lies in close proximity.
Wander idly along the riverfront past the imposing **Portales de la Marquesa★**,

Donkey ride by the Magdalena River

© Richard McColl/MICHELIN

enjoying the breeze and a cold juice before arriving upstream at the **Bosque Santander,** where a resident family of howler monkeys regularly spends the afternoon, shattering the lazy calm with their gutteral calls.

The most curious church in town is the **Iglesia Santa Barbara**★★ *(Calle 14, Plaza de Santa Barbara),* built in 1613, with its independent octagonal tower and balconies, yellow façade, Masonic imagery close to the altar and Moorish feel.

Other churches of note include the well-preserved **Iglesia San Agustin**★ *(Calle Real del Medio, between Calles 16 and 17),* **La Concepción** *(Calle 18)* and **San Juan del Dios** *(Calle Real del Medio, between Calles 19 and 20),* the oldest one (1564) being the red-painted **Iglesia San Francisco**★ *(Calle 20)* that stands proudly in the market area, in front of the river.

The **Iglesia de la Concepción** borders the north end in the old marketplace, where the **Casa de la Aduana**★ *(Plaza Real de la Concepción)* is located.

It is an unfortunate reality that the old **Customs House** is seemingly in a permanent state of abandon, when

Semana Santa

Austere and chaotic, the **Easter celebrations** in Mompox are rivaled in Colombia only by those of **Popayán** (☞*see POPAYÁN*), and are recognized as some of the most famous in the Americas. Nazarene **pilgrims** in heavy purple tunics march two paces forward and one pace back, carrying heavily ornate displays in the heat in processions that start in the late afternoon and go on until the early hours of the following day. What makes these Easter celebrations so special is that they truly belong to the people of Mompox and surrounding towns who come and display heart-felt devotion and religious tradition. For a fuller appreciation of the celebrations, be sure to arrive on Wednesday to experience the *Miércoles Alumbrado,* when the town's people dress up formally, visit the cemetery at night and place candles on the tombs of their friends and loved ones, while the band plays a solemn serenade. On many of the nights, there are street competitions to create **religious artwork** from sawdust and colored sand.

it should be the center of the tourism sightseeing circuit, because of its steps that lead straight down into the river. Imagine the amounts of gold, silver and contraband that must have passed along these neglected walls.

Save the **Iglesia Santo Domingo** *(Plaza de Santo Domingo)* until last, and after dusk, since in the plaza here at nightfall there are **juice vendors** creating any number of fresh-fruit concoctions from the region, such as *corozo* or *guayaba agria*. Such a refreshing beverage can be rewarding at the end of a long, hot day of sightseeing.

ADDITIONAL SIGHTS

Do not miss the town's **cementerio**★★, with its brightly whitewashed tombs and busts that are home to heroes of the independence movement, immigrants from all over as well as the forefather of black South American poetry, the *Mompósino* **Candelario Obeso**.

In most colonial towns, people were buried near the churches, but given the geography of Mompox, this cemetery was placed away from the river, and therefore removed from the churches.

There are enough points of interest in Mompox to keep you here a few days. You can visit additional colonial buildings such as the **Casa de la Cultura** *(Calle Real del Medio;* ◷ *open Mon–Fri 8am–5pm;* ☞ *2,000 COP;* ✆ *5 685 6044)*, eat with the locals in the **Plaza Santa Domingo**★ in the evening, and perhaps make a short visit to the informal **Jardín Botánico El Cuchubo** *(Calle 14;* ◷ *open daily; knock on the gate for a tour;* ☞ *contribution requested)*. While the owner speaks no English, he will happily walk you through his gardens.

The **Colegio Pinillos** *(Plaza Santo Domingo, Calle 18)*, located between the Plaza Santo Domingo and the **Plaza Bolívar**, is also worth a mention, as it was the first university on the Colombian coast, known at the time as **Antiguo Colegio Universidad de San Pedro Apóstol**. Work began on this fine two-story building in 1794. Completed in 1809, it has served as a high school for a long period of time.

At the time of writing, the building was undergoing major restoration work. In 2011 it is scheduled to reopen as both a university and a high school.

A couple of blocks back from the river, on **Calle Cuarta**, there are several workshops, for visitors interested in crafts or looking for authentic souvenirs from Mompox, where internationally renowned silver filigree jewelry called **Filigrana Momposina** (☞ *see sidebar p79)* is routinely coiled— painstakingly—into shape. The process is fascinating to watch.

Also for a destination that appeals to **ecotourists**, Mompox benefits from its location in wetlands because of the wealth and diversity of flora and fauna they provide. Boat trips out to the swamps, called **ciénagas**★★, around the town can be easily arranged; during the voyage, the boat plies through the **channels** dug in pre-Columbian times that were designed to help combat area flooding. Passengers will enjoy sightings of many types of birds, including **egrets** and **herons**, while the boat passes small riverside villages.

As these villages are fishing communities where the locals look for catfish and the local *bocachico*, the inhabitants spend just as much time in the water as they do on land, which has led Gabriel García Márquez to label them in his works as "amphibious."

Making silver filigree

Proexport Colombia

285

ADDRESSES

🏠STAY

$ Casa Viena – *Calle San Andres # 30-53, Cartagena.* 📞*(5) 664 6242. www.casaviena.com. 9 rooms.* Service is their pleasure at family-run Casa Viena, where the staff can provide information about Cartegena as well as travel in South America. Though the hostel sits on a noisy street in Getsemani, it is safe and clean. Wi-Fi access, coffee and local calls are free, but they don't accept reservations.

$$ Casa Relax – *Calle del Pozo # 25-105, Barrio Getsemani.* 🏊 📞*(5) 664 1117. www.cartagenarelax.com. 11 rooms.* Located within easy reach of the center of town, this reasonably priced bed and breakfast is also close to the Trinidad Church in Getsemani. The restored colonial property has a large pool, a sunny kitchen and social area, and breakfast is included in the rate.

$$ Casa Villa Colonial – *Calle de la Media Luna # 10-89, Barrio Getsemani, Cartagena.* ✖️📞*(5) 664 5421. www. hotelvillacolonial.com. 13 rooms.* This hotel in central Getsemani lies near the old part of Cartagena. A sound midrange option, Villa Colonial has spotless rooms that accommodate one to four people, plus a small kitchen for guest use. The helpful staff will organize everything from day trips to pizza delivery.

$$ La Casa Amarilla – *Carrera 1 # 13-59, La Albarrada con el Callejon de Cocosolo, Mompox.* 📞*(5) 685 6326. www.lacasaamarillamompos.com. 10 rooms.* Opened in 2008, La Casa Amarilla occupies a restored 17C house in front of the river. The owner, a journalist from London, promotes the cultural and ecological attractions in town and ushers people up to the roof terrace to watch the migrating birds. Air-conditioned rooms have been lovingly decorated and sit around a cloister-style garden. If you fancy real luxury, request the master suite **($$$)** with its own balcony and sitting room.

$$$$ Capilla del Mar – *Corner of Carrera 1 and Calle 8, Bocagrande, Cartagena.* ✖️🏊 📞*(5) 650 1500.* *www.capilladelmar.com. 203 rooms.* This high-class hotel boasts a revolving rooftop bar and a 22nd-floor swimming pool overlooking the sea. It's 10 minutes from the airport and 5 minutes from the walled city, and has its own beach area. Renovated rooms are outfitted with Wi-Fi access, safe deposit boxes and AC. Downstairs, there's a beauty salon, travel agency and Internet cafe.

$$$$ Cartagena Millennium – *Avenida San Martín # 7-121, Bocagrande, Cartagena.* ✖️🏊 📞*(5) 665 8711. www.hotelcartagenamillennium.com. 51 rooms.* Both business and leisure travelers feel at home in this modern hotel in the city's tourist zone. All the airy rooms are tastefully decorated; business suites provide a work desk, while deluxe suites add living and dining spaces. Relax at the pool or the bar on the rooftop terrace, or take a dip in the indoor pool on the first floor. In the restaurant, the menu stars Creole cuisine.

$$$$ Casa La Fe – *Calle Segunda de Badillo # 36-125, Centro, Cartagena.* 📞*(5) 664 0306. www.casalafe.com. 14 rooms.* This friendly B&B is proud to have been mentioned twice in the **New York Times**. Renovated in 2005 by its English and Colombian owners, Casa La Fe is decorated with religious art. More expensive rooms have views of Plaza Fernández de Madrid. Enjoy breakfast in the lush courtyard, and access to a small gym.

$$$$$ Charleston Santa Teresa – *Carrera 3 #31-23, Plaza Santa Teresa, El Centro, Cartagena.* ✖️🏊 Spa 📞*(5) 664-9494. www.hotelcharlestonsanta teresa.com. 89 rooms.* Now a hotel, the former Convento de Santa Teresa surrounds two bougainvillea-draped courtyards. Some of the rooms offer sea views. Guests can work out in the well-equipped gym, then kick back by the rooftop pool, or indulge themselves at the spa.

$$$$$ Hotel Caribe – *Carrera 1 # 2-87, Bocagrande, Cartagena.* ✖️🏊 📞*(5) 665 4042. www.hotelcaribe.com. 363 rooms.* A majestic four-story Spanish Colonial-style hotel, the Caribe opened in 1941. Three different wings hold a variety of well-appointed, high-ceilinged rooms, done in bright white with vibrant accents. The Caribe's grounds include beaches and gardens, and its restaurants provide both indoor and beachside dining options. Kids will enjoy the miniature golf course.

�‖/EAT

$ El Bistro – *Calle Ayos # 4-46, Centro Historico, Cartagena. ☎(320) 551 3587. http://el-bistro-cartagena.com.* At this casual bistro, continental cuisine incorporates tastes of the Caribbean. The blackboard menu changes daily to reflect market-fresh products. Breads and pastries are all made in-house, and there's an extensive list of beers, wines and cocktails. **European**.

$ La Dulceria – *Carrera 2 # 6-53, Bocagrande, Cartagena. Lunch only. ☎(5) 655 0281.* This pleasant small cafe is a good option if you're looking for a quiet lunch spot. Enjoy a wide variety of dishes on the inner patio, and be sure to save room for dessert. With a name that means The Sweet Shop, the restaurant specializes in homemade cakes and pastries. **Middle Eastern**.

$ La Mulata Cartagena – *Carrera 9 # 36-32, Barrio San Diego, Cartagena. Lunch only. Closed Sun. ☎(5) 664 6222. www.restaurantelamulata.com.* The appealing set menu at this hip restaurant is a great deal, but note that popular items run out fast. Caribbean cuisine with a Colombian twist stars here; the daily lunch menu lists five entrées and five grilled items. For a refreshing treat, try an *agua fresca* (fruit-juice drink). **Colombian**.

$$$ Club de Pesca – *Manga, Av. Miramar, Fuerte del Pastelillo, Cartagena. ☎(5) 660 4594. www.clubdepesca.com.* Affluent gourmands love this chic place, where they can arrive by land or sea and dine on the deck overlooking the marina. Club de Pesca is located inside San Sebastian del Pastelillo Fort, one of the most important forts of the colonial era. Modern seafood fills the menu, along with a great selection of wine. **Seafood**.

$$$ 8-18 – *Calle Gastelbondo # 2-124 local 8, Centro Historico, Cartagena. ☎(5) 664 2632. www.restaurante8-18.com.* Intimate and trendy, 8-18 provides a varied menu of coastal cuisine. The restaurant is normally full, so reserve your table in advance. **International**.

$$$ El Santísimo – *Calle del Torno # 39-62, Barrio San Diego, Cartagena. ☎(5) 660-1531. www.restaurante elsantisimo.com.* You'll be welcomed by the warm, attentive staff at this upscale eatery in the Barrio San Diego. Carefully prepared contemporary Colombian fare here is paired on the menu with a suggested wine. Use the warm fresh bread to soak up the juices in *obatala* (marinated beef stew). **Colombian**.

🛒 SHOPPING

Prices are higher in Cartagena than in the rest of Colombia. Head for the walled center to find upscale boutiques; go to Getsemani for inexpensive wares.

Las Bovédas – *Between the forts of Santa Clara and Santa Catalina, in the walled city.*

Upalema Handicrafts – *Calle San Juan de Dios, Edificio San Andres # 3-99, El Centro, Cartagena. ☎(5) 664 5032 www.upalema.com.*

Caribe Plaza – *Pié de La Popa, Calle 29D # 22-108. ☎(5) 669 2332. www.cccaribeplaza.com.*

🏃 RECREATION

Buzos de Baru – *Hotel Caribe, Local 9, Bocagrande. ☎(5) 665 7675. www.buzosdebaru.com.* This scuba-diving school has an environmental slant.

Diving Planet – *Calle Estanco del Aguardiente # 5-94, Cartagena. ☎(5) 644 2171. www.divingplanet.org.* Snorkeling and scuba dives and lessons are available at Diving Planet.

Café Havana – *Corner of Calle del Guerrero & Calle Media Luna, Getsemani, Cartagena.* This club features excellent local musicians and great Cuban cigars.

Barranquilla and Surroundings

Atlántico, Magdalena

Located between Cartagena and Santa Marta, Barranquilla is the capital of the department of **Atlántico**, and the country's fourth-largest city. Strategically positioned at the mouth of the Magdalena River, it is Colombia's main Caribbean port. A true cultural melting pot, "La Arenosa" (the Sandy City) is also home to the second-largest carnival celebration in the Americas. Birthplace of Colombian hip-shaker and songstress Shakira, and fundamental to the writings of Gabriel García Márquez, Barranquilla is a contemporary cultural heartbeat on the Colombian Caribbean coast, where fine dining, sophisticated shopping and literary haunts are among the many attractions.

▶ **Population:** 1,112,889.
🕭 **Michelin Maps:** pp 290–291.
ℹ **Info:** Parque Cultural del Caribe, Calle 36 # 46-66, ✆(5) 372 0581. Comité Mixto de Promoción del Atlántico, Antiguo Edificio de la Aduana, ✆(5) 330 3300, www.cultura caribe.org.
☺ **Don't Miss:** A trip to the outstanding Museo del Caribe to enjoy the exhaustive insights into music, literature, cooking and the history of the region.

A BIT OF HISTORY

At the time of the arrival of the Spanish, the area was inhabited by the **Kamash Indians**. Founded around 1629, Barranquilla became an **encomienda labor** outpost. Under this system, deserving subjects of the Spanish Crown were granted a certain number of native inhabitants in a particular area; in return for protecting them and instructing them in the Christian faith, Spanish colonists could require them to pay tribute in the form of work, goods or gold.

In 1825 Juan Bernardo Elbers brought the first **Mississippi steamboats** to Colombia, and with these new forms of transportation plying their trade on the Magdalena River, Barranquilla took off. The town became the seat of modernity, fashion and industrialization in Colombia at the turn of the 19C. In 1919 Colombia's national airline **Avianca** was created here in Barranquilla, albeit under a different name, and the city's airport was the first to be completed in South America. By the 1940s, with the **mass** immigrations taking place from Europe and Asia, Barranquilla had grown to Colombia's second-largest city behind Bogotá, with vast communities of British, German, Italian, Arabic and Jewish settlers. After the post-war expansion, Barranquilla went into decline, and was overtaken by Cali and Medellín. Recently, Barranquilla's stock has risen once again as a major seat of commerce and **cultural activities**.

TOWN

Aside from a major port system, you will not find any real **coherence** in this **urban landscape**—which is part of the city's interest. Do not expect any colonial center, but rather some neighborhoods displaying **ultra-modernity**, while others boast Neoclassical **Republican** elements. The city itself is too large and chaotic to walk from one place to another, so your best bet is to hop in a taxi and head up to the neighborhoods and sights most likely to interest you.

CENTRO★

For a glimpse of the traditional Barranquilla that belongs to the people of **Afro-Colombian** descent, head to Downtown Barranquilla, which is also called **Barrio Abajo**. Low houses with high pavements that protect the locals

GETTING THERE

BY AIR - **Aeropuerto Internacional Ernesto Cortissoz** (BAQ),www.baq. aero, 11km/7mi south of the city center, is served by most Colombian carriers, with direct flights that include Bogotá, Cali, Medellín, San Andres, Panama City, Venezuela, and Miami. A **taxi** (unmetered) should cost about 2,000 COP to get into town (negotiate your rate before getting into the cab). Buses to/from the airport and city center are clearly marked *aeropuerto* (1,300 COP).

BY BUS - Direct bus routes to the city include Bogotá (18hrs 95,000 COP), Medellín (12 hrs; 85,000 COP), Santa Marta (2 hrs; 10,000 COP) and Mompox. Barranquilla's main **bus terminal** (www.ttbaq.com.co) sits at the southern edge of the city, about 7km/4mi from city center. Bus trips to the center take about an hour; a taxi ride (1,500 COP) takes 30min.

GETTING AROUND

BY PUBLIC TRANSPORTATION - The new (2010) **Transmetro** articulated bus system (www.transmetro.gov. co) services the city and the larger metropolitan area. **Intercity buses** are inexpensive and relatively reliable; the bus network provides good coverage. The main bus terminal (*see BY BUS opposite*) is about an hour bus ride away; a taxi (1,500 COP) takes 30min. Other cities can be reached by bus such as Cartagena (2 hrs; 10,000 COP), Santa Marta (19,000 COP 2hrs), and via Santa Marta, Riohacha (4 hrs from Santa Marta; 34,000 COP).

BY TAXI - Taxis are unmetered, so negotiate your rate before stepping into the cab.

from street floods in the rainy season and a village-like feel have created this community within the city.

Many residents feel that this is the real heart of the **carnival** festivities (*see sidebar p 000*).

Museo del Caribe★★★

Calle 36 # 46-66. ⏰*Open Mon–Fri 8am –5pm, Sat–Sun and public holidays 9am –6pm.* ⏰*Closed first Mon of the month.* ⬛*2,000 COP (tour guide in English* ⬛*10,000 COP).* ☎*(5) 372 0581. www.culturacaribe.org.*

Designed and built to regenerate a run-down area of the Downtown, this modern edifice of a museum (22,000sq m/236,800sq ft) was opened in 2009. With its rooms dedicated to local music, theatre and literature, it stands as a huge recognition of the cultural achievements of the region. This is really the greatest possible celebration of the **cultura costena** that is so strong here, and a source of much pride for the region's population.

Here, every theme is presented and developed, from the historical aspects

Museo del Caribe

Samuel D. Tcherassi Barrera/Proexport Colombia

BARRANQUILLA
EL PRADO
0   500 m

© Instituto Geográfico Agustín Codazzi, 2010
74°48'

May not be reproduced either in its entirety or partially without
the authorization of the Instituto Geográfico Agustín Codazzi - IGAC

of the coast and its population to the environment that has given rise to such a strong sense of regionalism.

Pay close attention to the room dedicated to the **gente**, or people of the region, since an in-depth look into the **pre-Hispanic origins** of this land is provided here.

Marvel Moreno (1939-1995)

This former Queen of the Carnival at Barranquilla holds a significant place in the literary sphere of her Caribbean world. Born to an upper middle-class family in Barranquilla's El Prado neighborhood, she wrote several interesting short stories and novels, including *En diciembre llegaban las brisas* (The Breeze Came in December), which she referred to as the "Bible of Barranquilla."

The **Mediateca Macondo** is an entire room dedicated to the life and works of the Colombian Caribbean coast's most internationally lauded son, **Gabriel García Márquez**.

If you have ever wanted to know the real meaning of **bullerengue**, **chalupa**, **fandango**, **cumbia** or **porro**, then head to the exhibit dedicated to all of these musical forms that help give the coast its identity.

In its second phase *(currently under construction)*, the museum will also house a **modern art** annex, which will make it the epicenter of all things cultural on the Caribbean coast.

Iglesia de San Nicolás de Tolentino
Carrera 42 # 33-45.

The Gothic Revival Catedral Metropolitano overlooks the **Plaza San Nicolás**. Its construction began in the 17C, but took almost 300 years to be completed. The surrounding streets around the cathedral have become bric-a-brac

BARRANQUILLA CENTRO

0   500 m

74°47'

N

EL PRADO

Carrera 50

Calle 47

Murillo Toro

Antigua Estación
de trenes Montoya

Av. Olaya Herrera

CENTRO COMMERCIAL
PORTAL DEL PRADO

UNIVERSIDAD
LIBRE

Carrera 50

Vía 40

CATEDRAL
METROPOLITANA

PLAZA DE
LA PAZ

Edificio de
la Aduana

Calle 59

Calle 57

Carrera 44

Calle 53

Calle 50

Carrera 45

Museo del
Caribe

Av. Olaya Herrera

La Cueva

Avenida 20 de Julio

Calle 47

Carrera 45

Calle 36

TUBARÁ

10°59'

Calle 56

Calle 57

UNIVERSIDAD
DEL ATLÁNTICO

Murillo Toro

Calle 42

Carrera 44

10°59'

PARQUE
SIMÓN
BOLÍVAR

Carrera 41

Calle 48

Calle 44

Avenida 20 de Julio

Calle 54

Los Estudiantes

Iglesia de
San Nicolás
de Tolentino

Calle 52

Carrera 41

Carrera 40

Plaza San
Nicolás

Calle 53

CEMENTERIO
UNIVERSAL

PARQUE
UNIVERSAL

Carrera 38

Calle 38

Calle 34

Carrera 34

Calle 47

Carrera 36

Los Estudiantes

CEMENTERIO
CATÓLICO
CALANCALA

Calle 50

Murillo Toro

Calle 51

Carrera 35

Avenida Boyacá

Carrera 33

74°47'

© Instituto Geográfico Agustín Codazzi, 2010

markets, with stalls set up to sell all kinds of wares.

☞*Be sure to keep an eye on your belongings while here.*

BARRIO EL PRADO★

Located between Carrera 54 and Calle 53.
This neighborhood really defines **modern Barranquilla**, inasmuch as the Cen-tro defines its roots. Most of the **theaters**, **museums**, **hotels** and literary sites can be found in this barrio.

In this part of town, you can clearly see what the architects and designers had in mind. They intended to create broad, leafy avenues and stately mansions with well-tended gardens. When this idea was actualized in brick in the

Houses in Barrio el Prado

291

1920s, it was completely unheard of and revolutionary.

Teatro Amira de la Rosa★

Carrera 54 # 52-258. ⏰*Open Mon–Fri 8am–noon, 2pm–6pm.* ☎*(5) 349 1117. www.lablaa.org.*

This iconic structure was completed in 1982. It is the venue for regular cultural offerings, including opera, ballet, childrens' programs, concerts, poetry presentations and a **jazz festival**.

In the interior, be sure to catch a glimpse of **Alejandro Obregón**'s large painting that represents the story of the local myth of the Hombre Caimán.

Museo Romántico

Carrera 54 # 59-199. ⏰*Open Mon–Sat 8:15am–noon, 2pm–6pm.* 🎫*5,000 COP.* ☎*(5) 344 4591.*

Discover books and tales about Barranquilla's founding and growth in this museum, housed in a Republican-style mansion.

Estadio Roberto Meléndez

Avenida Murillo. ⏰*Check website for schedule.* ☎*(5) 360 0338. www.juniorbarranquilla.com.*
A hulking monument to the wonders of cement, this stadium is the largest in Colombia (58,000 capacity). It is home to the local **Atlético Junior** football club, and has hosted some thrilling matches, not least as the erstwhile home of the **Colombian national team**. With a devoted and unforgiving fan base, **Los Cafeteros** were hard to beat on their home turf in Barranquilla, especially since they preferred to play their games in the stifling heat of midday. Life has not been so rosy since they moved their home games to Medellín, an altogether more forgiving locale. Hopefully soon the national team will return to Barranquilla, as is expected, and this move will result in a change in the nation's football fortunes.

The city's remarkable archives include photos, historical documents (old newspapers, Simón Bolívar's letters, etc.), and even the typewriter on which Gabriel García Márquez wrote *La Hojarasca* (Leaf Storm), a short novel set in the mythical town of Macondo.

Casa del Carnaval★★

Located within the museum, the House of Carnival displays a colorful collection of **costumes** and **masks**.

You can always find someone here to recount a tale or two about the parades and processions, which actually start and finish at this location (🔖*see sidebar opposite*).

Hotel del Prado★

Carrera 54 # 70-10. ☎*(5) 369 7777; www.hotelelpradosa.com.*

Considered a National Landmark, this fine example of the Neoclassical **Republican style** was built in the 1930s. Large columns, marble floors and the vast entry hark back to more affluent times for the establishment.

Walk past the lobby into the peaceful courtyard, and you will find yourself transported to another era.

Museo de Arte Moderno de Barranquilla (MAMB)★

Carrera 56 # 74-22. ⏰*Open Mon 3pm-7pm, Tue–Sat 9am–1pm, 3pm–7pm.* 💬*Guided tours available for the temporary exhibits.* 🎫*Price varies with each exhibition.* ☎*(5) 369 0101. www.mambq.org.*

Founded in 1996 in the heart of the El Prado district, this museum has an interesting collection of modern and contemporary works from national and international artists, the focus being largely on Colombian Caribbean modern art from the second half of the 20C.

Paintings, sculptures, drawings, prints and conceptual pieces by Carlos Cruz Díez, Beatriz González, Jorge Páez Vilaró, Alejandro Obregón, Enrique Grau, Edgar Negret, Eduardo Ramírez Villamizar, Pedro Alcantara Herran, Luis Caballero and Pedro Alcántara, to name a few, are on view.

Marimondas, Carnaval de Barranquilla

Proexport Colombia

Carnaval de Barranquilla

In 2003 Barranquilla's carnival celebrations were recognized by **UNESCO** as part of the **Oral and Intangible Heritage of Humanity**. What began in the 19C, possibly around 1805, has now become a world-renowned party.

As the **second largest carnival** in the Americas, behind that of **Rio de Janeiro**, the Carnaval de Barranquilla actually runs for much longer than the prescribed dates of the three days prior to Ash Wednesday *(usually at the end of February or beginning of March)*, with pre- and post-carnival fiestas.

The Barranquilla Carnaval has been extensively studied, and is believed to be far more folkloric and true to its roots than that of Rio in that it wears its anthropological importance proudly. It started as an **indigenous parade**, demonstrating and celebrating the original inhabitants of these lands. Over time, it evolved to include people of **African descent**. This party is the result of a profound **fusion of cultures**: African, indigenous and white **European**.

The dances and music are all blended, as African **music** and **rhythms** are mingled with those from Europe and the Americas. The result is a fascinating take on the evolution of the nation of Colombia and its identity. The **congo** from Africa by way of Cartagena; the **garavato** from Spain that arrived in Ciénaga; the **paloteo**, also from Spain, that came to Yadira; and the **cumbia** from Tamalameque and El Banco have all been used inclusively.

And, in keeping with these social statements, the **marimondo**, a key figure in Carnaval, is traditionally a poor man protesting against the former ruling classes. He is vulgar and indecent. He is also critical of the oppression by the upper classes, and more recently, by corrupt politicians. Supposedly, the carnival here is a social leveler, but this is not true, since the class structure becomes more defined. What it grants, though, is permission to shrug off and ignore the social norms, and cut loose for a few days.

Barranquilleros are proud of their Carnaval, which is becoming so popular that it is gradually moving away from the organizers and becoming an even bigger **street party**.

In 2008 an estimated half-a-million revelers filled the streets of Barranquilla and romped in 75km/46mi worth of parades. *Prices rise steeply for carnival period, so reserving in advance is highly recommended.*

Barranquilla's Ruta Gastronómica

Barranquilla has grown as a city of **immigrants**. With such a rich, multicultural background, it is rightly up there in Colombia as one of the key **culinary hot spots** in the country. One can dine very well here and enjoy different styles of food, mixing Colombian Caribbean influences (both Amerindian and African) with those from Europe and the Arabic World.

For this reason, officials in the city have launched the "Ruta Gastronómica de Barranquilla" to showcase the traditional cooking done here. Be warned, there's a heavy emphasis on fatty foods, and much of what you will be offered is often *frito* or fried. The town hall, responsible for the creative touristic route, has selected four destinations in which to try **costeño specialties**, although many more can be found for those who would rather discover new places for themselves.

Approved by the mayor's office, rustic establishments such as **La Tiendecita** *(Calle 62 with Carrera 44)*, **Narcobollo** *(Carrera 43 with Calle 84)*, **El Proveedor** *(Las Flores)* and **El Merendero** *(Carrera 43 with Calle 70)* are on the list. In these eateries, you are invited to sample typical regional dishes such as *arepa`e huevo*, empanada meat pies, blood sausage, shellfish stew, pork chops and other delicacies.

Museo de Antropólogía Universidad del Atlántico

Calle 68 # 53-45. Call for hours. ℰ (5) 360 5922. www.uniatlantico.edu.co.
Home to a comprehensive collection of **pre-Columbian** archaeological exhibits, this museum includes objects from the Guane, Calima, Tayrona, Tumaco and Puerto Hormiga cultures, among others.

Edificio de la Aduana

Via 40 # 36-135. ◷ Check website for events. www.clena.org.
Demonstrating Barranquilla's impressive commercial and population growth in the 19C, the large and ornate yellow-painted Customs House was constructed after a fire destroyed the original building in 1915. Left in a state of decay until 1994, it was restored and now houses a library and the archives for the department of Atlántico.

Fundación Botánica y Zoológica de Barranquilla

Calle 77 # 68-40. ◷ Open daily 9am–5pm. Wed–Mon ⦿7,500 COP, ⦿Tue 5,000 COP. ℰ (5) 360 0314. www.zoobaq.org.
This foundation hosts some 500 animals from 140 different species. It focuses principally on the flora and fauna native to Colombia, in particular those species under threat of extinction, such as manatees and spectacled bears.

La Cueva★

Carrera 43 # 59-03. ℰ (5) 379 2786. www.fundacionlacueva.org.
To sample the literary heritage that is so prevalent in Barranquilla, head to a favorite watering hole for *literati*, artists and musicians such as **Gabriel García Márquez**, the vallenato composer **Rafael Escalona** and the artist **Alejandro Obregón**, who were once referred to as the "Grupo de Barranquilla."
From the mid-1950s to the late 1960s, this venue—the only one in a series of bars and clubs to survive—was a restaurant, a gallery and a haunt for intellectual discussions. Currently La Cueva is used as a center for cultural activities and workshops.

Montoya Railway Station

Located at the north end of Edificio de la Aduana.
The station was inaugurated in 1871. Trains used to connect the city to **Puerto Colombia** and to the **Bocas de Ceniza**, where the Magdalena River meets the Caribbean.

One of the old engines is on display, and a touristic train, the **Tren Ecoturístico de Las Flores** (*runs Mon–Sat 2:30pm, Sun & public holidays 11:30am & 2:30pm; Mon–Sat 8,600 COP, Sun & public holidays 14,000 COP; (5) 371 4583; www.cajacopi.com*) transports passengers to the mouth of the Magdalena River and back.

SURROUNDINGS
La Soledad
3km/2mi SE of Barranquilla via Carretera 90 and Avenida Soledad.

Simón Bolívar actually never made it to Barranquilla, but he did spend time in this nearby town (Pop. 455,796). Recognized for its **music** and its culinary delights such as the sausage-like **butifarra**, La Soledad makes an interesting side trip.

Casa de Bolívar
Carrera 26 # 18-10. Closed for restoration indefinitely; (5) 342 0207.
The Great Liberator resided here for a short time and composed 23 letters before leaving for **Santa Marta**, where he died in December 1830.

EXCURSIONS
Puerto Colombia
14km/9mi W of Barranquilla along Carretera 25.

The coastal highway leads to this town (Pop. 26,932), recently immortalized in the novel *Memories of My Melancholy Whores* (2004) by **Gabriel García Márquez**.
Over time, Puerto Colombia fell into decline, but with the recent refurbishment of the **Pradomar Hotel Climandiaro** (*Calle 2 # 22-61; (5) 309 6011*), and the opening of traditional **restaurants** offering good **seafood** dishes, the town has become a tourist attraction and weekend escape for visitors.
There are swimming **beaches** in the vicinity, and for history buffs, **Castillo de Salgar,** an old Spanish fort built in 1815 (*Corregimiento de Salgar, between Puerto Colombia and Puerto de Sabanilla; closed to the public; (5) 371 4545; www.cajacopi.com*).

Muelle de Puerto Colombia
Extending into the **Bay of Cupino**, Puerto Colombia's famous **jetty** is a national monument.
Conceived by Cuban engineer **Francisco Javier Cisneros** in 1888, it was reputedly the second-longest of its kind in the world (roughly 1,300m/4,264ft) at the time of construction. Thousands of immigrants disembarked here in search of a better life, Puerto Colombia being then a Colombian version of Ellis Island. In 2009, high waves brought down a section of the poorly maintained structure, which was consequently closed.

El Morro
7km/4mi W of Puerto Colombia along Carretera 25.

In this township is an indigenous reserve with **pre-Columbian petroglyphs** showing zoomorphic and anthropomorphic shapes along the Cajoru River. Nearby are also some good **beaches**.

Tubará
23km/14mi SW of Barranquilla along Carrera 38.

Situated on a leafy hilltop, with houses covered with palm-thatched roofs, Tubará (Pop. 10,602) was originally inhabited by the **Mocaná** people and discovered by **Pedro de Heredia** in 1533. It is here that one can find the traditional indigenous **Gaita flutes**, an important musical instrument on the Caribbean coast. With a stem made from a hollowed-out cactus, a beeswax and charcoal head and a feather's quill for the mouthpiece, these flutes are a real curiosity; they emit a most captivating sound heard during the Barranquilla Carnaval celebrations.

Ciénaga
59km/37mi E of Barranquilla by Carretera 90.

Situated along the coastal highway, Ciénaga (Pop. 100,908) is a town associated with the massacre of **banana workers** in 1928.
Before his writing career took off, Gabriel García Márquez worked here as a mobile book vendor.

A Recovering Lagoon

Severely affected by the construction of **roads** and **dikes** that severely disrupted the delicate hydrologic equilibrium among the different bodies of water, the **Ciénaga Grande**'s ecosystem started showing severe signs of deterioration years ago. The ensuing **hyper-salinization** process, combined with **contamination** due to untreated industrial and domestic waste, led to massive **death** of the **mangroves forests** and **marshes**, with dire consequences on biodiversity. Projects have been implemented to gradually recover the lagoon system. As a result, salinity levels have decreased, and mangroves are starting to show some signs of recovery.

Ciénaga Grande de Santa Marta Biosphere Reserve

Proexport Colombia

Ciénaga's Republican architecture is worthy of interest, but it is the vast coastal **wetlands** nearby—actually some of the largest in Latin America—that are the real attraction of the area.

Ciénaga Grande de Santa Marta Biosphere Reserve

Ciénaga Grande is Colombia's largest and most important **coastal lagoon**, an intricate network of **marshes**, **swamps** and **channels** connected to the Magdalena River and ultimately to the Caribbean Sea. It is one of the five Colombian reserves listed with **UNESCO**'s Man and Biosphere program. Its main ecosystems include **mangroves** and **coral reefs**.

Despite environmental threats to this delicate system, the area still has a number of habitats supporting a great variety of fauna and flora. Representative of the deltaic system of the Magdalena River, the following sanctuaries are part of the Ciénaga Grande Biosphere Reserve:

Santuario de Fauna y Flora de la Ciénaga Grande de Santa Marta

Accessible via canoe from Puente de la Barra, Carretera 90. ℘(5) 420 4504. *www.corpamag.gov.co.*

Created as a nature preserve in 1977, this lagoon and associated protected area cover some 23,000ha/56,834 acres. Only accessible by boat, **fishing villages** built on stilts, such as Nueva Venecia, Trojas de Cataca and Pueblo Viejo, are found in the periphery of the sanctuary. These communities live off small-scale fishing and subsistence farming.

Via Parque Isla de Salamanca

▶ *9km/6mi E of Barranquilla along Carretera 90.* ⏰*Open daily 8am–4pm. www.parquesnacionales.gov.co.*

Because it crosses the coastal highway, this unique Colombian **road park** makes it possible to view the wetlands from the road.

Trails in the mangrove forests, **boat rides** *(near the toll booths at Tasajera, small boats offer guided trips)*, **bird-watching** (some 199 species, including migratory birds) and walks along the beaches are some of the possible activities here.

Colombians Making a Difference

In recent history two men, and their larger-than-life personalities, have dominated Colombian politics, gaining worldwide attention as well as popularity within their own country. From overcoming violence to improving traffic, former president Álvaro Uribe and former Bogotá mayor Antanas Mockus helped modernize Colombia, inspire its people and attract more visitors.

Álvaro Uribe, the 58th president of Colombia, served two terms, from 2002 to 2010. His motivation to serve his country was deeply personal: while Uribe was mayor of Medellín (1982-1984), his father was killed during a failed kidnapping attempt by the Revolutionary Armed Forces of Colombia (known as FARC), the main guerrilla group that has used violence to try to control illegal drugs in Colombia since the 1960s. A lawyer by training, Uribe held elected positions in his home state of Antioquia, rising from a city council member to senator and governor. As president, Uribe instituted strong actions against FARC, resulting in many senior FARC commanders being killed, as well as FARC's releasing several hostages. Uribe offered peace talks, but only if the guerrilla groups would disarm. It is estimated that, due to the increase in military and police actions under Uribe, FARC membership shrank by half, from some 16,000 in 2001 to 6,000-8,000 in 2008. In 2003 Uribe negotiated a peace deal with paramilitary members (illegally armed right-wing fighters) that led to the disarming of 31,000 men. His determined and unflinching fight against Colombia's drug cartels has greatly improved the life of Colombians and the reputation of the country, and has more than doubled the number of tourists and tourism dollars. In April 2010 President Uribe was on hand to inaugurate Barranquilla's new TransMetro public transportation system centered on modern, articulated buses—an especially triumphant moment for Uribe, who narrowly escaped an assassination attempt in this city when a bomb exploded on a local bus in 2002. After leaving office with an approval rating of around 70 percent, he accepted a teaching position at Georgetown University's Walsh School of Foreign Service in the US and is serving as vice president of a United Nations' investigatory panel.

Former Bogotá mayor **Antanas Mockus** reinvigorated a previously unsafe, chaotic and filthy capital city during his two terms in office (1995-1997 and 2001-2003). The son of Lithuanian immigrants, Mockus studied mathematics and philosophy before becoming rector (president) of Bogota's Universidad Nacional. With no previous political experience, he ran for office in 1995 while Bogota was suffering from violence, corruption, gang activity and a general sense of apathy and contempt among its residents. He won Bogotanos over with his eccentric manner and public antics, including wearing a spandex superhero suit to walk the streets as "Super Citizen," expounding by example the value of being civil. Among his many creative solutions to spur social change, Mockus hired some 400 mime artists to control Bogota's unruly traffic by embarrassing those who broke rules; took a brief shower on television to encourage water conservation; and created a night for women to safely go out on the town while men stayed home to care for the children. His unusual campaigns, aimed at increasing knowledge through the use of art and humor, resulted in dramatic decreases in homicides and traffic fatalities, as well as an increase in the number of proud, pro-active and responsible citizens who better embody the civilized culture expected of a great capital city. Perhaps the most surprising example of this new pride is that more than 60,000 inspired citizens agreed to pay a voluntary tax to support their city's services. Mockus, who was recently diagnosed with Parkinson's disease, ran for president under the banner of the Green Party in 2010, but lost the election to former defense minister Juan Miguel Santos.

ADDRESSES

🛏 STAY

$ Hotel Colonial Inn – *Calle 42 # 43-131, Barranquilla.* ✗ ⌂ ☎ *(5) 379 0241. 38 rooms.* The pleasing lobby of this centrally located hotel gives the impression that the place has known better days. Comfortable rooms come with TV and en-suite bathrooms.

$ Hotel Skal – *Calle 44 # 41-35, Barranquilla.* ✗ ⌂ ☎ *(5) 351 0241. 38 rooms.* Backpackers love this converted 1930s residence for its budget accommodations and safe location next to the police station. Rooms are equipped with private baths, cable TV and a choice of AC or a fan. The pool makes a relaxing place to lounge.

$$ Hotel Pradomar – *Calle 22 # 22-61, Puerto Colombia, Barranquilla.* P ✗ ☎ *(5) 309 6011. www.ucrostravel.com/ pradomar.php. 10 rooms.* Located about 15 minutes outside Barranquilla, and about half an hour from the airport in the municipality of Puerto Colombia, this hotel is popular with folks attending the surfing and windsurfing schools in nearby Puerto Velero. It is also convenient to the hot mud baths in Totumo and the car-racing circuit at Turipaná.

$$ Howard Johnson Hotel Versalles – *Carrera 48 # 70-188, Barranquilla.* P ✗ Spa ☎ *(5) 368 2183. www.hojo.com. 80 rooms.* In the heart of Barranquilla's business district, the Versalles lies within easy walking distance of other sites of interest, including the El Prado area. Airy lounges, outdoor dining and a helpful staff enhance a stay here. Each room has phone, cable TV, private bath and 24-hour room service; for guests' convenience, check-out isn't until 3pm.

$$$ Hotel Barahona 72 – *Carrera 49 # 72-19, Barranquilla.* ✗ ☎ *(5) 358 4600. www.hotelesbarahona.com. 29 rooms.* This property is one of a chain of Colombian hotels offering good value for the money, including attentive service and clean rooms. It is located at the beach of Barahona, which is considered particularly beautiful. Some of its larger rooms have been recently renovated and have private saunas.

$$$ Hotel El Prado – *Carrera 54 # 70-10, Barranquilla.* P ✗ Spa ☎ *(5) 369 7777. www.hotelelpradosa.com. 193 rooms.* A converted 1920s-era Republican mansion, Barranquilla's oldest hotel is filled with spacious rooms done in soothing pastels with luxurious details such as flowing draperies and crown moldings. A national monument, El Prado is a place for romance—complete with its own art gallery, spa and tropical pool area.

$$$$ Hotel Puerta del Sol – *Calle 75 # 41D-79, Barranquilla.* P ✗ ☎ *(5) 330 1000. www.puertadelsol.com.co. 109 rooms.* Located in north Barranquilla, in the town's financial and commercial district, this hotel was reopened in 1992 after a complete renovation. Special extras include a *menu de almohadas* (pillow menu), in-hotel medical assistance, secure parking, and local newspapers and magazines available in each room.

$$$$$ Hotel Dann Carlton – *Calle 98 # 52B-10, Altos de Riomar, Barranquilla.* P ✗ ⌂ Spa ☎ *(5) 367 7777. www.dann carltonbarranquilla.com. 142 rooms.* With two bars, one of which offers live music, a cafe and two restaurants, this luxury chain hotel offers plenty of extras. Work out at the gym, then relax on the tropical terrace. For business travelers, the executive floor houses 14 deluxe rooms with access to the hotel's business center. Shoppers will appreciate the Dann Carlton's proximity to the town's largest mall.

$$$$$ Hotel Barranquilla Plaza – *Carrera 51B # 79-246, Alto Prado, Barranquilla.* ✗ ⌂ ☎ *(5) 361 0333. www.hbp.com.co. 176 rooms.* Located in the exclusive Alto Prado neighborhood, this hotel has excellent access to upscale shopping centers, restaurants and bars. When you're not in your air-conditioned room, the restaurant/bar on the 26th floor provides a stunning panoramic view of the city.

EAT

$ Nena Lela – *Carrera 49C # 75-50, Barranquilla. ℘(5) 368 0020. www.nenalela.com.* This pleasant, family-friendly restaurant, which dates back to 1930, was one of the first in Barranquilla to serve Italian cuisine. The house lasagna, made with bacon, two kinds of cheese and fresh tomatoes, is always a hit, as is the three-pasta combination plate. Come Thursday for discounts on house wines. **Italian.**

$$ Árabe Gourmet – *Carrera 49C # 76-181, Barranquilla. ℘(5) 360 5930.* Arab and international cuisine draw diners to Árabe Gourmet. Inside, Moorish elements and arches adorn the trendy eatery, where kibbeh, stuffed grape leaves, almond rice, tabbouleh, tahini and *kofta* (meatballs) number among the menu choices. **Middle Eastern**.

$$ La Cueva Foundation – *Carrera 43 # 59-03, Esquina, Barranquilla. Closed Sun. ℘(5) 379 2786. www.fundacionla cueva.org.* A national icon, La Cueva was the meeting place of the Barranquilla Group (composed of luminaries including author Gabriel García Márquez, painter Alejandro Obregón and journalist/filmmaker Alvaro Cepeda Samudio). Diners will enjoy Caribbean dishes such as *posta negra* (a local version of marinated pot roast), as well as the display of artwork by local and national artists. **Colombian**.

$$ Moys – *Carrera 52 # 74-107, Barranquilla. Dinner only. Closed Sun. ℘(5) 358 4309.* There's always a party at Moys, where locals come to rumba until the wee morning hours. To keep up their stamina, they chow down first on the likes of grouper, sea bass, and aged pork à la Dijon. **Colombian**.

$$ Naia – *Carrera 53 # 79-127 Norte, Barranquilla. Closed Sun. ℘(5) 368 8060.* Locals love to see and be seen on Naia's front patio. All you need for a night can be found at this bar/restaurant, including a great corozo martini (made with nuts from the corozo palm). Overall, the mood is soothing, and the cuisine incorporates local ingredients (Mero in guava sauce; langostino with corozo and pistachio). **Colombian**.

$$ Varadero – *Carrera 51B # 79-97 Norte, Barranquilla. ℘(5) 378 6519.* The decor and music here reflect the Cuban resort town from which the restaurant takes its name. Try the grouper Imperial (grouper filet in pesto sauce with shellfish) or the shrimp ceviche, both good choices. **Cuban**.

RECREATION

Estadio Metropolitano Roberto Melenez – *Av. Murillo, Barranquilla. ℘(5) 360 0338. www.juniorbarranquilla.com.* South of the center of town, the multi-use stadium is home of Atletico Junior, Barranquilla's local soccer team. Buy tickets for local soccer games at the gate.

Museo del Caribe – *Calle 36 # 46-66, Barranquilla. ℘(5) 372 0581. www.culturacaribe.org. Closed first Monday of the month.* Located in the Caribbean Cultural Park, the first stage of the Museum of the Caribbean opened in 2009. Displays focus on the history of Colombia's north coast and showcase local food, culture and music.

Parque Cultural del Caribe – *Calle 36 # 46-66, Barranquilla. ℘(5) 372 0581 www.culturacaribe.org.* Located in Barranquilla's historical center, the park promotes the natural, cultural and historic heritage of the Colombian Caribbean, with displays on environmental, historical and socio-cultural topics.

Via Parque Isla de Salamanca – *9km/6mi east of Barranquilla along Carretera 90. www.parquesnacionales.gov.co.* Between Barranquilla and the jurisdiction of Sitio Nuevo in Ciénaga, this park occupies the former Magdalena River estuary. Beaches, swamps, lagoons and mangrove forests fill the reserve. It's ideal for a day of turtle- and bird-watching.

Fundación Ecoturística Usiacurí Verde – *Carrera 18 # 17A-44, Usiacurí. 38km/24mi southwest via Carretera 90 and Baronoa. ℘316 313 3703. http://s1.webstarts.com/fundacionecoturisticausiacuriverde.* This agency offers guided tours to sites like Agua Fría, Luriza and Arroyo del Pueblo, and works with both ecotourists and educational institutions.

Santa Marta★★ and Surroundings

Magdalena

Situated between the crystal clear waters of the Caribbean Sea and the snowy summits of the Sierra Nevada—the highest coastal mountain range in the world that rises abruply from the Atlantic shore—the city of Santa Marta is blessed with incomparable natural riches. Populated first by pre-Columbian cultures, the town became a bastion of Royalist support during the colonial era, and is steeped in history. As the capital of the department of Magdalena, it is an important port and commercial hub. It has also become a major tourist destination for visitors keen on hiking its parks and enjoying its fauna, discovering its archaeological vestiges or simply soaking up some sun in one of the most beautiful parts of the Colombian Atlantic coast.

A BIT OF HISTORY

Founded in July 1525 by **Rodrigo de Bastidas**, Santa Marta was the first **permanent settlement** in Colombia.

> ▶ **Population:** 414,387.
> ◔ **Michelin Maps:** p270 and p303.
> ▤ **Info:** Casa de Madame Agustine, Calle 17 # 3-210, ✆ (5) 438 2777. www.santa martaturistica.org.
> ◉ **Don't Miss:** Parque Nacional Natural Tayrona, and its 15,000ha/37,065 acres of beautiful beaches located a little more than an hour outside Santa Marta.

Long before the arrival of the Spanish, indigenous people favored this area that was the seat of power of the **Tayrona** people and their ancestors, the **Arhuacos** and **Koguis**. Published in 1530 the chronicles written by **Pedro Marty Angheira** describe the Tayrona civilization as expansive and developed, and speak of densely populated valleys, fishing villages and well-established commerce. A multi-day hike to the mythical **Ciudad Perdida** (Lost City), on the foothills of the Sierra Nevada, provides insight into this advanced, yet extinct civilization. A bridge between Spain, Santo Domingo and the New World, Santa Marta quickly

Santa Marta

Aviatur/Proexport Colombia

GETTING THERE

BY AIR - Santa Marta's **Aeropuerto Simón Bolívar** (SMR), 16km/10mi south of the city, handles domestic flights only. Direct flights from Bogotá and Medellín are frequent. Avianca (www.avianca.com), Satena and Aerorepublica (www.aerorepublica. com) airlines fly into Santa Marta. City **buses** marked *Aeropuerto* reach Carrera 1C downtown in about 45min. A **taxi** takes 30min to downtown.

BY BUS - Buses arrive daily from Bogotá (17hrs; 95,000-120,000 COP) and Medellín (15hrs; 122,000 COP) and more regularly from Barranquilla (2hrs; 10,000 COP), Cartagena (4 hrs; 23,000 COP) and Bucaramanga (9hrs; 83,000 COP) at the **bus station** called Variante Gaira-Matamoco Transport Terminal (*5 430 2040*), about 20min south of Santa Marta.

GETTING AROUND

BY BUS - *Colectivos* and city buses ply Carrera 1C, the main thoroughfare along the beachfront. Minibuses depart often for nearby Taganga and El Rodadero (about 1,200 COP; 20min).

BY TAXI - Taxis (unmetered) are readily available, especially between Carreras 1 and 5.

BY MOTORBIKE - Motorbike taxis are cheap and fast but not recommended at all since they are illegal and unsafe.

GENERAL INFORMATION

PERSONAL SAFETY - Watch your belongings carefully in this large seaport city, especially on the beach. If you must be out after dark, be especially alert and stay with crowds.

---

played a major role in the colonization of the country. Through the 16C and 17C, the town became the target of constant attacks from French, English and Dutch pirates, which led many of its inhabitants to move to safer places such as Cartagena, Mompox and Ocaña.

In the 19C, when the winds of **independence** first blew through Colombia, Santa Marta remained loyal to the Spanish Crown, putting it at odds with its neighbors along the coast. **Simón Bolívar**, on his long final journey, actuallly died here. Towards the end of the 19C, **banana fever** ran high, and Santa Marta found itself at the center of this industry. The bonanza lasted a while, and brought with it American and English sailors; the latter introduced **football** (soccer) to the region.

By the end of **World War II**, the banana industry had collapsed. The focus rightfully moved to **tourism**, and even though this industry is now thriving here, Santa Marta has suffered at the hands of narco-traffickers, due to its position as a key port.

The city also had to face the fallout from the Colombian armed conflict in the Sierra Nevada, experiencing an influx of internal refugees from the affected zones in its midst.

Bananatown

Until recently it seemed that the citizens of Santa Marta would always look wistfully to the sea for entertainment and wealth, but by the mid-19C, their income came from another source, and constructions such as Bananatown *(Calle 25 with Carrera 4)* represented this change.

Look for the **Barrio Prado** or the **Barrio de los Gringos**, and you will be pointed in the direction of the **United Fruit Company**'s headquarters for the entire region.

The architecture and grid pattern design gives it all away, and the houses look similar to a retirement community in Southern California or Florida. Imagine this compound as it was back then, complete with its own railway, walled community for the staff and their families, and a fully functioning clinic.

A Football Legend

The most internationally recognized of Colombian footballers is unquestionably **Carlos "El Pibe" Alberto Valderrama** (b. 1961) for his sporting prowess—he is the most capped Colombian player, with 111 games for the national side under his belt. He also played for Montpellier (France), Tampa Bay, Colorado and Miami (the US), and Valladolid (Spain). He is known, too, for his mop of permed blond hair that made Valderrama stand out from the crowd. His vision on the pitch is legendary, and he was named by Pelé as one of the top players of the 20C.

Valderrama retired in 2004 after 22 years in the game, and in 2007 tried his hand at coaching one of his former clubs, **Junior of Barranquilla**. His most memorable achievement as coach was to walk out on the pitch during a game and wave a wedge of peso bills beneath the nose of the referee, accusing the official of taking a bribe. His coaching stint was not a success, and currently he busies himself with advertising gigs, and spends a good deal of time in his native Santa Marta, helping out people in his home *barrio*, the rundown Pescaito. There is a 22ft-tall **statue** in his honor outside Santa Marta's stadium.

TOWN

Some years ago, strolling through Downtown would have been warned against, but now it is almost the norm. Betting heavily on this newfound security, small exclusive hotels, fine restaurants and chic boutiques are popping up, whereas before, they would have moved to safer locations such as the former fishing village of **Taganga**, a long time tourist haunt, and **Rodadero**, the traditional Colombian beach resort.
Santa Marta is undergoing a long-overdue **makeover**, and with the renovation and restoration of its **colonial center**, visitors can now tour points of interest in a carefree manner.

●●WALKING TOUR
Catedral de Santa Marta
Carrera 5 # 16-03.
It took just under 30 years (1766-94) to build this imposing, white colonial church. Referred to as the **Basílica Menor** and "the mother of all churches in Colombia," the edifice marks the final resting place of **Rodrigo de Bastidas**, the founder of the city. Between 1830 and 1842, the cathedral also held the remains of **Simón Bolívar**, before being moved to the Pantheon in Caracas.
The well-preserved interior shows off Italian chandeliers and marble floors.

Plaza de Bolívar★

Surrounded by fine colonial buildings, this plaza is the ideal place to pause in the heat of the day and enjoy a refreshing juice beverage at the café before deciding where to head next.

Casa de la Aduana
Carrera 2 and Calle 14 # 2-7.
Believed to date back to 1531, Santa Marta's Customs House is supposedly the oldest building in the Americas. It survived fires and earthquakes, and has kept its typical external colonial balconies and traditional rooftops.
In colonial times it controlled the goods, wares and merchandise that came through the port.
Now it houses a small museum.

Museo de Oro Tayrona
🕐 *Open Mon–Fri 8:30am–noon, 2pm –6pm, Sat 9am–1pm.* 🕿 *(5) 421 4181. www.banrep.gov.co.*
The museum houses a full display of pottery and **gold** pieces from the Tayrona civilization, as well as Kogi and Arhuaco artifacts. Visitors learn about the agricultural practices of these early peoples. Not to be missed is the **model** of **Ciudad Perdida**, especially if you plan on doing the hike there (🕮 *see sidebar p308*).

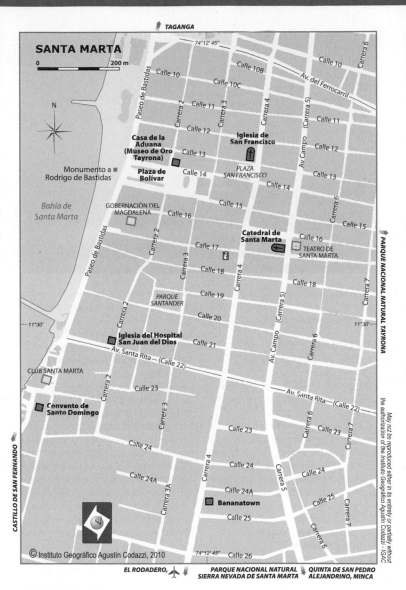

SANTA MARTA

0   200 m

N

TAGANGA

74°12' 45"

Calle 10

Carrera 6

Calle 10

Av. del Ferrocarril

Calle 10B

Paseo de Bastidas

Calle 10

Calle 10C

Carrera 2

Calle 11

Carrera 3

Calle 11

Carrera 4

Carrera 5

Calle 11

Calle 12

Av. Campo

Calle 12

Casa de la Aduana (Museo de Oro Tayrona)

Calle 13

Iglesia de San Francisco

Monumento a Rodrigo de Bastidas

Plaza de Bolívar

Calle 14

PLAZA SAN FRANCISCO

Calle 13

Bahía de Santa Marta

Calle 14

Calle 14

GOBERNACIÓN DEL MAGDALENA

Calle 15

Carrera 6

Calle 16

Carrera 2

Catedral de Santa Marta

Calle 16

Calle 15

Carrera 3

Calle 17

Carrera 4

TEATRO DE SANTA MARTA

Calle 18

Paseo de Bastidas

Calle 18

Carrera 7

Carrera 5

Calle 19

PARQUE SANTANDER

Calle 20

11°30'

Carrera 2

Iglesia del Hospital San Juan del Dios

Calle 21

Av. Campo

Carrera 6

11°30'

Av. Santa Rita—(Calle 22)

CLUB SANTA MARTA

Calle 23

Carrera 2

Carrera 3

Av. Santa Rita—(Calle 22)

Convento de Santo Domingo

Calle 24

Calle 23

Carrera 6

Carrera 7

Calle 23

Calle 24A

Calle 24

Carrera 4

Calle 24

Carrera 3A

Carrera 5

Calle 25

Carrera 6

Carrera 7

Calle 24A

Bananatown

Calle 25

Calle 25

74°12' 45"

Calle 26

© Instituto Geográfico Agustín Codazzi, 2010

CASTILLO DE SAN FERNANDO

PARQUE NACIONAL NATURAL TAYRONA

May not be reproduced either in its entirety or partially without the authorization of the Instituto Geográfico Agustín Codazzi – IGAC

EL RODADERO,

PARQUE NACIONAL NATURAL SIERRA NEVADA DE SANTA MARTA

QUINTA DE SAN PEDRO ALEJANDRINO, MINCA

Camellón

Just a few steps away lies the Caribbean Sea and its popular beachfront boulevard, known also as the **Paseo de Bastidas**. Do as the *Samarios* (citizens of Santa Marta) do and amble, all the while contemplating the bay, the city's sights and the history therein embraced. At one end of the boardwalk, a small **monument** has been erected to the Tayrona culture.

Despite all of the restoration going on in Santa Marta, only a few original religious buildings remain, in addition to the cathedral. These include the low, yet solid-looking Colonial **Iglesia de San Francisco** *(Calle 13 # 3-77, Plaza San Francisco),* built in 1597 and formerly surrounded by a marketplace; the **Iglesia del Hospital San Juan del Dios** *(Calle 22 and Carrera 2),* dating back to 1746; and the 18C **Convento de Santo Domingo**, almost completely restored

Casa Principal and statue of Simón Bolívar, Quinta de San Pedro Alejandrino

Juan Miguel Bonilla/Museo Bolivariano de Arte Contemporáneo

in its entirety, and now the seat of Santa Marta's Academy of History *(Carrera 1A # 16-15;* ⛔ *closed to the public).*

ADDITIONAL SIGHT
Castillo de San Fernando
Batallón Córdova, Carrera 1C, at the western point of the city. 🕐*Permission to access must be obtained from the naval base.* ✆*(5) 421 0520.*
As you can imagine, in order to try and quell the pirate threat, Santa Marta was fortified in places, but only this fort (1725) exists today. A special pass is required to visit since it is located within the naval battalion's compound.

SURROUNDINGS
Quinta de San Pedro Alejandrino★★
▶ 5km/3mi SE of Santa Marta in the barrio of Mamatoco. Avenida del Libertador, Sector San Pedro Alejandrino. 🕐*Open Dec–Jan, Easter week & mid-Jun–late Jul daily 9am–6pm. Dec 24 & 31 9am–2pm; Feb–early Jun & Aug–Nov daily 9:30am–5pm. Last entry 30min before closing.* 🕐*Closed Jan 1.* 🎟*10,000 COP.* ✆*(5) 433-1021. www.museobolivariano. org.co.*
This national monument, located on the outskirts of the city, is one of the most-visited sights in Northern Colombia, and a must see for any history enthusiast or

individual desiring to understand the development and independence of South America.
On these sprawling grounds are a hacienda, a museum, a garden, a monument to Simón Bolívar and other points of interest.

Antigua Hacienda
In 1830, after Gran Colombia dissolved and **Simón Bolívar** resigned from the presidency, he was invited to stay at this estate by a fervent patriot named Joaquín De Mier. It is in the **casa principal** (1608) that the Great Liberator of Northern South America died on December 17, 1830. Visitors will see the bedroom where he took his last breath, the library, the chapel and other rooms with period furniture. Also on the grounds are dependencies such as the **distillery**, that were part of the De Mier's family hacienda, dedicated to the cultivation of **sugarcane.**

Museo Bolívariano de Arte Contemporáneo
Do not miss the museum's collection of Bolívar's **portraits** by known artists such as Alejandro Obregón, Jorge Elias Triana, Gustavo Zalamea, Patricia Tavera, Germain Maripaz Tessarolo and Jaramillo. And take a look at the **sculptures** by Edgar Negret, Eduardo Ramírez Villa-

mizar, Lydia Azout and Carlos Chacin, displayed in the gardens.

Altar de la Patria

Located on the **Plaza de Banderas** (1980), this impressive Republican-style **monument** was built in 1930 to commemorate the 100th anniversary of Bolívar's death.

Jardín Botánico

Stroll through this peaceful, 22ha/54 acre garden that is home to humming-birds, iguanas and parrots, and discover some of the most characteristic ecosystems of the Colombian Caribbean.

El Rodadero

▶ *13km/8mi SW of Santa Maria via Carretera Ziruma.*

This resort destination has the highest concentration of **hotels** in the vicinity. The resort's **beach** is very busy in high season, and offers opportunities for water sports and a good *ceviche*.

At night, Rodadero turns into a hedonistic playground lively with restaurants, bars, discos and plenty of dancing.

Even a day trip here makes a pleasant change, but plan on coming to Santa Marta and Rodadero during the **Fiestas del Mar** (*celebrated here Jul 29 to Aug 4*), and be prepared to reserve your space on the beach.

Acuario Mundo Marino

Carrera 2 # 11, 68 Edificio Mundo Marino. ⏱*Open Dec–Jan, Easter week, mid-Jun–Jul daily 9am–10pm. Feb–early Jun, Aug –Nov daily 8am–noon, 2pm–6pm.* ⌖*10,000 COP.* ✆*(5) 422-9334.*

This aquarium is an updated version of South America's first aquarium, run by Bogotá's Jorge Tadeo Lozano University. It presents a series of underwater exhibits that display the submarine flora and fauna around Santa Marta. A large section is dedicated to marine conservation and environmental protection.

Mamancana Natural Reserve

▶ *14km/9mi S of Santa Marta via Carretera 45.* ⏱*Open daily 8am–6pm.* ⌖*10,000 COP.*

This 600ha/1,482 acre area of tropical dry forest is located just off the highway between the Santa Marta airport and the city. It is now a **nature park** and **adventure center**, with trails for hiking, mountain biking and horse riding, as well as facilities for hang gliding and rock climbing, among other pursuits.

Taganga

▶ *5km/3mi NE of Santa Marta via Carrera 2.*

This idyllic **fishing village** can be reached by a 10min-taxi ride from the Plaza de Bolívar in Santa Marta up and over **scrub desert**. Views take in a turquoise blue bay, brightly painted fishermen's cabanas and rustic boats. The whole setting looks like a paradise, but the arrival of foreign tourism is bringing change.

While Taganga is an excellent and economical place to learn to **scuba dive**, the charming luster has dimmed with an explosion of backpacker hostels.But, for this reason, Taganga also makes a good **base** for trips to **Tayrona** and the **Ciudad Perdida**, since these lodgings have the most up-to-date information. If you are short on time, head here for a lunch of red snapper, and then wander around the bay and the **Playa Blanca**, which is preferable to the beach at Taganga. However, the local government in Santa Marta is committed to cleaning up Taganga's image, and has

Mamancana Natural Reserve

Proexport Colombia

A Literary Detour to Aracataca

The birthplace of **Gabriel García Márquez** lies an hour-and-a-half drive from Santa Marta *(88km/55mi S of Santa Marta along Carreta 45)*, and at this moment in time is a destination for the hardcore literary fan only.

Aracataca is not without its charms, and any visitor will receive a friendly welcome, be shown around and will be able to observe the inspiration for the fictional town of **Macondo** of *100 Hundred Years of Solitude*. Nothing of colonial interest remains here; the old movie house is a hardware store now. But the Colombian government has created a **museum** in the home of Márquez' grandparents, entirely dedicated to the author. The museum was the victim of a little "Magic Realism"—García Márquez's literary trademark— since its opening was delayed because of an internal argument as to whether it should resemble the home of the author's grandparents or the Buendía family of the novel.

Should you make the detour to Aracataca, note that there are places to swim in the nearby **Aracataca River**. You will also notice the new era of environmental exploitation. Where once there were bananas, now there are African palms.

invested funds for a beachfront promenade that will make a pleasant division between the beach and the road.

EXCURSIONS
Ciénaga Grande de Santa Marta
(see BARRANQUILLA Excursions)

Parque Nacional Natural Tayrona★★★

▶ *Main entrance at El Zaino, 34km/ 21mi E of Santa Marta along Carretera 90.*
🕐 *Open daily 8am–5pm.* 🎟 *21,000 COP.*
☏ *(5) 420 4504. www.parques nacionales.gov.co.*

This national park is possibly the busiest national park in Colombia, and for good reason. Tayrona's **beaches** are legendary. They are among the most scenic and breathtaking in the world. Perhaps it is this unique blend of glorious stretches of white sand and clear blue water, extreme biodiversity and indigenous Tayrona culture that makes this park so special. Located on the road to Riohacha, the main entrance to the park can be reached by a short taxi ride from Santa Marta.

Arrecifes
To get to this first pristine beach requires a 45min walk over rolling jungle terrain. Or you can hire a **donkey** to bring you in if the walk sounds too long, or if rain has

made the path impassable. The beach at Arrecifes is stunningly beautiful, but has a snarling **current** that throws up a surf that crashes on immense sun-bleached **boulders**. Unfortunately, the current here, which is too strong to permit swimming, has claimed more than one life.

La Piscina
A 15min walk farther from Arrecifes leads to the place called *La Piscina* (the swimming pool). It is surrounded by a natural barrier of **corals**, where the still waters are ideal for swimming.

El Pueblito
Several good hikes in the park lead to the pre-Columbian ruins at El Pueblito. Also known as **Chairama**, El Pueblito resembles a miniature Ciudad Perdida. The on-site **Archeological Museum** (🕐 *open daily 8am–noon, 2pm–5pm;* 🎟 *790 COP;* ☏ *(5) 420 4504)* is worth a visit.

Additional Sights in the Park
With more time and definitely more energy, visitors can hike to farther, less frequented beaches like **Bahía Concha**, which fronts a dry, scrub forest.

In **Bahía Neguanje**, located in the central coastal part of the park, you will discover Tayrona's largest bay. Beyond **Playa Cañaveral**, there is even a nudist beach with crystal-clear, calm waters that is rarely visited.

Parque Nacional Natural Sierra Nevada de Santa Marta★★★

The highest coastal mountain range on earth is part of one of the five Colombian reserves listed with **UNESCO**'s Man and the Biosphere program. The mountains of the Sierra Nevada oversee not only a 383,000ha/946,413 acre park, but also the mythical "Lost City" of the **Parque Arqueológico Ciudad Perdida - Teyuna** (☙ *see sidebar p308*), managed by the Colombian Institute of Anthropology and History.

The Sierra Nevada de Santa Marta is home to some 30,000 local inhabitants of the **Kogui**, **Wiwa**, **Arhuaco** and **Kamkuamo** tribes, who cultivate mostly cocoa, plantains, sugarcane, coffee and potatoes, and sometimes raise cattle and sheep.

The park starts at sea level, and then climbs to the highest points in the country, with the peaks of **Colón** and **Bolívar** reaching comparable heights of 5,775m/19,000ft.

Within the park's boundary is an amazing mix of tropical **rain forest, sub-Andean and Andean forest, páramo** and **snowline** systems, which are habitats for a great variety of plants such as *frailejones*, as well as animals, including tapirs, pumas, otters, jaguars and all kinds of birds.

Minca★★

☙ *20km/13mi SE of Santa Marta via Carretera 66.*

One of the best ways of gaining access to this unbelievable cornucopia of natural wonders is to make a bumpy side trip to the village of Minca, sitting at 600m/1,970ft above sea level. Blessed with a favorable climate and exuberant vegetation, Minca makes a good starting point for treks to crystalline, cool waterfalls.

A 15min walk from the village leads to stunning rock formations called **Las Piedras**. The rocks hold a favorite spot where the river's swirling whirlpools offer a relaxing soak or swim.

The **Arimaka waterfall**, an ancient, sacred place for the Kogui, is reachable by a 40min excursion, but it is best to have a guide since falls are not easy to find.

Visitors interested in **archaeology** will appreciate the elaborate network of **stone paths** built by pre-Columbians; some sections are still visible around Minca.

The Sierra Nevada offers one of the best **birding** options in the country. Due to their geographical isolation, the surrounding mountains have recorded an unparalleled degree of endemism, with 36 species of birds unique to this area, including the Santa Marta Mountain Tanager *(Tangara Serrana)*.

Parque Nacional Natural Sierra Nevada de Santa Marta

Proexport Colombia

Arhuaco girls weaving mochila bags

Julian D'angelo/Proexport Colombia

Parque Arqueológico Ciudad Perdida - Teyuna★★

Within the lush Sierra Nevada mountains and the reward for a tough, but not gruelling, 5-6 day hike of 40km/25mi is the unforgettable **Lost City**. Constructed around AD 700 (600 years before Machu Picchu), **Buritaca** or **Teyuna** as it is known by local tribes, is a collection of leveled **terraces** cut into the foothills of the Sierra Nevada. The **Arhuacos**, **Koguis** and **Asario** have all declared that the surrounding area and the constructions are of sacred importance to their beliefs. The Ciudad Perdida was most likely a political and economic center for the indigenous tribes here, and its population apparently fluctuated between 1,400 and 3,000 inhabitants spread over the **250 terraces** thus far uncovered. What little knowledge there is has been gleaned from the scant information divulged by the understandably suspicious local tribes, and from knowledge acquired when looters and grave robbers scoured the area, taking anything of value in 1972. To say that the Ciudad Perdida is a collection of ruins would be inaccurate, because all around here are **indigenous dwellings** and **populations**. The terraces, found between 950m/3,120ft and 1,300m/4,265ft above sea level, are better described as **living ruins**.

Some visitors have expressed disappointment with the Lost City in that it is not a Colombian Machu Picchu, but the entire experience should be considered: the mysterious city at the end of a three-day hike uphill amid some thunderous tropical downpours; the opportunity to pass through traditional villages and interact with the local people; the flora and fauna; washing off the dirt and grime each evening in fresh water from jungle pools and streams; then, camping out in a hammock beneath the stars; and finally the thrill of knowing that you have arrived at the last challenge before

Proexport Colombia

Terraces of the Ciudad Perdida

reaching the Ciudad Perdida when, after crossing a river for the umpteenth time, you are faced with 1,260 rock steps that lead up to the settlement.

This trip is becoming more commonplace, but it is imperative that you go with an organized tour. There are two official tour companies: **Turcol** (*℘5 421 2256; www. buritaca2000.com*) and **Sierra Tours** (*℘5 421 9401; www.sierratours-trekking. com*). You also need to be fully aware of the security situation beforehand.

⊘This area of the Sierra Nevada still has a reputation for coca and marijuana cultivation, and is constantly fought over by warring guerrilla and paramilitary groups.

ADDRESSES

🛏 STAY

$$ Hotel El Caribe – *Carrera 3A # 5-74, El Rodadero.* 🅿✕🌐*(5) 422 9418. 14 rooms.* Although the El Rodadero area is on the whole very expensive, this hotel is as reasonably priced as you're likely to find here. A rather kitschy character describes the decor, and the rooms are small but clean with big beds. A friendly front-desk staff and a location two blocks from the beach are more reasons to stay here.

$$ Hotel Nueva Granada – *Calle 12 # 3-17, Centro Historico, Santa Marta.* 🌊🌐*(5) 421 0685. www.hotelnueva granada.com. 21 rooms.* The waterfront is just a short walk away from this mid-range hotel, where you'll get a lot of value for your money. Small clean rooms come with either fans or air-conditioning and have adequate showers. There's a small swimming pool, a Jacuzzi, a pretty flower-filled courtyard, and coffee is complimentary.

$$$ La Casa Hospedaje –*Calle 18 # 3-52, Santa Marta.* 🌊🌐*311 390 4091. www.lacasasantamarta.com. 3 rooms.* Built at the end of the 18C and restored in 2007, La Casa is a lovely small lodging with original tile floors and sensitively chosen local artwork. It's run by a woman who has worked with the indigenous Afro-Caribbean and Sierra communities for over a decade, and she has decorated each room as a tribute to them. Breakfast includes organic produce from the Sierra. Ask to arrange yoga workshops and bird-watching trips to Minca.

$$$$ Tamacá Beach Resort – *Torre Beach, Carrera 2a # 11A-98, El Rodadero.* ✕🌊🌐*(5) 422 7015. www.tamaca.com.co. 141 rooms.* Built over an ancient Gaira Indian worship site, Tamacá (meaning "the big house on the beach" in a local indigenous dialect) is a beachfront hotel with modern facilities and rooms that afford a good view overlooking El Rodadero's bay. The hotel restaurant offers a buffet and an à la carte menu; those seeking an alfresco cocktail can visit the outdoor bar located in the pool area.

$$$$$ Hotel Complex Irotama – *14km/ 9mi south of Santa Marta on the road to Ciénaga.* ✕🌊🌐*(5) 438 0600. www.irotama.com. 322 rooms.* Set on 23 hectares/56 acres of grounds in a lush and biodiverse rain forest, this mega-resort/eco-complex boasts a private beach, 10 restaurants (meals are included in the rate) and several pools. Many rooms face the ocean, and the resort generates its own electricity and desalinates its own water. All this plus friendly and efficient staff, impressive amenities and good security just 5 minutes away from the local airport.

$$$$$ Tayrona Ecohab – *Parque Nacional Natural Tayrona.* ✕🌐*(5) 438 0600. www.colombiatravelab.com; (57) 317-6381441, or www.diversitours. com; 🌐(57) 320 691 8556. 14 huts (max 4 people); 6 cabins (max 4 people).* Offering a secluded tropical getaway, these eco-huts overlook a pristine beach *(90min walk to swimming area).* Two restaurants provide meals, and spa treatments are available. The spacious, two-level thatched-roof huts are quite modern inside, with electric lighting, double beds and en-suite bathrooms with hot showers; amenities include a safe, mini-bar refrigerator and plasma TV. **Cabins ($$$$$)** are less expensive. Campers can book a **hammock ($)** with mosquito netting at a much lower cost.

$$$$$ Zuana Beach Resort – *Av. Tamacá, Carrera 2 # 6-80, Bello Horizonte, Santa Marta.* 🅿✕🌊🌐*(5) 432 0652. www.zuana.com.co. 185 rooms.* All rooms are suites in this huge all-suites hotel complex facing the ocean. When you tire of sunbathing on the beach, tennis, squash, table tennis and even a bowling alley await you at the hotel. There's also an evening show. Large brightly colored tropical-style rooms have tile floors and pale wood furniture. This place even has its own supermarket and travel agency.

🍴 EAT

$ Ben & Joseph's – *Carrera 1 # 18-67, Santa Marta. Closed Sun.* 🌐*317 280 5039. www.parkhotelsantamarta. com.* This restaurant and bar, owned by expatriates, serves up enormous portions of thick steaks. Attached to the Park Hotel, Ben & Joseph's is independently run and is easily the best of the waterfront options. If you want an outdoor table on the weekend, it's advisable to call ahead. **International**.

$ Los Baguettes De Maria – *Calle 18 # 3-47, Taganga (in front of the football field). Lunch only. Closed Sat & Sun. ℰ(5) 421 9328.* Many locals favor this eatery for its inexpensive and tasty food. The menu of sandwiches, salads, juices, and fruit shakes is varied and always fresh. Get there around 11am for freshly baked warm bread. **Colombian**.

$ Ostras El Juancho – *Carrera 1 between Calle 22 & 23, # 18-67, Santa Marta.* This tiny street stall, next to the Gino Passcalli Store, has been serving loyal clients for more than 30 years. It is open for breakfast, lunch and dinner, starring ceviche as the signature dish. **Colombian**.

$$ Basilea Gourmet – *Carrera 3 # 16-24, Santa Marta. Closed Sun. ℰ(5) 431 4138.* This eatery is an intimate Mediterranean restaurant that serves French and Italian dishes with a Caribbean influence. Beautifully decorated and smoothly operated, Basilea lists fiery red pepper steak on its menu, which is translated into French. **Mediterranean**.

$$ Burukuka – *Via al Edificio Cascadas, del Rodadero (behind the Cascadas building in El Rodadero). ℰ(5) 422 3080. www.burukuka.com.* A terrific steak restaurant overlookingthe beach, Burukuka takes its name from the original indigenous Indians who lived in the same hills where the restaurant is now located. Crowds jam this popular spot not only for steaks, but for the big rumba (all-night party) that takes place here *(Thu–Sun)*. Come for a sunset drink, and the late-night party. **Colombian**.

$$ Casa Holanda – *Calle 14 #1B-75, Taganga. ℰ(5) 421 9390. www.micasa holanda.com.* Three meals a day are served at this guesthouse, whose staff speaks English and Dutch. The kitchen emphasizes fresh local ingredients— organic when possible—and loads of vegetables. For night owls, the little bar stays open until midnight, and there's a happy hour daily at 9pm. **International**.

$$ Donde Chucho
Calle 19 # 2-17, Santa Marta; ℰ(5) 421 4663. Second location at Carrera 2 # 16-19, El Rodadero; ℰ423 7521. Both closed Sun. In a quiet corner across from the parque de los Novios, Donde Chucho, one of Santa Marta's best restaurants serves great seafood. There are six types of noodles, eight sauces and much more. Try the signature salad (shrimp, octopus, calamari and manta smoked in olive oil) or the *robalo au gratin* (mozzarella and parmesan). Two-for-one cocktails from 6pm–9pm, Monday to Thursday. **Seafood**.

⚡ RECREATION

Academia Latina – *Calle 14 # 1B-75, Taganga. ℰ(5) 421 9390. www.academia-latina.com.* Located inside the new 12-room Casa Holanda, the Dutch-run language school offers classes for a minimum of 10 hours a week. Part of the 160,000 COP fee (25 percent) goes to Foundation Más, which helps the underprivileged children of Taganga and Santa Marta.

Aquantis Dive Center – *Calle 18 # 1-39 Taganga. ℰ(5) 421 9344. www.aquantisdivecenter.com.* Taganga is a popular scuba-diving center with several schools and extremely competitive rates. This school is friendly and professional. Aquantis offers a bed-and-PADI-diving-certification package with breakfast for 580,000 COP in comfortable rooms at the dive center.

Diving with Aquantis Dive Center

Aquantis Dive Center

La Guajira Peninsula★★★

La Guajira

Bordering Venezuela to the east, Colombia's northenmost department is an intriguing land of deserts, folklore and tales of contraband. Its vast, arid plains are home mostly to the Wayúu, a fiercely independent people deeply anchored in its traditions and values, who have managed to survive in this harsh environment. The mysterious, sparsely populated Guajira Peninsula is defined by the dramatic color of deserts and empty beaches along the Caribbean coast. With such natural beauty, the area is set to become a major destination for ecotourism and ethnotourism since international visitors are starting to look for more adventurous travel options off the beaten track.

A BIT OF HISTORY

Prior to the arrival of the Spanish, the northern part of present-day La Guajira was peopled mainly by **Wayúus**, while **Arhuacos**, **Koguis** and other ethnic groups inhabited the South. Archaeological digs have unearthed evidence of settlements dating back to 10 BC. In the Upper Guajira, Wayúu groups such as the **Guajiros**, **Macuiros** and **Cuanaos** were all hunter-gatherers and fishermen, while in the Lower Guajira, the peoples related to the Arhuacos were semi-sedentary and cultivated crops. **Alonso de Ojeda** was actually the first Spaniard to sight the hostile lands along the Guajira Peninsula in 1498.

In 1510 the conquistadors would utimately locate the first, ill-fated European settlement on the South American mainland, nearby present-day Urabá.

In colonial days the Spanish Crown and its conquistadors hardly made an impression on the fierce aboriginal tribes who inhabited the isolated, unforgiving peninsula. Because of the Wayúu's **resistance** to colonization, the area of the Upper Guajira was largely left

◔ **Michelin Maps:** pp 314–315.

▯ **Info:** Dirección Operativa de Turismo, Avenida de La Marina, Riohacha, ℘(5) 727 1015. www.laguajira.gov.co. There are also various tour agencies in Cartagena and Riohacha that can provide up-to-date information.

◉ **Don't Miss:** It is strongly recommended that you take an organized tour with a reputable company with experience in the region, and head to the Punta Gallinas to enjoy some of the best views in the continent. Awesome sunsets, starry nights, unspoiled beaches and lobster dinners await.

alone by the Spanish, as they focused on exploiting the riches to the south.

In 1535, while the whole territory was nominally under the jurisdiction of **Santa Marta** and Rodrigo de Bastidas, **Martín Fernández de Enciso** founded the settlement of "Nuestra Señora Santa María de los Remedios del Cabo de la Vela". Now simply referred to as Cabo de la Vela, the town became an easy target for pirates such as the Englishman Sir **Francis Drake** and the Frenchmen **Nau** and **Lafitte**. It also suffered frequent attacks by the indigenous populations.

Quite soon afterwards, the town of Cabo de la Vela, where **pearls** were once abundant and heavily exploited by the Spanish, was abandoned. This settlement in the Guajira was relocated farther to the west, in current-day **Riohacha**, founded by **Nikolaus Federmann** in 1544.

Between 1701 and 1769, the state of semi-permanent war between the Spanish and the Wayúus—who had never been subjugated—escalated into violent **uprisings**, resulting in the burning of

311

GETTING THERE

BY AIR - **Aeropuerto Almirante Padilla** (✆5 727 3914) sits 3km/1.8mi southwest of Riohacha. Transportation by *colectivos* and taxis (7,000 COP) to Riohacha is available. Flights from Bogotá arrive once a day. Avianca Airlines has an office in Riohacha (✆5 727 3624; www.avianca.com).

BY BUS - The **bus terminal** (Avenida El Progreso at Carrera 11) is located some 11km/7mi from the town's center. A **taxi** costs about 3,500 COP. Direct **buses** arrive from Baranquilla (5hrs; 20,000 COP), Bogotá (18hrs; 80,000COP), Cartagena (7hrs; 35,000 COP) and Santa Marta (2.5hrs; 15,000 COP).

GETTING AROUND

BY TAXI - Taxis are available in Riohacha (3,000 COP to cross town).

DESERT TOURING

It is strongly recommended that you go with a pre-arranged tour headed by a reputable outfitter. The challenges here in the desert are very real, namely: lack of **water** and **food,** flash **floods**, exposure to the sun, shortage of **fuel**, unmarked or unmapped **roads** and **insecurity**. Tourists have been stranded for hours in the blazing sun and even into the night. With a Wayúu or Guajiro driver who knows the land, has connections and is prepared, you should not encounter such problems. One company with experience in the region, and who uses only local operators, is **Aventure Colombia** in Cartagena (✆5 664 8500; www. aventurecolombia.com). Ask at the tourist office about other companies.

Spanish settlements to the ground and the killing of some of the Capuchin friars. In 1871 the Guajira was formally separated from the Magdalena department and became a **department** in its own right. In more contemporary times, because of its remoteness and strategic location on the Caribbean coast, the Guajira has been attracting armed groups and other criminal groups

Festival de la Cultura Wayúu

Wayúu Yonna dance

Pablo Henao Mejía/Proexport Colombia

In 2006 this three-day festival was declared the **Cultural Heritage of the Nation**. It takes place every year, in either May or June, in the city of **Uribia**, the indigenous capital of the Guajira. The festival demonstrates the power and richness of the indigenous culture of this region, and the strength of the Wayúu identity and family ties. Traditional **music** is played with instruments such as the **taliraai** *(tubular flute)* or **wootoroyoi** *(a sort of clarinet)*. **Dances** are performed in traditional **costumes**, and you will find countless *mochilas* (bags), *chinchorros* (hammocks) and other hand-made **Wayúu products** for sale. This event is an opportunity for the Wayúu people to share their traditional **cuisine**. *Friche* is a goat-meat dish—goats being a key component of the Wayúu economy and culture— seasoned with salt and served fried or stewed. Iguana stews with coconuts, turtle meat cooked in a variety of ways, *iguarayas* (fruits from the cactus) and *mazamorra* (a corn-based beverage) are other classics.

controlling the illegal drug trade, and many Wayúus have been caught in the crossfire.

Today, the local economy largely depends on the coal-mining operation at **Cerrejón**, but due to the porous nature of the border with Venezuela, **bootlegging** and the transportation of **contraband** also play a significant role that cannot be ignored. Adventure travel is slowly taking hold here, and tour guides and companies are setting up shop for visitors desiring to take a guided trek through the desert.

LOWER GUAJIRA
Riohacha
⊙ *60km/99mi NE of Santa Marta via Carretera 90.*

In colonial times Riohacha was a key **port** and a source of **pearls** for the Spanish empire. Today, it is the **official capital** of the Guajira department, with a population of 169,311.

There is a bit of a Wild West feel to this laid-back town, sitting an hour from the Venezuelan border. While away a day or two here before touring the Upper Guajira. Stroll the beachfront along the **Paseo de la Marina** (or **Malecón**) and walk the pier, known as the **Muelle Turístico**.

In the daytime, Wayúu vendors sell finely woven **mochilas** (*see sidebar p316*). At sunset the place livens up when vendors gather their wares strung along the pier, making for quite a spectacle. The **seafood** found in Riohacha's restaurants is first class.

Catedral de Nuestra Señora de los Remedios
Calle 2 with Carrera 7.

To get a feel for the Spanish elements here, head first to the cathedral, with its 16C Gothic and marble architecture.

Inside this sanctuary are the remains of Admiral **José Prudencio Padilla,** a naval hero of the Colombian and Venezuelan wars of independence.

Seek refuge from the merciless sun under the trees of the **Parque de Almirante Padilla**, a popular evening meeting point.

Capilla de la Divina Pastora
Calle 1 with Carrera 2.

This structure is another local religious building worth noting. It belonged to the **Capuchins**, a creed that certainly suffered in their attempts to bring religion to the Wayúu.

Centro Cultural Municipal Enrique Lallemand
Calle 3 # 5-49. ⊙*Open Mon–Fri 8am-noon, 2pm–8pm.*

This starkly modern construction occasionally hosts shows and exhibitions about the Wayúu culture that will help visitors gain a better understanding of their indigenous ways.

EXCURSIONS
Santuario de Flora y Fauna Los Flamencos★
⊙ *25km/16mi SW of Riohacha along Carretera 90, in the town of Camarones.* ◷*31,000 COP.* ✆*(5) 423-0752.* *www.parquesnacionales.gov.co.*

Located at the mouth of the Tapias River, this 7,000ha/17,297acre park contains many tributaries and four marshes separated from the Caribbean by sand bars: Ciénaga de Manzanillo, **Laguna Grande,** Ciénaga de Tocoromanes and **Ciénaga del Navío Quebrado**.

Venture out onto the **trails** that take you close to the fauna. The **swamps**, **mangroves** and **tropical dry forest** provide an ideal habitat for anteaters, opossums, foxes and a wide variety of birds.

If you want to see spectacular flocks of **pink flamingos** (*Phoenicopterus ruber ruber*), you have come to the right place. Taking a stroll around the park will bring you into close proximity with their spectacular **nests** made of mud that reach up to 60cm/24in in height. **White egrets** can also easily be viewed year-round, in addition to **migratory species** that pass through here in accord with the seasons.

The marine area next to the sanctuary is a migratory corridor.

Stop by the **Centro de Educación e Investigación de Tortugas**. Located on the sand bar across Ciénaga del Navío Quebrado, the center is dedicated to the

313

LA GUAJIRA PENINSULA

0   50 km

CARIBBEAN SEA

Manaure
Musichi
El Pájaro
Mayapo
Riohacha
La Gloria
★Santuario de Fauna y
Flora Los Flamencos
Cucurumahana
Camarones
Palomino
Dibulla
Tigrera
Matita
Arroyo
Arena
Monguí
Carraipía
Mingueo
Cerrillo

May not be reproduced either in its entirety or partially without the authorization of the Instituto Geográfico Agustín Codazzi - IGAC

Wayúu Rancherías

A visit to the **Los Flamencos Sanctuary** (*see p313)* may be the occasion to spend some time with the Wayúu in one of their nearby traditional hamlets, usually isolated from one another. The Wayúu live in small groupings of huts with other members of their clan. Their small houses, called **piichi** or **miichi,** can either be semi-circular or rectangular. The **wattle-and-daub** walls are made of hay, mud and a dry timber wood called **yotojoro**, produced from a large columnar **cactus** *(Stenocereus griseus)* found in the Caribbean.

This small beach community between Riohacha and Santa Marta is on the verge of being discovered, as travelers look for the next laid-back, bohemian destination along Colombia's Caribbean coast. Nestled in the foothills of the Sierra Nevada de Santa Marta, and surrounded by generous forests, Palomino is the ideal place to relax after the **Ciudad Perdida** trek (*see sidebar p308)*. It lends itself perfectly to a drinking a cocktail at sunset and idling away the hours in a hammock. Life here is tranquil.

Many, if not all, of the places do not have reliable sources of electricity, so visitors adapt to the local custom of rising at dawn and settling down for the night not long after dusk.

protection of **marine turtles** such as the Atlantic loggerhead *(Caretta caretta).*

Palomino★

 80km/50mi E of Santa Marta via Carretera 90.

Manaure

 63km/39mi NE of Riohacha along coastal road off Carretera 90 via Uribia.

Nicknamed "La Novia Blanca" (the White Bride), the coastal town of Manaure (Pop. 68,578) is home to Colombia's

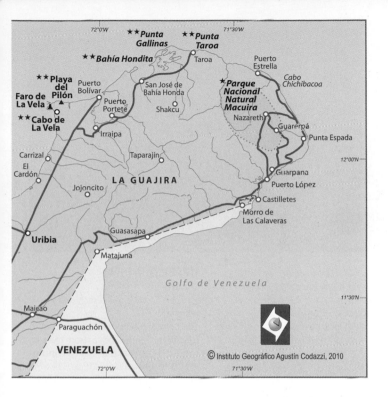

largest salt flats or **salinas** (4,000ha/ 9,884 acres). Stark reminders are massive white piles stacked at the sea front. Around town, the exploitation and processing of salt for export is visible on an **industrial** scale.

You will also see **artisanal** salt mining, vital to the local Wayúu people, in spite of grueling work in the scorching sun and paltry earnings. Yet, the turquoise blue of the sea that graduates to a darker hue, the blinding white of the mountains of salt awaiting refinement at the port, and the reddish-beige color of the desert all contrast to create a photographer's paradise.

Manaure's salt flats

Proexport Colombia

Cabo de la Vela

Proexport Colombia

The town itself is of no real interest. However, if you have time, stop by the Catholic church to look at the mosaic of **Wayúu cosmology**. Nearby, there are a couple of worthwhile beaches at **Musichi** and **El Pájaro**.

UPPER GUAJIRA
Uribia

▶ *92km/57mi NE of Riohacha via Manaure.*

The railway tracks used to ship coal to the port of Puerto Bolívar from the vast mine at El Cerrejón pass near the **indigenous capital** of Uribia (Pop. 116,674). This crossroads town is not a tourist

Wayúu Crafts

Wayúu mochilas

Proexport Colombia

High-quality Wayúu handicrafts are coveted throughout Colombia, and sold at exorbitant prices outside the Guajira, so take full advantage of your trip here and bring some of these lovely products home with you.

The **mochilas** or *Bolsos tipico Colombiano*—a type of low-slung woolen shoulder bag—have become incredibly fashionable in recent years, and come in many combinations of colors and designs. It takes approximately **40 hours** for a woman to create such a bag. They are meticulously, tightly woven by hand in cotton. The tighter the the *mochila's* weave, the better the quality and the higher the price. Famed for their broad and intricate designs, **hammocks** or *chinchorros* are colorful, woven works of art that literally take months to create, so the Wayúu cannot be blamed for the high prices.

You can find the best selection of Wayúu handicrafts in **Riohacha**. There is little for sale in **Cabo de la Vela**, aside from the usual bracelets, so either buy from those vendors on the seafront, or find out where their family store is. Whatever your choice, you will be buying from the source.

destination, but a commercial hub and service center: it's a place to stock up on provisions before setting out on a tour into the Upper Guajira.

All products here have arrived from **Venezuela**, given that the Wayúu have dual citizenship and the border is notoriously porous. You will notice canisters and plastic tanks full of cheap Venezuelan gasoline lining the roads. It is an odd situation, but it is evidence of how the region functions.

The Festival de Cultura Wayúu (*see sidebar p312*) is the most significant event in the area. For local color and a candid view of the Wayúu world, the early **morning market** is worth a visit. Be forewarned that the slaughtered goats there are a marked contrast to the desert colors and the bright robes of the local people.

Wayuunaiki-Spanish, Bilingual Dictionary

Part of the **Arawak** linguistic family, the **Wayuunaiki** is the language of the Wayúu people, with some regional variations among the southern, central and northern parts of the Guajira Peninsula.

In 2006, after many years of work, the first Wayuunaiki-Spanish, Spanish-Wayuunaiki dictionary was introduced. It is a 47-page illustrated document meant to be used as a teaching tool in ethnic educational institutions of the department of La Guajira. This document is available online at *www.sil.org/americas/colombia/pubs/guc/WayuuDict_45801.pdf.*

Cabo de la Vela★★

160km/100mi NE of Riohacha, north of the Manuare and Uribia crossroad.

The landscape of Cabo de la Vela—a remote and tranquil fishing village on a beautiful bay—has been likened to that of the moon, for its grayish sands and barren feel. With the constant winds here, the night skies are clear enough for stargazing, and the **sunsets** are breathtaking along the 8km/5mi stretch of open beach (unfortunately littered in

some places). The water in the shallows, while clear and inviting, hides a sludgy, not sandy floor, and does not lend itself to swimming. On the sea side, palm-thatched, open-sided shelters called *enramadas* are ideal places to spend the night in a hammock, while listening to the sound of the bay.

For an even better view of the sunset over the open ocean, walk for nearly an hour, or drive 10min up to the view-

Bahia Hondita

Proexport Colombia

point at **Faro de la Vela,** a lighthouse at the northernmost tip of the bay. Just around the point lies the picturesque, rust-orange **Playa del Pilón**★★, backed by craggy cliffs.

At the tall promontory called **Pilón de Azúcar**, there is a shrine to the Virgen of Fatima *(15min hike; be sure to hold on, since the winds are strong)*. Fittingly, from here one can see the wind turbines of the **Parque Eólico Jepirachi**, which generates between 60,000 and 75,000 megawatts.

Nearby are small mangrove swamps and the **Laguna de Utta**, a seasonal haven for flamingos, herons and sandpipers.

Punta Gallinas★★

◗ *75km/47mi north of Cabo de la Vela.*

Public transport is available as far as Cabo de la Vela, but to get to Punta Gallinas, the **northernmost point** on the South American mainland, it is strongly recommended that you join an organized tour.

Punta Gallinas has that special end-of-the-world feel. A short walk in any direction will lead to the ocean, but the calm **bay** nearby harbors fascinatingly earthy colors scarcely seen or experienced elsewhere in such a vivid sense.

If you have come this far, visit the **flamingo** communities in the small inlets and around the islands, and take a boat trip to the stunning beach of **Bahía Hondita**★★, frequented by shrimp

fishermen. At **Punta Taroa**★★ vast **dunes** slide from great heights into the sea.

Parque Nacional Natural Macuira★

Trek from Nazareth, a Wayúu settlement on the periphery of the park, ◗ *115km/ 71mi NE of Riohacha via Manaure.*
◔*Accessible Nov–Feb (dry season). Park must be visited with a guide to insure that you do not get lost.* ✆*(1) 243 1634. www.parquesnacionales.gov.co.*

Although most visitors never get as far as the park, preferring instead to stay in Cabo de la Vela and Punta Gallinas, a visit to the park is strongly recommended. Here you will find yourself in an unexpected **oasis** of animal life, and exuberant vegetation growing at 865m/2,838ft above sea level, just a few miles from a semi-desert area.

One of the most striking features of this 25,000ha/61,776 acre park is its dwarf **cloud forests** of perennials. Once the strong winds of the Guajira blow the rain clouds over this region, the rain is swept up into the thick vegetation and permits the growth of an abundance of bromeliads, ferns and mosses.

In addition to a rich flora, the park is home to an estimated 140 species of **birds**, some endemic to the region, and to some important populations of frogs, toads and iguanas, not to mention amphibians and reptiles.

Parque Nacional Natural Macuira

© Giovanny Pulido/Archivo Parques Nacionales Naturales de Colombia

ADDRESSES

🛌 STAY

$ Hotel Almirante Padilla – *Carrera 6 # 3-29, Riohacha.* ✆ *(5) 727 2328. 25 rooms.* Rooms in this high-rise hotel may be bland and some could do with renovation, but all are clean and have air-conditioning and TV. The popular beachfront area is just a block away from the hotel; and guests have access to a bar and Internet on-site.

$ Hotel Primavera – *Calle 14 and Carrera 11A, Riohacha.* ✆ *301 767 6859. 5 rooms.* Located right beside the bus terminal, Hotel Primavera is a clean, cheap and convenient place to stay, especially if you're a backpacker enroute to other places. Rooms are small but adequate, with one caveat: because buses park in the street outside the hotel, bringing earplugs is advisable. Otherwise the noise from the buses, which begins very early in the morning, combined with the exhaust fumes, can easily interfere with your good night's sleep.

$$ Hotel El Castillo del Mar – *Calle 9A # 15-352, Riohacha.* ✆ *(5) 727 5043. http://hotelcastillodelmarsuites.blog spot.com. 11 rooms.* Nondescript on the outside but quite nice on the inside, this comfy hotel is located right on the beach. Pleasant but slightly run-down rooms reside in large white-washed cabanas connected by paths that can get slippery. It's a short walk into town from the hotel.

$$ Hotel Majayura – *Carrera 10 # 1-40, Riohacha.* ✆ *(5) 728 8666. 36 rooms.* Reasonably priced for Riohacha, the Majayura sits close to Parque Jose Prudencio Padilla, just back (100m/328ft) from the shoreline and near the pier. The hotel's restaurant serves decent food, but the TV is always blaring in the dining room and the hotel staff are largely indifferent. No need to fret, however: there are a number of pleasant small bars and good restaurants nearby.

🍴 EAT

$ Hospedaje y Comidas Luzmilla – *Punta Gallinas, La Guajira.* ✆ *312 647 9881.* Maintained by the local primary-school teacher, this is one of the few dining options located in the northernmost point of the landmass of South America. Patrons are given the option of enjoying the Wayúu seafood cuisine in nearby beachside hammocks. **Regional Colombian**.

$ Marino's Junior – *Calle 1 # 10-97, Riohacha.* ✆ *310 705 0117.* The chef/owner of this charming cafe-restaurant cooks according to his passion for hot dogs and sausages. He claims to be able to make more than 50 different types of hot dogs, including the all-beef Suizo. If you're feeling daring, try the Italian (with mozzarella), the Mexican or the Hawaiian, all of which are served in a jiffy with chips to boot. **Colombian**.

$ Refugio y Restaurante Pantu – *At the northern end of El Cabo de la Vela, La Guajira. Dinner only.* ✆ *(5) 725 1405. http://elcabodelavela.com.* This posada's claim to fame is that it was chosen by former president Álvaro Uribe as his holiday destination in 2005. An above-average dining choice in an ecotourism destination, Restaurante Pantu features seafood dishes served alongside *arepas* and *patacón* (deep fried batter-crusted plantains). After dinner, stop by the on-site disco for a cocktail and dancing. **Regional Colombian**.

$$ La Tinaja – *Calle 1 # 4-59, Riohacha. Open for breakfast, lunch and dinner.* ✆ *(5) 727 3929.* This restaurant and bar features an innovative mix of typical Colombian and Guajiran dishes with seafood as their focus. Staff is friendly and helpful, and will even explain the cooking methods and recipes in detail if you are interested. Try the *cazuela de Mariscos*, a fish and shellfish stew. **Regional Colombian**.

San Andrés y Providencia★★

Over the years, any number of people—Puritan settlers, pirates, empire builders, Colombians and Nicaraguans—have wanted to get their hands on the Caribbean archipelago of San Andrés and Providencia. These two island groups really could not be more dissimilar. Flat with thin, yet enticing beaches, San Andrés has now become the tax-free, package tourist destination for Colombia. Providencia, volcanic, rugged and scenic, can be visited independently and will appeal to nature lovers and beach loungers alike.

A BIT OF HISTORY

San Andrés and Providencia are located some 775km/480mi northwest of Colombia's mainland coast. They are a mere 220km/136mi north of Nicaragua, which filed claims with the International Court of Justice (ICJ) over the **maritime boundary** in 2001. This ongoing conflict poses challenges to the Caribbean zone as it raises questions of **sovereignty**. The islands' location is central to their intriguing history. Unwittingly their geo-political importance involved the first occasional inhabitants, Central Ameri-

▶ **Population:** 59,573.

◔ **Michelin Maps:** p270, p322 and p325.

▤ **Info:** For San Andrés: Ministry of Tourism, House Fiscal diagonal Yacht Club, ✆(8) 512 5058; Airport Tourist Office, ✆(8) 512 1149; Kiosco tourist information, Avenida La Playa, Also check www.san andres.gov.co/turismo and www.sanandres.com *(both with English versions).*

⊛ **Don't Miss:** Renting a scooter and traveling around Providencia on your own, stopping at Roland's Bar on Playa Manzanillo for a truly laid-back Caribbean experience.

ca's **Miskito Indians**. Next came **New England Puritans**, Dutch freebooters and a assortment of pirates—including **Henry Morgan**, who used Old Providence as his base to sack Panama—as well as the **Spanish**, who occupied the islands from 1641 to 1677.

Had everything gone according to the plans of 17C English colonists and **Oliver Cromwell**'s Western Design (Britain's attempt to reduce Catholic influence

San Andrés Island

Proexport Colombia

GETTING THERE

BY AIR - **Gustavo Rojas Pinilla International Airport** (ADZ) is a 10-15min walk northwest of San Andrés town's commercial center. There are direct flights from Baranquilla, Bogotá, Cali, Cartagena, Medellín and Providencia (20min flight). Satena and Searca airlines also operate a shuttle between San Andrés and Providencia. Upon arrival, you must buy a **tourist card** for the island and present it upon **departure**. When checking in for your return flight, watch luggage restrictions and reconfirm your return flight, or your seat may be reallocated.

GETTING AROUND

BY BOAT - For those able to stomach a 5hr rough sea crossing, **cargo boats** take passengers on their route between Providencia and San Andrés (40,000 COP); bring your own food, water and something to sit or lie on. Tours by **lancha** (small boat) leave from Aguadulce.

BY BUS - Unless you walk, **local buses** are the cheapest way to get around. They encircle Providencia and ply the inland road to El Cove as well as all major attractions. The bus marked *San Luis* that services the east coast road and the bus marked *El Cove* that runs along the inner road through La Loma can be boarded near the Hotel Hernando Henry on San Andrés.

BY TAXI - Taxis are pricey; touring San Andrés costs about 50,000 COP.

BY OTHER - **Bicycles** (half day 10,000 COP or full day 20,000 COP) and **golf carts** (80,000 COP) can be rented on Avenue Newball in Providencia. Scooters (40,000 COP) are rented only for a full day.

---

in the Spanish West Indies), today's Providencia would perhaps not have the sleepy charm of contemporary Caribbean island life.

What exists today, though, is not a Puritan-linked enterprise run from London by aristocrats cashing in on **tobacco**, **cotton** and **indigo**, and celebrating a shared history with their kin in Jamestown, USA, but a set of islands that make up part of an anomalous Colombian territory in the Caribbean.

SAN ANDRÉS ISLAND★★

Blighted by massive chain hotels capitalizing on this tax-free zone, San Andrés (Pop. 55,426) is the larger and more populous of the two major islands that make up the archipelago. Long and narrow, it consists of three urban centers. The principal one is the disorderly **El Centro** (also called **North End**), where the majority of the businesses and hotels are located, as well as the beach of **Playa de Spratt Bight**, known as **Bahía Sardinas**.

Situated on the highest part of San Andrés, more or less in its center, is **La Loma** (or **The Hill**), a traditional Caribbean village of brightly painted wooden houses offering unrivaled **views** of the multicolored ocean. Since La Loma sits inland, as much as it can be here, you won't find beaches, but a few points of interest such as the **Iglesia Bautista Emmanuel** (1847) and farther south, **La Laguna**, an ideal habitat for birdlife. Those who wish to get away from it all, lounge on a beach, and empty their minds of stress should head for **San Luis**★. Located on the eastern side of the island, it is more traditional, far less hectic, and much more laid-back than El Centro.

Visit

There are two ways to see the sights in San Andrés. The first and most frequent is the **all-inclusive tour** that stops at all the key points of interest. It is relatively difficult to come here independently as so much is set up through your hotel, or included in your trip package.

Secondly, you can rent a **golf cart**, **moped** or **car** and take the route yourself at your own speed around the 32km/20mi-long road that rings the coastline.

SAN ANDRÉS ISLAND

0 _____ 2 km

N

Punta Norte

Cayo Sucre ★
(Johnny Cay)

Bahía Sardinas
San Andrés

Aeropuerto
Internacional
Gustavo Rojas Pinilla

Bahía de San Andrés

Cayo Santander

Parque Regional de
Mangle Old Point

Casa Museo
Isleña

Iglesia Bautista
Emmanuel

Evans Point

La Loma

Cayo El Acuario
(Rose Cay)

La Cueva
de Morgan

Laguna
Big Pond

Cayo Córdoba
(Haynes Cay)

Schooner
Bight

Coconut
Museum

Sterthenberg Point

El Cove

San Luis ★

West View

Bahía Sonora
(Sound Bay)

CARIBBEAN SEA

La Piscína

Carretera Circunvalar

Punta Rocosa

© Instituto Geográfico Agustín Codazzi, 2010

Hoyo Soplador

South End

MAINLAND COLOMBIA

La Cueva de Morganaa

▶ *Carretera Circunvalar at KM 8, 3km/
2mi S of La Loma.* *Open daily dawn–
dusk.* 2,000 COP. (8) 512 2316.

La Cueva de Morgan is one of San
Andrés' most visited tourist attractions.
You can step into a large hollowed-out
cave that weaves its way back through
the coralline foundations of the island.
Apparently, the famed pirate **Henry
Morgan** left some treasure here, and
the locals will regale you with tales of
the famed booty. In truth, everything
here feels a little bit fabricated in order
to amuse the tourist, but take this in
stride and you will enjoy yourself, since
there is no way to know whether Morgan ever placed any treasure here, left
any behind on Providencia or even buried some on the Pacific coast resort of
Tumaco.

The neighboring **Coconut Museum** (*same hours and fee as La Cueva de Morgan*) displays artifacts that offer enlightenment on life on the island, local customs and lore.

At **West View**, 1km/0.6mi south of La Cueva de Morgan, there is a sheltered natural pool, ideal for bathing or snorkeling.

El Cove

Continuing south from here, you should reach this deep anchorage, the major **port** for the Colombian navy and the international cruise ships that pass through San Andrés periodically.

Halfway between El Cove and Hoyo Soplador lies **La Piscína**, which has a depth of 5m/16.5ft, but seems a lot shallower due to the clarity of the water. La Piscinita is a good place for paddling and feeding fish.

Hoyo Soplador

The next stop is this popular **blowhole**, in the part of the island known as **South End**. Surrounded by various restaurants and bars, all taking full advantage of this natural formation, this place is always crowded, so you may want to think twice about coming here. In any case, when the tide is right, the jet of water spurting through the blowhole at times reaches heights of 10m/33ft to 20m/66ft.

OFF ISLAND

The sea around San Andrés is more than inviting, with its array of various shades of blue. For this reason, the waters here are often referred to as being of **seven colors**. They are still and refreshing, and lend themselves to **water sports** such as diving, snorkeling, windsurfing, kite surfing, sailing, waterskiing, jet skiing and deep-sea fishing.

Johnny Cay★

Nobody visits San Andrés without making a trip to this small island, visible from El Centro. Make no mistake, Johnny Cay is a palm-lined paradise of white sandy beaches and coconuts meant for relaxation. However, plan your trip for midweek to have the place to yourself, if you

The Raizales

Descendents of **slaves** from Jamaica and the Miskito coast of Nicaragua and **English Puritans** who settled the territory in the 17C, the **native islanders** are a Protestant Afro-Caribbean ethnic group with a very distinct culture and set of traditions. Raizales speak the **San Andrés Creole**, an English-based Creole which shows significant similarities with the Belize Kriol and other related varieties in Jamaica and Central American Creole communities. Many of its expressions derive from the **Kwa**, **Ibi**, **Ewe** or **Twi** African languages. As the influx of mainlanders on the archipelago is increasing, so is the pressure of **Spanish** on the Creole-speaking population.

are seeking peace. The weekend crowds are prone to partying. Many operators lining the beachfront in El Centro offer excursions to Johnny Cay.

Additional Sights

Haynes Cay and **Acuario** are spits of brilliant and fine white sand located to the east of the city; they are ideal for novice snorkelers.

PROVIDENCIA ISLAND★★

Located 90km/56mi north of San Andrés, Providencia may well be the Caribbean's best kept secret.

Life on this little volcanic island may seem monotonous, but there is plenty to do here, whether it be lounging on a beach, scuba diving, hiking, fishing, exploring, or attending a beachfront horse race.

Public transport does exist on Providencia, but the service is distinctly Caribbean, so it's advisable to rent a moped or bicycle and explore the sights at your own pace along the 20km/12.5mi of **road** ringing the island.

The following are some suggested attractions to see:

Providencia Island

Agenda del mar/Proexport Colombia

Bahía Aguadulce★

This hub is the foremost tourist center on Providencia, but by no means does it resemble the concrete mangle of El Centro in San Andrés. It is quaint, well-ordered and pleasant to visit.

Bahía Suroeste★

This little neighborhood lies about 2km/1.2mi south of Bahía Aguadulce.

Seaflower Biosphere Reserve

In 2000, the islands of San Andrés, Providencia and Santa Catalina and their associated coastal mangroves, swamps, dry tropical forests and coral reef ecosystems were listed on **UNESCO**'s Man and the Biosphere program. This huge marine reserve, which encompasses one of the largest coral barriers in the Western Hemisphere and concentrates 78 percent of Colombia's coral areas, covers about 10 percent of the Caribbean Sea or a staggering 250,000sq km/96,526 sq mi. Out of these, a **Seaflower Marine Protected Area** (MPA) of 65,000sq km/25,097sq mi was identified in 2005. Its coral reefs, mangroves, seagrass beds, beaches, and deep water are on the **UNESCO World Heritage** tentative list.

The beach here, a blanket of silky white sand, is more attractive than that of Bahía Aguadulce, and more often than not, you will have it to yourself. It is here, on Saturdays, that impassioned **horse races** are often held along the stretch of beach in front of the cabañas.

Playa Manzanillo★★

For the true Caribbean experience, do not miss this beach on the southern tip of the island. The water here is calm, lapping gently at the sand, the beach is shaded, and your own amateur photographs will look as if they have sprung from the pages of a vacation catalog.

Hiking Trails

For the adventurous and athletic types, there are trails starting in **Casabaja** or **Aguamansa** that take hikers inland up to **The Peak** (or **El Pico**) at 360m/1,180ft above sea level. From this old volcano, you can enjoy spectacular **views**★★ of the island. Your hike will take you through almost perfectly preserved **Caribbean jungle**.

Parque Nacional Natural Old Providence McBean Lagoon★

Open daily 8am–5pm.
21,000 COP. (5) 420 4504.
www.parquesnacionales.gov.co.
Located on the northeastern tip of the island, this park hosts amphibious trees of the **mangrove forest** (37ha/91 acres),

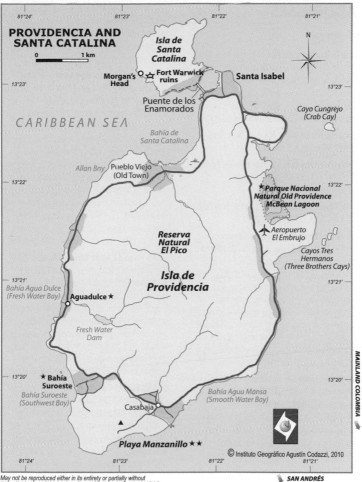

and a variety of resident and migratory birds. For a walk through a **tropical dry forest**, follow the trail to **Iron Wood Hill**.Kayaking in the reef-encircled lagoon is another way to discover the park, but your best option may well be to **snorkel** and **dive** among the coral formations, as it will provide an opportunity to observe the submarine landscape, with **coral pinnacles** rising to 8m/26ft.

SANTA CATALINA ISLAND

From **Santa Isabel,** to the north of Providencia, a 180m/580ft **walking bridge** called **Puente de los Enamorados** takes visitors to tiny Santa Catalina. Both islands were separated by an artificial canal created in the 18C by pirates in order to protect their lair.

Once on the islet, a **walkway** around Santa Catalina takes you past a few highlights such as **Morgan's Head**, a large volcanic rock; the vestiges of the pirate legacy at **Fort Warwick** (*free access),* where there are still some old cannons in place; and all of the well-maintained and brightly painted wooden **Caribbean-style houses**. Some of the bloodthirsty and cruel pirate history is shared here by way of descriptive signs illustrating what took place in Santa Catalina's past, such as the execution of Dutch pirates.

ADDRESSES

🛏 STAY

Las Posadas Nativas – At the low end of the budgetary scale is an excellent home-stay program called Las Posadas Nativas. For more information, contact the tourist office: ℘*(8) 512 1149; www. posadasturisticasdecolombia.com.*

$ Carson's Place – *El Cove, San Andrés.* ℘*(8) 513 0352. 3 rooms.*

$ Nativa Licy (Licy's Place) – *La Loma Flowers Hill 39-19, San Andrés.* ℘*(8) 512 3972. 5 rooms.*

$ William's Paradise – *Sector San Luis, San Andrés.* ℘*(8) 513 2119.*

$$ Hotel Flaming Trees – *Center of Santa Isabel, Isla de la Santa Catalina.* ✕℘*(8) 514 8049. 9 rooms.* An ideal choice for this part of the island, Flaming Trees sits by a picturesque bay and affords stunning views of Santa Catalina. While the area seems quite commercial, it is not yet on most tourist maps. The hotel offers spacious, comfortable rooms, each with AC, refrigerator, TV and local artwork.

$$ Hotel Hernando Henry – *Av. Las Americas # 4-84, San Andrés Town.* ✕℘*(8) 512 3416. 26 rooms.* The advantage of this hotel is that it doesn't rely on the local government for its provision of water or electricity. Most rooms have balconies; all have their own private bath. An Internet cafe adjoins the hotel.

$$$ Hotel Sirius – *South West Bay, Providencia.* ✕℘*(8) 514 8213. www. siriushotel.net. 8 rooms.* This small, well-run hotel, which has been owned by the same folks since its inception in 2007, incorporates a dive center on its grounds. Standard rooms have small balconies, while balconies off the suites are larger and claim ocean views. All rooms have AC, mosquito netting and hammocks on the balconies. Breakfast is included in the rate.

$$$$ Cabañas El Recreo – *Bahía Agua Dulce, Providencia.* ✕℘*(8) 514 8010. 15 rooms.* Divers will love the simple, clean, cabin-style rooms in a peaceful spot right next door to Felipe's Diving Shop. The friendly staff and the location near one of the best sandy beaches for swimming in this area make up for what this member of the Decameron chain lacks in terms of luxury.

$$$$ Decameron San Luis – *17km/ 10.5mi along the Carretera Circunvalar, San Luis.* ✕🛏℘*(8) 513 0295. www.decameron.com. 233 rooms.* Of the four huge all-inclusive beach resorts on the island, Decameron San Luis is the most attractive, owing to its bright island-style architecture. Rooms are scattered amid landscaped gardens, and on-site recreation includes tennis, volleyball, windsurfing, kayaking, snorkeling, and a 24-hour bar. The complex is open so safety is an issue, both on the beach and on the grounds.

$$$$ Posada Miss Elma – *Agua Dulce Bay, Providencia.* ✕℘*(8) 514 8229. 4 rooms.* Forested hills climb behind this charming posada, set right on the bay. Comfortable rooms sport a country style, and are either fan-cooled or air-conditioned. The common areas are bright and cheerful, and the covered deck morphs into a game room for guests in the evening.

$$$$$ Hotel Casablanca – *Av. Colombia # 3-59, San Andrés.* ✕℘*(8) 512 4115. 50 rooms. www.hotel casablancasanandres.com. 57 rooms.* With 11 modern, fully equipped bungalows and 39 large, comfortable rooms, this hotel—one of the first in the area—still prides itself on being a big property that is run like a small one. Check out the tempting seafood menu at the Casablanca's restaurant.

🍴 EAT

$$ Bamboo – *Santa Catalina Island; turn left after the footbridge from Providencia.* ℘*(8) 514 8398.* Grab a table on the deck in front of the restaurant for a peaceful view of the harbor, and take advantage of Bamboo's reasonably priced local dishes and attentive service. Even though it's not indicated on the menu, this is one of the few eateries on the island that offers vegetarian meals. **Seafood**.

$$ Café Studio – *Bahia Suroeste, San Andrés.* *(8) 514 9076. Closed Sun.* Known as the island's best restaurant, this place is run by a Canadian and her husband, who share the cooking. You won't be disappointed by any of the seafood dishes, including conch in Creole sauce made with wild basil, or anything with wild garlic. **Regional Colombian**.

$$ Roland Roots Bar – *Bahia Manzanillo Beach, Providencia.* *(8) 514 8417.* At this iconic island open-air bar, you will see people basking in the shade of coconut palms or in bamboo booths while listening to the loud reggae music that cancels out quiet conversation. This is the place for all-night fun fueled by *cocos locos* (pina coladas served in coconuts). The kitchen also kicks out some reasonably priced fried food. **Regional Colombian**.

$$$ El Rincon de la Langosta – *Carretera Circunvalar, Sector Schooner Bight KM 7, San Andrés.* *(8) 513 2707. www.rincondelalangosta.com.* A San Andrés tradition since 1994, this restaurant specializes in lobster—served any way you want, with a choice of sauces. Eat in one of four areas, one of which is a breezy tropical terrace that boasts stellar sunset views. Garlic octopus, stuffed crab, and a selection of fresh island fish are all winners, but the lobster steals the show here. **Seafood**.

$$$ Gourmet Shop Restaurant – *Av. Newball in front of Parque la Barracuda, San Andrés.* *(8) 512 9843. Closed Sun.* Dine on wooden tables made from reclaimed barrels while surrounded by an impressive cellar of global wines. Shelves are packed with herbs, spices and bottled provisions. A respite from the touristy chaos of the Caribbean, the restaurant features a menu that includes fine cheeses, smoked meats and foreign breads on its menu. **International**.

$$$ La Regatta – *Club Naútico, Av. Newball, San Andrés.* *(8) 512 3022. http://en.restaurantelaregatta.com. Closed Mon.* Wine bottles hang from trees and line the walkway to La Regatta. Shuttered windows enclose the dining area, and the interior decor follows a nautical theme, with sultry lighting come evening. Seafood heads the menu, with the likes of curried lobster tails, and seafood stew with seasoned coconut rice. Reservations required. **Seafood**.

$$$$ Miss Elma – *In the Miss Elma Hotel, Bahía Agua Dulce, Providencia.* *(8) 514 8229.* Convenient to many island hotels, Miss Elma, which opened in 1968, has garnered a reputation for its tasty island food. The signature dish is the House Crab, but the lobster is also worth ordering. **International**.

🛒 SHOPPING

Avenida Providencia, San Andrés – Make this avenue your first stop for shopping in San Andrés. Check out La **Riviera**, a favorite for duty-free high-end cosmetics and designer perfumes. For discount designer duds and brand-name sporting goods, head to **President Fashion** and **Madiera**.

🏃 RECREATION

DIVING
Good underwater visibility, warm waters and calm currents make the barrier reef off San Andrés a diver's paradise.

Banda Dive Shop – *Hotel Lord Pierre L-104, San Andrés.* *(8) 513 1080. www.bandadiveshop.com.*

Sharky's Dive Shop – *13km/8mi on the Carretera Circunvalar.* *(8) 513 0433. www.sharkydiveshop.com.*

PARKS AND RECREATION
El Reserva Natural El Pico – *Providencia.* Begin your hike from Casabaja to reach the highest point on Providencia (a guide is recommended).

Parque Nacional Natural Old Providence McBean Lagoon – *Northeast of Providencia. www.parques nacionales.gov.co.* On the northeast side of the island, the park covers a coastal mangrove system and offshore islands.

Paradise Tours – *Aguadulce, San Andrés.* *(8) 514 8283.* This agency offers tours and other services including bicycle rental, tours to El Pico, horseback riding, kayaking and boat trips.

Overlooked by most travelers visiting Colombia, the Pacific region is long overdue some attention, and is slowly but surely opening up to ecotourism. In the north, bordering Panama, this awe-inspiring terrain includes the impenetrable tangle of the Darien, a notoriously lawless area blessed with outstanding biodiversity. The Pacific coast stretches southwards through protective mangrove swamps and bays of crystalline waters, favored by migrating humpback whales. The shore continues all the way along the ports of Buenaventura and Tumaco before reaching the border with Ecuador. The Colombian Pacific region is one of the rainiest on earth, and its fiercely tropical climate and ecosystem, combined with the problems of the armed conflict here, have seriously inhibited successful development of a capable and inclusive infrastructure. However, the Pacific is gradually being placed on the map as a tourist destination. The local populations, of Afro-Colombian and indigenous descent, have set about creating ecolodges geared toward nature lovers, and national parks such as Gorgona, Sanquianga and Utría are receiving more visitors every year.

Highlights

1 Go wreck diving at **Bahía Solano** (p331)

2 Discover some of Colombia's best unspoiled surfing spots around **Nuquí** (p336)

3 Watch the annual migration of the humpbacks near **Juanchaco** and **Ladrilleros** (p342)

4 See baby sea turtles hatch on the beaches of **Sanquianga** (p345)

5 Put on your snorkeling gear and enjoy the exuberant marine life at **Isla Gorgona** (p347)

Adventure vs. Reality

Whether one's idea of recreation involves hiking, fishing, bird-watching, surfing or wreck diving, all nature lovers will be awed at the sight of frolicking dolphins and breaching whales rising up out of the water off the Pacific coast. There is no doubting that the Pacific's attractions are primarily for the **ecotourist**. Such sights draw a certain type of adventure traveler unaffected by rocky boat trips over open water or journeys on a small prop plane landing on makeshift airstrips, as if sliced with a machete and only momentarily clearing the jungle. Never underestimate the power of nature here, as the storm clouds roll in and a **deluge**, for which this region is famous, soaks you to the skin. Hikes to pristine, clear waterfalls or empty hot springs usually include spotting en route some of the several species of poison dart frog. Around the towns of Nuquí, El Valle and Bahía Solano, the jungles tumble into the Pacific Ocean, and the division between land and water seems delineated only by the piles of driftwood strewn along the beautiful, unsullied beaches.

Making the Pacific more accessible, but no less adventurous, is a new breed of **ecolodges**, often award-winning, springing up and promoting travel in the area by providing up-to-date information and intricate travel details. While **Nuquí** is gaining fame among surfers for its breaks, **Bahía Solano**, **Tumaco** and **Buenaventura** have garnered fame in recent years for other reasons. Bahía Solano, at the mouth of the Jella River, gives the opportunity to see migrating whales and birds, and is a base camp for ecological adventures, sports fishing, and scuba-diving trips to the wreck of a former navy vessel. Tumaco and Buenaventura are major ports on the Pacific coast, and with this role come all of the unfortunate realities of the drug trade and the armed conflict. In all of the Pacific regions of the departments of the **Chocó**, **Valle del Cauca**, **Cauca** and **Nariño**, prospective visitors need to get up-to-date information about **security conditions** here before making any travel plans.

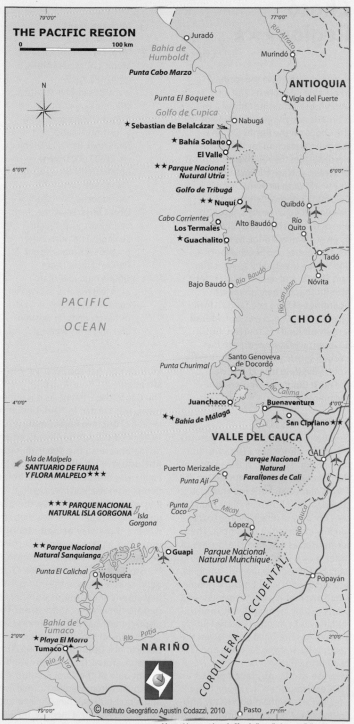

THE PACIFIC REGION

0   100 km

N

Juradó

Bahía de Humboldt

Punta Cabo Marzo

Murindó

Punta El Boquete

ANTIOQUIA

Vigía del Fuerte

Golfo de Cupica

Nabugá

★ **Sebastian de Belalcázar**

★ **Bahía Solano**

El Valle

★ ★ **Parque Nacional Natural Utría**

Golfo de Tribugá

★ ★ **Nuquí**

Quibdó

Cabo Corrientes

Los Termales

Alto Baudó

Río Quito

★ **Guachalito**

Tadó

Río Baudó

Bajo Baudó

Nóvita

CHOCÓ

PACIFIC

OCEAN

Punta Churimal

Santo Genoveva de Docordó

Río Calima

Juanchaco

Buenaventura

★ ★ **Bahía de Málaga**

★ **San Cipriano** ★ ★

VALLE DEL CAUCA

Isla de Malpelo

SANTUARIO DE FAUNA Y FLORA MALPELO ★ ★ ★

Puerto Merizalde

Parque Nacional Natural Farallones de Cali

CALI

Punta Ají

★ ★ ★ **PARQUE NACIONAL NATURAL ISLA GORGONA** ★ ★ ★

Isla Gorgona

Punta Coco

Río Micay

López

Río Cauca

★ ★ **Parque Nacional Natural Sanquianga**

○ **Guapi**

Parque Nacional Natural Munchique

Punta El Calichal

Mosquera

CAUCA

Pòpayán

Bahía de Tumaco

★ **Playa El Morro**

Tumaco

Río Patía

NARIÑO

Río Mira

CORDILLERA OCCIDENTAL

Pasto

Chocó Region★★★

Chocó

Bursting with life in the form of pristine rain forests and an abundance of marine animals, the dramatic and rugged coastline of the Chocó off the Pacific Ocean is the main attraction for the visitor. Here, despite the relative difficulties of access, you are transported to a world unto its own. One of Colombia's poorest and least developed departments, it is also one of its most beautiful, acting as an ecological bridge between North, Central and South America. You will be greeted by spectacular rain forests and dense, resplendent growth that harbors unknown quantities of flora and fauna. Until recently, the Chocó was considered largely off-limits to tourism, but an intense military presence has pushed security concerns elsewhere. Now is the time to visit one of the most biodiverse regions on the planet.

○ **Michelin Maps:** p329 and p332.

▯ **Info:** Bahía Solano: Palacio Municipal, Ciudad Mutis; ℘(4) 682 7049; www.posadasturisticasde colombia.com. Nuquí: Oficina de Cultura y Turismo, Palacio Municipal, Barrio La Unión; ℘(4) 683 6005; www. hotelesmarselva.com. Also check www. territoriochocoano.com.

◉ **Don't Miss:** Enjoy the sheer beauty of this bird-rich ecological treasure-trove packed with magnificent flora and fauna. Here, simple mud-and-thatch huts teeter along the Pacific coastal waters that provide fertile grounds for dolphins and migratory whales.

A BIT OF HISTORY

Originally populated by indigenous tribes, the Chocó has a contemporary history that starts with the arrival of the Spanish, and is centered on its **Afro-Colombian heritage** and related struggles. The Afro-Colombians found in the Chocó are of direct lineage to those forcibly exported to Colombia. These former slaves escaped the duress of other regions of Colombia, including working in the gold mines in Antioquia, and along with local **Embera** people, found that the only way to maintain and preserve their cultural identity and traditions was by living in isolated jungle areas. It has not been easy, given the geography, warring factions and lack of infrastructure.

Because of this displacement to an isolated, "forgotten" territory, there is a feeling among the modern-day Afro-Colombian *Chocoano* community that their region has received very little attention.

The Chocó department, as it is known today, was created in 1944. Under the regime of **Gustavo Rojas Pinilla** (1900-1975), it was due to be eliminated and divided between the departments of **Antioquia** and **Valle del Cauca,** but Pinilla was overthrown in 1957 before this division ever became a reality.

Beginning in the mid-1990s, the tranquillity of the department was shattered when a three-way **armed struggle** broke out among warring guerrillas, paramilitaries and government forces. The violence that has strafed the Chocó region has resulted in the internal displacement of enormous numbers of people fleeing the aggression. This displacement has put severe pressure on the already troubled capital of the department, **Quibdó** (Pop. 109,121).

Despite armed factions preventing the people of the Chocó, neutral to the conflict, from leading normal lives, and seriously threatening their cultural, ethnic and historical identity, the local

GETTING THERE

BY AIR - Satena has four weekly flights from Medellín to **Bahía Solano** 's Aeropuerto José Celestino Mutis, 3km/2mi south (☏ *4 682 7039; http:// portal.aerocivil.gov.co*). ADA flies less frequently from Medellín, Cali and Pereira. Planes are often delayed due to weather, so it's unwise to book connections for the same day you're booked to leave. **Nuquí** is served by direct flights from Medellín (45min; 85,000 COP), Quibdo (15 min; 35,000 COP) and Pereira (1hr; 95,000, COP).

BY BOAT - Weekly **cargo boats** from **Buenaventura** also ferry passengers occasionally. **Nuquí** can be reached by 1hr boat trip (16,000 COP) leaving from Arocia, near Guachalito. For travelers coming in from Nuquí or **El Valle**, small boats with outboard motors can be hired.

BY ROAD - There is no road from Nuquí to Bahía Solano. An unpaved 18km/11mi road from El Valle to Bahía Solano is accessed each morning by 4x4 vehicles (10,000 COP) or motorbike (20,000 COP).

GENERAL INFORMATION
SECURITY ISSUES

Considered a central part of the Zona roja, the Chocó department is key in the conflict between various warring factions and the cocaine trade. In recent years the government has made progress in securing the area. Do not be overwhelmed by the amount of military personnel in Bahía Solano. If they pull you to one side on the main street and ask you a few routine questions about where you are staying and ask to see your ID, they are here for your benefit. Yet, **caution** should be exercised and **local advice** should be sought before visiting, and when in, the region.

population is well aware of the **natural wealth** that lies within their realm. Successive waves of prospectors, both domestic and international, have arrived to exploit the gold, timber, energy and marine resources found within this strategic geography of the Pacific Coast.

BAHÍA SOLANO★

Formerly known as **Puerto Mutis**, Bahía Solano (Pop. 8,785) possesses a kind of other-worldly feel. Some months bring **migrating whales**, others **migrating birds**. The town itself is a bit run-down and feels as if it is eternally waiting for

Bahía Solano

Avia-ur/Proexport Colombia

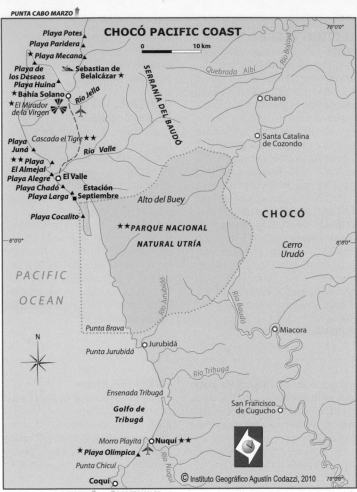

PUNTA CABO MARZO

CHOCÓ PACIFIC COAST

Playa Potes
Playa Paridera
Playa Mecana
Sebastian de
Playa de Belalcázar ★
los Deseos
Playa Huina
★ Bahía Solano
★ El Mirador
de la Virgen
Río Jella

SERRANÍA DEL BAUDÓ

Quebrada Albí

○ Chano

Cascada el Tigre ★★
Río Valle

Playa Juná
★★ Playa
El Almejal
Playa Alegre ○ El Valle
Playa Chadó
Playa Larga
Estación
Septiembre

○ Santa Catalina
de Cozondo

Alto del Buey

CHOCÓ

Playa Cocalito

★★ PARQUE NACIONAL
NATURAL UTRÍA

Cerro
Urudó

PACIFIC
OCEAN

Río Jurubidá

Río Baudó

Punta Brava

○ Miacora

N

Punta Jurubidá

○ Jurubidá

Río Tribugá

Ensenada Tribugá

Golfo de
Tribugá

San Francisco
de Cugucho ○

Morro Playita ○ Nuquí ★★
★ Playa Olímpica
Punta Chicuí

Río Nuquí

© Instituto Geográfico Agustín Codazzi, 2010

Coquí ○

GUACHALITO   LOS TERMALES *May not be reproduced either in its entirety or partially without the authorization of the Instituto Geográfico Agustín Codazzi - IGAC*

0   10 km

the long-promised, now abandoned, plan for a full highway linking it to Medellín. While it has little of aesthetic value, the town makes an ideal jump-off point for **ecological adventures**, and visitors interested in getting up close to nature will appreciate what the vicinity has to offer. Beyond the wooden fishing shacks and fishing nets awaiting repair are delightful ecological marvels waiting to be discovered.

A Bit of Geography

A thin strip of land located between the **Baudó** mountain range and the **Pacific Ocean** and ringed by jungle, Bahía Solano is, as its name suggests, a bay at the mouth of the **Jella River**. This large, semi-circular bay has become a favored spot for **humpback whales** to calf and nurse their young before migrating elsewhere. Such a remarkable sight has made the town a tourist destination in its own right for people eager to catch a glimpse of the whales.

Long before the fleeing Afro-Colombians settled here, or the opportunists from Medellín came, scenting a tourism boom that never materialized, the area was a preferred fishing spot for the native **Embera Indians**.

Since the arrival of a large military presence to combat the town's role as a key narcotics transshipment point, security has improved and **sports fishing** enthusiasts and **scuba divers** have been attracted to these abundant waters.

Beaches

In the town of Bahía Solano, there is no truly enticing beach, but nearby there is an abundance of riches.

For all of these beaches, in particular those visited by hiking along the coastline, check in advance with the locals about tides so that you do not become stranded.

A 2hr walk *(or 15min boat ride)* leads to **Playa Huina** *(NW of Bahía Solano)*, a wild stretch of unbroken beach with its own set of tourist resorts, hotels and restaurants.

Wander along jungle pathways that reveal pristine brooks and small waterfalls ideal for a dip and arrive an hour and a half later at **Playa Mecana**★ *(NE of Bahía Solano)*, unless you choose to get there by boat *(10min ride)*.

Other beaches at **Playa de los Deseos** *(30min boat ride, NW of Bahía Solano on the Punta Huina)*, **Playa Cocalito** *(4hr trek S via El Valle, in the Utría National Park*, **Playa Potes** *(25min boat ride, NE of Bahía Solano)* and **Playa Paridera** *(20min NE of Bahía Solano)* can also be visited.

🚶 Hiking Trails

Behind the town, a short but steep walk uphill leads to **El Mirador de la Virgen**★, from which unrivaled **views**★★ of the town and bay are permitted, as well as spectacular **sunsets**.

With appropriate footwear, and well worth the effort, a scramble upriver takes you over fallen trees and slippery rocks to arrive at the **Cascada Chocolatal** *(W of Bahía Solano)*. Allow the cool waters of this waterfall to pummel down upon you.

Remember that since it rains every day, the waterways remain full, and you should always err on the side of caution.

Whale-Watching Tours★★★

See sidebar on etiquette p334.

From July through October, Bahía Solano becomes one of the key focal

---

Chocó Endemic Bird Area (EBA)

The amazing endemic area that traverses the length of Colombia and Ecuador, is about 60,000sq km/23,166sq mi wide. With up to 1,600cm/630in of rain per year, it is arguably the wettest place on earth, with exceptional richness and endemism in a wide range of animals, including over 50 endemic bird species. This abundance is due to the fact that when the Andes were formed, the Chocó region was cut off from the Amazon rain forests, leading naturally to a divergent **evolutionary path**.

While in Bahía Solano or Nuquí, look for the Chocó Toucan (Ramphastos brevis), Rose-faced Parrot *(Pyrilia pulchra)* and Turquoise Dacnis-Tanager *(Pseudodacnis hartlaubi)*.

---

points In Colombia for tourists eager to witness the breaching and crashing of the formidable **humpback whales** and their young.

Passage on a **boat tour** that goes out into the bay and beyond can be arranged through any hotel. You can embark on a tour independently, once you have arrived in Bahía Solano, since there will be any number of operators offering tours, but you can guarantee that most people will be here on a package deal.

Diving Site★

Just moments offshore, but for experienced scuba divers only, there is the tantilizing treat of descending 34m /110ft to the **wreck** of the *Sebastian de Belalcázar*.

This scuttled former navy boat has a fascinating history in that it survived the attacks at **Pearl Harbor** and intercepted an arms shipment destined for the guerrillas. You can swim into some of the portholes. Enormous grouper, sharks, dolphins and whales frequent the artificial reef, so it is an excellent

Federico Puyo/El Tiempo/Proexport Colombia

Whale-Watching Etiquette

Once you start investigating which outfitter to use for your whale-watching trip, speak to your hotel owner and other tourists for their feedback. It is important that you go with a reputable firm that will respect these remarkable creatures and insure that they will continue to frequent these waters for the foreseeable future. For the most part, the environmental **WWF** (Worldwide Fund for Nature) has been working vigorously with the community here to provide training to boat drivers and guides. Please keep in mind that there are rules these operators should adhere to, and do not be afraid to mention them.

◆ Slowly approach whales from the side, never from the front or rear.
◆ Never cross the path of a whale or a pod of whales, especially to facilitate a closer encounter: they will most likely feel chased and avoid staying in the same area of the boat.
◆ Slow down to "no-wake" speed, and maintain a steady direction. The whales should feel less threatened, and the probability of a close encounter will be higher.
◆ Never position the boat so that it splits a pod or group of whales.
◆ Be aware of other boats in the surroundings. Whales should never feel encircled, and it is sensible to leave the area if it happens to be busy already.
◆ Be especially aware of the presence of female whales and their calves.
◆ Never spend more than 20min with whales, unless they want to spend a longer time with you.
◆ Never feed whales, which may cause problems in the long run. It is vital not to disturb their natural feeding habits.
◆ Try to make as little noise as possible.
◆ Be aware of possible signs of distress, and leave the area at very low speed if you notice any.

place to view the fauna up close and in their own habitat.

Sports Fishing★★
Heading north 3hrs by boat reveals the rocky inlets, crystalline pools and plentiful marine life of **Punta Cabo Marzo**. In the 1980s and early 1990s, the open waters offshore became a preferred fishing spot for big-name tourists hop-

ing to snare a **blue marlin**, **tuna** or **amber jack**. Unfortunately, the area, recognized for its concealed entrances and still waters, was coveted by the country's warring groups as the ideal place to receive shipments of arms and offload illicit goods. The situation has since improved, but check with local authorities before planning a trip here. Boats carrying suspicious shipments come under scrutiny of the Colombian navy, and smugglers occasionally toss their cargo (cocaine) overboard.

EL VALLE

Access by boat from Nuquí, but there is no connecting road between the two towns. There is an 18km/11mi unpaved road from El Valle to Bahía Solano that is served by early morning 4x4s that fill up fast.

El Valle could be described as the Pacific coast's one-horse town, but in addition to its central street, this fishing, farming and timber community is blessed with incredible beaches and access to the amazing **Parque Nacional Natural Ensenada de Utría**★★, with its palm-lined beaches, mangroves and plentiful birdlife.

Visit

The town itself, which has little infrastructure, sees virtually no tourism in the off-season, and many of the hotels close then. Its charming, brightly painted yet basic **wooden slat houses** give the place a rustic feel.

A standard by which all Colombian ecoresorts should be measured, the **El Almejal** ecolodge *(Calle 49A N # 65A-51; ℘(4) 230 6060; www.almejal.com.co)* is strongly committed to nature, conservation and education, as demonstrated by its own **whale-watching tower**, **butterfly garden** and **marine turtle sanctuary**. It also provides access to some of the nicest beaches along this coast such as **Playa Alegre** *(1km/.6mi NW of El Valle, before Playa El Almejal)*, **Playa Larga** *(2km/1mi SW of El Valle)*, **Playa Chadó** *(along the Vía Marítima pathway from El Valle towards the Río Chadó)* and **Playa Juná** *(2hr walk NW of El Valle)*.

Additional Sights
Playa El Almejal★★

2km/1mi NW of El Valle along the Vía Marítima pathway. Technically part of the Utría National Park.

Broad and 2km/1.25mi long, this beach is perhaps the ideal beach, with its dramatic crashing waves that have made it a popular haunt for the homegrown **surfing** crowd, and its calmer waters are suitable for **swimming**.

Estación Septiembre

Playa La Cuevita, approx. 5km/3mi S of El Valle. ⌘2,000 COP. ℘(1) 245 5700. *www.natura.org.co.*

During **turtle season** *(Sept–Dec)*, this turtle-nesting sanctuary offers ringside seats for this wonder of nature at **Playa Cuevita**.

Excursions
Cascada el Tigre★★

Technically part of the Ensenada de Utría Park. An easy 2hr walk north of El Valle brings you to these **waterfalls** which are well worth a visit if simply for the **jungle trail** that leads you here.

Parque Nacional Natural Ensenada de Utría★★

Reached after crossing a rickety suspension bridge and moving S from El Valle (30min by boat) or from Nuquí (1hr by boat). ⌚Open daily 8am–5pm. ⌘34,000 COP. ⌘Guided tours *organized by the Corporación Mano Cambiada del Municipio de Nuquí. ℘311 872 7887. www.nuquipacifico.com.*

Home to no less than seven types of **mangroves** (33ha/81acres), the park also boasts a **tropical rain forest** characterized by tree species that can reach

Mangrove forest, Parque Nacional Natural Ensenada de Utría

David Páez/Archivo Parques Nacionales Naturales de Colombia

The Exotic Morpho

If you dream of colorful butterflies flitting by, come to El Valle during high season *(Dec–Jan, Jun and Easter)*. Boat trips in **dugout canoes** are organized along the **Río Valle** to enable sightings of the silvery **Blue Morpho** butterfly *(Morpho menelaus)* and birds such as **kingfishers** that swoop down low over the water before taking up on the riverbanks.

45m/148ft in height, and by a large number of **bromeliads**.

An ideal stopping point for **migratory birds** such as the Blue Cotinga *(Cotinga nattererii)*, the White-necked Puff bird *(Notharchus hyperrhynchus)* and the Fulvous Vented Euphonia *(Euphonia fulvicrissa)*, the park is definitely a hot spot for birders.

If you are really dedicated and fortunate, you may glimpse the **Olive Ridley turtle** *(Lepidochelys olivacea)* hauling herself onto the beach to lay her eggs, but be sure to keep your distance. Other turtles, such as the **Leatherback** *(Dermochelys coriacea)* and the **Hawksbill sea turtle** *(Eretmochelys imbricata)* have also been observed, either on the beaches of the park or in the coral formations of the estuary.

In season, and with the necessary information, you may want to follow some of the **interpretive trails** that allow for trekking in the park and near the bay. These walks are ideal for observing birds, of course, but also snakes, frogs, insects and all kinds of mammals.

If you come here independently, be prepared to negotiate rickety bridges and river crossings.

Visiting with a **guide** is strongly advised though, since you may enjoy views of an unspoiled natural beach with coconuts strewn haphazardly about, but you are unlikely to know how to spot the **endemic wildlife**, or indeed where to look for it, on your own.

NUQUÍ★★

Found 50km/31mi to the south of Bahía Solano, Nuquí (Pop. 6,295) is accessible by boat from El Valle, Buenaventura or Bahía Solano. However, it is most easily reached by air from **Medellín** and **Quibdó** *(Aeropuerto Reyes Murillo, 2km/1mi SW of Nuquí; ℘(4) 863 6001; http://portal.aerocivil.gov.co)* with airline companies such as **Satena** *(flights on Mon, Wed, Fri & Sun; ℘(1) 605 2222; www.satena.com)* or **Aexpa** *(℘01 8000 116288; www.aexpa.com.co)*.

Given the ease with which the traveler can reach Nuquí and the extent of the accommodation possibilities, the area is an ideal jumping-off point for expeditions and adventures along the Chocó coastline.

Nuquí is becoming an adequate base for **whale-watching tours** and **diving** trips, for it is here that the Chocó is well compensated with internationally cel-

A World Away

Why talk about beautiful **Capurganá**★★ here, since it is located on the westernmost tip of Colombia's **Caribbean** coastline? Well, because this resort town is actually part of the **Chocó** department and so mentioned in this chapter. Close enough to nudge the border with Panama and sitting alongside the famously lawless **Darien Gap**, Capurganá cannot be reached by road from either the Caribbean or Pacific coasts, but requires a tumultuous **boat ride** from the dangerous port city of **Turbo**, or a **direct flight** with ADA airlines from **Medellín**. Given the difficulty of arriving here, you will not be surprised to find true paradise, shared between the towns of Capurganá and **Sapzurro**★★ (closer to Panama). There are lovely, undeveloped beaches that offer tranquillity as well as opportunities for adventure **ecotourism**.

Check with authorities for local security updates.

Nuquí's dense landscape

Proexport Colombia

ebrated **ecolodges** (*see ADDRESSES below*) located by a short boat trip either north or south of the town.

Visit

The small traditional town of Nuquí still belongs to the fishermen who ply the waters of the **Gulf of Tribugá,** but things are changing.

The area is becoming known to eco-aware travelers who want a full immersion in all things *Chocoano* and in reasonable style, as attested by one of the notable lodges in the area, the **Morromico**, ideally located in the gulf itself *(45min N of Nuquí by boat; 100,000 COP return trip; guided tours of the rain forest 90,000 COP; (8) 521 4172; www.morromico.com).*

ADDITIONAL SIGHTS
Playa Olimpica★

W of Nuquí. Guided tours organized by the Nuquimar Hotel. 27,000 COP. (4) 683 6194. http://nuquimarhotel.com.
This 5km/3mi-long beach lends itself to water sports such as **windsurfing** and **kite-surfing**, but it is mostly famous for having Colombia's best waves and therefore attracting a surfer crowd.

Coquí

8km/5mi SW of Nuquí, 20min boat ride.
Take a trip in a dugout canoe through the **mangroves** of Coquí.

Stop by the **indigenous village** of the same name, and catch sight of several endemic bird species.

EXCURSIONS
Los Termales

25km/16mi SW of Nuquí. 4,000 COP. More info available from the local lodge of Los Termales. (4) 683 6474. www.posadasturisticasdecolombia.com
This is a fairly nearby settlement with an adjacent **hot springs**.

Guachalito★

Guachalito definitely deserves investigating, and could easily be the entire focus of your trip to the Chocó.
Here you are treated to naturally gray sandy beaches, small inlets and some of the better ecolodges found in the region, such as **El Cantil** *(35min boat ride SW of Nuquí; 4 252 0707; www. elcantil.com)*, **Piedra Piedra** *(1hr boat ride SW of Nuquí; 315 510 8216; www. piedrapiedra.com)* and **Pijiba** *(35min boat ride SW of Nuquí; (4 474 5221; www.pijibalodge.com)*.
As you stroll into the encroaching forests, orchids, heliconias and all manner of birds come into close proximity. Whale-watching trips can be launched from here, as can scuba and snorkeling expeditions. There are also opportunities for surfing and kayaking.

ADDRESSES

🛏STAY

In recent years, forward-thinking entrepreneurs, mainly from Medellín, have constructed award-winning **ecolodges** to entice the more intrepid traveler to these lands. While there are some notable lodges in other areas, such as El Almejal in El Valle *(see below),* in Nuquí you have several choices. North of Nuquí is the highly recommended Morromico Lodge. South of town, you can choose any one of several fabulous destinations such as El Cantil, Piedra Piedra and Pijiba. What makes these places special is their dedication to the conservation of the environment. They educate their guests about the fragility of this diverse area, while making sure patrons get the most out of their trip here. Low-impact activities are proposed, such as hikes through different communities, during which you will have the opportunity to speak to the locals, perhaps spot a brightly colored tree frog, and wash off the day's dust in the ocean.

$ Hotel Palmas del Pacífico – *One block behind the main road leading to the airport, Northern sector, Nuquí.* ✗ ✆*(4) 683 6010. 20 rooms. www.facebook.com.* Cabanas in this coral-colored hotel are adequate, even if a bit worn. As with most hotels in this region, the Palmas del Pacífico caters to tourists coming in from Medellín, so two meals—plus an option for the flight from Pereira—are included in the room rate.

$$ El Almejal – *Playa El Almejal, 14km/ 9mi (40min by jeep) towards El Valle from the Bahia Solano airport.* ✆*(4) 230 6060. www.almejal.com.co. 12 cabins.* Cabins at this relatively luxurious ecolodge are designed to take advantage of sea breezes by allowing guests to open shutters on the opposite walls of the sitting area. Each cabin has two bedrooms, a private bath, and a terrace. There's a man-made swimming hole on-site, along with a turtle-breeding facility and a lookout point from which you can sometimes spot whales off the coast.

$$ Posada Vientos de Yubarta – *1km/.6mi north of Nuquí center along the beach.* ✗ ✆*312 217 8080. www.posada sturisticasdecolombia.com. 6 rooms.* Nestled amid palm trees 100m/328ft from the beach, this new hostel can accommodate up to 12 people. The use of local materials gives this place character, while the bamboo and wood beds enclose sturdy, comfortable mattresses. Some rooms have TV and overlook the sea. Accessible by moto-taxi along the inner beach road, this posada has become a favorite place for locals to stay.

$$$$ Piedra Piedra Lodge – *15km/ 9mi south of Nuquí center between the headlands of Terco and Terquito.* ✗ ✆*315 510 8216. www.piedrapiedra.com. 7 rooms.* Piedra Piedra Lodge provides accommodations in comfortable cabanas that are wood-and-thatch huts built from materials all sourced from the region. Four bedrooms are spread over three floors in each, housing a maximum of 17 people (meals included in rate). Each room has a bathroom and a large deck. Close to beaches, rivers, waterfalls, thermal springs and jungle trails, the lodge is particularly popular with birders and whale-watchers. The hotel also organizes catch-and-release sport fishing, marine and jungle safaris, and bird-watching expeditions.

$$$$$ El Cantil Ecolodge – *Quebrada Piedra Piedra, Vereda Termales, Municipio de Nuquí ; 35min south of Nuquí by boat.* ✗ ✆*(4) 252 0707 or 352 0729. www.el cantil.com. 7 rooms.* This 10-year-old ecolodge has seven large, comfortable rooms, with a maximum capacity of six people in each. Every room has a well-equipped bathroom, a stunning jungle view, and there's a lovely communal terrace facing the ocean. The hotel itself is built with tempered wood and a shingled roof. Guests are generally picked up at the airport and taken directly to the hotel by the owners' powerboat. For individual boating fun, there are kayaks, bodyboards and surfboards on hand for guests to use. All meals are included in the room rate.

$$$$$ Pijiba Lodge – *Playa de Terquito, Termales; or one hour south of Nuquí, along the coast by boat.* ✕ ✆*(4) 474 5221. www.pijibalodge.com. 6 rooms.*
In order to harmonize with the natural landscape, palm fronds and other local materials were used to construct the cabins here. Three duplex cabins without electricity each have two rooms with beds for eight people. There are hammocks on the deck, windsurfing gear and surfboards for rent, and the staff will organize whale-watching or scuba-diving trips. Sample tasty local fare for breakfast, lunch and dinner at the Pijiba's restaurant (meals are included in the room rate).

♟/EAT

Private Residences in El Valle – Hotels serve food only for large groups in Nuquí, but a number of local women cook Colombian fare for tourists in their homes, both for lunch and dinner. Reservations are required.

$ Residencia La Coti – ✆*(4) 682 7948.* Here you will dine on local dishes, not all of which consist of fish and rice. Give her advance warning and she'll also make you local specialties such as *jaiba con coco* (crayfish in coconut milk).

$ Residencia Dona Pola – ✆*(4) 683 6058.* This residence sits on a side street near the hotels of Nuquí. Dona Pola cooks up enormous quantities of traditional local food and usually needs about a two hour notice from guests.

$$$ El Mirador – *Just past El Almejal on the main beach, Playa El Almejal; 14km/ 9mi (40min by jeep) towards El Valle from the Bahia Solano Airport.* ✆*(4) 230 6060.* You'll find El Mirador atop a rocky outcropping. On Fridays and Saturdays, you can sit at the tables drinking rum while listening to the bar's reggae band, complete with the sound of the waves crashing in the background. **Regional Colombian**.

🏃‍♂️RECREATION

Turtle Watching at Estación Septiembre – *Playa Cuevita (5km/3mi south of El Valle).* ✆*(1) 245 5700. www. natura.org.co.* This is the only place on the Colombian Pacific coast where you can see multiple species of marine turtles, which lay their eggs on the beaches between September and December. **Estación Septiembre**, a national sanctuary, provides inexpensive rooms if you want to stay. With a beach that's too steep to land a boat, the sanctuary is most easily accessible by bike or on foot. Ask your hotel staff to recommend a guide for a nighttime turtle walk from El Valle.

Parque Nacional Natural (PNN) Utría – *1hr south of Nuquí by boat. Tours organized by Corporación Mano Cambiada del Municipio de Nuquí.* ✆*311 872 7887. www.nuquipacifico.com. 34,000 COP entrance fee.* One of the best places to see whales from land is from a narrow mangrove-lined cove in this national park, which encompasses three distinct ecosystems: rain-forest jungle, mangrove swamp and coral reefs.
Mano Cambiada in Nuquí runs the park concessions, including cabins and boat transportation between Nuquí and El Valle or Bahia Solano. They can also organize a guide to take you on foot to Lachunga, from which you can reach the visitor center at Jaibana.

Hiking around Bahia Solano – Hike upriver 30minutes from the Quebrada Chocolatal (at the southern end of town) through towering jungle to the lovely Cascada Chocolatal. Or walk to Playa Mecana, a pristine beach strewn with coconut palms, at low tide. For more ambitious guided walks, contact **Rocas de Cabo Marzo** (✆*4 682 7525; www.posadasturisticasdecolombia.com).*

On the Water – *For more information, contact the tourist offices in Nuquí* (✆*4 683 6005) or El Valle* (✆*4 682 7049).* Whether by kayak or guided wooden boat, navigating the park's waterways to the area's many waterfalls offers great rewards. In the offshore waters, sport fishermen catch record-breaking blue marlin and sailfish from a zone that extends to Panama. For surfing, contact Memo at El Cantil *(opposite page),* a veteran surfer and the most knowledgeable person about the breaks in these parts.

Pacific South Coast★

Valle del Cauca, Cauca, Nariño

The southern Pacific region in Colombia comprises the three sizable and well-populated departments of Valle del Cauca, Cauca and Nariño. Yet, the coastal strip remains largely unsettled due to logistical difficulties, lack of infrastructure and the armed conflict. The absence of modern advancements in this part of the country has left the region fairly free of large-scale tourism, and has preserved the integrity, authenticity and beauty of its coastline. Isla Gorgona, a former penal island, is a perfect example of such tranquillity, and is a coveted and protected natural reserve. It is not all idyllic though, as the Colombian internal conflict has severely affected life in the key port towns of Tumaco and Buenaventura, two smuggling access points and major gateways to the Pacific.

◔ **Michelin Maps:** p329 and p343.
▯ **Info:** Buenaventura: No formal tourist office, but tour companies on the Muelle Turístico, in the port; ✆(2) 241 9120; www.labuenaventura. com. Guapi: Oficina Guapi Gorgona, Hotel Rio, Carrera 2 and Calle 11; ✆(2) 840 0196. www.aviatur.travel. Tumaco: Oficina de Turismo, Office 302, 3rd Floor, Edificio Alcaldía, Calle 11 and Carrera 9; ✆(2) 727-1201; www.tumaco. com.co. Also check www. colombiatudestino.com.
☺ **Don't Miss:** Turtle hatching or birthing season in Parque Nacional Natural Sanquianga; Isla Gorgona's preserved ecosystem; and for expert divers only, UNESCO World Heritage Site Isla de Malpelo.

A BIT OF HISTORY

Situated on the island of **Cascajal,** the city of **Buenaventura** was founded in 1540, making it the older of the two major cities on the Pacific. **Tumaco** was founded a century later, in 1640. It is the area of Tumaco, however, closer to the border with **Ecuador**, that has yielded significant **archaeological discoveries** such as gold nose **jewelry** and **ceramic figurines**, particularly around the mouth of the San Juan River.

Spanish conqueror of the Inca empire, **Francisco Pizarro** passed through the area of the **Tumas**, whose territory extended through **Esmeraldas** in Ecuador. The rapid population of the region was due to the discovery of **gold** and **platinum**. Over time, the area suffered the same misfortune from periodic marauding raids by English **pirates**. Currently the inhabitants of these fertile lands are confronting similar threats as their neighbors face in the Chocó Region

due to the **internal conflict**. Both ports represent key points for the exportation of Colombian **cocaine**, a fact that has unfortunately rendered theses ports quite dangerous and unsafe.

In addition to the socio-economic problems afflicting the region, a great number of **environmental challenges** face the central government and the inhabitants of these regions. **Deforestation** of mangrove swamps has left some communities unprotected from Pacific storms and without a source of food, since the **mangroves** hold resources of benefit to the area's inhabitants.

BUENAVENTURA

▷ *142km/88mi from the city of Cali (NW via Lobo Guerrero and Dagua).*
Buenaventura (Pop. 324,207) resembles a sort of tropical Gotham of the Batman comics, lawless and dangerous, with severe poverty, high levels of crime and

GETTING THERE

BY AIR - Guapi is served by **Aeropuerto Juan Casino Solis** (📞840 0188) with direct flights from Cali and Popayán or charter service. Airlines include AEXPA (www.aexpa.com.co), Satena (www.satena.com).

BY BOAT - Buenaventura is reached by tourist **speedboats**, which go both north and south from the tourist wharf and by **cargo boats** departing from El Pinal. Tourist boats from the muelle turistico in Buenaventura also go to Guapi (3-4hrs; 80,000), and Juanchaco (1.5hr; 50,000 COP return) from which it's possible to walk the 2.5km/1.5mi to Ladrilleros or take a **motorcycle** (5min; 2,000 COP). Groups can haggle with **jeep** drivers who wait for them at the end of the Juanchaco Beach (around 25,000 COP). Other boats take passengers between Guapi and Charco (50min; 35,000 COP) and from there to Tumaco (3.5hrs; 85,000 COP). Asturias (tourist speedboat) 📞242 4620 or 313 767 2864. Pacifico Express 📞241 6507 or 313 715 3335.

GETTING AROUND

ON FOOT - Walking to tourist sights and on the beaches of these towns is possible, but much caution should be taken. The area's extreme poverty and smuggling activity add up to potential danger for the unsuspecting traveler. It's advisable to use the services of a guide or travel with a **reputable tour company**. Get reliable advice about where is it safe to go.

There has been considerably more police presence and army patrols in the area, but travelers should check the situation before planning a visit to Buenaventura.

homicide as the guerrilla, paramilitaries and emerging groups jostle for control of this key port.

Hot and **humid**, with an average year-round temperature of 28ºC/82ºF, it is a disorganized and architecturally barren town. Its stained buildings degrade in the humidity, as if ready to be reclaimed by the tropical elements. Easily reached by bus from **Cali** and regular flights from **Bogotá**, it is not without its positive aspects though, such as being an ideal **starting point** for excursions in the region.

San Cipriano★★

The inaccessible town of San Cipriano sits just inland, off the **Cali-Buenaventura road**. Locals have connected their hometown—unreachable by road—to nearby Córdoba by what is known as the *brujita* (little witch), a small motorbike and gravity-powered, no-frills railway service. Visitors pay a small fee and hop onto the open trolley platform for a **daring**, yet picturesque ride along the Pacific side of the mountain range. In San Cipriano, you can float **inner tubes** along the clear waters of the nearby river, swim in the pools of **waterfalls** and enjoy an area rich in such **fauna** as bears, monkeys, toucans and hummingbirds. SE of Córdoba, between Buenaventura and Buga. Rail trolley approx. 🚃10,000 COP round-trip. Haggling required.

Riding the brujita

© Luis Robayo/AFP/Getty Images

Visit

Visitors are reminded to use common sense and stick to the main tourist areas, including the **Muelle Turístico**, a floating wharf at the center of Buenaventura port. *4,000 COP.* *(2) 241 9120.* *www.labuenaventura.com.*

EXCURSIONS
Bahía de Málaga★★

20km/12mi NW of Buenaventura (1hr by boat).

Home to both indigenous and Afro-Colombian communities, the area around the bay is also the site of Colombia's most important **naval base** in the Pacific, responsible for interdiction efforts across some 336,700sq km/130,000sq mi. Bahía de Málaga, recently declared a national park, is famous for its extravagant **plant life**, but the real star attraction here is the **humpback whales** that come in large numbers to the bay to breed, give birth and nurse their young.

With an ideal average temperature of 25°C/77°F, the warm coastal waters of Bahía de Málaga have recorded the highest reproductive rate in the Colombian Pacific, and one of the highest birth rates in the world.

Needless to say, this location makes an excellent point to start a **whale-watching excursion**, while touring the hundred or more islands and rocky promontories offshore.

For most visitors, favorite places to visit close by include the two cascades of **Las Sierpes** *(where Bahía de Málaga meets the Río Bonguito)*, **La Piscina** waterfall *(close to Las Sierpes)*, and the beaches of **Playa Dorada** and **Chucheros** *(southern end of the Bahía de Málaga).*

For local culture, head to the community of **La Plata** *(NE part of the Bahía de Málaga, on the Archipiélago de La Plata)* to listen to some traditional **currulao** music and perhaps even dance a little.

Juanchaco

Located within Bahía de Málaga, just 1hr north by boat from the Muelle Turístico in Buenaventura.

This town is atypical of Colombian coastal communities in that tall speakers have been set up to blare music at brief intervals in an attempt to attract more tourism. It is, however, an excellent spot for **whale watching**.

Ladrilleros

NW of Buenaventura, at the southwestern tip of Bahía de Málaga via Playa La Barra.

Ladrilleros can be reached by boat directly from Buenaventura, but a good option is to alight in Juanchaco, and walk there *(45min-1hr)*. First you

Coast near Juanchaco, Bahía Málaga

Miky Calero/Proexport Colombia

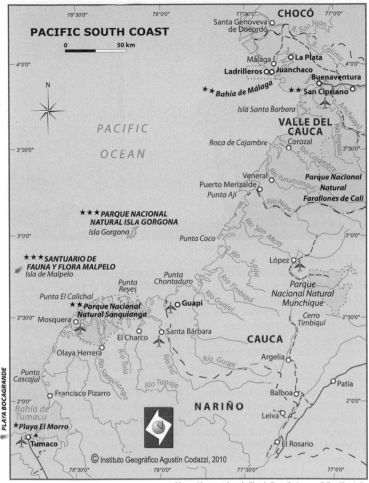

PACIFIC SOUTH COAST

0   50 km

PACIFIC

OCEAN

will enjoy ocean **views** from the flats near Juanchaco. Then, as the terrain steepens, it yields impressive **cliffs** near Ladrilleros.

Of course, **whale-watching excursions** are available here as well, but more enticing are the **canoe trips** into the thick mesh of tidal **mangrove** jungles.

GUAPI

🔾 *4km/2mi E of Aeropuerto Juan Casiano Solís.* ℘ *(2) 840 1167. http://portal.aero civil.gov.co. Accessed by daily flights from Cali and twice weekly flights from Popayán. Satena* ℘ *(1) 605 2222; www.satena.com.*

Just 6km/4mi away from the Pacific Ocean, the town of **Guapi** (Pop. 28,649) is little more than a staging point for trips to **Isla Gorgona** (🔾 *see below*). Founded in 1772, this **fishing town** saw its population increase dramatically when **gold** deposits were found nearby.

Tourists passing through can buy intricately handwoven goods, gold jewelry and **musical instruments**.

One of the most important pastimes in the department of Cauca is the *currulao*, an event that involves playing and dancing to **marimba** (wood xylophone) music.

Parque Nacional
Natural Isla Gorgona

Proexport Colombia

EXCURSIONS
Parque Nacional Natural Isla Gorgona★★★

▶ *46km/30mi NW of Guapi.*

🕐 *Boat trips depart daily from either Guapi (1hr30mn) or Buenaventura (cargo boats up to 12hrs; express boats 4hrs).* 🚍*34,000 COP entry fee. Check website for current prices of package tours.* 👣*Guided tours and accommodations organized by Aviatur ✆(1) 607 1597; www.concesiones parquesnaturales.com.*

This island was originally inhabited by people of the Tumaco, Tolita and Kuna cultures. In 1527 **Francisco Pizarro** fittingly named it "Isla Gorgona" in reference to the Greek goddess with hair made of snakes.

Once Colombia's equivalent of Alcatraz, the island held a former maximum-security **prison** (1960). In 1985 the island was turned into a protected national park for all to enjoy.

Blessed with a lake and 25 freshwater streams running across its 9km/5.5mi length, the ancient **volcanic** island hosts abundant fauna, its forest being home to **sloths** and the **blue lizard of Gorgona** (Anolis gorgonae).

A 5km/3mi nature trail called **Playa Palmeras** passes through a series of idyllic **beaches** such as Playa Blanca and La Azufrada *(SW of El Poblado)*, and actually ends at Playa Palmeras *(SW cor-*

ner of the island). A shorter trail called **Arbol del Pan** leads to El Problado and its **archaeological hall** (👣*guided tours organized by park rangers; ✆(2) 840 0190)* displaying artifacts from the pre-Columbian cultures who first settled the island.

It is possible to visit the **historic penitentiary** (👣*guided tours organized by park rangers daily upon request until 5pm; ✆(2) 840 0190),* but when walking, in particular after dusk, always keep in mind that the island literally crawls with **venomous snakes**.

The shoreline and offshore waters bubble with marine life, offering rewarding opportunities for **snorkeling** and **skin-diving**. Given the absence of shipping routes near the island, the surrounding ocean serves as a platform for observing **humpback whales**, killer whales, marine turtles, manta rays and other species drawn here to raise their young.

Santuario de Fauna y Flora Malpelo★★★

▶ *490km/304mi W of Guapi.*
Only 5 live-aboard diving ships are presently allowed access to Isla de Malpelo (including 3 based in Buenaventura), and only one ship is permitted to go out at a time. For details on the various options, contact the Oficina de Ecoturismo in Bogotá ✆(1)

353 2400 ext. 138; www.parques nacionales.gov.co. 46,000 COP for park entry fee plus 82,000 COP for diving permit.

This **UNESCO World Heritage Site**, Colombia's most distant territory, some 36hrs by boat out to the west in the Pacific Ocean, deserves mention, but only as an enticing trip for intrepid and highly **advanced divers**.

TUMACO

Reached overland from Pasto via Ipiales (300km/186mi NW of Pasto, following the Carretera 10 SW from Pasto) on a major highway.

There are twice daily flights on carrier Avianca, between Cali and nearby La Florida Airport (4km/2mi NE of Tumaco via the Puente del Morro); (2) 321 3434; www.avianca.com.

You will notice a significant military presence in **San Andrés de Tumaco** (Pop. 161,490), the second largest port on the Colombian Pacific.

Ecuador lies south of the city, but crossing the border here, while possible, is not recommended due to the high concentration of armed factions and traffickers.

Tumaco was built over three main islands: **El Morro**, **La Victoria** and **El Pindo**. It is not an unpleasant city, although some of its former glory has rubbed off. A visit to see the **iguanas** inhabiting the trees around the **Parque Colon**, near the cathedral, makes an interesting diversion.

SIGHTS
Casa de la Cultura

Calle Mercedes. Open Mon–Fri 8am–noon, 2–6pm. (2) 727 1201.

Here a small museum presents the history of the city and information about the surroundings as well.

Playa El Morro★

Near the airport, at the northern end of Isla Morro.

This black sand beach has a natural **arch.** It is supposedly the place where 17C pirate **Henry Morgan**, famous for daring feats of stealing Incan gold from the

Spanish, buried some **treasure**. Watch out for **stingrays** in the shallows here. Near the beach is the **Asociación de Artesanos** *(opposite Hotel Reynolds),* which shows various musical instruments, jewelry and crafts made from natural products in the Tumaco area.

ADDITIONAL SIGHTS

A 30min boat trip from the docks in Tumaco lies **Playa Bocagrande** *(W of Tumaco),* perhaps the principal attraction near to the city. In addition to the crystalline sea and fine silvery sand, there are the wetlands of **Papayal** and **Vaquería,** which abound with tropical vegetation and smaller beaches.

Check up-to-date security information about the areas around Playa Bocagrande as there is known coca cultivation here.

EXCURSION
Parque Nacional Natural Sanquianga★★

Boats can be contracted at the pier on Calle de la Merced, close to Calle del Comercio, to arrive at Playa Mulatos. (1) 353 2400. www.parques nacionales.gov.co.

A 4hr boat trip from Tumaco is well worth the time to get to this marine protected area.

Sanquianga contains no less than 30 percent of all of Colombia's Pacific **mangroves**, making it a key section of this amazingly biodiverse region. Composed of five rivers, the estuary delta system is an enormous alimentary source for numerous species such as **seabirds**, marine turtles, fish, crabs, sloths, **anteaters** and **caimans**.

To allow the species to recover somewhat, there is a protected **turtle hatchery** here to insure that the eggs and newly born marine turtles are prevented from being devoured by local fishermen, dogs or crabs.

Well-tended **trails** provide background information on the flora and fauna seen, and there are calm **beaches** for swimming as well as small indigenous and Afro-Colombian communities that can be visited.

ADDRESSES

STAY

$ Hotel Rio Guapi – *A block away from the point of departure for the Aviatur boat, Guapi.* ✕ ℘*(2) 840 0983. 40 rooms.* Probably the best hotel in town, this four-story lodging sits on the main street, close to the river. Simple rooms are accented with tile floors and concrete walls, and each has a bathroom, TV and ceiling fan. The on-site restaurant is known for its *ceviche guapense.*

$ Hotel Titanic – *Calle 1A # 2A-55, Buenaventura.* ✕ ⌥ ℘*(2) 241 2046. 37 rooms.* Close to Buenaventura's tourist wharf, this mid-range hotel occupies a five-story building in the safer part of the city. Each of the hotel's 37 rooms has cable TV, mini-bar, private bathroom, phone, Ethernet outlets and AC, but many of the rooms have no windows. The rooftop bar/restaurant affords good ocean views.

$$ El Morro – *Ladrilleros Beach.* ✕ ℘*(2) 334 2998. 40 rooms.* Stay here and you'll feel you've escaped the world. This tiny hotel has fantastic sea views, but no Internet access. Basic rooms have private bathrooms and fans. The bar, which is open to the public, is a wonderful place to sip a cold drink while watching the sun go down.

$$$ Concesión Gorgona – *El Planchon, Isla Gorgona; 46km/ 29mi (or 1hr 30min by boat) from the coast of Guapi.* ✕ ⌥ ℘*(1) 607 1597. www.concesionesparquesnaturales. com.32 rooms.* These government-sponsored accommodations feature rooms that sleep four. In the interest of maintaining as pristine an environment as possible on the island, a number of stringent prohibitions have been placed on visitors. They include animal and plant material, pets, various types of equipment and even loud music. Facilities include lovely communal areas, a swimming pool, Jacuzzis and hammocks, in dwellings that are smack in the middle of a stunning landscape.

$$$ Hotel Estelar Estación – *Calle 2 # 1A-08, Buenaventura.* 🅿 ✕ ⌥ ℘*(2) 243 4070. www.hotelesestelar.com. 75 rooms.* Opened in the Roaring 20s, this charming hotel is built in the Neoclassical style. Relax in deluxe rooms with verandas and panoramic sea views. The staff can hook you up with tours and whale-watching packages in season, and the hotel pool is open to the public from 9am to 6pm.

▯/EAT

$ La Galeria – *Barrio Pueblo Nuevo, Buenaventura.* Buenaventura's market is a bustling chaos of food stalls selling meat, fish and produce; there is a prepared-food area on the second floor. Costeña (from the coast) grandmothers make local dishes such as *sancocho de pescado* (fish in coconut milk) in the same way their families have done for generations. You can get here by taxi from the tourist wharf (3,000 COP), but take extra care with your belongings. **Regional Colombian.**

$$ Isla Gorgona Restaurant – *In the Concesión Gorgona hotel, Isla Gorgona.* ℘*(1) 607 1597. www.concesionesparquesnaturales.com.* The only restaurant on the island, this rustic place provides three meals a day—served at set times, so don't be late.A variety of hot and cold snacks, juices and non-alcoholic drinks (alcohol is not permitted on the island) are available for 25,000 COP per day (meals are included in the rate for hotel guests). Fish and rice figure prominently on the dinner menu. Strict island regulations limit what you can bring to and take from the restaurant. **Regional Colombian.**

$$ Las Gaviotas – *Calle 2 # 1A-08, Buenaventura.* ℘*(2) 243 4070. www.hotelesestelar.com.* Matching the style of the Hotel Estelar Estación in which it is located, this restaurant is noteworthy for its pleasant columned dining room as well as its carefully prepared regional Colombian seafood, peppered with international accents. **Seafood.**

🏃 RECREATION

WATER SPORTS

Canoeing through Parque Nacional Natural Sanquianga – *4hr boat trip from Tumaco. Boats can be hired from the pier on Calle de la Merced.* ✆*(2) 353 2400. www.parquesnacionales.gov.co.* Located in Colombia's Nariño Department, this park holds 30 percent of Colombia's Pacific mangrove forests. With a total of 80,000ha/197,684 acres, the park was created to protect a complex estuary formed by the Sanquianga, Patía, La Tola, Aguacatal and Tapaje rivers. PNN Sanquianga holds the highest concentration of birds on the Colombian Pacific coast and is a primary nesting ground for many of them. Travel with a guide or a tour agency (you'll find them on the pier in Tumaco) and expect to see the brown woodrail, gull-billed tern and neotropical cormorant among others. The labyrinthine estuary also harbors some 11,000 indigenous and Afro-Colombian communities.

Surfing – *Cabana Villa Malaty, Sector Villa Paz, Hacia La Barra.* ✆*320 666 2491.* From August to November is the best time to pursue ocean sports. You can rent surfboards (15,000 COP per hour), kayaks (30,000 COP per hour), and bodyboards (5,000 COP per hour) from Pedro Romero. You will find him on the beach at Ladrilleros (an hour's boat ride north of Buenaventura) on weekends and holidays or at his office during the week.

ISLAND FUN

Isle of Bocagrande – *30min by boat west of Tumaco.* A small island in the mangrove estuaries near Tumaco, Bocagrande is a magical place. Silvery sand and a mean temperature of 27°C/80°F await visitors here. While there are no offshore coral reefs, the area attracts birders who come to see the host of waterfowl that reside here. Get to the island using Transmart, which you'll find in Tumaco at the junction of Calle la Merced and Calle del Comercio (✆*316 682 7243).* Boats run to the island only during high season.

White-headed Capuchin, Parque Nacional Natural Isla Gorgona

Archivo Parques Nacionales Naturales de Colombia/Margarita Ramos

Parque Nacional Natural Isla Gorgona – *About 46km/29mi (or 1hr 30min by boat) off the coast of Guapi.* ✖ ✆*(1) 607 1597. www.concesionesparquesnaturales.com.* Within easy access of Buenaventura by boat, this former prison island and pirate's lair is covered by a dense tropical rain forest. Named for the number of poisonous snakes that make their home here, Isla Gorgona harbors myriad other creatures, including lizards, monkeys, bats, turtles and caimans. Natural beauty abounds on the island, whose waterways encompass some 25 freshwater streams, sheltered lagoons, and beaches that serve as turtle-nesting sites. Some of the old prison buildings have been converted into a research center, lodgings *(opposite page)* and a restaurant.

Exploring the island is only possible with a (free) guide, who will provide you with Wellington boots to protect your feet from snakes. The island's dive shop offers great tours, PADI courses and equipment for rent.

Take everything you might need as there are no shops or services on the island. All visits must be pre-booked through Aviatur on behalf of the PNNs de Colombia based in Cali *(www. concesionesparquesnaturales.com).* It's better to make your reservations as early as you can since these popular trips often get overbooked. There's a 34,000 COP fee to enter the park, and the cost of an overnight stay can be found on the park's website.

As one of Colombia's great expanses of topographical diversity, the Inner Southwest region is characterized by striking, contrasting terrain. Among dramatic altitudinal and climatic variations, lush tracts of jungle lead to snow-topped mountains, cactus-scattered sands and plunging valleys. Here dusty pastoral towns give way to whitewashed colonial settlements and some of Latin America's most amazing pre-Columbian archaeological sites. Sparkling mountain waters nurture the region's sugarcane, cotton, tobacco, soy and coffee crops across vast swaths of countryside. Subdued religious prayer sites, pilgrim trails and other-worldly stone-carved deities honor ancient gods and spirits. Cali, the region's capital and Colombia's third-largest city, is recognized by its ultra-modern sprawl of futuristic high-rise towers. Dubbed "Salsa City," Cali boasts a rich and rhythmic salsa tradition and is proud of the sashay, sway and sizzle found in its dozens of urban dance halls.

Highlights

1 Visit **Zoológico de Cali**, Colombia's finest zoo, with its special emphasis on endemic South American species (p356)

2 Witness **Popayán's Holy Week celebrations**, upholding a tradition said to be the most authentic outside Seville (p367)

3 Explore landscapes of lakes, marshy jungle lowlands, rugged rocks and snowy peaks at **Parque Nacional Natural Puracé** (p371)

4 Gaze at hundreds of ancient rock-carved figurines at **Parque Arqueológico de San Agustín**, Colombia's archaeological capital (p385)

5 Admire the unusual sight of a sanctuary straddling a verdant canyon on a long twin-arched bridge at **Las Lajas** (p397)

The Land and Its People

In terms of sheer geography, this is a land of striking contrasts indeed. Here the country's three cordilleras become separate, opening up to two great fertile valleys occupied by some of the nation's most vital waterways: the **Cauca** and **Magdalena Rivers**.

Topping 4,000m/13,123ft, eruptive mountains such as the **Puracé**, one of the most active volcanoes in Colombia, and the ominous **Galeras**, 2010's major volcanic threat, are an omnipresent component of the landscape. *Lagunas* or altitude lakes sometimes encased in mysterious cloud forests like Laguna de la Cocha, near the city of Pasto, occasionally lighten up the landscape. A true oddity, caused by Andean rain shadow, the spectacular cactus-clad **Tatacoa Desert** emerges from an otherwise fertile surrounding like a kind of miniature Grand Canyon, with monoliths á la Monument Valley, though smaller in scale. **Climate** in the Inner Southwest region varies dramatically by altitude and local conditions. Nowhere is this variation better exemplified than in Cali, a city with a tropical savanna climate that records significantly different amounts of precipitation between its southern and northern portions due to a sizable change in altitude of about 2,000m/6,560ft from one end of town to the other.

The Inner Southwest is home to a wide variety of people, most apparent at the Pasto's World Heritage Carnaval Negros y Blancos that celebrates the country's ethnic and cultural differences.

This multifaceted mix of influences is reflected in human habitats that range from isolated indigenous communities tucked away in the folds of the Andes to Cali, a bustling metropolis of some 2 million people and an academic center that has attracted a dazzling mélange of Middle Eastern, European and African populations. Preserved colonial cities, such

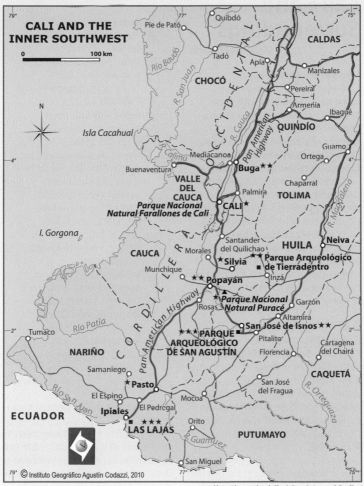

CALI AND THE INNER SOUTHWEST

0   100 km

Pie de Patá
Quibdó
CALDAS
Tadó
Apía
Manizales
Río Baudó
CHOCÓ
Pereira
Armenia
Ibagué
QUINDÍO
Isla Cacahual
Guamo
Ortega
Mediacanoa
Buga ★★
Buenaventura
VALLE DEL CAUCA
Palmira
Chaparral
TOLIMA
Parque Nacional Natural Farallones de Cali
CALI ★
I. Gorgona
Santander del Quilichao
HUILA
Neiva
CAUCA
Morales
★ Silvia
★★ Parque Arqueológico de Tierradentro
Munchique
Inzá
★★ Popayán
Garzón
Rosas
Parque Nacional Natural Puracé
Altamira
Río Patía
Tumaco
San José de Isnos ★★
Cartagena del Chairá
★★★ PARQUE ARQUEOLÓGICO DE SAN AGUSTÍN
Pitalito
Florencia
NARIÑO
Samaniego
★ Pasto
San José del Fragua
CAQUETÁ
El Espino
Mocoa
Ipiales
El Pedregal
ECUADOR
Orito
★★★ LAS LAJAS
PUTUMAYO
San Miguel

79° © Instituto Geográfico Agustín Codazzi, 2010

May not be reproduced either in its entirety or partially without the authorization of the Instituto Geográfico Agustín Codazzi - IGAC

as world-renowned Popayán, exhibit Baroque and early Colonial religious architecture, while sanctuaries such as Las Lajas form impressive landmarks.

The region's rich past surfaces spectacularly in unique archaeological sites like **Tierradentro** and **San Agustín**, which remained isolated and virtually unknown for centuries, but now bear witness to the creeds and hopes of long-vanished civilizations.

Great **religious events**, such as Popayán's Easter processions, draw massive national and international crowds.

Like everywhere in Colombia, **music** has a central role in the area's cultural life, but nowhere better than in Cali, self-declared salsa dance capital of the world. The Feria de Cali in December should by no means be missed.

The strong police presence noticeable in this part of the country offers considerable peace-of-mind for travelers to the must-see major sights, since the region remains troubled by the convulsions of Colombia's inner conflict.

Cali★ and Surroundings

Valle del Cauca

Sensual, sassy Santiago de Cali—Colombia's third-largest metropolis—pulsates with music and dance rhythms as the nation's Capital of Salsa. Holding court over the city, the lofty Torre de Cali soars 42 floors into the clouds as Colombia's tallest urban skyscraper and third-highest building. Needle-thin spires and space-age structures dot the sugar-rich fields and spiny ridges of the Cordillera Occidental and Cordillera Central ranges. As the prosperous capital of the fertile agricultural Valle del Cauca, hot and muggy Cali forms a stark contrast to the surrounding pastoral landscape in character, climate and culture.

A BIT OF HISTORY

Cali was founded in 1536 by Spanish conqueror **Sebastián de Belalcázar**. In the 20C, the population of the city grew rapidly from 20,000 to over 2 million people because of its strategic location close to the **mining regions** of Antioquia, Chocó and Popayán, the port city of Buenaventura and the arrival of the railroad.

Livestock, sugarcane, beef, coffee, fruit, cheese and dairy products formed the bedrock of Cali's economy as the city's

▶ **Population:** 2,075,380.

⊙ **Michelin Maps:** p349, pp 354–355 and p359.

▌ **Info:** Tourist information points (PITs) at Cali's Terminal de Transporte, Calle 30N # 2-29; Centro Cultural de Cali, corner of Carrera 4 and Calle 6. ℘(2) 885 6173. www.caliturismo.com.

☺ **Don't Miss:** The Juanchito district and its dozens of salsa joints, bars and dance halls; the historic Plaza de Cayzedo and the San Antonio colonial district; a fiercely-fought football (soccer) match between Cali's two home teams, America de Cali and Deportivo; a ride aboard the atmospheric Tren Turistico Café y Azucar, journeying through rolling countryside to La Cumbre and La Tebaida.

industrial sector experienced steady growth.

Though largely a newly developed city (and proud of it), some of its **historical architecture** has been retained to showcase fine old buildings along with the new. Before hosting the Pan Amer-

View of Cali from San Antonio district

© Richard McColl/MICHELIN

GETTING THERE

BY AIR - **Alfonso Bonilla Aragón International Airport** (CLO) (*2 280 1515; www.aerocali.com.co*) lies 20km/12mi northeast of Cali, in Palmira. Avianca provides frequent flights from Bogotá, as well as flights from Guapi, Cartagena, Pasto and Tumaco. **Shuttle buses** leave the airport every 10min (daily 5am–9pm) for the city's bus terminal *(see below)*. A **taxi** ride to the city center takes about 30min but is more expensive than a bus ride. **BY BUS** - The city's **bus terminal** sits near Chipichape, a 25min walk north of the city center (www.terminalcali.com). **Long-distance buses** arrive from cities near the Pacific and Caribbean coasts and from Bogotá (12 hrs), Medellin (9 hrs) and Pasto (9 hrs).

BY TAXI - Taxis are metered. For safety, have your hotel call the cab and give you the taxi number or code; get in only that taxi. When you step into the cab, check the meter.

GETTING AROUND

BY PUBLIC TRANSPORTATION-MIO (Masivo Integrado de Occidente) is a mass-integrated public transportation system that connects 77 stations across 243km/151mi, and centers on **articulated buses** that move in dedicated lanes. Cost per ticket is about 30 COP. MIO operates 18hrs a day (5am–11pm). **SECURITY** - Exert caution when exploring quieter neighborhoods away from police patrols, and apply common sense.

---

ican Games in the 1970s, Cali was the focus of considerable construction. Since then, Colombia's political instability and violence have resulted in urban growth in fits and spurts, but today's expanding population continues to stretch the city at the seams.

Essential to former president Álavaro Uribe's crackdown on Colombia's criminal elements was an uncompromising, hard-line approach to Cali's mightiest drug cartels. In recent years, many of the most powerful drug lords have been extradited to the US for trial. In 2006 the jailing of the "godfathers" of the **Cali Cartel**, Gilberto Rodriguez Orejuela and his brother Miguel, marked the end of the longest running and most important investigation in US Drug Enforcement Agency history.

A Sporting Tradition

Cali was the first Colombian city to host the **Pan American Games** in 1971, and today, it continues to reap the rewards of a strong sporting heritage. The city is home to two of the nation's most successful **soccer** clubs: **Deportivo Cali** *(www.deporcali.com)* and **America de Cali** *(www.america.com.co)*.

As often is the case in South American football (soccer), a fierce rivalry exists between the two clubs, which are divided by clear class distinctions.

An affluent upper class supports Deportivo Cali, while fans of America de Cali tend to be from working class neighborhoods on the rundown outskirts of the city. In the past, tensions have erupted into violence during derby matches.

The city's many football fans flock to two large stadiums, the **Estadio Deportivo Cali** (built in 2007, capacity 58,000) and the **Estadio Olímpico Pascual Guerrero** (built in 1937, capacity 45,625). Other sports disciplines also benefit from Cali's sporting infrastructure. The city is home to a covered arena called **El Pueblo**, mainly used for national **basketball** events.

Several major **international** sports competitions have taken place in Cali, including the Games of the Pacific, the World Basketball Championship, the World's Roller Hockey Championships, various women's basketball and swimming events, the Pan American Speed-Track Cycling Championships and the World's Roller Speed Skating Championship, to name a few.

⊙ Photo Tips ⊙

For unrivaled photographs of Cali, take a taxi to **Monumento Las Tres Cruces**★★ *(on Cerro de las Tres Cruces, reached by Avenida 4 Oeste and Vía Normandía)*. As the focus of an annual Easter pilgrimage, the site dates back to 1937 and was built to counteract a legend relating to a devil's curse. At 480m/1,575ft, the monument towers over Cali, and the summit affords stunning **views** across its urban sprawl. Another option is a trip to the top of the **Torre de Cali** *(Avenida De Las Americas)*, Cali's highest skyscraper, at 183m/600ft.

CITY CENTER

A stroll around Cali's relatively small center and a little beyond will allow you to see most places of interest and soak up the atmosphere of Cali's architectural mix—a real insight into the growth and development of Colombia's "third city."

☙❧WALKING TOUR

◐ *Start from Plaza de Cayzedo, between Calles 11 and 12 and Carreras 4 and 5.*

Plaza de Cayzedo★

Soaring palms dominate the center of the plaza topped by a statue of independence leader **Joaquín de Cayzedo y Cuero**. Born in Cali in 1773 and quite the homespun hero, Cayzedo led the cry for independence on behalf of his city as a patriot soldier. He died in battle, and is honored by Cali in this prominent plaza as a martyr and a man of great courage and conviction.

Here under the trees of the plaza, all manner of people surround the monument, from hawkers, lottery ticket sellers and food vendors to business leaders, students and shoeshine boys.

Catedral San Pedro★

Corner of Calle 11 and Carrera 5A.

Located on the southern corner of the Plaza de Cayzedo, Cali's principal place of worship is a statuesque white structure that was built by prison labor. Its first stone was laid in 1772, but the church was not completed until 1841. Over the years, **earthquake damage** has caused erosion to the towers and façade, now patched up with modern materials.

However, the **interior** remains original and spectacular, with carved wood altars painted blue and gold, ornate shrines, etched white marble, hammered silver, stunning murals and dazzling crystal chandeliers.

◐ *From there, make a short detour by the river to see another much-visited Cali landmark.*

Iglesia de la Ermita★

Corner of Carrera 1A and Calle 13.

Housed inside this early 20C church is an 18C painting, **El Señor de la Caña** (Lord of the Sugarcane), which is said to have produced many miracles—hence the lines of Catholic **devotees**.

While in this area, take a look at **Puente Ortiz**, straddling the river. Located between Carrera 1 and Calle 12, this handsome bridge was built between 1840 and 1844. With distinctive stone arches, it is another major landmark in Cali. The bridge has been converted into a traffic-free **pedestrian walkway** that connects the northern part of Cali with the Downtown area.

◐ *Retrace your steps to the cathedral. Walk one block down Carrera 5, and turn left one block up Calle 10.*

Complejo Religioso de San Francisco

Between Carreras 5A and 6A and Calles 9A and 10.

Directly under the towering presence of the **Gobernación Building**, this compound comprises a set of 18C and 19C religious buildings that include the

Colombia's Salsa Capital

As the nation's self-proclaimed Capital of Salsa, Cali shimmies to an irrepressible rhythm that pulses through almost every arterial of this modern urbanscape. City-wide **bars**, **restaurants**, **studios**, **cafes** and car **radios** throb with a percussive Latin beat. More than 100 salsa CD vendors, 150 salsa orchestras, 5,000 salsa students and a host of frenzied maraca players add to Cali's musical character.

La Feria de Cali

Proexport Colombia

Visitors anxious to absorb Cali's energetic salsa **nightlife** will require plenty of stamina because when Cali's party people come out to play, they play hard. Expect to hear a wealth of good homespun salsa alongside imported classics from Cuba and Puerto Rico. There will be an occasional musical foray into samba, rumba and the syncopated ta-tum-ta-tum beats of natty bossa nova.

Yet it is Colombian salsa that truly energizes Cali's hip-swaying salsa-lovers—and on almost any given night, you'll find **dance halls** packed with crowds of sashaying, sassy movers in Downtown **salsotecas** (salsa bars). Be prepared to break out in a sweat as the pulsating sounds of bass, bongos, bells and brass accompanied by hypnotic strobe lights take hold.

Salsa club in Cali

Proexport Colombia

Join the throng of gyrating, weaving and swirling salsa fans in **Juanchito**'s 100-plus hottest dance halls, where more than 2,000 locals pour into this eastern suburb to party 52-weeks of the year. Listen for the vibrant non-traditional sounds of **Jairo Varela** and the **Grupo Niche** or other artists like **Lisandro Meza**, **Kike Santander**, **Joe Arroyo** and **Eddy Martinez**—Cali favorites with a sound as hot as the city itself.

Cali is also home to **La Feria de Cali**, a week-long salsa festival—the largest such homage to salsa on the planet—celebrated since 1957, from December 25 to December 30. This legendary hedonistic **music and dance marathon** saturates and exhausts the city, running from dawn until dusk and attracting partying salsa die-hards from all over the globe. After a full year of frenzied planning, the entire city surrenders itself to a mammoth celebration that paralyzes almost every street. Expect fiercely-fought dance-offs, showcase extravaganzas, leading salsa dance acts from all over the world and every dance, music and cultural venue packed to the rafters. For more information, access www.feriadecali.com.

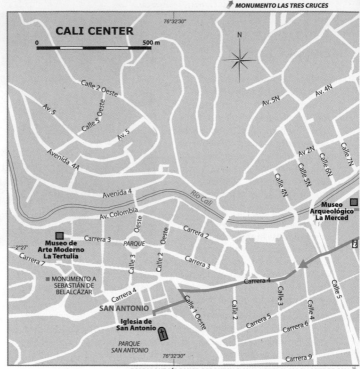

MONUMENTO LAS TRES CRUCES

CALI CENTER

0   500 m

N

76°32'30"

Calle 2 Oeste
Av. 5
Calle 5 Oeste
Av. 5
Avenida 4A
Avenida 4
Av. Colombia
Carrera 3
PARQUE
Carrera 7
Museo de
Arte Moderno
La Tertulia
2"27'
MONUMENTO A
SEBASTIÁN DE
BELALCÁZAR
Carrera 4
SAN ANTONIO
Iglesia de
San Antonio
PARQUE
SAN ANTONIO
76°32'30"

Río Cali
Av. 5N
Av. 4N
Av 2N
Calle 6N
Calle 7N
Calle 5N
Calle 4N
Museo
Arqueológico
La Merced
Calle 3
Calle 2
Oeste
Oeste
Carrera 2
Carrera 3
Carrera 4
Calle 1 Oeste
Calle 2
Carrera 5
Carrera 6
Carrera 9
Calle 3
Calle 4
Calle 5
Calle 5

ECOPARQUE RÍO PANCE, PARQUE NACIONAL NATURAL FARALLONES DE CALI

Convento San Joaquín, the **Iglesia de San Francisco**—a Neoclassical church with brick masonry and an altar in the Spanish Renaissance style—and the **Capilla de la Inmaculada**.

Parque de los Poetas★

Found between the Iglesia de la Ermita and the Teatro Jorge Isaacs (*Calles 12 and 13*), this park was built in 1995 in tribute to the **poets** of **Valle del Cauca**. Today, as a venue for cultural presentations, it remains a gathering point for **poets** and **writers**. On the last Thursday of each month, you'll find poetry lovers here en mass for **recitals** by new and established local talent in the spirit of Jorge Isaacs, Ricardo Niero, Carlos Villafañe, Antonio Llanos and Octavio Gamboa—all immortalized in the park's construction.

Museo Religioso y Colonial de San Francisco

Calle 9 # 5-59. ⓘ*Open Mon–Fri 9am–11am, 3pm–5pm. Advance reservations required.* ✆*(2) 884 2457.*

In echoed chambers, more than 350 pieces of priceless religious works of art are displayed in all their glory, from communion items and gilded paintings to grandiose high altars, statues and monuments.

Torre Mudéjar★

Corner of Calle 9 and Carrera 6.

This San Francisco complex also houses a magnificent relic of Arabic culture that is undoubtedly Cali's best-preserved architectural treasure and one of South America's most impressive. It is the city's only example of **Neo-Mudéjar art**—a resplendent 23m/75ft domed **bell tower**, constructed in patterned brick of geometric design.

This fine residue of the Arabic-influenced Spanish era was built in 1772. Spanning four sections, the building's **dome** itself

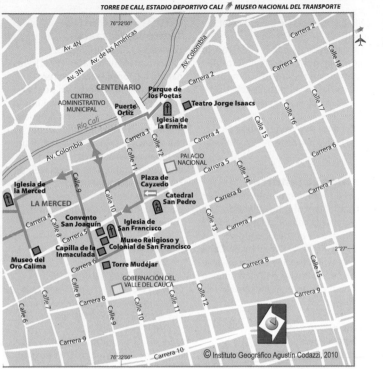

TORRE DE CALI, ESTADIO DEPORTIVO CALI ● MUSEO NACIONAL DEL TRANSPORTE

© Instituto Geográfico Agustín Codazzi, 2010

May not be reproduced either in its entirety or partially without the authorization of the Instituto Geográfico Agustín Codazzi - IGAC

is the true highlight: an opulent structure covered in **glazed tiles** and topped with a **wrought-iron cross**.

▷ *From the Complejo Religioso de San Francisco, proceed three blocks down Calle 9 before turning left for two blocks into La Merced district.*

Iglesia de la Merced
On the corner of Carrera 4 and Calle 7.
This edifice is Cali's oldest church, dating back to 1545, just nine years after the founding of the city. It is a charming whitewashed building in the Spanish Colonial style. Its simple interior of wood and stucco contains a heavily gilded Baroque **altar** topped by the *Virgin de las Mercedes* and a long, narrow nave.

Museo Arqueológico La Merced
Carrera 4A # 6-59. ◑*Open Tue–Sat 9am –6pm.* ◉*4,000 COP.* ✆*(2) 885 4665. www.museoarqueologicolamerced.org.*
Housed in the former La Merced Convent, this museum displays a com

prehensive collection of more than 11,000 pre-Columbian artifacts.
Among the highlights is an impressive sample of **ceramics** that belong to the diverse cultures of the Calima, Nariño, Quimbaya, San Agustín, Tolima and Tumaco, including ornate goblets decorated with bird and animal motifs. Carved wooden deities and construction materials typical of the ancient civilizations of Southern Colombia as well as later Colonial and Republican styles are exhibited. Also note the scale model of Cali.

▷ *Walk south on Calle 7 until you come to the Banco de la República's Gold Museum.*

Museo del Oro Calima
Calle 7 # 4-69. ◑*Open Tue–Fri 9am– 5pm, Sat 10am–5pm.* ✆*(2) 684 7754. www.banrep.gov.co/museo.*
Since its opening in 1991, the museum has focused on 8,000 years of history across the region, in particular on the

Calima people before the arrival of the Spanish.

Its excellent, if small, collection of Colombian gold and pre-Columbian pottery draws the crowds. Temporary exhibits depict various aspects of the Calima's metal-working heritage.

▷ *Continue west along Carrera 4 across Calle 5 and on to the San Antonio district.*

San Antonio District★★

Located southwest of the city center, this traditional **colonial** neighborhood has retained the feel of Cali's bygone era. Once part of the Downtown, it is now neatly self-contained by **La Calle Quinta**, which has helped to conserve its charm. Set on a hill, with San Antonio Park on the summit, it makes a lovely area for a stroll.

Iglesia de San Antonio★★
On Cerro Antonio.

This hilltop church, well-cared for by a team of dedicated nuns, was built in 1757 and contains some highly valuable 17C *tallas quiteñas* (carved-wood statues). Outside, a stall selling religious art stands close to a bench shaded by leafy trees—a great place to relax and soak up **views** of Cali.

Iglesia de San Antonio

Proexport Colombia

ADDITIONAL SIGHTS
Teatro Jorge Isaacs
Carrera 3 # 12-28. ℰ(2) 889 0320.

This handsome theater (1931) was named for **Jorge Isaacs Ferrer** (1837-1895), a famous Colombian poet and writer, whose romantic novel *María* has become a classic in Latin American literature. The theater was bought by the municipality in 1986 as part of the re-urbanization of the city's Downtown, and considerable care was placed on restoring its **Neoclassical** features.

It is now a venue for concerts, dance performances, theater and stand-up comedy.

Museo de Arte Moderno La Tertulia
Avenida Colombia # 5-105 Oeste.
◷*Open Tue–Fri 9am–1pm, 3pm–7pm, Sat 10am–1pm, 3pm–5pm. ⬮4,000 COP for temporary exhibitions.*
ℰ(2) 893 2942.

Housed in a modern building, this museum is home to the city's best art-house cinema, and hosts an ever-changing calendar of temporary exhibits of **contemporary paintings** and **photographic design**.

The museum contains a small theater that stages well-attended outdoor concerts, a highly regarded cinematic library with a number of Colombian film classics, and exhibit space for its huge body of works by national and international contemporary artists.

Upon leaving the museum, take a look nearby at Cali's **obelisk**, sculpted by Giovanni Fisher in 1929.

Zoológico de Cali★★
Corner of Carrera 2A Oeste & Calle 14 Oeste. ◷Open daily low season 9am–4:30pm, high season 9am–5pm. ⬮9,800 COP, child 6,800 COP. ℰ(2) 892 7474 ext 220. www.zoologicodecali.com.co.

This zoo is, without a doubt, Colombia's finest zoo, and one of the best in Latin America. An excellent collection of species native to Colombia and a magnificent host of lush, green gardens occupy some 10ha/25 acres. Approximately

Lemur, Zoológico de Cali
© Carlos Ortega/epa/Corbis

1,200 animals representing some 180 species enjoy a setting around lakes and mature shrubs.

An extremely pleasant place to spend the day, the zoo features picnic areas, cafes, restaurants and walking **trails** around numerous enclosures in eight special zones: insects, aquatics, avian, primate, reptile, butterfly, amphibian and turtle.

SURROUNDINGS
Museo Nacional del Transporte

◗ 16km/10mi NE of city center, close to the Aeropuerto Alfonso Bonilla Aragón, Vía Zona Franca Palmaseca. ◷Open Mon–Fri 8am–4pm, Sat–Sun & public holidays 9am–5pm. ◉10,000 COP. ℘(2) 270 5008.

This transport museum contains an impressive collection of motorbikes, helicopters, classic cars, steam trains, old planes and other means of transit, including carts typical of the rural areas of southwestern Colombia.

Wall-mounted narratives outline the history of transportation across the region, from the arrival of the railway to the building of Cali's airport, just a stone's throw away.

Ecoparque Río Pance

◗ 12km/8mi S of Cali via the road to La Voragine. ℘(2) 889 9407. Facilities include restaurants, cafes, shops, bridge-straddled pools, swimming baths, hiking trails and camping sites. Located along the clean waters of the **Río Pance** between the mountains and the plains of the Cauca River Valley, this highly popular eco-park (more than 72ha/178 acres) attracts hordes of families on weekends.

The park offers places to picnic, relax by the river, fish in the lake and stroll the bloom-filled trails of a well-stocked **botanical garden**.

Parque Nacional Natural Farallones de Cali

◗ 28km/17mi S of Cali via the road to Pichindé. At the corner of Carrera 11 and Calle 11. ◷Open daily 8am–5pm. ◉19,000 COP. ⬥Guided tours organized by the Oficina de Ecoturismo in Bogotá. ℘(1) 353 2400 ext. 138. www.parquesnacionales.gov.co.

Home to an important hydroelectric plant generating power for the city of Cali, this 200,000ha/494,210 acre leafy green park feels a world away from the urban hustle and bustle. It contains various ecosystems characteristic of the Andes, the Pacific Coast and the Cauca River, and is notable for its **endemic**

For Diehard Soccer Fans

Estadio Deportivo Cali – Located 8km/5mi NE along Carretera 25 en route to Palmira. Check website for schedule. Tickets (◉5,000-55,000 COP) may be purchased from several vendors including Licores Saney, Calle 15 # 3-10; Almacen Saturia, Calle 19 # 5-26; or Los Millán, Carrera 31 # 22-54, Palmira ℘(2) 518 3000 ext. 306.

Estadio Olímpico Pascual Guerrero – Located on Carrera 34 # 29-86, Barrio Versalles. Check website for schedule. Tickets (◉8,000-40,000 COP) may be purchased from several vendors including Sede Administrativa, Avenida 3 # 17-77; and Caseta La María, SE corner of the stadium, ℘(2) 513 0417 ext. 105.

Hacienda El Paraíso

Miky Calero/Proexport Colombia

species (monkeys, bears, eagles, snakes, peccaries, deer, pumas) and vast array of **birds**. Thick forests and springs can be found at altitudes that range from 200m/656ft to 4,100m/13,451ft above sea level.

Two popular **hikes** lead upward to **Pico Pance** and **Pico de Loro**, where scenic summits boast fine **views**. Indigenous groups, such as the Cholos Chocó, Paez, Nasa and Inga Embera-Chami, inhabit the park environs, many in the cliff-top regions, not far from the traffic-heavy streets of the metropolis of Cali.

EXCURSIONS
Tren Turistico Café y Azucar★

⊙ *Estación del Ferrocarril, Avenida Vásquez Cobo # 23N-47, 2km/1.2mi from Cali's Downtown.* ⊙*Departs for La Cumbre or La Tebaida on various days, call for exact times. La Cumbre.* ⊷*46,000 COP, La Tebaida.* ⊷*65,000COP.* ℰ*(2) 620 2326.*

Aimed squarely at day-trippers, this scenic railway ferries passengers from Cali to **La Cumbre** and **La Tebaida**. Part of the schedule is a "rumbero" option—a party train packed full of drinking revelers that leaves at 8pm and returns to the city at 3am, having completed a large loop with music blaring.

Hacienda Piedechinche★

⊙ *42km/26mi NE of Cali, in Amaime.* ⊙*Open Mon–Fri 9am–4pm, Sat–Sun & public holidays 9am–4:30pm.* ⊷*Guided tours (1hr 45min).* ⊷*5,000 COP.* ℰ*(2) 550 6076.* *www.museocanadeazucar.com.*

This handsome Colonial building is home to the **Museo de la Caña**, claiming to be the only **sugarcane** museum in the world, although several in the Caribbean would dispute the claim.

Dedicated to all things connected with sugarcane production and consumption, the property sits in the heart of the region's sugarcane plantations and offers rides through fields of sugarcane in open-topped trains and carts.

Hacienda El Paraíso★

⊙ *36km/22mi N of Cali via Carretera 25, close to El Cerrito.* ⊙*Open Tue–Sun & public holidays.* ⊙*Closed Tue after Monday bank holiday.* ⊷*4,500 COP.* ℰ*(2) 514 6848.* *www.inciva.org.*

Surrounded by scenic water canals, extensive sugarcane plantations and gigantic saman trees, this restored hacienda is a favorite destination for lovers of **Jorge Isaacs'** writings, as it was the setting for the writer's famous romantic novel *María*, considered a Latin American

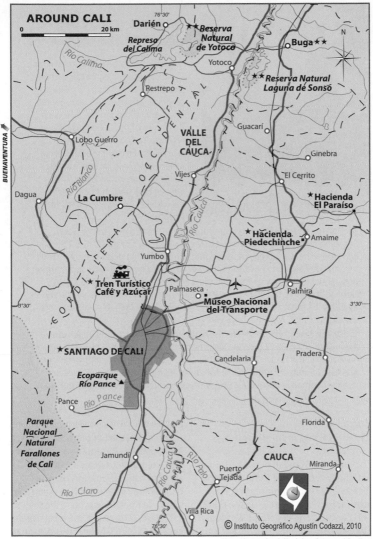

AROUND CALI

0   20 km

Darién ○ — ★★ **Reserva Natural de Yotoco**

Represa del Calima

Río Calima

Yotoco

Buga ★★

Restrepo

★★ *Reserva Natural Laguna de Sonso*

Lobo Guerro

VALLE DEL CAUCA

Guacarí

Ginebra

Vijes

El Cerrito

Dagua

La Cumbre

Río Blanco

Río Cauca

★ **Hacienda El Paraíso**

★ **Hacienda Piedechinche**

Amaime

Yumbo

🚂 **Tren Turístico Café y Azúcar**

Palmaseca

Palmira

● **Museo Nacional del Transporte**

★ **SANTIAGO DE CALI**

Ecoparque Río Pance ▲

Candelaria

Pradera

Pance

Río Pance

Parque Nacional Natural Farallones de Cali

Florida

Jamundí

Río Cauca

Río Palo

CAUCA

Miranda

Puerto Tejada

Río Claro

Villa Rica

BUENAVENTURA

3°30'

3°30'

76°30'

76°30'

© Instituto Geográfico Agustín Codazzi, 2010

literary classic. Built between 1816 and 1828 by a cattleman and former mayor of Buga, El Paraíso was purchased by Jorge Isaacs's father in 1828.

As an excellent example of the traditional architecture in the region, the hacienda boasts large accommodations with high ceilings and breezy balconies overlooking flower-filled gardens.

Transformed into a fine **house-museum**, it presents exhibits and displays that mirror the plot of the book,

with bedrooms allocated to its **main characters**. Stroll through Efrain's room where he placed freshly picked blooms from the garden in remembrance of María; the study where he taught María and her sisters; the living room where the women did embroidery; María's room; Efrain's father study where important household decisions were made; and the oratory where the priest conducted three masses each Sunday for the family, associates and slaves.

Miky Calero/Proexport Colombia

Basílica del Señor de los Milagros★★

Buga is undoubtedly best known for a miracle recognized by the Catholic church that draws some 3 million pilgrims each year. The story centers on a poor indigenous laundress on the shores of the Guadalajara River, who was saving money to buy a crucifix. When word reached her of a man being held by two Spanish soldiers for an unpaid debt, the woman took pity and paid the man's bill with her savings, earning him his freedom.

Back on the shores of the river, she spotted a crucifix floating in the water. Scooping it up, she looked around to see if anyone had dropped it. Seeing she was alone, she wondered if it was a gift from God for her good deed, and took it home. However, she noticed that it was strangely growing each day. Alarmed, the woman took it to the priests in the city and shared her tale. At first, they were disbelieving, but once they witnessed the crucifix for themselves, they declared it a miracle. Soon Catholic devotees built a church to commemorate the event.

Today, the Basílica del Señor de los Milagros (*Carrera 14 # 3-62;* ◷*open daily 6am–7pm;* ☎*2 228 2823; www.milagrosodebuga.com*) is visited by worshippers from all over the country on public holidays and Sundays, when those attending mass ask for miracles from the *Señor de los Milagros*. An adjoining museum depicts the many miracles that Buga has played a part in over the centuries.

Buga★★
▶ *57km/36mi NE of Cali along Carretera 25.*
Known as the "Cuidad Señora," for its nationally recognized Colonial architecture and religious importance, this lovely town (Pop. 111,487) on the north of El Cerrito is one of Colombia's oldest Spanish settlements, dating back to 1555. It is also notable for visits from **Simón Bolívar** during the fight for independence.

Lago Calima
▶ *108km/67mi N of Cali via Carretera 25, and then W from Buga to Darién.*
Water sports organized by the Jean Paul Liechti Uribe Windsurfing School, close to Llanitos on the north side of Lago Calima. ☎*315 554 2131. www.windsurfingcalima.com. There are cabins, camp grounds, hotels and hostels close to the lake.*

Built in 1961, this scenic **hydroelectric reserve** is actually Colombia's largest artificial lake. A popular out-of-town day excursion, it is geared to windsurfing, fishing, boating, kitesurfing, paragliding, waterskiing, jet-skiing and diving. Temperatures around the lake (at 1,500m/4,921ft above sea level) rarely exceed 17°C/63°F, and the national **kitesurfing** championships are staged here, an indication of just how windy it can get.

Darién
▶ *On the northern bank of Lago Calima.*
The village of Darién was founded in 1912. With its narrow streets and pretty little plaza trimmed by a handful of family-owned restaurants, bars, kiosks and bakeries, it is well worth a visit on the basis of charm alone, but also make time for its small archaeology museum.

Museo Arqueológico Calima

Calle 10 # 12-50. ⏱*Open Tue–Fri 8am–noon, 1pm–5pm, Sat– Sun & public holidays 10am–6pm.* ⌾*2,500 COP.* ☎*(2) 253 3121. www.inciva.org.*

Well-conceived exhibits of artifacts from regional pre-Columbian cultures convey 10,000 years of history across several **Calima** groups, including the **Llama**, **Yotoco**, **Sonso** and **Malagana** tribes. Used as a research resource for Colombian archaeologists, the museum also narrates southwestern Colombia's history of *guaqueros*, treasure hunters who unlawfully acquired these ancient relics through any means.

Museo Arqueológico Calima

Milky Calero/Proexport Colombia

Reserva Natural Laguna de Sonso★★

▶ *10km/6mi SW of Buga on the road to Loboguerrero. http://lagunasonso. tripod.com.*

This reserve is a major migratory point for a large number of **birds** such as greyish piculets, Blue-winged teals and flycatchers. A remarkable variety of mammals, fish and reptiles have also made their home in this 2,450ha /6,054 acre expanse whose marshlands and floodlands are rich in deposits and sediment from the **Cauca River**. With 90 percent of its terrain being wetlands, Laguna de Sonso is a long-established important stop for international bird watchers anxious to add rare Colombian species to their bird list.

Reserva Natural de Yotoco★★

▶ *18km/11mi SW of Buga on the road to Madriñal and Buenaventura.*
⏱*Open daily 7:30am–6pm with prior reservations. Email pablo-emilio.florez@ cvc.gov.co for visitor permit.* ☎*(2) 228 1922. http://bosqueyotoco.tripod.com.*

As one of the region's most important state-managed woodland reserves, Yotoco stretches over 560ha/1,384 acres and contains almost all of the 3,000 Colombian endemic **orchid species** and more than 1,000 **howler monkeys**, numerous **butterfly** species and all kinds of **insects**. It is a crucial base for conservation studies in Colombia.

Guides take visitors over 2hr-long scenic **trails** through pine trees, cedar and bamboo thickets.

Reserva Natural Laguna de Sonso

Milky Calero/Proexport Colombia

ADDRESSES

🛏 STAY

$ Café Tostasky – *Carrera 10 # 1-76, Barrio San Antonio, Cali.* 📞*(2) 893 0651. www.cafetostaky.blogspot.com. 11 rooms.* The French-Colombian couple who run this hostel in the heart of the San Antonio district (a distance from downtown Cali) want their guests to feel at home. To that end, there's a communal kitchen, free Internet and cable TV, and a pleasant cafe *(5pm–11pm)* that serves good coffee and crepes—a nod to the owner's French heritage.

$ Guest House Iguana – *Av. 9N # 22N-46, Barrio Granada, Cali.* 📞*(2) 660 8937. www.iguana.com.co. 15 rooms.* Offering large clean rooms, a shared kitchen, a small garden and free Wi-Fi in a quiet residential neighborhood, this little budget lodge is a favorite with backpackers. The friendly owner, who speaks English and German, can also arrange salsa or Spanish lessons. If it's nightlife you seek, the Iguana is a few blocks away from restaurants and clubs.

$$ Posada San Antonio – *Carrera 5 # 3-37, Barrio San Antonio, Cali.* 📞*(2) 893 7413. www.posadadesanantonio.com. 12 rooms.* In the heart of historic San Antonio, this Spanish Colonial-style mansion dates back to 1902. Rooms, which face the light-filled interior courtyard with its bubbling fountain, have private baths and TV. Historical artifacts and local handicrafts decorate the common areas. Although there's no air-conditioning, windows open to allow fresh air to circulate.

$$$ Four Points by Sheraton Cali – *Calle 18N # 4N-08, Cali.* 🅿✕🛁🆂🅿🆄 📞*(2) 685 9999. www.starwoodhotels.com. 181 rooms.* Located in the north end of Cali, within easy reach of the commercial and gastronomic zones, this member of the Sheraton chain offers all the comforts of home. Amenities include electronic safes and iron/ironing boards in each room, an on-site hair salon, and transfers to and from the airport.

$$$ Hotel Intercontinental Cali – *Av. Colombia # 2-72, Cali.* 🅿✕🛁🆂🅿🆄*(2) 882 3225. www.ichotelsgroup.com/intercontinental/en. 299 rooms.* Río Cali borders this luxury hotel, set on the edge of San Antonio. Done in gold hues and honey-toned woods, rooms come complete with coffeemakers, mini refrigerators, work desks and high-speed Internet. Amenities include five restaurants, a fitness center, a spa, tennis courts and a casino next door.

$$$ Hotel Valle Real – *Av. 3 Norte # 17-25, Barrio Versailles, Cali* 🅿✕🆂🅿🆄 📞*(2) 685 1212. www.hotelvallereal cali.com. 43 rooms.* All the rooms in this contemporary boutique hotel are suites, the most modest of which still has a kitchen, a dining/living area and a private bathroom. Each is decorated in soothing neutrals with plenty of natural light. The hotel's business center caters to the needs of executive guests.

$$$ Mercure Hotel Cali, Casa del Alférez – *Av. 9 Norte # 9N-24, Cali.* 🅿 ✕ 📞*(2) 661 8111. www.accorhotels.com. 60 rooms.* Located in one of the best parts of exclusive Granada, 10 minutes from the city center, the Casa del Alférez is decked out in elegant Colonial style. Whirlpool baths and air-conditioning come in every room; spacious suites have their own balconies and living areas. **Ginger N Garlic restaurant** serves a mix of Asian and Mediterranean fare.

$$$$ NOW Hotel – *Av. 9A Norte # 10 N-74, Cali.* ✕📞*(2) 488 9797. www.now hotel.com.co. 19 rooms.* This trendy, ultra-modern hotel in Cali's Zona Rosa crows about its "eco-friendly intelligent" rooms that boast state-of-the-art technology and custom-designed contemporary European furnishings. Enjoy breakfast on your own private balcony, or have a meal downstairs in **Restaurante Go**, which features organic ingredients and is open 24 hours.

$$$$ Radisson Royal Hotel Cali – *Carrera 100B # 11A-99, Cali.* ✕🛁 📞*(2) 330 7777. www.radisson.com/calico. 146 rooms.* Located in a quiet residential area, next to the Trade Center Corporate Complex, this hotel is still convenient to downtown. Standard rooms have city views, complimentary newspapers, safes, Wi-Fi and VCR; suites look out over the mountains. A gym, business center, and airport transport service complete the amenities. Reservations are required in December.

⍟EAT

$ Restaurante Granada Faró – *Av. 9N # 15AN-02, Barrio Granada, Cali. ℘(2) 667 4625. www.granadafaro.com.* One of a chain of restaurants, the Great Lighthouse (as its name translates) resides in a landmark building whose decor and furnishings recall Spanish Granada. The chef/owner whips up the likes of salmon lasagna, coq au vin, prawns Thermidor and veal osso bucco on his eclectic menu. **Mediterranean**.

$$ Restaurante Vegetariano Sol de la India – *Carrera 6 # 8-48, Centro Sector Plazoleta de San Francisco, Cali. Closed Sat & Sun. ℘(2) 884 2333.* Even meat-lovers will like the inexpensive and flavorful vegetable curries offered at this modest restaurant. The menu also lists many options that will appeal to vegans. Don't pass up the breads and the deep-fried *pakoras*, a snack made with a variety of vegetables. **Indian**.

$$$ Restaurante Faró El Solar – *Calle 15 Norte # 9N-62, Barrio Granada, Cali. ℘(2) 653 4628. Closed Sun.* Tasty Italian food and a relaxing atmosphere attract diners to Faró El Solar. For a real treat, dine alfresco on the umbrella-shaded patio. The attentive staff, consistently good cuisine, and menus in both Spanish and English are just a few more reasons to come here. **Italian**.

$$$ Platillos Voladores – *Av. 3 Norte # 7-19, Barrio Centenario, Cali. Closed Sun. ℘(2) 668 7750. www.platillos voladores.com.* Honing in on the authentic dishes of northern Colombia, this eatery—whose name means Flying Saucers—is no alien when it comes to good food and attentive service. Guava shrimp, kiwi mango fish, and banana lomo (made with veal) will give you an idea of the Thai-inspired fare. Get the party started with a lychee martini. **International**.

🛒 SHOPPING

Parque Artesania Loma de la Cruz – *Calle 5, between Carrera 14 and 17, Cali. www.lomadelacruz.com.* Also known as Parque Artesanal, this place sells authentic handmade goods from the Amazon, Pacific coast, southern Andes and Los Llanos in particular.

Centro Comercial Chipichape – *Calle 38 Norte # 6N-35, Cali. ℘(2) 659 2199. www.chipichape.com.co.* One of the area's best malls, this huge complex is constantly crowded. Here you'll find everything from CDs to perfume.

🏃 RECREATION

Blues Brothers Bar – *Av. 6AN # 21-40, Barrio Santa Mónica, Cali. ℘(2) 661 3412. www.caliblues.net.* Owned by an Irishman, Blues Brothers Bar emphasizes the blues, but you'll also hear genres such as salsa and rock, depending on the night of the week. A good-size crowd of expatriates frequents this place, where there's always a party going on.

Changos – *3km/2mi east of Cali along the road to Cavasa (Juanchito). ℘(2) 662 9701. www.chango.com.co.* Changos has been around for a while, but the place still delivers. The rumba is hot, the dance floor stays packed, and the music is eclectic. Juanchito has a reputation for carnival celebrations, so things can get wild around here; the club, however, prides itself on its reputation for safety.

Delirio – *Carrera 2A Oeste # 13-34, Barrio Santa Teresita, Cali. ℘(2) 893 7610. www.delirio.com.co.* Delirio is supported by the nonprofit Fundación Delirio, whose objective is to promote Cali's contemporary culture and the city itself as the capital of salsa. This club stages a huge variety of acts and is the place to go to catch Cali's unique style of salsa dancing.

La Sexta Avenida – This Cali avenue is jam-packed with bars and discos, almost all of which have their own dance floor. Among the nightclubs on this avenue, Kukaramakara *(Calle 28 Norte # 2Bis-97; www.kukaramakara.com)* is a good bet for salsa, rock and pop

Popayán★★ and Surroundings

Cauca

In the hearts of the Colombian people, the capital of the Cauca department is held in fond regard and known as "La Ciudad Blanca," meaning The White City for its many whitewashed buildings. Surrounded by the lush green curves of the Valle de Cauca at an altitude of 1,737m/5,699ft, Popayán epitomizes simple, colonial charm with its quaint streets and pretty cobblestone plazas. Numerous churches reflect the religious heritage of the town where one of Colombia's oldest and most important Holy Week parades draws crowds from all over the country. Miracles abound here as the history books bear out, and Popayán is all the more intriguing for having survived earthquake devastation on a massive scale in the early 1980s, a true modern-day marvel.

A BIT OF HISTORY

Founded in 1537 by conquistador **Sebastián de Belalcázar**, Popayán takes its name from the indigenous *po* (meaning two), *pa* (meaning straw) and *yan* (meaning village)—a reflection of

▶ **Population:** 258,653.

◔ **Michelin Maps:** p349, p366 and p373.

▤ **Info:** Popayán Oficina de Turismo, Carrera 5 # 4-68, ℰ(2) 824 2251. http://popayan-cauca.gov.co.

☺ **Don't Miss:**
The treasures of the Museo Arquidiocesano de Arte Religioso, with jewel-encrusted artifacts, paintings and statues gathered from churches all over the region; Popayán's poignant Holy Week processions, held since 1556; Tierradentro, one of Colombia's two main archaeological sites, located in a fittingly remote spot in a land stripped bare by the cold, where subterranean chambers and standing stones await.

its rustic beginnings as a collection of humble straw-roofed houses.
Very little is actually known about the pre-Hispanic history of Popayán, although the ancient burial site named **El Morro de Tulcán** (◔*see Photo Tips opposite page*) is thought to pre-date the arrival of the Spanish.

Puente del Humilladero

Proexport Colombia

GETTING THERE

BY AIR - The local **Guillermo León Valencia** (PPN) airport is easily accessible since it is next to the bus terminal, about 1km/.6mi north of the city center, a 20min walk away. Direct flights arrive Bogotá and Guapi, but it's best to book seats in advance. Avianca (Bogotá) ℘2 256 5810, *www. avianca.com*. Satena www.satena.com (Bogotá) ℘2 423 8530. Minibuses to the center city cost about 2,000 COP; a taxi to the center is about 8,000 COP.

BY BUS - The **bus terminal** (www. terminalpopayan.com) sits close to the airport (*see BY AIR above*). **Long-distance buses** arrive from Armenia (7hrs; 42,000 COP), Cali (3hrs; 12,00 COP), San Agustín (5hrs; 18,000 COP) and Tierradentro (5hrs; 18,000 COP). It should take 15-20min to walk to the center of Popayán from the station.

GETTING AROUND

BY BUS - The city is well-served by minibuses, which are inexpensive to ride, and plentiful..

BY TAXI - Taxis are available, but walking is encouraged(*see below*).

ON FOOT - The city is laid out mostly on a grid, and sights are concentrated around Plaza Mayor, on the south bank of Río Molino, so walking is a good option for getting around.

GENERAL INFORMATION

AMENITIES - Popayán being a university town, there are Internet cafes and **ATMs** in the city center. Be watchful when using ATMs as well as when in the markets and near bridges.

In the colonial era, Popayán provided a strategic stop-off between **Quito** (Ecuador) and the **Caribbean Coast** for the transfer of riches bound for Spain.

As a university town, Popayán has a youthful feel to it. Synonymous with enlightened, progressive free-thinkers and intellectuals, it is home to the **Universidad del Cauca** (1827), one of the nation's oldest and most distinguished institutions of higher education.

Popayán is renowned for having produced more **presidents** than any other city, 17 to date, as well as poets, painters, playwrights and composers.

One Big Shock

When a violent **earthquake** shook Popayán's foundations to the core in 1983, moments before the annual much-celebrated Maundy Thursday procession, more than 10,000 buildings suffered severe damage.

Though the quake, measuring 5.4 on the Richter scale, lasted just 18 seconds, it proved highly destructive, razing much of Popayán's historic center to the ground and causing fatalities. Restoration work took more than 20

years to complete—but the results are stunning, with few signs of lasting damage evident in Popayán's streets today. As a national architectural treasure, it joins Villa de Leyva and Cartagena as Colombia's most beautiful colonial-era cities, so be sure to pack a camera when you visit.

HISTORIC CENTER★★

Picturesque whitewashed buildings edge the narrow streets of Popayán's old center where all of the city's main sites of historic interest are contained within an easy-to-walk **10-block area**. In the colonial era, Popayán's religious communities were a mix of Jesuits, Dominicans, Franciscans, Carmelites, Camerons, Augustines and Bethlemites who left behind a rich architectural legacy for all to enjoy.

Parque Francisco José de Caldas★

Between Calle 4 & 5 with Carreras 6 & 7. Many of Popayán's Holy Week celebrations center on this pleasant, leafy park dating back to 1537. This park makes a good place to start exploring the

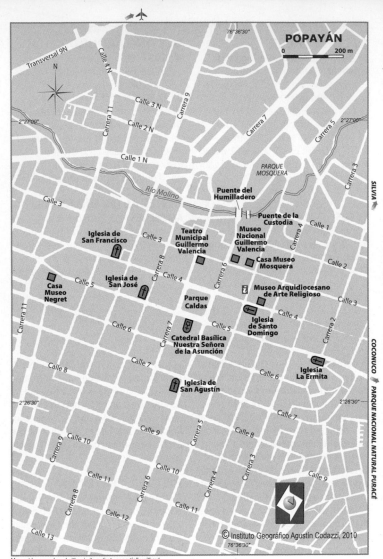

POPAYÁN

0 ────── 200 m

city's many religious sites, since several churches clustered around, or not too far from, this central point.

Catedral Basílica Nuestra Señora de la Asunción

Calle 5, between Carreras 6 and 7.
Built between 1859 and 1906 after a quake razed the previous Colonial church to the ground, this whitewashed Neo-classical structure is actually Popayán's newest religious building. It boasts the clean lines of Roman architecture, with an impressive **dome** designed by architect **Adolfo Duenas**.

Just prior to the 1983 earthquake, the church was embellished and restored again by Bishop Silverio Buitrago Trujillo. Afterwards, the dome was displaced, but has now been reinstated.

© Caros Duran/epa/Corbis

Semana Santa Processions

Every year, tens of thousands of people from all over Colombia descend on Popayán to watch its famous Holy Week celebrations, said to be the most authentic outside Seville in Spain. Honored since 2009 with a **UNESCO** Intangible Cultural Heritage award, this tradition was passed on from the early Spanish colonists and perpetuated without interruption since 1556, as if untroubled by the upheavals of the times.

Held in March or April, according to the liturgical calendar, the processions snake through the streets after dark in grand style, following a route of 54 stopping points across town during the five-day event. Wooden **holy statues**, weighing 500kg/1,102 pounds each and representing the different stages of Jesus Christ's Passion, are painstakingly carried by townsfolk for hours and hours across 20 blocks, while people walk alongside, carrying flickering candles in a solemn fashion. Meanwhile, choir boys and flower carriers in elaborate costumes, capes and flowing robes transport garlands. Particularly poignant, the **Holy Friday** procession represents Jesus before his crucifixion, an event that centers on the image of death as a skeleton, with all-male participants carrying hammers, chisels and other tools to symbolize the removal of Jesus' body from the cross.

During Holy Week, Popayán also hosts the **Festival de Música Religiosa**, a modern tradition that was launched in the 1960s by Edmundo Troya Mosquera. Staged in venues throughout the city, the event attracts choirs, soloists and artists from around the world, specializing in sacred music. For more information, access www.semanasantapopayan.com.

In Popayán, the cathedral is renowned for the resonating deep tones of its magnificent church **organ**.

Iglesia de San Agustín
Corner of Carrera 6 & Calle 7.
This church and convent was founded by **Jeronimo Escobar** in the late 17C. Reconstructed after the 1736 quake with contributions from notables of the city, the church required further restoration work following the severe earthquake in 1983.

Highlights include an ornately carved **altar** covered in gold leaf, an **expository** of Baroque silver and an image of *Virgen de los Dolores*.

Iglesia de Santo Domingo
Corner of Calle 4 and Carrera 5.
Designed by Spanish architect **Antonio Garcia**, this church was largely rebuilt.

367

It is notable for its lavish **stonework** depicting flora and fauna, and elegant **altar** and fountain. It also boasts a fine early-19C **pulpit** that was drawn by **Francisco José de Caldas** (1768-1816), an illustrious son of Popayán executed in the Reconquest's regime of terror.

Iglesia La Ermita★

Calle 5, between Carrera 2 & Carrera 3.
As the oldest church in the city, this venerable building dates back to 1546. It was built on the site of a thatched church dedicated to Santa Catalina and Santa Barbara. Due to its small compact design, La Ermita was able to withstand the impact of earthquakes between 1736 and 1906.

Over the years the church has been altered with a new façade, new roof and added embellishments to the side chapel.

Iglesia de San José

Corner of Calle 5 & Carrera 8.
Replacing the humble church that used to stand on the present site, this edifice was commissioned after the earthquake of 1736. However, violent aftershocks seriously affected its structure, as did the quakes of 1885 and 1906 when the church's west tower was destroyed. Damage during the 1983 earthquake was also severe, necessitating extensive restoration.

Although largely emptied of the rich art treasures that once decorated the interior—they were confiscated to fund General Mariño's military campaigns in the 19C—the church is still notable for its stunning **altar** of the Sacred Heart of Jesus, dating from 1736.

Iglesia de San Francisco★

Calle 4, between Carrera 9 and Carrera 10.
Popayán's largest Colonial church is a handsome building with an elaborate high altar inside. San Francisco was actually built on the site of a previous church, the latter having been destroyed in the 1736 earthquake.

The present church was designed by Spanish architect **Antonio Garcia**, who also worked on the construction

of Cali's Catedral San Pedro. Since it took two decades to construct the church, in frustration, officials blessed it when it was only half completed in 1787.

Today, the building's facade has been hailed as the best example of **Baroque style** throughout Colombia. A tower houses a famous **bell**, donated by Don Pedro Agustín de Valencia. The interior of the church features a resplendent **altar**.

Museo Arquidiocesano de Arte Religioso★★

Calle 4 # 4-56. Open Mon–Fri 9am–12:30pm, 2pm–6pm, Sat 9am–2pm. 3,000 COP. (2) 824 2759.
There is no better place to end your tour of Popayán's main churches than here, in this outstanding museum.

Housed in an attractive colonial building (1763) set around a paved courtyard dotted with trees, the museum holds gem-studded religious deities, glittering chalices, and paintings and holy statues, many from the 17C and some as old as 1580.

ADDITIONAL SIGHTS
Casa Museo Negret★

Calle 5 # 10-23. Open Tue–Sun 8am–noon, 2pm–5pm. Guided tours available upon prior request. 2,000 COP. (2) 824 4546. http://museonegret.wordpress.com.
Widely considered one of Colombia's finest living sculptors, **Edgar Negret** was born in this house (1781) in 1920. A tribute to the abstract sculptor's brilliant career, this museum exhibits part of his private collection.

Much of Negret's work is in aluminum, and a fine array of pieces reflects his fondness for this material. Of special interest is the model of **Simón Bolívar**, conceived as a commemorative monument for the 150th anniversary of his death. Widely criticized by historians and academics, the controversial piece elicited such vehement reactions that it ended up here, in the confinement of this museum, rather than in Bogotá's Parque Simón Bolívar, its intended location.

Teatro Municipal Guillermo Valencia

Corner of Calle 3 and Carrera 7.
📞(2) 822 4199. www.festivalpopayan.org
This Republican-style building (1915-1927) is the venue for religious music concerts, opera, choral performances and theatrical productions. Be sure to peek inside the lavishly **restored** 900-seat theater.

Next door, the **Panteón de los Próceres** *(Carrera 7 # 3-55, between Calle 3 and Calle 4)* provides a final resting place for Popayán's most illustrious talents.

Museo Nacional Guillermo Valencia

Carrera 6 # 2-69. ⏰Open Tue–Sun & public holidays 10am– noon, 2pm–5pm. ⊙2,000 COP. 📞(2) 820 6160.
A leader of the Modernist movement, **Guillermo Valencia** (1873-1943) was known for his subtle verses such as those found in *Ritos* (1898). Housed in a Renaissance-style building with a cloistered courtyard and park overlooking the tomb of the poet, this museum pays tribute to his works and life.

Casa Museo Mosquera

Calle 3 # 5-14. ⏰Open Mon–Fri 8am–noon, 2pm–6pm, Sat–Sun & public holidays 8am–noon, 2pm–5pm. ⊙2,000 COP. 📞(2) 824 0683.
General **Tomás Cipriano de Mosquera** (1798-1878), president of Colombia between 1845 and 1867, was born in this Colonial-style residence (1780-88). A bust of him by Italian sculptor Pietro Tenerani takes pride of place together with military uniforms, documents and a range of personal artifacts.

Popayán's Bridges

Two bridges span the Río Molino: the **Puente de la Custodia** and **Puente del Humilladero** *(at the top of Carrera 6, after the turn for Calle 2).*
The former, and smaller of the two, was built in 1713. The larger, constructed 160 years later, is a more robust structure at 178m/584ft, arching under the gaze of the town's grassy hill, the **Cerro del Morro**.

SURROUNDINGS
Las Ardillas★

▶*8km/5mi S of Popayán (Vereda La Martica, close to Timbío, on the road leading S from Popayán). ⏰Open Mon–Fri 8am–6pm. Activities include canopy climbing ⊙18,000 COP, swimming ⊙5,000 COP, sauna ⊙5,000 COP, climbing wall. ⊙5,000 COP. 🐾Guided ecotours available upon request. 📞(2) 830 5555. www.canopylasardillas.com.*
This private nature reserve has a lot to offer for visitors who love thrilling challenges.

Here you will find **canopy lines** that zip through the treetops at considerable speed, offering a bird's-eye view of the countryside. There are also **tube rides** amid crashing waterfalls along the beautiful **Río Honda**, as well as opportunities to cross suspension bridges over ravines and navigate climbing walls.

Nature trails loop through wetland **conservation zones** rich with wildlife, especially butterflies, frogs and birds.

EXCURSIONS
Circuito del Maiz★★

By organized tour, bookable at the tourist office in Popayán, Carrera 5 # 4-68, 📞(2) 824 2251, www.popayantourism.com.
This popular gastronomic tour of the region to the west of Popayán allows visitors to sample local specialties and produce. Recipes vary dramatically from village to village, and this tour is a great way to learn about the regional **culinary traditions** of El Charco, Santa Ana, Cajete and Balneario La Lajita in the spirit of Popayán's centuries-old gastronomy.

Expect to learn about soups, dough mixing, corn pancakes and *chicha* (fermented corn drink) in an exploration of food culture that has been passed down through oral tradition through many generations.

Fruit marinades are commonplace in the region's rustic *platos de las abuelas* (grandmother's dishes), with hearty pork, beef, chicken and rice dishes featured during religious holidays, such as Holy Week.

Circuito Ancestral★

▶ *15km/9mi NE of Popayán.*
Allow 4hrs. Organized tour, bookable at the tourist office in Popayán, Carrera 5 # 4-68, ℘(2) 824 2251, www.popayan tourism.com.

This **hiking** circuit, which can also be done on **horseback**, will please nature lovers, since it follows bird-rich **ecological paths** along historic trails. The tour explores the region east of Popayán, passing through La Union, Santa Helena, Problazón and Santa Barbara.

Silvia★

▶ *59km/37mi NE of Popayán, via Piendamó, after traveling along Carretera 25.*

This charming settlement (Pop 30,826) is the heartland of the **Guambiano people**, a very traditional indigenous group. Dressed in customary blue and red, the Guambiano live in remote mountain villages and descend on Silvia via sloping paths each **Tuesday** to sell their handicrafts, fruits and vegetables at a colorful weekly market.

Visitors should take an opportunity to visit Silvia and peek into the **church** topping a hill—from this vantage point, the **panorama** of the area is simply astounding.

Also take a look at the **Museo de Artesanias** *(Carrera 2 # 14-39, Casa Turística;* ⏰*open daily 8am–8pm;* 💰*2,000 COP;* ℘*2 825 1034; www.hotelcasaturistica. com),* a small museum featuring a range of locally made handicrafts.

From Silvia, several tour operators offer a trip along the **Ruta Etno-Ecoturis-**

Guambiano women in traditional dress, Silvia

©Michael Runkel/Photoshot

tica—a scenic loop on nature trails through indigenous villages that culminates in the Guambiano settlement of **La Campana** *(for details, ask at the Casa Turística;* ℘*(2) 825 1034).*

Coconuco★★

▶ *35km/22mi SE from Popayán, on the road to San Agustín (S of Parque Nacional Natural Purace).*

The village of Coconuco is famous for its curative **hot thermal springs**, often visited by hikers after a full day exploring the wind-swept trails of Purace National Park (💧*see opposite).*

Choose from steaming, communal-sized pools of **Agua Herviendo** *(1km/0.6mi from Coconuco;* ⏰*open Tue–Sun;* 💰*3,000 COP; details at the Hostería Comfandi Coconuco;* ℘*2 827 7014),* with piping-hot water gushing out of the ground

---

Popayán, First UNESCO City of Gastronomy

It's well known that Popayán's 16C-initiated Semana Santa processions were awarded UNESCO status in recent years. But did you know that Popayán was also appointed the first UNESCO City of Gastronomy, in recognition of its unique, centuries-long **culinary tradition**? Launched in 2004 by UNESCO, the **Creative Cities Network** is designed to promote the social, economic and cultural development of cities by acknowledging their **innovative talent** in the areas of Literature, Film, Music, Crafts and Folk Art, Design, Media Arts and Gastronomy. To date, only one city other than Popayán has been nominated in the field of gastronomy: **Chengdu** (China).

Parque Nacional Natural Puracé

Proexport Colombia

at 90°C/194°F, or journey farther up the valley to **Thermales Aguas Tibias** *(4km/3mi S from Coconuco on the Paletará road;* ⏱ *open Tue–Sun;* 🎟 *5,000 COP; details at the Hostería Comfandi Coconuco;* 📞 *2 827 7014).* At an altitude of 2,560m/8,400ft, this hillside boasts spectacular surrounding scenery with tranquil views and soothing therapeutic mud baths.

Parque Nacional Natural Puracé★

▶ *45km/28mi SE of Popayán (entrance at Pilimbalá, 1km/.6mi from El Crucero).* ⏱ *Open daily 8am–6pm. 19,000 COP.* 💬 *Guided tours organized by the Oficina de Ecoturismo in Bogotá.* 📞 *(1) 353 2400 ext 138. www.parques nacionales.gov.co.*

Sectors of this 83,000ha/205,097 acre park overlap with reservations and ancestral lands of the Kokonuco and Yanacona peoples. Crossed by mighty rivers such as the Cauca and Magdalena, Puracé is notable for its incredible biodiversity. Sitting at an altitude of between 2,500m/8,200ft and 5,000m/16,404ft above sea level, its striking terrain rises from marshy **jungle lowlands** to rugged, **snowy highland peaks**.

Hiking trails pass a bubbling geothermal wonderland, gushing waterfalls and 50 lakes. In the past, **landmines** made traversing the park dangerous.

Widespread clearance has opened trails to the active **Puracé volcano** (4,580m/15,026ft). The **Pan de Azúcar**, with its 5,000m/16,404ft high permanently snow-capped peak, and the 9 craters called **Cadena Volcanica de Coconuco** are accessible, but caution is advised.

Caves, **woodlands** and **pasture** are rich with frogs, birds, butterflies and insects. Andean condors, spectacled bears, pumas and mountain tapirs also frequent the park.

☺ Photo Tips ☺

Don't miss an opportunity to capture the charming whitewashed **Capilla de Beléna**, a simple Spanish-style church set atop a hill to the east of the city's central core (accessed via a leafy trail from the Calle 4 and Carrera 1 intersection). It offers wonderful views across Popayán from a flower-filled courtyard.

Another must-visit for views is the **El Morro de Tulcana** (by Carrera 2A and Calle 1A, at the NE end of the town), a pyramid-shaped tomb dating back to approximately AD 500-1600, on a hill crowned with an equestrian statue of Popayán's founder.

PARQUE ARQUEOLÓGICO DE TIERRADENTRO★★

Located in a fittingly remote spot, this park is the lesser-visited of Colombia's two main archaeological sites (&see SAN AGUSTÍN).

It is a perfect illustration of, in some civilizations, earthly life solely as a preparation for the afterlife, with death being the ultimate journey.

Difficult to access in anything other than perfect weather, Tierradentro ("the Land Inside") is reached by a long, slow journey over water-logged roads punctuated by puddles and mudslides. Bridges wobble, routes erode, and it isn't uncommon for the bus to grind to a premature halt with a few miles left to go.

Well off the standard tourist trail, this intriguing archaeological site can be reached by road from either **Popayán** to the west *(100km/62mi, with paved road until Gabriel López, half way, then dirt road; bus transport regularly starts from Popayán's Terminal de Transportes; jeep tours may also be arranged from that city)* or **Neiva** to the northeast *(126km/78mi of paved road to La Plata, then 36km/22mi of dirt road).*

However, the rewards are definitely worth the trip. Visitors arrive to discover an amazing number (as many as 78) of open **shaft-and-chamber tombs** and a variety of **standing stones**, outstanding examples of complex ancient architecture and decoration, each directly carved from sheer **volcanic rock**.

A BIT OF ARCHAEOLOGY

A **UNESCO** World Heritage Site under the tutelage of the Colombian Institute of Anthropology and History (ICANH), Tierradentro's remarkable **necropolis** is still shrouded in mystery, although recent research indicates it may have an age somewhere between 600 and 800 years ago, and was probably built by the people living in the San Andrés de Pisimbalá, Ullucos and Rionegro basins. This spectacular site is famous for its **statues** of human figures and mammoth **hypogea**. Characterized by huge underground burial caves (many up to 12m/39ft wide), sometimes decorated with motifs of **birds**, **animals** and **geometric designs**, Tierradentro reveals much about the social complexity and cultural wealth of Colombia's north-Andean pre-Hispanic societies. Most of the underground tombs face west, plunging 5-8m/16-26ft into the earth, and bear some similarities to the chambers in San Agustín.

& Check **www.tierradentro.info** for maps, updated information and an excellent selected bibliography.

The tiny village of **San Andrés de Pisimbalá** *(8km/5mi from Inzá)* serves as a base from which to explore Tierradentro. The archaeological **trail** itself is 14km/9mi long. You can also hire a **horse** to get around the site *(available by request from La Portada Hospedaje at the park entrance; &311 601 7884; http://laportadahotel.com).*

Burial chamber, Alto de Segovia

© Diego Lezama Orezzoli/Corbis

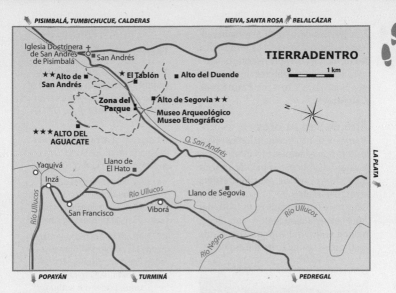

PISIMBALÁ, TUMBICHUCUE, CALDERAS   NEIVA, SANTA ROSA   BELALCÁZAR

Iglesia Doctrinera
de San Andrés
de Pisimbalá   San Andrés

TIERRADENTRO

0   1 km

★★ **Alto de
San Andrés**

★ El Tablón   ■ Alto del Duende

**Zona del
Parque**   ■ Alto de Segovia ★★

Museo Arqueológico
Museo Etnográfico

★★★ **ALTO DEL
AGUACATE**

Q. San Andrés

LA PLATA

Yaquivá   Llano de
El Hato

Inzá   Río Ullucos   Llano de Segovia

Río Ullucos   San Francisco   Viborá   Río Ullucos

Río Negro

POPAYÁN   TURMINÁ   PEDREGAL

VISIT

🕐 *Open daily 8am–4pm.*
💰 *15,000 COP, including entrance to
museums (🕐 same hours; ☎ (2) 825
2903; www.icanh.gov.co). ☎ 312 495
5516. www.tierradentro.info.*

Located at the entrance of the park,
two fine museums offer visitors another perspective, one with an archaeological focus and the other with an
ethnographic bias. Decorated pottery
forms the centerpiece of the collection
at the **Museo Arqueológico,** while the
Museo Etnográfico houses an exhibition of Nasa Indian artifacts.

Towering stone statues of various sizes
and shapes are clustered around the
four main archaeological zones that
tend to be visited in the following order
as a natural progression.

👁 *To fully enjoy the beauty of these tombs
and the park's viewpoints, bring a flashlight and binoculars with you:*

Alto de Segovia★★

Segovia is a very comprehensive site,
one in which most of Tierradentro's
technical studies actually take place.
Because of its close proximity to the
entrance of the park, it is also the most
visited burial site.

It contains some of the best-preserved
chambers, including the only ones that
allow in light. You will discover 25 different tombs decorated with sculptures
and paintings in varying styles.

Alto del Duende

Close to Segovia, this site has five burial
tombs. When combined with the first
alto, it provides a good overview of
Tierradentro for visitors whose time is
limited.

😊 Finding Your Way 😊

There is no detailed map of the
Tierradentro archaeological zone,
but the museum staff will kindly
furnish visitors with a hand-drawn
diagram to serve as a guide around
the tombs, statues and waterfalls.
You may also find it useful to print
some of the maps contained on the
www.tierradentro.info website
in advance and take them with
you. Once you enter the park, you
will find the occasional signpost
along the trails that weave around
some 100 tombs ranging from
collapsed holes in the ground to
well-preserved chambers. In each
location, a security guard unlocks
a kind of trap door leading below
ground, waiting for visitors to
descend a set of large steps, some
high and awkwardly spaced and
nearly impossible to navigate.

From El Duende, a scenic 5km/3mi walk leads to the indigenous village of **Santa Rosa**, with its friendly people, beautifully restored colonial church, and eye-popping views across the **Páez River Canyon**★★.

Alto de San Andrés★★

A series of six richly painted tombs offers visitors fine examples of subterranean funerary chambers—with lofty lookout points that provide excellent **views** across San Andrés.

From here, a trail leads to the Alto del Aguacate—a demanding slog along muddy paths, but with great rewards for those prepared to do the legwork.

Burial site, Alto del Aguacate

© Diego Lezama Orezzoli/Corbis

Alto del Aguacate★★★

The **view** from this alto, sitting high on a mountain ridge, is utterly awesome—a fitting setting from which to depart for the afterlife.

A recent report stated that 41 of the Aguacate's 42 chambers open to the public required urgent, much-needed conservation work.

Seismic activity due to the **Nevado del Huila** volcano (*see NEIVA*) is believed to have caused many of them to col-

The People of Tierradentro

An estimated 60,000 people live around Tierradentro, a province of the Cauca department with two municipalities, **Inzá** (Pop. 27,172) and **Páez** (Pop. 31,548).

◆ 2 percent of **Afro-Colombians** live in the municipality of Paéz (in and around Belalcázar).

◆ 41 percent of **Mestizos** live in rural neighborhoods *(veredas)* and towns of the municipality of **Inzá** such as San Andrés de Pisimbalá.

◆ 57 percent of American Indians, mostly **Nasa people** (formerly called Páez) are dispersed across communally held lands *(resguardos)* under the authority of traditional indigenous leaders *(cabildos)*. It should be noted that the Nasa of Tierradentro do not consider themselves descendants of the builders of the mysterious megalithic statues and hypogea.

lapse and disappear over the centuries. Most of the chambers that have survived are painted with an outstanding combination of geometric abstractions and images of wildlife and flowers.

Although not quite as complex as the other three altos in terms of structure, Alto del Aguacate is home to one of Tierradentro's most famous tombs, known as the **Tomb of the Moons** (also called "Tomb of the Salamanders").

This tomb is laid out as a symmetrical oval, with a rectangular staircase of steps arranged irregularly and a wall and vault divided in two parts, high and low, by a strip of black, red and ochre lines. Representing the best of the pictorial tradition, the style of this tomb is so different from the one found on Tierradentro's other altos that viewers may be inclined to think it belonged to another local tradition or another time period.

ADDRESSES

STAY

$ Casa Familiar Turistica – *Carrera 5 # 2-07, Popayán.* ℘*(2) 824 4853. www. hosteltrail.com/casafamiliarturistica. 4 rooms.* This concrete building on the edge of the colonial old town is a low-budget, dog-friendly hostel. The management staff are helpful and strive to maintain a comfortable family atmosphere. Guests have a choice between dormitories or double rooms; all are clean and safe, with shared baths and access to a communal kitchen and laundry. Breakfast is available for an additional charge.

$ Hosteltrail – *Carrera 11 # 4-16. Centro Historico, Popayán.* ℘*(2) 831 7871. www.hosteltrail.com/guesthouse. 14 rooms.* Owned by a Scottish couple, Hosteltrail guesthouse is the backpackers' choice in the area and attracts travelers from all over the world. Although accommodations are basic, they're large and clean, and the owners have gone out of their way to make things comfortable. There's free Wi-Fi throughout the building, and computers are available for a fee in case you need one. If you're interested in exploring, the knowledgeable owners offer a tour to the nearby thermal springs.

$$$ Hotel La Plazuela – *Calle 5 # 8-13, Popayán.* 🅿✕℘*(2) 824 1084. http://hotellaplazuela.com.co. 27 rooms.* Graceful arcaded piazzas face the interior courtyard in this handsome whitewashed structure, located across the road from Iglesia San José. The charming hotel dates back to 1742 and was renovated after the 1983 earthquake. Period furniture and original artwork fill the rooms, all of which have cable TV, mini refrigerators and private baths. Ask for a room facing the courtyard if street noise disturbs your sleep.

$$$ Hotel Los Balcones – *Carrera 7 # 2-75, Popayán.* ℘*(2) 824 2030. www.hotellosbalconespopayan.com. 11 rooms.* Originally built for Don Joaquín Mosquera y Figueroa, who was president of Colombia from 1830-1831, this renovated 18C mansion is elegantly decked out with plush leather furniture and eclectic art in the common areas. There's no restaurant on-site, but given sufficient notice, the staff is happy to cook for guests. Rooms are large with TV and free Wi-Fi; groups or families can rent the adjacent apartment.

EAT

$ Restaurante Vegetariano Naturaleza y Vida – *Carrera 8 # 7-19, Centro Historico, Popayán. Closed Sun.* ℘*(2) 822 1118.* Cheap and cheerful, this restaurant offers fresh and tasty vegetarian fare in the form of soups, entrées and desserts. The menu changes regularly, and seating is family-style at long wooden tables and benches. **Vegetarian**.

$ Madeira Café – *Calle 3 # 4-91, Popayán. Closed Sun.* ℘*300 788 6508.* A local favorite, Madeira Café sports a subtle earth-toned dining space, outfitted with wood and wrought-iron tables. This coffee shop makes an ideal spot to stop for a cup of coffee and sweet pick-me-up during a break from sightseeing, or to warm up with a *canelazo* (liquour-spiked coffee) on a chilly night. Seek out the adjoining shop for handicrafts made by local artisans. **Colombian**.

$$ Restaurante El Quijote – *Calle 10N # 8-14, Popayán.* ℘*(2) 823 4104.* A short taxi ride outside Popayán, this restaurant serves a menu of succulent grilled meat and a variety of oversize salads. On weekends, you can eat on the large outdoor patio facing a small park, while you listen to live guitar music. **Colombian**.

$ La Cave – *Calle 4 # 2-07, Popayán. No dinner Sat & Sun.* ℘*316 753 7670.* Located in one of the quieter parts of the historical center of Popayán, this restaurant cooks up consistently well-prepared French cuisine. The staff can be a bit patronizing at times, but you can overlook that in favor of spit-roasted chicken, delicious crêpes and freshly baked desserts. There's a set menu at lunch. **European**.

Neiva and Surroundings

Huila

This modern regional capital seems at odds with the olden, folksy character of the Huila department it represents, yet Neiva remains a bastion of tradition. Lying close to the equator, Nuestra Señora de la Limpia Concepción del Valle de Neiva—its full name—is characterized by hot, dusty lowlands and the creamy torrents of the mighty Río Magdalena.

The river serves as an important staging post for local farmers reliant on freighting rice, corn, beans, cotton, potatoes, sesame, tobacco and bananas to the markets of Bogotá. Engulfed by vast expanses of cattle plains and arid moorlands, with the snowy Nevado del Huila looming to the west, Neiva makes an ideal base for exploring the cacti-dotted Tatacoa Desert and archaeological wonders of San Agustín.

A BIT OF HISTORY

Opitas, as people from Huila are known, are mostly of Spanish descent or *mestizo*. Before the arrival of the Spaniards in the 16C, Huila was populated by native warrior groups: the **Paeces**, **Yalcones** and

▶ **Population:** 315,332.
⚬ **Michelin Map :** p349.
▤ **Info:** Policía Turismo Neiva, Centro Cultural José Eustasio Rivera, Carrera 5 # 21-82. ℘(8) 875 3042.
☺ **Don't Miss:** An opportunity to listen to *bambuco* music and watch a local folkloric dance, complete with traditional costumes; the mesmerizing lunar landscape of the La Tatacoa desert, a paleontologist's dream land of red-rock formations and sun-baked sands, even more beautiful in the late afternoon hours when the area is swarming with birds and the lighting enhances color contrasts. Get your camera ready.

Pijaos. They fiercely opposed the Spanish expansion in the region.

After **Juan de Cabrera**'s failed attempt to establish a settlement on the right bank of the Magdalena River in 1539, **Juan de Alonso y Arias** tried his luck farther to the north, on the present site of Villavieja; his settlement ended up being destroyed by the Pijaos in 1560. The city was finally founded in 1632 by **Diego de Ospina y Medinilla**.

Río Magdalena, Huila

Proexport Colombia

GETTING THERE

BY AIR - Flights arrive from Bogotá, Cali, Medellín and other destinations at Neiva's **Benito Salas Vargas Airport** (NVA) just north of city center. A **taxi** to the city center takes 5min.

BY BUS - Buses arrive from Bogotá (6hrs; 5,000 COP), San Agustín (5.5hrs; 12,000 COP), Popayán (11hrs; 19,000 COP) at the **bus terminal**, the Terminal de Transportes (Carrera 7 No 3-76S), about a 30min walk from city center of town, or 5min taxi ride.

GETTING AROUND

BY BUS - 🖱 *See above for address of bus terminal.* Local buses service the city. To access the **Tatacoa Desert,** take a collectivo from the bus terminal to Villavieja. To get to San Agustín's **archaeological zone**, take one of the frequent minibuses from Neiva (5hrs; 11,000 COP), or one of San Agustín's battered taxis if you're unwilling to walk what is less than 3km/1.8mi to the site.

ON FOOT - Though Neiva is a sizable modern city, several sights of interest cluster in the vicinity of Parque de Santander and along Carrera 5 and 7, so walking is an option, if you avoid the heat of the day.

GENERAL INFORMATION

ACCOMMODATIONS - While Neiva's own attractions are limited, the city makes a good base for exploration of outlying sights such as San Agustín and the Tatacoa Desert. Reserve lodgings well in advance if you plan to visit Neiva during its major **fiesta** *(Jun)*. 🖱 *See ADDRESSES at end of the chapter.*

Today, as the capital of Huila, Neiva not only plays a major role in the region's economy, but also upholds the department's unique cultural identity and strong **folkloric tradition**, mainly by staging a trio of annual fiestas famous for their colorful regional costumes *(🖱 see sidebar p378)*. Throughout the city, an authentic song and dance tradition called *sanjuanero, rajalena and bambuco*—the so-called "rhythm of Huila"—remains very much alive.

A Treasure Trove

Bordered by the departments of Tolima, Cundinamarca, Meta, Caquetá and Cauca, Huila is wedged between the Eastern and Central Cordilleras and blessed with many rivers. The **Río Magdalena**, which supports varied ecosystems, also drains a fertile valley and is a vital resource for domestic, industrial and agricultural needs. Well-nourished **farmlands** produce significant amounts of Colombia's **coffee**, **cocoa** (for chocolate), **cassava** and **livestock**.

An abundance of **oil** and **minerals** such as **phosphate rock** are an added geological facet of the landscape. Subsoil areas contain deposits of **natural gas**, **gold**, **silver** and **quartz**.

Other surprises awaiting discovery include some spectacular paleontological, archaeological and geographical features, from rust-colored outcroppings and grayish sand dunes studded with **fossils** to huge other-worldly standing stones. Towering at 5,365m/17,602ft, the great **Nevado del Huila** ranks as Colombia's highest active volcano—a beautiful, yet threatening mass of seismic energy that continues to spew molten rock into the Páez River

Long on Atmosphere

Neiva isn't renowned for its wealth of sightseeing opportunities, though the city has invested in a number of well-run and well-funded museums.

However, visitors will enjoy soaking up the atmosphere of this little-visited regional hub. It makes a good base from which to explore Huila's farthest reaches.

Grab a cup of coffee and people-watch from Neiva's **Malecón Río Magdalena**, a cosmopolitan stretch of city space that boasts cafes with outdoor seating and pleasing waterfront vistas.

Bambuco dancing

Proexport Colombia

Reinado Nacional del Bambuco

The highlight of Neiva's **Fiestas de San Juan y San Pedro** *(Jun)* is a beauty-queen pageant wherein the **National Queen of Bambuco** is crowned.

By tradition, only childless Colombian-born maidens who have lived in the area for 10 years may enter. Prospective queens also need a college education and should be 18-25 years of age. Entrants are judged on their dance skills—the local **sanjuanero folk dances** are a serious business—and on their cultural attributes, beauty, punctuality and popularity. The Huilense place great emphasis on interpreting the *sanjuanero* in its purest form to honor the origins of the distinctive **bambuco** rhythms and the culture of the Colombian Andes region.

Played with three typical instruments—the **bandola**, the **tiple**, and the **guitar**—songs, as well as choreography, are also awarded crucial marks in the bid for the crown. Much drinking and carousing accompanies a succession of raucous *bambuco* showcases, prompting great applause and fervor during colorful, noisy parades in June and July. Entrants are also given marks for the authenticity and quality of their **regional costume**: potential queens are adorned in a richly embroidered colorful frock of layered petticoats, swirled for dramatic effect.

SIGHTS
Parque de Santander
Neiva's central square is a popular gathering point. It is flanked by a few buildings worthy of interest, including the Gothic Revival **Catedral Inmaculada Concepción** (*Calle 7 # 4-52*), erected between 1917 and 1957, and the **Templo Colonial** (*Carrera 5 # 7-98, corner with Calle 8),* a fine 17C structure notable for its original stone floors, wooden ceilings and mud walls.

Museo Arqueológico Regional del Huila
Centro Cultural José Eustasio Rivera, Carrera 5 # 21-81. ○*Open Mon–Thu 8am–12:30pm, 2pm–5pm.* ☎*(8) 875 3070.*
En route to San Agustín or Tierradentro, stop by this small museum to see its collection of lithic tools, ceramics, carvings and jewelry.

These pre-Columbian artifacts were found in and around Neiva, San Agustín, Tesalia and **Santa Ana**. Located on the banks of the Cabrera River, some 165km/102mi from Neiva, this archaeological zone has revealed prehistoric cemeteries, anthropomorphic sculptures and various objects made in tumbaga (an alloy of gold and copper).

Museo de Arte Contemporáneo del Huila★
Centro Cultural José Eustasio Rivera, Carrera 5 # 21-81. ○*Open Mon–Fri 9am–noon, 2pm–6pm by previous appointment.* ▰*Guided tours available.* ☎*(8) 875 3042.* *http://artemach.blogspot.com.*
This small museum is jam-packed with artwork, almost all by local artists. The sculpture is particularly exciting, made from diverse materials including natural stone, forged metal, scrap items, card-

board, household objects and fabric. One of the temporary exhibits organized by the museum showcased the work of great Colombian painter and sculptor **Omar Rayo**, just before his death in June 2010.

Museo Geologíco Petrolero

Facultad de Ingeniería, Universidad Surcolombiana, Avenida Pastrana Borrero. ⏰*Open Tue 8am–10am, 2pm–6pm, Fri 8am–noon, 2pm–6pm,* 👈*Guided tours upon request for a small fee.* ✆*(8) 875 4753 ext 301. http://museousco.neivap.com.*
Located in the School of Engineering at the University of South Colombia, this museum narrates the history of the petroleum industry in this part of the country. If you plan on visiting La Tatacoa Desert, you might enjoy the exhibits on mineralogy and paleontology.

Neiva's Monuments

Standing 16m/52ft high and 12m/39ft wide, the **Monumento a la Gaitana** *(Avenida Circunvalar with Carrera 1)* is a poignant sculpture created by **Rodrigo Arenas Betancur**. It skillfully shows the two sides of **Caciqua Gaitana**, a Pijao woman who led an Indian rebellion in the 16C—one loving, motherly and tender, and the other, a fierce warrior, avenging the death of her son **Timanco**.

Another handsome statue, the **Monumento a los Potros** *(Avenida la Toma and Carrera 2)* is a tribute to Neiva's illustrious son **José Eustasio Rivera** (1888-1928), famous for his widely acclaimed novel *La Vorágine* (The Vortex, 1924), in which he denounced the hardships of the Amazon rubber workers.

Parque Islas de Aventura★

Cable car from the Torre del Mohán, Avenida Circunvalar and Calle 9, alongside the Río Magdalena.
👉*Park closed for renovation until 2011.*
Cross the **Magdalena River** by cable car at 236m/774ft or by riverboat to reach this popular island getaway. Covered with dense, humid tropical forest, it is a pleasant place amenable to outdoor

The Petroglyphs of Huila

Widely regarded as a form of **shamanic visionary art**, petroglyphs are found in nearly all areas of Colombia. The unknown artists who engraved these mysterious symbols in the rock were most likely the *jeques* or high priests, who could talk to the spirits of dead ancestors, bring rain, heal the sick and predict the future.

In the department of Huila alone, beside the magnificent rock at **Aipe**, there are several places where petroglyphs can be seen, generally near water sources or channels that have now disappeared. Here are a few:

◆ Acevedo ◆ Agrado ◆ El Tambillo
◆ Garzón ◆ Pitalito ◆ Saladoblanco
◆ Suaza ◆ Timana ◆ Villavieja.

pursuits such as hiking, horseback riding, cycling, bird watching, sport fishing, rafting, canoeing, kayaking and canyoning.

EXCURSIONS
Rivera★

▶ *20km/12mi S of Neiva, off Carretera 45.*
This pretty town (Pop. 16,654) boasts a curative health source, given its large number of underground thermal springs. Over the years, a variety of establishments such as **Termales de Rivera** *(*⏰*open Tue–Fri 4pm–midnight; Sat–Sun & public holidays 10am–midnight;* 🎫*14,000 COP;* ✆*8 838 7147; www.comfamiliarhuila.com/termales. html)* have sprung up to capitalize on the therapeutic benefits of the local waters. Several traditional healers use the sulfur-rich properties in their treatment of fatigue, aches and joint stiffness.

Piedra Pintada de Aipe

▶ *In Aipe, 32km/20mi N of Neiva via Carretera 45.*
Just 30m/98ft off the main road to Bogotá, this gigantic rock (6m/20ft long by 3m/10ft high) is etched with **petro**

glyphs carved by pre-Columbian **Pae-ces** and **Pijaos** peoples, representing birds, animals and hunting scenes. The rock is located in an area believed to be a former sacred burial ground.

Villavieja★★

36km/22mi N of Neiva, off Carretera 45.
Located close to the La Tatacoa Desert, this town (Pop. 7,314) is renowned as "Colombia's Paleontological Capital." It offers some handsome examples of Colonial architecture and an interesting museum.

Capilla de Santa Bárbara

Calle 3 # 3-05.
This 1630 edifice boasts the distinction of being the oldest church in the Huila department. It is worth seeing for its ornate **altar** alone.

Museo Paleontológico★

Casa de la Cultura, Calle 3 # 3-04.
Open Mon–Fri 7:30am–1pm, Sat–Sun 7am–6pm. 2,000 COP.
(8) 879 7744 ext. 110.
This museum has a fine collection of fossils from the La Tatacoa Desert, including mollusks, turtles, mice and even giant armadillos, many recovered by the local people.
Boasting close links with several American universities, the museum has been instrumental in collecting some extraordinarily well-preserved crocodile skulls, fossilized ground sloths and other endemic South American mammals—a study that helped highlight a striking bio-geographic difference between the tertiary faunas of Colombia and Patagonia.

Desierto de la Tatacoa★★

About 40km/25mi N of Neiva, by way of Villavieja. Guided tours organized by Andarríos (1) 606 4557; http://andarrios.com.co. To visit the Tatacoa Desert, it is advisable to get an early start (7am is ideal), as temperatures here can be positively Sahara-like, reaching a harsh 50°C/ 122°F. Be sure to wear long trousers, a long-sleeve shirt, hat and hiking shoes. Bring sunscreen and carry plenty of water.
Located in the middle of the upper course of the **Magdalena River**, this awesome desert lies in a rain shadow, and receives little precipitation, although it is surrounded by moist montane forests. It is actually the second-largest semi-arid area in Colombia after the La Guajira region, on the northernmost tip of the Caribbean coast. At Tatacoa, a unique ecosystem of eroded **cliffs** and crumbling **gullies** lying at depths of 20m/66ft is home to **scorpions** and **rattlesnakes**, with goats and cattle grazing on patches of scrub nourished by the reserves of the wetter months of April, May, October and November. With a backdrop of **high mountains**, this once lush garden terrain is all dried

Desierto de la Tatacoa

Proexport Colombia

up and withered. Spanning an area of 330sq km/127sq mi, it offers huge, open stretches of rust-colored sand peppered by sun-parched rocks and patches of arid scrub. Strange **cacti**, isolated **wind-gnarled trees** and other alien-looking plants evoke the feeling of a landscape from another planet. The **Cuzco** sector, in particular, comprises an eerie, ochre-toned labyrinthine valley riddled by lunar-like walking paths.

For a change of scenery, visit the grayish sand dunes of the **Los Hoyos** area.

Observatorio Astronómico de la Tatacoa★★

Guided tours daily 6:30am–9:30pm 5,000 COP high season, 4,000 COP low season. (8) 879 7584. www.tatacoa-astronomia.com.

Dry, clear conditions at Tatacoa are ideal for **stargazing** and observing **meteor showers**. Without moisture in the air, the sky is exceptionally visible. In daylight, it is cloud-free, but occasionally dotted with swooping hawks and eagles.

Anyone who enjoys the night sky will definitely relish some time at this observatory. After dark, the surrounding blood-red arid soil fades to a golden orange. Several telescopes are set up along an open terrace to make full use of a terrain free of any light pollution whatsoever.

San Agustín★★★
(*see SAN AGUSTÍN*)

Tierradentro★★
(*see POPAYÁN*)

Parque Nacional Natural Cueva de los Guácharos★★

Accessible from Neiva by way of Carretera 45 to Pitalito (183km/114mi SW), then via the road to Palestina (22km/14mi S) through some lovely rural scenery, then onto La Mensura (8km/5mi S), and finally to the park's entrance at Sector Cedros (8km/5mi S), a 5-6hr drive. Open daily 8am–4pm. Permission to enter must be obtained from the park administration center

---

The Elusive Guácharo

Otherwise known as the **oilbird**, the *guácharo* lives in caves and hollows, and emits a distinctive mournful call in the dark. Entering a cave with a light especially provokes these piercings **calls**, which are uttered when the birds prepare to emerge from a cave at dusk. Slim, long-winged and small footed, the *guácharo* is a **seasonal migrant**, moving from its breeding caves in search of **fruit** trees. It clings to vertical surfaces and navigates restricted areas of caves with nimble dexterity, using its powerful **hooked bill** to forage. Reddish-brown in color, with white spots on the nape and wings, the birds nest on cave ledges (the nest being a heap of droppings), usually over a stream.

---

in Palestina, Calle 3 # 3-12. 32,000 COP. (8) 831 5702. Guided tours organized by the Oficina de Ecoturismo in Bogotá; (1) 353 2400 ext 138. www.parquesnacionales.gov.co.

Colombia's oldest national park (1960) was named after the nocturnal bird found in the western face of the Cordillera Oriental.

Straddling the departments of Huila and Caquetá, it covers an area of 90sq km/35 sq mi and comprises high-elevation **cloud forests** and neo-tropical ecosystems.

The park is home to one of the last remaining undisturbed **oak forests** in the country. A maze of canyons, ravines and **rocky caves** carved by the waters of the **Sauza River** and its tributaries include the Cueva del Indio, Cueva del Hoyo, Cabaña la Ilusión and Cueva de los Guácharos.

The **Cascada Cristales** and **Cascada Quebrada Negra** are among the highlights, along with a **natural bridge** across the Sauza River and a perfectly-located **observation point** for views of forests filled with **birds** (some 300 species).

ADDRESSES

🛏STAY

$$ Hosteria Matamundo – *Carrera 5 # 3 Sur 51, Neiva.* ✕ ⌷ ☎*(8) 873 0202. www.hosteriamatamundo.com. 22 rooms.* The walls of this restored Colonial mansion are white, the rooms and communal areas are light and airy. All rooms have air-conditioning, free Wi-Fi and cable TV. If you eat in the hotel's restaurant, you'll have your pick between indoor and outdoor seating. The poolside bar features live music many nights.

$$ Hotel Pacandé – *Calle 10 # 4-39, Neiva.* ▣✕ ☎*(8) 871 1766. www.hotelpacande.com.co. 27 rooms.* Cozy and comfortable, this white-washed boutique hotel attracts guests with its host of amenities. Rooms face the small interior courtyard, which centers on a bubbling fountain. Safe deposit boxes, a gym, and high-speed Internet connection (at no charge) number among the modern conveniences. The hotel's restaurant provides room service.

$$$ Hotel Neiva Plaza – *Calle 7 # 4-62, Neiva.* ✕ ⌷ ☎*(8) 871 0806 or 871 0498. www.hotelneivaplaza.com. 90 rooms.* Located in the heart of Neiva, close to Parque Santander, the stylish and contemporary Neiva Plaza ranges over four floors, the top three of which contain rooms. Much of the original architecture has been preserved in this landmark 1956 building, which now contains a soda fountain, a restaurant and a sprawling terrace. Potted palms line the refreshing courtyard pool.

$$$ Hotel Tumburagua Inn – *Carrera 5 # 5-40, Neiva.* ▣✕ ☎*(8) 871 2470. www.htumburagua.com. 36 rooms.* Given its location in the financial zone, near the Banco de la Republic, this small hotel caters to business travelers. A business center, conference room, and audio-visual setups provide all the fittings for a successful meeting. Recently renovated, rooms have air-conditioning and private baths.

🍴EAT

$ Delicias de Fortalecillas – *Malecón del Río Magdalena, Neiva. Lunch only.* ☎*316 634 4617.* With its pleasant setting amid lush vegetation on the bank of the River Magdalena, this is a relaxing place to pass the time and people-watch. While you're at it, enjoy tasty dishes such as *huilense parrilla* (grilled pork) as well as grilled beef, chicken and fish. **Regional Colombian**.

$ Super Jugos La Ñapa – *Carrera 5 # 12-26, Neiva.* ☎*(8) 871 2251. Closed Sun.* Though not much to look at on the outside, this budget eatery is nonetheless worth a visit—especially if cost is an issue. This is the place to sample an array of the exotic local fruit, which is squeezed here into refreshing fruit drinks. Sandwiches and snacks are also served. **Colombian**.

$$ La Casa del Folclor – *Calle 33 # 5P -59 (by the road to Bogotá), Neiva.* ☎*(8) 875 3040. http://lacasadelfolclor.com.* Casa del Folclor's laid-back atmosphere provides the perfect setting in which to savor satisfying *opita* (the local name for the people of this area) cuisine. The menu cites a wide variety of local fish and meat dishes, and recommends juice squeezed fresh from the cholupa, a sweet and sour fruit grown in the Huila region. For a traditional treat, try the signature Huila grilled platter, a mouth-watering mixture of meats that may make you wish you had grown up in these parts. **Colombian**.

$$ Restaurante Hotel Los Manguitos – *11km south of Neiva on Carrera 45 (the road to San Agustín).* ☎*(8) 870 5050. www.losmanguitos.com.* A collection of local memorabilia—costumes and musical instruments—adorns this family-owned restaurant, which has been in the same hands for 35 years. Its warm atmosphere and location just outside the city keep folks coming back for more. **Regional Colombian**.

San Agustín★★★ and Surroundings

Huila

As the undisputed "Archaeological Capital of Colombia," San Agustín boasts a wealth of ancient treasures scattered around the picturesque landscapes of the Upper Magdalena River Valley. Not long ago, this rural town wasn't easily accessible because of security problems, but today the situation is wholly different. Roads are safe and tourism has more than doubled in what is fast becoming one of the most-talked-about historical attractions in the Americas. Declared a UNESCO World Heritage Site in 1995, the Parque Arqueológico de San Agustín is a magical place, with hundreds of silent standing stones, impressive statue-guarded crypts, distinctive funerary mounds and elaborate monuments for visitors to discover.

A BIT OF HISTORY

In search of El Dorado, conquistador **Francisco García de Tovar** and his men were the first Europeans to make their way to this high valley where mounds of earth promised untold riches. Yet, no record was made of any finding.

The first description of San Agustín was made by **Juan de Santa Gertrudis,**

▶ **Population:** 29,699.
  Michelin Maps: p349 and p386.
  Info: Oficina Municipal de Turismo, Calle 3 and Carrera 12; Oficina de Policía de Turismo, Carrera 3, # 11-86. ℰ(8) 837 3062. www.icanh.gov.co. www.sanagustintravel.com.

  Don't Miss: The builders of these monumental statues definitely chose scenic sites to bury their dead. Provided that you have time, venture beyond the unparalleled Parque Arqueológico de San Agustín and explore some of the surrounding countryside, which offers great scenic views and interesting burial mounds such as the Alto de los Ídolos (near San José de Isnos), one of the best preserved funerary complexes in the region.

a monk from Majorca who visited the region in 1756. The entire area made such an impression on him that he recorded his observations in a chronicle entitled *Maravillas de la Naturaleza* (not published until 1956). San Agustín was

Fuente de Lavapadas

© G. Bludzin/Michelin

383

GETTING THERE

BY AIR - There is no air service to the village of San Agustín. It is best to fly into Neiva (see NEIVA) or Popayán (see POPAYAN) and take a bus to San Agustín from there (see BY BUS).

BY BUS - Long-distance buses arrive from Bogotá (12hrs overnight; 45,000 COP), Neiva (4hrs; 4,000-11,000 COP), Popayán (8hrs; 13,000 COP) and Pitalito (45min; 5,000 COP) at the **bus offices** in the area known as Cuatro Vientas on the corner of Calle 3 and Carrera 11 in the town of San Agustín.

GETTING AROUND

BY BUS - Buses and minibuses are available in the town of San Agustín. The archaeological park is 3km/1.8mi

from the town; bus transport (from corner of Calle 5 and Carrera 14) to the park costs about 1,000 COP.

BY TAXI - Fixed rates apply outside of town as well as in and are clearly shown inside the vehicles. A taxi ride to the park costs about 5,000 COP.

ON FOOT - The town sights and the archaeological park are within walking distance. Since you will be on your feet for 4-5hrs in the park, consider taking a bus or taxi to/ from the park.

GENERAL INFORMATION

ACCOMMODATIONS - Lodgings are quite basic in San Agustín; if you choose to stay outside of town, chivas and vans can take you to and from your hotel.

---

then visited in 1797 by **Francisco José de Caldas**, a famous Neo-Granadine scientist who called attention to the historical importance of its stunning statuary.

In 1857 Italian geographer **Agustín Codazzi** visited the southern region of Huila. He did some mapping of the zone, and even drew a few hypothetical reconstructions of the ruins. In the 20C San Agustín's archaeological vestiges finally became the delight and fascination of archaeologists such as **Konrad Theodor Preuss**, the first to lead scientific investigations in 1913, only to draw a blank. Archaeological excavations did not start until the 1930s. Luis Duque Gómez and Julio César Cubillos led particularly intensive explorations in the 1970s.

In spite of all this work and ongoing research, little is known about the mysterious statue builders except that the area was settled as early as 3300 BC. The "classic" Agustinian period (200 BC-AD 800) was characterized by the construction of large burial mounds and the production of zoomorphic and anthropomorphic stone carvings and statues. By the 16C, this distinct culture had disappeared.

Archaeological Zone

Although not all the region's fine archaeological treasures are contained within the limits of the **Parque Arqueológico de San Agustín**, it is arguably home to many of the most significant ones. Spanning an incredible 500sq km/193sq mi, the park is considered the largest of pre-Columbian sites in South America. Visitors should be prepared to cover a fair amount of ground to discover its full gamut of stones, as they are scattered on both sides of the mighty **Río Magdalena Gorge**, around the municipalities of **San Agustín** and **San José de Isnos**.

Ideally, visitors should see the vestiges located around both towns, keeping in mind that San Agustín does remain the primary site. Should you be pressed for time and unable to travel farther afield, there are plenty of rock-carved figurines to enjoy right there. And these account for only a small portion of the ancient ruins that lie buried in the area and surrounding valley.

Today San Agustín's ceremonial statues seem unperturbed by time, which is nothing short of miraculous considering that the entire zone was affected by the Colombian internal conflict for many years.

SAN AGUSTÍN

Apart from San Agustín's archaeological gems, the town itself is a pleasant place to spend time in and soak up southwest Colombia's rural ambience.

A few simple churches are worth a look such as the **Iglesia Nuestra Señora de Lourdes** (*Calle 1 # 10-11*) and **Iglesia San Agustín** (*Carrera 14 # 2-45*). The **Museo Arqueológico Julio César Cubillos** (*Carrera 11 # 3-61;* ⏰*open Mon–Fri 8am–noon, 2pm–6pm;* ✆*8 837 3007*) contains some interesting artifacts, though it isn't as well-stocked as the collection in the park's museum (✆*see below*).

Yet for many, it is the **Piscina Municipal Las Moyas** (*Calle 5, on the way to Parque Arqueológico*) that is San Agustín's most welcoming attraction. A swim in its clear, sparkling waters is much appreciated after a long, muddy day hike out to the statues and monuments.

PARQUE ARQUEOLÓGICO DE SAN AGUSTÍN★★★

▶ *3km/1.8mi W of San Agustín.*
⏰*Open daily 8am–4:30pm.*
☞*15,000 COP,* ☞*25,000 COP combined with Parque Arqueológico Alto de los Ídolos y Alto de las Piedras.* ✆*(1) 561 9700. www.icanh.gov.co.*
✎*To do the park justice, arrive with a few hours to spare and wear comfortable clothing appropriate for walking on sloping grass and unmarked paths.*

Museo Arqueológico y Sala Etnográfica★

Located at the entrance to the park.
⏰*Open daily 8am–4:30pm.*
☞*included in park entrance fee.*
✆*(1) 561 9700 ext 109.*
www.icanh.gov.co.

This museum provides an overview of the Agustinian culture as it is understood today. Various statues, stone artifacts and pottery from different time periods are on display. An ethnographic section exhibits pieces of clothing, feather art, headdresses and necklaces of various Colombian ethnic groups.

Once you've entered the gate and visited the museum, you'll start to get a feel for the lay of the land. Among artificial banks and earthworks, there is a mind-boggling succession of megalithic monuments, dolmenic tombs, caryatids supporting large slabs of stones, big monolithic sarcophagi, petroglyphs and of course, those famous Agustinian statues (✆*see sidebar p387*), some more than 6m/20ft high, with iconographic features.

Mesitas★★★

In the Agustinian culture, the ordinary man was buried under the floor of his hut. Elaborate tombs with monumental architecture housed the remains of important people. In order to build those tombs, hills were leveled, and funeral monuments were in turn placed on little mounds.

The park encompasses four of these man-made **esplanades** or *mesitas*. They contain distinct groupings of statues, crypts and figurines dating from

---

El Purutal-El Tablon Trail★

Lying fairly close to one another, the following sites may be visited all in one trip. This being a popular 15km/9mi hike, you may decide to walk, unless you prefer to arrange a horseriding trip with your local hostel and follow the passable, well-marked horse trail, an excellent opportunity for sightseers in the saddle to revel in the scenery.

El Tablón★ – A set of statues presumably dedicated to a moon deity.

La Chaquira★ – A sacred site where sacrifices were performed, with petroglyphs carved onto large rocks overlooking the impressive Río Magdalena gorge.

La Pelota★ – More statues, including one of an eagle devouring a snake.

El Purutal★ – Some of the rare examples in the region of statues with polychrome paint.

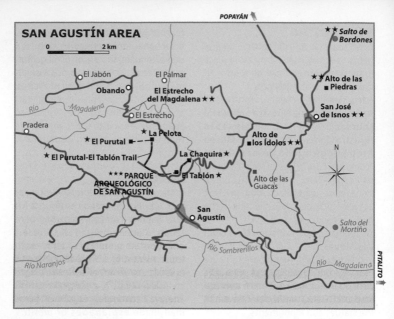

SAN AGUSTÍN AREA

2C BC–AD 10C. The well-tended paths connecting each area can get muddy during the wetter months.

Mesita D
Located in the museum's garden, this small group of graves, less complex than those found in the other *mesitas*, dates from 2C BC, 2C AD and 5C AD, and contains a few pits with a chamber.

Mesita B
You will see the famous 4m/13ft high statue of an eagle grasping a snake with its claws at this site, which houses a most interesting collection of tombs (1C BC) characterized by three artificial burrows, each containing a main burial area at its center.

Mesita A
These two impressive **dolmenic tombs** and various statues date to 2C-3C AD.

Mesita C
This small group of **dolmenic tombs** (3C AD-7C AD) is located near the sacred spring of Lavapatas, the next stop.

Fuente de Lavapatas★★
This picturesque riverside maze of **canals** and **terraced pools** is thought

to be a sacred site for religious ceremonies and **ritual baths** in the ancient San Agustín culture. It consists of some 30 monuments carved on-site in the bedrock of the stream, depicting lizards, snakes, salamanders, iguanas, toads, chameleons and turtles with human faces and shapes, forming a complex sculpture on a grand scale. Water flows through the ditches to intertwine with the other parts of the maze, symbolically evoking the journey of life.

Alto de Lavapatas★★
At the end of a muddy track, San Agustín's oldest site (3300 BC) tops a hill, affording unforgettable **views**★★★ of the countryside. The tombs here are guarded by impressive **anthropomorphic** and **zoomorphic** statues, including a good example of the *Doble Yo* or "double self" style (possibly a reference to a common form of ritual dance in ancient America, where it was customary to wear the skin of an animal).

Bosque de las Estatuas★
A pleasant walk along a winding path leads past a collection of statues originally found in remote areas, some abandoned by looters, and now set in natural woodlands.

Agustinian Statuary

Known as **chinas**, San Agustín's mysterious statues are mostly rectangular or oval in shape. They were carved in blocks of tuff and volcanic rock, and came in various sizes, the most impressive being more than 6m/20ft high and weighing several tons. Most statues were originally painted yellow, red, black and white, but these colors were preserved only in those that have remained underground or under cover. In among the megalithic tombs, dolmens, caryatids and burial chambers, some of the most mysterious sculptures clearly

Eagle with snake statue, Mesita B
© Richard McCole/Michelin

represent **reincarnation** themes, and the imagery is strongly associated with the spiritual power of the dead and more generally, the **supernatural world**.

The statues predominantly represent **anthropomorphic male figures**, sometimes bearing feline features (linked to the image of masculine force), sometimes hovered over by a double figure. Adorned with various styles of clothing, hair and accessories, they share common features such as a disproportionately large head, **blank eyes**, a rigid posture, and thin arms bent at the elbows, ending in **claws** rather than fingers. When flanked by guardians or warriors, the statue of the deceased gains even greater importance. Although the exact symbolism of the carved stones of San Agustín may never be known, studies in what appear to be similar cultures and sacred depictions have offered some credible suggestions.

 www.sanagustinstatues.org/english.html provides in-depth information on the sculptural iconography at San Agustín. It contains an amazing catalog with downloadable drawings of more than 450 statues, and for each statue, a corresponding information card: a must for anyone interested in archaeology.

This walk is a fitting way to conclude your visit of the park, since it illustrates the four major styles found in Agustinian statuary: archaic, naturalist, expressionist and abstract.

SURROUNDINGS
El Estrecho del Magdalena★★

 10km/6mi NW of San Agustín on the San Agustín to El Estrecho road.
For a picnic and an escape to total tranquillity, head to El Estrecho, the point at which the Río Magadalena is at its narrowest—a beautiful section of river at just 2.2m/7ft wide, where waters rush through on their way to the Caribbean Sea.

Obando
Cross the Magdalena narrows at El Estrecho, and follow the road to Obando.
On your way, you will pass a trail leading to some **petroglyphs**. The village of Obando itself is approximately 3km/2mi past this point.

Museo y Parque Arqueológico de Obando

 Open Tue–Sun 8am–1pm, 3pm–6pm.
 (1) 837 3133.
This set of painted burial tombs, dating from 11C-2C BC, is somewhat reminiscent of Tierradentro (*see POPAYÁN).*
It now forms part of a park that includes a small museum displaying some grinding stones, ceramic pots and other utensils.

Tomb, Alto de los Ídolos

Proexport Colombia

SAN JOSÉ DE ISNOS★★

▶ *Located across the Río Magdalena, 26km/16mi NE of San Agustín, 40km/ 25mi on the road from Pitalito.*

Nestled in rugged terrain at an altitude of 1,400m/4,593ft-1,800m/5,905ft, San José de Isnos (Pop. 23,756) is a charming, flourishing **coffee-producing** community. While in town, you might see coffee being dried under sheltered patios to protect the beans from unexpected showers—common in San José de Isnos. All the local farms here are small holders in size, and the growers say their coffee has the aroma of raisins, nuts and chocolate, very caramel-like and sweet. Local coffee is sold by roadside vendors and brewed by local cafes, so be sure to ask for a cup when passing through. San José de Isnos is certainly not just a jumping-off point for the region's archaeological treasures. Yet, it makes a great base for reaching two lesser-visited Agustinian sites, also part of the UNESCO World Heritage list and every bit as fascinating as their counterparts in San Agustín.

SURROUNDINGS

🚙 All-day **jeep tours** run from San José de Isnos to Alto de los Ídolos, Alto de las Piedras and Salto de Bordones—a recommended way to experience the sector (*guided tours organized by Nueva Lengua Tours; ℘1 753 2451; www. nuevalenguatours.com*).

PARQUE ARQUEOLÓGICO ALTO DE LOS ÍDOLOS Y ALTO DE LAS PIEDRAS

🕐 *Open daily 8am–4:30pm.*
💰*15,000 COP,* 💰*25,000 COP combined with Parque Arqueológico de San Agustín. ℘(1) 561 9700. www.icanh.gov.co.*

Alto de los Ídolos★★

▶ *4km/3mi SW of San José de Isnos.*
This crescent-shaped site consists of 37 tombs and funerary monuments dating from 1C BC to 6C AD, some with traces of color still visible.

Alto de las Piedras★★

▶ *7km/4mi N of San José de Isnos.*
Nine burial mounds are set among an abundance of orchids. Admire sun gods and other deities, some with touches of red, yellow and black, and one most interesting statue representing a creature with large fangs.

Salto de Bordones★★

▶ *9km/6mi along the same road.*
Just outside the village of Bordones, this 300m/984ft high **waterfall**, said to be Colombia's highest, is set among spectacular jungle reached by a rough downhill trail *(1hr)*.

ADDRESSES

🏠 STAY

$ Hospedaje Cambi – *Carrera 13 # 3-36, San Agustín.* ✆*(8) 837 3357. 13 rooms.* Half a block from Parque Bolívar, this budget hostel provides clean, simple rooms in an old Colonial building. All except three of the rooms have a TV and private bath, though if you stay in one of the accommodations that shares a bath, you'll save money and you won't be disappointed. The beautifully maintained back patio invites relaxation with its bright flowers and comfortable seating.

$ La Casa de François – *Carrera 13 Vereda la Antigua, San Agustín (just off the junction of the roads to El Tabion and La Antigua.* ✆*(8) 837 3847. www.lacasadefrancois.com. 4 rooms.* Choose among private rooms, dorms or the campsite at this farmer's cottage turned backpackers' lodge. Located just outside town atop a small hill, the hostel can hold 16 people in the main building and two cabins. The knowledgeable and helpful French owner—François, of course—will pick guests up in San Agustín's center and bring them here. Although the hostel has no restaurant, delicious fresh homemade bread and jams are always on sale.

$$ El Maco – *Finca El Maco, 2km/1mi to the right of the municipal swimming pool, San Agustín.* ✕✆*(8) 837 3437. www.elmaco.ch. 7 rooms.* A good option for backpackers, this Swiss-run hostel sits amid landscaped grounds close to the archaeological park. Care has been taken to construct the building out of local wood and other materials. If you don't want to cook your own meals in the communal guest kitchen, treat yourself to a meal in the hostel's restaurant *(see restaurant listings, under EAT on this page)*.

$$ Finca el Cielo – *Via del Estrecho, 3km/2mi from San Agustín on the road to Huila.* 🅿✕✆*313 493 7446. www.fincael cielo.com. 5 rooms.* Located in the San Agustín archaeological park, this five-bedroom bamboo farmhouse boasts a panoramic view out over the Andes. The friendly owners can facilitate a wide number of extreme and adventure activities, including trekking and horseback riding (you can rent the farm's own horses). When you want to take a dip, there's a swimming pond on the grounds; and the terrace restaurant serves home-style dishes.

🍴 EAT

$ El Fogón – *Calle 5 # 14-30, El Centro, San Agustín.* ✆*(8) 837 3431.* If you want to eat where the locals eat, head for this modest restaurant in the center of the city. Steaks and chops head the à la carte menu (there's a fixed menu too), along with the likes of fried plantains. At lunch, the set menu is a great value. **Colombian**.

$ Restaurante El Maco – *Finca El Maco hostel, 2km/1mi to the right of the municipal swimming pool, San Agustín.* ✆*(8) 837 3437. www.elmaco.ch.* The hostel's restaurant wins local raves for its Thai cuisine. The Swiss owner of the property farms part of his land, and the restaurant profits from his organic produce in many of the dishes served here. **Colombian**.

$$ Donde Richard – *Calle 5 #23-45, San Agustín; on the road leading to the Parque Archeológico.* ✆*(8) 837 9692.* On the outskirts of town, Donde Richard wins high marks for its carefully seasoned meat and fish dishes as well as its local specialties. For a tasty regional treat, try the restaurant's signature *lomo de cerdo* (marinated pork loin). **Colombian**.

$$ Restaurante Italiano – *Vareda El Tablón, San Agustín.* ✆*(8) 837 9650. www.restauranteitalianosanagustin. vitriniando.com. Closed Mon.* For something out of the ordinary in southwestern Colombia, go for a pizza or a plate of pasta at this two-story restaurant across from the Iglesia de San Francisco. You'll be assured of getting authentic cuisine here, since the place is run by an Italian. **Italian**.

Pasto★ and Surroundings

Nariño

Set in the fertile Valle de Atriz, in Colombia's most southwesterly department, San Juan de Pasto is the capital of an agricultural region specialized in the production of dairy products. Nestled at the eastern base of Volcán Galeras, the country's most infamous spurting crater, the city has managed to retain some of its colonial charm, despite suffering earthquake and volcano damage. Dubbed "La Ciudad Teológica," Pasto boasts numerous churches and narrow cobbled streets. It is a popular jumping-off point for cross-border travel to Ecuador and for discovering nearby villages and natural parks.

▶ **Population:** 383,846.
🕭 **Michelin Maps:** p349 and p394.
🛈 **Info:** Oficina de Turismo, Calle 18 # 25-25 Centro. ✆ (2) 723 4962. http://turismocultura. pasto.gov.co and www. turismonarino.gov.co.
☺ **Don't Miss:** A stroll around Pasto's charming churches; a hike through Isla de la Corota Sanctuary, amid an abundance of bromeliads and orchids; a picnic on the shores of Laguna Verde, in a setting of bubbling waters and fumaroles; and the Gothic style church of Las Lajas, straddling the dramatic gorge of the Guáitara River.

A BIT OF HISTORY

Pasto was originally founded by Sebastián de Belalcázar in 1537, and was moved to its present location by **Lorenzo de Aldana** two years later. During the wars of independence, it became a **Royalist** stronghold, and led a fierce armed opposition to the Republican armies under the leadership of *mestizo* **Agustín Agualongo** (1780-1824). In the 19C, during the conflicts that pitted Liberals against Conservatives, Pasto became the capital of the Republic for a short few months. When the department of **Nariño** was created in 1904, it was then named its capital. Today, Pasto's deeply hybrid ethnicity, celebrated during its famous Carnival, has created a wholly distinct fusion of cultures, beliefs and flavors, quite unlike any other Colombian city.

Pasto and Volcán Galeras

© Roger Ressmeyer/Corbis

GETTING THERE

BY AIR - **Aeropuerto Antonio Nariño** (PSO), 35km/21mi north of Pasto, has direct flights from Bogotá and Cali. Buses and *colectivos* serve Pasto and connect with **Ipiales**, (80km/50mi southwest of Pasto), which has its own airport, Aeropuerto San Luis (IPI) with flights to Cali. There are no direct flights from either airport to Ecuador.
BY BUS - From Pasto's **bus terminal** (Carrera 20A and Calle 17), 2km/1mi from the city center, buses arrive from Bogotá (22hrs; 90,000 COP), Cali (9hrs; 38,000 COP) and Ipiales (2hrs; 8,000 COP) and will drop you off at Popayán which is en route. Ipiales' **bus terminal** is less than 1km/.6mi from its center. Buses have the best views if you sit on the right on the way from Ipiales. Buses also run to/from Bogotá (25hrs; 100,000 COP), Cali (10hrs; 68,000) as well as Popayán (8hrs COP) which is en route. At night this route attracts opportunistic bandits.

GETTING AROUND

BY BUS - Urban buses serve the city.
BY TAXI - A taxi (10min) to Pasto's bus terminal costs about 4,000 COP.

GENERAL INFORMATION

SAFETY - Drugs and gang violence haunt Pasto. Dense jungles in the area camouflage rivers along the Colombia-Ecuador border, making it a most difficult area for frontier control. Guerrilla activity has remained high, with the border notorious for narcotics and contraband. Pasto should be safe during daylight hours, but should be avoided after sundown.
COLOMBIA-ECUADOR BORDER - If crossing to Ecuador, be cautious. The border is linked by a road bridge with the Colombian and Ecuadorian immigration offices on their respective sides. On arrival, present your passport to the immigration office of the country you're leaving to collect your **exit stamp**. Walk across the bridge to the immigration office of the country you're entering and to collect your entry stamp.
Be sure to stop at both booths, in and out. Exit stamps are particularly easy to miss, a potential major problem for travellers later on. From Ipiales, buses run to the border from the corner of Calle 14 and Carrera 10.

Charming Survivors

Although a sizable number of its buildings have been destroyed by successive earthquakes, Pasto is still surprisingly inviting for visitors seeking to explore its highlights.
A number of ornate churches and fine museums share the city with pleasant parks that attract families on weekends, when all the shops are closed. Swings, slides and climbing frames at the **Parque Infantil** *(Carrera 30 and Calle 18)* are covered with children, while joggers and dog owners claim the paths, and picnickers spread out blankets to relax, eat and read among the trees.

SIGHTS

An important religious center since the colonial times, Pasto boasts a significant amount of churches for a town of its size.

The following are a few major ones, but for more details on Pasto's religious heritage, visit this website:
http://turismocultura.pasto.gov.co.

Catedral de Pasto

On Carrera 26 # 17-23, at the corner of Calle 17.
Consecrated in 1920, Pasto's cathedral is a rather austere redbrick building consisting of three large naves.
Inside, in the presbytery's apse, note the exquisite gilded **altarpiece** with a central niche holding the statue of the Sacred Heart of Jesus, framed by four Corinthian columns on each side.
Much of the cathedral's elaborate decor was due to Nariñense artists such as Isaac Santacruz, Luis Pazmiño, Lucindo Espinoza, José León Erazo and Miguel Astorquiza.

Proexport Colombia

Carnaval Negros y Blancos

Each January, one of the single most significant celebrations of ethnic and cultural difference in the country takes place in Pasto: a carnival proclaimed by **UNESCO** as one of the Masterpieces of the Oral and Intangible Heritage of Humanity in 2009.

This Carnival of Blacks and Whites is a mix of various influences, including the agrarian indigenous cultures of the **Pasto** and **Quillasinga** Indians, who held celebrations in honor of their moon goddess as a way of pleading protection for their crops. More modern origins stem from the slave-trade era, with a number of events that draw on the relationship between slave and Spanish master and the dynamics of power. Numerous up-tempo street processions and drum-based music fill the corners of the city during this two-day festival. Celebrated since the time of Spanish rule, the festival is awash with the eye-catching costumes and painted faces of the participants. The noisy, high-energy event culminates in the merry messiness of **black paint** (el Dia de Los Negros, January 5) and showers of **flour and talc** (El Dia de Los Blancos, January 6), said to foster tolerance and respect.

The **Museo del Carnaval** (Calle 19 and Carrera 42, Centro Cultural Pandiaco; open Tue–Sun 8am–6pm; ✆ (2) 731 4598) houses a permanent exhibit containing colorful puppets, costumes, masks, and elements of monumental floats from the carnivals.

Iglesia de San Juan Bautista★

Calle 18A # 25-17.

Pasto's only Colonial religious relic, and the city's former cathedral, this church occupies a prime location on **Plaza de Nariño**, the main square. The original building (c.1539), affected by earthquakes, was demolished and replaced by this one (1669), renowned for its pure Mozarabic style.

San Juan Bautista houses the remains of the city's first settlers and contains a few interesting pieces, including a **Baroque pulpit** and **La Danzarina**, a colorful statue of Virgin Mary by Bernardo de Legarda, a famous 18C Ecuadorian artist.

Iglesia de Cristo Rey★

Corner of Calle 20 and Carrera 24.

In the 1930s the original 16C Dominican church that stood on this site was replaced with this yellow-and-beige brick church, undoubtedly one of

Pasto's highlights. A stunning example of the High Gothic Revival style, Cristo Rey reveals an elegant façade framed by twin towers topped with angels. Inside, a monumental statue of Christ the King greets visitors as they come in. Note two large paintings by Isaac Santacruz, and as a background to the **main altar**, an impressive series of 19 **wood carvings**, crafted by Ecuadorian artists and by Alfonso Zambrano, a talented local sculptor. The skilled **guilding** on the altars was done by Alfonso Chaves Enríquez, yet another artist from Pasto. **Stained-glass windows** add the final touch to this harmonious interior.

Iglesia Nuestra Señora de Las Mercedes

On Carrera 22# 18-24.

The two churches that preceded this one, including a sanctuary erected in 1609, were both destroyed by eathquakes. The present one—a fine piece of Neo-

Romanesque architecture—dates from the early 20C. This church is the most visited church in town, as it houses the much revered statue of **La Virgen de las Mercedes**, the patron saint of Pasto, holding the baton of Royalist Colonel Basilio Garcia, who fought against Simón Bolívar in the 19C. Las Mercedes is famous for its extremely rare example of a **spiral staircase** without a central axis pole.

ADDITIONAL SIGHTS
Museo Taller Alfonso Zambrano Payán
Calle 20 # 29-79, Barrio las Cuadras. ⏰*Open Mon–Sat 8am–noon, 2pm–4pm.* ✆*(2) 731 2837.*
This museum was named after a 20C local sculptor who became particularly famous for his religious wood carvings and for his artistic contributions to the Pasto Carnival's floats. The eclectic collection includes religious artwork (with some fine pieces from the Quito School), musical instruments and pre-Columbian artifacts from the Quillasinga, Pasto and Tumaco cultures.

Museo del Oro Nariño
Calle 19 # 21-27, Centro Cultural Leopoldo López Alvarez. ⏰*Open Tue–Sat 10am–5pm.* ✆*(2) 721 5777. www.banrep.gov.co/museo.*
The permanent collection consists of some 400 pre-Columbian artifacts from the cultures of the southern Altiplano (**Capulí, Piartal** and **Tuza**) and the Pacific coastal plains (**Tumaco**). Workshops, talks and presentations are also held in a modern auditorium.

Museo Juan Lorenzo Lucero
Calle 18 # 28-27. ⏰*Open Mon–Fri 8am–10am, 2pm–3:30pm.* ✉*2,000 COP.* ✆*(2) 731 4414.*
Named for the 17C Bishop of Quito and Popayán, the museum displays religious artwork from the Quito School, but also folk art, musical instruments, and archaeological and ethnographic collections. An on-site library has a comprehensive collection of literary works by regional authors.

Museo Madre Caridad Brader Zahner
Calle 18 # 32A-01. ⏰*Open Mon–Fri 8am–11:30am, 3pm–5pm.* ✉*500 COP.* ✆*(2) 731 2092.*
In addition to the section devoted to the Franciscan Mother's life and work, the highlights of this museum are its archaeological and ethnographic exhibits, with indigenous ritual objects, jewelry, textiles and baskets, and various artifacts from the Calima, San Agustín and Pasto cultures, to name a few.

Museo Taminango de Artes y Tradiciones Populares de Nariño
Calle 13 # 27-67. ⏰*Open Mon–Fri 8am–noon, 2pm–4pm, Sat 9am–1pm.* ✉*2,000 COP.* ✆*(2) 723 5539.*
Housed in a Colonial mansion built in 1623, this museum shows different regional art techniques such as the pre-Columbian **barniz de Pasto**, a famous glaze made of vegetable resin extracted from the mopa-mopa tree, used to decorate wooden bowls, plates and boxes.

Circumvalar de Galeras

Also known as the **Ruta Dulce de Nariño** (Sweet Route of Nariño), this popular tour transports visitors through some particularly gorgeous countryside to several **colonial villages** around the foothills of the Volcán Galeras. Not only does the Circumvalar de Galeras run through **Nariño, La Florida, Sandoná, Consaca, Yacuanquer** and **Tangua** before looping back to Pasto, it also provides an opportunity to snap up **handicrafts** en route. At 48km/30mi NW of Pasto (via the Pasto-Sandoná road), Sandoná is famous for its palm-woven **Panama-style hats,** and Consaca is renowned for its colorful **Saturday market**. *Book through the tourist office or local hotel.* ✆*(2) 723 4962.* ✉*2,000 COP entrance fee.*

Don't miss the little garden full of traditional medicinal plants.

SURROUNDINGS

Volcán Galeras★

Hiking trail from Pasto via the western road off Carretera 25, leading to one of the two ranger stations: Sendero el Frailejonal and Sendero el Achichay. *Trail open daily 8am–5pm under normal circumstances. During periods of volcanic activity, the trail is closed; check current conditions with the local tourist board at http://intranet.ingeominas. gov.co. If conditions permit, guided tours are available via the Pasto tourist office; (2) 723 4962; 2,000 COP entrance fee; http://turismocultura. pasto.gov.co.*

As Colombia's most active volcano, Galeras has erupted frequently since the Spanish conquest, with the first eruption recorded on December 7, 1580. However, it has almost certainly been active for at least a million years, with very few periods of complete dormancy.

In 2010 Volcán Galeras began spewing smoke and ash, forcing the evacuation of 8,000 people—the 10th such eruption of the volcano in a 12-month period. Assuming that conditions are safe, a guided trek to the summit *(8km/5mi)* around this volatile terrain, ascending a path to 4,276m/14,029 ft, is well worth the slog for the truly unforgettable panoramic **views**★★, and for the Andean páramo and sub-páramo ecosystems that you will discover on the volcanic slopes.

Laguna de la Cocha★★

25km/16mi SE of Pasto (via El Encanto, located along Carretera 45). Given the lake's close proximity to the Putumayo department, a hotbed of guerrilla activity and an active drug production center, an organized excursion is considered the safer option. Trips may be booked with a local tour operator that include lunch and fishing gear.

As Colombia's second-largest lake, the Laguna de la Cocha is 14km/9mi long by 4.5km/2.8mi wide. It is, without a doubt, one of the most spectacular lakes in the Andes, set amid alpine vegetation at an elevation of 2,760m/9,055ft. With its pure air, pristine sparkling waters (good for trout fishing) and stunning colors, this water body occupies a resplendent setting that evokes the magic of Scandinavia.

There will be lakeside **trails** for you to explore, but mostly an island botanical garden right in the middle of the lake, which should not to be missed.

Macizo Colombiano

Proexport Colombia

The Road to Ecuador

To journey along the **Pan-American Highway** from **Popayán** to **Ipiales** is to experience some of Colombia's most magical landscapes. Between Popayán and Pasto, a vast mountainous knot known as the **Macizo Colombiano** (Colombian Massif) denotes the divergence of the Eastern, Western and Central cordilleras from the main Andean chain. Unfurling like a fan, the road radiates over deep, plunging valleys and precipitous gorges to crisscross crests lined with volcanoes up to 4,600m/15,100ft high. It skirts the hulking shadows of the Western Cordillera and its mighty textured folds to offer breathtaking **views**★★ of verdant gullies. Dense cloud forest cloaks rugged slopes as the headwaters of Colombia's two main rivers—the **Magdalena** and **Cauca**—slice their way through a jumbled landscape. On their long journey to the Caribbean, these rivers will cross rocky crevices, deep ravines, banana and sugarcane fields, canyons, rows of maize and towering vegetation—and for the next 6 to 9 hours, so will you.

The **Valle del Patía** marks the crossing of the provincial border between Cauca and Nariño at 550m/1,804ft above sea level. The thick, muggy, cloying air of this low-lying terrain is stifling, but the ascending mountain road soon brings relief as it climbs up to 1,000m/3,281ft and 1,500m/4,921ft through planted fields of tufted coffee. Even the constant noise of thundering trucks can't distract from the captivating beauty of the terrain of Carretera 25. From the Nariño departmental border, Pasto lies just 80km/50mi away in the **Valle de Atriz**, at the foot of **Volcán Galeras**, where the road twists and turns in some chaotic doglegs prior to another long climb. Follow it from the spectacular Guáitara gorge (at 1,700m/5,577ft) to Ipiales (at 2,900m/9,514ft)—a kaleidoscope of picturesque highland scenery guaranteed to invoke an involuntary intake of breath.

Santuario de Fauna y Flora Isla de la Corota★★
Boat departs from Puerto del Encanto (10min). ☎14,000 COP boat trip; ☎1,000 COP park entrance fee. ☏Guided tours organized by the Oficina de Ecoturismo in Bogotá. ☏(1) 353 2400 ext. 138. www.parquesnacionales.gov.co.

This offshore island reserve is officially the smallest of Colombia's national parks. La Corota is a 75m/247ft-deep expanse of low mountain humid forest, where important scientific research is conducted under the auspices of the University of Nariño. From the park's **observation point** above the lake, you can view a large diversity of birds

(32 species of fowl alone roost here), amphibians (newts and frogs) and some 500 plant species. A **nature trail** crosses the island amidst an abundance of epiphytes, including bromeliads, orchids and anthuriums. Two other **paths** circle La Corota in its entirety, allowing visitors to take a close look at the **aquatic habitat**, with its reeds, rushes and tall grasses, attracting coots, grebes and black-crowned night herons.

The island is also home to a small **chapel** dedicated to the adoration of the Virgin of Lourdes, the object of an annual pilgrimage.

Reservas Naturales de la Cocha★

Information available from the Pasto tourist office, Calle 18 # 25-25 Centro. ℘(2) 723 4962. http://turismocultura. pasto.gov.co.

Once a place of sacred rituals for the **Mocoa** and **Quillasinga** cultures, La Corota island is surrounded by small farming communities, active in conservation, that have set up more than 50 **private nature reserves**.

They collectively protect the prime forest areas and ecosystem of the **Guiamués River**, a tributary of the Río Putumayo, while practicing sustainable agriculture. Some provide interpretative trails for **bird watching** and other ecotourism-oriented activities.

EXCURSIONS
Túquerres

▶ *72km/45mi SW of Pasto (off the Carretera 25, the turn before El Pedregal).*
Authentic souvenirs, such as *ruanas* (woolen ponchos typical of the altiplano), might be for sale at the local weekly **Thursday market**.

Set among stunning highlands scenery, Túquerres (Pop 41,205) sits at an elevation of 3,051m/10,001ft and is a great base from which to explore the craggy foothills of a semi-active stratovolcano (see below).

Though agricultural settlements, potato crops and extension of cattle-ranching have modified some of Túquerres' natural habitat, the beauty of its overall setting has in no way diminished.

Laguna Verde★★

▶ *About 15km/9mi from Túquerres.*
The easiest access is to have a taxi drop you directly at the cabaña de Corponariño (the regional environmental agency). From this point, a 6km/3.7mi walk is necessary to reach the shores of Laguna Verde.

Rising to 4,070m/13,353ft amid fertile soils, **Volcán Azufral** (4,070m/13,353ft) displays a striking array of vascular plant species, thought to number some 470. Now part of the **Reserva Natural del Azufral** (*open to the public because of the low level of seismic activity*), the Azufral is particularly famous for its spectacular Laguna Verde (3,765m/12,353ft), the largest of its three **crater lakes**, owing its special color to sulfur and iron in the waters.

The trail weaves through the *frailejón* and *chupalla* plants of the páramo, and leads to the rim of the crater, offering great **views**★★ of the Azufral's lakes, all boasting ethereal qualities. Weather permitting, you might see as far as Cayemba (northern Ecuador) to the south, and Volcán Galeras to the east.

Nourished by sulfur springs, Laguna Verde occupies the northwestern side of the caldera. An 800m/2,625ft trail heads down to the shores of the lake, where sulfuric rocks, bubbling water and fumaroles are gentle reminders that this is not an extinct volcano.

Reserva Natural La Planada★

▶ *100km/62mi NW of Túquerres, 7km/ 4mi from Ricaurte, off the Carretera 10 towards Tumaco. Guided tours by calling the reserve. ℘(2) 775 3396. Maps and details about nature trails are available at the visitor center.*

This private reserve is a 3,200ha/ 7,907 acre expanse of lush cloud forest containing one of the densest concentrations of **endemic bird species** in South America.

At the heart of the indigenous **Awá territory** of Colombia, La Planada is situated on a rocky plateau between 1,850m/6,070ft and 2,300m/7,546ft above sea level.

© Michael Major/Dreamstime.com

Basílica Santuario de Nuestra Señora de Las Lajas★★★

▶ *7km/4mi SE of Ipiales via the road to Potosí.* ⏲*Open daily 6am–6pm; museum open daily 7am–noon, 2pm–6pm.* ☏*(2) 775 4490.*

History for some, legend for others, has it that the image of the **Virgen del Rosario**, venerated by Catholic pilgrims from all over Colombia and Ecuador, was discovered by an Indian woman in the mid-18C, etched on a stone slab in a **cave** by the **Guáitara River**. As reports of miracles spread throughout the region, devotion to the mysterious image soon grew and a humble chapel of wood and thatch was built. In 1795 local people started building a second chapel in brick and stone. It took seven years of hard work to complete the 7m/23ft long by 6m/20ft wide structure. In 1853 the chapel was widened under the guidance of Ecuadorian architect Mariano Aulestia, but it was still too small to accommodate the increasing number of pilgrims who came here. A last phase of construction, started in 1915 and completed in 1949, finally gave birth to Las Lajas as we know it today.

Framed by stark mountains and waterfalls, this stunning sanctuary is a daring example of **Gothic Revival** architecture. The gray and white grand basilica is a symphony of towers and spires, rose windows, buttresses and pinnacles. It straddles the verdant plunging gorge of the **Guáitara River** on a long, ornate **twin-arched bridge** (50m/164ft high by 17m/56ft wide and 20m/66ft long) linking both banks of the canyon. The originality of the main building, divided into three naves, is that it was designed so as to rest against the rock of the canyon, the **image** of the **Virgen del Rosario** forming the **altarpiece** of the central nave.

Under the care and administration of the Franciscan Sisters of Mary Immaculate, Las Lajas is a venue for regular religious worship. Upon entering the sanctuary, you will notice the large amount of *ex-votos* and plaques from grateful devotees who often arrive on foot from Ipiales, Pasto, Túquerres and nearby villages, or from Ecuador, often after walking 12 hours or more.

Perhaps most distinctive is the reserve's abundance of **orchid** and **bromeliad species**, one of Colombia's most impressive. The rich, unspoiled natural habitat is also home to a variety of amphibians (frogs and salamanders). A program of managed reintroduction of the **spectacled bear** has had some notable success.

Ipiales

80km/50mi SW of Pasto via Carretera 25.
Sitting at an elevation of 2,897m/9,505ft
on the banks of the **Río Guáitara**, mist-
shrouded Ipiales (Pop. 109,865) can be
cool and chilly, so sightseers will need
to prepare for colder Colombian climes.
Almost everyone stopping off in Ipiales,
located just 2km/1mi from Ecuador, is
here to cross the border or go to **Las
Lajas Sanctuary** (*see sidebar p397*),
a massive Gothic Revival church famed
for its many miracles, which attracts
pilgrims from all over Colombia and
Ecuador.
Like most border towns, Ipiales isn't
particularly blessed with beauty. Yet it
boasts one of Colombia's finest Indian
markets (held here each Friday). While
major attractions are lacking, a small
number of sights should be visited. Most
are centered on two parks at the heart
of city life.

Parque de la Independencia

Between Carreras 5 & 6 and Calles 8 & 9.
You'll find a collection of buildings
around this park, including the **Catedral
Bodas de Plata** (*Carrera 6 and Calle 13*).
Its rather uninspiring redbrick exterior
(1823) hides an impressive inner space,
featuring imposing columns, inlaid
wood, gilded chapel screens and huge
clerestory windows.
Outside, a needle-thin column dominates the center of the park, topped by
Lady Liberty riding on the back of a flying condor.

Parque La Pola

Between Carreras 5 & 6 & Calles 13 & 14.
This central plaza is edged by an endless
succession of banks, ATMs and money
changers, with buses zipping to and
from the border amid tooting horns.
In the midst of this traffic, a statue of
Policarpa Salavarrieta (1791-1817)
depicts the heroine of independence
breaking free from the chains that tether
her to a post. Overlooking the park, the
white and blue **Iglesia de San Felipe
Neri** (*Plaza La Pola and Carrera 5*), built
about 1825, is distinctive for its dome-
topped campaniles.
But perhaps more exciting are the scat-
tering of **indigenous communities**
within a stone's throw of Ipiales, some
of which have weekly **markets** of fresh
produce, handicrafts and **local art**.

Cumbal★★

15km/9mi NW of Ipiales via Carretera 10.
This municipality (Pop. 22,418) was
named in honor of **Cacique Cumbe** of
the Pasto Nation who, back in in 1529,
founded a *pueblo* at the foot of **Volcán
Nevado del Cumbal** (4,764m/15,630 ft),
between the Río Blanco and the Riochi-
quito. A trip to Cumbal is rewarding, not
only for its picturesque Saturday market, but also for the amazing **views**★★ it
affords of its own Volcán Cumbal and the
nearby snow-capped **Volcán Nevado
Chiles** (4,748m 15,577ft).
Trails snake to the summit of Volcán
Cumbal, where locals harvest ice and
sulfur. It's a hard uphill climb, but worth
it for the **views**★★ of Ecuadorian snowy
peaks to the south and the glittering
Pacific Ocean to the west. While in Cumbal, explore the following sights.

Piedra de Machines

*2km/1.2mi from Cumbal, on the path
leading to Volcán Cumbal.*
Located on an ancient place of worship
for the Pasto people, this big rock
(2.5m/6.5ft long by 2m/8.2ft high) is
etched with **petroglyphs**.
Among anthropomorphic and zoomorphic figures, notice the star-shaped symbol that anthropologists have called *Sol
de los Pastos*.

Laguna de la Bolsa o Cumbal

*6km/3.7mi past the Piedra de
Machines, at the foot of Volcán Cumbal.*
Rainbow trout thrive in the cold waters
of this pretty **lake** (5km/3mi long by
2km/1.2mi wide), set at an elevation of
3,036m/9,961ft.

ADDRESSES

🏠STAY

$ Koala Inn – *Calle 18 # 22-37, Pasto. ℘(2) 722 1101. 15 rooms.* Although nondescript from the outside, the Koala Inn is a great starting point for backpackers exploring the area. Inside, the decor is pleasant, with a common TV room for socializing. A 15-minute cab ride from the bus station, this hostel provides all the essentials: a book exchange, laundry and an American-style breakfast for 4,000 COP. Guests have a choice of room size, view and private or shared bath.

$$ Hotel Cuéllar's – *Carrera 23 # 15-50, Pasto. ✕℘(2) 723 2879. www.hotel cuellars.com. 53 rooms.* One of the larger hotels of the area, Hotel Cuéllar's enjoys an excellent reputation for its helpful and accommodating staff. It is located in the center of Pasto about four blocks from Plaza de Nariño. Large, bright earth-toned rooms have all the standard amenities: phone, work desk, safe, hairdryers and private bathrooms.

$$ Loft Hotel – *Calle 18 # 22-23, Pasto. ✕ Spa ℘(2) 722 6733. www.lofthotel pasto.com. 24 rooms.* Located in the city's business zone, this minimalist hotel is designed for peace, luxury and rest. Clean lines distinguish the rooms and suites, which sport a slight Asian vibe in their design. Soft lighting, varnished wood floors, king-size beds, and free Wi-Fi access are what you can expect in the rooms. Loft's spa includes a sauna, Turkish baths and a massage room.

$$$ Hotel Morasurco – *Calle 20 & Carrera 40, Av. de los Estudiantes, Pasto. ✕ Spa ℘(2) 731 3250. 60 rooms.* Attention to detail shines at the Morasurco, where rooms are large, comfortable and modern, with excellent private bathrooms. Most rooms have great views, and a stunning panorama unfolds from the "wet zone," the rooftop terrace where the sauna, Jacuzzi and Turkish bath are set. Always happy to help, the hotel staff is friendly and efficient.

🍴EAT

$ Mestizo Peña-Bar – *Calle 18 # 27-67, Pasto. ℘(2) 723 7754. Dinner only. Closed Sun.* Although a good selection of low-priced food and snacks is served in this warm bamboo-paneled space, it's not the food that draws folks here. It's the large dance floor where locals sway to booming Andean music from Thursday through Sunday nights. Come for dance classes on Wednesday at 6pm. **Regional Colombian**.

$ Picantería Ipiales – *Calle 19 # 23-37, Edificio Ariel, Pasto. ℘(2) 723 0393. Closed Sun.* Conveniently located close to the post office, this restaurant is one of a chain that has branches in Pasto and Bogotá. Typical Nariño dishes of southern Colombia, especially pork, are the focus of the kitchen here. On the menu of delicious home-style items, the *lapingachos* (fried potato and cheese pancakes), the *hornados* (roast pork) and the *maíz tostado* (a blend of corn and pork rinds) all stand out. **Regional Colombian**.

$ Tienda del Café del Parque – *Carrera 24 # 18-62, Pasto. ℘300 657 7115. Closed Sun.* If you're looking for good coffee, head to this cafe next to the Plaza Casino. They make their java from organic beans grown in Nariño, and serve an assortment of pastries, snacks and sandwiches. Art hangs on the walls, and there's a second-floor bar with balcony seating for watching the sunset. **Colombian**.

$$ Tipi Cuy – *Calle 18 # 51-110, Torobajo. ℘(2) 731 7604. www.tipicuy.com.* Established in 2003, this modest restaurant has the capacity to seat 100 people inside its vivid lime-green-colored dining space. Tipi Cuy's kitchen staff prides itself on serving hearty and simple country fare. On weekends, live music entertains diners here. **Colombian**.

Together, Los Llanos (the Plains) and Amazonia (the Amazon) cover more than half of Colombia's territory, yet contain less than three percent of its population. As two very different wilderness regions, they have few common characteristics. Located east of the Andes, Los Llanos is an expansive stretch of rolling tropical grassland nourished by the Orinoco River and reaching out into Venezuelan territory. In contrast, the Colombian Amazonia is wet, lush jungle and represents a small, yet complex and varied part of the whole basin region. Located in the far southeastern part of the country, this muggy flatland expanse is particularly susceptible to the ebb and flow of the Amazon River. An equatorial climate and heavy rainfall nurtures dense plant growth that supports an inconceivable list of rare and unusual wildlife and botanical species. Scattered indigenous communities rich in tradition, language and culture, such as the Nukaks, Ticunas, Tucanos, Camsás, Huitotos, Yaguas and Ingas, can also be found in riverside settlements.

Highlights

1 Eat smoke-flavored, fire-grilled meats in the Llanero palm plantation town of **Cumaral** (p407)

2 See the vast pampas of Los Llanos on horseback from **Puerto López,** including cattle fields and cowboy ranches (p409)

3 Buy handicrafts in the jungle frontier towns of **Leticia** and **Tabatinga**, amid the bustle of travelers passing through to the depths of rain forests (p412)

4 Explore the awesome untamed wilds of the **Parque Nacional Amacayacu** (p418)

5 Journey along the magnificent **Río Yavari** to spot the Amazon's pink river dolphins (p422)

Ecological Heartlands

A world away from Bogotá, these two great hinterlands face considerable modern-day environmental and societal challenges that continue to place customary lifestyles and family structures under threat.

One of Colombia's most traditional regions, Los Llanos remains highly reliant on livestock and agriculture, with entire communities devoted to **cattle rearing**. The *llaneros* (plains folk) in this slow-paced "Cowboy Country" are faced with the dilemmas of modern farming,

from forest erosion and the widespread use of agro-toxins, to the draining of sizable wetlands and a continued imbalance between drought and flood. Vast sweeping alluvial savannas lay studded with occasional clumps of vegetation that are prone to flooding from the heaviest rains (May to October).

The Amazon is a vital environmental component of the planet, absorbing carbon dioxide at a phenomenal rate. Unlike neighboring Brazil, where widespread commercial logging has decimated the landscape, Colombia's resplendent **watershed** remains undisturbed by deforestation. The jungle's indigenous communities make scant use of axes for tree-felling, preferring to employ machetes for selective small-scale needs. Human threats to the natural resources of the Amazon region are therefore less prevalent in the Colombian terrain. Yet, rising waters and flooding do place a strain on the resources of the low-lying Colombian Amazon, where riverside villages can be engulfed by the river in the **wet season**.

Water levels can rise by up to 15m/49ft and swallow large tracts of jungle in the tide. Though much of the Amazon lowlands benefit from this prolonged soaking in terms of nutrient-rich plant matter, the disruption that this uncontrollable riparian swelling causes can be immense.

The wettest period occurs between the end of December and the end of June, with levels reaching their highest level in March, April, May and early June.

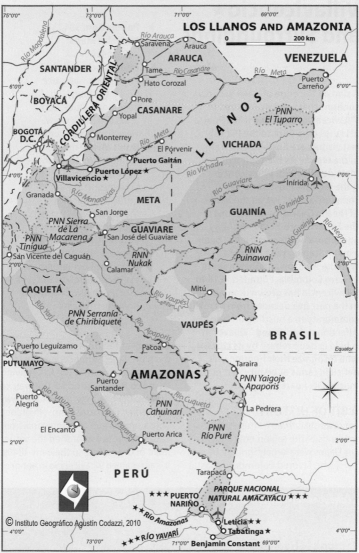

LOS LLANOS AND AMAZONIA

Cultural Heritage

Both Los Llanos and the Amazon are considered Colombia's great heartlands of **folklore**.

The plains folk are renowned throughout Latin America for the marked sounds of their traditional music (using harp and *cuatro*) and regional dance (*joropo*). Festivals celebrate the cowboy culture of the savannas, from the region's cattle-roping traditions to the all-important Los Llanos skills of horsemanship. In the Amazon numerous distinctive jungle communities continue to rely on wood-carved boats or canoes to navigate the river and its many tributaries.

Shamanic rituals and sacred plants still play an important role in Amazon culture, and its poetry, song, music and dance reflect and incorporate more than 180 regional linguistic styles and the dozens of dialects found in the region.

401

Villavicencio★ and Surroundings

Meta

A sign on the edge of town proudly confirms that you have arrived in Villavicencio, declaring it "La Puerta al Llano" (The Gate to the Plains), lest visitors are unsure of its status in the region. As the capital of the Meta department, Villavicencio is the region's most important commercial hub. Set on the banks of the Río Guatiquia, at the foot of the Eastern Cordillera in a grassy agricultural wilderness, it has been a major staging post for trade with the Amazon and the Andes in eastern Colombia. Founded in 1840 Villavicencio has grown dramatically in the past five decades from a small community to a bustling metropolis. Affectionately dubbed "Villavo," it is held in deep regard by its citizens, who recognize their hometown's deficit in terms of beauty, but make much of its heart and soul.

A BIT OF HISTORY

For more than three centuries, the barren lands of the region now known as Los Llanos were largely ignored by settlers, who favored Colombia's coastal

▶ **Population:** 384,131.
◔ **Michelin Maps:** p401, p406.
▤ **Info:** Edificio Alcaldía Primer Piso, Calle 40 # 63-44. ◷Open Mon–Fri 8am–noon, 2pm–6pm. ✆(8) 670 3975. www. vivevillavicencio.com.
☺ **Don't Miss:** The Monumento de Cristo Rey—Villavicencio's own version of Rio's *Cristo Redentor* (Christ the Redeemer)—with its unparalleled city view; a musical journey through Llanera music and dance at the Casa del Joropo; the exuberant acrobatics of pink river dolphins downstream from Puerto Gaitán.

plains over the **hostile landscape** of the hinterland. Significant geographical obstacles, such as the fast-flowing **Orinoco River**, stood in the way of development. Muggy, oppressive **heat** also served to dissuade most migrants, until a small group of farming folk from eastern Bogotá established the settlement of **Gramalote** in the early 1840s. It was renamed Villavicencio in honor of

Coleo competition, Villavicencio

Proexport Colombia

GETTING THERE

BY AIR - Two airlines, Aires and Satena, offer regular flights from Bogotá and Medellín to Villavicencio's **La Vanguardia Airport** (VVC), about 4km/2.5mi northeast of city center, across the river.

BY BUS - Bolivaríano runs several buses to and from Bogotá (*1 424 9090; www.bolivariano.com.co*) as do Auto Llanos (*1 263 0799*), and Macarena (*1 425 4900; www.flotamacarenna.com*) at a cost of about 25,000 COP or higher a person (about a 2hr ride). The **bus terminal** lies 7km/4mi east of city center.

GETTING AROUND

BY BUS - Buses serve the city, and depart regularly for nearby Restrepo.

BY TAXI - Taxis are readily available. If traveling some distance or through areas about which you have no knowledge, consider taking a taxi. Always have your hotel phone ahead for a cab or ask the management of the location you're visiting to call for one; you may not be able to distinguish a licensed taxi from a less safe, illegitimate one.

BY CAR - Having your own vehicle is ideal for exploring Los Llanos. Consider hiring a car and driver. Three routes (*see EXCURSIONS below*) lead east into the plains from Villavicencio.

GENERAL INFORMATION

ACCOMMODATIONS - *Fincas* and bed and breakfasts of varying levels of comfort can be found on the town's outskirts. In rural settings, they may be difficult to locate, so get directions from the local tourist office. *See ADDRESSES at the end of the chapter.*

Antonio Villavicencio, an early advocate of the struggle for independence from Spain. Parcels of **subsidized** or **free land** were offered to relocating farming families by the Colombian government, anxious to set up a staging platform for trade. New **roads** helped ease access into the savanna's farthest reaches, enabling the efficient shipment of produce, crops and cattle to the markets of Bogotá.

Early settlers in Los Llanos were formidable **horsemen** with legendary equestrian skills. They fought for Spanish **Royalists**, then joined Venezuelan and Colombian freedom-fighters during the war of independence, crossing the Andes with **Bolívar** to take the Spaniards by surprise in 1819.

Modern Development

Today, with most residents employed in the local **cattle-raising**, **distilling**, **rice-milling** and **saddle-making** trades, large numbers of agricultural traders pass through this bustling commercial hub. They usually arrive in one of the many exhaust-spewing trucks that rumble along the dusty roads from the northeastern and southern parts of the Meta department.

Villavicencio is now connected by a **modern highway** (*see sidebar p410*) that links to Bogotá, 90km/55mi to the northwest—a three-hour journey and a far cry from a decade ago when the road was so poor that it was a 10-hour haul. The city has also been earmarked for sizable redevelopment, with new retail sectors, large malls and dozens of small outlets slated to open in 2011.

Yet, alongside this modern growth, Villavicencio retains the feel of a city longing to hold on to bygone traits. A lengthy tradition of oral storytelling remains a cultural backbone of the local society, and the city is home to several seasoned narrators and storytelling events held in parks, schools and plazas.

In the heat of the day, a searing haze rises above Villavicencio's hodgepodge of **disorderly streets**, a legacy of poorly managed development.

A ramshackle maze of **slum-like housing** on the city's outskirts congregates around makeshift **markets** and upscale **retail zones** close to the swankest **residential streets**.

Monumento a Cristo Rey★★

Cerro el Redentor, off Calle 40.
Set high atop a hill overlooking the city, this stunning monument offers an unrivaled **view** that sweeps across Villavicencio to encompass a truly pleasing scenic mix of rural and urban aspects.

It was undertaken by artist **Elisha Achury Pedro Garavito** and completed in 1954. Capturing the essence of ethereal quietude, the monument is a much-photographed city icon, and the city's equivalent of Rio de Janeiro's *Christ the Redeemer* statue atop Corcovado Mountain in Brazil.

To reach the summit, take the steps along the **Caño Parrado** to enjoy a scenic uphill walk *(30min)* through lovely terrain—and don't forget to bring your camera.

SIGHTS

Catedral Metropolitana Nuestra Señora del Carmen★

Calle 39, Carreras 32 and 33.
This fine old church (1845) was one of the first buildings in the newly founded town of **Gramalote**. It was commissioned by priest **Ignacio Osorio**, who gave the job to the local congregation—a decision he was later to regret. Crudely constructed, the building required significant re-working. A fire ravaged it in 1890, but it was painstakingly restored.

Step inside the Gothic style **interior**, a dramatic design of ornate arches.

Casa de la Cultura Jorge Eliécer Gaitán★

Carrera 32 # 39-62. ◐*Open Mon–Fri 8am–noon, 2pm–6pm, Sat 8am–noon.* ℘*(8) 662 6327.*
This bastion of culture opened in 1971 to promote the unique heritage—past and present—of the region. Housed in a single-story orange and yellow-painted building, the facility includes a public library, exhibition space and the **Cine Club Villavicencio**, a small movie theater that shows films on a cultural theme.

Casa del Joropo★

Calle 44 # 56-21 Galan. ◐*Open Mon–Sat 8am–noon.* ◉*18,000 COP.* ℘*(8) 664 3000. www.corculla.com.*
This showcase of traditional **Llanera music** and **dance** offers visitors an opportunity to interact with artists from the prairies during exhibits, workshops on instruments, and other events. Staff dressed in typical costumes of the plains guide visitors on a journey around the musical exhibits and narratives.

SURROUNDINGS

Monumento a las Arpas★

▶*Carretera 65, 2km/1mi from the city en route to Vanguardia Aiport.*
This striking 10m/33ft-high monument dominates the **Via Marginal de la Selva** roundabout. It features a trio of metal prong-like structures and a dazzling **illuminated waterfall** that cascades to the sound of the Llanero harp, an eye-popping sight after dark.

Parque Los Fundadores★

▶*Corner of Avenida 40 and Via a Bogotá.* ◐*Open daily dawn–dusk.*
On weekends, dozens of *Villavicense* families gather in this leafy space on the south side of Villavicencio to picnic and hang out.

Set around a central masterpiece—*El Monumento a los Fundadores,* created by renowned Colombian sculptor **Rodrigo Arenas Betancur**—the park is also known for its spectacular **illuminated fountain** with stunning cascades. Lush parklands are neatly divided by small paved plazas that are home to domino-playing elders, street theater, food vendors and handicrafts stalls.

Parque Las Malocas★

▶*Vía Kirpas.* ◐*Open Tue–Sun 9am–5pm.* ◉*7,000 COP.* ℘*(8) 671 6666.*
Villavicencio's **Rodeo Theme Park** is a venue for the celebration of cattle-roping and horsemanship, where the life, work and culture of the Llanos cowboy are showcased in thrilling style.

Joropo dancing

Aviatur/Proexport Colombia

The People of the Plains

The **Llaneros**, plainsmen from the Venezuelan-Colombian savanna, are proud of their distinct culture, taking their name from the cattle-strewn Los Llanos grasslands. Ethnically part **Spanish** and **Indian**, they boast strong, rugged facial features and thick, black hair. They have a strangely poetic style of speech and a nasal, tonal **dialect** with dialogue peppered by phrases unchanged from the idioms of the Spanish colonists in the 16C and 17C.

This style is particularly prevalent in the **romantic laments** of the Llaneros distinctive form of **music**. Lyrics are poignant and accompanied by the melodic strum of the **cuatro** (4-string) **guitar** or **harp**, telling of heartache on the lonesome rolling prairies and the bitter hardships of rearing cattle. Harp-led melodies in traditional *joropo* style blend *machismo* desires with big-hearted passion that captures the essence of these vast flatlands. Joyous, rhythmic verbal contests called **contrapunteo** are often part of this musical tradition.

From the cradle to the grave, Llaneros are dedicated **cowboys**, moving mammoth droves of cattle over many thousands of acres. During the rainy season, the cattle are driven to higher ground to escape the flooded plains resulting from poor drainage in the lowlands. In the drier months, the herdsmen guide the cattle toward wet areas where grass is more fertile. **Coleo competitions** (similar to rodeos) provide frequent opportunities for the Llaneros to demonstrate their cattle-roping skills, of which corralling, ranging and lassoing are the lifeblood of Colombia's "Cowboy Country." Long days are spent in the saddle in extreme heat and high winds, yet these gaucho-like ranchers are happiest simply doing their job.

Donning the traditional clothes of the region, a **poncho**, **straw hat** and **cotizas** (rope-soled sandals), Llaneros relax and enjoy a provincial culture rich in music, dance, folklore, legends and stories.

Llaneros are highly superstitious, with ancient **legends** and **myths** continuing to form an important part of modern society. Some of the most prevalent include the *Leyenda de Diablo,* a devil's offer of untold riches and all the women in the world in return for a man's soul; *Bola de Fuego,* balls of fire of such ferocity that they can chase people into their homes; and *Jente sin Cabeza,* a headless, machete-wielding rider on horseback who appears only at night-time gatherings.

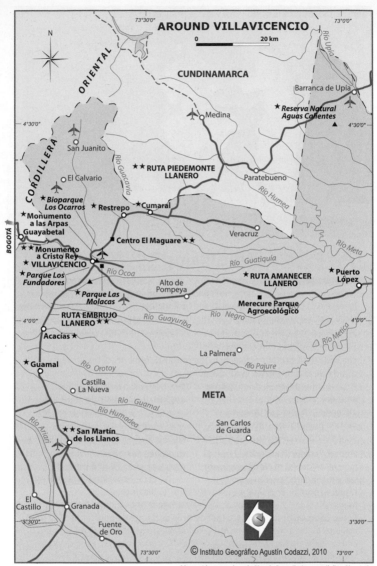

AROUND VILLAVICENCIO

0   20 km

CUNDINAMARCA

CORDILLERA ORIENTAL

★ Reserva Natural Aguas Calientes
Barranca de Upía
Río Upía
Río Meta

San Juanito

● Medina

★★ RUTA PIEDEMONTE LLANERO

Paratebueno
Río Humea

● El Calvario

★ Bioparque Los Ocarros   ★ Restrepo   ★ Cumaral
Río Guacavía

★ Monumento a las Arpas
Guayabetal

■ Centro El Maguare ★★

Veracruz

★★ Monumento a Cristo Rey
★ VILLAVICENCIO

■ Río Ocoa
Río Guatiquía

★ Parque Los Fundadores

Alto de Pompeya

★ RUTA AMANECER LLANERO   ★ Puerto López

★ Parque Las Molacas

■ Merecure Parque Agroecológico

RUTA EMBRUJO LLANERO ★★
Río Guayuriba   Río Negro

Río Metica

★ Acacías ★

La Palmera ○   Río Pajure

★ Guamal
Río Orotoy

Castilla
La Nueva ○
Río Guamal

META

Río Humadea

San Carlos de Guarda

★★ San Martín de los Llanos
Río Ariari

El Castillo ○   ○ Granada

Fuente de Oro

© Instituto Geográfico Agustín Codazzi, 2010

BOGOTÁ

Browse permanent exhibitions of the horse world, and visit reconstructions of typical **Llanera houses**, livestock pens and agricultural lands for the cultivation of cassava and plantain.

Large **arenas** attract the crowds for highly popular **rodeo competitions**, races and contests. A small **museum** on the premises is dedicated to the region's important industry and its 90,000 head of cattle. Featured here are informative displays about milk production, meat production and the heroes and legends of Los Llanos.

EXCURSIONS

A trio of **touristic roads** lead from Villavicencio deeper into the Eastern

Plains, providing some options for visitors ready to explore the surrounding rural area.

RUTA PIEDEMONTE LLANERO★★ *(running northeast)*
Bioparque Los Ocarros★

Carretera 65, 3km/2mi NE of Villavicencio. Open Mon–Fri 9am–4pm, Sat–Sun 9am–5pm. 10,000 COP, child 7,000 COP. (8) 670 9094. To get the most from a visit, arrive in the morning before the heat of the day, or go in late afternoon when animal feedings take place as the day starts to cool.

This natural zoo and botanical reserve is dedicated to the species endemic to the **Orinoco River Basin.** Set on 5.7ha/14 acres, it contains 181 species, from **waterfowl** and **caimans** to **monkeys** and **jaguars**—all rescued from traffickers or donated as abandoned pets.

Signs give excellent explanations of the ecological importance, status and habitat of each animal. Many creatures have also been given pet names and are available to stroke, cuddle and feed.

Centro Cultural Etno Turistico El Maguare★★

Carretera 65, 2km/1mi NE of Los Ocarros. Guided tours organized by Hotel del Llano in Villavicencio. (8) 671 7000. Open daily (phone for hours). 5,000 COP. (8) 664 8105.

The **Huitoto** (wuh-toe-toe), also spelled Witoto or Uitoto, are recent arrivals in Los Llanos, a region without any surviving indigenous peoples from the pre-colonial era. One of Colombia's largest indigenous groups, the Huitoto hail from a principal territory in the **La Chorrera** in the Amazon jungle, and have had a presence in Los Llanos for only a few years.

Artistically talented people, they make **masks**, **rattles** and **blowguns** as well as a range of **jewelry** made from bark cloth, seed and nuts colored with vegetable dye.

At the Huitoto settlement, visitors can experience the **dance**, **rituals** and handicrafts of this fascinating community, with talks about ancestral homelands, marginalization and traditional ceremonies.

You may be treated to a typical Huitoto **meal** of grilled meats, plantains and rice, served in a banana leaf and washed down with a tumbler of maize drink.

Restrepo★

10km/6mi NE of Villavicencio along Carretera 65. www.restrepo-meta.gov.co.

This town (Pop. 10,112) is recognizable by a well-maintained twin-towered church called **Santuario Inmaculada Concepcion★**. A central feature of the town's main plaza, the church has been the setting for many of the region's local celebrations and religious festivals. Inside, marvel at the **frescoes** painted by **Patricia Corzo.**

In general, soak up the ambience of the town's rural charm. The plaza is also home to a **Casa de Cultura,** where folkloric exhibits and events promote the music, dance, languages and traditions of the region.

Cumaral★

26km/16mi NE of Villavicencio along Carretera 65. www.cumaral-meta.gov.co.

Cumaral (Pop. 16,634) is crisscrossed by five rivers and a trio of canals.

Founded in 1901, the original town was relocated to higher ground after illness nearly wiped out the entire population. Today, Cumaral is an important palm-growing town, actually named after the **Cumare palm**, whose fibers are used to make baskets, rope and hammocks.

It has a reputation for its many places to eat **fire-cooked meat**, something that should be tried at least once if you are a meat-eater.

Each December, the town plays host to the **Festival Internacional el Cumare**, a celebration of its palm-fiber heritage. The community is also renowned for its **coleo** (rodeo). During the year several fiestas draw big crowds of spectators from all over Los Llanos.

☺ Don't Miss ☺

Las Tradicionales Cuadrillas de San Martín

If you happen to be around San Martín de Llanos in November, do not miss this impressive choreographed **horse ballet** performed to the rhythm of the **joropo**, as it celebrates with great enthusiasm the legendary equestrian tradition of Los Llanos and the myths and legends of Colombia's Eastern Plains.

Reserva Natural Aguas Calientes★

◐ Near Barranca de Upía, 107km/67mi NE of Villavicencio along Carretera 65.
◀◕ Guided tours in Spanish organized by Chivas y Parrando; ◉55,000 COP; ℘(8) 661 0451; www.chivasyparrando.com.
This luxuriant forest conceals spring-fed **pools** and **waterfalls** set among warm, gin-clear basins under the trees. Underground wells are believed to have curative properties for all manner of ailments. **Ecological trails** around the pools allow visitors an opportunity to learn about the medicinal heritage.

RUTA EMBRUJO LLANERO★★
(running south)
Acacías★

◐ 21km/13mi SW of Villavicencio along Carretera 65. www.acacias-meta.gov.co.
This town (Pop.54,753) offers a scenic **river walk** along a leafy trail, and stages a popular **Torneo Nacional de Música Llanera y de Toros Coleado** (music of the plains and bull-roping tournament). Scenic surrounding countryside reveals livestock **farms**, steer **ranches** and rolling fields of grazing cattle.

Guamal★

◐ 43km/27mi S of Villavicencio along Carretera 65. www.guamal-meta.gov.co.
During the peak holiday month of December, many thousands of domestic tourists descend on Guamal (Pop. 8,933), a popular vacation spot on the shores of the **Río Humadea**. The town is distinc-

tive for its German-influenced culture, as many of Guamal's settlers in the 1920s arrived in Colombia after fighting for **Germany** in WW1.
Guamal boasts a reputation for curative healing by its thermal waters. The year-round temperatures here of 26°C/79°F make bathing in several natural dipping **pools**★ a popular pastime all year.

San Martín de los Llanos★★

◐ 66km/41mi S of Villavicencio along Carretera 65.
http://sanmartin-meta.gov.co.
Founded in 1585 the region's oldest city (Pop. 21,511) is widely considered the spiritual heart of Colombian rodeo and cattle-rearing. Tournaments take place in its Hernando Rodriguez Solano arena, one of the best in the Meta department, and traditional fairs and fiestas such as the **Festival Internacional Folclórico y Turístico del Llano** *(Nov)* lure ranchers and cowboys region-wide.
Most visitors come to San Martín to meander around the town's colonial streetscape, across cobbled plazas and down narrow backstreets flanked by stately 16C architecture.
Friendly locals might invite you to enter their houses to marvel at the courtyards and woodwork—it's not uncommon to leave with a bag of freshly plucked fruit or a home-baked cake.

RUTA AMANECER LLANERO★
(running east)
Merecure Parque Agroecológico

◐ 47km E of Villavicencio along Carretera 40. ◒Open Feb–mid Jun & Aug–mid-Dec Thu–Sun & public holidays 9am–5pm. Holy Week, mid Jun–Jul, school holidays & mid-Dec–Jan daily 9am–6pm. ◉Day pass 33,000 COP, child 20,000 COP. Quad biking (1hr) ◉60,000 COP; fishing (2hr) ◉7,000 COP; ◀◕guided walks ◉3,000 COP; jet-skiing (30 min) ◉80,000 COP; horse riding ◉25,000 COP. ℘(8) 682 3636. www.merecure.com.co.
As the biggest agro-ecological park (600ha/1,483 acres) in Latin America, this popular family vacation spot draws

A Rich Ecosystem

Today the Venezuelan and Colombian Llanos form about 17 percent of South America's 29 million ha/72 million acre **savanna ecosystem**, of which 17 million hectares/42 million acres are found in Colombia. Comprising a single eco-region, the Colombian-Venezuelan expanse of grasslands is covered mainly by savanna vegetation and ranks among the world's richest tropical grassland.

Pink river dolphin

Óscar Orlando Díaz Jaimes/Proexport Colombia

A mix of dry forests, undulating grassy lowlands and seasonally flooded plains teem with **wildlife**, and a river delta of bogs and coastal mangroves serves as the habitat for more than 100 mammal species and 700 species of birds. The endemic **Orinoco crocodile**—one of the world's most critically endangered reptiles—can be found in Los Llanos. Other endangered species include the **Orinoco turtle**, the **giant river otter**, the **ocelot**, the **giant armadillo**, the **black-and-chestnut eagle** and several species of **catfish**. The **jaguar**, the largest American felidae, has been severely hunted in the Llanos, both for sport and the protection of cattle.

Pink river dolphins or *botos*, found in Los Llanos and the Amazon, deserve a special mention. Though one of the most common river species, they have been listed as **endangered** by the International Union for Conservation of Nature, as freshwater habitats are under threat from **pollution**, **damming**, **boat traffic**, and **hunting**. Actually born gray, *botos* become pinker as they age, and will flush from a rose-pink to a brighter pink as they become excited. With a long, powerful beak and small eyes, the slow-swimming *botos* have unique molar-like teeth and chew their prey. Their brain is 40 percent larger than a human brain. As a solitary species, *botos* rest on the bottom of muddy, stagnant tropical rivers. During the rainy season, they move onto flooded forests, where they weave through trees in search of prey.

In Los Llanos, pink river dolphins can be sighted at **Puerto Gaitán** (Pop. 15,475), 150km/93mi east of Puerto López, where the **Río Meta** and **Río Yucao** meet the **Río Manacacias**.

lovers of **camping** and **outdoor** pursuits. Amenities include large **lakes**, man-made **beaches**, rolling meadows, stone-built cabins, restaurants, bars, volleyball courts and a small church.

Puerto López★

▶ *83km/52mi E of Villavicencio along Carretera 40.*
http://puertolopez-meta.gov.co
As the principal port on the **Río Meta**, Puerto López (Pop. 28,922) has always played a crucial role in shipping produce. In recent years, it has made inroads into tourism, especially with river **boat tours**.

Shady picnic spots permit river and savanna views. Numerous charters run **fishing excursions** along the river, where there are **horse-riding trails** rich in **birdlife**. Plenty of guides offer ecological hikes and camping trips out across the plains.

Prior to arrival, most visitors take time to marvel at the 30m/98ft-high **Alto de Menegua obelisk** on the town's outskirts.

Marking the geographical center of Colombia, this needle-thin structure is surrounded by a handicraft market *(daily)* and a handful of food stalls selling sizzling empanadas and arepas.

Cowboy of Los Llanos

Aviatur/Proexport Colombia

Road Trip to the Gateway to the Plains

Journeying to Villavicencio from **Bogotá** on a modern highway offers spectacular **views**★★ along a route that climbs higher than 3,100m/10,170ft before several dramatic plunges. Reaching your destination requires crossing no less than 50 bridges and snaking through five tunnels.

Splendid vistas unfold en route to the **Parque Nacional Natural Sumapaz** (⚘ *see AROUND BOGOTÁ*), across lush grassy verges and stunning verdant valleys clad with towering palms and cascades of tumbling water. Once a sacred place for the Muiscas, the Sumapaz Páramo forms a striking backdrop to the nation's capital.

Heading southeast, the road sweeps past curbside dairy vendors selling yogurt, cream and smoked cheese from makeshift, wooden stalls. At the small town of **Chipague**, it curves around a string of family-owned shops and food joints before diving into a stunning valley flanked by amber-colored rocks. Just yards from grazing herds of cattle, clusters of plastic chairs and tables are set up outside a rustic wood-fired grill serving giant slabs of freshly cooked beef.

Next up is the pit-stop town of **Abasticos**, little more than a row of snack stalls on the left of the road, where the aroma of sizzling *chorizo* fills the air. On the outskirts of town, the **Quebrada Blanco** trickles down a deep ravine.

Before long, the rock-strewn terrain is transformed by a blanket of what Colombians call **Spoon Trees**, with patches of spongy grass home to rope-tethered grazing bulls. Next comes the Tunnel de Quebrada Blanca before the road trundles through the town of **Guayabetal**. Behind, an Andean forest nourished by crystal-clear, gushing mountain streams casts a spectrum of colors. A custard-yellow bridge denotes the fact that Bogotá lies 70km/44mi distant—look out for the narrow crumbling remains of the old road hidden beneath a tangle of mossy creepers.

A collection of maroon-colored farmhouses signifies the start of the 10km/6mi run into Villavicencio. Those who make the challenging ascent of **Alto de Buena Vista** do, indeed, witness its "good" views of thick vegetation, pretty **fincas** and the **Río Meta**—have your camera ready.

ADDRESSES

🛏 STAY

$$ Hotel Sunrise – *8km/5mi southeast of Villavicencio along Carretera 40 (the road to Puerto López).* ✕🌐 ☎(8) 672 1144. *www.sunrisellano.com. 42 rooms.* Great for families traveling wtih children, this hotel is located inside an aqua park that features pools, tennis, miniature golf, beach volleyball, soccer and more. The recreational complex also includes restaurants and bars.

$$$$ Hotel Campestre El Campanario – *2km/1mi east of Villavicencio along the road to Catama.* ✕🌐 ☎(8) 661 6666. *www.hotelcampestreelcampanario. com.co. 50 rooms.* Attached to the convention center, this upscale hotel offers a host of amenities, including a pool, a gym and a children's playground. Tastefully decorated rooms all have Internet access, plasma TV, and a work desk. Bathrooms come with a separate shower and Jacuzzi tub.

$$$ Hotel del Llano – *Carrera 30 # 49-77, Barrio el Caudal, Villavicencio.* ✕🌐 ☎(8) 671 7000. *www.hotel delllano.com. 115 rooms.* Located in a residential area in the north part of Villavicencio, this hotel boasts modern, spacious, light-filled rooms, which provide all the standard amenities. Hotel del Llano's best feature is its well-situated Olympic-size pool, which has a separate shallow area for children.

$$$ Hotel Don Lolo – *Carrera 39 # 20-32, Barrio Camoa, Villavicencio.* ✕ ☎(8) 670 6020. *www.donlolohotel.com. 60 rooms.* Rooms at this traditional hotel, in the tourist sector of the Meta, vary in size from singles to triples (some are extremely small). For the best views, ask for a corner room with two walls of windows overlooking the city. One of the most popular area hotels, Hotel Don Lolo fills up quickly in peak seasons.

$$ Hotel Maria Gloria – *Carrera 38 # 20-26, Barrio Camoa, Villavicencio.* ✕🌐 ☎(8) 672 0197. *www.hotel mariagloria.com. 60 rooms.* A popular hotel that prides itself on its modern interior design and ample room size, the Maria Gloria even has a business center. Natural woods and warm colors fill the peaceful rooms.

$$ Hotel Napolitano – *Carrera 30 # 36-50, Villavicencio.* ✕ ☎(8) 662 8470. *www.hotelnapolitanovillavicencio.com. 68 rooms.* This mid-size family-run hotel comprises basic but comfortable and attractive rooms, along with four special-event areas that can be used for conferences and business meetings. A convenient location in the center of town is another reason to stay here.

🍴 EAT

$$ Asadero El Amarradero del Mico – *2km/1mi northeast of Villavicencio along Carretera 65 to Restrepo; close to the toll booth to Vanguardia airport.* ☎(8) 664 8307. One of a chain, this thatched-roof restaurant traces its origins back to Pozo Azul 57 years ago. The menu reflects dishes typically served on the Llano, the vast tropical grassland that covers this area, such as grilled meat, churrasco and beef tongue, as well as traditional soups. **Colombian**.

$$ El Llano y sus Hayacas – *Carrera 24A # 37-62B, Villavicencio.* ☎(8) 671 6896. *www.elllanoysushayacas.com.* This largerestaurant and adjoining cafe specializes in Llano-style *hayacas* (tamales wrapped in plantain leaves). Alternate menu options include oysters, tropical fruit salad with cheese, and a tempting variety of desserts. **Regional Colombian**.

$$ Restaurante Cofradía – *Calle 15 # 371-10, Villavicencio.* ☎(8) 663 2183. A popular upscale restaurant with its own parking lot, this eatery specializes in fish and shellfish. Restaurante Cofradía is open for breakfast, lunch and dinner. Expect to dress up for dinner. **Seafood**.

$$ La Fonda Quindiana – *Carrera 32 # 40-4, Villavicencio.* ☎(8) 662 6857. One of the oldest restaurants in the area, La Fonda Quindiana has a bustling ambience. It serves local and traditional dishes, focusing on Creole cuisine. Its sizzling grill is fired up constantly, since the restaurant serves three meals a day. **Regional Colombian**.

Leticia★★ and Surroundings

Amazonas

As the capital of the Colombian Amazonas, Leticia is the jumping-off point for most visitors entering the region at the borders of Colombia, Brazil and Peru. Situated at just 96m/315ft above sea level, the town is a steamy lowland settlement centered on the river where wooden canoes piled high with sacks of rice, plantains and stings of fish ferry goods downstream. Leticia is characterized as a melting pot of linguistic, cultural and gastronomic ethnicities. Domestic migrants from Cali, Medellín and Bogotá who set up home here in the 1950s live among neighbors from several dozen indigenous Amazon communities, plus a mix of citizens of Peruvian and Brazilian descent.

▶ **Population:** 32,450.
🕭 **Michelin Maps:** p401, p417.
🔲 **Info:** Decameron Decalodge Ticuna, Carrera 11 # 6-11. ☎(8) 592 6600. www.decameron.com
🐾 **Don't Miss:** Exploring the character-packed frontier towns of Leticia, Tabatinga and Santa Rosa. Be sure to allow time to journey along the Amazon and its tributaries in order to experience the vast might of this powerful watershed and its amazing biomass. Look out for rose-colored river dolphins on beautiful Lake Tarapoto, with its backdrop of vine-tangled jungle and a sprinkling of mangrove isles.

A BIT OF HISTORY

Leticia was named in honor of a Leticia Smith, said to be a young female resident of Iquitos, Peru's Amazonian riverside city.

The town was founded in 1867 by Captain **Benigno Bustamante**, then governor of the Peruvian department of Loreto. Relations between Colombia and Peru soon soured when, in 1829, a bilateral treaty failed to accurately pinpoint the true geographic coordinates of the **colonial boundary**. In 1930 a second agreement was dismissed by Peru as biased toward Colombian interests. Four subsequent treaties in 1906, 1909, 1911 and 1922 proved ineffective, despite arbitration.

Leticia and the Amazon River

© Nik Wheeler/Danita Delimont/Alamy

GETTING THERE

BY AIR - Aeropuerto internacional Alfredo Vásquez Cobo (LET) is north of Leticia: all non-residents must pay 15,500 COP **tourist tax** upon arrival. Direct flights arrive here from Bogotá (300,000 COP one-way). Brazil's nearby Tabatinga International Airport has flights to Manaus (600,000 COP one-way). Leticia's *colectivos* marked "comara" will drop you near Tabatinga.

GETTING AROUND

BY BOAT - Although there are no roads into or out of Leticia, it is well-served by water transport. It's best to use a tour operator who is a member of the Fondo de Promocion Ecoturistica del Amazonas. Navigation is easier in the drier months (Jul-Aug). **BY BUS -** *Colectivos* (1,000-5,000 COP) serve Leticia and link it with Tabatinga and villages north of Leticia's airport. **BY TAXI -** Standard taxis are on the expensive side. (15,000 COP). Motor-taxis, (big red motorcycles) are cheap: the base rate is 1,000 COP, but they are often unlicensed and recklessly driven. **BY SCOOTER -** Scooters can be rented (30,000 COP plus petrol); rental shops in Leticia stay open during the week. **ON FOOT -** Walking is a good means of mobility, even to Tabatinga, Brazil.

TRI-BORDER FORMALITIES

Leticia skirts the borders of Brazil and Peru. The "tri-border community" moves around without the hindrance of an overly fussy frontier. **COLOMBIAN-BRAZILIAN BORDER** - Between **Leticia** (Colombia) and **Tabatinga** (Brazil) there are normally no passport checks or guards. If visiting Brazil **beyond Tabatinga**, you will need to go through immigration. **COLOMBIAN-PERUVIAN BORDER** - The border lies along the river in the Peruvian village of **Santa Rosa**, a 5min boat journey from Leticia. Trans-border formalities are **casual**. You don't need stamps to cross for the day, but always carry your **passport.**

In 1911 **troops** from both countries moved into Leticia and things took a turn for the worse. By 1922 the situation had stabilized enough for another treaty to be drawn up, although Peru refused to ratify the boundary for six long years. In 1930 Colombia finally took **formal possession** of Leticia, but Peru didn't fully withdraw its troops until 1932, requiring another show of might from the Colombian army. Several months of diplomatic spite followed before both parties agreed on bringing the conflict to a close.

A provisional **peace treaty**, brokered by the League of Nations, was signed in May 1933, followed by yet another bilateral agreement in June 1934. This latter agreement resulted in Leticia's finally being returned to Colombian control, and Peru's issuing a formal apology for the 1932 invasion.

Since the agreement was ratified in September 1935, Colombian-Peruvian relations have remained cordial.

Amazon Tourism Boom

As a hard-to-reach port town, many miles from Bogotá's prying eyes, Leticia used to make a convenient **base** for the **narcotics trade**. Drugs were bought and sold in broad daylight, and shipments were made by drug cartel employees via cargo boats and kayaks along the Putumayo River. Plans by drug barons to construct a highway to facilitate transportation by truck as far as Tarapaca made good progress, with 12km/7mi carved out of the jungle before police made significant arrests. Today Leticia is enjoying much improved safety. Since former president Uribe's **crackdown** on illegal drug trafficking, tourism has become Leticia's economic bedrock. Several resort chains have expressed an interest in establishing **hotels** in Leticia, while a growing number of **airlines** fly daily from Bogotá to Leticia, aiding the Colombian Amazon tourism boom.

Pirarucú, Leticia

© Hervé Collart/Corbis Sygma

El Pirarucú de Oro

Held in Leticia in late November to early December, this **International Festival of Amazonian Folk Music** is an annual event that celebrates the music, culture and traditions of the Amazon jungle. Three days of merriment witness indigenous communities from all over the region converging on Leticia in tribute to Amazonian folk music, rituals, values, heritage and customs. Shows and concerts take place in venues across the city, and the tri-border region, to honor the integration of three cultures and the peoples of the Colombian, Brazilian and Peruvian territories of the Amazon River Basin.

First staged in 1987, El Pirarucú de Oro is named after a local species of tropical **freshwater fish** that is important to all three communities. *Pirarucús* can weigh up to 300kg/660 pounds and grow up to 2.5m/8.2ft, and are found on restaurant menus throughout the region.

A World Away

There is a certain charm about Leticia's humid streets and its melee of motor-bikes and road battles for control of rush-hour traffic. With a backdrop of wild, inaccessible jungle, Leticia boasts plenty of the colors of nature, albeit faded by the searing heat in parts.

Wind along a jumble of restaurants, shops and painted houses set on a neat grid of **pavement-lined streets** that have expanded considerably in recent years to include an eclectic collection of tourist-friendly bars and hotels.

Yet, as bustling as it is, Leticia remains very much an **isolated frontier town**, stretching south of the Putumayo River and seemingly lost in time. Despite good flight connections with Bogotá, in Leticia the rest of country seems far away, with the nearest Colombian highway a 804km/500mi trudge.

SIGHTS

Parque Santander★

Avenida Vasquez Cobo, Calles 10 and 11. Leticia's bustling social hub is famous for its colorful flock of tiny resident **parrots**. Every day, at dawn and sunset, the entire plaza becomes a cacophony of sound as several thousand screeching *pericos* (small parrots) entertain park-goers with a magnificent, swooping display.

Every aspect of daily life plays out in the Parque Santander, which serves as a meeting place, playground and teen-age hangout, place of courtship and stage for local gossip.

Museo Freí Antonio Hoover Lamaña★

Carrera 11, Calles 9 and 10. ◯ *Open Mon–Fri 8:30am–11:30am, 1pm–5pm, Sat 9am–1pm.* ✆ *(8) 592 7729.*

This small but fascinating collection of artifacts contains some household items, tools and implements gathered from a number of indigenous communities in the region. A narrative on display boards explains the origins of the artifacts and their importance in the lives of the Amazonian people over the ages.

Biblioteca Banco de la República★

Carrera 11 # 15. ◯ *Open Mon–Fri 8am–noon, 2pm–6pm, Sat 8am–noon.* 🐾 *Guided tours in Spanish available.*

(8) 592 7783. www.lablaa.org/ banrep_leticia-galeria.htm.
Part of the Colombian national bank's social pledge several decades ago was a program of investment to promote the country's historical and indigenous heritage.
As a result, this fine, if rather small, collection gathered mainly from the Amazon's **Ticuna** and **Huitoto** tribes found a place in the bank's ultra-modern complex.
It includes carved masques, ceramic pots and various instruments.

Museo Alfonso Galindo

Calle 8 # 10-35. Open Mon–Sat 8am–noon, 2pm–6pm, Sun and public holidays 9am–noon. (8) 592 7056.
Peer beyond the souvenirs and handicrafts of Leticia's **Galería Arte Indígen** and you will spot an impressive **ethnography** and **zoology collection.** Among the items displayed are preserved animals, turtle shells, snake skins, dead insects, pickled birds and various artifacts.

SURROUNDINGS
Jardín Botánico Zoológico Francisco José de Caldas
Avenida Vásquez Cobo, Vía al Aeropuerto Open daily 8am–5pm. 2,000 COP. 9819 25759.
This tired-looking collection of caged animals is in need of a bit of paint and some TLC, but it continues to attract the tourists.
Specializing in Amazonia, the zoo showcases such species as the mammoth **anaconda,** tapir, ocelot, owl, eagle, macaw and monkey. Feeding schedules that run throughout the day allow visitors to get up close to some of the resident wildlife, especially the snakes.

Tabatinga★ (Brazil)
4km/2mi from Leticia via Faja Central (between centers, towns virtually merge on the outskirts).
Though it lacks the quaint charm of its Colombian sister city, Tabatinga has an inviting collection of bars, restaurants and street markets that make it well

Brazilian Influence

Leticia and Tabatinga have no clear border controls. They are conjoined with no discernable individual identity and with easy pedestrian and vehicular access that insures constant movement between the two. As a result, a steady stream of **cross-border cultural influences** continues to deluge Leticia. So, expect to find lots of joyous **samba** (originally from Rio de Janeiro), love-inspired **pagode** (from Salvador Bahía), fast-paced **forro** (from Brazil's northeast) and traditional **boi bumbá** (from the north of the Brazilian Amazon). You'll also find powerful **Brazilian cocktails** on every menu, together with plenty of typical **Brazilian grilled meat** restaurants serving plates of mouth-watering smoky *churrasqueira* that are standard Letician fare, much like the usual Colombian cuisine.

worth a visit. Tabatinga (Pop. 45,293) is the largest of the *tres frontiers* Amazonian trio.
Though this busy border outpost is less focused on tourism than Leticia (the Brazilian port city of Manaus farther up the river fulfills this role), Tabatinga does have a schedule of **daily boat** departures to Iquitos, Manaus and **Benjamin Constant**, and is a popular point from which to explore the indigenous communities along the **Yavari**, **Curuca** and **Quixito** rivers.
As a result, the town appears to be in a permanent state of movement, as motorbikes roar around congested streets filled with bars, discotheques and passers-by. Stalls sell trinkets, hammocks, woven bags and bootlegged CDs from Rio de Janeiro, while cafes pump out samba music.
Tabatinga shares easy pedestrian and vehicular access with neighboring Leticia. Both frontiers have been inextricably linked with **narcotic trafficking** in

Chagras

In recent years conservation groups have promoted activities and programs aimed at increasing the role of local indigenous communities, such as the ones around **Lago Yahuarcaca**, in land management, thereby encouraging them to be proactive in the protection of their environment. Around the lake, you will see several examples of *chagras*, **traditional small farms** with crops of great nutritional and medicinal value, that have been supported by the Colombian government. Such initiatives are becoming increasingly important in sustaining indigenous communities. They do not have any adverse effect on the environment, since they do not involve the devastating, large-scale clearing of forest land commonly taking place in the Brazilian part of the Amazon Basin.

the past, and Tabatinga is rumored to still have some 100 *bocas* (cocaine outlets). In 2008 a coca production plant in cleared jungle close to the city was discovered by drug enforcement agents. Shipments of **contraband** are also managed and controlled by highly organized Tabatinga operatives working from the city's two ports.

Santa Rosa de Yavari★ (Peru)

▷ *2km/1mi SW of Leticia.*
This small, laid-back Peruvian **island** in the Amazon is just a 5min jaunt by boat from Leticia. Like Tabatinga, Santa Rosa (Pop. 10,000) is free from immigration formalities unless you travel farther into Peru.
Santa Rosa is considerably smaller than Leticia and Tabatinga, and quite different in character. Set around one long, wide main street that is only the merest concession to tourism, it is every inch the **rustic beach town** wholly devoted to the island's **fishing tradition**.
Stretches of sand and simple shipyards contain hundreds of boats of all shapes

and sizes undergoing an overhaul or refit. During the day, men repairing outboard engines sip from bottles of **Inca Cola**, while a flimsy breeze offers little respite from the heat and humidity. Outside rows of simple wooden huts, men gather to mend nets on the sands while fishing boats unload their glistening daily hauls.
From here, regular **departures** *(lanchas)* sail out almost daily to towns along the **Amazon River** and its **tributaries**.

Lago Yahuarcaca★★

▷ *4km/2mi NW of Leticia.*
A fixture on every standard day tour from Leticia, this picturesque lake island is a photographer's dream.
Multi-colored **heliconias** and **palms** grace the water's edge as well as vast numbers of parrots, but save your film for shots of the spectacular **giant lilies** *(Victorias Regias)* found here.
Named after England's Queen Victoria, the world's largest water lily has a unique 93-day lifecycle and coexists with the dreaded piranha fish.

Reserva Tanimboca★

▷ *8km/5mi from Leticia. Various tour packages available upon request.* 📞*(8) 592 7679. www.tanimboca.org.*
Located on the trail to **Tarapaca**, a Huitoto Indian village, this pristine jungle reserve offers a complete package of adventures, including a 45m/148ft **platform** amid the trees that affords spectacular Amazon **views**★★.
Climb to the highest part of the tree canopy and let yourself **slide** 80m/262ft from tree to tree through the forest while companioned by lizards, birds and monkeys. Visitors also get an opportunity to go on a nocturnal **caiman-spotting** excursion on the Río Tacana and even catch a piranha—safely, that is.

Serpentario Armero-Guayabal

▷ *11km/7mi from Leticia.* 🕐*Open daily 8am–4pm.* 🎫*7,000 COP.* 📞*(8) 592 7679. www.nativa.org.*
This well-run project is dedicated to conservation and environmental edu-

AROUND LETICIA

0 — 10 km

70°0'0"

AMAZONAS

★★★ PARQUE NACIONAL
NATURAL
AMACAYACU

★ Mirador
Nai Pata

San Martín

○ PUERTO NARIÑO ★★★
Centro Natütama ★★

○ Palmeras

Isla Cacao

Islas
Loreto

○ Mocagua

Zaragoza

N

RÍO AMAZONAS

Santa Sofía

4°0'0"

4°0'0"

Isla de
los Micos

Islas
Santa Sofía

© Instituto Geográfico Agustín Codazzi, 2010

Nazareth

★ Reserva
Tanimboca

★★ Lago
Yahuarcaca

○ San Jorge

AEROPUERTO
ALFREDO
VÁSQUEZ COBO

Av. Vásquez Cobo

○ Leticia ★★

Jardín Botánico
Caldas ■

LETICIA

○ Tabatinga ★

★ Santa Rosa de Yavari

BRASIL

★ Parque
Santander ■

Calle 11

Av. Internacional

PERÚ

Calle 9
Calle 8

Calle 6

★ RÍO AMAZONAS

Reserva Natural Zacambu ★★

Río Amazonas

★★★ RÍO YAVARÍ
Benjamin Constant

○ Tabatinga ★

★ Reserva Natural Palmari ★
★ Reserva Natural Heliconia ★

BRASIL

70°0'0"

LAGO DE TARAPOTO

cation, and is owned and managed by
the non-profit organization, the Nativa
Foundation.

The Amazon region is famous for its
many species of **snakes**, which slither
and coil and haunt the rivers. Of the
nearly 300 species in Colombia, some
50 snakes are poisonous.

Here, visitors are able to observe up
close an array of snakes of all patterns,
sizes and colors.

ALONG THE AMAZON RIVER★★
UPSTREAM
Isla de los Micos

▶ 35km/22mi NE of Leticia, along
the Amazon River. ↝Guided tours
organized by the Decameron travel
lodge in Leticia; ☎ (8) 592 6600;
www.decameron.com.

Scientists admit that they may ne[...]
record every Amazon rain forest m[...]

Boating on the Amazon River, Parque Nacional Natural Amacayacu

Proexport Colombia

key species, so great are their numbers. Visitors hoping to interact with **pygmy marmosets** should find that these 450ha/1,112 acres of primary forest are definitely the right place.

Monkey Island's former owner was arrested for cocaine smuggling in 1989, which gave it a controversial reputation. Today, however, it has become a regular stopping-off point for Amazon tours operating out of Leticia.

The place is primarily home to **capuchin monkeys**. It is also rich in **bird life** and has several **ecological hiking trails**, with walks to Huitoto and Ticuna settlements.

Parque Nacional Natural Amacayacu★★★

▶ 60km/37mi NW of Leticia.
🕐 Open daily 7am–6pm. 💰21,000 COP. ☞ Guided tours organized by Decameron Explorer 📞(8) 522 2890; www.decameron.com.

This 293,500ha/725,254 acre expanse of rain forest occupies a large part of the Amazon trapezoid and is accessed by an exhilarating boat ride to the **Quebrada Matamata**, at the edge of the park. Once the ancestral land of more than a dozen indigenous Amazon communities, only the **Ticunas** remain in this magnificent jungle stretch where two very different landscapes are a major characteristic.

Rolling and relatively dry **scrubland** supports a wealth of vegetation, including an array of trees that can reach up to 40m/130ft in height. Mammoth **ceiba trees** need up to 30 people to fully encircle their girth. Other species—such as red and white cedar, mahogany, rubber, balsam, caoba and uvo—flourish on drier terrain.

In the boggy **wetlands**, the spectacular **Victoria lily**, and capiron and munguaba trees are typically found, along with 150 mammals and dozens of reptiles and snakes, including the caiman (*Caiman crocodilus*), boa snake, **anaconda** and coral snake, as well as **jaguars**, otters, **pink dolphins** (*boto*), black alligators, monkeys and the world's largest **freshwater tortoise**.

Fish at Amacayacu also make up a diversified group; they are found in abundance in waters rich with gray and pink dolphins and hovering insects and butterflies.

Puerto Nariño★★★

▶ 15km/9mi SW of Amacayacu.
http://puertonarino-amazonas.gov.co.
Named after famous Colombian general **Antonio Nariño**, who fought in the war of independence against the Spanish, the Amazonian town of Puerto Nariño (Pop. 6,816) sits at the confluence of the **Amazon** and the **Loretoyacu** rivers. Founded in 1961, it is home to about

5,000 people of an ethnic mix of **Ticuna**, **Cocoma** and **Yagua** peoples.

Today the city is renowned throughout Colombia for its pro-environmental stance and **eco-friendly** initiatives. Beautifully maintained, Puerto Nariño is a neat, traffic-free jungle town, quite unlike any other in the country. Rather improbably, "green" issues are at the fore in this **pioneering community**, possibly because of the many biologists, ecologists and conservationists who have passed through over the years. Sustainable living projects focus on community-based **waste management** and **rainwater collection**.

Puerto Nariño is also the only place in Colombia where **recycling** has been embraced as a citizen-led initiative—everybody plays a part in one way or the other. Fishermen from Puerto Nariño help conservationists transfer turtle eggs laid at night to the safety of the

Amacayacu's Birds

Some 468 species of birds, including flocks of brightly colored **macaws**, can be seen in the park. You may also get a glimpse at the Grey-winged Trumpeter, the Red-throated Caracara, the Amazonian Umbrella bird and all kinds of anhigas, egrets and herons.

Enthusiastic **birdwatchers** may find useful insider tips on bird sightings through the Red Nacional de Observadores de Aves de Colombia (RNOA) at **www.rnoa.org**

Natütama beach, and protect trees important for **heron nesting**.

They also survey **river dolphins** and **manatees** and educate hunters in other communities about the importance of

😊 Practical Hints for an Amazonian Trip 😊

Pack carefully to insure that you have everything you need that isn't available in Leticia, such as specific prescription **medicines**, effective **mosquito spray**, **camping gear** (from tent pegs to rain forest-ready sleeping bags), **clothing** (waterproof rubber-soled boots, sunglasses, loose cotton jungle-wear and sun hats), **maps**, **mobile phones** and **GPS equipment**.

♦ Do as much **research** as you can about what you want to see and where you want to go—if you are deviating from the standard tourist trail, you will need to plan ahead. Most expeditions use **local guides**, **porters** and **boatmen**—practiced explorers who are adept at navigating the currents and tidal flows of the Amazon River and its many tributaries. However, the more information you gather about your destination, the better equipped you will be to handle any unforeseen circumstances that may arise. Pick up a decent **map**, plot a suitable **route** and make a note of **visa requirements** to enter neighboring Peru and Brazil.

♦ Prepare your trip according to the **time of year** you visit. In the **dry season**, the rivers will be low and jungle trails parched and dusty; in the **wet season** rivers are high with heavy showers, a daily occurrence. Wildlife and camping can be more enjoyable in the dry season; rivers aren't fast-flowing and prone to flooding, and equipment is less likely to get damp. Yet, in the rainy season, you are unlikely to encounter an exposed riverbed—a major hindrance to exploration by boat that makes getting from A to B hard-going. **Dugout wooden canoes** are the most common means of travel on Amazonian rivers.

♦ No matter how you travel, be sure to pack **binoculars**, **camera** (with spare film or memory card), **first-aid kit** (including rehydration salts) and a **change of clothing** (everything you own will, at some point, get wet).

🌿 Walking Trails

From Puerto Nariño, you can hike to the nearby indigenous villages of **San Martin de Amacayacu** and **20 de Julio**. This walk is a good occasion to learn about traditional medicine, indigenous plants and local customs.

Three trails lead out of the town's outskirts to offer great **bird-watching** and **hiking** through plant-rich terrain:

- ◆ **Sendero Ecologico** is a leafy forest path that is renowned for its medicinal plants, curative barks and flowers.
- ◆ **Sendero Ecologico Mitologico** is a winding trail that focuses on the ecology and mythology of the Amazon region.
- ◆ **Sendero Interpretativo Nama Araku** is a bird-filled track that shows the ancestral use of plants in indigenous cultures.

these species to the eco-balance of the Amazon region.

Centro de Interpretacion Natütama★★

▶ *Near Puerto Nariño.*
🕐 *Open Wed–Mon 8am–noon, 2pm–5pm.* ✺*Contribution suggested.*
✆ *313 411 2872. www.natutama.org.*
This center is run by **Natütama**—a non profit organization (NGO) set up to work with local communities to protect the Amazon's wildlife and habitats.

A fine range of 70 life-size **wood carvings** of Amazonian fauna and flora provides a glimpse into the **underwater world** of the **Amazon Basin**. River dolphins, manatees, pirarucu (the world's biggest freshwater fish), otters, turtles and numerous fish species are depicted swimming among the flooded trees and roots of the rain forest during the high-water season.

As the Amazon is so sediment-rich, waters appear cloudy and opaque, making it impossible for many locals and visitors to see the incredible diversity of animals and plants that flourish below the surface.

A second exhibition centers on a **night-time scene**. Hand-sewn dark blue squares of cloth are set with stars and a moon that look down on a river where a fisherman is guiding a leaping river dolphin into his net. Nearby, exposed mud flats are home to a mammoth caiman. On the riverbank, turtle hatchlings are scampering down to the safety of their nest. Also depicted are a capybara, a turtle and a heron in the bushes and an array of Amazonian vegetation.

♿ *In June each year, workshops take place on specific environmental themes dedicated to the protection of species such as river dolphins, manatees and turtles.*

Puerto Nariño and the Amazon River

Aviatur/Proexport Colombia

Casa Museo Etnocultural Ya Ipata Ünchi—Ya Ipata Ünchi★

Carrera 7 and Calle 5. ⏰Open Mon–Fri 7am–noon, 2pm–5:45pm. ☞Guided tours in Spanish. ✍Contribution suggested. ✆313 885 2237.

You will find a wide array of artisan exhibits depicting the cultures of the **Ticuna**, **Cocama** and **Yagua**. Artifacts gathered from communities in and around Puerto Nariño help narrate the special heritage of this fertile region, which sits at the convergence of the Amazon and the Loretoyacu rivers.

Mirador Nai Pata★

▶ *Near Puerto Nariño.*
☞*Guided tours organized by Mahatu Hostel in Leticia ✆(8) 592 7384; www.mahatu.org.*

A must for every visitor, this climb up to the top of a wooden **lookout tower** affords breathtaking **views**★★ over the west of the town and the Loretoyacu River flowing into the Amazon.

Lago de Tarapoto★★

▶ *10km/6mi W of Puerto Nariño.*
Surrounded by enormous Ficus trees, this sacred lake for local indigenous communities is steeped in ancient myths and legends. It is often visited by tourists seeking to spot rare **pink river dolphins** (👁see sidebar p409). Lake Tarapoto is also home to feeding **manatees**, and is rich in **giant lilies**.
Many local legends relate to the lake's mystical depths. One tells of a strange green light that illuminates the night sky, a sight that prompts fishermen to pack up their nets and head home at speed. Fishing overnight under the green haze is said to bring doom to fishermen—rumor has it that their bodies are found headless as the sun rises over the lake.
Other legends relate to pirates who ascend suddenly from the water to kill unsuspecting fisherman as the green light shines.
The magical **boto** (pink river dolphin) is also believed to undergo a metamorphosis into human form in the Lago de Tarapoto's myth-shrouded depths.

DOWNSTREAM
Benjamin Constant (Brazil)

▶ *40km/24.8mi S of Tabatinga.*
In sharp contrast to the Colombian Amazon, the Brazilian segment has been subjected to extensive **deforestation** by commercial loggers. Tours from Leticia often visit **sawmills** located along the river to understand the history of the lumber industry in the Amazon Basin.
Benjamin Constant (Pop. 29,268) is very much the outpost town. It is built around a busy port frequented by **boats** departing downstream to **Manaus**, carrying cargoes of latex, resin and paying passengers. Named after **Benjamin Constant Botelho de Magalhães** (1836–91), a military man and political thinker, this Brazilian settlement holds a small anthropology museum.

Museo Magüta

Avenida Castelo Branco 396.
✆ *(97) 3415 6077. www.laced.mn.ufrj.br.*
One of Brazil's most populous indigenous groups, the **Ticuna** live in some 95 villages scattered along the banks of the **Upper Solimões River** and its tributaries. Reflecting this, the compact museum contains interesting artifacts relating to Ticuna culture, including some rare books and scripts.

Jungle Reserves

In recent years, a number of small **private reserves** (👁see p416 and p422) have sprung up along the Amazon and Yavari rivers. Most specialize in adventure activities with the services of a guide, from **nocturnal hikes** and nighttime **caiman-watching** to birding, fishing and **jaguar trekking**.

Rooms tend to be simple mud-and-thatch with hammocks and a washroom, and food included in the cost of your stay. Tours and transfers are extra, though border formalities are often taken care of as part of the package.

ALONG THE YAVARI RIVER★★★

This powerful **tributary** of the Amazon extends into exquisite rain forest, providing incredible **wildlife-spotting** opportunities.

In its entirety, the Río Yavari runs from the border between Brazil and Peru's Loreto department, flowing northeast 870km/541mi. Since it joins the Amazon River near Benjamin Constant, visitors will need to make passport/**border control** inquiries prior to travel. Shortly after leaving Leticia, watch for the region's **pink river dolphins** (boto) and the silver colored **tucuxis** (Sotalia fluviatili).

Have your binoculars at the ready for squirrel monkeys, **black-mantle tamarins**, night monkeys, brush-tailed rats, black agoutis, **Amazon dwarf squirrels**, pygmy marmoset and **white-fronted capuchin**.

There is also a plentiful supply of the **woolly monkey**, monk saki, red howler, titi monkey, collared peccary, tapir, oncilla, **giant armadillo**, sloth, **jaguar**, ocelot and **giant otter**.

Some 3,200 types of **Amazon fish** have been identified, from armored pleco catfish to goliath pirarucú—although the true figures may be around 3,900, at least.

Amazon-Friendly Websites

http://worldwildlife.org/amazon/
Discover the World Wildlife Fund's (WWF) vision and initiatives regarding the protection of the world's richest rain forest and the development of a sustainable forest economy.

www.ethnobotany.org/
The site of the Amazon Conservation Team is full of information regarding the forests and people of the Amazon, and contains all kinds of documents on ethnobiology, ethnobotany, conservation and research.

Reserva Natural Zacambu★★ (Peru)

▶ 60km/37mi NW of Leticia on the Yavari River. Guided tours organized by Amazon Holidays ✆(8) 592 6692; www.amazon-holidays.com.

Set among lowland flooded forests on the **mangrove**-hemmed bank of Lake Zacambú, this small wooden lodge offers simple accommodations.

Walk along **butterfly-rich trails** to the sound of dolphins frolicking in the water, or canoe from a boardwalk dock to spot **caimans** several feet in length.

Reserva Natural Palmari★ (Brazil)

▶ 110km/68mi SW of Leticia on the Yavari River. Guided tours organized by the Palmari Jungle Lodge ✆(1) 610 3514; www.palmari.org.

Located on a bend in the river where pink and gray dolphins are often sighted, this sprawling lodge is famous for its **views** of dolphins and boasts a **tower** to insure unrivaled vistas.

As the reserve is a **research facility**, all excursions have an ecological focus. An impressive bird tally—more than 541 species at last count—covers 60 bird families (quite a record) across three Amazonian ecosystems: dry, semi-flooded and flooded.

Reserva Natural Heliconia★ (Brazil)

▶ 95km/59mi SW of Leticia on the Yavari River. Guided tours organized by the Heliconia Reserve ✆(8) 592 5773; www.amazon heliconia.com.

For forays by foot to discover the river, creeks and jungle, this reserve makes an ideal base amid palms and other trees on 15ha/37 acres of preserved jungle. Almost every activity— birding, hikes, river trips and **ecological walks**—support the native cultures that inhabit the lodge's surroundings.

The wide range of options includes **dolphin-spotting**, kayaking, fishing, **canopy exploration** and bird-watching (the lodge actually has its own **observation towers**).

The Amazon's Extraordinary Wildlife

Ascertaining exactly what creatures inhabit the Amazon rain forest isn't easy, with new species still being discovered all the time. As yet, the full tally of insect species could be anything up to several million, even though only 20,000 have so far been identified. What is known is that

Kinkajou
© Daniel Heuclin/NHPA/Photoshot

the Amazon is the home of more than 300 species of **mammals**, around 3,900 of freshwater **fish**, tens of thousands of **trees** and nearly a hundred thousand other **plant species**. In a single acre of forest, as many as 100 arboreal species have been counted. At least 7,500 species of **butterfly**, more than 1,800 **birds**, and almost 2,000 species of **reptile** and **amphibian** have been recorded, but this count is just the tip of the iceberg, because the Amazon contains a staggering 10 percent of all flora and fauna species found on the planet. In fact, scientists doubt they will ever be able to catalog everything in the lifetime of the world—a mind-boggling thought.

Capybaras
Amazon leaf frog
© NHPA/Photoshot
© Ken Klotz/iStockphoto.com
Victoria water liliy
Froexport Colombia
Yellow-billed Jacamar
Juan David Ramírez/Proexport Colombia

ADDRESSES

🛏 STAY

$ Hotel La Frontera – *Av. Internacional # 1-04, Leticia. ☎(8) 592 5600. 16 rooms.* True to its name, this hotel lies only steps away from the Brazilian border. It's a pleasant place, and each of the 16 clean rooms has a bath, air-conditioning and cable TV. From the airy rooftop terrace, you can look out over both Brazil and Colombia.

$ Hotel Los Delfines – *Carrera 11 # 12-85, Leticia. ☎(8) 592 7488. 10 rooms.* This is a small, family-owned hotel that is about a 10-minute walk from the center of Leticia. Spacious but basic rooms come with beds and hammocks and overlook a flower-filled courtyard. Rooms have private bathroom and a fan, and the hotel even has its own water-treatment facility.

$$ Hotel Malokamazonas – *Calle 8 # 5-49, Leticia. ✕ ☎(8) 592 6642. www.hotelmalokamazonas.es.tl. 9 rooms.* Surrounded by native fruit trees, Malokamazonas claims to be the only boutique hotel in Leticia and boasts of its position on the border of Colombia, Brazil and Peru—a site reflected in the hotel's decor. The work of local artisans and furnishings made of indigenous wood decorate the rooms in this charming lodging, while personalized service caters to guests' comfort. Rooms, which are not air-conditioned, are sited to take best advantage of the jungle breezes.

$$ Hotel Yurupary – *Calle 8 # 7-26, Leticia. ✕ ☎(8) 592-4743. www.hotelyurupary.com. 29 rooms.* Airy, well-appointed, air-conditioned rooms open onto a lush courtyard at this hotel in the center of Leticia. Indicated by a red and yellow sign set back from the road, the hotel offers a large buffet breakfast each morning, along with good lunch and dinner options and a well-stocked bar. If you must go out to eat and are watching your pennies, the Yurupary is just steps from a good and incredibly cheap 24-hour diner.

$$$ Waira Suites Hotel – *Carrera 10 # 7-36, Leticia. ✕ ☎(8) 592 4428. www.wairahotel.com.co. 28 rooms.* If you're looking for a good level of service and comfort in the awe-inspiring setting of the Amazon jungle, Waira Suites Hotel is for you. Near Vásquez Cobo International Airport and the river port, this hotel offers bright, contemporary, air-conditioned rooms with LCD TV and mini-bar. Suites add extra living space, while connecting rooms are perfect for families.

$$$$ Hotel Anaconda – *Carrera 11 # 7-34, Leticia. ✕ ☎(8) 592-7119. www.hotelanaconda.com.co. 50 rooms.* The Anaconda Hotel, once considered the best in Leticia, is located in the heart of the city and 10 minutes from the Vásquez Cobo airport. Equipped with Wi-Fi and air-conditioning, rooms look a bit the worse for wear these days, but some have lovely river views. The courtyard pool and alfresco dining at the restaurant make a stay here worthwhile.

$$$$ Hotel Decameron Decalodge Ticuna – *Carrera 11 # 6-11, Leticia. ✕ ☎(8) 592 6600. www.decameron.com. 28 rooms.* Part of the Decameron hotel chain, Decalodge Ticuna makes an ideal perch from which to explore the amazing biodiversity of Amazon region. Rooms and cabanas mix contemporary style with Amazonian accents, and don't spare any modern conveniences.

Hotel Decameron Decalodge Ticuna

Proexport Colombia

Guided walks through town and bike rides around the area are offered for guests, and the Decalodge restaurant serves fine Peruvian cuisine.

$$$$$ Casa Flotante Amazonas – *1hr 30min by boat from Leticia to Casa Navegante on the Amacoyacú River. Organized by Aviatur* 📞*(1) 382 1616. www.concesionesparquesnaturales. com. 1 room, accommodates 5 guests.* A luxurious floating hotel that sleeps five, Casa Navegante puts a new twist on ecotourism. The two-story houseboat moves at a leisurely 10mph to enable its guests to admire the jungle, swamps, marshes and wildlife. A fully equipped kitchen, a deck strewn with lounge chairs and hammocks, and a private bath with hot water are among the amenities you can expect. Reservations required.

⍾/EAT

$ La Casa del Pan – *Calle 11 # 10-20, Leticia. Breakfast and lunch only.* 📞*(8) 592 7660. Closed Sun.* A bright, bustling and popular bakery, La Casa del Pan is a good place to start your day. You can enjoy eggs, bread, coffee and fruit juice for 3,500 COP, with a view of Parque Santander to boot. Drop by in the afternoon for a snack or a coffee pick-me-up. **Bakery**.

$ Las Margaritas – *Calle 6 # 6-80, Barrio Comercio, Puerto Nariño.* 📞*311 276 2407.* The fact that Las Margaritas is obscured from view by its thick thatched roof and picket fence has no bearing on its popularity. Locals flock here to dine on delicious—and generously portioned—set meals that include local fare such as pirarucu and *carne asada* (grilled steak). The restaurant is open for breakfast, lunch and dinner. **Amazonian**.

$ Mimo's – *Carrera 11 # 7-26, Leticia.* 📞*8-592-5129.* A plethora of different flavors and sizes of ice cream are a welcome sight for anyone with a sweet tooth who passes by Mimo's. In addition to the option of relaxing by Parque Orellana on the outdoor terrace, the establishment also sells take-away tubs of ice cream so you can get a sugar high throughout the day or night. **Ice cream**.

$ Restaurante El Sabor – *Calle 8 # 9-25, Leticia. Closed Sun.* 📞*(8) 592 4774.* This well-known hole-in-the-wall diner is a Leticia landmark. El Sabor serves set meals—no *comida corriente* (à la carte menu)—that feature grilled meat and local fish. Vegetarian dishes and fruit salads are also available. Whether you sit on the outdoor thatched-palm patio in front of the restaurant or in the dining room inside, you'll won't go away hungry. All meals come with soup, salad and unlimited fruit juice. **Amazonian**.

$$ La Cava Amazonica – *Carrera 9 # 8-22, Leticia.* 📞*(8) 592 4935.* This open-air restaurant is a lunchtime favorite with the locals. Set meals include huge bowls of soup, salad, meat dishes and a side of vegetables for around 7,000 COP. The place gets quite crowded during the weekday lunch rush, so it's best to time your meal slightly before or after the noon hour. **Amazonian**.

$$ Tierras Amazónicas – *Calle 8 # 7-50, Leticia.* 📞*(8) 592 4748. Closed Mon.* With its walls covered in kitschy Amazonia souvenirs, this restaurant might seem like a tourist trap at first glance, but don't let that deter you from coming here. It's a great place for a fun meal, and fish—especially the pan-grilled pirarucu—is the thing to order. There's also a full bar and romantic music most nights. **Amazonian**.

$$$ Restaurante Wayaguru – *Decameron Decalodge Ticuna, Carrera 11 # 6-11, Leticia.* 📞*(8) 592 6600. www.decameron.com.* Set alongside the agreeable grounds of the local Decameron hotel, Restaurante Wayaguru offers its diners a choice between local or more standard international dishes. There is also an accompanying terrace bar adorned with rustic decor overlooking the swimming pool. **Colombian**.

INDEX

INDEX

INDEX

INDEX

INDEX

MAPS AND PLANS

MAP LEGEND

	Sight	Seaside resort	Winter sports resort	Spa
Highly recommended	★★★	‹‹‹	✳✳✳	‡‡‡
Recommended	★★	‹‹	✳✳	‡‡
Interesting	★	‹	✳	‡

Selected monuments and sights

	Tour - Departure point
	Catholic church
	Protestant church, other temple
	Synagogue - Mosque
	Building
■	Statue, small building
	Calvary, wayside cross
◎	Fountain
	Rampart - Tower - Gate
	Château, castle, historic house
	Ruins
∪	Dam
☼	Factory, power plant
☆	Fort
∩	Cave
	Troglodyte dwelling
	Prehistoric site
▼	Viewing table
Ⱳ	Viewpoint
▲	Other place of interest

Sports and recreation

	Racecourse
	Skating rink
	Outdoor, indoor swimming pool
	Multiplex Cinema
	Marina, sailing centre
	Trail refuge hut
	Cable cars, gondolas
	Funicular, rack railway
	Tourist train
◆	Recreation area, park
	Theme, amusement park
	Wildlife park, zoo
	Gardens, park, arboretum
	Bird sanctuary, aviary
	Walking tour, footpath
	Of special interest to children

Abbreviations

G, POL	Police (Federale Politie)	**P**	Local government offices (Gouvernement provincial)
H	Town hall (Hôtel de ville ou maison communale)	**P**	Provincial capital (Chef-lieu de provincial)
J	Law courts (Palais de justice)	**T**	Theatre (Théâtre)
M	Museum (Musée)	**U**	University (Université)

Additional symbols

	Tourist information	⊠	Post office
	Motorway or other primary route	◎	Telephone
❶ ❶	Junction: complete, limited		Covered market
	Pedestrian street	·×·	Barracks
	Unsuitable for traffic, street subject to restrictions	△	Drawbridge
	Steps – Footpath	∪	Quarry
	Train station – Auto-train station	✕	Mine
	Coach (bus) station	Ⓑ Ⓕ	Car ferry (river or lake)
	Tram		Ferry service: cars and passengers
⊜	Metro, underground		Foot passengers only
P	Park-and-Ride	③	Access route number common to Michelin maps and town plans
♿	Access for the disabled	Bert (R.)...	Main shopping street
		AZ B	Map co-ordinates

437

You know
the Green Guide

...DO YOU REALLY KNOW **MICHELIN**?

• Data 31/12/2009

The world No.1 in tires
with 16.3% of the market

A business presence in over **170 countries**

A manufacturing footprint
at the heart of markets

In 2009 **72** industrial sites in **19** countries produced:

- **150** million tires
- **10** million maps and guides

Highly international **teams**

Over **109 200** employees* from all cultures on all continents

including **6 000** people employed in R&D centers

in Europe, the US and Asia.

*102 692 full-time equivalent staff

The Michelin Group
at a glance

Michelin
competes

At the end of 2009

Le Mans 24-hour race
12 consecutive years of victories

Endurance 2009
- 6 victories on 6 stages
in Le Mans Series
- 12 victories on 12 stages
in American Le Mans Series

Paris-Dakar
Since the beginning of the event,
the Michelin group has won
in all categories

Moto endurance
2009 World Champion

Trial
Every World Champion title
since 1981 (except 1992)

Michelin, established close to its customers

○ **72 plants in 19 countries**

- Algeria
- Brazil
- Canada
- China
- Colombia
- France
- Germany
- Hungary
- Italy
- Japan
- Mexico
- Poland
- Romania
- Russia
- Serbia
- Spain
- Thailand
- UK
- USA

● **A Technology Center spread over 3 continents**

- Asia
- Europe
- North America

● **Natural rubber plantations**

- Brazil

Our mission

To make a sustainable contribution to progress in the mobility of goods and people by enhancing freedom of movement, safety, efficiency and the pleasure of travelling.

Michelin committed to environmental-friendliness

Michelin, world leader in low rolling resistance tires, actively reduces fuel consumption and vehicle gas emission.

For its products, Michelin develops state-of-the-art technologies in order to:
- Reduce fuel consumption, while improving overall tire performance.
- Increase life cycle to reduce the number of tires to be processed at the end of their useful lives;
- Use raw materials which have a low impact on the environment.

Furthermore, at the end of 2008, 99.5% of tire production in volume was carried out in ISO 14001* certified plants.

Michelin is committed to implementing recycling channels for end-of-life tires.

*environmental certification

Passenger Car
Light Truck

Truck

Michelin
a key mobility enabler

Earthmover

Aircraft

Agricultural

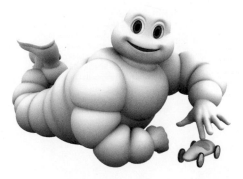

MICHELIN
plays on balanced performance

Two-wheel   **Distribution**

Partnered with vehicle manufacturers, in tune with users,
active in competition and in all the distribution channels,
Michelinis continually innovating to promote mobility today
and to invent that of tomorrow.

Maps and   **ViaMichelin,**   **Michelin**
Guides   travel   **Lifestyle,**
                    assistance   for your travel
                    services   accessories

MICHELIN
plays on balanced performance

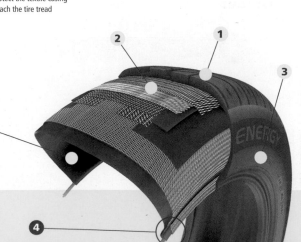

● **Long tire life**

● **Fuel savings**

○ **Safety on the road**

... MICHELIN tires provide you with the best performance, without making a single sacrifice.

The MICHELIN tire pure technology

1 **Tread**
A thick layer of rubber
provides contact with the ground.
It has to channel water away
and last as long as possible.

2 **Crown plies**
This double or triple reinforced belt
has both vertical flexibility
and high lateral rigidity.
It provides the steering capacity.

3 **Sidewalls**
These cover and protect the textile casing
whose role is to attach the tire tread
to the wheel rim.

4 **Bead area for attachment to the rim**
Its internal bead wire
clamps the tire firmly
against the wheel rim.

5 **Inner liner**
This makes the tire
almost totally impermeable
and maintains the correct inflation pressure.

Heed
the MICHELIN Man's advice

To improve safety:

- I drive with the correct tire pressure
- I check the tire pressure every month
- I have my car regularly serviced
- I regularly check the appearance of my tires (wear, deformation)
- I am responsive behind the wheel
- I change my tires according to the season